Consumer and Commercial Credit Management

Consumer and Commercial Credit Management

ROBERT H. COLE, Ph.D.

Professor of Marketing
University of Nebraska

FOURTH EDITION · 1972

RICHARD D. IRWIN, INC. *Homewood, Illinois 60430*
IRWIN-DORSEY LIMITED *Georgetown, Ontario*

658.88
C 689b
c. 2

Fourth Edition

First Printing, March, 1972

Library of Congress Catalog Card No. 77-172966
Printed in the United States of America

To
Mary Rose
Robb
and Rick

Preface

More and more each day we live in a World of Credit. And this is true, whether we are talking about retail credit, service credit, cash loan credit, commercial credit, financial credit, or public credit. Thus there exists a continuing need for a better understanding of this activity which is so vital in the lives of all of us. Likewise, the importance of this understanding of credit is bound to increase in the years ahead, as it will become even more necessary for everyone to know what credit is, what it does, what it can do, and what it cannot do.

This fourth edition has been designed to meet the needs of people who are now—or who will be—involved with the management of credit and collection activities of their own affairs or of those business concerns with whom they are associated.

As in previous editions, consumer credit has been given coverage comparable to that of the business credit field, especially commercial credit activities. The organization of the material has been planned to give the reader an appreciation of the economic and social implications of credit and to reveal to him the specific types of credit available. Once again the chapters have been placed in a sequence that corresponds to the actual performance of credit activities in a consumer or commercial credit department.

The reader will find many changes have taken place in this fourth edition. Perhaps the most obvious is the tremendous impact that federal legislation has had upon credit activities, particularly those in the consumer credit field. These laws, which were enacted in the late 1960s and early 1970s, include the Truth-in-Lending Act, the Fair Credit Reporting Act, the Credit Card Issuance Act, and the Credit Control Act. The importance of these laws is so great that the major provisions of the Truth-in-Lending Act and the entire Fair Credit Reporting Act are shown in Appendix B. In addition, coverage of the enactment on state levels of the Uniform Commercial Code and the Uniform Consumer Credit Code appears in this revision.

The place of these enactments in this "Age of Consumerism" has been explored and explained, along with an analysis of the increasingly dominant role played by the American consumer as a vital factor in the level of business activity.

Again, as in the third edition, footnote references have been expanded in order to give the reader a workable source of reference materials on a wide range of topics and from all possible sources.

The growing importance of bank credit card plans (especially Master Charge and BankAmericard) has been recognized, and their activities have been explained in detail. In addition, attention has been directed again to a closer look at the possible ramifications of a "cashless-checkless" or a "less-check" society of the future.

The option-terms revolving credit plan has been recognized for its importance in the consumer credit field, and the open charge account has been relegated to a somewhat less important position in this revision. The confusion regarding the validity of interest charges in excess of state usury laws has been pointed out—an area that probably will be of even greater importance in the revolving credit and the bank credit card fields in the years to come.

The impact of the Fair Credit Reporting Act upon credit bureaus and other types of reporting agencies has been explained in detail. The subject of automated credit bureau reporting has been developed to reflect current and proposed changes.

Once again the material on credit scoring plans has been expanded in the chapter devoted to the problems of decision making, and the material covering automated approaches to credit control (in both consumer and commercial credit operations) has been updated to reflect present-day thinking on this rapidly changing topic.

Other areas in the consumer credit field that have been expanded include the increasing importance of service credit, the use of credit by the low-income market, the growing importance of the student loan market, the increasing but still limited use of the variable interest rate in home mortgages, the changed procedure in figuring true annual rates of interest under the Truth-in-Lending Act, and the growing importance of payments systems such as Giro in foreign countries.

Extensive revision has occurred in the chapter on Dun & Bradstreet, Inc., reflecting the major changes installed as of May 1, 1971. Such changes include a more realistic Key to Ratings, as well as extensive revision of the principal activities of The Mercantile Agency. Likewise, the special mercantile agencies that are Dun & Bradstreet subsidiaries—Credit Clearing House and National Credit Office—have made significant changes in their operations, and these changes have been recognized in this revision.

The reader also will notice that the International Consumer Credit Association and the National Association of Credit Management have extensively revised their educational requirements for their professional certification programs.

Recognition also has been given to the growing importance of the Small Business Administration as a source of cash loans to business concerns. Likewise, expanded treatment has been given to a discussion of the importance and possible problem areas in the use of commercial paper as a source of funds in business operations.

Such an extensive revision of *Consumer and Commercial Credit Management* would not have been possible without the helpful ideas and suggestions of teachers, credit association and other business executives, and students. I am especially grateful to Professor Lewis E. Davids of the University of Missouri who reviewed the entire book and who gave many valuable suggestions which have been included in this edition. Of course, recognition is given to the work of Professor Robert S. Hancock, Chairman of the Marketing Department, University of Arizona, who coauthored the first two editions of the book. Professor Phillip McVey, my Marketing Department Chairman, provided encouragement during the trials of this revision, and Professor John Brash, also of the University of Nebraska, offered many valuable recommendations.

And of course, any and all suggestions from the readers of this edition will be most welcome in order that the book may continue to tell the complete and full story of the management of credit and collection activities.

February, 1972   ROBERT H. COLE

Contents

PART I

Background to the Field of Credits and Collections

1

Credit—What It Is
and What It Does

Ours is a credit world. Credit has become an integral part of our everyday lives, and it appears that in the future its importance will grow even greater. Thus it is vitally necessary for all of us—whether we be individual consumers, retailers, service concern operators, wholesalers, manufacturers, financial executives, or individuals involved in running our governmental units—to have a fully complete and clear understanding of what credit is, what it does, what it can do, and what it cannot do. Not only is it valuable for us to know its many advantages and benefits, but it also is necessary that we recognize the possible limitations to the use of credit. Likewise it is vital that we understand the legal framework, both federal and state, within which our credit operations are conducted. Only through such a complete background of unbiased knowledge can we learn to benefit from this activity which permeates every phase of our economy and will do so more and more in the years ahead, as we become even more credit-oriented.

During the last decade, the federal government, state and local governments, and business enterprises greatly expanded their use of credit to carry on their many and varied operations. Likewise, American consumers used credit widely and extensively to purchase homes, to buy automobiles and the ever-widening array of consumer goods, to repair and improve their residences, and to obtain the services needed and desired to live in this 20th century. Thus the terms installment credit, revolving credit, open charge credit, service credit, cash loan credit, commercial credit, financial credit, and public credit have become familiar to most of us.

This increased use of credit can be attributed to several major factors. First, it is important to recognize that the consumer's attitude toward credit has changed substantially over the years, and the incurring of individual debt has attained a relatively new

3

respectability. Second, the enhanced financial security experienced by an increasing proportion of consumers has permitted them to satisfy wants and desires far in excess of their basic needs. While such financial security—resulting from high employment levels, social security, unemployment benefits, and health and pension programs—does not always suffice for outright cash purchases, it still has proved sufficient to cover a series of payments and interest charges resulting from credit purchases of the ever-increasing array of goods and services.

Third, this increase in credit has become an important factor in the growth of our economy. The attitude of more and more retailers and service concern operators has become increasingly favorable toward the use of consumer credit, as they have discovered that the acceptance of credit from consumers can be a powerful competitive device by which to expand sales, profits, and market share. This attitude is reflected backward through the channels of distribution and has had its favorable effect upon the operations of wholesalers, manufacturers, and finanacial institutions.

The emotions of many people, however, have been and continue to be stirred when they hear the word "credit." In fact, some individuals condemn all types of credit, and particularly installment credit, without stopping to analyze just what our nation would be like without credit. The simple fact is that the United States runs on credit. If all credit activities were stopped right now, the wheels of business as we know it would come to a screeching stop. Just how many manufacturers, wholesalers, retailers, and service concern operators would be able to stay in business without credit? Not many. Just how many individuals would be able to buy homes, cars, and appliances without some form of credit? Not many. Just how many people would be willing to pay cash each time to the paper boy (at 6 A.M.), or the milkman, or to pay for their utilities such as gas, electricity, water, and telephone on a strictly cash basis? Not many.

Thus credit has become one of the many social inventions with which we are familiar and which we use more and more, whether we be the family, the retailer, the wholesaler, the financial institution, the manufacturer, or any one of the many other institutions engaged in the marketing of goods, services, and money.

WHAT CREDIT IS

The term "credit" has been defined in many ways and by many writers. When analyzed, however, many of the proposed definitions[1]

1 / Hewitt Rogers, "The Fundamentals of Consumer Credit," *Credit World*, December 1969, p. 10.

are simply descriptions of credit or statements as to the use of credit, rather than definitions of credit itself. To contribute to an understanding of what credit is and what it does, the following definition will be followed throughout this book: *credit is a medium of exchange of limited acceptance.* The diagram shown in Figure 1-1 illustrates this definition.

FIGURE 1-1
How Credit Works

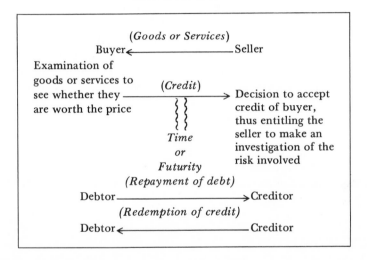

Medium of Exchange

In the diagram, it is seen that credit acts as a medium of exchange in that it facilitates the passage of goods or services from seller to buyer. Just as money is recognized in our economy as a medium of exchange permitting the easy passage of goods or services between seller and buyer, so is credit recognized.

Early in the development of trade it was found very inconvenient to exchange material things by the process of barter. The use of money, in the form of metallic coin, was a great improvement over barter but was not entirely satisfactory. Paper money was invented centuries ago and was a further improvement of the medium of exchange. At times it is a token, the representative of the metallic money which is held in reserves at a central point; at other times it is simply government credit. Thus paper money represents an attempt to facilitate the marketing process by the use of a medium of exchange which is more convenient than barter or than metallic money and which is easily recognizable.

Even paper money left something to be desired as a medium of exchange. Hazards were (and still are) involved in carrying large amounts of money while pursuing trading ventures. Thus a further improvement in our exchange media was attained by the development of credit. Such credit is not a monetary medium of exchange, although it is created for the same purpose—that of facilitating the passage of goods or services from seller to buyer. Although the use of credit goes back into the dim, dark ages before recorded history, the increased extent of its use in modern times has led us to speak of our times as being a credit era.

Credit, viewed as a medium of exchange, does have particular characteristics. It is a medium of exchange which is created at the time of the transaction and which arises for the purpose of facilitating that particular exchange. It is a medium of exchange which, after being issued, does not close the transaction; there is a promise that at some future time a further step will take place, that the credit will be redeemed by the process known as payment.

The creation of this medium of exchange brings into existence certain rights and privileges. With this thought in mind, we may point to the fact that credit is given by the buyer to the seller, and the seller exchanges goods or services for the buyer's credit. It is only after agreeing to accept the buyer's credit that the seller transfers the goods or services.

Limited Acceptance

When a customer offers a merchant $10 today in exchange for a hat priced at that figure, the retailer does not stop to analyze whether the $10 should be accepted (except perhaps for caution against counterfeiting) but takes the money, knowing that he in turn will find others highly willing to accept it from him. Thus our metal money and paper money today have a characteristic that can be called "unlimited acceptance." Therein lies the main difference between credit, which is generally considered to have limited acceptance, and money, which has unlimited acceptability.

This limited-acceptance concept of credit is perhaps more clearly understood when reference is made again to the diagramed definition. While it is true that the buyer has the option of examining the goods or services to see whether they are worth the price asked by the seller and whether to offer his credit for them, the seller also has the right to make an investigation of the buyer and to decide whether to accept the individual as a credit risk. For, in every credit transaction, there is a passage of time before repayment of the debt occurs. It is because of these two elements, "risk" and "time," found in every credit transaction, that credit has limited acceptance.

When the two parties to a transaction exchange goods or services for credit, we call them "buyers" and "sellers," but after the exchange we can and do use the legal term indicative of their continuing relationship, namely "debtor" and "creditor." The exchange does not end their relationship, which continues into the future and links them until the credit is redeemed by the exchange of money for the credit of limited acceptability first offered by the buyer and accepted by the seller. Upon payment, the buyer then has his credit returned to him, and he is in a position to reuse this credit in purchasing other goods or services if he can find a seller willing to accept the credit offered.

Credit as a Power

Credit may be thought of as a power inherent in all of us—the power to create a medium of exchange. The quantity of this power which each of us can issue depends upon the acceptance we can obtain for it; upon how many persons we can induce to accept our credit and in what amount. Thus for all practical purposes credit as a power cannot be measured.

Quality, however, cannot be separated from quantity—the question is always of acceptable quality for what amount. Relative to quality the question must always be raised concerning the certainty of redemption in accordance with the conditions under which the credit is accepted. The standard of quality is necessarily a variable which ranges from virtual certainty without reasonable doubt to the barest possibility that redemption will be in accordance with the agreed-upon conditions. Obviously the greater the certainty, the more readily the credit will be accepted and in larger quantity. Everyone, however, has a quantity limit which is raised by the inability to convince others that additional credit should be accepted in exchange for the goods or services sought.[2] Redemption of outstanding credit is likely to enhance the power to issue additional credit, and an excellent record for redemption in accordance with the previously determined conditions increases the acceptability and the quantity.

Since credit involves the prospect of future performance, acceptability rests on confidence—the confidence that future performance will be consistent with current promises. Such confidence must necessarily rest on an appraisal of available information and a forecast of future circumstances. In any such appraisal we are necessarily limited by the availability of information

2 / Wilbur T. Blair, "The Power of Credit," *Credit and Financial Management*, June 1970, p. 18.

and the correctness of our interpretation of the information at hand.

The sources of data available to the credit manager to secure accurate, complete, speedy, and reasonable information are numerous. These sources are discussed in detail in several of the subsequent chapters and include information supplied by the credit applicant himself on application forms or through personal interviews, data from direct investigation, facts from in-file ledgers, financial statement analysis, and information from local retail credit bureaus, the Retail Credit Company, banks, Dun & Bradstreet, Inc., credit interchange bureaus, specialized credit bureaus, and other miscellaneous sources.

The power to issue credit is thus limited by the extent to which we can convince others of its acceptability. The credit record we make as consumers or as businessmen is the most significant contribution to the enhancement of our power to issue acceptable credit. And an important contributor to this record is the character of our past credit dealings. Past redemption in accordance with agreement is a significant portion of this record, but it is importantly modified by the forecast of our future ability to adhere to our promises. No matter how good our record may be, it remains sterile unless others can be persuaded to validate it by accepting the credit offered them. It is this willingness to accept our credit power which we say rests on confidence.

Debtor-Creditor Relationship

When discussing credit it is easy to forget that credit is also debt. As we have seen, once credit is accepted we can call the parties to the transaction by their technical names, *debtor* and *creditor*. The credit outstanding is a debt, an obligation to pay at some future time. The obligation may be highly formal and embodied in a contract which details the rights and duties of the parties. The obligation may be quite informal, relying upon statutory law and common law, as well as equity, to determine the rights and duties of the parties only when the situation requires formal legal action. But regardless of the formality or informality of the agreement, the fact remains that a debt exists. This debt must remain until it is discharged by payment or by the acceptance of a new agreement.

The semantics of our language tend to make "credit" a rather pleasant term and "debt" a somewhat unpleasant term. In retail work the credit department may be called the Department of Credit Sales, not the Department of Debt Collections, but the latter term is equally descriptive of the duties. We can refer to statistics of credit outstanding, but we would be equally correct to refer to the debts unpaid. Our banker friends have succeeded in an interesting semantic switch when they concentrate attention on their deposits as though these were a source of strength when really they represent the obligation, debts, of the banks to their customers.

In order to keep our analysis clear we will speak of the "issuance of credit" or the "acceptance of credit," meaning thereby the exchange of credit for other values, but we must remember that the party issuing the credit which is accepted thereby becomes a debtor and thus is in debt; he has a liability to pay.

Is Credit Wealth or Capital?

Credit is often confused with wealth or with capital. Since it is intangible, it can be neither, because of the definitions used for wealth and capital.[3] Wealth is usually defined as scarce material goods that are transferable and useful; capital is usually defined as wealth that is used for the purposes of further production. Thus credit, being an intangible, is neither wealth nor capital. But credit does transfer wealth and capital. In the process of transferring wealth or capital, it may make them more productive, that is, more useful than they would otherwise be. A saver, a person having no productive use for the wealth he accumulates, would find that wealth, so long as it remains in his hands, is unproductive. Through credit it is possible to transfer this wealth to a businessman who desires to use it productively. The wealth thus becomes more socially useful than it otherwise would be.

Because credit facilitates the transfer of wealth, it enables wealth to be put to more productive uses. In the process of bidding for the right to use wealth, those borrowers who are best able to use it will be able to bid higher prices for it or offer greater certainty of future redemption. This bidding is done through the payment which they offer for the privilege of using the wealth of others and through the certainty of redemption which they can provide. The premium paid for the use of wealth is in itself a stimulus to the additional accumulation of wealth through saving. Wealth which is accumulated and remains idle is unproductive and has no earning power; thus it does not encourage further savings. When wealth can be loaned to others and a return thus obtained, there is more encouragement for an additional expansion of savings and a resulting increase in capital resources. Since in a modern economy the enlargement of

3 / From the point of view of the individual, however, credit may be considered by him as part of his "wealth." For example, if a person has a note receivable that has been given to him in a credit transaction, he will normally consider this as part of his wealth. The confusion here lies, of course, in the definition commonly given to the term wealth.

productivity is dependent upon the use of capital, credit is productive even though it is not itself wealth or capital.

Effect on Purchasing Power

A question often discussed is whether credit increases or decreases purchasing power. To set the proper frame of reference it is necessary, of course, to determine whether the question involves an individual consumer or a business concern. Likewise involved is the question of time, whether a short-run or long-run period of time is being considered.

Taking the individual consumer, it is obvious that if the money runs out before the end of the month and the grocery purchases are made on credit in order to eat, purchasing power for the short run is increased. However, at the end of the month payment is due, and if an interest charge is placed upon the account, the purchasing power of the consumer is correspondingly less than if purchases had been delayed. In connection with food, however, the alternatives are not very attractive.

Another view deserves consideration. In their efforts to obtain many of the desirable material things in a very short period of time, many people agree to large installment payments, too large, in fact, to be met out of their regular paychecks. Thus, the wife takes a job and the husband starts "moonlighting" (holding a second position) in order to meet the monthly payments. In a sense, then, the need to meet the scheduled payments necessitates harder work and results in a larger purchasing power than the family would otherwise have had if credit commitments had not been made. This larger purchasing power is reduced, however, by the amount of the interest charges placed upon the account.

In connection with business concerns, it should be recognized that their use of credit is generally viewed as facilitating the production of goods and services at a hoped-for profit, which in turn can be used to liquidate the indebtedness and to increase the purchasing power of the firms for future activities.

Documents as Credit Instruments

Credit is itself an intangible; it may, however, be represented by a tangible document. The document is not credit; it is merely a credit instrument which is evidence[4] of the intangible. These various credit instruments are the concrete, visible representatives of the intangible. They make the promise more definite and specific and more readily transferable. These representatives may be considered more desirable

4 / Rogers, *op. cit.,* pp. 10 and 14.

because they carry with them certain legal rights and thus confer certain powers. Although they give exactness and definiteness to the promise, they should not be confused with the credit transaction itself.

From time to time, as we discuss credit operations, we shall refer to various documents.[5] Each type has its specific legal definition and its proper use. But the task of credit evaluation must concentrate on the quality of the promise rather than on the document itself.

Should a check be considered as a credit document? In everyday business operations, checks have become so commonplace that they are viewed generally in the same light as paper money. It should be remembered, however, that in the promise behind every check there are inherent the two elements of limited acceptance—risk and time. True, these elements vary widely in extent and application. But to the merchants who cash worthless checks, these elements are forcefully apparent. Although no factual data or experience statistics are available to make accurate predictions, some sources recently have placed the annual loss from forged and fraudulent checks at somewhere between $400 million and $1 billion.[6] It is evident that as more and more checks are being written each year, this amount will increase.

WHAT CREDIT DOES

For Our Entire Economy

Ours is a mass-producing, mass-distributing economy. It has been said that credit is the lubricant that makes our system work. Mass production is not possible without mass distribution, and mass distribution is not possible without credit. But the credit involved must be the type that is soundly analyzed and appraised before it is accepted; it must be the type that does not place a burden upon the people and businesses faced with future repayment—a burden that in some instances is so heavy as to remove all benefits and joys from the goods and services received.

The vast majority of all transactions between businesses are carried on through credit. The manufacturer sells to the wholesaler on credit; the wholesaler in turn sells to the retailer on credit. The manufacturer, the wholesaler, and the retailer all borrow at some time from some type of financial institution to help carry on their business operations. This is a continuous day-by-day action. Unfortunately, no statistics are available on the extent to which credit is used in transactions between business concerns, but it is

5 / Documents are described in some detail in Appendix A.
6 / Don S. Lintvet, "Fraud is Your Worst Enemy," *Credit World,* February 1970, p. 20.

estimated that approximately 90 to 95 percent of these transactions involve credit of some type.

On the other hand, we do have figures (see Table 1-1) on the dollar volume of consumer credit outstanding at the close of the year from 1929 to the present time. These refer, of course, to those transactions in our economy that involve individual consumers. One has only to view these figures to visualize easily the growing importance of credit as a device that makes our vast distribution system run, and run smoothly. In this world of credit, nearly all consumers regularly use credit in some form or other to obtain goods, services, and money (which is in turn used to pay for goods and services).

TABLE 1-1
Consumer Credit
(millions of dollars)

End of Year	Total	End of Year	Total
1929	6,444	1959	51,544
1935	4,911	1960	56,141
1939	7,222	1961	57,982
1941	9,172	1962	63,821
1945	5,665	1963	71,739
1951	22,617	1964	80,268
1952	27,520	1965	90,314
1953	31,393	1966	97,543
1954	32,464	1967	102,132
1955	38,830	1968	113,191
1956	42,334	1969	122,469
1957	44,971	1970	126,802
1958	45,129		

Note: Consumer credit data have been revised at various times, for various series, and for various periods of years. (For the latest, most comprehensive revision, see "Revision of Consumer Credit Statistics," *Federal Reserve Bulletin,* December, 1968, p. 983.) Hence, the consumer credit data cannot be considered to be strictly comparable for every year from 1929 to the present. The data shown are exclusive of home mortgage loans.

Source: Board of Governors of the Federal Reserve System.

For the Consumer

The individual consumer uses credit basically for one of the following reasons: (1) because of a desire to raise his standard of living or to increase his enjoyment, (2) because of the convenience offered by the use of credit, or (3) because of the pressure of necessity.

Unhappily, consumer credit and its use appear to stir emotions, and it is difficult to consider its use without emotional involvement.

For centuries, the use of credit by the consumer was condemned by religion and by ethics. It still is regarded by some as being neither respectable nor legitimate. It would not further our present purpose, however, to examine the arguments about consumer credit which were so much a part of the doctrine of the early scholars nor to trace the history of its gradual approach to respectability. Suffice it to say that while the journey is not yet complete, developments in recent years have brought the use of consumer credit to a place where it is considered respectable, legitimate, and highly desirable by the vast majority of our American consumers.

Human nature being what it is, the consumer has a desire to raise his standard of living and to gain more enjoyment from life by having more of those goods and services which contribute to these ends. True, these may be obtained by a regulated program of saving, but it is difficult to imagine a high-consumption economy such as ours in which everyone saved a sufficient amount to purchase his home without the use of credit. Likewise, it is hard to imagine the present volume of automobile ownership unless some system of "pay as you ride" was available. This is in no sense saying that credit should be used indiscriminately and without care and caution,[7] but it is saying that a credit system such as we have devised has provided the American consumer with the highest standard of living as measured by material goods and services that any civilization has ever known.

Convenience also is a vital reason why consumer credit has come into almost general acceptance. The ease of buying goods and services without the need for the consumer to carry the money with him to pay for his purchases has been a large factor in his desire for credit. This convenience is making its influence felt more strongly at the present time in the marketing of services than ever before.

Credit as a medium of exchange may well be much more convenient than purchase with cash. Goods can be ordered by telephone or by telegram without bothering to send a remittance with the order. Mail orders also are more convenient when the order can be charged. Goods purchased with credit can be received, checked, and inspected before payment.

Payment also may be more convenient when it is settlement of an open account than when it is made for each individual transaction. Many consumers make frequent purchases from the same retail or service concern. It may be more convenient for them to be able to pay for a number of purchases at one time rather than to make payment for each transaction separately. Of course, this also applies to revolving credit transactions, as well as to certain types of installment credit arrangements.

7 / Robert P. Shay, "Marketing Consumer Credit in the Present and Future," *Credit World*, March 1968, p. 7.

Necessity does not apply to all types of consumer credit, as many purchases that are bought on credit could be handled on a cash basis, except perhaps for the convenience involved. But in the purchase of higher priced consumer goods, credit is practically a necessity for a consumer if the sale is to be made. Likewise, loans to consumers by personal finance companies and commercial banks often fall into the category of necessity, especially when the cash loan is made to permit the family to have the necessary medical and hospital care. Nor should we forget that at times the pay check runs out before the month does. When this happens, the credit purchase of items such as groceries takes on the necessity aspect.

For the Retailer and the Service Concern Operator

Credit for the retailer or for the service concern operator serves a threefold purpose. First, it enables him to sell more of his goods or services by allowing his customers to purchase these items by offering their credit in exchange. Second, it permits him to purchase his own goods on terms that will normally allow him to resell these goods and thus have the money with which to make payment. Third, it provides an avenue in the form of cash loans from a commercial bank or some other type of financial institution that will enable him to meet certain expenses and even to expand his business operations through additional investment of funds.

Why should the retailer or service operator prefer, or at least elect, to use credit when as a medium of exchange it may be somewhat more risky than other mediums which might be used? One obvious explanation is the desire to sell more goods or services. Since the buyer prefers this medium, it becomes somewhat of a patronage inducement to be willing to accept his credit. In fact the extent to which the merchant lowers his standard of credit acceptability will often determine the extent to which he can enlarge his market opportunity. By the acceptance of credit he is able to get a larger volume of business from those customers whose financial resources are limited and who often would not be in a position to make the purchases they desire without the use of credit.

Credit also enables the retailer or service operator to purchase his goods and services on a time basis and to pay for them at some future date. Thus the importance of commercial credit appears, as most merchants desire to exchange their credit for the stock of goods which they plan to sell in the future. When by means of credit they are able to stock additional goods, they can bring into their establishments more merchandise than their cash resources permit them to pay for at the present moment. By deferring the time of payment they can obtain funds from the sale of these goods, either in part or in total, before the time of payment arrives. This, of course, enables them to do more business than they could do if their transactions were limited to their present cash resources. Likewise, the importance of commercial banks and other financial institutions appears, as these provide funds generally needed by most business establishments.

It should be recognized that certain services, such as medical, dental, legal, appliance repair, and many others, are normally provided the customer who pays for these services at a later time. This has become a customary method of doing business for these people offering their services to the customer.

For the Manufacturer and the Wholesaler

Manufacturers and wholesalers depend upon credit arrangements to sell their goods to their customers. Over the years this has become the customary way of doing business, with the credit terms varying widely depending upon the character of the goods, the nature of the credit risk, the class of customer, competition, financial resources of the manufacturer or wholesaler, economic conditions both national and local, and many other factors.

With many manufacturers and wholesalers, the problem is to make certain that their merchandise has the maximum exposure to consumers—more sales will follow when the goods are offered in a large number of outlets. Thus a device that enlarges the number of sellers stocking the line will increase sales. Also, a manufacturer seeking entry into a market in which he is unknown has to overcome the lack of confidence in his merchandise and in himself. Since confidence is likely to generate confidence, or nonconfidence generate nonconfidence, his offer to show confidence by accepting the buyer's credit is more likely to develop acceptance of himself and of his line. The acceptance of credit is likely to generate a series of transactions rather than termination of the relationship with a single sale. Thus credit relations are more likely to be continuing relations.

To be realistic, consideration also must be given to another major factor in a manufacturer's accepting credit: that is, competition with other manufacturers. Some companies that have believed they were the undisputed leaders in their particular industries or fields have on occasion attempted to tighten credit terms. They have discovered, when competition did not similarly reduce terms, that they were forced because of lost business to return to the former, longer credit terms.

It also should be pointed out that both the manufacturer and the wholesaler make widespread use of commercial credit in their own buying from sources of supply. Likewise, they are concerned with the availability of all types of cash (financial) credit. In total, they are vitally concerned with all phases of business credit, but they are not directly involved with consumer credit unless they are distributing goods to the ultimate consumer.

For the Financial Institution

Perhaps instead of saying what credit does for the financial institution, we should say what the financial institution does for credit. Financial concerns—commercial banks, consumer and commercial finance companies, industrial banks, credit unions, savings and loan institutions, sales finance companies, insurance companies—all are filling the vital need of providing cash to consumers and business concerns that are offering their credit in exchange. This may be long-term borrowing, or short-term borrowing, or borrowing for a period between these two. It may be buying accounts receivable and notes receivable, thus providing needed capital to various types of business concerns. But the point to remember is that financial institutions are credit institutions and are accepting their customers' credit in order that these customers may use the cash received to buy goods and services and to carry on their own personal and business transactions.

Dangers in Using Credit

Although properly used credit is an efficient medium of exchange and an aid to the productive use of wealth and capital, its use also is associated with some dangers. There are, for example, times when the use of credit permits the capital of savers to be allocated to nonproductive rather than to productive uses. Thus, accumulation of savings may be lost by unwise acceptance of credit.

At times the use of credit can lead to the creation of an excessive or redundant medium of exchange. This may lead to overstimulation of business activity, to inflation and boom, to be followed by a corrective action. Such errors of judgment have widespread repercussions. Because credit joins all units of the economy together intimately, the entire economy suffers as a result of the errors of those who make mistakes in their use of credit. Just as credit benefits all members of the economic community, it can cause all to suffer.

Because there are dangers resulting from abuses and excesses in the use of credit, it is necessary that this social device be used with care. This means that buyers and sellers, borrowers and lenders, debtors and creditors, credit men and sales managers should all strive to use rather than to abuse the services which credit offers. Each creditor and each debtor should recognize his individual responsibility and try, so far as sound judgment permits, to avoid the mistakes which interfere with receiving the benefits which are otherwise gained from the use of credit.

Better understanding of the nature of credit and the role which it plays in our marketing and credit economy will contribute to the care with which credit is used. Debtors who understand the benefits which may be obtained from the use of credit, and the consequences which may follow its abuse, will use their credit more intelligently, more carefully, in a sounder manner. Credit managers who understand the principles which contribute to the safe use of credit will be more effective and will do a better job of controlling their acceptance of credit.

CLASSIFICATION OF CREDIT

Credit has been defined as a medium of exchange of limited acceptance. We have explained how credit differs from money and have pointed out that credit also may be viewed as a potential in the hands of users as well as a debt once the credit is accepted. The differences between credit and wealth and capital have been noted, and the dangers inherent in the use of credit have been discussed. But throughout this entire introduction, credit has been viewed primarily as one concept and no clear distinction has been made between the various and diverse types of credit that appear in our economy today. Thus it should be recognized that even though credit in general may be defined as a medium of exchange of limited acceptance, the specific aims and results of the different types of credit are multifold. While many classifications are possible and many have been used by other writers in this field, the following classification[8] is advanced with the view that it permits a workable examination of credit as it is in our present economy.

It will be noted that credit has been divided into two main classifications according to the form of the debtors' responsibility— private credit and public credit. The names given to these two major groups are indicative of the parties involved. Private credit is concerned with credit of individual ultimate consumers and with credit of private business concerns. It is with the field of private credit that this book is primarily concerned.

8 / This classification has been changed slightly from that shown in previous editions. Changes have been made to reflect the shifts in importance in the various types of credit plans.

Private Credit
  Consumer Credit
    Merchandise (Retail)
      Revolving
      Installment
      Open Charge
    Service
      Open Charge
      Revolving
      Installment
    Cash (banks, personal finance companies, etc.)
      Conventional Installment
      Other Types of Installment
      Single Payment
  Business Credit
    Merchandise and Services (Commercial or Mercantile)
    Cash (Financial) (banks, finance companies, factors, insurance companies, etc.)
      Long-Term Borrowing
      Intermediate-Term Borrowing
      Short-Term Borrowing
Public Credit (federal, state, and other governmental units.)

Public credit, on the other hand, involves the credit activities of the federal, state, and other governmental units. Whereas only limited space is devoted to the study of public credit, it must be recognized that private credit cannot be considered as operating in a vacuum, that is, completely separated and apart from public credit. The reason for this is that the use of credit by the various governmental units and by the institutions established to administer public credit has an important influence on the amount and types of private credit found in the economy. In the United States we have numerous governmental bodies—federal, state, and local—and the local become even more diffuse, such as municipal, school districts, sanitary districts, park boards, counties, townships, and similar units. A common characteristic of their credit is that it generally is not self-liquidating but is expected to be retired from payments made by the citizens. In the case of the federal government some agencies are given authority to borrow money; in the case of some states, road and bridge authorities and port authorities have this right. The quality of this credit and its acceptance by citizens ultimately rests on the ability of the governing body to service the debt by the collection of tax revenues, in other words the income of the citizens.

Consumer Credit

While the study of credit as a vital function of business was begun early in the 1900s, the attention that has been directed to consumer credit can be considered a present-day development. This phase of credit may be defined as the medium of exchange that an individual consumer may offer to a seller of goods or services or to a lender of money in order to obtain these items at the present moment on the promise to repay at some future time. In most texts on the subject of credit, the study of consumer credit has been relegated to a decidedly secondary position, with business credit, and in particular commercial credit, occupying the top position. Such an approach does not seem practical, as almost every student of credit—in fact practically every person in America—will at some time in his life come into contact with some phase of consumer credit. The extent to which a consumer uses his credit will vary, of course, with some individuals perhaps buying only the barest minimum on credit, such as utilities of gas, water, electricity, and telephone, as opposed to other persons who start using their credit extensively early in life and remain in a state of indebtedness throughout their lifetime. Such is not the case with business credit, as many individuals will never have occasion to come into contact with commercial credit and the other types of business credit.

Merchandise (Retail) Credit. This type of credit is concerned with the sale of goods on the retail level to the ultimate consumer. This sale may take place as a revolving credit, an installment, or an open charge transaction.

Retail Revolving Credit. This type of credit is a relatively new development in the field of consumer credit and has some of the characteristics both of an open charge account and of an installment account. Under the most common type of plan a customer is allowed to purchase goods and in return agrees to pay for them within some 25 to 30 days after statement closing date without a carrying charge. However, if total payment is not made, the customer agrees to make a monthly payment in which is included an interest charge for the privilege of using this type of credit. So long as the balance due is below the amount that the retail store believes the customer should not exceed, the customer is automatically eligible without any further investigation by the store to make additional purchases on her revolving credit account. Variations of this type of plan have appeared in many stores over the country. The use of revolving credit has had a very rapid growth, and today in many stores revolving credit has become the most important credit arrangement with customers.

Retail Installment Credit. Perhaps the type of consumer credit that has received the greatest attention over the years in the form both of praise and of criticism is retail installment credit. It is this form of credit that is involved when an agreement is reached between the buyer and seller by which payment for the goods is extended over a considerable period of time and by which a carrying charge is levied on the customer for this privilege of delayed payment. It generally involves the purchase of only one item and the installment account may be secured by some additional legal agreement. Retail installment credit, which takes many forms and is called by many different names, has become a permanent and integral part in facilitating the movement of the higher priced durable goods into the hands of the American family, thus providing a means of mass distribution needed by a mass-producing economy.

Closely connected with the retail installment field is the sales finance company, which has appeared in response to the growing demand for installment credit and the financing needs of retailers making installment sales. Likewise, commercial banks are important institutions as holders of installment paper sold to them by retail dealers.

Retail Open Charge Credit. Until the advent and growth of revolving credit, open charge (or as it is sometimes called, 30-day or regular or normal) credit was the type that the average housewife would think of first when she was asked what the term "credit" meant to her. Today, however, this type of credit has become almost universally restricted to the small retail establishment serving a limited clientele. This type of account enables the customer to purchase goods now and to pay for them usually 30 days later without any carrying charge or expense to the buyer. Any number of purchases may be made, provided that the combined dollar total does not exceed the credit limit that the store feels it can accept from that one individual. Many modifications of this type of credit are found in the retail establishments of the nation, with many similar plans appearing under widely varying names.[9]

Service Credit. This type of credit is often neglected or over-looked in any discussion of consumer credit, but it has rapidly become a customary method of doing business between consumers and business concerns and businessmen dealing in services. The doctor, the dentist, the lawyer—to name only a few—have become

9 / In some areas—particularly the West Coast—some retail firms have started honoring a club membership "cash" card and allowing discounts from their stated prices for cash payments. In effect, then, the quoted price is actually the credit price. See Claudia H. Deutsch, "Consumer Groups for Cash Buying," *Stores,* February 1971, p. 12.

accustomed to billing their customers for the services rendered. Today, more than ever before, the traveling American is using credit arrangements to pay for his hotel or motel accommodations and is encouraged to "charge" his air, bus, and rail transportation costs. The use of credit for utilities (gas, electricity, water, and telephone) is almost accepted without thought by most consumers. In this field of service credit, the three arrangements of open charge, revolving, and installment credit are found.

Cash Credit. Not only does credit facilitate the movement of goods and services to the consumer, but there is another whole field of credit activity in the loaning of *money* directly to the consumer. This money may be repaid under one of three arrangements: (1) conventional installment, (2) other types of installment, and (3) single payment. Although borrowing for personal use has occurred throughout history, cash loan credit as we know it today is a development of the past 50 years. Today we find consumer finance companies (or as they are sometimes called, personal finance companies or small-loan companies), commercial or industrial banks (personal or consumer loan departments), credit unions, savings and loan associations, insurance companies, and other types of lenders serving the needs of their customers through the loaning of money which consumers in turn agree to repay. An interest or carrying charge is almost always included in the amount repaid. The development and rapid expansion of this type of credit has been in response to the definite need for places to which consumers can go to obtain funds to meet emergencies and other vital requirements and which they can trust will not entangle them in such a mesh of legal terminology that repayment is almost an impossibility, with the skyrocketing borrowing costs characteristic of a "loan shark."

Although there is some controversy as to whether home mortgage loans should be considered a form of cash credit to consumers to be repaid in installments over an extended period of time, consideration will be given in this text to this type of credit which has been badly neglected in the credit literature. The tremendous upsurge since World War II in home building and in home buying urgently calls for a reappraisal and clear understanding of this type of credit. The American family in deciding to purchase a home is almost always committing a larger portion of its future income for this one good than for any other good that it will purchase. The amount borrowed generally will be the largest amount for which the family will offer its credit, and the repayment period certainly will extend over a period of time much longer than that involved in the purchase of any other good.

Business Credit

The second major field of credit appearing in our classification is that of business credit. It will be recalled that consumer credit was defined as a medium of exchange which an individual consumer may offer to a seller of goods or services or to a lender of money in order to obtain these items at the present moment on the promise to repay the debt incurred at some future time. This same definition applies equally well to business credit, if the word "business" is simply substituted for the word "consumer." Business credit is one of the principal means by which businessmen can translate into reality their interpretation of the opportunities that exist to carry on productive ventures. It thus gives businessmen a valuable means by which they may obtain goods and services (or money with which to purchase goods and services) vital to the successful operation of their business activities. Having performed their customary functions upon these goods and services obtained, the businessmen then endeavor to sell their products for a profit, thus enabling them to repay the debts created. Thus it may be said that business credit is self-liquidating.

The classification of business credit contains a two-way breakdown: (1) commercial (or mercantile as it is sometimes called) credit, and (2) cash (or financial as it is often called) credit.

Commercial Credit.   This form of credit is the type that enables a business firm to buy goods and services from another business concern and to pay for these items at some future time. If a firm sells both to consumers and to other business firms, only the credit sales to other firms are considered to come under the commercial credit classification. Commercial credit is perhaps the outstanding example of how the economy operates on a self-liquidating credit basis, with an estimated 90 to 95 percent of transactions between commercial and industrial concerns being carried on through the medium of credit exchange.

Cash (Financial) Credit.   As is true with consumers, business concerns also experience the need to borrow money to be repaid at some future time. The sole use of commercial credit would leave most business enterprises short of other capital requirements. Most businesses use their credit power to borrow cash to acquire both current assets and fixed assets and agree to repay the amounts borrowed on a long-term (over five years), an intermediate-term (one to five years), or a short-term (less than one year) basis. The principal sources of business loans are commercial banks, investment companies, insurance companies, factors, commercial finance companies, and individuals.

The first form of credit generally needed by a business firm starting operations is long-term (over five years) credit through which funds are obtained by the concern to enable it to purchase necessary plant and equipment. This long-term credit also is often needed by going concerns to refinance long-term obligations and to secure capital goods for replacement or for expansion purposes. It should be recognized, moreover, that most business concerns have need for additional investment capital for what is called an "intermediate" period of one to five years to meet the growing needs of a going operation.

Rounding out the needs of a business concern for money is that of short-term borrowing. The principal sources for this are commercial banks and commercial finance companies. In general, short-term loans from these sources are available to businesses for periods of less than one year and frequently for a maximum of two or three months and are designed to meet the current needs of businessmen for funds that will permit the completion of the production and marketing functions being performed.

HOW CREDIT IS STUDIED

There are many approaches that may be taken in the study of credits and collections. Most of the previous ones have tended to give greater emphasis to business credit, and in particular to commercial credit, and to view consumer credit in the light of a necessary but secondary activity. A quick glance at the table of contents of this book will show that the approach used here is one which recognizes that consumer credit has come of age and accordingly is awarded its true place of equal significance with business credit.

The social and economic problems connected with credit operations also are discussed. In this connection, attention is directed toward credit as an aid to mass production, mass distribution, and full employment. Likewise, the influence of consumer motives, habits, attitudes, and expectations on consumer spending is explored. The actions of the disorganized masses, the consumers, who are coming to be recognized as powerful forces in this age of consumerism, also are discussed. In addition, a summarization is made of the influence of credit on the business cycle.

A growing volume of legislation, particularly on the federal level, has been directed toward the credit field, and particularly toward consumer credit. Whereas a few years ago the credit industry operated practically untouched by state or federal legislation, this is not the case today. The most important of these legislative enactments are explored and explained as to their effects on present and future credit operations.

In the discussion of consumer credit, the descriptive approach has been followed first in order to present a picture of present-day credit arrangements that are available between the customer and the retailer, the service concern, and the financial institution. Too often there is the belief that since many of our more common forms of consumer credit have been in force for years, everyone knows about them and understands their operations. Experience has shown that this is anything but true, especially among people who are being exposed to a study of credit for the first time. In this descriptive matter attention also has been directed to the newer types of consumer credit that have appeared or have gained importance in recent years—for example, retail revolving credit, credit card plans, and various types of cash loan plans. More emphasis has been placed on service credit than has been the practice of other authors, as it is believed that this field of credit has grown in stature and importance in recent years and that it will show even greater strides in the future. The tremendous field of home mortgage loan credit is described, because of the vital place it occupies when any study is made of the debt of the American consumer.

After this preliminary descriptive approach, we then move to a general discussion of the problems and objectives of consumer credit management. This is designed to place credit activities in proper perspective in terms of the operations of the entire institution— retailing, service, or financial—and to relate these credit activities to the overall question of costs and profits. Management of credit operations is no different than management in any field of business. It consists of applying sound principles of management, which are general to all management problems, to the special technical or operational conditions of credit operations. Thus the good credit manager must know the technical aspects of credit work as well as the general management principles.

It is desirable at this point to emphasize the fact that while this book treats the problems of credit operation and management of the large firm, in no way is the small businessman neglected. It is recognized that in many instances the owner of the business is the buyer of the goods, the principal salesman, and the credit manager; there is not sufficient business nor adequate funds to establish any form of full-fledged operations. Yet this merchant has his problems of how to carry on his credit transactions in a profitable manner just as much as the large competitor next door with his computerized credit operations. Once a concern decides to embark upon a credit arrangement and decides to introduce such a policy, it has to decide what type or types of credit to accept, what standards it will use to judge the credit offered, what and how much investigation of the risk it will conduct, where it will secure the information on which to base the credit decision, what guideposts or warning signals it will use in determining the amount of credit to accept, how the credit department will be organized and what techniques of operation will be introduced, what types of salesmanship will be applied by the credit department, and how the collection policies and practices will implement the credit management techniques. It also should be emphasized that not only is the question of *what* action to take covered, but of equal or perhaps greater importance is the discussion of *why* such techniques, practices, and policies are adopted.

Practically the same approach is taken in the discussion of the commercial phase of business credit. This is done with the recognition that some duplication may occur. For example, there are certain principles and objectives in collection operations that are common to both consumer and commercial credit, but to take up a general discussion of collections after all other phases of consumer and commercial credit are discussed would defeat the plan of following through the consumer credit activity and the commercial credit transactions from the beginning to the logical and final conclusion—payment. While some duplication may result from this approach, the actions taken in these two major types of credit vary widely in many instances. For example, the wage assignment as a method of collection often appears in consumer credit but has no application in commercial credit.

In conclusion, attention then is directed toward those tools or measurements that are available to test the success or failure of a credit and collections system. By use of these techniques, credit management can endeavor to determine whether its operations have proved to be a "credit" to the firm.

REVIEW AND DISCUSSION QUESTIONS

1. Explain why we live in a credit world.
2. What is meant by the statement that credit is a medium of exchange?
3. Why is credit considered to have limited acceptance, while money is said to have unlimited acceptance?
4. What is the difficulty involved in defining credit as a power?
5. Discuss why credit is often confused with wealth and with capital.
6. Do you believe that credit increases or decreases a person's purchasing power? Explain your answer.
7. Explain the importance of credit in our mass-producing, mass-distributing economy.
8. Explain how the necessity of meeting installment payments may result in a family taking action to increase its purchasing power. Do you believe that this point of view is realistic or theoretical? Why?

9. Discuss how the individual consumer may use credit to raise his standard of living.
10. Distinguish between a retailer and a service concern operator.
11. What dangers can you see in the use of credit?
12. What are two main subdivisions of private credit?
13. What type of activities does public credit involve?
14. Distinguish between short-term, intermediate-term, and long-term borrowing.
15. Explain why retail open charge credit has become less important over the recent years.
16. Distinguish carefully between consumer credit and business credit.
17. Explain the most important differences between conventional installment cash loans and other types of installment cash loans.
18. Explain why some retail firms have started honoring a club membership "cash" card.
19. Discuss the trend in the growth of consumer credit, as shown in Table 1-1.
20. Propose another order in which the chapters of the book might be arranged.

2

The Economic and Social
Concepts of Credit

As the playwriters and musicians have told us that this is the "age of Aquarius," so have many writers and speakers told us that this is the "age of consumerism." And credit—particularly consumer credit—is one of the major topics to appear in the forefront of the discussion that has "attributed consumer unrest to rising public standards of business conduct and social responsibility brought about by increasing education and sophistication."[1]

Much has been written about the good and the evil of credit as a force in the social and economical development of our country. In this connection, the following comments of Professor Reavis Cox are very pertinent and revealing:[2]

When the country's output of goods and services grows rapidly, most people rejoice. The heads of the Federal agencies that compile statistics on national income find it expedient to announce their findings through the White House rather than through their own news bureaus. It will be the President himself who announces the glad tidings that gross national product has climbed to a new record high, that more people are employed than ever before, and that the greatest flood of purchasing power ever known is pouring into and out of the pockets of consumers. Everyone is happy.

Not so when, as is to be expected at such a time, consumer credit grows along with everything else in the economy. That this should be happening often seems to worry some otherwise optimistic observers. The fact that it is happening in the midst of booming prosperity seems actually to increase such concern. There is conjecture lest fair economic skies may be leading consumers to overextend themselves seriously. In gloomier moods they may even express a nagging fear

1 / Robert O. Herrmann, "Consumerism: Its Goals, Organizations and Future," *Journal of Marketing*, October 1970, p. 55.

2 / Reavis Cox, *Consumers' Credit and Wealth* (Washington, D.C.: National Foundation for Consumer Credit, 1965), p. 7.

that the prosperity so evident in the statistics rests upon a questionable foundation.

Sooner or later, must not consumers come to the point where they cannot afford to expand their debts further? Are they not making the whole economy vulnerable? If they run into even a small reduction of their incomes, may not a wave of defaults follow that will bring the whole edifice of prosperity crashing down?

As is true in many segments of our economy, it is no longer satisfactory to speak in terms of millions or billions when we are discussing what Americans owe. As seen in Table 2-1, Americans in 1970 owed each other 1.8 trillion dollars. Of this total, federal, state, and local governments owed approximately 26 percent; corporations, about 42 percent; and individuals and unincorporated businesses, approximately 32 percent. Of course, it should be remembered that every debt not only is owed by someone, it also is owed to someone. Thus there are actually two sides to each credit transaction.

TABLE 2-1
Debt Structure of the United States, 1940-70
(in billions of dollars)

	1940	1950	1963	1966	1969	1970
A. Net public and private debt:						
Public debt	61	240	349	388	451	483
Corporate debt	76	142	376	506	716	774
Individual and noncorporate debt	53	104	346	447	556	583
Total	190	486	1,071	1,341	1,723	1,840
B. Public debt by types:						
Federal debt	45	218	265	283	320	339
State and local debt	16	22	84	105	131	144
Total	61	240	349	388	451	483
C. Individual and noncorporate debt by types:						
Farm debt	9	12	33	42	56	59
Mortgages	26	55	199	252	305	321
Consumer	8	21	72	98	122	127
Commercial and financial	10	16	42	55	73	76
Total	53	104	346	447	556	583

Source: U.S. Department of Commerce, *Survey of Current Business,* May 1969, May 1970, and May 1971.

IS CREDIT PRODUCTIVE?

Despite the close relationship between government credit, business credit, and consumer credit and their foundation in our modern capitalistic system, there is no unanimity of opinion as to the economic significance of each type of credit. These differences in opinion are partly the result of regarding business credit and government credit as essentially *productive* in use and consumer credit as essentially a *consumptive* type of credit. Attempts to compartmentalize the types of credit by the use of the terms *productive* and *consumptive* and to regard only "productive credit" as beneficial to the economic welfare of the nation often lead to fallacious reasoning. Unfortunately, this very approach to credit matters is still practiced in some circles.

Some people hold the following views: business credit is productive in the sense that this type of credit facilitates the production of goods and services at a profit, which in turn liquidates the indebtedness; government credit, which is not self-liquidating, does, however, give rise to the production of goods and services and frequently sets the wheels in motion which produce the conditions for debt liquidation; and consumer credit is only consumptive in that it is used to acquire things for consumptive purposes. This view of consumer credit has led some people to regard the use of credit by consumers with reservation and even as ill-advised.

Another view, to which your author subscribes, is that *all* credit—government, business, and consumer—is productive and to view it otherwise is an economic fallacy. Consumer credit, which has been an instrument in raising our material standard of living, affording a host of consumer satisfactions and resulting in the creation of utility, cannot be regarded as anything but productive. There is no question that consumer credit serves a need of the American consumer and stimulates the economy in many ways. The tremendous program of building up great masses of consumer capital assets as undertaken by American consumers has been described as follows:[3]

Millions of individuals, each working for himself, have assembled the assets required. The result is a vast accumulation of wealth but, strangely, one that until recently has been overlooked by students of our economy because it produces services for direct use by consumers rather than something to be sold in the market place.

The piling up of this wealth in turn has been facilitated and speeded up by the liberal use of credit. We all know that there is no closely automatic correspondence between the times when consumers need things of this sort and the time when they have readily available the capital sums required to pay for them. Fortunately, many, while they could not conveniently pay lump sums for them, have been able to pay something down and agree to pay the rest in instalments. Because they wanted to mechanize their households quickly, they have been willing to pay something over and above the cost of the goods for the privileges of immediate possession with payment over time as consumption

3 / Cox, *op. cit.*, pp. 10-12.

proceeds. A result has been two simultaneous processes—accumulation of a great mass of consumer capital assets and the building up of a corresponding structure of intermediate and short-term debt to finance it.

Only in recent years have economists attached significance to the important place of credit in our economy. The reason for this is that several types of credit were of little or no significance in the marketplace until the middle or late 1920s. For example, consumer credit is a phenomenon of only the last four or five decades, but with enormous growth since World War II. In fact, the broadened scope of credit activities by financial institutions serving the credit needs of both consumers and businesses is of quite recent origin. Despite the prolonged use of some types of credit throughout the history of commerce and the importance of credit as a device for financing governments, few types of credit were used in the past in sufficient proportions to register an impact on business and consumer life.

Even though each type of consumer credit and each type of business credit represent highly specialized business activities, they nevertheless have far-reaching effects on the social and economic aspects of our nation. The same may be said for any of the public credit used by governmental bodies. Throughout this book the social and economic aspects of consumer credit and business credit are specifically emphasized so as to permit a keener appreciation of the role of credit.

THE ROLE OF CREDIT IN OUR ECONOMY

One way of appreciating the importance of credit in our economy is by examination of Figure 2-1. This chart shows the flow of goods and services from point of manufacture into the hands of consumers. Money and credit are exchanged for these goods and services as they progress through the channels and are finally purchased by consumers. While it is perhaps impossible to depict accurately the role of credit by means of a flow chart, it is desirable to sacrifice precision for the concept. The chart does, however, show the close interdependence which exists between consumer credit and much of the business credit used in producing and distributing the nation's goods and services.

Economists are not in agreement as to the particular forces which generate economic activity. For the purpose of our discussion, we take the view that the chain of events shown in Figure 2-1 commences when consumer demand is stimulated and consumer purchases materialize. Rather than pay cash, either because of greater convenience or because of necessity, many consumers will satisfy their material needs by use of their credit, or in other words, exchange their credit for goods and services. Retailers of goods and

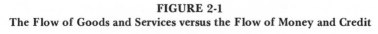

FIGURE 2-1

The Flow of Goods and Services versus the Flow of Money and Credit

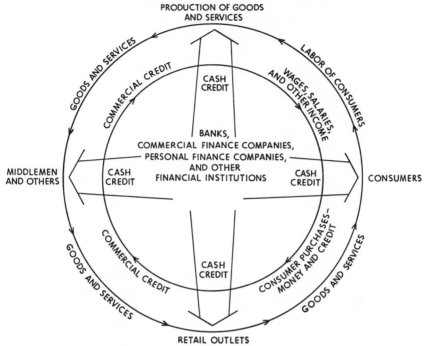

services then are *holders* of consumer credit, and in turn they finance their inventories and other working capital needs by using their business credit. Retailers' inventories are usually financed by middlemen and manufacturers as they *hold* the retailers' credit. This same chain of events repeats itself again and again with the multiplicity of transactions throughout the entire productive, distributive, and consumptive processes.

Financial institutions such as commercial banks, commercial finance companies, insurance companies, and personal loan institutions feed cash credit into the various segments of our production and distribution systems. This is also shown in Figure 2-1. Funds which are loaned to either businesses or consumers are utilized in any number of ways. Businesses may require additional cash for long-term needs such as financing plant and equipment, or for short-term needs such as financing inventories and other current assets. Likewise consumers have similar long-term and short-term cash needs, such as financing real estate purchases and durable goods such as automobiles and major appliances. The channeling of cash, or cash credit, into the various segments of the economy registers an impact on each using segment. In fact the economic segments are subject to the impact of cash credit supplied by financial institutions as well as the impact of that merchandise credit held by virtue of the flow of goods and services in the distribution channel. This "broad-broom" type of analysis indicates the interrelationships and interdependence of the various kinds of credit. Without this concept of the role of credit, an intelligent understanding of its importance is difficult to attain.

It is now desirable to point out that credit in our economy is best visualized as follows:[4]

As an Aid to Mass Production. Credit makes possible the productive genius of the nation's enterprises by providing the means by which manufacturing opportunities can become a reality. As markets for goods and services expand or contract, a manufacturing firm's credit stands ready as a flexible device to finance its operations. When businesses forecast profitable and expanding market opportunities, the need for business credit expands in order to finance at least a portion of the larger operations. Conversely, as the business outlook and opportunity appear to be declining, the need for credit declines, but the proportion of the business financial burden carried by credit may increase. Thus the attitudes and expectations of businessmen play a vital role in this connection. Local, state, national, and international conditions influence the hopes and fears of the business community. Confidence in governmental action can add to optimism, while distrust of governmental action can tend to produce the opposite effect.

As an Aid to Mass Distribution. Without mass distribution, its counterpart—mass production—would not be possible. A mass-distribution system is an essential to the objectives of a mass-production system, and again credit plays an important role. It is not enough that vast quantities of goods and a great variety of goods move through the marketing channels. The goods, services, and the marketing institutions themselves must be financed in one way or another. At each successive stage of distribution larger inventories and expanded business operations must parallel the accomplishment of the mass-distribution task. Credit's role is to provide the financial means, thereby permitting businessmen to take advantage of expanded market opportunities, both at home and in foreign markets. Larger inventories, for example, can be financed by commercial credit transactions between suppliers and resellers. Payment for the broader and deeper inventory lines is deferred until such time as the merchandise is sold. Consequently, middlemen can be more flexible in their decisions to take advantage of market opportunities not possible with the use of their own limited financial resources. Time

4 / See the Suggested Readings at the end of the chapter.

purchasing, especially in the case of automobiles, appliances, boats, and mobile homes, is a vital necessity in the movement of these goods along the trade channels to the hands of the consumer. The simple fact is that if credit were not available for mass distribution, mass production of these goods would not occur.

As an Aid to Full Employment It was not until 1946 that our federal government passed the Employment Act, which formalized its area of responsibility in promoting economic stability and so-called "full employment." This act proclaimed:

> The Congress hereby declares that it is the continuing policy and responsibility of the Federal Government to use all practicable means consistent with its needs and obligations and other essential considerations of national policy, with assistance and cooperation of industry, agriculture, labor and State and local governments, to coordinate and utilize all its plans, functions, and resources for the purpose of creating and maintaining, in a manner calculated to foster and promote free competitive enterprise and the general welfare, conditions under which there will be afforded useful employment opportunities, including self-employment, for those able, willing, and seeking to work and to promote maximum employment, production, and purchasing power.

In our attempts to attain the goals set forth in this act, we must recognize the important place that credit occupies in both government and private business efforts to provide full employment, despite the different interpretations that have been given to this term. The employment of labor to produce goods and services is, of course, largely dependent upon businessmen's forecasts of future market expectations, which are in turn importantly influenced by consumers' desires and their ability to fulfill these desires. Consumer credit is a vital link between mass production and mass distribution, because it functions to give most consumers the power to buy goods and services over and above their limited cash resources. Likewise, business credit is an aid to expanded employment inasmuch as it permits businessmen to expand their operations, and expanded business operations often have as their counterpart the employment of more labor.

Credit in the hands of consumers does not entirely influence the level of their consumption, but it does give them the potential of registering a significant impact on the quantity of goods and services consumed. Most American families depend on credit to help them acquire many high-priced goods and services, and their great inclination to use credit influences the level of employment. Today, for example, the *major* proportion of new homes and new automobiles is financed by means of installment credit, and a *substantial* proportion of all other "high-ticket" items is acquired in the same way. Quite obviously, if the families of today were required to pay cash for their homes and other high-priced consumer items, the demand for these products would be sharply curtailed, and the demand for labor in the producing firms would be reduced.

This subject of full employment has been clearly discussed by Professor Henry Kester as follows:[5]

> The level of employment in an economy is one of the indicators of its overall operating efficiency. As such, it is a relative term—like so many of those used by economists—and its use more or less reflects the view at any point in time as to the degree of total utilization of all economic resources. Therefore, when we talk about a fully-employed economy, we are merely indicating that in so far as it can be measured, we are using all of our resources at the highest level of efficiency. In many respects, it's like driving an automobile with the accelerator pushed to the floor-boards; and the economy—just like the car—is travelling at a rate of productivity consistent with the goal resources available or put into it—just as a car travels at a rate consistent with its total horsepower, as well as the level of head-power of its driver.

It also should be remembered that government itself is a large user of labor, both civilian and military. Under its obligations of the Employment Act of 1946, our federal government has at times used its credit to provide positions "for those able, willing, and seeking to work."

As an Aid to a Higher Standard of Living. American families enjoy the highest material standard of living in the world, and much of it is attributed to the abundant use of credit. The mass demand for consumer durables, stimulated by consumer credit, could have become a reality only by a change in attitudes toward credit. It was not until the mid-1920s that businessmen generally recognized consumer credit as an effective tool for increasing sales of high-priced items; and similarly, consumers changed their philosophies with regard to their use of credit to acquire the "better things in life." Today, rather than forgo the enjoyment of a higher standard of living, families use their credit to acquire durable goods. In this way they enjoy the goods and the higher level of living, and pay for them by means of "forced savings."

The widespread acceptance of credit as a socially desirable and safe medium with which to purchase durable goods has undoubtedly made possible the present scale of production of automobiles, refrigerators, automatic washers and dryers, television, and many other durable products. Business credit as the device which aids the mass production and flow of goods in the channels of distribution, and consumer credit in the hands of consumers, have made it possible for almost all families to share the products of our industries.

5 / From an address given by Dr. Henry I. Kester, Graduate School of Business Administration, University of Colorado, at the Nebraska Consumer Finance Association meeting, Omaha, Nebr., September 28, 1966. Also see Henry I. Kester, "Financing the Consumer in a Fully-Employed Economy," *Credit World,* February 1967, p. 18.

The tremendous extent to which American families have acquired these durable goods is shown in Table 2-2. This extensive use simply would not have been possible without credit.

It must be recognized that while the great mass of American consumers has been able to share in this rising standard of living, there still exists in many areas the situation of hopelessness, unemployment, and underemployment which all converge upon the low-income area resident to intensify the feeling that he may be

TABLE 2-2

Homes with Various Electrical Appliances

(as of January 1, 1970)

WIRED HOMES WITH			WIRED HOMES WITHOUT	
number	%		%	number
23,011,000	36.7	ROOM AIR CONDITIONERS	63.3	39,688,000
29,782,000	47.5	BED COVERINGS (ELEC.)	52.5	32,917,000
19,876,000	31.7	BLENDERS	68.3	42,823,000
27,086,000	43.2	CAN OPENERS	56.8	35,613,000
54,172,000	86.4	COFFEE MAKERS	13.6	8,527,000
14,860,000	23.7	DISHWASHERS	76.3	47,839,000
25,268,000	40.3	DRYERS, CLOTHES (ELEC. & GAS)	59.7	37,431,000
14,358,000	22.9	DISPOSERS, FOOD WASTE	77.1	48,341,000
18,559,000	29.6	FREEZERS, HOME	70.4	44,140,000
34,610,000	55.2	FRYPANS	44.8	28,089,000
15,110,000	24.1	HOT PLATES & BUFFET RANGES	75.9	47,589,000
62,386,000	99.5	IRONS (TOTAL)	.5	313,000
54,611,000	87.1	IRONS (STEAM & STEAM/SPRAY)	12.9	8,088,000
51,225,000	81.7	MIXERS	18.3	11,474,000
62,511,000	99.7	RADIOS	.3	188,000
24,014,000	38.3	RANGES, FREE-STANDING (ELEC.)	61.7	38,685,000
9,029,000	14.4	RANGES, BUILT-IN (ELEC.)	85.6	53,670,000
62,574,000	99.8	REFRIGERATORS	.2	125,000
61,884,000	98.7	TELEVISION, B & W	1.3	815,000
23,951,000	38.2	TELEVISION, COLOR	61.8	38,748,000
57,056,000	91.0	TOASTERS	9.0	5,079,000
56,868,000	90.7	VACUUM CLEANERS	9.3	5,831,000
57,620,000	91.9	WASHERS, CLOTHES	8.1	5,079,000
18,559,000	29.6	WATER HEATERS, (ELEC.)	70.4	44,140,000

All figures based on 62,699,000 and farm electric customers.

Source: *Merchandising Week*, February 23, 1970, p. 24. Reproduced with permission of *Merchandising Week*, a Billboard Publication.

forever denied the economic fruits of this society. As one speaker has put it, the following are examples of what the poor believe:[6]

1. With an income barely above the subsistence level, credit is almost unavailable to them for appliances.

2. Low-income credit applicants are treated discourteously—the more wealthy get the noticeably better treatment.

3. Many low-income residents use lay-by plans to purchase clothes, but by the time payment has been completed, many times the item is out of style.

4. Most of the time these community residents pay a higher price for purchasing less than a certain quantity.

5. The poorest quality of meats and fresh foods is sold at premium prices.

6. Where the grocer does extend credit, usually the prices for food are higher.

7. Ghetto merchants are viewed as over-selling their merchandise, and selling old merchandise as new.

8. Loan agencies charge a higher interest rate that bleeds the community of its resources and perpetuates poverty.

The interest of the federal government in this situation resulted in a Federal Trade Commission study which was based on a survey of 96 District of Columbia retailers of household furnishings and appliances with annual sales of at least $100,000. This survey of installment credit and sales practices was released in March 1968, and has resulted in a variety of actions and reactions. In an address given before the 1968 American Industrial Bankers Association's Public Affairs Conference, Commissioner Mary Gardiner Jones made the following closing remarks:[7]

There is little doubt that the low-income market is substantial. It is obvious that the disparities of opportunities and options available to the low-income consumers can no longer be tolerated. All of us must stop and re-examine our own responsibilities and obligation to determine whether there are areas in which we can take action now towards eliminating these disparities. I have suggested one such area. Others may prove more fruitful. My plea is only that the private sector, as one possible avenue for corrective action, re-examine its credit policies toward both the individual consumer and the low-income market retailer. The private sector must make certain that it is not arbitrarily denying credit to persons who in fact may be excellent credit risks and by the same token depriving itself of the opportunity to make its services available to this market to the maximum extent possible.

At approximately the same time, the following comments appeared in *The Credit World:*[8]

It is apparent that the solution to the problem of instalment credit for the poor requires a variety of actions. A requirement that finance charges be clearly

6 / John M. Warder, "How One Small Bank is Helping the Low-Income Consumer," *Industrial Banker,* April 1970, p. 8.

7 / Mary G. Jones, "Credit and Low-Income Consumers," *Industrial Banker,* May 1968, p. 14.

8 / "FTC Report on D.C. Credit Sales Practices," *Credit World,* April 1968, p. 11.

and conspicuously stated is a necessary but not a sufficient solution to the problem of instalment credit for those consumers who are considered poor credit risks and are unsophisticated buyers. Among the complementary steps which might be considered are the following: (1) make reasonable credit more accessible, perhaps through expansion of local credit unions; (2) provide counseling services which will encourage customers to practice comparison shopping; (3) equalize the legal right of buyers and creditors in instalment credit transactions, particularly with respect to garnishments and repossessions; (4) encourage additional businesses to enter the low-income market to intensify competition and bring lower prices; and (5) expand consumer protection activities on both federal and local levels to eliminate fraud and deceptions in advertising and offering credit.

In an attempt to start remedying this situation, retail firms and financial institutions[9] have become more active in trying to provide credit arrangements for low-income consumers. It should be recognized, however, that there is not complete agreement as to exactly what action to take and how to take it.[10]

CREDIT AND THE BUSINESS CYCLE

All credit, whether consumer credit, business credit, or government credit, can function as an activator or stimulant of business cycle fluctuations. Contrariwise, credit may also function to aggravate contracting phases of the business cycle.

In recessions and during periods of marked business declines, business purchases and consumer purchases are contracted to a level more in keeping with general economic conditions. As buyers (business and consumer) decide to reduce their purchases the need for their use of credit declines, and accordingly the volume also declines. On the other hand, during the recovery phases and prosperity phases of the business cycle, general optimism prevails among businessmen and consumers. The optimistic outlook results in increased purchases, and the use and volume of both business credit and consumer credit begin to increase.[11] During sustained periods of prosperity the influence of the high level of economic activity is generally reflected by a continuing high or increasing volume of credit.

Business credit and consumer credit also play some part in weakening economic forces during recessive stages of the business cycle. During the recession stages, credit men are torn between two opposing considerations. On one hand they would like to aid in

9 / See the Suggested Readings at the end of the chapter.

10 / "Spanish Harlem Furniture Seller Provides Credit, Plus High Prices and Hard Dunning," *Wall Street Journal,* August 28, 1970, p. 22.

11 / D. C. Sutherland, "How Will Our Recent Financial Problems Affect Credit in the Future?" *Credit and Financial Management,* August 1967, p. 20.

maintaining sales volume and even help to increase sales by relaxing their credit standards, but this adds to the risk of an already poor situation. So, on the other hand, they also are influenced by conservatism, the need to reduce risk, and generally they regard their customers as a deteriorating lot. Theoretically, the expansion of credit during the declining phases of the cycle will contribute to a softening of the trend downward. Practically, however, credit men, and for that matter their companies' managements, are not willing to act as public benefactors during this time. Instead they tend to adopt a policy of "tightening standards, limiting extensions, and pressing for collections." There is no question that this attitude tends to reduce sales (consumer and business) to a level much lower than safety might dictate. Perhaps most affected by these policies are the weaker buyers. The financial restraints placed on weak business concerns can be so great that they fail for want of financed working capital.

In a later stage, as general economic recovery prevails, credit men reverse their policy and now aid in increasing sales volume by accepting the credit of marginal buyers. The upswing of business conditions may be considerably exaggerated by credit men who now become overconfident and tend to evaluate customers' credit standing generously.

During sustained periods of business prosperity it is perhaps true that credit men, their standards of acceptability, and their thinking with regard to risk taking approach greater normalcy. What the norms should be is very difficult to establish, because each creditor is heavily influenced by his own operating and financial condition. But it is perhaps accurate to state that a higher degree of credit objectivity and normalcy will prevail during periods of sustained economic optimism.

Considering only one type of credit, consumer installment credit, we find the relation of this type of credit to economic stability has been of interest to the general public and to economists for many years. During the 1920s, when the first phase of discussion was taking place, consumer installment credit was growing fairly rapidly. During the depression and mild recovery years of the 1930s, a second phase developed, and consumer installment credit was viewed in light of the economic conditions then prevailing. A third phase began in 1941 with the wartime regulations of consumer credit and extended through the period of postwar regulation. A fourth phase is in full swing, in which the growing importance of the consumer as the key to economic activity is recognized. In fact, in this fourth phase the entire area of consumer credit and the recent legislative actions to regulate it have become subjects of vital interest, and their place in the age of consumerism is discussed in the following section.

THE PLACE OF CREDIT IN THE AGE OF CONSUMERISM

Consumerism has been a subject of increasing interest in recent business literature.[12] And credit is at the very heart of the present consumer movement, as evidenced by the passage on the federal level of the Consumer Credit Protection Act (popularly known as the Truth-in-Lending Act); the Fair Credit Reporting Act and the Credit Card Issuance Act (amendments of the Consumer Credit Protection Act); the Credit Control Act; and, on state levels, of the Uniform Commercial Code and the Uniform Consumer Credit Code.[13] As an illustration of the importance of credit in the current consumerism movement, Title I of the Consumer Credit Protection Act zeroes in on credit transactions and credit advertising. In its explanation of this act, the Commerce Clearing House made the following observations:[14]

Its purpose is to provide for a complete and conspicuous disclosure of credit charges in dollars and cents and as an annual percentage rate. The annual percentage rate will become the uniform standard of measurement in credit cost comparison. To make the rate meaningful, the Act contains a comprehensive definition of a finance charge so that there will be no doubt as to the component items that must be disclosed and reflected in the rate calculation.
. . . .
The basic philosophy behind the advertising mandates of Truth-in-Lending is all-of-it or none-of-it. You cannot tell part of the story of your credit terms without telling all.

In the Fair Credit Reporting Act, the interests of the consumer also were recognized as reported in the purpose of the act:[15]

There is a need to ensure that consumer reporting agencies exercise their grave responsibilities with fairness, impartiality, and a respect for the consumer's right to privacy.
It is the purpose of this title to require that consumer reporting agencies adopt reasonable procedures for meeting the needs of commerce for consumer credit, personnel, insurance, and other information in a manner which is fair and equitable to the consumer, with regard to the confidentiality, accuracy, relevancy, and proper utilization of such information in accordance with the requirements of this title.

12 / See the Suggested Readings at the end of the chapter.
13 / These laws are discussed in detail in the subsequent chapters.
14 / *Truth-in-Lending* (Chicago: Commerce Clearing House, Inc., 1969), pp. 6 and 45.
15 / Section 602 of the Fair Credit Reporting Act (amendment of Consumer Credit Protection Act), effective April 1971.

Various definitions of consumerism have appeared in the literature. One of the most commonly quoted (but perhaps narrow)
definitions has been offered by Peter Drucker:[16]

Consumerism means that the consumer looks upon the manufacturer as
somebody who is interested but who really does not know what the consumers'
realities are. He regards the manufacturer as somebody who has not made the
effort to find out, who does not understand the world in which the consumer
lives, and who expects the consumer to be able to make distinctions which the
consumer is neither willing nor able to make.

Another definition of consumerism has been given by Mrs.
Virginia H. Knauer, special assistant to the President for consumer
affairs, who pointed out that the watchword for the new consumer
agitation is simply, "Let the seller beware," in contrast to the old
statement of *caveat emptor* or "Let the buyer beware."[17]

When one begins to analyze the relative importance of the various
segments of the economy, he is struck by the dominant role played
by the behavior of the American consumer. It is amply implied in
Chapter 1 and to this point in this chapter that the consumer is the
most important single factor in determining the level of American
business activity. It has been only in recent years, namely since
World War II, that consumers' reactions in the marketplace have been
recognized as playing the dominant role of setting the pace and level
in the production and distribution of goods and services.

Writing on the importance of the consumer, Dr. S. Lees Booth of
the National Consumer Finance Association made these observations:[18]

Sociologists and economists have recognized in recent years the changing role
played by the consumer sector in the socio-economic pattern of America. At
various times in the past, the overwhelming developmental role in the economy
has been assumed as primarily a function of government or business enterprise or
a joint effort of the two. But with the maintenance of near full employment and
the increase in personal income since World War II, there has been a greater
discretionary role played by the consumer. In this role, he shifts the pattern of
his money outlays not only among various types of current expenditures but
also between investment in consumer durables and liquid savings. This ability to
ration expenditures for various purposes places the consumer sector in the
position of providing more funds for economic development and thus wielding
greater influence on economic growth and stability than was true when the
consumer was living on a near subsistence wage. Thus, social scientists, especially

16 / Peter Drucker, "Consumerism in Marketing," a speech to the National Association
of Manufacturers, New York, April 1969. The reader is also referred to Clifton H. Kreps, Jr.,
"The New Consumerism: Implications for Business," a speech to the Council on Trends and
Perspective of the Chamber of Commerce of the United States, Washington, April 15, 1969.

17 / "The Consumer Revolution," *U.S. News & World Report,* August 25, 1969, p. 43.

18 / *1966 Finance Facts Yearbook* (Washington, D.C.: National Consumer Finance
Association, 1966), pp. 2–3.

economists, are taking a new view of the consumer sector—not as a passive sector but one which provides much of the impetus for economic growth.

During recent years consumer purchases of durable goods, nondurable goods, and services account for approximately 60 to 65 percent of the gross national product. This has been true throughout the recent years, despite heavy government purchases and expenditures for national security. Another valuable observation is the fact that for more than three decades American consumers have spent more than 90 percent of their disposable income (personal income less taxes). The only exceptions to this are the depression years of 1932 through 1934, when they spent more than they earned, and during the World War II years, when savings rose rapidly because only limited goods were available. In general, consumers can be relied upon to spend a heavy proportion of their incomes on goods and services. In Figure 2-2, the personal income and consumer expenditure dollar in 1970 is shown, and the figures given bear out the previous statement that consumers tend to spend a large proportion of their income for personal consumption of goods and services.

Writing in his book *The Mass Consumption Society,* George Katona has pointed out that:[19]

The past few decades have seen the rise, here in America, of a new and unique phenomenon in human history, the mass consumption society. It is unique by virtue of three major features:

Affluence. Not a few individuals, nor a thin upper class, but the majority of families now have discretionary purchasing power and constantly replace and enlarge their stock of consumer goods.

Consumer power. Cyclical fluctuations, inflation or deflation, and the rate of growth of the economy—all now depend to a large extent on the consumer.

Importance of consumer psychology. In our economy, consumer demand is no longer a function of money alone. Discretionary demand, which has assumed a decisive economic role, is influenced and sometimes even determined by consumers' willingness to buy. In turn, the willingness to buy is a reflection of consumer motives, attitudes, and expectations.

This view, along with many others similarly expressed, supports the belief that the more modern approach is to regard business behavior as a product of consumer behavior. In other words, the quantities of goods and services purchased for industrial use and the eventual flow of finished goods through the channels of distribution are based on businessmen's forecasts of what the consumer is expected to do. In this country, where the consumer has the freedom to choose how he spends his income (to pay for current purchases or to pay for prior purchases made under some credit arrangement) and also the freedom to shift his purchases from product to product, the consumer is the *key* to business health.

19 / New York: McGraw-Hill Book Co., Inc., 1964, p. 3. Used by permission of McGraw-Hill Book Co.

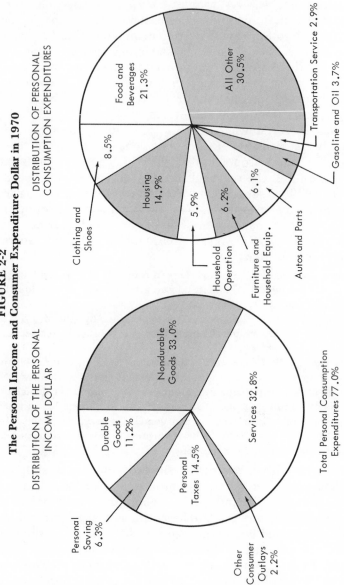

FIGURE 2-2
The Personal Income and Consumer Expenditure Dollar in 1970

DISTRIBUTION OF THE PERSONAL INCOME DOLLAR

DISTRIBUTION OF PERSONAL CONSUMPTION EXPENDITURES

Personal Saving 6.3%

Durable Goods 11.2%

Nondurable Goods 33.0%

Personal Taxes 14.5%

Services 32.8%

Other Consumer Outlays 2.2%

Total Personal Consumption Expenditures 77.0%

Total Personal Income in 1970— $801.0 billion

Clothing and Shoes 8.5%

Food and Beverages 21.3%

Housing 14.9%

5.9%

Household Operation

6.2%

Furniture and Household Equip.

6.1%

Autos and Parts

All Other 30.5%

Gasoline and Oil 3.7%

Transportation Service 2.9%

Total Consumption Expenditures in 1970— $616.7 billion

Source: U.S. Department of Commerce and 1971 *Finance Facts Yearbook* (Washington, D.C.: National Consumer Finance Association, 1970), p. 35.

THE CHANGING ROLE OF CREDIT AND THE NEED FOR EDUCATION

Despite the important role played by credit in our economy, there is little agreement as to its effects and its desirability. Many consumers still view the use of credit in acquiring material things as dangerous and imprudent. Some of these same attitudes and beliefs are held by various writers because of their refusal to regard the consumption function as the dominant objective of economic activity. Furthermore, commercial credit, which is emphasized in the last half of this book, has often been overlooked as an important device for financing the short-term needs of businessmen. It is believed that in the future a growing amount of emphasis and economic significance will be given to both consumer credit and commercial credit. If this does occur, many of the views stressed in the preceding pages will be more universally understood.

It is believed that credit will play an increasingly important role in our economy. Those who refer to ours as a "credit economy" are apparently accurate in their description of its role, inasmuch as credit has replaced to a marked degree the use of cash as a medium of exchange. This is true for an increasing proportion of transactions by government, business, and the consumer. There are also a number of underlying techniques to expand the opportunities for consumers to buy on credit. Almost every conceivable line of merchandise and most consumer services appear destined for purchase by means of credit.

Recent predictions[20] have been made that American business (particularly banking and retail credit), as it is now operating, may not exist a decade from now. Electronic data processing, it is claimed, is on the verge of changing the very nature of money, and checks and credit cards as we presently know them are on the way out. It is predicted that within a few years, money transfers will be made instantaneously through electronic impulses and computers and that the impact on all segments of our economy will be staggering. Other aspects of this predicted "cashless-checkless" society of the future will be discussed in subsequent chapters.

In view of the increased and changing use of consumer credit, a spontaneous interest has arisen in education to help the consumer understand credit in its many forms and varieties and to use credit more intelligently and judiciously.

Writing in the *Industrial Banker,* Dr. Ernst A. Dauer, Director of Consumer Credit Studies for Household Finance Corporation, discusses the following objectives that the Consumer Education

20 / See the Suggested Readings at the end of the chapter.

Curriculum Development Committee of the State of Illinois developed to guide the consumer education of students early in their lives:[21]

... (1) to understand the role of the consumer in our economy; (2) to develop the ability to make rational choices among alternatives; (3) to introduce sources of information which can aid the student as a consumer throughout life; (4) to recognize and learn to avoid certain pitfalls that could greatly reduce real income; (5) to develop skills needed to solve new consumer problems as they arise; (6) to show the relevance of economic principles to personal economic competence and develop basic economic understanding, a requisite for responsible citizenship; (7) to become aware of the dependence on society for consumption and of reciprocal responsibilities to obtain greater satisfaction and benefits through proper utilization of economic resources.

It is becoming more and more apparent each day that[22]

education of both the users of credit and those who grant it is more urgently needed and more important now than it ever was. Understanding of the problem, and a whole-hearted dedication to a sane and effective solution—on the part of all segments of business and society—is also now of greater priority than it has ever been.

REVIEW AND DISCUSSION QUESTIONS

1. What is meant by the title of the chapter, The Economic and Social Concepts of Credit?
2. Do you believe that credit is productive? Why or why not? Explain.
3. Why has the significance of credit been stressed only in recent years?
4. In what ways are the various types of consumer credit and the various types of business credit interdependent?
5. Why would an economist look at credit in a different light than a marketing executive would? Under what circumstances would they have practically the same ideas about credit?
6. Explain how personal consumption expenditures affect the economic activity of the nation.
7. As a businessman, what advantages do you see in the intelligent use of business credit? What disadvantages?
8. Explain how credit functions as an aid to mass production, to mass distribution, to full employment, and to a higher standard of living.
9. What was the basic purpose of the Employment Act of 1946?

21 / "Consumer Credit Education," *Industrial Banker,* April 1969, p. 7. Also see D.D. Lintvet, "Consumer Education Begins Early," *Credit Management Year Book, 1968-69,* p. 87; and Robert Dolphin, Jr., "Education of the Financially Distressed," *Quarterly Report,* Winter 1970, p. 8.

22 / S. C. Patterson, "Educating Consumers About Personal Credit," *Credit World,* March 1968, p. 24. Also see "Consumer Credit Information and Education Is Vital," *Industrial Banker,* December 1969, p. 9; and "Credit Education," *Management,* October 1969, p. 3.

10. How would you measure the standard of living of an individual?
11. Why don't credit men attempt to expand credit during the recession phase of a business cycle when it is perhaps most needed?
12. What are some of the more important social implications of the widespread use of credit?
13. Discuss the problems involved in accepting the credit of the low-income individual.
14. What is meant by the "age of consumerism"?
15. What evidences of the consumer movement are apparent in the business concerns of your community?
16. Prepare your own definition of consumerism.
17. What educational courses in credit are given in the public school system of your community?

SUGGESTED READINGS

Role of Credit in the Economy

Genser, Harold A. "Consumer Credit as a Tool for Economic Democracy," *Credit World,* July 1967, p. 19.
Jones, Mary G. "Role of Business Government," *Industrial Banker,* January 1969, p. 5.
Miller, Herman P. "Tomorrow's Consumer," *Journal of Consumer Credit Management,* Summer 1970, p. 22.
Rogers, Hewitt. "The Fundamentals of Consumer Credit," *Credit World,* December 1969, p. 10.
Watkins, Henry C. "Consumer Credit in the 1970s," *Industrial Banker,* December 1969, p. 13.

Credit for Low-Income Consumers

Bowditch, Nathaniel R. "Developing the Black Market," *Journal of Consumer Credit Management,* Fall 1969, p. 41.
"Credit Extension to the Low-Income Consumer," *Department Store Management,* February 1970, p. 21.
O'Brien, William M. "Credit Unions to Serve Low-Income Families," *Credit World,* January 1969, p. 15.
Petrof, John V. "Black Men's Attitudes Toward Credit Practices," *Journal of Consumer Credit Management,* Winter 1970, p. 88.
"Ward's Credit for Welfare Recipients; S.M.I.'s 'Conflict' Seminar," *Chain Store Age,* March 1970, p. E2.
"Where Negro Business Gets Credit," *Business Week,* June 8, 1968, p. 98.

Credit in the Age of Consumerism

"And Now, a Message from the Consumers," *Fortune,* November 1969, p. 103.
"Business Responds to Consumerism," *Business Week,* September 6, 1969, p. 94.
Buskirk, Richard H. and Rothe, James T. "Consumerism—An Interpretation," *Journal of Marketing,* October 1970, p. 61.

Day, George S. and Aaker, David A. "A Guide to Consumerism," *Journal of Marketing,* July 1970, p. 12.

Herrman, Robert O. "Consumerism: Its Goals, Organizations and Future," *Journal of Marketing,* October 1970, p. 55.

Jones, Mary G. "The Role of the FTC in Increasing Consumer Awareness and Meeting Consumer Credit Problems," *Consumer Finance News,* March 1971, p. 8.

Lavidge, Robert J. "The Growing Responsibilities of Marketing," *Journal of Marketing,* January 1970, p. 25.

The Changing Role of Credit

Appell, Allen L. "Does the Public Really Want a Cashless Society?" *Bankers Magazine,* Spring 1970, p. 48.

"Money Goes Electronic in the 1970s," *Business Week,* January 13, 1968, p. 54.

Reistad, Dale E. "Electronic Money Makes Its Bid," *Savings and Loan News,* September 1970, p. 36.

——. "Tell It Like It Is," *Credit World,* March 1970, p. 13.

——. "The Implications of the Checkless Society," *Credit World,* November 1967, p. 9.

——. "Vestibule Banking," *Credit World,* June 1970, p. 19.

PART II

Understanding
Consumer Credit

3

Growth, Regulation, and Use of Consumer Credit

Contrary to common belief, consumer credit dates back to ancient times. This may come as a surprise to many people, who tend to regard the growth and use of consumer credit as a present-day business development and operation. However, it is quite true that most of our modern-day credit institutions, as we know them, are of fairly recent origin. Likewise, the story of the development of consumer credit, like so many other business phenomena, is one of dramatic change and growth. Accompanying this change and growth has been the changing attitude of government, both federal and state, toward controlling the use of consumer credit.

Thus it is important to discuss the growth, regulation, and use of consumer credit in order to increase our understanding of its importance today.

GROWTH OF CONSUMER CREDIT

Early Days of Consumer Credit

The buying of goods to be paid for at some later date and the borrowing of money to be repaid sometime in the future are prehistoric practices. There is much documentary evidence that consumer credit played an important role in ancient societies. Some of this evidence has been uncovered by archaeologists, while the Bible provides us with numerous references to creditor practices, credit regulations, and the actions of debtors. Writers of history tell us of many early uses of consumer credit. For example, Paul Einzig, an English monetary authority, points out: "Credit existed on a fairly extensive scale long before the stage of money economy was reached."[1] He makes reference to the fact that in many primitive societies, with no trace of a medium of exchange, transactions involving credit in kind played an important part in the life of primitive communities. Even before the development of barter, credit existed because of discrepancies between the values in goods or services traded or because deliveries had to be deferred because of natural conditions. Typically, a creditor would loan seed to a debtor who would repay his debt out of the next harvested crop. Primitive man appears to have used his credit for other reasons too. Rents for land and shelter were fixed in kind over long periods of time, and loans were made to enable debtors to pay ". . . ransom fines, tribute, blood money, bride money . . ." and to carry on trade.[2]

Turning now to the early history of the United States, we find much interesting evidence of consumer credit practices. One example is Wilbur C. Plummer's informative study of consumer credit in colonial Philadelphia.[3] In this early period of United States history, Philadelphia merchants were accustomed to sales on credit for all kinds of commodities and services. Plummer's examination of professional and business records shows conclusively that it was common to transact the major proportion of business on credit. In fact, he writes ". . . it seems certain that credit rather than cash was the rule."[4]

It is impossible to draw reliable conclusions on the volume of consumer credit during these early periods. Reliable data were not gathered on this subject until 1930 by the U.S. Bureau of the Census. Despite this limitation of data, several types of consumer credit-granting institutions are known to have developed in the period from 1800 to the Civil War. The merchant, the physician, and the pawnbroker were the principal agencies of consumer credit. Business records and advertisements of some early businesses and professional men are available in museums and certain libraries. These sources of data permit historical researchers to make reliable generalizations on the growth and uses of consumer credit during the formative years of the United States.

Merchants prior to the Civil War not only sold merchandise on the open-book account, but they sold pianos, organs, sewing machines, stoves, and other items on the installment plan. Service credit was granted principally by physicians and dentists. Credit extended by physicians was the earliest type of service credit, and much of it was uncollectible. This was caused by the ethics of the medical

1 / *Primitive Money* (London: Eyre & Spottiswoode, 1949), p. 372.

2 / *Ibid.*, pp. 372-73.

3 / "Consumer Credit in Colonial Philadelphia," *Pennsylvania Magazine,* October 1942, p. 385.

4 / *Ibid.*, p. 409.

profession, which provided services without regard to ability to pay. Pawnbrokers were the first agency to make cash loans to the consumer in this country. By 1800 they were operating in New York City, Philadelphia, and Boston on an extensive scale. In certain respects the pawnbroker is not a consumer credit agency, because his transactions involve no explicit promise to pay. His claim is against the property which is pledged in exchange for the cash loan. Technically, the transaction is a conditional purchase of the "borrower's" personal property. In this respect the pawnbroker resembles a merchant more closely than a consumer credit agency.[5]

Consumer Credit between 1860 and 1920

During this period of United States history, dramatic economic changes took place. Large numbers of people were drawn from farms to industrial cities; manufacturing industries became firmly rooted and prosperously large; the interior territories of the country grew rapidly; and many department stores and chain retail institutions had their origins during this period. Paralleling these developments were the more widespread extension of installment credit, the rise of the small loan business, and the origin of several important consumer credit institutions and associations.

The credit policies that characterized the period prior to 1860 were liberalized shortly thereafter, and goods of many descriptions were commonly sold on the installment basis. Pianos, organs, melodeons, and stoves were sold on liberal terms and low down payments. Nugent writes, "By 1870 furniture dealers in the principal industrial cities had begun to sell goods on small down-payments and long-term contracts to wage-earners of very modest incomes."[6] Newspaper advertisements of retailers in the larger cities offer much evidence of a general liberalization of credit terms during this period.

The small loan business had its origin in Chicago about 1870 and spread rapidly to the principal cities of the East and Middle West. Household Finance Corporation, the largest personal loan company in the nation, was established in 1878. Other well-known companies in this field originated at about the same time. The more successful personal loan companies organized chains of offices which operated over wide geographical areas. This type of consumer credit grew so rapidly that by 1910 the two largest companies had more than 100 offices in operation, and several companies had more than 30 offices.

5 / Rolf Nugent, *Consumer Credit and Economic Stability* (New York: Russell Sage Foundation, 1939), pp. 42-64. The first several chapters of this book are an excellent reference for the reader who desires an authoritative account of the early growth and development of consumer credit in the United States.

6 / *Ibid.*, p. 66.

A large number of single-office companies had started operations by 1910. Small personal loans to wage earners were the outgrowth of the sociological changes of the times. Wage earners, out of necessity, required personal loans to pay debts, meet emergency needs, and to compensate for differences in income and expenses. The origin and rapid growth of the small loan business are testimony to the fact that a large proportion of American families and individuals had no source of funds with which to meet emergencies. For the most part this group of cash lenders loaned money on the security of chattel mortgages on household furniture, wage assignments, or unsecured promissory notes. It was many years later that banks of the United States recognized cash loans to consumers as a legitimate phase of their operations.

In 1907 and 1908 the Russell Sage Foundation financed studies of the personal loan business, which had attracted many lenders who charged exorbitant rates of interest, practiced deception, and utilized questionable collection practices. After careful investigation, the foundation concluded that the most effective way of combating questionable practices was to legalize an interest rate on small loans that would be sufficient to attract reputable businessmen into the business. In 1911 Massachusetts enacted a consumer loan law based on the findings and recommendations of the Russell Sage Foundation. One state after another enacted the Uniform Small Loan law. This law was originally drafted by those lenders willing to submit to regulation. The law has since served as a model and basis for legislation in most states. Today a majority of these states have adopted legislation based on the original provisions of the Uniform Small Loan law.

With the growing demand for small loans and the need for legitimate organizations to meet the demand, the credit union and industrial bank developed in the United States. The first credit union was organized in 1909 in Manchester, New Hampshire, and within several years 142 credit unions were operating in six states. Paralleling this rapid development was the growth of the industrial bank. Credit unions are cooperative associations, while industrial banks are business corporations. Further discussion of these cash lending associations will be found in Chapter 8.

The growth of consumer credit reporting agencies closely accompanied the growth of consumer credit granting. As early as 1906, 30 credit reporting bureaus banded together to provide for an interchange of information. This amalgamation arose from the need for credit information as to the extent of obligations existing at any one time against an individual. Singular developments of this nature could not have occurred except for the rapid and widespread use of consumer credit in our economy.

Consumer Credit between 1920 and 1930

The automobile, the electric washing machine, the vacuum cleaner, and other household goods made great strides during this period. Consumers began to enjoy a wider variety of goods, many of which contributed to an increased enjoyment of life. The widespread use of such merchandise called for even greater utilization of credit arrangements. Several hundred sales finance companies were established during this period. Many of them grew to large proportions in a matter of a few years.[7] Paralleling this development, other consumer credit institutions had similar growth and development, as the greater variety of goods found their way into American homes. Merchants who formerly had regarded installment selling with skepticism now began to regard time payment plans as an integral part of their merchandising programs. While this type of selling was enjoying a rapid growth and was gaining a more respectable place in the American economy, the cash lending institutions were also registering dramatic change. From 1923 to 1929 the number of regulated small loan offices increased from about 600 to approximately 3,500. The services of these institutions were in such great demand by American households that they increased their loan balances sixfold.[8] This rapid growth followed closely after the enactment of small loan laws in many states. Credit unions, industrial banks, and the personal loan departments of commercial banks underwent rapid growth and their loan balances increased in similar proportions. In 1928 the National City Bank of New York organized a personal loan department. This step, by the then largest bank in the world, met with mixed reaction in banking circles. Soon thereafter, however, many other banks took the same step and actively entered the consumer loan field.

The developments cited in this section indicate in general a decreasing prejudice against installment selling and small loan operations. The retail charge account expanded to greater proportions during this period. This type of consumer credit was accepted by more stores, and a greater number of families began to enjoy its benefits. As the retail charge account came into widespread use, retail merchants began to recognize credit accommodation as a competitive force. It took only the short span of years during this period for credit to become firmly established as a retail promotional device. Retail store customers in increasing numbers began to "expect" this service.

It was generally apparent toward the end of this period that consumer credit had become an important force in the American

7 / Thomas W. Rogers, *The Development of the Sales Finance Industry in the United States* (Chicago: American Finance Conference, 1954).

8 / Nugent, *op. cit.*, p. 99.

economy. The first organized attempt to collect and analyze consumer credit statistics was made by the Bureau of Foreign and Domestic Commerce of the U.S. Department of Commerce. These studies were undertaken at the request of the National Retail Credit Association (now the International Consumer Credit Association). The first published analysis of consumer credit statistics revealed that a sizable proportion of total retail sales were credit sales. Table 3-1 is a summarization of the data for January-June 1930. The economic importance of consumer credit, which had been claimed by many students of the subject, now became a realistic fact as shown by these data. Hence, this period was one in which consumer credit became a common occurrence for many American families, as more and more merchants adopted the policy of selling merchandise for credit as well as for cash.

TABLE 3-1
Methods of Payment as Percentages of Total
Sales in Various Stores
(January-June 1930)

		Credit	
Type of Retail Store	*Cash*	*Open*	*Installment*
Department	47.4	45.6	7.0
Furniture	8.5	27.8	63.7
Jewelry	24.0	56.4	19.6
Men's clothing	42.4	54.6	3.0
Shoes	58.4	41.6	. . .
Women's specialty	42.7	56.5	.8
Electrical appliance	12.7	16.3	71.0

Source: *Retail Credit Survey, January-June 1931,* U.S. Department of Commerce, Domestic Commerce Series No. 53, p. 2.

Consumer Credit since 1930

The American economy has been subjected to a series of strenuous tests since 1930. In September 1929, the stock market collapsed and the so-called Great Depression ensued. After a brief period of recovery the United States was plunged into World War II. After almost four years of intensive war effort, 1946 marked the beginning of a period of great prosperity and inflation. These diverse conditions affected the growth and use of consumer credit in many ways. A study of the pattern of consumer credit during these periods is both interesting and revealing to the student and practitioner.

An analysis of consumer credit statistics shows that fluctuations in the volume of consumer credit are closely related to general economic conditions. All types of consumer credit are somewhat deflated during prolonged depressions and conversely inflated when the nation is prosperous. From the graphic presentation in Table 3-2, it can be seen that the volume of consumer credit reflects to a marked degree general business conditions. During the period of the Great Depression, it will be noted that charge account and service credit deflation were moderate as compared to installment accounts and single-payment loans. This may be accounted for by the fact that installment credit and single-payment loans are utilized for different reasons than service credit and the charge account. The latter two types of consumer credit are primarily a convenience to the customer, whereas the former types come into use by virtue of necessity. Another fact which may explain this phenomenon is that during hard times consumers have a greater tendency to cut back rapidly on merchandise of high unit value. Further, it may be added that charge account credit and service credit represent a relatively small volume of the total credit, and they are generally considered nonpromotional forms of credit. It is quite obvious from these data that consumers drastically adjusted downward their purchases of durable goods during the early 1930s. Purchases of automobiles, radios, household appliances, and other items of high unit value could well be postponed, whereas the purchase of merchandise or services for "everyday living" could not be as readily delayed.

The rapid deflation of consumer credit continued until 1934 when an upturn in general business conditions began. By 1936 and continuing through 1941, the recovery from the Great Depression had come about. Relatively prosperous times followed the depression, as the United States became an arsenal for its allies who were involved in the early stages of World War II. It is well to note that installment credit, which resulted principally from the sales of new and used automobiles, led the expansion of consumer credit just as it led the earlier deflation.

The World War II period was characterized by a scarcity of consumer goods. The mass production facilities of the entire nation were quickly converted to production for a wartime economy. Consumer durable goods of all types virtually disappeared from the retail stores, as the raw materials used in their manufacture were diverted to war goods. Only the essential consumer goods remained available, often at a sacrifice of quality. Here again installment credit led the deflation of consumer credit. Even though the American worker had increased earnings to spend, he found little on which to spend his money. It should be noted that charge account credit and service credit volumes increased during the war. The higher levels of charge account credit which were attained may be explained by the increased ability of consumers to maintain a high-level consumption

TABLE 3-2
Volume of Consumer Credit by Major Types
(millions of dollars)

End of Year	Total Consumer Credit	Install- ment	Single- Payment Loans	Charge Account	Service Credit
1929	6,444	3,151	1,112	1,602	579
1930	5,767	2,687	1,037	1,476	567
1931	4,760	2,207	772	1,265	516
1932	3,567	1,521	549	1,020	477
1933	3,482	1,588	450	990	454
1934	3,904	1,871	493	1,102	438
1935	4,911	2,694	575	1,183	459
1936	6,135	3,623	707	1,300	505
1937	6,689	4,015	797	1,336	541
1938	6,338	3,691	777	1,362	508
1939	7,222	4,503	787	1,414	518
1940	8,338	5,514	800	1,471	553
1941	9,172	6,085	845	1,645	597
1942	5,983	3,166	713	1,444	660
1943	4,901	2,136	613	1,440	712
1944	5,111	2,176	624	1,517	794
1945	5,665	2,462	746	1,612	845
1946	8,384	4,172	1,122	2,076	1,014
1947	11,570	6,695	1,356	2,353	1,166
1948	14,398	8,996	1,445	2,673	1,284
1949	17,305	11,590	1,532	2,795	1,388
1950	21,395	14,703	1,821	3,291	1,580
1951	22,617	15,294	1,934	3,605	1,784
1952	27,520	19,403	2,120	4,130	1,867
1953	31,393	23,005	2,187	4,274	1,927
1954	32,464	23,568	2,408	4,485	2,003
1955	38,830	28,906	3,002	4,795	2,127
1956	42,334	31,720	3,253	4,995	2,366
1957	44,971	33,868	3,364	5,146	2,593
1958	45,129	33,642	3,627	5,060	2,800
1959	51,544	39,247	4,129	5,104	3,064
1960	56,141	42,968	4,507	5,329	3,337
1961	57,982	43,891	5,136	5,324	3,631
1962	63,821	48,720	5,456	5,684	3,961
1963	71,739	55,486	6,101	5,903	4,249
1964	80,268	62,692	6,874	6,195	4,507
1965	90,314	71,324	7,671	6,430	4,889
1966	97,543	77,539	7,972	6,686	5,346
1967	102,132	80,926	8,428	6,968	5,810
1968	113,191	89,890	9,138	7,755	6,408
1969	122,469	98,169	9,096	8,234	6,970
1970	126,802	101,161	9,484	8,850	7,307

Note: Consumer credit data have been revised at various times, for various series, and for various periods of years. For these reasons, the consumer credit data cannot be considered to be strictly comparable for every year from 1929 to the present. The data shown are exclusive of home mortgage loans.

Source: Board of Governors of the Federal Reserve System.

of those goods which were available in retail stores. The service credit increase seems to reflect the ability of the American consumer to seek professional services which might have been postponed during the previous decade.

Since the end of World War II the growth of consumer credit has been phenomenal. In one decade, from the end of 1946 to the end of 1956, consumer credit expanded more than five times. The postwar prosperity saw the vast production facilities of American industry turned to the production of consumer goods. Not only did American industry produce consumer goods at an unparalleled pace, it also provided a greater variety of goods than the American consumer had imagined possible. Since 1950, the vast majority of consumers have bettered their standard of living by purchasing the outputs of industry. Automobiles were purchased at an unprecedented rate; black-and-white or color television became a reality to the vast majority of American households; dream kitchens and completely modernized household laundries have relieved the housewife of much of the drudgery of the homemaking tasks; stereos, deepfreeze units, and large and small appliances of every description became commonplace in millions of American homes. Consumer credit facilitated the mass distribution of these goods, inasmuch as the major proportion of consumer durable goods were purchased through consumers' utilization of their credit. Future expansion of living standards and consumer markets will most certainly be accompanied by additional surges of consumer credit.

CONSUMER CREDIT RELATIVE TO BUSINESS ACTIVITY

Inasmuch as the absolute dollar amounts of consumer credit outstanding do not show its growth in proper perspective, it is necessary to relate consumer credit to other important economic factors. Other important relatives to the volume of consumer credit are retail sales, disposable personal income, and personal savings. Table 3-3 shows these important economic factors in two ways. It will be noted that when the data are not adjusted for the influence of higher prices, the percentage increase reaches great magnitudes. Hence, the unadjusted percentage increase of consumer credit from 1941 to 1970 is 1,278.3 percent, while retail sales, disposable personal income, and personal savings registered increases for the same period of 559.3 percent, 638.7 percent, and 356.4 percent, respectively. Another and perhaps more objective approach to the analysis of these data is to adjust them for changes in the consumer price index and hence remove the influence of higher prices. The consumer price index from 1941 to 1970 (using 1967 as 100 percent) rose from 44.1 to 116.3, an increase of 163.7 percent. When

TABLE 3-3
Growth of Selected Economic Factors, 1941 and 1970
(dollars in billions)

Economic Factor	1941	1970	Increase	Percent Increase
Consumer credit*				
Unadjusted	$ 9.2	$126.8	$117.6	1,278.3
Adjusted	20.9	109.0	88.1	421.5
Retail sales				
Unadjusted	55.3	364.6	309.3	559.3
Adjusted	125.4	313.5	188.1	150.0
Disposable personal income				
Unadjusted	92.7	684.8	592.1	638.7
Adjusted	210.2	588.8	378.6	180.1
Personal savings				
Unadjusted	11.0	50.2	39.2	356.4
Adjusted	24.9	43.2	18.3	73.5
Consumer price index				
(1967 = 100)	44.1	116.3	. .	163.7

*End of year figures.
Source: *Federal Reserve Bulletin,* June 1971, pp. A54 and A62. *Survey of Current Business,* May 1971, pp. S-2 and S-5.

this adjustment is made, it is seen that consumer credit actually increased 421.5 percent; retail sales, 150.0 percent; disposable personal income, 180.1 percent; and personal savings, 73.5 percent.

The economic factors analyzed in Table 3-3 are all relevant and important to the growth of consumer credit. That is, the American consumer has responded to the purchase of a greater quantity and variety of goods as his income and savings registered increases. Consumer credit is a direct result of the interrelationship of these data. When consumer credit is seen in this way, we find that its growth is closely associated with the general economic growth of the economy. Even though consumers used their credit to a greater extent, as indicated by the 421.5 percent increase (adjusted), several facts should be remembered. First, during recent years, it was possible for consumers to purchase a greatly increased variety of goods with their credit. Second, consumers greatly increased their standard of living and actually purchased a greater variety of goods as their incomes rose with the expanding economy. Third, the increased number of households on the American scene also has influenced the ability of manufacturers to market their increased outputs. When analyzed in this manner, the growth in consumer credit is seen as an integral part of a greatly expanded economy.

A principal limitation to the preceding analysis concerns the use of aggregate data in regard to consumer credit. Credit practitioners and students should not lose sight of the fact that a debtor-creditor relationship exists in each and every credit transaction. Aggregate data, while depicting an inherent soundness of our credit structure relies on the worthiness of the credit applicant. The ability of a consumer to meet his credit obligations satisfactorily is to a large extent dependent on a balanced relationship between his income and his debts. When disposable personal income declines, a consumer has less with which to meet his fixed obligations. It seems essential that each debtor-creditor relationship be analyzed closely so that forecasted changes in income, prices, and individual desires do not put a strain on the continued good relationship of the debtor and the creditor. If the soundness of the total volume of consumer credit is to prevail for individual accounts, it is necessary that credit granters not lose their technique of applying basic fundamentals.

REGULATION OF CONSUMER CREDIT

As background for an understanding of American experiences with consumer credit regulations, it is important that we consider briefly some of the objectives that such regulations have attempted to achieve. It should be recognized, however, that there is a lack of general agreement as to the primary purposes of these regulations. Some of the earlier views, as they pertain to regulating consumer installment credit, were summarized in the Federal Reserve System's 1957 study on installment credit:[9]

> Many observers who have supported the idea of regulation have based their endorsement on the belief that it would help to moderate instability in the economy.
> . . . .
> Installment credit regulation has been advocated in periods of national emergency, when circumstances make it necessary to curtail production of consumer durable and other goods. . . .The regulation of consumer credit, while not an ideal rationing device, is considered to be helpful in keeping the effective demand for consumer durables in tolerable balance with the reduced supply.
> . . . .
> Another objective is protection of the quality of the credit structure.
> . . . .
> A somewhat related objective, but one that probably is prompted by different motives, is the policing of trade practices in order to protect borrowers, vendors, and lenders. Sometimes the underlying concern is with sales practices, such as hidden charges in installment sales contracts, which have nothing to do with credit terms.
> . . . .

9 / Guy E. Noyes, "Experience with Consumer Instalment Credit Regulation," *Consumer Instalment Credit*, Report of Board of Governors of the Federal Reserve System (Washington, D.C.: U.S. Government Printing Office, 1957), Part I, Vol. 1, pp. 286-87.

On the basis of experience, some groups accept regulation as an essential part of the implementation of a major defense or emergency effort but reject it as a continuing tool of monetary policy.

On the other hand, some writers on the subject of regulation of consumer credit have emphatically opposed any controls on the federal level. Speaking before the June 1965 conference of the National Retail Merchants Association, Credit Management Division, Edward V. Long (then United States senator from Missouri) stated:[10]

> I am firmly convinced that federal intrusion in the field of consumer credit is unwise, unwarranted and unworkable. Each and every transaction is essentially a local arrangement between buyer and seller or a borrower and lender. Literally billions of these transactions could never and should never be supervised by any federal agency.

Another writer opposing federal control of consumer credit has pointed out:[11]

> Even in the absence of federal legislation, there are at least two significant factors which provide considerable protection from abuses for those consumers using installment credit: (1) the existence in 40 states of legislation specifically requiring disclosure on installment of all pertinent information; and (2) normal or "competitive" practices of honest, reputable business firms.

On the other hand, speaking before the Workshop on Consumer Credit in Family Financial Management sponsored by the American Home Economics Association, a Federal Trade Commissioner made the following comments:[12]

> The essential need today, therefore, is for the development of adequate regulations to protect consumers against fraud and deception in the field of credit transactions and to ensure that consumers have sufficient information about the cost to them of credit to enable them to function rationally in the market-place.
>
> In light of the state of today's credit market, there is little the consumer can rationally do to educate himself either as to the absolute cost of credit to him or as to the relative cost of various credit alternatives open to him. Thus, while education is frequently an effective and indeed in many instances a preferable alternative to government regulation of business practices, this alternative is not really available today with respect to credit transactions.

Thus, as in most matters, there has been and still is a wide area of

10 / Edward V. Long, "The Regulation of Consumer Credit—Whose Job?" *Stores,* June 1965, p. 28.

11 / Ray McAlister, "Is Federal Regulation of Credit Really Necessary?" *Credit World,* June 1965, p. 10.

12 / Mary G. Jones, "The Role of the FTC in Consumer Credit," *Credit World,* December 1967, p. 9. Also see Mary G. Jones, "Role of Business and Government," *Industrial Banker,* January 1969, p. 5.

disagreement as to the need for, and the type and extent of, regulation of consumer credit.

Federal Regulation

Experience with federal regulation of consumer credit in the United States has been limited to four particular time periods: during World War II and the reconversion period immediately following; from September 1948 to June 1949, at which time fear of inflation prompted Congress to vote a limited degree of regulation; during the Korean crisis; and during the recent period of the late 1960s and early 1970s. In the first three of these periods, the federal regulation involved was Regulation W. In the last period, an assortment of federal legislation has been passed.

Regulation W. During World War II, all areas of consumer credit were covered by Regulation W. The most important phases of the regulation dealt with: (1) the amount of down payments and the length of the repayment periods in installment selling, and (2) prohibition of continued activity of charge accounts which were past due for a specified period of time. In considering only the down payment provisions as applied to installment sales contracts, any regulation which establishes the down payment requirement can also affect the amount of credit created. Regulation W first established the down payment on new automobiles at 33 1/3 percent. While many sellers in the automobile trade had previously subscribed to the principle of one third down, this field is one which is usually harassed by many sellers offering very lenient terms. To illustrate the effect of increased down payment requirements, let us assume a potential new car customer has saved $700, or has a comparable amount of equity in his present car. Either cash or equity can be used for the down payment on a new car. The amount of credit created by our new car customer as he uses his $700 cash or the comparable equity as a down payment under varied down payment percentages would be as follows:

Down Payment		*Maximum*	*Credit*
Cash-Equity	*Percent*	*Price*	*Created*
$700	10%	$7,000	$6,300
700	20	3,500	2,800
700	33 1/3	2,100	1,400

In the above example, the new car purchaser would, under the provisions of Regulation W, have been restricted to the purchase of a $2,100 automobile, and hence $1,400 of installment credit would have been created.

When the length of installment sales contracts is regulated, the obvious effect is to shorten the repayment period and consequently increase the amount to be repaid per installment. During much of World War II the maximum repayment period on automobiles was 15 months. A repayment period of this duration has a particularly negative influence on the lower income groups and those households with relatively heavy financial obligations. As a result, by the regulation of the down payment requirements on installment sales contracts and the shortening of the repayment period, the quantity and quality of credit were supposedly regulated.

While the intended effect of Regulation W has been illustrated, the actual results are open to question when one examines other aspects of the control periods. During World War II few consumer durable goods were available in retail stores, and consumer income was unusually high. Consequently, those goods which came under Regulation W registered sales declines for reasons other than the curbing regulation. During the same time, savings rose to a high level and a great pent-up consumer demand existed at the close of World War II. The effect of regulation during the postwar period and the Korean conflict was mild. It may be that only those of the lower income groups and those with heavy obligations on their incomes were obliged to delay purchases of durable goods. For the major portion of consumers, their incomes were high enough and their savings sufficient to meet the regulatory standards. Further, a scarcity of goods prevailed for several years after World War II, and by the time the United States was involved in the Korean conflict the ineffective results of the previous regulations were well understood. Regulation during the Korean conflict was mild and applied only to the down payment and length of the repayment periods on installment sales contracts. And in this instance the goods under regulation were very limited, while all other goods were free of controls.

Credit Control Act. This is one of the many new federal enactments relating to the field of credit that appeared during the late 1960s and early 1970s. This (S. 2577) legislation, which was signed into law on December 24, 1969, empowered the President "at any time at his discretion to authorize complete and total control of all forms and types of credit by the Federal Reserve Board—even over rates and licensing."[13] To enforce the provisions of this act, the Federal Reserve Board is empowered, with permission from appropriate courts, to issue permanent or temporary injunctions or restraining orders against violators or suspected violators, and to

13 / Wm. Henry Blake, "Credit Control Act Authorizes Total Control of All Credit Forms," *Credit World,* January 1970, p. 9.

assess civil penalties or bring criminal charges against willful violators.

As of this writing, none of these new powers for compulsory credit controls, similar to those of Regulation W, has been used by the President, but the possibility of such action of course remains.

Consumer Credit Protection Act. In 1960, a serious but unsuccessful attempt at federal regulation of credit activities was made in the form of a "Consumer Credit Labeling bill" (S. 2755), which among other things would have required the statement of total finance charges in dollars and cents and of the "simple" annual rate to accompany every consumer credit transaction. According to its sponsors, this bill was drawn to "assist in the promotion of economic stabilization by requiring the disclosure of finance charges in connection with extension of credit." This bill was again introduced in 1961 under the interesting title, "Truth-in-Lending bill" (S. 1740), and its leading spokesman was Paul H. Douglas (then United States senator from Illinois). Extensive hearings were held on this and similar bills introduced during the early years of the 1960s. In January 1967 William W. Proxmire (United States senator from Wisconsin) introduced his version (S. 5) of the so-called Truth-in-Lending bill. This was subsequently passed, was signed into law, and became effective July 1, 1969.

As originally passed, the Truth-in-Lending act is Title I of the Consumer Credit Protection Act; Title II deals with extortionate credit transactions; Title III is concerned with wage garnishment; and Title IV provides for the creation of a National Commission on Consumer Finance. For most consumer-business transactions, compliance with the law will be under the general supervision of the Federal Trade Commission, which has been given part of the responsibility of enforcing Regulation Z. This regulation, which implements the Truth-in-Lending law, was issued by the Board of Governors of the Federal Reserve System and is designed to tell businessmen how to comply with the law. It also adds substantive requirements necessary to carry out the disclosures required by the law. One interesting provision of the regulation is that the Board may exempt from federal disclosure requirements certain transactions within a state if it determines that the state law imposes substantially similar requirements and adequate enforcement is provided. Regulation Z, however, spells out the detailed procedures a creditor must follow if he decides to comply with any provisions of a state law which are inconsistent with the federal disclosure requirements.

The main purpose of the Truth-in-Lending portion of the law is to assure a meaningful disclosure of credit terms so that the consumer will be able to compare more readily the various credit terms available to him and to avoid the uninformed use of credit. The

Truth-in-Lending act is simply a disclosure law[14]; it does not set maximum interest rates. It does specify, however, that the most important credit terms—the finance charge and the annual percentage rate—be disclosed to the customer.

Other pertinent provisions of the Truth-in-Lending law include the following:

> The Truth in Lending law and Regulation Z give a customer the right to cancel a credit transaction within three business days when the creditor acquires or retains a security interest in the customer's principal residence. No such cancellation right is afforded for first mortgages to finance purchase of a residence itself. But the right of rescission does apply when a residence is otherwise used as collateral for a consumer loan. The regulation specifies the notice the creditor must give a customer when the right of rescission can be exercised.
>
> . . . .
>
> In general, no advertising offering credit may state that a specific amount of credit or installment can be arranged unless the creditor customarily arranges such types of credit. No one specific credit term—that is, the down payment, finance charge, and so forth—can be advertised unless all the terms are stated clearly and conspicuously.[15]

There is widespread disagreement as to the accomplishments of this law. Comments as to its effect include the following:

> The consumer who wants to ascertain credit terms, according to a Federal Reserve Board report, must go from store to store and shop for credit. These authors find, however, that going from store to store soliciting information from credit personnel yields as much incorrect information after Truth in Lending as before. The major change brought about by Truth in Lending was the transformation of store literature and contracts from seductive sales pieces to informative disclosures. Retail organizations must train their personnel to read their own credit documents. Consumers should rely on the printed literature only and not on retail store personnel.[16]
>
> It thus appears that Regulation Z has not affected retail charge account usage patterns. Future research, using more detailed data, may reverse this conclusion.[17]
>
> To answer the question, what have been the effects . . . I could almost say that the answer to this question is: expensive to the lenders. However, to stop

14 / Unfortunately, some business firms have used this law as a basis to start charging interest on their credit accounts. Following is a paragraph of a letter sent by a retailer grocer to his customers: "We also must reluctantly announce that at the same time we are forced to start charging a service charge under the provisions of the Federal Truth in Lending Legislation which became effective July 1, 1969. This charge will be 9% per annum, or 3/4 of 1% per month for any account not paid in full within a 30 day period. . . . " This is, of course, false and misleading, and such action should be condemned whenever it occurs.

15 / "Truth in Lending," *Federal Reserve Bulletin,* February 1969, p. 102.

16 / Marilyn M. Max and Richard L. D. Morse, "Retail Open End Credit Disclosures Before and After Truth in Lending," *Quarterly Report,* Fall 1970, p. 122.

17 / C.W. Lee, "Effects of Regulation Z on Charge Account Sales," *Credit World,* June 1970, p. 15.

here would not be fair, even though it would be totally correct. To answer this question, we could all have to keep in mind that of all the years involved since the Great Depression, we could not have possibly picked a time where disclosures to consumers and borrowers would have been less effective than this year of 1969. Inflation has reached an all-time high. The demand for money has surpassed the supply in most parts of the country. Shopping for a mortgage of a potential home is just one of the things of the past. Before you can be quoted a rate, you have to find someone willing to loan long-term money.

. . . .

What are the effects of Truth-in-Lending? What has Truth-in-Lending accomplished? Personally, I am confused on both points and I am still searching for the answers and finding new ones everyday. Like all things in our society, each problem is a special one with different solutions. Each business is different. Each problem is different.[18]

For a detailed discussion of the law, please refer to Appendix B. Likewise, throughout this book, reference is made to the provisions of the Consumer Credit Protection Act when discussion is centered on topics that are covered in the act.

Fair Credit Reporting Act. This amendment (Title VI) to the Consumer Credit Protection Act became law in April 1971. The provisions of this act affect all granters of consumer credit and all local retail credit bureaus. One of the major requirements on credit granters is the provision which makes it mandatory for the business firm to inform the consumer whenever credit is refused on the basis of a credit report and, further, to inform him of the name and address of the bureau making the report. If credit is denied on the basis of information received from a source other than a credit bureau, the business firm must inform the consumer of his right to request in writing the nature of the information on which the denial was based.

The act places new restrictions upon credit bureaus as to the inclusion of obsolete information in any consumer report released by the bureaus; spells out the conditions under which bureaus must disclose in-file information to consumers; prescribes the procedure to follow in case of dispute about the accuracy of information contained in a report; places certain restrictions on investigative consumer reports; and sets forth the liability of the bureaus in connection with their operations.

The law places similar responsibilities on all those who either issue or use reports on consumers in connection with insurance transactions and employment practices.

More details of the act will be covered in the chapter on local retail credit bureau operation. Appendix B shows the entire act.

18 / J. L. Holloway, "Effects and Accomplishments of Truth-in-Lending," *Credit World*, April 1970, pp. 9 and 11.

Credit Card Issuance Act. In October 1970, a new federal law on credit card issuance became effective. Under this law (Title V of the Consumer Credit Protection Act), no credit card may be issued except in response to a request or application. This requirement, however, does not apply to renewals or substitutions for previously accepted cards.

Previously—on May 18, 1970—the Federal Trade Commission had issued a Trade Regulation Rule on unsolicited mailing of credit cards, but it was determined that the FTC rule did not apply to banking institutions. The new law, however, applies to all card users, including banks, oil companies, entertainment firms, and others.

In addition to stopping the mailing of unsolicited cards, the law also limits to $50 the card holder's liability in those cases where his card is used without his permission. Under the law, the card holder would not even be liable for the $50 liability if the issuer had not complied with certain requirements. One of these requirements is that the card issuer must provide the card holder with a self-addressed, prestamped notification to be mailed by the card holder in the event of the loss or theft of the credit card.

The law states that it is now a federal offense when a credit card is used for the theft of goods and services with a retail value of $5,000 or more and provides a maximum $10,000 fine and a five-year prison sentence for persons convicted of violating this provision.

Regulation Q. Interest rate ceilings on deposits at commercial banks which are members of the Federal Reserve System are established under Federal Reserve Regulation Q. Ceilings at insured nonmember banks are set by a regulation of the Federal Deposit Insurance Corporation and are the same as for member banks. The Banking Acts of 1933 and 1935 are the basis of these regulations. Until 1966, there were no explicit nationwide regulations on interest and dividend rates at savings and loan associations and mutual savings banks. In that year, legislation brought rates paid by federally insured mutual savings banks under the control of the Federal Deposit Insurance Corporation; rates paid at savings and loan associations which are members of the Federal Home Loan Bank Board were placed under control of the Board.

This regulation will be explained in more detail in subsequent chapters.

State Regulation

Until recent years, the overwhelming belief throughout most of the United States was that a business firm might sell its goods and services at one price for cash and at a higher price on time without violating the interest and usury laws. The reason for this view arose from the generally accepted idea that a sale of goods and services was involved and that a loaning of money was not connected with the transaction. This was based on a judicially created doctrine which originated in England in 1774. The English court at that time ruled that the words "loan" and "forbearance" were used to designate transactions to which the usury law applied and that a sale of merchandise on time by a merchant was neither a loan of money nor a forbearance of a debt.

Recent legislative and court actions in various parts of the country, however, have raised pertinent but confusing questions as to the applicability of interest and usury laws to the sale of goods on a time basis. The first deviation from the time-price doctrine was in 1957 in the Arkansas *Sloan* v. *Sears Roebuck and Co.* case (308 S.W. 2d 802). Here the court decided that the usury law in Arkansas was not limited to finance charges on loans or forbearances but covered credit sales as well. In 1963 the second deviation from the time-price doctrine occurred in Nebraska in the case of *Lloyd* v *Gutgsell* (124 N.W. 2d 198), in which the court held that usury laws applied to credit sales where financing was arranged through and by a third party finance company.

Opposition to the time-price doctrine has been further advanced by those who argue that the so-called open-end credit account (such as the option-terms revolving credit account) is not a true time sale and thus is different from the closed-end contract (such as the installment contract) in which the customer chooses in advance the number of months over which he will make payment and the service charge is added to the cash price at the time of sale.

Toward the end of the 1960s, almost all of the states had statutes, special or regular, relating in a direct and material way to spelling out in detail the cash price-time price concept. In other states, the fundamental issue still involved was simply whether a finance charge or service charge was to be considered an interest charge. However, the confusion as to whether a revolving credit account came under the time-price doctrine further clouded the legal issue. As an indication of this problem as it exists at the state level, the following quotation from *Women's Wear Daily* is given:

> In at least 20 states retailers suddenly are aware that revolving credit could come crashing down upon them with possibly millions of dollars in class action suits to reimburse customers retroactively for "usurious" service charges.
> . . . .
> The validity of the revolving credit service charge hinges partly on statutes, partly on common law. Some 30 states now have laws specifically authorizing retailers to impose a specified rate of service charge on revolving accounts.
> . . . .

But in 19 states and the District of Columbia no such law exists.

· ·

In these states, retailers for years have relied on the "time-price doctrine" to justify imposing a 1 or 1.5 per cent monthly service charge on revolving accounts. The doctrine has been upheld by the courts of almost all states, but only for closed-end credit. But the applicability of the time-price doctrine to open-end (revolving) credit has not until now been specifically passed upon by state courts.[19]

During 1971, however, ten more states joined the ranks of those having specific legislation on revolving credit accounts and passed enabling legislation specifying the maximum rate that can be assessed on revolving credit accounts. The maximum rates set in nine of these states was 1½ percent per month, and 1 percent per month in one of them.

Thus, it is clearly evident that the cash price-time price concept strikes at the very heart of our entire credit system.

Uniform Consumer Credit Code (UCCC). The UCCC has been defined as:

An Act to establish a Uniform Consumer Credit Code, thereby consolidating and revising certain aspects of the law relating to certain loans, sales and leases of goods, and sales of services and interests in land to consumers; limiting certain judicial remedies of creditors and creating certain judicial remedies of debtors; providing for administrative regulation of certain consumer credit transactions including the granting of powers to issue administrative orders and initiate judicial proceedings; revising the law relating to usury; providing for regulation of certain practices concerning insurance in certain consumer credit transactions; making uniform the law with respect thereto; and repealing legislation inconsistent therewith.[20]

As of this writing, only a very few states have adopted the UCCC as a law covering consumer credit transactions. As is to be expected, its backers insist the code should be looked on as a boon to consumers, but certain consumer groups "denounce the UCCC as a finance-industry-backed attack to keep the federal government from taking over the regulation of consumer credit."[21]

Uniform Commercial Code. The Uniform Commercial Code is a uniform body of rules designed to deal, from start to finish, with all

19 / "Fear a Credit Blowup Over 'Usury' Suits," *Women's Wear Daily,* October 29, 1970, pp. 1 and 34. Reprinted by permission from *Women's Wear Daily,* copyright 1970, by Fairchild Publications, Inc. For additional references see the Suggested Readings at the end of the chapter.

20 / *Uniform Consumer Credit Code* (Chicago: Commerce Clearing House, Inc., Instalment Guide No. 176, May 13, 1968), p. xiii.

21 / "Battle Breaks Over Buying on Time," *Business Week,* March 29, 1969, p. 80. For additional references see the Suggested Readings at the end of the chapter.

situations ordinarily arising in the handling of a commercial transaction (including installment transactions). It was promulgated by the National Conference of Commissioners on Uniform State Laws and the American Law Institute, with the endorsement of the American Bar Association. Passed at the state level, this law affects all commercial transactions and has made many important changes in the consumer credit field.

A more detailed look into these state laws[22] will appear in the subsequent chapters dealing with revolving credit, installment credit, and sales finance institutions.

THE INDIVIDUAL'S USE OF CREDIT

When an individual uses his credit, a debtor-creditor relationship is established. The principal motivation of the creditor in the relationship is to gain a profit. Different motivating forces influence the customer in this transaction. It is generally recognized that credit is used by individuals for one or more reasons. In most instances, close observation will reveal the motivating influence as an attempt to *increase satisfactions from life, convenience,* or *necessity.* In some instances, the individual may be motivated by a combination of these reasons.

Use of Credit to Increase the Satisfactions from Life

Primarily the individual uses credit in order to increase the satisfactions which he can obtain from life. Credit enables him to have and enjoy things now, rather than postponing the purchase and use of these things until some indefinite future time. By means of credit he is able to obtain the use of goods or services and defer payment until the future. The alternative would be for him to accumulate funds—doing without now in order to save for the future. This, to him, is not nearly as attractive a proposition as buying now and deferring payment until some future time when, optimistically, he thinks his ability to pay will be greater than it is at the present moment.

Because he can use credit as a means of payment rather than having to save and accumulate funds, the range of goods which are available for his choice is considerably increased. There are certain commodities which have a high unit value. Very rarely will he be able

22 / One of the outstanding studies in this field was made by Barbara A. Curran, *Trends in Consumer Credit Legislation* (Chicago: University of Chicago Press, 1965). Barbara Curran was research attorney for the American Bar Foundation at the time of the study.

to accumulate cash in advance so that he can pay for them immediately. One of these is a home. Most homes are purchased through credit and paid for over a long period of years. In the development of our modern economy, a number of other commodities of this same type have been added to the customary scale of living. Generally these are durable goods with a high unit value. Frequently, these items are purchased on the installment plan of payment. If this credit device were not available to the individual consumer, very few of the low- and middle-income groups would be able to use and enjoy these commodities. Once they have committed themselves to the purchase, they are impelled to make regular payment by the terms of the contract which they have signed. Were they not under contract and instead attempting to save in advance of the purchase, it is rather doubtful if they would be able to accumulate the necessary funds. It is more likely that day-to-day temptations would arise and they would dissipate their funds in what might be called "nonlasting" purchases.

Use of Credit as a Convenience

Another important reason for using credit is simply convenience. It is far more convenient, when shopping, to be able to say, "charge it, please" than to have to carry the cash which otherwise would be necessary. Also, when credit is available at one or more of the local stores, other members of the family may be sent to the store without worrying about the cash. It may also facilitate the process of household budgeting to have the merchant assume part of the responsibility for keeping the household accounts. Many people pay their bills only once a month, although their bank account is ample throughout the month, so that they could well pay cash.

In noting the use of credit as a convenience, recognition should be given to the growing number of credit plans that have expanded rapidly in recent years. Among the most important of these are the revolving credit plans that have appeared across the nation. Also, bank credit cards are being promoted on the basis that one may purchase many items from many different stores and make a single payment to the bank for the variety of purchases. Similar illustrations arise from the increasing use of credit cards for goods and services, such as the gasoline company credit cards, the Diners Club, and the American Express Credit Card—to name a few.

Use of Credit as a Necessity

A third reason why many a consumer is impelled to use credit can be described as a necessity. There is something which presses upon him so strongly that to do without is quite an undesirable choice.

Under these circumstances, he does not pay cash but resorts to credit. The ordinary affairs of life are responsible for many of these occasions: birth, death, sickness, and similar events which demand a large immediate outlay. Not having a reserve sufficient for the occasion, the individual is pressed by what he regards as an emergency to secure a loan or to use his credit for goods and services. Occasionally, of course, there may be some difference of opinion as to what constitutes an emergency. Very often credit is resorted to under emergency conditions when the funds obtained are spent for purposes which the outsider would scarcely regard as an emergency. The use of credit in order to pay off other bills may be classified as an emergency need. Frequently, items purchased on the installment plan impose payments greater than the current revenue will meet. The collector is pushing hard for his money and unless paid promptly threatens some dire consequences, such as repossession of the article bought on the installment plan or perhaps suit, garnishment, or some legal action. This being clearly an undesirable event, the individual resorts to the use of credit to avoid less desirable consequences. Generally, the form of credit used under these circumstances is the cash loan, made from one of the various cash lending agencies.

Wise and Unwise Use of Credit

The question may be raised as to whether the individual is wise or unwise in his use of credit. The use of credit often imposes a cost. Installment buying generally is accompanied by carrying charges which place the cost of the credit directly upon the person who uses it. Charge account credit, frequently, means trading at stores which may have a slightly higher price than would be available if the purchase were made at the so-called strictly cash store or the cash-carry store. Borrowing from cash lenders generally results in the payment of interest charges. Is the payment of these additional amounts justified? It is difficult to set any definite criterion by which we can judge whether the individual has been wise or foolish in using credit. About the only criterion we can cling to with any degree of certainty is the individual's own judgment. If he actually knows what it is costing him, if he still makes the decision to use credit, and if he feels that the additional satisfaction obtained by the use of credit is greater than the cost of the credit, then we must conclude that it has been a good bargain from his standpoint. To do otherwise is to attempt to substitute our judgment for that of the individual. This is not in accordance with the principles of a society in which the individual enjoys freedom of choice.

Is it true that all cash buyers are intelligent shoppers? Frequently, impelled by the urgency of the salesman, or just because of insufficient willpower, or because of lack of foresight and inability to appraise correctly the need for the article as against the usefulness of the purchase being considered, cash buyers may make an unwise decision and find the satisfaction obtained is not as great as they expected it to be at the time of purchase. When credit is used as a medium of exchange, there is probably more opportunity for errors of this sort than when the purchase is made for cash. Credit is a very easy way to purchase. It is necessary for the individual using credit to make two calculations as to future circumstances. First, the future enjoyment he will obtain from the things he is getting now; and second, the future difficulties and disutilities he will suffer from the necessity of having to make payment at some time in the future—both of these must be considered.

There is a natural tendency to exaggerate the pleasures of the present and to minimize the difficulties of the future. This leads to unwarranted optimism. It seems to the individual that it will be quite easy to make payment in the future. Surely, his circumstances at that time will be better than they are now. Surely his income will increase, and he will find it easier to pay then than it is now. Also, we all are inclined to feel that present pleasures are better than postponed pleasures. For that reason, we are quite anxious to have the thing we are considering purchasing and it seems that it will be quite easy to pay when the time comes.

These occasional errors in the use of credit may be considered abuses rather than necessary results. Too often the entire credit device is condemned because of occasional abuses and errors. The abuses may be on the part of the buyer; they may be on the part of the seller. Certainly, it is not the part of good judgment to criticize the entire credit mechanism and condemn all individuals' use of credit because occasionally some individuals use it not wisely, but too freely.

Changing Pattern of Use—Summary

The widespread use of consumer credit, and particularly of consumer installment credit, is a characteristic of recent decades. Since the turn of the 20th century, fundamental changes in our industrial output and in consumer behavior have been closely associated with the rapid growth of consumer credit.

Authoritative evidence of the present-day widespread use of consumer credit is available from the *Survey of Consumer Finances* conducted by the Survey Research Center of the University of Michigan. The 1969 *Survey of Consumer Finances*[23] carried forward

23 / George Katona, William Dunkelberg, Gary Hendricks, and Jay Schmiedeskamp, *1969 Survey of Consumer Finances* (Ann Arbor: University of Michigan, 1970).

basic trend data on installment debt; housing; automobile purchases and ownership; household durables, vacations, and recreation items; financial assets; financial transactions; and income changes.

According to this 1969 survey, the average amount of installment debt per family in early 1968 was $1,370. By early 1969, it had risen about 12 percent, to an average of $1,540. In addition, the proportion of families with debt rose from 48 to 51 percent. Since incomes rose substantially during 1968, many families decided that they could afford a larger debt obligation. This change is reflected in the fact that in early 1968 only 27 percent of all families were devoting 10 percent or more of their disposable income to repay previously contracted obligations; one year later this 27 percent had increased to 30 percent.

Among the different groups, those in the $7,500-$9,999 and the $10,000-$14,999 groups had the largest increases in debt. Thus it is evident that not the poor but the fairly well-to-do have been responsible for the growth of installment debt.

Age is also an important factor to consider in connection with installment debt. In the 25-34 age group, some 20 percent had debts of $2,000 or more in 1969; in the 35-44 age group, some 21 percent had debts of this size in 1969. The major increases in debts of $2,000 or more were among married families under 45 years of age, particularly those with older children.

The changing attitudes and behavior of consumers[24] thus have had their counterpart in the changing array of consumer goods and in the revolution that has occurred in the ways in which to produce and to finance these goods. Thus, there has been an interlocking of influences between the appearance of new products, new methods by which to purchase them, and new and changing consumer tastes and desires.

REVIEW AND DISCUSSION QUESTIONS

1. Explain the basic differences between a credit economy, a money economy, and a barter economy.
2. Trace the changes in the consumer credit field between 1860 and 1920; between 1920 and 1930.
3. Why was the Russell Sage Foundation established? What do you believe was its principal contribution to the field of consumer credit?
4. How do you account for the fact that commercial banks entered the consumer credit field many years after the small loan companies had been operating in this area?
5. Why does Table 3-2 start with the year 1929?

24 / For references on this topic, see the Suggested Readings at the end of the chapter.

6. Using the figures shown in Table 3-2, explain why the volume of consumer credit has expanded so rapidly since the close of World War II.

7. Discuss why an analysis of the consumer credit field must take into consideration the trend of other factors, such as retail sales, disposable personal income, and personal savings.

8. Discuss the limitations to the use of the data shown in Table 3-3.

9. Explain what Regulation W was and discuss the effect it had on the volume of consumer credit outstanding.

10. Discuss the arguments for and against the control of consumer credit.

11. Explain why a President of the United States might be reluctant to invoke the Credit Control Act.

12. Review the summarization of the Truth-in-Lending Act that is contained in Appendix B.

13. What do you believe are the most important provisions of the Truth-in-Lending Act? Why did you choose the ones that you did?

14. Discuss the provisions of the Fair Credit Reporting Act with the manager of your local retail credit bureau.

15. What was the main purpose of the Credit Card Issuance Act?

16. What are the interest rates now in effect under Regulation Q?

17. What is the status of the Uniform Consumer Credit Code in your state?

18. Should the consumer be protected from using his credit unwisely? If you answered yes, how would you propose doing this?

19. What are the three motivating forces that are connected with an individual's use of credit? Distinguish carefully between these.

20. Read the latest *Survey of Consumer Finances* and comment on the most important changes that are described.

SUGGESTED READINGS

State Regulation of Credit

Rosen, Stuart M. "The Wisconsin Decision: Implications for Retailing," *Stores,* January 1971, p. 28.

"Wisconsin Supreme Court Service Charge Decision Against J. C. Penney Starts Chain Reaction," *Quarterly Report,* Winter 1970, p. 26.

Uniform Consumer Credit Code

Butler, Nathaniel E. "A Summary of the Uniform Consumer Credit Code," *Credit World,* August 1969, p. 9.

Dunham, Allison. "Consumer Protection Under the UCCC," *Credit World,* February 1969, p. 8.

Johnson, Robert W. "Uniform Code for Consumer Credit,'" *Harvard Business Review,* July-August 1968, p. 119.

Robinson, W. F. "The Uniform Consumer Credit Code," *Quarterly Report,* Fall 1968, p. 118.

Changing Attitudes of Consumers

Dyle, J. S. "The New Consumer—And Total Credit," *Industrial Banker,* September 1968, p. 5.

Penner, Irvin. "Penetrating the College Market," *Credit World,* February 1970, p. 13.

"Youth Buyers," *New York Times,* November 22, 1970, p. 5.

4

Types of Consumer Credit—
Retail Revolving Credit

That credit is a persuasive salesman has been pointed out in the previous chapters. Sellers for credit are in a position to tempt their customers at any time and in many ways, whereas sellers for cash must bring about buying when their customers have the money in hand. And in an economy such as ours there is an ever-expanding assortment of goods and services which continuously fight for the consumer's attention—and his credit or his pocketbook. In the assortment of credit plans being offered, one of the newest is the retail revolving credit plan; and the most important type of revolving credit plan is the option-terms plan. Revolving credit should be considered as a hybrid between installment credit (to be discussed in Chapter 5) and open charge account credit (to be discussed in Chapter 7).

The first revolving credit plan offered in the United States for the sale of soft goods to the consumer was introduced in 1938 by Wanamaker's of Philadelphia. This plan, which was quite different from the revolving credit plan commonly in effect today, called for complete liquidation of the account in four monthly payments, and no service or extra charges were posted to the account. Shortly thereafter, Filene's in Boston, Bamberger's in Newark, and Bloomingdale's in New York introduced plans of their own that offered terms with a service charge added each month on the unpaid balance. During World War II, Regulation W, in requiring down payments on all purchases over $10, acted as a strong deterrent to the expansion of this type of retail credit; but with the lifting of this regulation, department and specialty stores—both large and small—have actively utilized this type of plan.

OPTION-TERMS REVOLVING CREDIT PLAN

Most of the larger department stores and specialty stores over the country have recently been adopting what has been commonly called in the trade the option-terms type of revolving credit plan. A representative option-terms plan is shown in Table 4-1.

It was in May 1956 that J. L. Hudson's Department Store in Detroit first introduced its "30-Day Account with Optional Terms." As established, this plan provided for repayment in full in 30 days without service charge; or the customer could pay as little as one fourth of the balance each month with a minimum monthly payment of $10 if the balance was $50 or less. If the customer chose to extend his payments past 30 days, a service charge was added.

TABLE 4-1
Representative Option-Terms Revolving Credit Plan

If Customer's Balance Is—	Monthly Payment Is—*
$ .01-$ 10	Balance
10.01- 100	$10
100.01- 150	15
150.01- 200	20
200.01- 250	25
250.01- 300	30
300.01- 350	35
Over 350	1/10 of account
*Including carrying charge.	balance

The option-terms plan in effect today in most of the retail stores is a replacement for the so-called basic plan which was the first type of revolving credit plan to be introduced. Under the basic plan, the customer was afforded the opportunity to buy primarily apparel and other soft-goods items on a deferred payment basis. The customer determined the monthly payment best suited to his needs. This monthly payment multiplied by the number of months that the store chose to run its revolving credit plan determined the credit limit that was established for the customer. A service charge, which usually was based on the brought-forward balance, was generally included as part of the agreed monthly payment, rather than considering it as an additional amount due.

Although the basic form of revolving credit plan was the first type to be introduced, it has fallen into disfavor and has been replaced almost universally by the option-terms arrangement. Under this type of arrangement, the customer is given the option of paying his bill usually within 25 to 30 days (from billing date) without the addition of any service charge. The plan, of course, also provides a schedule of payments for amounts carried beyond the prescribed time period.

For each range of unpaid balances—as, for example, $10.01-$100, and so on—there is a specific monthly payment of $10, $15, and so on, due. In the example shown in Table 4-1, when the account balance is over $350 the monthly payment is one tenth of the account balance. The service charge is included in this monthly payment. The payment that is due is predicated on the balance owing, thus providing for reduced monthly payments as the balance outstanding declines.

Following are the most important features of a typical option-terms revolving credit plan:

1. The customer ordinarily makes a series of purchases—in fact the retail store would consider its sales promotion program faulty if this were not the case.
2. There is no down payment.
3. If the account is not paid within the prescribed time period, a series of recurring payments are made over a period of time.
4. There is a finance charge if the account is not paid within the prescribed time period.
5. In most states, revolving credit transactions are governed by the provisions of a state law.
6. Under the federal Truth-in-Lending law, disclosure procedures are spelled out for open-end (including revolving credit) credit transactions. See Appendix B for details of the law.

The option-terms revolving credit plan has become the answer for many stores because this plan is believed to be more adjustable to the customers' needs. Examples of the plans adopted by two of the larger retail organizations are shown in Figures 4-1 and 4-2. The option-terms plan tends to place the responsibility for control of the account on the customer himself, although the store determines the credit limit of the customer. According to some credit executives, the distinct advantages of the option-terms type of account include the following: increased sales, simplified billing, convenience to the customer, increased service charge income, uniform collection procedure, and savings in supplies. On the other hand, some credit officials point out that there are disadvantages to this type of plan and that these include: increased average outstanding balances, which result in more capital being tied up in accounts receivable, and more difficulty in controlling some accounts.

In many classifications, revolving credit has been considered as simply a modified form of installment selling. In fact, the statistical data on consumer credit that appear in the monthly issues of the *Federal Reserve Bulletin* include most of the revolving credit sales volume as part of the installment credit sales. For this reason, it is not possible to arrive at the national importance of this type of credit.

FIGURE 4-1

Sears Revolving Charge Account and Security Agreement

SEARS, ROEBUCK AND CO.

In consideration of your selling merchandise and services for personal, family or household purposes to me on my Sears Revolving Charge Account I agree to the following regarding all purchases made by me or on my Sears Revolving Charge Account Identification.

1. I have the privilege of a Charge Account, in which case I will pay the full amount of all purchases within 25 days from the date of each billing statement.

2. If I do not pay the full amount for all purchases within 25 days from the date of each billing statement, the following terms shall be in effect:

    (A) I will pay the Deferred Payment Price for each item purchased consisting of:

    (1) The cash sale price, and

    (2) A FINANCE CHARGE, which will be an amount determined by applying a periodic rate of 1.5% per month (ANNUAL PERCENTAGE RATE of 18%) to the first $500.00 of "previous balance" and a periodic rate of 1% per month (ANNUAL PERCENTAGE RATE of 12%) to any part of the "previous balance" in excess of $500.00. FINANCE CHARGE is based upon account activity during the billing period preceding the current billing period, and is computed upon the "previous balance" ("new balance" outstanding at the end of the preceding billing period) before deducting payments and credits or adding purchases made during the current billing period.

    (B) I will pay for all purchases in monthly installments which will be computed according to the following schedule:

If the unpaid balance is:	The scheduled monthly payment will be:	If the unpaid balance is:	The scheduled monthly payment will be:
$ .01 to $ 10.00	Balance	$350.01 to $400.00	$30.00
10.01 to 200.00	$10.00	400.01 to 450.00	35.00
200.01 to 250.00	15.00	450.01 to 500.00	40.00
250.01 to 300.00	20.00	Over $500.00	1/10 of account bal.
300.01 to $350.00	25.00		

I will pay each monthly installment computed according to the schedule as stated above upon receipt of each statement. If I fail to pay any installment in full when due, you may, at your option, take back the merchandise or affirm the sale and hold me liable for the full balance on my account which shall be immediately due. Ownership of the merchandise purchased on this account shall remain in Sears until I have paid the purchase price in full. My installment payments shall be applied as follows: in the case of items purchased on different dates, the first purchased shall be deemed first paid for; in the case of items purchased on the same date, the lowest priced shall be deemed first paid for. I have risk of loss or damage to merchandise.

    (C) You are to send me a statement each month which will show my previous balance (last month's new balance), new balance, scheduled payment, Finance Charge, purchases, payments and credits, and the amount of my monthly installment coming due.

    (D) I have the right to pay all or any portion of my account in advance.

3. You are authorized to investigate my credit record and report to proper persons and bureaus my performance of this agreement.

NOTICE TO BUYER: (1) DO NOT SIGN THIS CONTRACT BEFORE YOU READ IT OR IF IT CONTAINS BLANKS. (2) YOU ARE ENTITLED TO A COPY OF THIS CONTRACT. KEEP IT TO PROTECT YOUR LEGAL RIGHTS. (3) YOU HAVE THE RIGHT TO PAY IN ADVANCE THE FULL AMOUNT DUE.

DF99961-5 REV. 8-1-70

(Customer's Signature)   DATE

Courtesy of Sears, Roebuck and Co.

FACTORS AFFECTING A DECISION TO SELL ON REVOLVING CREDIT

In his decision to adopt a revolving credit plan, the merchant must take many factors into consideration. The most important of these factors include effect on profits, desires of customers, amount of capital, competition, type of goods, size of community, type of community, and legal restrictions.

Effect on Profits

Whether or not to introduce or to expand revolving credit activities depends primarily upon the effect on profits that the

FIGURE 4-2

J. C. PENNEY COMPANY, INC.   PENNEY'S CHARGE ACCOUNT AGREEMENT

With respect to my Penney's Charge Account, I agree with you that

1. I will pay the time sale prices of items charged to my account, consisting of (a) the cash sale prices, plus (b) **FINANCE CHARGES** computed by applying to the Adjusted Balance (the unpaid balance of the cash sale prices and any unpaid **FINANCE CHARGES** at the beginning of my monthly billing periods, less any payments and credits during the respective billing periods) monthly Periodic Rates of 1½% on the portion of the Adjusted Balance not exceeding $500 and 1% on any excess over $500. The corresponding **ANNUAL PERCENTAGE RATES** are 18% and 12% respectively.

2. If I pay the cash sale price of any purchase prior to my second monthly billing date following the purchase, I will pay no **FINANCE CHARGE** on that purchase.

3. I will, after each monthly billing date (which will be approximately the same day of each month pursuant to your then current billing schedule) and prior to the next monthly billing date, make a minimum installment payment in accordance with your then current minimum payment schedule, your present schedule, being as follows:

Minimum Payment Schedule

Unpaid Balance	$.01 -$11	$11 -151	$151 -201	$201 -251	$251 -301	$301 -351	$351 -401	$401 -451	$451 -501	Over $501
Monthly Payment	Balance	$10	$15	$20	$25	$30	$35	$40	$45	1/10 of Balance

You will advise me of any changes in your minimum payment schedule in accordance with applicable law. Payments will be applied to the time sale prices of purchases in the order of purchase. I understand that I may pay my unpaid balance at any time.

4. Upon any default by me, my entire balance shall at your option become payable.

5. You waive and disclaim the right to retain, acquire or enforce any security interest in any property to secure the payment of any credit extended under this account. This provision is not applicable to judgement liens.

6. You may limit or terminate my account as to future purchases. I will upon request return my account identification, which shall remain your property.

J. C. PENNEY COMPANY, INC.   **RECEIPT OF COPY IS ACKNOWLEDGED**

By   BUYER'S
                                                    SIGNATURE_____ DATE_____
Vice President and General Credit Manager

JCP-3505 (REV. 7/69) NEBRASKA   ADDRESS_____

Courtesy of J. C. Penney Co.

merchant expects such an action to have. Despite all the other factors that have been enumerated and that will be discussed subsequently, unless a merchant believes that increased sales accompanied by increased profits will result, or unless he is forced to offer or expand revolving credit activities to maintain his present profit level, he should not introduce or attempt to expand his revolving credit activities.

Closely connected with this aspect of profits is the method of tax accounting authorized by the federal government. Beginning in 1964 a retailer who regularly sells under an installment plan may defer federal income tax on the gross profit of installment type accounts until the year of collection. After long controversy with the Treasury Department, retailers have won approval to apply this installment method of reporting to sales made under plans of the revolving credit type.

Desires of Customers

The desires of the customers must be considered. Simply installing such a plan is no guarantee of greater sales and higher profits, unless the customers actually wish to purchase under such terms or can be persuaded that this arrangement is to their advantage.

Amount of Capital

The introduction of revolving credit may necessitate a large capital investment on the part of the retailer because of the time that is involved before an article is paid for completely. In addition, since revolving credit usually results in increased credit sales, this of itself calls for a larger capital investment. Consideration has to be given, however, to whether a firm plans to carry its own revolving credit transactions or to make arrangements to sell them to some other institution at a discount. This situation is discussed in detail in the subsequent section on the financing of revolving credit plans.

Competition

This factor has been especially important in revolving credit, because the first department store in a community that adopts such a plan seems to derive an important and often lasting competitive advantage with some customers over similar stores which may introduce such a plan in the future. Thus, if the store has a successful sales promotion program and keeps the customer buying, this buying may be heavily concentrated at this one store in which the customer first opened a revolving account. This is the hope of the store, of course; it can be accomplished only if the customer remains satisfied with the merchandise sold, the prices charged, and the services rendered.

Regardless of this possible initial advantage, competing stores often believe—and rightly—that they should offer equivalent credit opportunities, and thus they too install revolving credit arrangements. Their potential market for revolving credit customers includes people who have not opened a revolving account at the first store, as well as people who are members of the first store's plan.

Type of Goods

This factor plays an important role in the decision of many stores as to whether to adopt a revolving credit plan. If a store handles primarily "big-ticket" items (such as appliances, furniture, and similar consumer durables), a successful revolving credit plan must provide for a sufficiently long repayment period to permit reasonable monthly payments. It also should be recognized that with this type of goods, regular recurring purchases are not customary. Thus in many such instances the installment type of credit arrangement has proved more suitable. If the goods handled are of such a nature that they would be consumed, such as groceries, before they are completely paid for under a revolving credit plan, the characteristics for successful operation are not generally believed to be present. However, some firms are experimenting with the use of revolving credit plans even for the purchase of groceries.[1]

Size of Community

The size of a community, in itself, is no determinant of the success or failure of a revolving credit plan. To say that a plan automatically will be a success in a city of 100,000 persons and a failure in a town of 10,000 is failing to recognize the importance of the size of the store itself, the type and price of merchandise carried, the selection of goods available to customers not only in this particular store but also in competing stores in the same town and in towns attracting trade from some distance, and the availability of credit data on prospective customers.

Experience has shown, however, that stores in the larger communities have been the ones most often introducing such a plan, although more careful attention might be given by smaller town merchants to this credit arrangement as a possible means of holding more trade in the local area and of preventing regular customers from widely dividing their patronage. To accomplish this, the smaller town merchant will, of course, have to offer merchandise of quality, assortment, and price comparable to his larger community competitors. Revolving credit alone will not prevent a customer from shopping around for the best buy.

Type of Community

The success of a revolving credit plan is based primarily upon regularly recurring purchases and regular monthly payments on the part of customers. Thus another factor to be considered by the store contemplating the introduction of such a plan is the type of community in which it is located. Is the town one in which the inhabitants generally have a regular weekly or monthly source of income, relatively free from the seasonal income feature found in some agricultural areas and not subject to the irregularity of work

1 / "A&P Tries Credit Cards," *Business Week*, September 28, 1969, p. 42; "Food for Thought," *Management*, Januarv 1969, p. 18; Charles J. Stein, "A Community Credit Card Which Expires Monthly," *Credit World*, December 1968, p. 24.

due to strikes, layoffs, and cutbacks in industrial activities? This is not to say that such a credit arrangement is impossible in such communities, but it is imperative that in these areas merchants give long and careful consideration as to whether their customers—present and future—will be able to meet their regular monthly payments. This problem also exists, of course, in installment sales, but is involved only to a limited degree in open charge transactions.

Legal Restrictions

Careful consideration also should be given to the state laws that have been placed on the books regulating revolving credit transactions.[2] Many states have enacted specific regulations relating to the maximum amount of interest charge allowed, dollar amount permitted to be placed on the account, and other details[3] of the contract to be signed by the customer. And of course, compliance with the disclosure procedures of the federal Truth-in-Lending law is required. Appendix B contains the detailed provisions of the law.

As revolving credit has grown and expanded, so has a growing interest developed in the possible changes that might occur in the regulation of this type of credit plan. Merchant and consumer groups have developed this interest for a variety of reasons. For one thing, revolving credit agreements do not disclose the time price in dollars and cents to the customer. This is, of course, different from the conventional installment credit contracts. Thus it is a debatable point as to whether our courts will consider a revolving credit transaction as a bona fide time sale.[4] If they do not, then the possibility exists that merchants who have made these revolving credit agreements could be subject to state usury laws.[5] For this reason, more than half of the states have passed special legislation[6] to regulate revolving credit transactions. It should be pointed out that New York was the first state to pass such a law, the New York Retail Installment Sales Act,[7] which went into effect October 1, 1957 and which recognized that retail stores have different problems in handling revolving credit accounts, as opposed to other types of credit plans.

2 / Bronson LaFollette, "Revolving Credit Plans and the Law," *Credit World*, December 1967, p. 13.

3 / One point of contention has been whether interest charges should be figured on customer accounts after a payment is deducted or by computing interest using the "previous balance" method. See "Class Action Suits Hit Finance Charges of Michigan Units," *Women's Wear Daily*, August 24, 1970, p. 1.

4 / Bona fide times sales are discussed in detail in Chapter 5.

5 / "Charge-Account 'Finance Costs' of 1.5 Per Cent Under Court Attack," *National Observer*, October 26, 1970, p. 6. Also see the Suggested Readings at the end of Chapter 3.

6 / James B. Harper, *A Summary of Consumer Installment Credit Laws and Rules* (New York: Beneficial Corp., 1971).

7 / New York Retail Installment Sales Act, Personal Property Law—Ch. 41, Art. 10, as added by Laws of 1957, Ch. 599, approved April 17, 1957.

BENEFITS AND PITFALLS OF REVOLVING CREDIT

To introduce a revolving credit plan is not an automatic assurance of higher profits. The store must give careful consideration to the factors just discussed and should weigh the advantages and pitfalls of such a credit arrangement. It should be recognized that many of the advantages for the store become the reverse—that is, disadvantages—for the customers.

To the Customer

The customer who decides to purchase goods under a revolving credit plan is usually in the position of being able to charge a larger dollar volume of goods than under a regular 30-day arrangement because of the extended period of time over which payment may be made. Once the revolving credit account is established, the customer then is free to buy at any time (usually up to a limit previously determined by the store) without the need of having his credit rechecked with each purchase as is the case with the usual installment buying.

Despite the advantages, the customer encounters certain pitfalls when deciding to buy under such an arrangement. For one thing it may be too easy for the customer to buy, and thus he may find himself continually in debt to the store. In fact, it has been discovered that in some areas in which revolving credit has been actively sold to customers, these families have come to look upon revolving credit payments in the same light as income tax and other types of deductions.

Another factor for the customer to consider is, of course, the carrying charge involved in revolving credit. Thus, the customer is the one directly paying for the use of this privilege of continuous buying. With the most commonly used carrying charges running at 1½ percent per month on the unpaid balance, the customer is paying a true annual rate of approximately 18 percent.[8] As an offset to these carrying charges, it should be mentioned that the customer, under the federal income tax law,[9] is permitted to list as a deduction on his Form 1040 interest paid by him "equal to 6 percent of the average unpaid monthly balance under the contract" with the store.

8 / This rate will vary to some degree depending upon the time that the service charge is levied; that is, is the carrying charge added before giving credit for the current monthly payment and for returns and allowances, or after such credits are made to the accounts?

9 / At the time of this writing, a confrontation is shaping up between taxpayers and the Internal Revenue Service. The issue is whether a person can deduct his entire finance charge or whether he is limited to the 6 percent rule. See "Finance Charges: Are They or Aren't They Interest?" *Changing Times,* August 1970, p. 13; "Tax Report," *Wall Street Journal,* February 3, 1971, p. 1.

Another factor of importance to the customer—but often over-looked by him—is the statement that appears in some of the revolving credit agreements between customer and store. Typical of such a statement is the following:

Title to merchandise purchased on this account shall remain in you until I have paid the purchase price thereof in full. I assume and shall be responsible for all loss or damage to said goods after receipt.

Such a statement raises a question as to when merchandise bought under a revolving credit agreement is actually paid for completely and in full. Of course, no problem is involved if an account is completely paid and there is no balance owing. Under such a condition, it is obvious that title passes to the buyer. But the point in question does arise if the customer keeps a continuous balance owing to the store and if at any time the customer defaults in payment. In such a situation, just what goods if any has the customer paid for in full? In the soft-goods line, such a question is generally more theoretical than practical, since the ability to repossess soft merchandise and the advantage of doing so are obviously little. But the issue assumes greater importance as revolving credit arrangements are used more and more for hard-goods purchases.

To the Store

The primary purpose of a store in introducing revolving credit is to increase sales and, in turn, profits. If this type of credit arrangement is not productive in this manner, then the store should seriously reconsider this phase of its credit policy. Closely connected with this primary objective is the added income available to the store from the carrying charge levied on the customer. Another related advantage is the meeting of competition offered by other stores with similar plans, as well as the hope that through this plan customers of the store will be encouraged to make more of their purchases in this one retail establishment rather than divide their buying among many competing institutions. Many stores also have adopted this policy in the hope of decreasing bad-debt losses, in that customers can not only purchase more but can pay off the resulting amount owed much more easily through small but regular monthly payments.

While the store may benefit in the ways just described, it still experiences certain limitations in the use of revolving credit. This type of arrangement generally calls for more capital investment, in that payment is made over an extended period of time. Because of this time factor, some stores have found that bad-debt losses may tend to increase because of "skips." Thus the type of clientele, which may change with the introduction of revolving credit, may call for more careful and most costly credit investigation. It should be recognized that "calling for" a different type of investigation and actually "making" this more detailed analysis of the credit risks are two entirely different things. Thus some stores have continued to accept revolving credit on exactly the same basis as they accepted regular charge account credit. Another point worthy of comment is the additional bookkeeping, billing, and other related tasks that accompany revolving credit and add to the costs of its operation.[10]

FINANCING REVOLVING CREDIT PLANS

It has been pointed out that the introduction and expansion of the use of revolving credit involves the need for additional capital. This capital may be furnished by the store's reinvestment of earnings or by the investment of added funds secured from loans from commercial banks or other types of financial institutions. Either of these methods may enable the retail merchant to carry his own accounts until payments are received from customers.

The loans obtained may be based solely upon the unsecured credit position of the store, may be secured by the store's putting up certain assets as collateral for the loan, or may be obtained by the store's selling its accounts receivable outright. In the latter instance, the store may continue to collect the account and the customer generally is unaware that his account has been sold. It should be understood that these receivables are the result of previous credit transactions approved and established solely by the store.

Credit Card Plans

Another technique of financing revolving credit accounts is by means of the various credit card plans that are found in the economy today. In recent years, a rapidly increasing transfer of the activities involved in the granting and collecting of revolving credit accounts from retailers to commercial banks and private companies has occurred. This not only has been true in the United States but similar action, although more slowly, has taken place in the European way of life.[11] The credit card plans to be discussed here are the bank

10 / For an excellent study on the economic analysis of credit revenues and costs in department stores, see *Economic Characteristics of Department Store Credit* (New York: National Retail Merchants Association, 1969). For a comparison of marginal and functional cost allocations on revolving credit accounts, see page 20 of this NRMA report. Also see *Penney's Reports on the Costs of Its Credit Operations* (New York: J. C. Penney Company, Inc., 1971).

11 / "Europe's Reluctant Move Toward Credit Cards," *Banking*, February 1968, p. 45.

credit card plans and the credit card plans of the major oil companies.[12]

Bank Credit Card Plans. Bank credit card plans or, as they are sometimes called, charge account bank plans have become an increasingly important way available to retailers to carry on a credit business but to remain on a "cash" basis. These plans are relatively new, with very little mention of them found prior to 1950.[13] The Franklin National Bank in Franklin Square, New York, started the first of the current bank credit cards in August 1951. In the next two years almost 100 banks entered this field in the hopes that profits would be substantial, but about half of them discontinued this activity in a short period of time.

Tracing the history and characteristics of these plans, a Federal Reserve System report points out:[14]

A major stimulus to bank credit cards came in 1958 and 1959. By that time a number of banks had become convinced that credit cards could be profitable. The Bank of America introduced its program in 1958, and toward the end of the year Chase Manhattan Bank began credit-card operations.
. . . .
But as it turned out, the two largest banks ran into difficulty with their credit cards not long after the programs were initiated . . . .
. . . .
Bank interest has been renewed in all types of revolving credit plans in the past few years. Between 1961 and 1965, only a handful of plans came into existence, but in the summer of 1965 the two largest banks in Pittsburgh—Mellon and Pittsburgh National—introduced their credit-card programs. . . . Within a short time, reports in trade papers indicated that bankers were again becoming interested in credit-card programs.
. . . .
Until recently, bank credit-card programs were primarily local retail plans. Within the last two years, however, many practices have been introduced that have resulted in the spread of the cards beyond their former geographic limits. The Bank of America and two firms offering travel and entertainment cards—American Express and Carte Blanche—have been offering their programs to other banks for a fee. Bankers have been bombarded with ideas and proposals relating to card programs that would be national in scope. Banks in various

12 / Credit card companies, such as the American Express, Diners Club, and Carte Blanche, are discussed in connection with open charge credit transactions in Chapter 7.

13 / Robert H. Cole, *Financing Retail Credit Sales Through Charge Account Bank Plans* (Urbana: University of Illinois, Bureau of Business Management, 1955). Also see Fred D. Reynolds, *Bank Charge Plans: A Unique Form of Retail Financing* (University: University of Alabama, Bureau of Business Research, June 15, 1967); and William B. Davenport, "Bank Credit Cards and the Law," *Bankers Magazine,* Winter 1969, p. 35.

14 / *Bank Credit-Card and Check-Credit Plans* (Washington: Board of Governors of the Federal Reserve System, 1968), pp. 7-8. The Interbank group includes such plans as Master Charge, Midwest Bank Card, Firstbank Card, Marine Midland Card, Pittsburgh National, and Mellonbank Charge Service, to name just a few. The Bank of America credit card plan is known as BankAmericard.

regions have grouped together to study or introduce interregional plans. Some banks, such as the principals in the Midwest Bank Card program, have increased the coverage of their programs by signing correspondents on an agency basis. And various banking groups have agreed to interchange their cards, that is, to honor cards in the other's trade area. One example is the Interbank group.

Bank credit cards are used chiefly as a means of charging purchases in retail (and service) concerns. Credit cards are issued to consumers, who may or may not be depositors of the issuing bank. Generally, the larger banks have introduced their plans by an unsolicited—but not indiscriminate—mailing of cards to selected individuals.[15] There is no charge to the consumer for the card itself; the card entitles the holder to charge purchases at those firms that have signed with the plan. The bank bills the card holder monthly (usually on a cycle billing basis), and the card holder has the option of repaying the full balance within a specified period—usually 25 to 30 days—without any finance charge. If he does not pay in full within the prescribed time period, his account is placed on a revolving credit basis with a service charge added. The card plays the dual role of giving evidence to the merchant that a line of credit has been granted to the consumer and of being a convenient, accurate means of imprinting sales drafts. These sales slips are deposited by the merchant with the card-issuing bank or with one of its agents. In either case the merchant receives an immediate deposit (less a discount) in his own bank account. Many articles have been written on the subject of bank credit cards;[16] in these articles it appears that three main advantages are potentially available to a merchant participating in such a plan.

1. Increased Sales and Profits.   The bank plan has enabled many "cash" stores to adopt a credit policy for the first time, thereby opening the door to a new field of customers.[17] By far the greatest number of merchants enjoying this initial credit opportunity are smaller businessmen who have been limited to a cash operation because of a shortage of personal working capital and an inability to fill such a need from other sources. Thus, it appears that to some degree these charge plans are enabling smaller businessmen to compete (as far as a credit policy is concerned) with their better financed competitors. A second group of merchants involved includes store members who previously did a limited amount of credit business due to a shortage of capital or fear of loss but who

15 / This action has been modified, of course, under the Credit Card Issuance Act, effective October 27, 1970, under which no credit card may be issued except in response to a request or application. For articles on the subject of fraud in bank credit card usage see the Suggested Readings at the end of the chapter.

16 / See the Suggested Readings at the end of the chapter.

17 / See the Suggested Readings at the end of the chapter.

now may actively promote their credit business to authorized customers.

The development of neighborhood and outlying shopping areas is closely tied in with this phase of bank plan operation. It appears that in some localities these merchants are primarily the smaller type of business concerns that are often able to give only a limited amount of credit to a select group or to sell strictly on a cash basis. In attempting to continue to attract customers to their stores, many have been faced with competition on a credit basis from downtown department stores and their outlying branches. Bank charge plans have in some cases enabled these neighborhood stores to compete actively with their larger competitors, to hold old customers, and to attract new ones because of the credit-granting opportunity heretofore unavailable.

2. Conversion of Credit Accounts into Cash. One of the main advantages of these plans is the immediate cash returns for all credit sales, less the bank service charge. Thus, in a sense, the member stores can do a credit business on a cash basis. The merchant who handles all of his credit transactions through a bank has none of his money tied up in receivables and thus is in a better position to use his capital in taking cash discounts and improving the quantity and quality of goods and services offered.

3. Freedom from Credit Department Detail. In those stores that have never had a credit department or that have discontinued it upon joining the plan, this factor becomes of major significance. There is no need for the establishment, equipping, and development of a credit office, for the determination of credit and collection policies to follow, and for the hiring and satisfying of operating personnel. It is possible, however, that in many instances this advantage is overstressed. Most of the stores that have joined these plans are smaller concerns. The credit problems involved, if the stores were to handle their own credit, would be conducted usually by the owner or his wife. Thus, the need for an elaborate, well-equipped credit office simply does not exist in such stores.

Of course, there are two sides to the picture of bank credit cards, and disadvantages of the plan must be considered. These include the following:

1. Cost of Bank Service. The merchant must pay for the privilege of belonging to such a plan. Whether the cost of this privilege exceeds the benefits the merchant thinks he will derive from membership is a determining factor in his decision whether to join.

2. Loss of Store Traffic. This point appears to trouble a great many of the participating merchants and also is a strong factor in the decision of many stores not to join a plan. The importance of this factor varies by line of business and by type of customer served. If a store caters to a group that charges and pays primarily by check, then this factor is of little consequence. If payment is normally by cash within the store itself, then a distinct disadvantage of the bank charge plan appears, because the store loses the opportunity of making additional sales while the customer is within the confines of the store.

3. Other Disadvantages. In some localities, it has been found that many of the individual customers simply refuse to participate in such a plan. Some dislike letting the bank know all of their intimate credit dealings; others prefer to deal individually with the store of their choice; others do not like the methodical billing and follow-up procedure used by the bank but prefer the more informal approach between merchant and customer.

It also should be recognized that all participating stores are subject to the standard credit policy of the bank and do not have the freedom of selecting their own risks. If stores do not maintain their own credit departments and certain marginal credit customers are refused credit by the bank standards, then such customers are lost to the store unless they can be converted into cash customers.

Another objection often raised by merchants who have completely eliminated their own charge activities upon joining the plan or who have continued to carry both their own and the bank charge activities is the fact that under the bank plan they are sharing their customers with all other charge plan members. No longer does the customer feel that he belongs to a certain store where he has an account. Instead, he may feel only that he belongs to the XYZ Charge Plan.

There are indications that the bank charge plan will probably not strongly appeal to the following types of stores: those operating on the supermarket technique because the markup is too low; chain stores, which for the most part do not go along with the plan because it requires changes in their established operating policies; larger department-type stores that already have an established credit department and credit customers; and stores that are now extending credit and requiring weekly payments in the store.

Major Oil Companies. Over the years an outstanding example of the use of the credit card plan has been by the major gasoline companies (see Figure 4-3 for present-day application form). Initially these companies were very strict in their acceptance of individuals as credit risks, and only the items—such as gasoline, oil, tires, repairs—normally asked for in a service station were allowed to be charged by a card-carrying customer.

Until just recently, a consolidation of all of a customer's purchases over a period of time (generally 30 days) was made, and the

· **FIGURE 4-3**

CONTINENTAL OIL COMPANY — APPLICATION FOR RETAIL CREDIT CARD

NAME (PRINT)_____
(LAST)   (FIRST)   (MIDDLE INITIAL)   Do Not Write in These Blocks

ADDRESS: STREET_____ CITY & STATE_____ ZIP CODE_____

IF AT ABOVE ADDRESS LESS THAN ONE YEAR, GIVE FORMER ADDRESS BELOW: FOR OFFICE USE ONLY

STREET:_____CITY & STATE_____ NO. & TYPE

AGE_____MARRIED_____SINGLE_____ NUMBER OF DEPENDENTS (OTHER THAN SELF)_____ OWN HOME YES_____NO_____ EXPIRES

EMPLOYED BY_____FOR: YRS._____MOS._____

EMPLOYER'S ADDRESS:_____ PRESENT OCCUPATION_____

WIFE'S EMPLOYER_____FOR: YRS._____

ADDRESS OTHER THAN ABOVE WHERE MAIL WILL ALWAYS BE RECEIVED:

IN CARE OF_____

REFERENCES: BANK_____ BRANCH CHECKING ☐ SAVINGS ☐ LOAN ☐
(NAME AND ADDRESS)

CREDIT ESTABLISHED   SHOW CREDIT CARD NUMBER (IF ANY)

WITH: FIRM_____
(NAME AND ADDRESS)

FIRM_____
(NAME AND ADDRESS)

FIRM_____
(NAME AND ADDRESS)

NUMBER OF CARDS DESIRED_____To be charged to account carried in my name. If this Application is approved I agree to pay all charges upon receipt of monthly statement. Delinquent accounts are subject to a nominal service charge.

17-1-C REV. 5-1-67   DEALER'S NAME AND ADDRESS   DATE_____SIGNED_____

NOTE — ON APPROVED APPLICATIONS CREDIT CARDS SHOULD BE RECEIVED WITHIN APPROXIMATELY THREE WEEKS

customer was presented with one bill to be paid as a regular 30-day open account[18] with no finance charge, even for late payment. This situation has changed, however, and the major oil companies (see Figure 4-4 for a typical notice to a credit card customer) have adopted the revolving credit type of credit card plan.

Mention should be made of the "pirate" use of one oil company's card by another company. This strategy has been accomplished by such means as advertising that "We honor all major oil companies' cards" and then billing the customer directly for any purchases made. It should be pointed out that some major oil company stations also run their own credit plans in addition to the company plan. Such an arrangement, they tend to believe, holds their preferred customers to just their station, rather than encouraging them to buy at several different stations of the same major company.

Another significant development in this field has been the increasing range of items which a customer may purchase by using his gasoline credit card. These include rooms and meals at a wide variety of motels and hotels, insurance, car rentals, travel clubs, check cashing, to name only a few. Gasoline credit card holders also have been the subjects of an extensive direct-mail sales-promotion campaign to promote items that ordinarily are not associated with the typical operations of a major oil company. Such items include

18 / The regular 30-day open account is described in detail in Chapter 7.

FIGURE 4-4

STANDARD OIL
DIVISION OF AMERICAN OIL COMPANY

910 SOUTH MICHIGAN AVENUE   CHICAGO, ILLINOIS   60680

CUSTOMER SERVICES DEPARTMENT

Dear Standard Oil Credit Card Customer:

We are pleased to announce that beginning in April, we will offer our Standard Oil Revolving Charge Plan to our credit card holders. With this Plan, unique in the oil industry, we continue to pioneer new services which will better enable you to travel everywhere while enjoying the convenience of your Standard Oil credit card.

With our Revolving Charge Plan you will have a choice of how you wish to pay your bill. If the

Total Balance is:	Minimum Amount Due is:
Less than $10.	Total balance
Between $10. and $100.	$10. Plus current insurance premium, if any.
Over $100.	10% of new balance plus current insurance premium, if any.

Any insurance premium billed on your account is not included in the Revolving Charge Plan. At any time you may pay more than the minimum amount due, or even the entire balance if you wish.

A small service charge, referred to as a time price differential, will be applied only to the closing balance on each statement.

With your Standard Oil credit card, you may use the Revolving Charge Plan for all your usual and special motoring purchases, as well as for vacation travel. You may rent an auto, or truck from Avis or National Car Rental System, and enjoy fine food and lodging at Best Western, Quality Courts, and Albert Pick Hotels and Motels.

Since we have not had the pleasure of serving you recently, perhaps it is because you have misplaced your Standard Oil credit card. Just fill out the enclosed prepaid postage return card, mail it to us, and we will send you replacement or additional cards.

Through your credit card, we hope; that you will allow Standard Oil the opportunity not only to service your car, but also to serve you.

Very truly yours,

F. A. BROWN

silverware (see Figure 4-5),[19] socket wrench and tool sets, AM-FM radios, and many others. Time alone will tell how the consumer will continue to react to this new approach to credit selling.

19 / It will be noted that this technique also enables the oil company to obtain the signature of the customer to a revolving credit agreement. If a company does not have such a signature on file, the legality of a finance charge in excess of the state usury law is in question. For a good analysis of the changing picture of oil credit cards, the reader is referred to Paul S. Nadler, "A New Look at Oil Credit Card Profitability," *Credit World*, October 1969, p. 9.

FIGURE 4-5

Standard Oil 15 Day Free Trial Certificate

(STANDARD)

If you need a replacement or additional credit card, check here:
☐ Replacement Card   ☐ Additional Card

☐ **IMPORTANT!** Indicate here the initial you want hand-engraved on your Grandé tableware. (Remember, if not absolutely delighted, you may return the set even though it's hand-engraved with your initial.)

☐ **YES!** I accept your 15 day Free Trial. I want to see and feel the heavyweight Grandé 50-piece stainless steel service for 8 so I can evaluate both its design and quality for myself. If I'm not *completely* satisfied, I'm welcome to return it after using it for 15 days—even though my initial is hand-engraved on every piece—and owe *nothing*. Otherwise, you may add the low purchase price of $29.95 (plus $1.95 shipping and handling and any state or local taxes which may apply) to my Standard Oil Revolving Charge Account.

☐ Please send the 74-piece service for 12, for only $14.95 more (plus 65¢ additional shipping and handling and state or local taxes which may apply).

(If name or address is incorrect, please indicate corrections above)

SHIP TO (if different from address above):

Name_____

Address_____

City_____State_____Zip_____

I understand that a Revolving Charge Agreement must be signed by me. I have read the American Oil Company Revolving Charge Account Plan which is printed in the enclosed circular and agree to its terms and conditions. I also acknowledge receipt of an exact copy.

Please Sign Here_____

TODAY, REVOLVING CREDIT—TOMORROW, CASHLESS/CHECKLESS SOCIETY?

The impact of a cashless/checkless society on the consumer, on the retailer, and on the banker has in recent years been discussed extensively.[20] Many writers seem to feel that instant transfer of money and credit is a certainty of the computer age and its effect on the lives of all of us will be pervasive. "Technically speaking, the checkless society is virtually feasible now; the computer hardware is capable of handling it. But enormous problems remain, particularly in planning how the system will be instituted and financed, persuading the segments of the economic community to accept it, and showing them how to take advantage of it."[21]

One of the leading supporters of this development is Dale L. Reistad, president of Payments Systems Incorporated. Mr. Reistad has written and spoken extensively on this topic, and some of his more recent interesting and important ideas are shown below.[22]

The rapid rate of change in the evolution of Electronic Fund Transfer Systems (EFTS) is such that the charge account banking industry, which is at the heart of

20 / See the Suggested Readings at the end of the chapter.

21 / Robert L. Kramer and W. Putnam Livingston, "Cashing in on the Cashless Society," *Harvard Business Review,* September-October 1967, p 141.

22 / Dale L. Reistad, "Beyond the Credit Card," *The Bankers Magazine,* Spring 1971, p. 96.

these systems, is itself going through a metamorphosis. What is happening? What will instalment lending be like in the future? Will the changes be significant?

By carefully studying the trends in the evolving EFTS area, a number of predictions can be made—without going out too far on a limb:

The credit card will evolve into a "financial" or "bank" card, and every customer of every financial institution will carry one.

Financial accounts will be opened only after credit checking has been completed, and every account opened will include a "line-of-credit" feature.

Boundaries between commercial banks and other financial institutions will blur and nearly disappear. Services offered will vary only slightly between credit unions, S & L's, mutual savings banks, and commercial banks.

Instalment loans under $1,000 will be automatically generated by the "bank" card and will be automatically repaid through the line-of-credit/checking account.

Government subsidies and financial industry cooperative support will eventually permit the extension of the basic bank account, including the "line-of-credit" provision, to the lower income segment of the population.

The concept of a national bank card system will change dramatically as a result of arrangements between banks and "Travel and Entertainment" credit card organizations.

Implementation will have begun on terminal oriented electronic fund transfer systems, based on successful pilot tests conducted in the early 70's. Each major bank card system and each major computer company will be a participant in the implementation.

A combination of factors will lead to a trend toward bank data processing through facilities management contracts with data processing professionals. Chief among these factors will be one-bank holding company legislation and a shortage of high level data processing managers.

Considerable progress will have been made in automatic payment of bills through pre-authorization arrangements. Most instalment payments to banks will be handled sans paper through computer transfers. Banks will offer reduced service charges to customers willing to preauthorize in this manner.

It also seems quite probable that instalment credit departments themselves will undergo major structural changes, leading to the establishment of personal money management centers. In this respect, credit and lending experts will either change assignments or will shift to commercial lending areas of the bank.

Plastic Money. Consider the credit card. Its evolution can be seen all around us; it's almost being taken for granted. There is disagreement as to when, and under what circumstances an optimum system using the card will materialize. Just the same, plastic money will lead to something dramatic in this direction in the next five-year period—call it what you may, but it will have to do with the electronic transfer of funds.

In this connection, there does appear to be a general concern within the banking community over the present status of the credit card. Volume of both cards and retail outlets appears to be generally up, and card use appears to be growing. On the negative side, however, are such other factors as the cost of money, the continuing high percentage of convenience buying, the narrowing merchant discount levels, the high price of establishing interchange on the nationwide basis, fraud and credit losses, and the still unsolved problems of paper processing systems.

Looking at it one way, banking could be said to be "taking a bath" in developing a "credit-card system"—or it is paying a small fee for entering the era of the electronic fund transfer. If the credit card itself has been the goal, then the former would seem to be the case. But, if the card itself has been either a calculated or fortuitous step toward electronic fund transfers in anticipation of a marriage with a terminal oriented system, then the banking industry has made the smartest investment in its history.

It is now important to emphasize that the trends that seem to indicate the need for change in charge account banking are so obvious as to be discernable by most practitioners in the field. The bank credit card, with some notable exceptions, is experiencing considerable difficulty in getting established as a viable banking service. More expansion on that point isn't called for here. One has only to pick up the telephone and call a few credit card experts to become convinced that the problems with credit cards are many and involved.

A Period of Transition. This is not to suggest for one moment that banks give up on credit cards. Far from it. The card is indeed on its way to becoming the activator device for a variety of banking services in the future, the most obvious being the electronic terminal which will soon be starting to appear at the point-of-sale in place of the credit card embosser as we know it today.

What will this transition from card to activator be like? By mid-1971, standardization of credit card reading techniques will open the floodgate for the development of point-of-sale terminals by hundreds of electronics companies. The major thrust by banks at that time will involve the selection of terminals to replace embossers. This activity will be mainly the responsibility of the large bank credit card interchange and processing organizations, which will have grown by then into impressive repositories of fund transfer research and marketing capability.

Credit authorization will be of the zero dollar floor limit variety, and a few major retailers will move to direct billing from terminal-based transactions. This step will be watched carefully by retailers everywhere in much the same way that descriptive billing was watched nearly a decade earlier.

The major bank and retail credit card systems will coexist into the late 70's, both undergoing a transition to fund transfer activators—then there will be a blur, and almost overnight the retail card as we know it today will cease to exist.

The activator, or fund transfer card of the future, will look very much like today's credit card. It will probably even be of the BankAmericard, Master Charge or Uni-Card variety. On some part of the card, there will be an electronic activator which will meet standard specifications which will be even more rigid than the MICR standards today. It is too early to tell exactly what standard or standards will be selected for inter- and intra-industry use. The magnetic stripe appears to be a favorite of the airlines, but other approaches are also under consideration. What is required is a standard that will be near-fraud-proof, inexpensive to implement, and acceptable for use in point-of-sale terminals, cash dispensers, and airline ticketing machines among other devices.

With the addition of an electronic stripe or similar standard, the credit card begins to change into an activator card. It would be best if a bank's entire approach to credit cards or charge accounts change simultaneously. What this requires is to throw out the old rule book which called for mass distribution of cards, mass sign-ups of merchants, and hard sell to stimulate card usage, and reorient along the following lines:

1. Integrate the card into the basic account structure of the bank, preferably via the demand deposit account. (At least one major West Coast bank has already done this.) The future accounting structure of commercial banking seems to call for both card and check activators for fund transfer purposes.

2. Determine the premise role that the credit card is playing in your bank today and then, taking into consideration the trends in credit card technology, reappraise the role of the card in the next five year period.

¤ Will the credit card become a money card?
¤ Will terminals replace embossers?
¤ Will banks share terminals with other financial organizations?
¤ Will the card be an area card or national card?
¤ Will zero dollar floor limits be required?
¤ Will all of your customers be issued cards?
¤ Will the customer pay for the card?
¤ Will interest free periods be eliminated?
¤ Will the card be used for preauthorization purposes?
¤ Will the card have a single or multiple electronic standard (i.e.,stripe)?
¤ Will the card be used to activate cash dispensers and other robot-like machines?
¤ Will the bank permit interest free periods but not re-issue cards to convenience buyers?
¤ Will merchant discounts give way to transaction fees?

3. Develop a plan for moving from your present credit card base to the achievement of goals over the five year period. Estimate the magnitude of changes that will be taking place in terms of manpower requirements, economics, time frames, and impact on other banking services.

4. Begin to implement the plan.

A Matter of Time. Lest one think that time is not "of the essence," consider the events of recent weeks which touch on the changing role of the credit card:

¤ The American Bankers Association has sent out requests for specifications for fund transfer terminals, and is actively researching different approaches to credit card reading. This certainly is an indication that pressures are building at the A.B.A. for standards on a replacement unit for credit card embossers, hopefully to save the bank credit card.

¤ National Cash Register has finally announced its new line of electronic cash registers, which will have credit card readers and are adaptable to fund transfer purposes.

¤ J. C. Penney has issued Request For Proposals on 80-terminal, four store "bench mark" test for credit authorization. The RFP specifies "zero dollar floor limit" which is synonymous with electronic fund transfers.

¤ The Federal Home Loan Bank Board granted the savings and loan industry the right to make third party transfers. This paves the way for more sophisticated fund transfer accounts for S & L's, and the near term probability of the issuance of a form of credit card for membership use.

¤ *Bank Systems & Equipment* magazine, in a comprehensive article on payment systems progress, concluded that progress was indeed moving ahead on a number of fronts. The article contained as its lead story a prediction on the future of EFTS by PSI. In another article, Governor George Mitchell, of the Federal Reserve, stated, "Electronic technology now available and of proven capability can provide a vastly more efficient functional performance if permitted to slough off paper tracers and by-products. The needle in our paper stack that we need to find is the requisite incentive to motivate banks and others to install and accept the economies and conveniences of an electronic settlement system. Basically, we know the nature of the problem, and we know how to solve it—what is lacking is enough motivation to act."

The transition from credit cards to EFTS has indeed started. The changes now taking place are subtle, and if you don't watch for them carefully, they may not be noticed. There is the slight modification of the card itself that changes the credit card into the activator card. When the customer finally gets the modified card, there may be little or no sensation of change, and yet for that customer the EFTS era will have arrived. The J. C. Penney customer who finds out firsthand what zero dollar floor limit is all about may never know that anything happened differently from before. Again, the arrival of EFTS. When the card is used for cash dispensing, EFTS is there. Ultimately, when the card is requested by the merchant in lieu of a check—then and only then will the customer finally understand the significance of electronic fund transfer systems.

How close are we to the day of the electronic fund transfer at the point-of-sale? As noted earlier, the A.B.A. is already gathering data on the "Point-of-Sale Credit Card Terminals." A look at the section on "Features for Consideration" in their survey should reveal the kind of equipment they forsee:

1. "Size—Small, compact, fits easily on counter."
2. "Simple—Easy to operate, no special environmental requirements."
3. "Provide for mechanical or other back-up in event of power failure."
4. "Require minimum maintenance."
5. "Be reliable and accurate."
6. "Provide for voice referrals."
7. "Communications interface—Public network, dial up, touch tone, leased line, voice grade, unconditional lines."
8. "Modular and expandable."
9. "Provide for manual input of account number instead of from card."
10. "Read multiple issuer card conforming to the ANSI Standard."
11. "Transmit data on-line or capture data off-line."
12. "Ability to communicate with other CPU's."
13. "Imprinting capabilities for point-of-sale terminals, provide machine readable hard copy showing cardholder number, date authorization indicator, merchant, dollar amount and terminal I.D."

14. "Responses—Authorization approval or referral, error indication, amount verification, activate imprinter on approval; responses may be either voice display or print-out—indicate which."

The A.B.A. also asks the question, "Would production models be available within one year?" This should give some indication of the time frame of EFTS as one can interpret it from this survey from banking's major trade association group.

There is ample evidence today to discern that a clear path is being taken by both bankers and retailers in their search for a terminal approach to solving part, if not all, of the problems connected with the credit card. Several major retailers are pilot testing credit authorization terminals, and you can be certain that more than just J. C. Penney are aiming toward that zero dollar floor limit. Most major banks and banking groups are also searching for an electronic replacement for the embosser. At least one of the top five banks has already commissioned the design of a fund transfer terminal, and the Hempstead Bank in Long Island is said to be designing its second generation of fund transfer terminals while installing its first generation in a suburban Long Island pilot study. A number of banks have experimented with credit authorization terminals without print-out capability and have gathered valuable experience in the process.

Where does all this lead? Will there be a series of decisive steps by banks from embossers by Addressograph/Multigraph to electromechanical credit authorization terminals by Audac, Inc. to electronic cash registers of NCR and Pitney-Bowes-Alpex to the ultimate EFTS terminals? That would seem a rather expensive, and somewhat maddening, experience. Or, will certain banks take certain steps while other banks move in different directions vis-à-vis terminal orientation? This would be possible, but likely very disturbing to the retailers. Will all bankers agree then, at a single time, to a single standard and adopt a single machine to use? Possibly, but hardly consistent with the multidirectional marketing philosophies of bankers nationwide.

The problems in transition to EFTS are ten, even a hundred times greater than those the banking industry faced when it embarked on its great MICR journey. In order for banking to emerge unscathed and intact after the transition, it must be prepared to mount a massive effort in standards. There appears to be no alternative. For starters, there is the need for the standard for machine reading. That alone can "eat up" trade association budgets well into this decade.

Bankers will all have ample opportunity to participate in the era of EFTS. Since they are in the credit card business today, they should keep their technology quotient up and engage in some realistic short range planning in preparation for what is just around the corner. It is terribly important that they don't become the only credit card banks in town, after everyone else has made the shift to the new activator cards for EFTS banking of the future.

It is apparent that there is a great deal of uncertainty as to just what the cashless/checkless society of the future actually will be. However, it is obvious that a nationwide integrated payment system would embrace virtually every element of society: consumers, retailers, industrial firms, credit bureaus, financial institutions, and government.

REVIEW AND DISCUSSION QUESTIONS

1. What is the option-terms revolving credit plan?
2. What are the advantages of the option-terms plan to the store and to the customer? The disadvantages?
3. In his decision to adopt a revolving credit plan, a merchant must take many factors into consideration. What are these factors? Which one or ones do you believe are the most important? Why?
4. Discuss with an accountant the installment method of reporting taxable income. What is the application of this method to revolving credit transactions?
5. Discuss why the courts might decide that a revolving credit transaction is not a bona fide time sale.
6. What is usury? Discuss the usury law in your state with an attorney.
7. What are the characteristics of bank credit card plans? Is there such a plan in your community? If so, secure some promotional data on the plan and present the information to the class.
8. What are the advantages of bank credit card plans? The limitations?
9. If you were a retailer, would you join such a plan? Why or why not?
10. Discuss the recent trends in the use of gasoline credit cards to obtain goods and services.
11. What do you believe is the future of the revolving credit account?
12. What are your views on the possibility of a cashless/checkless society?

SUGGESTED READINGS

Fraud in Bank Credit Card Usage

Coha, Stephen P. "Credit Card Frauds," *Bankers Monthly Magazine*, June 15, 1967, p. 24.
McDonald, Hugh C. "Prevention and Cure of Credit Card Fraud," *Credit World*, August 1968, p. 11.
Taylor, Harold D. "The Chicago Bank Credit Card Fiasco," *Bankers Magazine*, Winter 1968, p. 49.
Watkins, Duane O. "Fraud Emerging as Major Credit Card Problem," *Credit World*, May 1970, p. 5.

Bank Credit Card Plans

"A Friendly Game of Cards," *Business Today*, Autumn 1970, p. 32.
Brennan, Jr., Edward J. "The Changing Face of Charge Account Banking," *Credit World*, September 1968, p. 21.
Breth, Robert D. "How to Make Credit Cards Profitable," *Banking*, February 1968, p. 51.
"Can the Stores Trump Bank Credit Cards?" *Business Week*, January 30, 1971, p. 62.
Doyle, Patrick E. "Small Bank Opportunities in Charge Card Banking," *Bankers Monthly Magazine*, June 15, 1969, p. 29.

Etzel, Michael J. "Merchants Look at Bank Credit Card Plans," *Credit World,* July 1970, p. 14.

Giblin, Thomas J. "Buying Accounts Receivable in Bank Card Plans," *Credit World,* February 1969, p. 14.

"Here Come the Bank Cards," *Forbes,* February 15, 1969, p. 39.

Nadler, Paul S. "Bank Credit Cards in the 1970s" *Banking,* September 1969, p. 45.

———."Evolving Implications of the Credit Card," *Banking,* October 1970, p. 3.

Rainey, Leo J. "Bank Credit Cards and Consumer Lending," *Credit World,* December 1968, p. 11.

Rodier, Jr., William I. "The Rush to Retail Banking," *Bankers Magazine,* Winter 1969, p. 106.

Roeling, Gerard H. "Bank Credit Cards: A New Force," *Management,* January 1970, p. 14.

Rogers, Nat. S. "Charge Cards—the New Face of Economic Communication," *Credit World,* January 1970, p. 18.

Rosefsky, Robert S. "When Credit Cards Take Over," *Banking,* April 1970, p. 38.

Savage, John A. "Bank Credit Cards—Their Impact on Retailers," *Banking,* July 1970, p. 39.

"Save Your Money; It Might Become Valuable," *Savings and Loan News,* June 1970, p. 37.

Stevens, William B. "Expanding Opportunities in the Bank Card Market," *Banking,* July 1970, p. 47.

———."The Expanding Role of Bank Charge Card Association," *Banking,* November 1969, p. 47.

"Store Credit: Bank Cards—No Cards or a Profitable Mix?" *Department Store Management,* March 1969, p. 24.

"The Santa Claus That Makes You Pay," *Business Week,* December 20, 1969, p. 76.

Weiss, E. B. "Must Department Stores Go Into Banking?" *Stores,* Spring 1969, p. 33.

Williams, Harold S. "Development and Problems for Bank Credit Cards," *Journal of Consumer Credit Management,* Summer 1970, p. 17.

Credit Card Behavior

Etzel, Michael J. "The Bank Credit Card's Forgotten Participant," *Journal of Consumer Credit Management,* Winter 1971, p. 81.

Mathews, H. Lee, and Slocum, Jr., John W. "Social Class and Commercial Bank Credit Card Usage," *Journal of Marketing,* January 1969, p. 71.

Penner, Irvin. "Credit Card Behavior of the Human Female," *Credit World,* September 1969, p. 17.

Slocum, Jr., John W. and Mathews, H. Lee. "Social Class and Income as Indicators of Consumer Credit Behavior," *Journal of Marketing,* April 1970, p. 69.

Cashless/Checkless Society

Appell, Allen L. "Does the Public Really Want a Cashless Society?" *Bankers Magazine*, Spring 1970, p. 48.

Brandemihl, Arnold. "Automated Bank System for Credit Verification," *Credit World*, December 1968, p. 15.

Hammerton, James C. "Is the Consumer Ready for 'Checkless Society'?" *Bankers Monthly Magazine*, November 15, 1967, p. 37.

Leos, Irving. "The Checkless Society? Retailers Have Reservations," *Stores*, February 1968, p. 30.

Mateer, William H. *The Checkless Society—Its Cost Implications for the Firm* (East Lansing: Graduate School of Business Admn., Michigan State University, 1969).

"Money Goes Electronic in the 1970s," *Business Week*, January 13, 1968, p. 54.

Reistad, Dale L. "Electronic Money Makes Its Bid," *Savings and Loan News*, September 1970, p. 36.

———. "Tell It Like It Is," *Credit World*, March 1969, p. 13.

———. "The Implications of the Checkless Society," *Credit World*, November 1967, p. 9.

Schannen, Henry A. "Consumers Begin to Speak Out on 'Less-Check Society'," *Bankers Monthly Magazine*, May 15, 1968, p. 41.

Vergari, James V. " 'Checkless Society' Revisited," *Bankers Monthly Magazine*, November 15, 1968, p. 37.

5

Types of Consumer Credit –
Retail Installment Credit

The retail installment account has been the subject of more praise and of more criticism than any other type of consumer credit. Since most American families use installment credit at one time or other, and use it primarily for the purchase of the more expensive items in the family budget, it is important to these families, to the business and financial institutions concerned, and to society in general that installment credit be used wisely and correctly.[1]

There is little doubt that consumer installment credit has played an important role in our expanding economy. It is this type of credit which is responsible for facilitating the possession of durable consumer goods and hence contributing to the material comfort and convenience of the American people. The rather recent adoption of installment credit by many service institutions will undoubtedly bring their higher valued services within the reach of the mass of middle-income families. As consumer markets for goods and services are expanded in the future, and the American people further increase their enjoyment of life, there is every reason to believe that consumer installment credit will continue to expand. The material in Table 5-1 shows the expansion that has taken place in the use of installment credit. In fact, if the production and distribution trends of today are to continue, an even greater growth in the use of installment credit must of necessity occur. Installment credit as a sales promotional tool has been so completely effective that today it is firmly rooted as a permanent part of our business structure.

1 / George Katona, "One Important Function of Instalment Buying," *Industrial Banker,* June 1970, p. 12; Mary G. Jones, "Business Responsibility in Retail Instalment Credit," *Credit World,* August 1969, p. 13; Milton J. Huber, "Installment Credit Problems Among Public Welfare Recipients," *Journal of Consumer Affairs,* Summer 1967, p. 87.

TABLE 5-1
Volume of Installment Credit by Major Types
(millions of dollars)

End of Year	Total Installment Credit	Auto-mobile Paper	Other Consumer Goods Paper	Repair and Mod-ernization Loans*	Personal Loans
1939	4,503	1,497	1,620	298	1,088
1940	5,514	2,071	1,827	371	1,245
1941	6,085	2,458	1,929	376	1,322
1942	3,166	742	1,195	255	974
1943	2,136	355	819	130	832
1944	2,176	397	791	119	869
1945	2,462	455	816	182	1,009
1946	4,172	981	1,290	405	1,496
1947	6,695	1,924	2,143	718	1,910
1948	8,996	3,018	2,901	853	2,224
1949	11,590	4,555	3,706	898	2,431
1950	14,703	6,074	4,799	1,016	2,814
1951	15,294	5,972	4,880	1,085	3,357
1952	19,403	7,733	6,174	1,385	4,111
1953	23,005	9,835	6,779	1,610	4,781
1954	23,568	9,809	6,751	1,616	5,392
1955	28,906	13,460	7,641	1,693	6,112
1956	31,720	14,420	8,606	1,905	6,789
1957	33,868	15,340	8,844	2,101	7,582
1958	33,642	14,152	9,028	2,346	8,116
1959	39,247	16,420	10,631	2,809	9,386
1960	42,968	17,658	11,545	3,148	10,617
1961	43,891	17,135	11,862	3,221	11,673
1962	48,720	19,381	12,627	3,298	13,414
1963	55,486	22,254	14,177	3,437	15,618
1964	62,692	24,934	16,333	3,577	17,848
1965	71,324	28,619	18,565	3,728	20,412
1966	77,539	30,556	20,978	3,818	22,187
1967	80,926	30,724	22,395	3,789	24,018
1968	89,890	34,130	24,899	3,925	26,936
1969	98,169	36,602	27,609	4,040	29,918
1970	101,161	35,490	29,949	4,110	31,612

*Holdings of financial institutions; holdings of retail outlets are included in "Other Consumer Goods Paper."

Note: Consumer credit data have been revised at various times, for various series, and for various periods of years. For these reasons, the consumer credit data cannot be considered to be strictly comparable for every year from 1939 to the present. The data shown are exclusive of home mortgage loans.

Source: Board of Governors of the Federal Reserve System.

FACTORS AFFECTING THE DECISION TO
SELL ON INSTALLMENT CREDIT

The decision to sell goods and services on installment credit is a major policy decision. This is so because any seller of goods or services who adopts the installment method of financing customer purchases cannot ignore the implications of this decision on his merchandising operations. His financial requirements, promotion policy, and services to customers are vitally affected by such a decision. The seller's personnel requirements become an immediate problem. Personnel who have a complete understanding of this type of credit are necessary in order to avoid many of the internal problems which can develop in the offering of this credit. To ease the impact of this decision, careful consideration should be given to the factors which influence the sale of goods and services on installment credit.

Financial Requirements

When a vendor adopts a credit policy, greater financial resources are required to offset the time element inherent in accounts receivable. A nominal strain on financial resources occurs when the vendor sells only on the open account type of credit. The turnover of accounts receivable is quite obviously more rapid when the accounts receivable are made up entirely of regular charge accounts. A different situation confronts the vendor when he adopts an install-ment credit policy. Larger sums and longer periods are involved in installment sales. Consequently the vendor's accounts receivable will turn relatively fewer times; and without additional working capital, it is quite probable that a shortage of working capital may occur.

Additional working capital may be provided by the owners of the business or by institutions which specialize in financing installment sales. Since their origin, sales finance companies have regarded the "buying" of consumer installment contracts as one of their major functions. In more recent years commercial banks increasingly have become more interested in accepting this same kind of business. Many vendors find it necessary and sometimes preferable to sell their installment contracts to one of these institutions. When this is done, the retail institution is free to channel its resources into its merchandising activities. A more detailed discussion of retailers' financing of their installment sales is reserved for Chapter 6.

Type of Goods

The degree to which the type of goods influences a vendor's decision to adopt an installment credit policy is difficult to measure. It is known, however, that the kinds of goods typically sold on installment credit have not been drastically altered in several decades. For example, before and during the early 1900s, household furniture was one of the lines of merchandise which was adapted to installment selling. By 1920 the automobile and a few household appliances were being sold on installment credit. Today, approximately two fifths of the total installment credit volume is made up of automobile paper. The vast majority of goods sold on installment terms are *durable,* of *high unit value,* and frequently possess some *repossession value.* Goods which possess these characteristics are more suitable to installment selling than other types of goods.

Competition

The policies adopted by competitors will most certainly influence other vendors' decisions. Credit is one of the most important services rendered by retailers to their customers. When this service is offered by the competition, retailers without credit service are in a weakened competitive position. The offering of durable goods to consumers without an installment credit (or in some instances, a revolving credit) plan represents a merchandising method contrary to the way in which such goods are commonly bought. The American consumer *expects* this arrangement—and chances are that he will buy his high-unit-valued items from those retailers who can satisfy this requirement. Retailers, when expanding their merchandise lines to include durable, high-ticket goods, have set the stage for their sale by adopting an installment credit policy. In this way they can compete with other retailers who offer credit.

Other Factors

Laws, passed and pending, are having an increasing influence upon retailers' decisions as to whether to introduce installment credit into their operations. The preferences of customers, certain sectional differences, and the size of a community also may influence decisions about adoption of an installment credit policy. At one time the geographical factors were more important than they are today; but as our travel and communication systems have developed, our concept of what is "local" has changed. The size of communities and the economic differences of some sections have greatly diminished in the past few decades.

DEVELOPMENT OF INSTALLMENT CREDIT

The development of all types of consumer credit was traced in Chapter 3. In many ways the evolution of installment credit parallels the development of other types of credit. It differs, however, in two important respects. First, installment credit as a business practice may have an earlier origin than other types of consumer credit. At least this type of credit transaction is more easily identified as a business practice in early literature. Second, in recent years this type of credit has registered a growth which is out of proportion to the other types. Its post-World War II expansion is greater than the combined growth of all other types of consumer credit (excluding home mortgage loan credit).

Professor Clyde W. Phelps, writing on the use of installment credit, had this to say on the development of installment credit:[2]

> Attitudes toward consumer instalment credit seem to exhibit three stages. Fifty years ago the position taken by most people regarding the use of instalment credit by consumers was one of flat condemnation.
>
> Later on, instalment credit moved into the stage of being merely suspect— rather than being condemned outright. That is to say, there developed a grudging acknowledgement that instalment credit did have some advantages. But the general attitude was to exaggerate its disadvantages, and to hold that every consumer really ought to always save and pay cash—except perhaps in buying a home.
>
> More recently, instalment credit has moved into the stage of respectability —at least in the United States. Its real advantages are coming to be more fully appreciated, while its evils are being seen in their proper proportion as characterizing only a minority of instalment credit transactions. In short, there is a gradual acceptance of the instalment plan as an important and useful tool, which may often be used to advantage, but should not be abused.

Origin and Early Use

Installment selling is indeed of very early origin. It is known that the Babylonians and Phoenicians financed marine insurance in this way. Another very early form of installment credit has been found in connection with real estate. Researches into the past reveal this device in the sale of real estate in ancient Egypt and Rome. Plutarch writes that Crassus made a profitable venture of buying up many houses in Rome during periods of conflagration and in turn selling them on the installment plan.[3] In the United States this method of financing purchases is known to have been applied to horses, carriages, and farm equipment during the 1780s.[4] One of the first retailers in the United States to adopt an installment credit policy was Cowperthwaite and Sons, founded in 1807. Nugent writes that

2 / *Using Instalment Credit* (Baltimore: Commercial Credit Company, 1955), p. *v*. The author recommends this and other volumes by Dr. Phelps. Some of the material in this and the following chapters is based on these studies. The author is indebted to him for his valuable and authentic contribution to this area of credit literature. Unfortunately, however, up-to-date revisions of these publications have not been forthcoming.

3 / R. A. Seligman, *Economics of Installment Selling* (New York: Harper & Bros., 1927), Vol. I, p. 10.

4 / Rolf Nugent, *Consumer Credit and Economic Stability* (New York: Russell Sage Foundation, 1939), ftn., p. 54.

this is "...reputedly the first specialized furniture store in the United States, [and it] began immediately after its organization to sell goods on instalment terms."[5] Within a few years pianos, sewing machines, household organs, and stoves were sold on installment terms. It is significant to note that American retailers and door-to-door agents were early in recognizing the shortcomings of any other type of credit if they hoped to sell durable goods in volume.

Prior to the Civil War, merchants who were selling high-priced durable goods devised special credit arrangements. They found that they could not expect their customers to pay for high-priced goods under the terms of the open account. Instead installment terms were encouraged to ease the impact of the debt burden and still liquidate the amount due within a reasonable period. However, prior to the Civil War, installment terms were short, down payments high, and only those who enjoyed an excellent credit reputation qualified for this "privilege."[6]

It remained for the post-Civil War period to witness the relaxed standards that permeated the installment device. Installment sales expanded in this period as merchants required smaller down payments, lengthened the contract terms, and began selling to the more marginal credit risk. The variety of goods which were sold on installment terms was also expanded. The automobile appeared to be doomed as a commonplace purchase by the early 1920s. Again installment credit came to the rescue of the American consumer, as increasing numbers of customers enjoyed private transportation on the time payment plan. Nugent contends that the expansion of installment sales of automobiles tended to reduce some of the stigma attached to this type of selling.[7] It appears logical that anything as dominant as the automobile in the American economy could have facilitated this change. With much of the stigma of installment sales removed, installment selling was expanded to additional lines of merchandise, and merchants who had at one time professed negative reaction began to adopt this method of selling. Installment credit today is a firmly established, respected, and volume-producing instrument of the retailing industry.

Increasing Frequency of Use

Installment credit alone is approximately four times greater than all other types of consumer credit (home mortgage credit being excluded) and thus has a tremendous impact upon the entire

5 / Ibid.
6 / Ibid. pp. 55-56.
7 / Ibid., p. 96.

economy. The Federal Reserve System statistics for the end of 1970 show installment volume of $101.2 billion, while noninstallment single-payment loans, charge accounts, and service credit totaled $25.6 billion. Automobile paper alone accounted for more than $35 billion of the installment credit volume. The breakdown of install- ment credit outstanding by type of credit for selected years which is shown in Figure 5-1 indicates clearly the increasing frequency of use. To what factors can we attribute the rapid growth in installment credit? It is believed that three primary factors account for the installment credit climate we see today. First, the productive geniuses of American industry have been successful in continually expanding the variety of consumer products which are particularly adaptable to installment selling; second, there is a changed attitude among consumers with respect to this type of credit; and, third, retailers have changed their attitudes with respect to this powerful selling tool.

Expanded Variety of Consumer Goods. Table 5-2 was constructed to illustrate the degree to which durable goods have expanded. This is only a partial listing of the small and large appliances offered in 1941 as compared with 1970, but it illustrates the variety of new products developed in a short span of years. Even though some of the appliances in the 1970 column were manufactured in 1941, they did not become important lines for vendors until recent years. Similarly plumbing and heating equipment, siding, insulation, roof- ing, and many other types of building materials are now typically offered on installment terms. Again, it was after World War II that building materials were introduced to a mass market of do-it-your- selfers.

The increased leisure time of Americans has opened the way for a greatly expanded market in sporting goods of all types. Installment credit sales of outboard motors, water craft, snowmobiles, motor- cycles, and camping trailers and equipment are commonplace today. The tremendous growth in the use of mobile homes[8] has been another vitally important contributing factor. New markets and opportunities for installment credit sales open up as rapidly as basic economic changes occur. All of this implies that manufacturers are alert to new market opportunities and have found success in developing markets as soon as favorable market climates develop. Increased income, home ownership, more leisure, larger families can mean only one thing—an expanded variety of goods.[9]

Changing Attitude of Consumers. Throughout the early develop- ment of installment credit, the sales techniques used by some

8 / The rapidly expanding market for mobile homes is discussed in Chapter 9.
9 / Katona, *op. cit.,* p. 12.

FIGURE 5-1
Installment Credit Outstanding by Type of Credit,
Selected Years 1950-70
(billions of dollars)

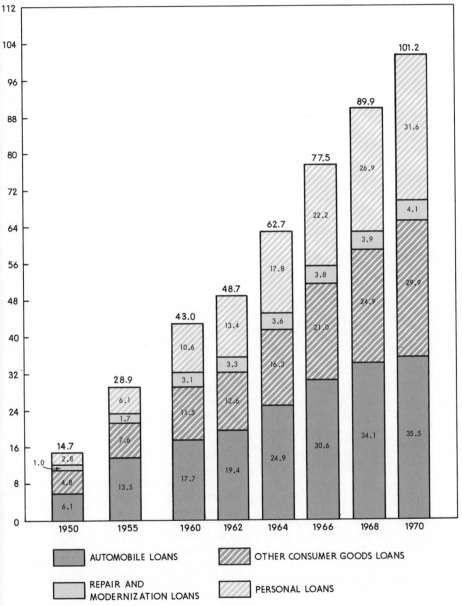

AUTOMOBILE LOANS   OTHER CONSUMER GOODS LOANS

REPAIR AND
MODERNIZATION LOANS   PERSONAL LOANS

Note: Items may not add to totals due to rounding.
Source: Board of Governors of the Federal Reserve System.

TABLE 5-2
The Small and Large Appliances of 1941
Contrasted with the Expanded Lines in 1970

1941 Appliances	*1970 Appliances*
Vacuum cleaners	Vacuum cleaners
	Built-in home vacuum systems
	Air conditioners
	Humidifiers and dehumidifiers
	Gas and electric power lawn mowers
	Riding power mowers
	Power trimmers, edgers, etc.
	Food waste disposers
	Waste compactors
Irons (dry)	Irons (steam, steam and spray)
Ironers	Ironers
	Automatic dishwashers
Radios and phono combinations	AM and FM radios; stereo combinations
	Tape recorders and players
	Radios (clock, portable, transistorized)
	Television (black and white, color, portable)
	Cassettes
Gas and electric ranges	Gas and electric ranges
	Wall ovens
	Infrared ovens
	Indoor, outdoor grills, rotisseries, etc.
	Counter cooking units
Washing machines (wringer)	Washing machines (wringer)
	Automatic washers
	Dryers
	Washer-dryer combinations
	Floor polishers, scrubbers, carpet shampooers
Water heaters	Water heaters
	Automatic coffee makers
Food mixers	Food mixers
Toasters	Toasters, broilers
	Blenders
	Can openers
	Automatic frypans and deep-friers
	Electric knives, scissors
	Ice crushers
Refrigerators	Refrigerators
	Food freezers
	Hair dryers and curlers; shavers
	Electric toothbrushes, oral hygiene sprays
	Reducing and exercising equipment

vendors were damaging to the goodwill created by installment sales. Exaggerated claims, misunderstanding between vendor and customer, and threats of force to accomplish collections contributed to the stigma which was associated with this type of selling. It was not until this stigma was removed that installment buying became commonplace for the majority of middle- and upper-middle-income groups. Fortunately the early abuses were short-lived, and industry recognized the goodwill of its customers as essential to its success. The statistics shown in Table 5-3 give a good picture of how the American family utilized its installment credit in 1969.

Changing Attitude of Retailers. Paralleling the changing attitudes of consumers is the changing attitude of retailers. Many retailers had built up the same prejudice against installment selling as consumers had against installment buying. Retailers shunned this type of selling because of the prevailing low standards of the industry, and because they failed to recognize it as a productive merchandising tool. However, as the changing attitude began to register among consumers, so it did with retailers. They observed the adoption of high standards by the sales finance industry[10] and soon were convinced of the sales possibilities of this type of credit. More and more retailers gained respect for this device and willingly accepted the installment customers as a valuable and sales-producing group. While it had been the tendency to assume a durable-goods customer as a cash or open account buyer in the early 1920s, merchants soon changed their assumption so as to regard all customers as potential installment buyers. Retailers who had formerly rejected this type of credit offered it in the sale of their durable goods and high-priced soft lines. By the middle 1920s retailers could openly promote installment credit without fear of damaging the goodwill of their customers. The trend for retailers to adopt installment selling continues to the present day. Retailers of many types, chains and independents alike, have instituted installment plans to facilitate the sale of their expanded lines of merchandise. Without question, the retailing industry now regards this type of credit as a necessary requisite. The success with which they have been able to merchandise installment sales is such that the customer who does not buy in this way at some time in his life is coming to be the rare exception.

In addition, the retailer has learned that the typical installment buyer does not stay in debt for long. The typical consumer, it is true, uses installment credit and goes into debt. But he also comes out of it with more wealth in the form of automobiles and other valuable durable goods than he had formerly. In Table 5-4 statistics are given for the years 1956 through 1970 showing the volume of the annual

10 / The sales finance industry is discussed in Chapter 6.

TABLE 5-3
Installment Debt on Automobiles, Household Durables, Additions and Repairs, and Others, within Income, Age, and Life Cycle Groups, 1969
(percentage of families in each group)

Group Characteristics	Families with Specific Type of Debt (Early 1969)			
	Automobiles	Other Durables	Additions and Repairs	Other
All families	30	20	6	23
Total family income:				
Under $ 3,000	4	8	3	10
$ 3,000– 4,999	14	19	1	18
5,000– 7,499	34	28	6	26
7,500– 9,999	43	27	7	28
10,000–14,999	45	25	8	33
15,000 and over	36	11	9	18
Age of family head:				
18-24	34	31	1	36
25-34	47	32	8	35
35-44	40	26	8	29
45-54	36	21	8	21
55-64	22	11	6	16
65 and older	7	5	3	7
Stage in family life cycle:				
Under age 45:				
Unmarried, no children	22	9	2	25
Married, no children	51	31	4	27
Married, children:				
Youngest under 6	46	36	8	39
Youngest 6 or over	46	29	8	35
45 years or older:				
Married, children	40	19	9	27
Married, no children:				
Head in labor force	27	14	7	15
Head retired	12	7	2	5
Unmarried, no children:				
Head in labor force	12	13	5	17
Head retired	3	3	4	5
Any age:				
Unmarried, children	21	28	3	20

Source: *1969 Survey of Consumer Finances* (Ann Arbor: Survey Research Center, University of Michigan, 1970), p. 29.

installment credit extended, of the annual installment credit repaid, and the net change occurring.

PRINCIPLES OF INSTALLMENT CREDIT

The foregoing sections of this chapter have pointed out some of the abuses of installment credit. These abuses came about because of

TABLE 5-4
Consumer Installment Credit
Extended and Repaid, by Type of Credit, 1956-1970
(millions of dollars)

Year	Extensions	Repayments	Net Change*
1956	39,866	37,056	2,810
1957	42,019	39,870	2,149
1958	40,110	40,339	-229
1959	48,048	42,603	5,598
1960	49,793	46,073	3,720
1961	49,048	48,124	924
1962	56,191	51,360	4,831
1963	63,591	56,825	6,766
1964	70,670	63,470	7,200
1965	78,586	69,957	8,629
1966	82,335	76,120	6,215
1967	84,693	81,306	3,387
1968	97,053	88,089	8,964
1969	102,888	94,609	8,279
1970	104,130	101,138	2,992

*Net Changes in credit outstanding are equal to extensions less repayments.
Source: Board of Governors of the Federal Reserve System.

a failure to exercise sound principles of management. It is not enough merely to adopt a credit policy and begin selling goods in exchange for credit. This activity, like other management decisions, must be governed by sound and proven principles of operation. One can observe these principles in action by a visit to a major retail establishment or by observation of the operating policies of many sales finance companies. Adherence to the following installment credit principles will successfully serve the vendor and the customer alike.

Type of Goods

Perhaps the first principle which may confront a vendor is the type of goods which he will sell on installment credit. It has already been shown that durable and high-unit-value goods are most susceptible to success. There is good reason to believe that installment sales should be confined to high-value lines. This means that any line of merchandise, whether hard or soft line, can be sold on installment credit provided it represents a major expenditure for the consumer. What is and what is not a major expenditure is a relative matter. A vacuum cleaner which sells for $79.95 may be a cash purchase for some families but an installment purchase for others. In general, goods of high unit value are consumed over a relatively long period. Consumers who purchase these goods by means of the installment plan have many months or years of enjoyment from the items. Their tendency to regard their responsibility to pay their debt is greater when they see the benefits conveyed to them by the merchandise. Long-standing obligations on goods immediately consumed place the vendor in a more difficult position from the collection standpoint.

Down Payment

The next principle of use and value to both the vendor and customer is the amount of the down payment. An accepted principle is that the down payment should be sufficient to create a sense of ownership. A sense of ownership creates pride of possession in the customer's mind and provides a safety margin for the vendor. When a sense of ownership is lacking, there is always the danger that the customer will become discouraged, hateful, and passive with regard to his obligation. While today there is a small minority of installment vendors who offer merchandise at "no money down," this policy is considered a violation of good business practice.

The amount of the down payment will of course vary with the type of goods financed. The customary down payment on new cars is from one fifth to one third of the original purchase price. Lower down payments are frequently available to those with excellent credit standings. Household furniture and appliances and many automobile accessories have a usual down payment of 10 percent. Some stores, rather than require a definite percentage down, state their requirements in dollars. Some stores advertise "no down payment" but still encourage customers to make a down payment of some amount. Down payments of some respectable amount also provide for the initial depreciation of the item. If the down payment is sufficient to do this, the payments can be somewhat lower but still adjusted to provide for more investment in the goods than depreciation.

The Amount and Schedule of Payments

The amount and schedule of payments are important in two particular ways. First, the amount to be paid must be relative to the income and other outstanding obligations of the customer. Second, it should be set up so that the unpaid balance is no greater than the resale value of the goods. With durable goods, it is a relatively simple matter to adjust the payments so that the unpaid balance is always less than the resale value of the goods. The amount of the payments should not be in excess of what is judged to be reasonable and prudently possible for the customer to meet, nor should the time of payment be set when difficulty in meeting the payments may occur. It behooves the merchant to correlate the time of payment with the receipt of income. If the customer is paid twice a month and he has a home mortgage and other obligations to meet on or about the first of each month, it would be well to charge additional installments to the income not so heavily obligated. The same procedure holds when the purchaser is paid weekly. When receipt of income is on a monthly basis, a date in the week following the receipt of income would be the logical choice.

Installment Terms

Installment terms and the amount and schedule of payments are closely related. The principle that *the unpaid balance should not be more than the resale value of the goods* is also a function of installment terms. Not only is this principle affected by the amount of payments, but it becomes a reality as the terms are adjusted in view of the useful life of an article. When terms are extended too far into the future, there is always the prevailing possibility that the owner's equity in the purchase will be too small and the item may be worth less than the amount owed on it. This presents a great risk to the vendor in that a few customers may want to be relieved of their obligation and simply surrender the article to the retailer. Avoidance of this risk may be brought about by adjusting the terms to a point within the useful life of the purchase.

In general, the terms of an installment contract should be as short as possible. When installment contracts are made to run for long periods of time, even though the customer could pay in a shorter time, an injustice is done the customer. Hence, each installment contract should be adjusted to the characteristics of the customer.

Carrying Charges

Carrying charges should be reasonable and adequate to defray the costs of installment transactions. The cost[11] of an installment business varies according to the size of the average sale and the volume transacted. In general, this is a decreasing-cost activity, inasmuch as the greater the volume, the less the unit cost. Some firms have a nominal minimum charge which appears to be an

11 / For an excellent study on the costs of installment transactions, see *Economic Characteristics of Department Store Credit* (New York: National Retail Merchants Association, 1969).

exorbitant rate when calculated against a small purchase. The principle is that the carrying charge should be sufficient to offset at least some of the costs, and that the customer gains the impression that he is "paying his own way."

The carrying charge should be expressed to the customer so that no misunderstanding develops throughout the relationship. This, of course, is covered under the Truth-in-Lending law, which is discussed in a subsequent section in this chapter. Furthermore, the customer should be truthfully advised as to his prepayment privileges and the refund rates if the balance is paid before maturity. Above all, a conscientious effort should be made by the seller to inform the customer of all aspects of the installment transaction.

Credit Investigation

The credit investigation is of unique importance in installment credit. transactions. Installment credit accounts usually represent a high average-sale figure and are extended over a relatively long time. A single-installment transaction results in the assumption of a sizable risk by the vendor or financing institution. In the sale of new automobiles, for example, the sum to be financed is quite large. The average sale of other merchandise lines adaptable to installment sales is also high. This fact alone accounts for considerable contribution to the risk factor. In addition, installment terms are frequently over long periods. It is commonplace that automobiles are sold on terms up to 36 months; and a large proportion of household furnishings and appliances are sold on terms of 12, 18, or 24 months. Extended terms are available when the size of the sale warrants this consideration. The large amount of the average sale combined with the terms present a risk peculiar to this type of credit. The principle created by these conditions is that the credit investigation should be so thorough in extent and penetration as to diminish the inherent risk. Even though it is sometimes true that the right of repossession offers considerable protection to the creditor, it must be remembered that profit in installment sales is really dependent on completion of the payments. Repossessions can be costly and even disastrous if they occur too frequently. It seems best to rely on the quality of the risk as revealed by the credit investigation rather than on other contingent factors.

It also should be recognized that frequently the resale or repossession value is lower than the amount of the note remaining at the time repossession is necessary. For this reason credit often is not granted on the basis of the value of the security at the time of necessary repossession and resale, but rather some credit personnel regard the value of the good itself as a psychological factor which keeps the customer paying on the debt. However, when the buyer's equity drops below what he owes, he too frequently feels he is paying for a "dead horse" and may be willing to permit the retailer or financing institution to repossess the item.

CHARACTERISTICS OF AN INSTALLMENT ACCOUNT TODAY

An installment account results when a consumer purchases an article for immediate use but promises to pay for it over a series of weeks or months in partial payments. It is an arrangement whereby the customer usually pays part of the purchase price at time of the sale. He agrees to a continuous series of payments at stated intervals, and he signs a written agreement as evidence of his intention to fulfill his obligation. These steps in the transaction will readily be recognized as the down payment, the amount and schedule of payments, and the installment contract. In addition to these characteristics, the purchaser will pay a larger sum for this privilege than had he paid cash for the article. This differential is known variously as the finance charge, carrying charge, service charge, or interest charge.

There are many variations in installment accounts. Retailers offer this type of credit under names such as deferred payment plan, divided payment account, budget account or budget plan, extended payment account, time plan, coupon account, convenient payment account, or simply installment account. Some of the above are merely different names for the same thing. In some instances actual variations from the installment account as described do exist. The principal differences lie in the lack of the requirement of a down payment and relatively short installment terms. Many of the above are in reality installment accounts, whereas others are a hybrid of other types of consumer credit with one or more characteristics of installment credit.

Secured Transactions—Uniform Commercial Code

The Uniform Commercial Code[12] is a uniform body of rules designed to deal, from start to finish, with all situations ordinarily arising in the handling of a commercial transaction (including installment transactions). This code, which has been adopted by 49 states, covers one of the essential characteristics of an installment account—that of the written agreement or contract accomplished by

12 / For good coverage of this code, see Arthur T. Wasserman, "How to Avoid Legal Entanglements in Credit," *Credit and Financial Management,* August 1968, p. 17.

the parties to the transaction. Commenting on this aspect of the code, the Commerce Clearing House pointed out:[13]

A variety of devices have come into existence over the years to meet special installment credit needs. Common devices used for obtaining a security interest in personal property include the pledge, the chattel mortgage, the conditional sales contract, the trust receipt and the factor's lien. Traditionally, these devices have been treated separately by the courts and the state legislatures, and separate bodies of law have grown up around each. Article 9 (Secured Transactions) of the Uniform Commercial Code, which has been adopted in a majority of states, abolishes distinctions based merely on form and refers to a "security agreement"—a term designed to embrace all security devices.

· ·

Article 9—Secured Transactions—is considered to be not only the most important part of the UCC but also the most novel. It is designed to cover all existing and future security devices and applies to all transactions which intend to create a security interest in personal property. The scope of the coverage of the Article is overshadowed only by the fact that for the first time there is an integrated branch of law designated "Secured Transactions." The Article replaces all previous laws enacted to govern security transactions. This includes laws relating to chattel mortgages, conditional sales, factors' liens, trust receipts and assignments of accounts receivable.

· ·

The fundamental purpose of the Secured Transactions Article is to provide rules under which commercial transactions may be completed with a maximum of simplicity and certainty. In line with this purpose, a completely new set of terms was chosen to avoid any implication of association with old laws. The new terms have no common law or statutory roots tying them to any particular form.

"*Security agreement*" is the agreement which creates or provides for a security interest. This replaces such terms as "chattel mortgage," "conditional sales," "assignment of accounts receivable," "trust receipts," and "factor's lien."

"*Debtor*" in all but a few cases is the person who owes the debt and the person whose property secures the debt. Where one person furnishes security for another's debt and where property is transferred subject to a secured debt of the transferor which the transferee does not assume, "debtor" may, depending upon the context, include either or both such persons. An "account debtor" is used where the collateral is an account, contract right, chattel paper or general intangibles. "Debtor" replaces conditional buyer, chattel mortgagor, trustee, or vendee.

"*Secured party*" is any person in whose favor there is a security interest. The term is used equally to refer to a seller retaining a lien on or title to goods, to a person whose interest arises initially from a loan transaction, and to an assignee of either. The seller is a secured party in relation to his customer, but the seller may become a debtor if he assigns the chattel paper as collateral. Formerly, the

13 / *Today's Instalment Credit Rules Highlighted* (New York: Commerce Clearing House, Inc., March 1966), pp. 3-5. For additional information the reader also is referred to the *Credit Manual of Commercial Laws,* prepared and published annually by the National Association of Credit Management.

"secured party" was called the chattel mortgagee, the conditional seller or vendor, the entruster, or the lender.

"Collateral" is the property subject to the security agreement. It is a general term for the tangible and intangible property subject to the security interest. Distinctions are made between different types of collateral for purposes of creating and enforcing security interests. Consequently, collateral which consists of tangible property is "goods," and "goods" are again subdivided into "consumer goods," "equipment," "farm products" and "inventory."

"Security interest" is the interest in the personal property or fixtures which secures the payment or performance of an obligation.

"Financing statement" is the new, brief UCC form which is filed to perfect the security interest. A copy of a security agreement may be filed in place of the statement.

The legal interpretations and certain remedies of the seller using installment contracts may appear to be harsh at times. In a few cases it is necessary for the creditor to exercise his rights as outlined herein. When fraud and misrepresentation appear, the creditor would do well to enforce his remedies with the strongest kind of remedial action. In the vast majority of cases, merchants are known to be very lenient in interpreting the provisions of their contracts. Vendors, sales finance companies, and banks recognize that continued profitable operations are dependent on their reputation and goodwill. Hence, great leniency prevails in most credit circles. Sickness, death, unemployment, and late payments are regarded as normal occurrences associated with the credit business.

Service Charges

Another characteristic of an installment account is that some consideration will be paid for the privilege of delayed payment. This may be called a service charge, carrying charge, finance charge, or interest charge.

The overwhelming rule for years was that a business firm could sell its goods and services at one price for cash and at a higher price on time without violating the interest and usury laws. This arose from the generally accepted idea that a sale of goods and services was involved and that a loaning of money was not connected with the transaction. Thus, interest and usury laws were interpreted over the years as applicable only to the lending of money. Carried one step further, it also was accepted in most instances that the sale of an installment contract by a business firm to a financial institution did not involve the interest and usury laws. Recent legislative and court actions in various parts of the country, however, have raised some highly pertinent questions as to the applicability of interest and usury laws to the sale of goods and services on a time basis.

Commenting on this, Professor Richardson of Arizona State University pointed out in his 1962 study:[14]

In this state and in all other states, except Arkansas, instalment sellers of automobiles, home appliances, boats, furniture, jewelry and a multitude of other goods, charge service or finance fees which, if they were converted to an annual interest rate, would exceed state usury laws. Yet, in no state, except Hawaii, are merchants licensed under small loan laws or subject to small finance charge limitations. This is because sellers of merchandise on time are not considered by the court to be making a cash loan and, therefore, there can be no forebearance or illegal interest. This ruling, called the time sale doctrine, which goes back to English Common Law, states that sellers may offer their wares for a time price which is greater than the cash price. The difference between the cash price and the time price, the time price differential or finance charge, in a *bona fide* time sale, is a matter for individual bargaining and not subject to usury restrictions.

Indiana in 1935 became the first state to pass this type of special legislation, and five other states had enacted similar legislation by 1945. Today more than 80 percent of the states and the District of Columbia have laws on their books to regulate the time sales of motor vehicles or other durable goods, or both. Provisions of these laws vary, but certain basic points are widely found. These provide:

1. State licensing of everyone in the business of buying time sale contracts.
2. Maximum limit on the time price differential, or finance charge.
3. Complete disclosure of all the contract terms, with signing of blank contracts prohibited.
4. Specific method of refunding to the customer who prepays his contract.
5. Penalties for violations.

Truth-in-Lending Law. As discussed in Chapter 3, the federal Truth-in-Lending act became effective July 1, 1969. It will be

14 / Barrie Richardson, "Regulation of Retail Revolving Credit Transactions," *Arizona Business Bulletin*, Vol. IX, No. 4 (April 1962), p. 3. Author's note: The Supreme Court of Arkansas, in a decision on December 23, 1957, held that an installment sale contract by Sears, Roebuck & Co. was usurious and void. This Sears case put Arkansas in the unique position in which merchants of the state must restrict their time price of goods to no more than the legal rate of interest above their cash price of the goods. In this particular case the contract showed "Total cash price $393.98" plus "Carrying charge $37.17." The total of $431.15 was payable in monthly installments of $22, and the carrying charge exceeded the maximum interest rate of 10 percent established by the Arkansas Constitution, which provided that "all contracts for a greater rate of interest than 10 percent per annum shall be void." In its decision the court noted that Sears has ". . . a splendid reputation for its dealings with the public; . . . but if we should hold that this contract is not usurious, it would be a precedent by which all the sellers of merchandise of every kind and description could add any amount to the cash price as interest, carrying charge, differential or what not, that those whom the Constitution and statutes were designed to protect would of necessity agree to pay. And Art. 19, par. 13, of the Constitution, prohibiting usury, would amount to nothing more than a scrap of paper."

remembered that the main purpose of this law is to assure a meaningful disclosure of credit terms (primarily the finance charge and the true annual percentage rate) so that the consumer will be able to compare more readily the various credit terms available to him and to avoid the uninformed use of credit. The installment transaction is considered under the law as a closed-end credit transaction, as opposed to the revolving credit transaction, which is considered an open-end credit transaction. For detailed provisions of the law the reader is referred to Appendix B, in which the law has been summarized.

An interesting piece of legislation foreshadowing this law was the Massachusetts Retail Installment Sales Act of 1966. This is the first statute adopted by a state to require that the service charge under retail installment sales agreement be expressed as a simple annual rate. Thus, Massachusetts became a laboratory for testing the workability of the requirement for disclosure of a simple annual rate as embodied in the Truth-in-Lending law.

Service charges and the actual cost of credit are seldom well understood by consumers. The cost of credit takes on significance for both the consumer and vendor, but for different reasons. Consumers should know the cost of credit so as to evaluate the alternatives open to them. Is the cost of the credit worth the enjoyment and service derived from this purchase? If the consumer knows this, he can accept or reject the installment credit or seek alternative ways to make his purchase. The vendor, on the other hand, must know the yield of his finance charge so that he is able to cover his costs and anticipated profit.

Methods of Converting Charges into Annual Rates

There are three terms that are important to understand in the process of converting charges into annual rates. These are: nominal rate, nominal annual rate, and true annual rate.

The nominal rate, sometimes known as the quoted rate, is simply the dollar amount of interest charge divided by the dollar amount of credit desired by the consumer. Since interest charges are normally thought of as on a yearly basis, the nominal rate must be converted to a nominal annual rate if the period of time is less than or more than one year. Since the consumer is making periodic payments in a retail installment transaction and thus does not have full use of the credit during the entire period involved, it is then necessary to convert the nominal annual rate to a true annual rate (sometimes called a simple annual rate). The interest charge in a retail installment transaction is figured on the total amount of credit desired by the consumer. However, since periodic payments are being made by the consumer, he does not have full use of this credit during the entire time period involved.

Let us take an uncomplicated example first. A person borrows $100 from a friend at 6 percent interest for one year and agrees to pay back $106 in one lump sum at the end of 12 months. In this example, the nominal rate is 6 percent; the nominal annual rate is 6 percent, since the period time involved is 12 months or 1 year; and the true annual rate is also 6 percent, since he had full use of the money in this transaction during the entire credit period of 12 months. It should be noted that this example (used for simplicity purposes) involves a loaning of money and not a retail installment sale of goods.

However, when a consumer makes a retail purchase on an installment plan and agrees to repay the principal amount throughout a series of stated intervals, he is going to pay a true rate of interest higher than the nominal rate or the nominal annual rate. The nominal annual rate does not take into account the fact that the debtor does not have use of the total principal for the entire duration of the contract. A debt of $1,000 repayable in 12 monthly installments means that the debtor actually uses the principal for six and one half months. A formula for determining this is simply $n + 1 \div 2$, where n represents the number of installments needed to discharge the debt. Hence, an installment account repaid in 10 payments means that the debtor has full use of the principal amount for five and one half months on the average. Clearly, this explains the need for computing the true rate on installment purchases. Inasmuch as the debtor has full use of the creditor's principal for slightly more than one half the total installment period, it may be already surmised that the true rate is approximately twice the nominal annual rate. For many years, in the finance field, the nominal rate per year times two was a rule-of-thumb method of computing the true annual rate. Today, under the provisions of the Truth-in-Lending law,[15]

the annual percentage rate should be determined by (1) the actuarial method of computation, prescribed in a series of formulas available from any Federal Reserve Bank; (2) the United States Rule, under which the finance charge is computed on the unpaid balance for the time the balance remains unpaid; or (3) using the charts and tables produced by the Federal Reserve Board or any other organization which has conformed its charts to Board Specifications.

The constant ratio method, which prior to the Truth-in-Lending law was the most common method in effect, may now be used only when the retailer is in the exceptional instance of not being able to use either the actuarial method or United States rule and if the retailer is not trying to evade the requirements of the law.

15 / *Truth-in-Lending* (Washington: American Retail Federation, 1969), p. 4.

Table 5-5 is a table for computing approximate annual percentage rates for level monthly payment plans.

To help the reader cope with some of the more difficult installment cases, a model method for approaching each case might be used. Such a model is presented below with an outlined step-by-step discussion. This form may be modified to the simplicity or complexity of individual installment cases.

```
a) Cash price  . . . . . . . . . . . . . . . . . . . . . $ _____
b) Less: down payment or trade-in  . . . . . . . . . $ _____
   Equals: remaining balance  . . . . . . . . . . . . $ _____
c) Plus: insurance, other purchases, etc.  . . . . . . $ _____
   Equals: balance to finance  . . . . . . . . . . . . $ _____
d) Plus: service charge  . . . . . . . . . . . . . . . $ _____
e) Equals: total amount of obligation  . . . . . . . . $ _____
```

a) Determine the cash price. The cash price of an article is the total amount that would be needed by a consumer to buy the item outright.

b) Deduct the cash down payment or an allowance for a trade-in. This line is used only when one or the other occurs in the transaction. The down payment or trade-in reduces the amount of the cash price to a remaining balance; or if no other additions are to be made, it becomes the balance to finance.

c) Add any insurance, other purchases, or "add-ons" which will increase the balance remaining so that a total balance to finance is arrived at. Insurance is a usual addition to an automobile installment account because this is a requirement of most financing institutions. Other purchases represent anything which the customer selects as an additional item to finance, such as accessory items and other small purchases. These, added to the former balance, result in the total amount to be financed.

d) Arrive at the service charge. If the charge is quoted as an annual rate, such as a 6 or 7 percent figure, merely multiply this figure by the balance to finance. Care must be exercised here so that one does not relate this nominal rate to the total amount of the obligation. It is the amount of credit sought to which the service charge applies.

e) The total amount of the obligation is the balance financed plus the total service charge. This figure is needed in order to set the amount to be paid in each installment. When the amount is not perfectly divisible by the time factor, it is customary to make all installments equal except the first or the last. In this way there is less risk of customer confusion being created.

To illustrate a complete installment transaction, the following problem is stated: an automatic washer and dryer are sold by a multiply by $100. This gives the finance charge per $100 of amount to be financed. That is, $38 ÷ $250 × $100 = $15.20. (Alternate method: Find the number of $100 units in the amount to be financed by setting the decimal two places to the left, for example, 2.50 units. Then, $38 ÷ 2.50 = $15.20.)

Step 2: Follow down the left-hand column of the table to the line for 24 months. Follow across this line until you find the two numbers between which the finance charge of $15.20 falls. In this example, $15.20 falls between $14.66 and $15.80. Read up between the two columns of figures to find the annual percentage rate. In this example it is 14%.

Approximate annual rate

: 14% :	15% :	16% :	18% :	20% :	22% :	24% :	26% :	28% :	30% :	33% :	36% :
(Finance charge per $100 of balance to be financed)											
$1.12	$1.21	$1.29	$1.42	$1.58	$1.75	$1.92	$2.08	$2.25	$2.42	$2.62	$2.88	$3.12
1.69	1.82	1.94	2.13	2.38	2.63	2.88	3.14	3.39	3.64	3.95	4.33	4.71
2.26	2.43	2.59	2.85	3.18	3.52	3.86	4.20	4.53	4.87	5.30	5.80	6.31
2.83	3.04	3.25	3.57	3.99	4.41	4.84	5.26	5.69	6.11	6.65	7.29	7.93
3.40	3.65	3.91	4.29	4.80	5.31	5.82	6.34	6.85	7.37	8.01	8.79	9.57
3.97	4.27	4.57	5.02	5.61	6.21	6.81	7.42	8.02	8.63	9.39	10.30	11.22
4.55	4.89	5.23	5.75	6.43	7.12	7.81	8.51	9.20	9.90	10.77	11.83	12.88
5.13	5.51	5.90	6.48	7.26	8.03	8.82	9.60	10.39	11.18	12.17	13.36	14.57
5.71	6.14	6.57	7.22	8.08	8.95	9.83	10.70	11.58	12.47	13.58	14.92	16.27
6.29	6.77	7.24	7.96	8.91	9.88	10.84	11.81	12.79	13.77	15.00	16.48	17.98
6.88	7.40	7.92	8.70	9.75	10.80	11.86	12.93	14.00	15.08	16.43	18.06	19.71
7.46	8.03	8.59	9.45	10.59	11.74	12.89	14.05	15.22	16.40	17.87	19.66	21.46
8.05	8.66	9.27	10.20	11.43	12.67	13.93	15.18	16.45	17.72	19.33	21.26	23.22
8.64	9.30	9.96	10.95	12.28	13.62	14.97	16.32	17.69	19.06	20.79	22.88	25.00
9.23	9.94	10.64	11.71	13.13	14.57	16.01	17.47	18.93	20.41	22.27	24.52	26.79
9.83	10.58	11.33	12.46	13.99	15.52	17.06	18.62	20.19	21.76	23.75	26.16	28.60
10.43	11.22	12.02	13.23	14.85	16.48	18.12	19.78	21.45	23.13	25.25	27.82	30.42
11.03	11.87	12.72	13.99	15.71	17.44	19.19	20.95	22.72	24.51	26.76	29.50	32.26
11.63	12.52	13.41	14.76	16.58	18.41	20.26	22.12	24.00	25.89	28.28	31.18	34.12
12.23	13.17	14.11	15.54	17.45	19.38	21.33	23.30	25.28	27.29	29.81	32.88	35.99
12.84	13.82	14.82	16.31	18.33	20.36	22.41	24.49	26.58	28.69	31.36	34.60	37.88
13.44	14.48	15.52	17.09	19.21	21.34	23.50	25.68	27.88	30.10	32.91	36.32	39.78
14.05	15.14	16.23	17.88	20.09	22.33	24.60	26.88	29.19	31.53	34.48	38.06	41.70
14.66	15.80	16.94	18.66	20.98	23.33	25.70	28.09	30.51	32.96	36.05	39.81	43.63
15.28	16.46	17.65	19.45	21.87	24.32	26.80	29.31	31.84	34.40	37.64	41.58	45.58
15.89	17.13	18.37	20.24	22.77	25.33	27.91	30.53	33.18	35.85	39.23	43.36	47.54
16.51	17.80	19.09	21.04	23.67	26.34	29.03	31.76	34.52	37.31	40.84	45.15	49.52
17.13	18.47	19.81	21.84	24.58	27.35	30.15	33.00	35.87	38.78	42.46	46.95	51.51
17.75	19.14	20.53	22.64	25.49	28.37	31.28	34.24	37.23	40.26	44.09	48.77	53.52
18.38	19.81	21.26	23.45	26.40	29.39	32.42	35.49	38.60	41.75	45.73	50.60	55.54
19.00	20.49	21.99	24.26	27.32	30.42	33.56	36.75	39.97	43.24	47.38	52.44	57.58
19.63	21.17	22.72	25.07	28.24	31.45	34.71	38.01	41.36	44.75	49.05	54.29	59.63
20.26	21.85	23.46	25.88	29.16	32.49	35.86	39.28	42.75	46.26	50.72	56.16	61.70
20.90	22.54	24.19	26.70	30.09	33.53	37.02	40.56	44.15	47.79	52.40	58.04	63.78
21.53	23.23	24.94	27.52	31.02	34.58	38.18	41.84	45.56	49.32	54.09	59.93	65.87
22.17	23.92	25.68	28.35	31.96	35.63	39.35	43.14	46.97	50.86	55.80	61.83	67.98
22.81	24.61	26.42	29.18	32.90	36.69	40.53	44.43	48.39	52.41	57.51	63.75	70.11
23.45	25.30	27.17	30.01	33.85	37.75	41.71	45.74	49.82	53.97	59.24	65.68	72.25
24.09	26.00	27.92	30.85	34.80	38.82	42.90	47.05	51.26	55.54	60.97	67.62	74.40
24.73	26.70	28.68	31.68	35.75	39.89	44.09	48.37	52.71	57.12	62.72	69.57	76.56
25.38	27.40	29.44	32.52	36.71	40.96	45.29	49.69	54.16	58.70	64.47	71.53	78.74
26.03	28.10	30.19	33.37	37.67	42.05	46.50	51.03	55.63	60.30	66.24	73.51	80.94
26.68	28.81	30.96	34.22	38.63	43.13	47.71	52.36	57.09	61.90	68.01	75.50	83.14
27.33	29.52	31.72	35.07	39.60	44.22	48.93	53.71	58.57	63.51	69.80	77.50	85.36
27.99	30.23	32.49	35.92	40.58	45.32	50.15	55.06	60.06	65.13	71.60	79.51	87.60
28.65	30.94	33.26	36.78	41.55	46.42	51.38	56.42	61.55	66.76	73.40	81.53	89.85
29.31	31.66	34.03	37.64	42.54	47.53	52.61	57.78	63.05	68.40	75.22	83.57	92.11
29.97	32.37	34.81	38.50	43.52	48.64	53.85	59.15	64.56	70.05	77.04	85.61	94.38
30.63	33.09	35.59	39.37	44.51	49.75	55.09	60.53	66.07	71.70	78.88	87.67	96.67
31.29	33.82	36.37	40.24	45.50	50.87	56.34	61.92	67.59	73.37	80.72	89.74	98.96
31.96	34.54	37.15	41.11	46.50	51.99	57.60	63.31	69.12	75.04	82.58	91.82	101.28
32.63	35.27	37.94	41.99	47.50	53.12	58.86	64.70	70.66	76.72	84.44	93.91	103.60
33.30	36.00	38.72	42.87	48.50	54.26	60.12	66.11	72.20	78.41	86.31	96.01	105.94
33.98	36.73	39.52	43.75	49.51	55.39	61.40	67.52	73.75	80.10	88.19	98.13	108.29
34.65	37.46	40.31	44.64	50.52	56.54	62.67	68.93	75.31	81.81	90.09	100.25	110.65
35.33	38.20	41.11	45.53	51.54	57.68	63.96	70.36	76.88	83.52	91.99	102.38	113.02
36.01	38.94	41.91	46.42	52.56	58.84	65.25	71.78	78.45	85.24	93.90	104.53	115.41
36.69	39.68	42.71	47.32	53.58	59.99	66.54	73.22	80.03	86.97	95.82	106.68	117.81
37.37	40.42	43.51	48.21	54.61	61.15	67.84	74.66	81.62	88.71	97.75	108.85	120.22
38.06	41.17	44.32	49.12	55.64	62.32	69.14	76.11	83.21	90.45	99.68	111.03	122.64

Source: The table was issued with Department of Defense Directive 1344.7.

TABLE 5-5
Table for Computing Approximate Annual Percentage Rate
for Level Monthly Payment Plans

EXAMPLE

Finance charge = $38   Total amount to be financed = $250   Number of
monthly payments = 24

SOLUTION

Step 1: Divide the finance charge by the total amount to be financed and

Number of level monthly payments	: 5%	: 5½%	: 6%	: 6½%	: 7%	: 7½%	: 8%	: 9%	: 10%	: 11%	: 12%	: 13% :
							(Finance charge per $100 of balance to be financed)					
1	$0.40	$0.44	$0.48	$0.52	$0.56	$0.60	$0.65	$0.71	$0.79	$0.88	$0.96	$1.04
2	.59	.66	.72	.78	.84	.91	.97	1.06	1.19	1.31	1.44	1.57
3	.79	.88	.96	1.04	1.13	1.21	1.29	1.42	1.59	1.76	1.92	2.09
4	.99	1.10	1.20	1.31	1.41	1.51	1.62	1.78	1.99	2.20	2.41	2.62
5	1.19	1.32	1.44	1.57	1.69	1.82	1.95	2.13	2.39	2.64	2.89	3.15
6	1.39	1.54	1.68	1.83	1.98	2.13	2.27	2.49	2.79	3.08	3.38	3.68
7	1.59	1.76	1.93	2.09	2.26	2.43	2.60	2.85	3.19	3.53	3.87	4.21
8	1.79	1.98	2.17	2.36	2.55	2.74	2.93	3.21	3.60	3.98	4.36	4.74
9	1.99	2.20	2.41	2.62	2.83	3.05	3.26	3.57	4.00	4.43	4.85	5.28
10	2.19	2.42	2.65	2.89	3.12	3.35	3.59	3.94	4.41	4.88	5.35	5.82
11	2.39	2.64	2.90	3.15	3.41	3.66	3.92	4.30	4.81	5.33	5.84	6.36
12	2.59	2.87	3.14	3.42	3.69	3.97	4.25	4.66	5.22	5.78	6.34	6.90
13	2.79	3.09	3.39	3.68	3.98	4.28	4.58	5.03	5.63	6.23	6.84	7.44
14	2.99	3.31	3.63	3.95	4.27	4.59	4.91	5.39	6.04	6.69	7.34	7.99
15	3.20	3.54	3.88	4.22	4.56	4.90	5.24	5.76	6.45	7.14	7.84	8.53
16	3.40	3.76	4.12	4.48	4.85	5.21	5.58	6.13	6.86	7.60	8.34	9.08
17	3.60	3.98	4.37	4.75	5.14	5.52	5.91	6.49	7.27	8.06	8.84	9.63
18	3.80	4.21	4.61	5.02	5.43	5.84	6.25	6.86	7.69	8.52	9.35	10.19
19	4.01	4.43	4.86	5.29	5.72	6.15	6.58	7.23	8.10	8.98	9.86	10.74
20	4.21	4.66	5.11	5.56	6.01	6.46	6.92	7.60	8.52	9.44	10.37	11.30
21	4.41	4.88	5.35	5.83	6.30	6.78	7.26	7.97	8.94	9.90	10.88	11.85
22	4.62	5.11	5.60	6.10	6.60	7.09	7.59	8.35	9.36	10.37	11.39	12.41
23	4.82	5.33	5.85	6.37	6.89	7.41	7.93	8.72	9.77	10.84	11.90	12.97
24	5.02	5.56	6.10	6.64	7.18	7.73	8.27	9.09	10.19	11.30	12.42	13.54
25	5.23	5.79	6.35	6.91	7.48	8.04	8.61	9.47	10.62	11.77	12.93	14.10
26	5.43	6.01	6.60	7.18	7.77	8.36	8.95	9.84	11.04	12.24	13.45	14.67
27	5.64	6.24	6.85	7.46	8.07	8.68	9.29	10.22	11.46	12.71	13.97	15.24
28	5.84	6.47	7.10	7.73	8.36	9.00	9.64	10.60	11.89	13.18	14.49	15.81
29	6.05	6.70	7.35	8.00	8.66	9.32	9.98	10.97	12.31	13.66	15.01	16.38
30	6.25	6.92	7.60	8.28	8.96	9.64	10.32	11.35	12.74	14.13	15.54	16.95
31	6.46	7.15	7.85	8.55	9.25	9.96	10.67	11.73	13.17	14.61	16.06	17.53
32	6.66	7.38	8.10	8.82	9.55	10.28	11.01	12.11	13.59	15.09	16.59	18.11
33	6.87	7.61	8.35	9.10	9.85	10.60	11.36	12.49	14.02	15.57	17.12	18.69
34	7.08	7.84	8.61	9.37	10.15	10.92	11.70	12.88	14.45	16.05	17.65	19.27
35	7.28	8.07	8.86	9.65	10.45	11.25	12.05	13.26	14.89	16.53	18.18	19.85
36	7.49	8.30	9.11	9.93	10.75	11.57	12.40	13.64	15.32	17.01	18.71	20.43
37	7.70	8.53	9.37	10.20	11.05	11.89	12.74	14.03	15.75	17.49	19.25	21.02
38	7.91	8.76	9.62	10.48	11.35	12.22	13.09	14.41	16.19	17.98	19.78	21.61
39	8.11	8.99	9.87	10.76	11.65	12.54	13.44	14.80	16.62	18.46	20.32	22.20
40	8.32	9.22	10.13	11.04	11.95	12.87	13.79	15.19	17.06	18.95	20.86	22.79
41	8.53	9.45	10.38	11.32	12.25	13.20	14.14	15.57	17.50	19.44	21.40	23.38
42	8.74	9.69	10.64	11.60	12.56	13.52	14.50	15.96	17.94	19.93	21.94	23.98
43	8.95	9.92	10.89	11.87	12.86	13.85	14.85	16.35	18.38	20.42	22.49	24.57
44	9.16	10.15	11.15	12.15	13.16	14.18	15.20	16.74	18.82	20.91	23.03	25.17
45	9.37	10.38	11.41	12.44	13.47	14.51	15.55	17.13	19.26	21.41	23.58	25.77
46	9.58	10.62	11.66	12.72	13.77	14.84	15.91	17.53	19.70	21.90	24.13	26.37
47	9.79	10.85	11.92	13.00	14.08	15.17	16.26	17.92	20.15	22.40	24.68	26.98
48	10.00	11.09	12.18	13.28	14.39	15.50	16.62	18.31	20.59	22.90	25.23	27.58
49	10.21	11.32	12.44	13.56	14.69	15.83	16.98	18.71	21.04	23.39	25.78	28.19
50	10.42	11.55	12.70	13.84	15.00	16.16	17.33	19.10	21.48	23.89	26.33	28.80
51	10.63	11.79	12.95	14.13	15.31	16.50	17.69	19.50	21.93	24.40	26.89	29.41
52	10.84	12.02	13.21	14.41	15.62	16.83	18.05	19.89	22.38	24.90	27.45	30.02
53	11.05	12.26	13.47	14.69	15.92	17.16	18.41	20.29	22.83	25.40	28.00	30.64
54	11.26	12.49	13.73	14.98	16.23	17.50	18.77	20.69	23.28	25.91	28.56	31.25
55	11.48	12.73	13.99	15.26	16.54	17.83	19.13	21.09	23.73	26.41	29.13	31.87
56	11.69	12.97	14.25	15.55	16.85	18.17	19.49	21.49	24.19	26.92	29.69	32.49
57	11.90	13.20	14.52	15.84	17.17	18.50	19.85	21.89	24.64	27.43	30.25	33.11
58	12.11	13.44	14.78	16.12	17.48	18.84	20.21	22.29	25.10	27.94	30.82	33.74
59	12.33	13.68	15.04	16.41	17.79	19.18	20.58	22.70	25.55	28.45	31.39	34.36
60	12.54	13.92	15.30	16.70	18.10	19.52	20.94	23.10	26.01	28.96	31.96	34.99

Note: The values in this table have been computed by the actuarial or annuity method, which conforms to the United States Rule.

department store for the combined cash price of $565. The down payment is 10 percent of the cash price, and the installment payments are extended over 18 months. A carrying charge of $61.02 is added to the contract. What is the true annual rate of interest involved in this retail installment transaction? What are the monthly installment payments the consumer will be asked to pay?

Cash price	$565.00
Less: down payment	56.50
Balance to finance	$508.50
Plus: service charge	61.02
Total obligation	$569.52

Following the instructions shown at the top of Table 5-5, divide the finance charge by the total amount to be financed and multiply by $100. This gives the finance charge per $100 of the amount to be financed. For the washer-dryer problem, the following computation should be made: $61.02 ÷ $508.50 × $100 = $12. As shown in step 2 of Table 5-5, follow down the left hand column of the table to the line for 18 months. Follow across this line until you find the two numbers between which the finance charge of $12 falls. Reading up between the two columns, you find that for the washer-dryer problem, the true annual rate is 15 percent.[16] Thus, the monthly installment payments can be 18 of $31.64 each.

The previous discussion has been based on what is known as the *actuarial* or *annuity* method as specified by the United States Rule set forth by the United States Supreme Court in 1839. Mention also was made of the *constant ratio* method which follows the practice of allocating a constant fraction of each monthly payment to the finance charge and to the principal amount of credit extended. Of course, many other formulas[17] are available, each of which has a different underlying assumption of the division of the monthly payments between the service charge and the unpaid balance of the principal. For example, in the *direct ratio* method the assumption is that any service charge for the use of credit is divided among the months in direct ratio to the total number of month-dollars in use during the month. This method is sometimes called the 78ths method, because on a one-year contract the digits from 1 through 12 total to 78. Thus 12/78 of the service charge would be absorbed in

16 / In using Table 5-5 it is not necessary to convert the nominal rate into a nominal annual rate. This is done automatically by the selection of the correct number of level monthly payments shown in the left-hand column.

17 / For a more detailed discussion of this topic, the reader is referred to M. R. Neifeld, *Neifeld's Guide to Instalment Computations* (Easton, Pa.: Mack Publishing Co., 1953); Robert W. Johnson, *Methods of Stating Consumer Finance Charges* (New York: Graduate School of Business, Columbia University, 1961); and Wallace P. Mors, *Consumer Credit Finance Charges* (New York: National Bureau of Economic Research, 1965).

the 1st month and only 1/78 in the 12th month. In addition, there are the *minimum yield* and *maximum yield* methods, which work on the assumption that the service charge should be deducted from the earliest or the latest payment. As a practical matter, the differences in the results obtained by using one method over another are negligible.

BENEFITS AND PITFALLS OF INSTALLMENT CREDIT

Few would deny that installment credit has been a profitable and effective sales-building tool for retailers and a means of creating much enjoyment and satisfaction in the life of consumers. The real danger in installment credit, as in so many other things, is not in its use but in its abuse. Consumers must be aware of the ease with which it is possible to overextend themselves with this type of credit. The consequences of this are that the consumer will fail to appreciate fully what the prudent use of installment credit can do for him. Numerous examples of the benefits of this type of credit are well known. There remains, however, a small number of consumers who have installment debts out of proportion to their ability to pay. This is damaging to the credit industry and presents a problem of consumer education in the use of credit.

From the standpoint of the installment retailer, he must be aware that the credit qualities of the customer are more crucial elements to the risk than the lien retained upon the article sold. Even though we are able to cite evidence of group success with installment credit, it does not mean that the retailer can offer credit unwisely. Some customers are imprudent, some impetuous, while others are dishonest. Adherence to sound principles of credit management will do much to avoid the individual who does not have the ability or character to pay.

SUMMARY

The discussion thus far has covered the factors that affect a merchant's decision to sell on installment credit, the development of installment credit, the principles of installment credit, and the characteristics of an installment account today. It has been pointed out that the installment plan is widely used in the United States and that installment buying has been instrumental in aiding the widespread ownership of consumer durable goods by American families of all income groups. But there is more to this subject—and this is a study of the financing of installment purchases and the kinds of institutions involved in this operation. This is the subject of Chapter 6 and certain parts of Chapters 8 and 9.

REVIEW AND DISCUSSION QUESTIONS

1. Why would a merchant decide to use an installment credit plan in his store rather than a revolving credit plan?

2. Why would a merchant decide to use a revolving credit plan in his store rather than an installment credit plan?

3. Discuss the factors that affect the decision of a retailer to sell on installment credit. Which of the factors do you believe is the most important? Why?

4. What is meant by the "changing attitude of consumers" toward installment credit? The "changing attitude of retailers"?

5. Can you think of any items that should be added to the list shown in Table 5-2?

6. What is meant by the Uniform Commercial Code? What impact has it had in your state on retailers and consumers?

7. What is meant by an installment credit principle? Do you believe that all of those shown are of equal importance?

8. Explain the provisions of the Truth-in-Lending law in connection with retail installment transactions.

9. What is meant by the true annual rate of interest in a retail installment transaction?

10. Why should you, as a consumer, be interested in knowing the true annual rate of interest?

11. How would you explain the benefits and pitfalls of installment credit to a newly married couple?

In computing the true annual rate of interest in the following problems, use Table 5-5:

12. An appliance store sold Mr. Brash a stereo for $495. A down payment of 10 percent of the sale price was required, and the payment period was set to cover 24 months. An interest charge of $60 was added. What is the true annual rate of interest paid by Mr. Brash? Would this rate be legal in your state?

13. The McVey family has just purchased a new television set. The cash price of the TV set is $300. The set was bought under the following arrangement: $30 down and a carrying charge of 12 percent of the balance. The payment period is 12 months. What is the amount of the note and monthly payments that Mr. McVey should agree to? What is the true annual rate of interest?

14. Mr. Curtis purchased a five-year old automobile for $950. He paid $325 down and made arrangements with his local bank to finance the balance by signing a note for $750, to be repaid in 18 monthly installments. The insurance premium was paid in cash directly to the insurance company. What true annual rate is involved in this transaction?

15. Would you say the true annual rates of interest that you figured in Problems 12, 13, and 14 are excessive? Explain why or why not.

6

Financing Retail Installment Transactions

The American consumer is making, and will continue to make, purchases of automobiles, appliances, and a wide variety of higher priced durable goods. For some of these goods, he will pay cash that he has earned or inherited. For other of these goods, he will borrow the money directly from some financial institution and will pay "cash" to the retail establishment. For still other of these products, he will make an installment arrangement with the retail seller. This retail seller may decide to carry his own installment paper until maturity or he may decide to sell it (or part of it) to a sales finance company, commercial bank, or some other type of consumer financial institution.

In this chapter, we shall be looking into the activities of the institutions, particularly the sales finance companies and the commercial banks, that are buying retail installment paper.

Consumer installment accounts may originate with the purchase of goods from a retail outlet. The retailer, whether he carries his own paper or not, takes the customer's credit information, executes the security agreement, and completes other forms and acts necessary for the establishment of the installment account. The retailer also will inform the customer as to the terms of the contract and remain ready to answer the customer's questions. Some retailers carry their own installment paper while others find it desirable to let a financial institution assume this burden. In Chapter 5 the problem of the retailer carrying his own paper was confronted. It was shown that in order to do this he would have to provide the necessary capital to compensate for a decline in his working capital turnover. Additional capital also will be needed if the retailer is successful in increasing his sales volume by offering installment credit services. In either instance a greater investment is required. The retailer who wants a faster turnover of his own capital and desires to shift much of the credit risk burden may sell his paper to a sales finance company, commercial bank, or other type of consumer finance institution. When a retailer does this he transfers the credit function to specialists in the installment credit field and frees his own organization for greater participation in the merchandising task.

Some indication of the relative importance of the installment paper carried by financial institutions as contrasted with that carried by retailers is shown in Table 6-1. It is interesting to observe that of

TABLE 6-1
Percentage Distribution of Installment Credit Outstanding by Holder
(selected years, 1950-70)

Year	Total	Com- mercial Banks	Finance Cos.*	Credit Unions	Mis- cellaneous Lenders*	Retail Outlets
1950....	100	39.4	36.2	4.0	0.7	19.7
1955....	100	36.7	41.0	5.8	1.0	15.6
1960....	100	38.8	35.9	9.1	1.5	14.7
1965....	100	40.6	34.0	10.3	1.4	13.7
1966....	100	40.4	33.6	10.6	1.4	13.9
1967....	100	40.4	33.0	11.1	1.3	14.1
1968....	100	41.1	32.4	11.3	1.4	13.8
1969....	100	41.1	32.3	11.8	1.4	13.4
1970....	100	41.4	30.8	12.4	1.5	13.9

*Finance companies consist of those institutions formerly classified as sales finance, consumer finance, and other finance companies. Miscellaneous lenders include savings and loan associations and mutual savings banks.
Note: Year-end data. Items may not add to totals because of rounding.
Source: Board of Governors of the Federal Reserve System.

the total volume of consumer installment debt, retailers were carrying only approximately 14 percent of it in recent years. Department stores, furniture stores, household appliance stores, and automobile dealers actually carry a very small portion of the debt which they have been influential in creating. Consequently, this table indicates that while the origin of installment accounts rests with retail outlets, they have a very great tendency to shift their credit burden to financial institutions. Commercial banks and finance companies are the dominant holders of installment paper, according to these data.

The paper held by finance companies accounts for approximately a third of the total installment paper and is made up principally of new and used automobiles and major household appliances. Among these finance companies, the sales finance company[1] has played, and continues to play, such a unique and important role in installment credit that particular attention is warranted for this type of institution.

DEVELOPMENT OF SALES FINANCE COMPANIES

The sales finance company is not to be confused with cash lending institutions such as small loan companies, consumer finance companies, and personal loan companies which are engaged in lending money directly to consumers and operate under special state legislation. Instead, the sales finance company is a specialized type of institution which engages primarily in buying consumer installment contracts from retail dealers and in providing wholesale financing for these dealers, and which charges rates competitive with those of commercial banks and other lenders for equivalent services.

Writing on *The Role of the Sales Finance Companies in the American Economy,* Professor Clyde W. Phelps made these excellent summary observations:[2]

1. The rise of the sales finance companies is an excellent illustration of two important principles: that institutions arise in response to social needs, and that when established institutions fail to meet the changing needs of society, new institutions come into being.

2. For many years after automobile production began, cars were sold only for cash. The limited financial resources of early car manufacturers made it impossible for them to sell vehicles on credit to automobile dealers, and they demanded cash on delivery from the latter. The dealers' financial resources were small and, therefore, they had to require cash for cars from the public.

3. As a result of this situation, the well-to-do and rich got automobiles and the masses did without. Furthermore, mass production and mass distribution of automobiles—which would make possible better cars, lower prices, increased opportunities for employment, and the advancement of the standard of living of the American people—appeared impossible.

4. The solution to this problem called for a new type of financing service which would do two things: provide wholesale financing to dealers, involving extremely large advances in proportion to their own invested capital; provide retail financing for consumers, involving instalment payments.

5. In the early years of this century, before the rise of our specialized financial institutions, the commercial banks were the established institutions

1 / As will be pointed out in a subsequent section, some sales finance companies "wear two hats." In addition to their regular sales finance operation of buying retail installment paper, they also carry on a small loan operation under state regulation. Thus "repair and modernization loans" and "personal loans" are part of the installment credit held by sales finance companies. Technically, when a sales finance company loans money directly to a consumer, it is not a sales finance company but a small loan company.

2 / Baltimore: Commercial Credit Co., 1952, pp. 9-10.

upon which society depended for financing the movement of goods from producer to consumer. The commercial banks were unwilling or unable to provide the new financing service required, and the institutions now known as finance companies came into being to meet the emerging social needs.

6. The sales finance companies pioneered in the creation and development of new financing services, and have made great contributions in the way of social benefits which are of interest to students of economics, history, sociology, and to the public generally. For one thing, the automobile revolutionized American life, and its rapid growth to the position of our No. 1 industry was dependent for its wholesale and retail financing upon the sales finance companies—banks and other institutions did not offer such financing until long after the automobile business had become our leading industry. Also, the early growth of other industries producing consumers' durables, such as radios and household appliances, was dependent upon the sale finance companies for its wholesale and retail financing.

The origin of the sales finance company dates back to the early 1900s. The *Saturday Evening Post,* in its March 31, 1900 issue, carried its first "horseless carriage" advertisement, but it was not until 1909 that the production of motor vehicles (both passenger cars and trucks) exceeded 100,000. While the first sales finance companies supplied working capital to manufacturers and wholesalers by buying open accounts and purchasing drafts and notes receivable, it was not until the increased acceptance of the automobile that the sales finance companies, as we know them today, were organized. The Commercial Credit Company began in 1916 to purchase automobile paper, and since that time the development and growth of sales finance companies have been almost without interruption. The rise of the sales finance companies parallels the growth of the automobile industry (see Table 6-2); hence the Great Depression of the 1930s and World War II were two periods in which they declined in relative importance. Three of the largest and best-known sales finance companies are Commercial Credit Company, C.I.T. Financial Corporation, and General Motors Acceptance Corporation. Each of these sales finance companies has several hundred branches throughout the United States. In addition to this vast network, there are many large regional sales finance companies and many hundreds of local companies. Many of these independent sales finance companies are members of a national association, the National Consumer Finance Association.[3]

3 / This association was formerly known as the American Industrial Bankers Association. In May 1971, consumer finance companies, sales finance companies, and industrial banks, through their respective trade associations, joined forces into one organization known as the National Consumer Finance Association. For an account of this merger, see "We have a Merger NCFA and AIBA Join Forces," *Consumer Finance News,* July 1971, p. 3.

TABLE 6-2
Rise in Automobile Registrations since 1900
(in thousands)

Year	Registrations	Year	Registrations
1900	8	1955	52,145
1910	458	1960	61,682
1920	8,131	1965	75,258
1930	23,035	1966	78,354
1940	27,466	1967	80,414
1945	25,797	1968	83,698
1950	40,339	1969 (est.)	86,560

Note: America's spectacular increase in car registrations has had only two major interruptions, the 1930s depression and World War II. Recovery and new highs quickly followed each time. Registration figures exceed the actual number of cars on the road because of continuing scrappage.
Source: *Statistical Abstract of the United States 1970*, p. 544.

In addition, during the 1950s and early 1960s the managements of a sizable number of the nation's largest nonfinancial corporations established subsidiary companies to hold notes receivable produced in connection with the parent corporation's sales. This action was taken primarily to raise needed debt capital. Writing on these so-called captive finance companies, Andrews pointed out:[4]

Overwhelmingly, the captives operating actively were and are concentrated in four of the Standard Industrial Classification (S.I.C.) industry groups—electrical machinery, nonelectrical machinery, transportation equipment and, to a lesser degree, retail trade. The roster of companies involved reads like a social register of corporations—General Electric, Borg-Warner, Philco, Motorola, Westinghouse, and others in appliances; Caterpillar, International Harvester, Koehring, and Allis-Chalmers in earth moving and other heavy machinery; John Deere and Massey-Ferguson in farm equipment; Clark Equipment, Pullman, and Fruehauf in truck trailers; International Telephone & Telegraph, Stromberg-Carlson, and General Telephone in telephone equipment; Cessna and Beech in small aircraft; Sears Roebuck, Montgomery Ward, Gamble-Skogmo, Macy, and Spiegel in retail trade; White Motor and Mack in trucks; and so on.

OPERATIONS OF SALES FINANCE COMPANIES

As stated earlier, the sales finance company is a specialized type of institution which engages primarily in buying consumer installment contracts from retail dealers and in providing wholesale financing for these dealers. Let us look now into some of the details of these operations.[5]

4 / Victor L. Andrews, "Captive Finance Companies," *Harvard Business Review*, July-August 1964, p. 82.
5 / For a discussion of the accounting aspects of these operations, see Robert M. Furman, "Financing Retail Credit Accounts Receivable," *Credit World*, June 1967, p. 13.

Financing Consumer Purchases

The usual procedure involved in the installment credit purchase of an automobile or some other type of higher priced durable item is to have the customer fill out an application form on which he gives fairly detailed information concerning his status, his employment, his income, and other pertinent factors. These application forms vary, however, from retail dealer to retail dealer. After the application is signed by the buyer, it usually is witnessed and signed by a salesman or the dealer himself. The usual contract is then prepared, and a negotiable promissory note is executed by the purchaser.

If the retail dealer then decides not to carry the paper until maturity, the contract may be offered to a sales finance company. Arrangements usually will have been made at an earlier date between the dealer and the sales finance company to provide for such transactions. It is usual procedure for the sales finance company to perform the credit investigation (although the dealer may do it at certain times), to make certain that all the documents are in order, and, if everything is found acceptable, to make the purchase. The customer's account then is opened, and the customer usually is notified of the purchase of the contract by the sales finance company. Payments then are made directly to the sales finance company. Upon final payment, many sales finance companies will send a form (similar to the one shown in Figure 6-1) to the customer.

In former years some sales finance companies were able to purchase paper under a so-called temporary repurchase plan which gave the sales finance company a short period of time to investigate the risk and to decide whether to purchase the paper. After

FIGURE 6-1

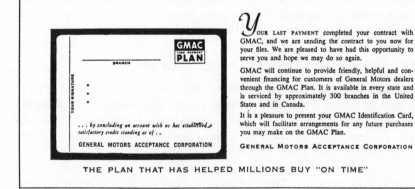

Courtesy of General Motors Acceptance Corp.

investigation, if the sales finance company decided it did not want to make the purchase, it could return the paper to the dealer, who then had to hold his own paper until maturity or locate some other buyer. This type of arrangement has become virtually extinct today, because of the press of competition.

Customer Default of Payment

The purchase of installment paper by sales finance companies comes under three major classifications: the nonrecourse plan of purchase, the recourse plan of purchase, and the repurchase plan. Under the *nonrecourse plan* of purchase, the dealer is not contingently responsible for the credit failure of the customer. Should the customer default in his payments, the dealer has no responsibility. Under this plan the sales finance company buys the paper solely on the credit quality of the installment purchaser. In the event of repossession, the sales finance company assumes the full responsibility of retaking, reconditioning, and reselling the vehicle. Under the *recourse plan* of purchase, the dealer is contingently responsible for the credit failure of the buyer. Should the buyer default for any reason, the dealer is liable to the finance company for the balance due. The dealer may repossess the vehicle on approval of the sales finance company, or the sales finance company may retake and deliver the property to the dealer. In either event the dealer is responsible for the balance due, reconditioning, and resale of the automobile. A third plan with several variations is known as the *repurchase plan.* Under the various repurchase plans the dealer is responsible for buying back the property for the unpaid balance after it has been retaken from the installment buyer. The sales finance company must first find and repossess the vehicle before it can require the dealer to repurchase it.

In sharing a contingent risk as under the recourse plan, the dealer is protected to some extent against losses by the *dealer reserve.* This fund, set aside by the sales finance company out of the finance charges, is held for refund to the dealer under specified conditions. The dealer reserve is used to cover expenses of repossession and other encumbrances against the vehicle. The reserve account is set up in the accounting records of the sales finance company. The dealer reserve ordinarily totals about 1½ percent on the amounts advanced on new automobiles, and approximately 2 to 3 percent on used cars. Payments are made periodically to the dealer in order that the retail dealer may be reimbursed on repossession from two regular sources, the car resale and the accumulated dealer reserve.

Wholesale Financing

Sales finance companies are engaged in a variety of financial activities which serve the manufacture and distribution of goods in this country. Their commercial financing involves the purchase of accounts receivables from manufacturers, wholesalers, mills, and converters. Their principal activity always has been and still is the buying of installment paper from retailers, and in particular from the automobile dealer. This same institution provides what has come to be known as *wholesale financing* to durable-goods dealers. Inasmuch as this service was first developed for the automobile dealer and he utilizes it to a great extent, wholesale financing of the automobile dealer serves as an appropriate example.

Automobile dealers are required to pay cash for automobiles delivered to them by manufacturers. The manufacturer draws a sight draft on the dealer, which is payable upon receipt of the automobiles. If dealers used their own capital to pay for the automobiles, many would have all of their working capital tied up in inventory and would be seriously limited in the quantity of automobiles they could purchase. Sales finance companies *floor plan* or *wholesale finance* the shipments from manufacturers by paying the manufacturer for the dealer. In exchange for this financing, the dealer delivers to the sales finance company the security of a trust receipt, or other form of lien. By virtue of the trust receipt, title vests in the sales finance company and the dealer retains possession of the automobiles. It is usual practice that the dealer uses the automobiles for display, storage, and demonstration. When the dealer sells an automobile listed on the trust receipt, he must immediately or within a stipulated period satisfy the sales finance company's lien. Sales finance companies charge a low rate of interest for this service, approximately half of 1 percent per month, because the risk is relatively low and the turnover of their capital rapid. In reality, the sales finance company desires that when the automobile is sold, the customer's installment paper will be offered to it.

Other Activities

The activities of sales finance companies have been changing and expanding over the years, and diversification has taken at least four different forms:[6]

The first involves retail instalment paper other than automotive such as mobile homes, boats, aircraft and farm machinery.

6 / S. Hayward Wills, "The Changing Role of Sales Finance Companies," *Industrial Banker*, January 1968, p. 13; also see "10th Annual Finance Industry Survey," *Industrial Banker*, June 1970, p. 14.

The second form of diversification involves moving into other types of financing, such as small loans and commercial lending.

A third form of diversification has been into new fields which may or may not be related to the finance industry. Here I am thinking of developments like the acquisition of a bank by C.I.T. and our own entry into manufacturing.

Finally we should mention the insurance subsidiaries of many independent finance companies.

OUTLOOK FOR SALES FINANCE COMPANIES

As consumer installment credit continues to expand, so will the sales finance companies. Consumer credit in all likelihood will expand with the growing population, the increased discretionary buying power of American families, and the expanded markets of American manufacturers. The trends of the past which have continued into the future mean an increasing amount of valuable and durable goods will be marketed. Sales of automobiles, appliances, and furniture, which have become a part of our daily living through installment buying, have every indication of continued growth. Because of the past great success of the sales finance companies in financing consumer durables, it is only natural to look for their continued future expansion.[7]

FINANCING BY COMMERCIAL BANKS

Commercial banks were late to enter into the activity of making installment loans directly to consumers or of buying installment paper from retail dealers, but they have rapidly taken an important place in this phase of consumer finance operation. Table 6-1 revealed that commercial banks held slightly more than 41 percent of the total installment debt. This represents paper purchased by the commercial banks from automobile dealers, department stores, furniture stores, and appliance stores. It also includes installment notes (to be discussed in Chapter 8) arranged directly with the installment loan department of a commercial bank. Durable-goods paper, and automobile installment paper in particular, make up the major portion of their holdings. In contrast with the sales finance company, which has little or no direct contact with the installment buyer at the time of purchase, the commercial bank may deal directly with the consumer in its installment loan department or indirectly by buying installment contracts from retail dealers. When

7 / Mention should be made in this connection of the envisioned arrangement called Packaged Universal Lifetime Credit (PULC) whereby "one institution will handle a consumer's financial needs from the cradle to the grave, from a real estate mortgage to a gasoline sale, and from life insurance to financing a boat. There will be several multi-division companies competing for every consumer's patronage." *Ibid.,* p. 15.

buying the installment contracts, the methods, contract forms, and procedures of the commercial banks are similar in many respects to those covered for sales finance companies. The interest rates of commercial banks versus the rate of sales finance companies are highly competitive in most communities.

The future undoubtedly will see even greater competition between the commercial bank and the sales finance company in the financing of retail installment transactions.

REVIEW AND DISCUSSION QUESTIONS

1. What is the primary reason for the existence of sales finance companies?
2. Explain the various ways retailers may finance their installment accounts. What factors should retailers consider in choosing one method over another?
3. How do you explain the changing pattern of the percentage distribution of installment credit outstanding by type of holder? See Table 6-1.
4. What is the National Consumer Finance Association?
5. Trace the development of the sales finance company in the United States.
6. Visit a local sales finance company office and discuss its activities with its manager.
7. Distinguish clearly between the nonrecourse, recourse, and repurchase plan of buying paper from retailers by sales finance companies. Which plan is best for the consumer? For the retailer? For the sales finance company?
8. What is floor plan financing? Why is it especially important in the automobile industry?
9. What is the primary purpose of a dealer reserve?
10. Discuss the main activities of captive finance companies.
11. Would you be interested in having your financial needs handled under some arrangement such as PULC? Why or why not?
12. Explain how the commercial bank may finance retail installment purchases through two different methods of operation.

7

Types of Consumer Credit –
Retail Charge Account Credit
and Service Credit

The businessman today uses credit to increase the profitable sale of his products or services and to improve his relations with his customers. However, his decision to introduce credit into his operations is entirely one of his own choosing, as there are no laws or regulations that force a businessman to offer his goods or services to his customers under some type of credit arrangement. His freedom of choice of the policy to follow in selling strictly for cash, strictly for credit, or under some combination of the two is influenced by his goal.

DECISION TO ADOPT RETAIL CHARGE ACCOUNT CREDIT

A well-managed store operates on the basis of sound policies predetermined to guide the courses of action that the store will follow. One such policy is the determination of whether or not to sell on credit. Credit policies cover a considerable variety of situations and are effective at a number of levels of importance. A discussion of the determination of consumer credit policies appears in Chapter 10, but at this point in our discussion we should realize that once the decision is made to sell on credit, then other corollary decisions must follow. One of these decisions is what type or types of credit to accept from the individual customers. One type is the retail charge account or, as it is often called, the open account or the 30-day account. Under this traditional retail charge account arrangement, the customer is allowed to make any number of purchases provided the total dollar amount purchased does not exceed the quantity the store desires to accept from this individual. No down payment is asked, and carrying charges are generally not involved, unless for late payment. Full payment is expected a few days after the bill is rendered by the store.

Traditionally, the retail charge account was the type that would have come to the mind of the American consumer when the word "credit" was mentioned. Today this has changed—particularly in the larger retail firms—and the revolving credit type of plan has become more or less synonymous with the word "credit" in the mind of the American consumer. However, for the smaller retail firm the retail charge account still is an important factor in its credit policies and practices.

Factors Involved in Decision

In his decision to adopt the retail charge account type of credit, the merchant must take many factors into consideration. The most important of these factors include effect on profits, desires of customers, amount of capital available, competition, type of goods, and location of community in which the store is located.

Effect on Profits. Whether or not to introduce or to expand charge account credit depends primarily upon the effect on profits that the merchant expects such an action to have. Despite all the other factors that were enumerated and that will be discussed subsequently in detail, unless a merchant believes that increased sales accompanied by increased profits will result, he will not introduce or will not attempt to expand his charge account credit activities. In some types of retail stores—for example, the grocery supermarket—the margin of profit generally is too small to permit the use of any kind of credit arrangement, and cash transactions are the rule.

Desires of Customers. The retailer must determine whether his customers actually desire the opportunity to buy goods and to pay for them some 30 days in the future, with no charge for this delayed payment. Of course, the fact that a store has a policy of accepting 30-day accounts has the reciprocal effect in that this policy attracts new customers who desire this established type of credit arrangement.

It is particularly true in the smaller retail establishments operating on a cash basis that the desires of customers often cause a change in policy and an introduction of the charge account. The smaller merchant finds his regular customers often asking him to trust them for a few days until they have the money to pay for the goods purchased, and in a short time he often finds himself doing a substantial share of his business on credit. Of course, there are firms that claim to be cash stores which carry the accounts of some of their "privileged" customers and thus should really be considered credit institutions.

Amount of Capital Available. To be able to operate a retail charge account arrangement, the merchant must realize that he automatically increases his capital needs. No longer is cash received immediately for every piece of merchandise sold; instead he is faced with the prospect of waiting 30 days (and longer) for payment of the goods sold. He is not given longer terms by his own suppliers simply because he is operating on a credit basis, and as a result is often faced with the prospect of having to borrow money to pay his own bills on time or of having to invest amounts of his own capital (if available) to meet the needs arising before customer payments are received for goods bought on account. The fact that this indebtedness is evidenced only by entries in ledger accounts handicaps the merchant in his attempts to secure loans, as he is not provided with a credit instrument that may be easily and customarily discounted at some financial institution. He must rely primarily upon his own credit standing in his attempts to secure loans for working capital to meet his recurring needs. All these points should be taken into consideration and weighed carefully by the retailer in his decision to sell his goods on a charge account arrangement.

Consideration should be given to those types of credit plans—those available under the American Express Company and the Diners Club, for example—under which the merchant does not have to provide his own capital (earned or borrowed) to carry his accounts, but rather sells his accounts receivable to the organization operating such a plan. The merchant thus continues to work on a "cash" basis but pays a fee or discount for this privilege. These will be discussed in detail later in this chapter.

Competition. Many retailers are faced with the situation that their competitors are offering charge account arrangements, and as a result they are forced to make equivalent types of credit accommodations. Of course, examples may be cited of retail stores that have grown and prospered with the adoption of a cash-carry policy, such as retail grocery supermarkets. But essentially these supermarkets are competing with similar stores selling under similar cash-carry arrangements. Only indirectly are the smaller retail grocers who offer services such as credit and delivery competing with these supermarket operators.

Type of Goods. The lines of merchandise carried by a retailer are a determinant in the advisability of adopting and actively utilizing a charge account system. Such a device is adapted primarily to merchandise that can be paid for easily by the customer within the normal 30-day repayment period. A retail store that stocks principally higher priced consumer durables such as refrigerators, stoves, and television sets—not to mention automobiles—will find that such merchandise is not adaptable in most instances to a 30-day credit arrangement. To handle such consumer goods on a credit basis requires some arrangement in which the customer is given a longer period of time to make payments.

Location of Community. The section of the country in which a retail store is located often exerts a considerable influence on the wisdom of a retailer's relying upon a 30-day charge credit system as his sole credit device. In some areas—primarily agricultural—income is not something that is received every Friday or Saturday night, but something that is dependent upon receipt of payment for various crops harvested and sold. Stores catering to such persons find that some type of credit other than the charge account is often more adaptable. In those communities, however, in which income received is a regular weekly, biweekly, or monthly occurrence, the charge account is readily usable.

DEVELOPMENT OF RETAIL CHARGE ACCOUNT CREDIT

Early Use

There is a strong belief on the most part of most of us Americans that consumer credit is a modern, present-day development. The fallacy of this concept is clearly seen in the following comments:[1]

While it is true that most of the agencies of consumer credit are new, consumer credit itself is extremely ancient. About a year ago Paul Einzig, a well-known English monetary authority, wrote a book on *Primitive Money*. He pointed out that the evolution of money tended to follow this pattern: first, barter; second, barter with credit to make barter more flexible; and third, money. Since primitive people make their economic plans on a day-to-day basis, and since they have little capital, their credit operations were largely for consumer goods. Consumer credit is prehistoric and many primitive people in remote parts of the world use it today.

What about consumer credit in our own early history? Professor Plummer of the Wharton School of the University of Pennsylvania has made a study of consumer credit in colonial Philadelphia. He concludes that a very large amount of the local trade was carried on, on a credit basis. That should not be surprising. There were no banks, and money was not always plentiful, at least dependable money was not. He says, "it seems certain that credit rather than cash was the rule." He cites the example of David Evans, a cabinetmaker who kept records over a 32-year period, 1775 to 1811. These showed 92 per cent of all sales on a credit basis. There were other similar cases. Collections were slow in those days. Samuel Powel, Jr., a linen merchant, expected that few if any customers would pay him in less than a year. Benjamin Franklin paid his bookseller, on the average, in nine and one-half months. Francis Hopkinson, who bought more

1 / Donald L. Kemmerer, "An Economic Historian Looks at Consumer Credit," *Consumer Credit Today* (Urbana: University of Illinois Business Management Bulletin No. 76, June 1951), pp. 6-8.

books than Franklin, took two and one-fourth years on the average to pay his book bill. Under such conditions the ratio of bad debts was high.

. . . .

Developments in consumer credit did not change radically in the two generations before the Civil War. Most consumer credit was probably still in the form of store charge accounts. . . . Lewis Atherton who wrote a study of pioneer merchants in the Midwest in this period says that credit extension constituted a serious probem for most merchants. . . . According to Professor Fred Jones of Illinois, well over a half of a western store's sales were on a credit basis. A frequent cause of failure was the injudicious granting of credit to customers. Merchants generally granted six months' credit without interest (those were the terms they got from wholesalers), and after six months they charged a stiff rate of interest.

Thus it appears that charge account credit in the United States dates back to the country general store in colonial days, although the present 30-day account did not appear until much later in our history. It was expected even in that time that purchases would be kept well within earnings accruing to the buyer of the goods, and that full settlement would be made upon receipt of income, however irregular that might be. In the rural areas, many of the farmers of those days found themselves in the position of possessing relatively little cash with which to make purchases. As a result, credit was employed to buy the goods needed, and harvest money was used to settle accounts for goods bought on time. This situation was not confined to the rural areas, however, and there is ample evidence that open-book credit was common in many cities in the early 1800s. All of these credit transactions were highly informal; credit was an accommodation extended to those customers who paid their bills as agreed; and the principal collection weapons were suspension of credit privileges and the pressure of public opinion.

In the commercial development period between 1860 and 1920, banks increased rapidly in number, and capital was becoming more plentiful. In the retail stores of the nation, the average length of time that open charge purchases were allowed to run was shortening, and the proportion of charge credit sales to cash sales was declining. The reason for these changes may be explained in part by the shortening of the credit terms extended to retailers, the introduction of more frequent pay days in industry, the expansion of installment credit in the purchase of higher priced consumer goods not adaptable to charge account credit, and the successful operation of many types of retail stores on a "cash sale only" basis. During this period of time, however, there appears to have been a rather consistent expansion of open account credit granting among department stores and among clothing, jewelry, and furniture stores other than those that had begun to sell their goods on the installment plan. Also during the latter part of this period, the development of retail credit bureaus provided a source of comprehensive and reliable information on individual consumers. More expert credit analysis was thus possible, permitting charge account credit acceptance with less fear of crippling bad debt losses.

Increasing Frequency of Use

In the years following the adjustment period after 1920, an expansion of charge account credit occurred, stimulated even more strongly by the active competition for the consumer's dollar between stores and between products in the same store. Credit accommodations became a vital factor in competition, and more liberal credit policies were the result. Products which faced the competition of other commodities sold under installment plans were afforded more liberal open account credit terms, and many merchants were highly hesitant in pressing good customers for prompt 30-day payments in fear of losing these desirable buyers to more lenient competing retailers.

The Federal Reserve Board has compiled a statistical series (Table 7-1) showing the dollar volume of retail charge account credit from 1929 to the present time. This series has been related percentagewise to the total volume of consumer credit (excluding home mortgage loans). An analysis of the dollar-volume statistics reveals that after reaching a low at the close of 1933, charge account credit expanded steadily until our active participation in World War II. After declining in 1942 and 1943, the dollar volume of charge account credit expanded rapidly, reaching new heights in almost each succeeding year. The general customer acceptance of charge account credit as a highly respectable transaction acceptable to all social circles, the expanding population (especially urban and suburban), the increasing level of retail prices—all these factors and others have contributed to this expanding dollar volume of charge account credit.

A decidedly different picture of retail charge account credit is revealed, however, when the percentages (charge account credit divided by total consumer credit) are analyzed. With the declining severity of the Great Depression, the situation arose in which the importance of charge account credit dropped rapidly as compared with the other types of consumer credit accepted. The growing importance of automobiles and other higher priced consumer durables resulted in rapidly expanding installment transactions. This situation was reversed temporarily throughout the World War II years, primarily because of the scarcity of such goods and secondarily as a result of government regulations (Regulation W) which

TABLE 7-1
The Changing Importance of Retail Charge Account Credit

| End of Year | Dollar Volume (in Millions) | | Charge Account as % of Total Consumer Credit |
	Charge Account Credit	Total Consumer Credit	
1929	1,602	6,444	24.9
1930	1,476	5,767	25.6
1931	1,265	4,760	26.6
1932	1,020	3,567	28.6
1933	990	3,482	28.4
1934	1,102	3,904	28.2
1935	1,183	4,911	24.1
1936	1,300	6,135	21.2
1937	1,336	6,689	20.0
1938	1,362	6,338	21.5
1939	1,414	7,222	19.6
1940	1,471	8,338	17.6
1941	1,645	9,172	17.9
1942	1,444	5,983	24.1
1943	1,440	4,901	29.4
1944	1,517	5,111	29.7
1945	1,612	5,665	28.5
1946	2,076	8,384	24.8
1947	2,353	11,570	20.3
1948	2,673	14,398	18.6
1949	2,795	17,305	16.2
1950	3,291	21,395	15.4
1951	3,605	22,617	15.9
1952	4,130	27,520	15.0
1953	4,274	31,393	13.6
1954	4,485	32,464	13.8
1955	4,795	38,830	12.3
1956	4,995	42,334	11.8
1957	5,146	44,971	11.4
1958	5,060	45,129	9.3
1959	5,104	51,544	9.9
1960	5,329	56,141	9.5
1961	5,324	57,982	9.2
1962	5,684	63,821	8.9
1963	5,903	71,739	8.2
1964	6,195	80,268	7.7
1965	6,430	90,314	7.1
1966	6,686	97,543	6.9
1967	6,968	102,132	6.8
1968	7,755	113,191	6.9
1969	8,234	122,469	6.7
1970	8,850	126,802	6.9

Note: Consumer credit data have been revised at various times, for various series, and for various periods of years. For these reasons, the consumer credit data cannot be considered to be strictly comparable for every year from 1929 to the present. The data shown for total consumer credit are exclusive of home mortgage loans.

Source: Board of Governors of the Federal Reserve System.

controlled the amount of down payment and the length of the repayment period on installment sales. With the reappearance of these consumer durables and with the increasing acceptance of revolving credit plans, retail charge account credit declined rapidly in importance as a contributing factor in the expanding overall consumer credit picture.

Present-Day Characteristics

Under the generic term "charge account," numerous plans[2] have been devised by retail merchants in their attempts to sell merchandise and to collect for these sales in a relatively short time. All of these plans have the same objective—to sell merchandise at a profit; each, however, represents some variation in the need or the ability of the merchant to meet competition and to carry the account until the customer pays the amount due the store.

Repayment Period. The words "30 days" have been used to describe the so-called "normal" period of time the retail charge account is to run. However, in actual practice bills may be outstanding for a somewhat longer period of time, depending upon general economic conditions, the season of the year, the type of store involved, and the type of customers to which the store caters.

Carrying Charges—to Use or Not to Use? This delayed payment has given rise to a problem that has troubled retail merchants for years, and continues to bother them—that of whether to charge a fee on accounts that are not paid by the end of the normal 30-day period. Undoubtedly most of the stores would prefer to add such a fee, but competition has at times proved to be a limiting factor. Also, simply because a store threatens to add a carrying charge if accounts are not paid within a certain specified time—often 60 days after receipt of statement—there is no guarantee that such a policy will be indiscriminately enforced. Many stores carefully screen their overdue

2 / In addition to the regular 30-day account, divided payment accounts may be found. It is debatable whether divided payment accounts should be classified as charge accounts or as installment accounts. Most retail merchants have recognized the fact that although their charge account terms are theoretically 30 days, in actual practice the customer may take a longer period of time to make complete payment. As a result, some retailers have used this situation as a sales promotional device and have informed their customers that they may charge higher priced goods, such as furniture, appliances, and carpeting, and make payments of one third in 30 days, one third in 60 days, and one third in 90 days. In most of these arrangements, no down payments are required, nor is any service charge made to the customer.

Another variation of the regular open charge account is the plan (virtually extinct today) which provides customers with scrip or coupons which are used to purchase merchandise within the issuing store. This plan permits a store to control the amount that a customer may purchase on credit by supplying new scrip to a customer each month only in an amount equivalent to his previous month's remittances.

accounts and are very careful not to offend their "good but slow" customers by imposing charges and by writing collection letters. If the decision is made to place a charge on late accounts, the further problem arises as to the amount to add to the account. Generally this is limited by the usury rate in the state involved.

Who Pays the Cost? It cannot be denied that the retail charge account involves a store in certain costs that are not found when a cash sale is made.[3] These costs are of several varieties. Bad debt losses occur despite the efforts made by most merchants to weigh the risk involved in increasing sales versus the possibility of nonpayment of the account. The retailer who accepts credit thus must walk the tightrope, deciding whether the acceptance of a certain account will add increased profits through increased sales while debating whether the risk is sufficiently good to offset the danger of expanding uncollectible accounts. In many stores, however, and in smaller stores in particular, pressure of personal friendship, lack of knowledge of general and local economic conditions, inadequate facilities to obtain and even lack of knowledge of how to secure credit information, pressure of other duties, and lack of adequate record-keeping—all these factors have combined to make retail credit acceptance a more careless operation than in any other type of business in which credit plays such a dominant role. Another cost factor involved is payment for personnel, equipment, and space to carry on the credit activities. If the proprietor devotes a share of his time to this function, it is apparent that he is limited in the time that he can devote to buying, selling, and other administrative duties. Another factor to consider is the cost of additional merchandise returns, which a charge account customer has come to look upon as a special privilege. In addition, if the store decides to carry the account for a period of time to secure full payment, the interest on the money tied up for this period is another cost item to consider.

All of these cost factors—and some stores consider other factors as well—lead to the question of who pays the added costs involved. It is often claimed that the store which accepts credit must charge more for its goods to cover these additional costs. This is not necessarily true, however. If these costs are spread over an increased volume of sales, the dollar amount of net profit may be larger without any increase in the selling price of the merchandise. In those instances where the price of the goods sold must be higher because of the involvement of credit, the customer should and usually does realize

3 / One of the valuable studies that have been made in this cost field is the *Economic Characteristics of Department Store Credit* (New York: National Retail Merchants Association, 1969). Costs involved in handling 30-day charge accounts, revolving credit accounts, and conventional installment accounts are covered in this study.

that he is paying this extra amount because of the added service which he is receiving.

Financing by Business Owner Himself. It has been pointed out previously that the introduction and expansion of the 30-day charge account involves the need for additional capital. This capital may be furnished by the store's reinvestment of earnings or by the investment of added funds secured from loans from commercial banks or other types of financial institutions. The loans obtained may be based solely upon the unsecured credit position of the store or may be secured by the store's putting up certain assets as collateral for the loan. It should be remembered that when financing is accomplished by the business owner himself, under the methods just described, the retailer will carry his own charge accounts until payments are received from customers.

Financing through Private Credit Card Companies. The 30-day charge has been the basis of many of the private credit card companies that have appeared in the last two decades. Despite all the humor on this topic that appeared in cartoons and storytelling, the private credit card industry did not have much to laugh about in the early years of its development. However, by the mid-1960s this situation had changed, primarily because of the increased use of automation, the elimination of poor credit risks, and the entrance into new areas of business opportunity.[4]

The American Express Company (see Figure 7-1 for American Express Card Application form), the Diners Club, and the Carte Blanche are among the leaders in this field. Different rates of growth have been experienced by these plans, with the Diners Club being the "granddaddy" of them, dating back to 1950. American Express entered the field in 1958.[5] Under these plans, the customer pays an annual fee (usually in the $11 to $15 range) to the organization, has the privilege of saying "charge it" at member establishments, and then receives just one itemized monthly statement of the charges. This gives the customer an itemized record of expenditures and travels through the monthly statement—this record serving as supporting proof of legitimate business expenses for tax filing

4 / For a good coverage of the changing pattern of the operations of these private credit card companies, see "The Trick is Managing Money," *Business Week,* June 6, 1970, p. 75; and "Shuffling Cards at Diners Club," *Business Week,* December 27, 1969, p. 20.

5 / The American Express Company (Amexco, as it is sometimes known) reluctantly entered the credit card business as a defensive move. However, in 1963 the company was badly hurt financially when the so-called salad-oil swindle shocked the company awake. In this swindle, salad oil was supposedly put into an American Express subsidiary's storage tanks in New Jersey and then money was borrowed on the receipts for the oil that wasn't there. The company was almost wrecked, and in its attempt to rebuild quickly the company decided to intensify its credit card business. The decision has proved to be a wise one. For a coverage of this unusual chain of events, see "Disaster Can Be Good For You," *Forbes,* February 1, 1969, p. 18.

FIGURE 7-1

AMERICAN EXPRESS CARD APPLICATION
Please print or type information

| C | P | | PP | B | | O | | FS | | H | | PH | | AI | | R | | |

PLEASE DO NOT WRITE ABOVE THIS LINE. FOR OFFICE USE ONLY

DO NOT ENCLOSE $15.00 ANNUAL FEE. WE WILL BILL YOU LATER.

PERSONAL ACCOUNT – MAIL BILL TO OFFICE ☐
PERSONAL ACCOUNT – MAIL BILL TO HOME ☐
COMPANY ACCOUNT – MAIL BILL TO OFFICE ☐

NOTE: If earnings shown are less than $7500, indicate source and amount of any other income, e.g. commissions, expense account, dividends, investment income. Fill in below)

PRINT NAME (First) (Middle) (Last) | AGE | SPOUSE (First Name)

HOME ADDRESS (Street) (City) (State or Country) (Zip Code)

TELEPHONE | YEARS AT PRESENT ADDRESS | OWN HOME ☐ RENT ☐ | NUMBER OF DEPENDENTS | SOCIAL SECURITY NO.

PREVIOUS HOME ADDRESS (Street) (City) (State or Country) HOW LONG

FIRM NAME OR EMPLOYER | NATURE OF BUSINESS

ADDRESS (Street) (City) (State or Country) (Zip Code)

POSITION | ANNUAL EARNINGS | YEARS WITH FIRM | TELEPHONE

ADDRESS (Street & City) IF BILLING IS TO GO TO A BUSINESS ADDRESS OTHER THAN MAIN OFFICE ADDRESS PLEASE SPECIFY (State or Country) (Zip Code)

PREVIOUS EMPLOYER (If employed by above less than 3 years) OR COLLEGE/UNIVERSITY IF RECENT GRADUATE | YEARS WITH FIRM OR YEAR GRADUATED

ADDRESS (Street) (City) (State or Country) (Zip Code)

BANK (When for Company Account show Company Banks)

ADDRESS | ACCT. NUMBER / TYPE ACCOUNT

BANK (When for Company Account show Company Banks)

ADDRESS | ACCT. NUMBER / TYPE ACCOUNT

OTHER CHARGE ACCOUNTS (Include other national credit cards)

The undersigned agree(s) that if this application is accepted and a Card issued, the individual and the company he represents, if this is a company account, will be bound by the terms and conditions accompanying the Card and any renewal or replacement card, unless he returns the Card immediately. The individual applicant and the company, if this is a company account, will be liable for all charges incurred with the Card and all supplementary Cards issued on the account. Each supplementary applicant will be liable for all charges incurred with the supplementary Card, jointly and severally with the holder of the basic Card.

DO YOU NOW HAVE ☐ OR HAVE YOU PREVIOUSLY HAD ☐ A PERSONAL ☐ OR A COMPANY ☐ ACCOUNT WITH AMERICAN EXPRESS?
IF YOU KNOW THE ACCOUNT NUMBER WRITE IT HERE

PLEASE SEND ME SUPPLEMENTARY CARDS FOR IMMEDIATE MEMBERS OF MY FAMILY AS FOLLOWS: (PRINT NAMES):
(First) (Middle) (Last) (First) (Middle) (Last)

(SIGNATURE of supplementary applicant) (RELATIONSHIP) (SIGNATURE of supplementary applicant) (RELATIONSHIP)

DO NOT ENCLOSE $10.00 ANNUAL SUPPLEMENTARY CARD FEE. WE WILL BILL YOU LATER.

In addition please send me _____ applications for supplementary cards for other immediate members of my family ☐ for other members of my firm ☐

NOTE: For Company Accounts, signatures of both applicant and authorizing officer are required.

X SIGNATURE OF INDIVIDUAL APPLICANT (ink only) _____ DATE _____

X COMPANY ACCOUNT AUTHORIZATION (ink only) _____
(Must be signed if company account) (Signature of Authorizing Officer) (Title)

purposes. Retailers who agree to honor the cards pay a stipulated percentage discount in order to be reimbursed immediately for the customers' charges.

The policies followed by the American Express Company and the Diners Club in connection with late payments by consumers are as follows:[6]

Diners Club: Our accounts are 30 day accounts. If a cardholder is late in payment the service is 1½%. Yes, our card is an international credit card, it can be used in purchasing airline tickets. An airline charge is the only thing that can be extended for payment, depending upon the amount the extension can go up to 24 months. Again, the service charge is 1½% of the unpaid balance of the charge.

6 / This material was obtained from personal correspondence with Diners Club dated February 5, 1971, and with American Express Company dated March 29, 1971.

American Express Company: Delinquency charges are assessed at 1.5% on accounts that are 90 days over-due. The charge is computed on the amount that is 60 days past-due. Airline charges can be deferred over 3, 6, or 12 months. There is a finance charge under our Extended Payment Plan of Sign and Fly based on an annual percentage rate of 12%.

SERVICE CREDIT

Although service credit is recognized as an important segment of the total consumer credit picture, it is a subject that has been practically ignored in the consumer credit literature. While the subjects of retail credit and cash loan credit have been closely followed and analyzed by consumer credit observers, only lip service has been paid to service credit. It has been considered sufficient to say that there is such a thing as service credit—even though the American consumer owes in excess of $7 billion for services he has received.

In the statistics reported monthly in the *Federal Reserve Bulletin* (see Table 7-2), service credit has been defined as "the amount owed by individuals to professional practicioners and service establishments."

Problems of Professional Credit

Credit is a customary method of doing business with members of the medical and dental professions. Under normal conditions, almost all private practitioners and clinics accept some credit from their patients, and most of them expect to collect the greater part of the amount due them for these services.[7] It should be recognized, however, that in some instances fees for some patients are entered as receivables on the books, even though it is known by the practitioner that the recipients of the service will be unable to pay at any time in the future.

Whereas the 30-day form of account is the most common type of credit involved in the medical and dental professions, it is also often advisable for the professional man to encourage those of his patients who so prefer to arrange installment payments for protracted treatments or services.

Credit arrangements also are found in the legal profession, in which services are rendered for a client who is billed at some later date for this professional service.

The vast growth of hospital, medical, and surgical insurance plans has permitted millions of people to take care of their vital health

7 / For a coverage of the articles recently appearing on the problems of professional credit, see the Suggested Readings at the end of the chapter.

TABLE 7-2
Service Credit, 1929-70
(in millions of dollars)

End of Year	Noninstallment Service Credit	End of Year	Noninstallment Service Credit
1929	579	1950	1,580
1930	567	1951	1,784
1931	516	1952	1,867
1932	477	1953	1,927
1933	454	1954	2,003
1934	438	1955	2,127
1935	459	1956	2,366
1936	505	1957	2,593
1937	541	1958	2,800
1938	508	1959	3,064
1939	518	1960	3,337
1940	553	1961	3,631
1941	597	1962	3,961
1942	660	1963	4,249
1943	712	1964	4,507
1944	794	1965	4,889
1945	845	1966	5,346
1946	1,014	1967	5,810
1947	1,166	1968	6,408
1948	1,284	1969	6,970
1949	1,388	1970	7,307

Note: Consumer credit data have been revised at various times, for various series, and for various periods of years. For these reasons, the consumer credit data cannot be considered to be strictly comparable for every year from 1929 to the present.
Source: Board of Governors of the Federal Reserve System.

needs on a "cash basis," by having paid in advance for this protection and thus being able to shift the financial burden—or a large part of it—for the services rendered to the insurance companies with which they have such arrangements.

Credit in Service Establishments

Basically, credit in a service establishment is like credit in an establishment that sells goods. In many instances it is difficult or practically impossible to separate the two, as there are thousands of retail concerns that sell goods on a credit basis and are at the same time offering repair and similar services that may be received by the customer and paid for in the future.

It should be clearly understood that when the word "service" is used it does not mean the various devices employed by a store to attract and hold customers, such as delivery of goods, credit arrangements, parking lots, baby-sitting, and all the other sales

152   *Consumer and Commercial Credit Management*

promotional devices found in retail establishments today. Rather the word "service" refers to an establishment that is providing some need for the person himself or is performing some operation or task on goods belonging to the customer. The term "service" may also apply to the individual who does not have a so-called "place of business" but who is handy with tools and has an ability for fixing things. This service person may operate from his own car or truck and have regular customers for whom he performs certain services and sends his bill at the end of the month for services rendered.

The number of these service establishments that cater to the consumer has been increasing rapidly over the years, and a large segment of this total is conducting its business on a credit as well as on a cash basis. It should be recognized that when a person heats his home with gas during the winter months and receives a bill for this utility service at the end of the month during which the service was received, credit is involved just as much as if this same customer had walked into a department store, bought a suit of clothes, and charged it.[8] Again, as in the medical and dental professions, it is a customary method of doing business. True, the credit time involved is usually short, and the installment method of repayment is not as commonly used in consumer service credit as it is in retail credit.

A great deal has been written on the "credit-card boom" in this country since the close of World War II. Observers have pointed out that millions of Americans are riding a magic carpet called the credit card and are using a pen instead of cash to obtain food and drink, shelter and clothing, sleep and entertainment, gas, oil, tires, and even travel to faraway places. This was referred to previously in this chapter, but the discussion centered on the obtaining of goods, not the securing of services on credit. Of course, it is difficult if not impossible to separate the two, as thousands of concerns are offering goods on credit to customers at the same time they are giving services under some credit arrangement. Hertz Rent-a-Car System, Avis Rent-a-Car System, and National Rent-a-Car System have their own charge cards. Telephone credit cards, especially valuable for long-distance calls while away from home, are being issued. Credit has become popular, especially with the group of people to whom traveling is a necessary part of their business life, in the purchase of "sleeping" services in motels and hotels and in the buying of transportation services on planes, buses, and railroads.

REVIEW AND DISCUSSION QUESTIONS

1. Distinguish carefully between a retail charge account and a retail installment account. Between a retail charge account and a retail revolving account.

8 / For a discussion of credit in the utility industries, see Frank N. Bien, "Checkless Payment of Utility Service," *Credit World*, March 1968, p. 12.

2. Discuss the characteristics normally found in the retail charge account.

3. What factors should a retailer consider in deciding whether to adopt the retail charge account in his business? Which factor do you think is the most important? Why?

4. How do you account for the changing importance of retail charge account credit, as shown in Table 7-1?

5. When do you believe that carrying charges should be used with regular retail charge accounts?

6. What are the important disadvantages in using carrying charges?

7. Who pays the cost of credit in a retail store? Support your answer with statements from leading merchants in your community.

8. Distinguish between divided payment accounts and regular 30-day charge plans.

9. Explain how the American Express Company, Diners Club, and Carte Blanche plans operate.

10. What is service credit, and why is it important that it be recognized and fully understood?

11. Discuss the problems of professional credit.

SUGGESTED READINGS

Problems of Professional Credit

Davids, Lewis E. and West, David A. "EDP and Medical Accounts Receivable," *Journal of Consumer Credit Management,* Fall 1969, p. 47.

Franklin, Max "A Pre-Admission Policy for Hospital Credit," *Credit World,* February 1971, p 18.

Gainsburgh, Martin R. "The Socio-Economic Outlook for the 70s," *Credit World,* September 1969, p. 14.

Grant, H. L. "Revitalizing the Patient Accounts Office," *Credit World,* May 1970, p. 18.

Herring, W. L. "Hospital Billing and Receivables Control," *Credit World,* October 1967, p. 14.

Rogers, Hewitt "Credit Department Communications," *Credit World,* June 1970, p. 28.

8

Types of Consumer Credit—
Cash Loan Credit

A vast system of financial institutions has been developed over the years to provide consumers with cash in exchange for their credit. In analyzing this area of consumer credit, it should be recognized that cash loan credit is credit in the form of money, as contrasted with other types which are credit in the form of goods and services.

The borrowing of money by consumers is not of recent origin, but it has occurred in all ages. Before 1900 all types of consumer credit were of only nominal importance in the United States, but since that time the expansion of cash loan credit has been almost as rapid and dramatic as installment credit. The need to borrow money today is much greater than it was in the past, because the American consumer has come to be increasingly dependent upon his ability to use his credit to fulfill his varied wants and desires. Just as the several forms of consumer credit developed in response to the diversity of credit needs of the American consumer, so did cash loan credit become an important segment in the consumer credit field.

The system of financial institutions which has evolved is one which supplies most persons with a wide variety of types of cash loans, much as they are supplied various types of credit in their acquisition of goods and services. Supplying the various types of cash loans to consumers are commercial banks, consumer finance companies, credit unions, industrial banks, and a number of other institutions such as philanthropic organizations and illegal lenders. The major proportion of all consumer loans is made by commercial banks, consumer finance companies, and credit unions. Table 8-1 shows the relative position of each of the several cash lending institutions by the volume of cash loan credit held. A discussion of home mortgage loans is reserved for Chapter 9, in which the

TABLE 8-1
Cash Loans Outstanding at Financial Institutions, by Holder
(in millions of dollars)

End of Year	Total Install- ment and Non- installment Loans	Installment Loans				Noninstallment Loans (Single-Payment Loans)		
		Total (1)	Com- mercial Banks (2)	Finance Com- panies* (3)	Credit Unions (4)	Total (5)	Com- mercial Banks (6)	Other (7)
1939	1,901	1,114	363	619	132	787	625	162
1941	2,219	1,374	471	705	198	845	693	152
1945	1,766	1,020	312	606	102	746	674	72
1950	4,834	3,013	1,037	1,386	590	1,821	1,576	245
1955	9,836	6,834	1,916	3,240	1,678	3,002	2,635	367
1960	17,013	12,506	3,577	5,006	3,923	4,507	3,884	623
1964	27,771	20,897	5,542	9,015	6,340	6,874	5,950	924
1965	31,585	23,914	6,357	10,233	7,324	7,671	6,690	981
1966	34,078	26,106	7,011	10,840	8,255	7,972	6,946	1,026
1967	36,714	28,286	7,751	11,563	8,972	8,428	7,340	1,088
1968	40,878	31,740	8,855	12,707	10,178	9,138	7,975	1,163
1969	44,486	35,390	9,735	14,061	11,594	9,096	7,900	1,196
1970	46,906	37,422	10,482	14,440	12,500	9,484	8,205	1,279

*Finance companies consist of those institutions formerly classified as sales finance companies, consumer finance companies, and other finance companies.

Source: *Federal Reserve Bulletin*, March 1971, pp. A54-55.

importance of savings and loan associations, life insurance companies, commercial banks, mutual savings banks, mortgage companies, and individual investors is covered.

USE OF CASH LOANS BY CONSUMERS

The consumer who borrows money from any one of the consumer financial institutions does so mainly for the purpose of consolidating his existing debts into one lump sum, the payment of emergency services, or the purchase of merchandise and services. Loans made to cover these broad purposes, for example, may be used for payment of medical and dental expenses, repair and modernization of homes, tax bills, and educational expenses, as well as for the purchase of furniture, appliances, and automobiles. Individual consumers not only have varied needs and desires, but they obviously differ greatly in their ability to satisfy their wants. Some borrowers will need nominal sums of money; others will require larger sums. Some will be able to repay their loan in a matter of 60 to 90 days; others will need more lengthy terms. Some will prudently compare interest and service charges; others will regard the receipt of immediate cash as more important than cost. A number of borrowers will need the security of a comaker, while others will be able to borrow sums on their signature alone. In addition to the varied characteristics of the consumer borrowers, they will differ in their ability to handle funds wisely. Consequently the cash-lending industry of this country is confronted with a different set of circumstances each time a loan is made. The numerous and varied uses of cash loan credit combined with the different consumer characteristics explain to a great extent the need for a wide variety of different types of loans.

Some businessmen use cash loan credit for the purpose of obtaining short-term working capital for their businesses. These loans, made particularly to small businessmen on their signature or with collateral, are included in the Federal Reserve Board's loan statistics.

The question might be raised as to why consumers borrow money to purchase goods and services when other types of credit could be used to make these purchases. Many consumers will calculate the cost of other types of credit, compare this cost with a personal loan, and use the cheapest money available to them. Prestige or conventional association with a particular financial institution may provide an additional explanation. Typically the professional and managerial groups have had long and pleasant associations with commercial banks, while these same services have not been as fully utilized by skilled and semiskilled workers until recent years. Consequently, individual preferences to deal with one financial institution and not another and the cost of money from one source versus another explain some of the apparent duplication of credit services. In some instances retailers themselves will suggest that the buyer arrange a loan from a financial institution rather than buy on the retailer's installment plan. Frequently retailers complete the necessary papers, take credit information incidental to a cash loan, and forward the papers to a financial institution for its acceptance and establishment of a loan. These procedures may be less formal from the retailer's standpoint than the selling of installment paper as carried on by some merchants. Furthermore, in the life of most consumers, a number of opportunities and situations arise which cannot be met except by cash loans.

CONSUMER CASH-LENDING INSTITUTIONS

Commercial banks, consumer finance companies, credit unions, and industrial banks are the principal sources of cash loans made to consumers. Each of these institutions was originated either to serve a particular consumer segment or meet some specific consumer needs not otherwise met by already existing credit facilities. The types of loans offered by the several lending institutions are so varied and numerous that relatively few American consumers have no ready source of cash credit. As the variety of cash-lending institutions is studied, it becomes readily apparent that they exemplify an effort to meet diverse consumer needs.

It may be well to regard the several cash-lending institutions as "sellers of money." This concept of cash-lending institutions clearly establishes them as *merchandisers* of credit. The supply and cost of money to the cash-lending institutions have their parallel in the supply and cost of goods for retail firms; their building of a customer group which seeks cash loans and the same group which will return when the need again exists has its counterpart in the goodwill, promotion, and repeat sales to satisfied customers so well understood by retailers of other commodities. Their interest rates and service charges represent the cost of money to the borrower as do prices of goods, and carrying charges represent costs to the buyer of goods and services. Furthermore, the profit motive attracts capital, institutions, and personnel to this field just as this same motive lends impetus to most economic activity. Consequently sellers of money are confronted with many of the same problems as other types of merchandising establishments, and the degree of their success will frequently hinge on the same or similar merchandising methods used by successful merchandisers of goods and services.

Commercial Banks

Commercial banks were slow in adopting the practice of lending cash to consumers. Before 1930 commercial banks were active in the real estate loan field but made only a few customer loans to individuals. The loans of this period were single-payment loans made to individuals with high incomes.

In late 1920s banks began to enter the field of consumer cash lending. By this time they were fairly well assured of the fact that consumer credit was a mature economic force, and more importantly they now could see the profitable experience of the pioneering sales finance and consumer loan institutions. The National City Bank of New York opened the first consumer loan department in 1928. Gradually the early stigma of consumer credit diminished, and cash lending to consumers became as accepted and commonplace as loans to businesses. Consequently, other commercial banks adopted the practice. The data in Table 8-1 show that commercial banks are dominant with regard to cash loan credit held, provided single-payment loans are combined with the volume of installment cash loans.

Types of Loans. Cash credit, as offered by commercial banks, has experienced considerable change in recent years. Such a wide variety of new credit plans has recently appeared that difficulty is experienced in trying to identify and to classify them. As late as 1964, it appeared that there were three types of plans: single-payment loans, conventional installment loans, and revolving check[1] (sometimes called "ready credit" or "instant check"). By 1967, however, the revolving check plan had declined in importance and in its place had come the so-called automatic loan plan (or, as sometimes called, the overdraft plan), and the combination credit card and traveler's check plan. With the recent growth of bank credit card plans, such as BankAmericard and Master Charge, the loaning of

---

1 / The Federal Reserve Bank of Philadelphia in its September 1959 *Business Review,* pp. 2-3, described this type of plan as follows:

The customer fills out an application stating the amount he can afford to repay each month. If the bank approves, this figure is multiplied by a fixed number of months—from 12 to 24, depending upon the bank's policy—to determine the maximum amount he may borrow. In other words, if it is decided that repayments of $50 a month can be handled and the bank's plan is for 20 months, the limit of the line is $1,000. The customer then receives a supply of checks which he may use just like any personal check. When one of these checks is written and comes back to the bank, it is charged to the revolving credit account and becomes a loan.

Monthly repayments begin once a debt is incurred. They are usually in the predetermined size regardless of the amount borrowed, although a few plans provide for payments as a fraction of the outstanding balance. The customer may continue to write checks until he reaches his maximum line. Once repayments bring his debt below the limit, he may start borrowing all over again.

There is no charge of any kind while the account is not in use. When the customer borrows, he must pay interest on the amount outstanding—generally around 1 percent a month. Some banks also levy a service charge on each check.

cash to card holders has become commonplace. In one of the publicity brochures of the BankAmerica Service Corporation, the question was asked: "Suppose I am short of cash. May I use my BankAmericard to 'charge' cash?" The following answer was given: [2]

You certainly may. This is another of BankAmericard's big advantages. You can walk into any one of the thousands of BankAmericard participating banks from coast to coast, present your BankAmericard, and for a small fee, charge cash instantly! You repay it the same as you repay your bill for purchases. That includes time payments, if you wish.

Similar arrangements are of course available under other bank credit card plans.

It appears that these present-day plans, while varied and ingenious, can best be classified into the following three forms of installment loan plans.

1. Single-Payment Loans. The expansion of single-payment loan credit from $625 million in 1939 to $8,205 million by the end of 1970, as shown in Table 8-1, indicates both the absolute and the relative importance of this type of loan to the loan portfolio of commercial banks. Single-payment loans are frequently made for 30, 60, or 90 days and longer periods such as six months, nine months, or even a year. The term "discount loans" is frequently used to describe these loans when the bank deducts the interest from the principal amount at the time the loan is made. With some banks it is the policy to collect the interest on the maturity date of the loan when the single payment of principal is made. If the former arrangement prevails, the borrower pays a slightly higher true rate of interest because he has use of the amount borrowed less the interest charges for the duration of the time stipulated. In the event the latter prevails, a quoted annual interest charge is also the true interest rate, inasmuch as the borrower has full use of the principal for the entire period of the loan. Mention also should be made of the so-called prime rate, which is nominally the rate banks charge their customers with the best credit standing. [3] In actual operation, it is the base price from which negotiations start, but each loan is a separate negotiation.

No data are available on the average amount of these loans, but it is known that the average is considerably larger than the average amount of installment loans by commercial banks. Most banks discourage single-payment loans of less than $100. When small loans of short duration are made, banks customarily make a flat charge rather than an interest charge.

2 / *Your Questions Answered About BankAmericard* (Lincoln, Nebr.: BankAmerica Service Corporation, undated), unnumbered.
3 / "What Is the Prime Rate?" *Industrial Banker,* September 1969, p. 14; "Why the Prime Loses Its Power," *Business Week,* December 13, 1969, p. 119.

These loans may be made on either an unsecured or a secured basis, depending on the overall quality of credit risk relative to the amount of the loan. The collateral, if requested, pledged as security on these loans is usually in the form of government bonds and other securities and of the cash value of life insurance policies, savings accounts, automobiles, and other personal property that may readily be converted into cash in the event of default by the debtor.

2. *Conventional Installment Loans.* A full appreciation of the growing importance of commercial banks in the installment loan field cannot be gained from Table 8-1. In addition to the installment cash loans made to consumers for a variety of purposes, other activities in the commercial banks have aided consumers in their installment purchases. An examination of Table 8-2 will reveal that commercial banks make direct cash loans for the purchase of automobiles and other consumer goods, as well as loans for home repair and modernization. It is apparent from data in Table 8-2 that commercial banks are purchasers of a large volume of installment paper representing the sale of automobiles, household goods, appliances, boats, and motors which have been sold by retailers. The column headed "other consumer-goods paper" represents purchased paper from retailers, sales finance companies, and some direct loans made for the purchase of such items. Most of these loans are secured loans. Because of some intermingling of direct loans with purchased paper in the data, it is difficult to estimate accurately the net importance of banks in the installment cash-lending field. It is clearly indicated, however, that commercial banks have been successful in capturing an increasing share of the cash loan market.

Additional characteristics of installment loans as made by commercial banks were revealed in a recent study conducted by the Instalment Credit Committee of the American Bankers Association.[4] The most common down payment (expressed as a percentage of the retail price to the consumer) and the most common maximum maturity terms (in months) reported by the study were:

Type of Loan	Down Payment	Maturity
Automobile—new	·29%	36
Home appliance	10	36
Boats—new	25	36
Boats—used	25	24
Mobile home—new	25	84
Mobile home—used	25	60
Modernization—own plan	...	60
FHA Title I	...	60

4 / *1968 Instalment Credit Survey* (New York: Instalment Credit Committee, 1970), pp. 14-16.

TABLE 8-2
Installment Credit Held by Commercial Banks
by Type of Credit
(in millions of dollars)

End of Year	Total Install- ment Credit	Automobile Paper Purchased	Direct*	Other Con- sumer Goods Paper	Repair and Moderni- zation Loans*	Personal Loans*
1939 . . .	1,079	237	178	166	135	363
1941 . . .	1,726	447	338	309	161	471
1945 . . .	745	66	143	114	110	312
1950 . . .	5,798	1,177	1,294	1,456	834	1,037
1955 . . .	10,601	3,243	2,062	2,042	1,338	1,916
1960 . . .	16,672	5,316	2,820	2,759	2,200	3,577
1964 . . .	25,094	8,691	4,734	3,670	2,457	5,542
1965 . . .	28,962	10,209	5,659	4,166	2,571	6,357
1966 . . .	31,319	11,024	5,956	4,681	2,647	7,011
1967 . . .	32,700	10,927	6,267	5,126	2,629	7,751
1968 . . .	36,952	12,213	7,105	6,060	2,719	8,855
1969 . . .	40,305	12,784	7,620	7,415	2,751	9,735
1970 . . .	41,895	12,433	7,587	8,633	2,760	10,482

*Predominantly direct cash loans to consumers.
Source: *Federal Reserve Bulletin*, March 1971, p. A55.

3. Other Types of Installment Loans. As previously mentioned, a wide variety of new types of installment loan plans have appeared on the banking scene. One of these is the automatic loan plan (sometimes called overdraft) which is normally used in conjunction with a customer's regular checking account. Under this plan a customer establishes a line of credit at the bank (for a maximum dollar amount mutually agreed to by the bank and the customer); if his checking account balance reaches zero at any time, the preestablished line automatically goes into effect. The customer repays any loan thus made on an installment basis, with repayments usually running not longer than two years and with an interest charge of 1 to 1½ percent a month.

Another new variation to appear is the check guarantee card plan,[5] which may be used to supplement a bank's overdraft arrangement. Under this plan, the bank would guarantee payment of a customer's check to a merchant, for example, charging the customer interest on the amount of any money overdrawn to make his purchase. The check may not exceed a predetermined amount, usually $100, and certain terms and conditions must be met. These may include the

5 / *American Banker,* March 22, 1967, pp. 1 and 16.

following: the check is printed with the card holder's name exactly as it appears on the face of the check guarantee card; the check is properly drawn and is signed by the card holder at the time it is delivered; the check is dated not later than the date it is delivered nor later than the expiration date of the card; and the check is presented to the bank for payment within 15 days after its date.

Mention has been made of the use of bank credit cards, such as BankAmericard and Master Charge, to obtain cash loans up to some predetermined amount. This is growing in importance, and only the future will tell the effect it will have upon the conventional installment loan activity of commercial banks (and of finance companies also).

Another variation is the combination credit card and traveler's check, of which Bancardchek is an example. Introduced in June 1966,

> Bancardcheks are unique, guaranteed checks (like Travelers checks) that are acceptable everywhere. They are issued in varying denominations and can be cashed for any amount up to the dollar limit on the face of the check. They are imprinted with the name of the person to whom they are issued and unlike ordinary Travelers checks, are not paid for in advance.[6]

Since the bank administering the plan guarantees to honor all of the traveler's checks the customer writes, the customer must agree to have enough money in his checking account to cover the checks cashed. Otherwise the bank is authorized to create a cash advance through its charge card service to cover the overage. A finance charge, usually at an annual rate of 18 percent, is imposed on the amount of the cash advance. A cash advance feature is also available to the customer, similar to that described in connection with bank credit card plans.

Another type of loan is found in the student loan market.[7] The major types of student loans break down into: federal government loans, state loans, United Student Aid Funds, Inc., college loan funds, and parental. Under the federally insured loan program, the student goes to a financial institution (such as a savings and loan association or a commercial bank) and secures the needed loan. The federal government is responsible for the payment of the interest charge (the present rate approximating 7 percent) while the student is in school. After graduation the student receives a free grace period, not to exceed one year, before repayment is required. The importance of this program is illustrated by the fact that in the fiscal year ending June 30, 1967, loans of this nature amounted to $248

6 / *Corporate Bancardchek* (Boston: First Group, 1969), unnumbered.

7 / "Why Banks Are Cool to Student Loans," *Business Week*, September 20, 1969, p. 142.

million; in 1968, $436 million; in 1969, $687 million; and in 1970, $840 million. Under the so-called National Defense Loans, which amounted to $236 million in the academic year 1970-71, the federal government sends the education institution a predetermined dollar amount; the school adds 10 percent and deposits the total with the state treasurer; and the school actually makes the loan to the student. The student is charged no interest while in school; after a free grace period of one year after graduation a simple interest charge of 3 percent is made on any balance remaining unpaid. Partial (or even total) cancellation of the amount of the loan may result if the student decides to enter such fields as teaching, nursing, and the armed forces.

These are simply some of the variations in installment loans that have appeared in recent years. Undoubtedly, more and more plans will appear as bankers decide to become even more of a competitive force in the consumer credit field.[8]

Interest Rates. An interest rate quoted, such as a 7 percent by commercial banks on single-payment loans, approaches the actual rate of 7 percent. Whether or not the 7 percent actually is the true rate is dependent upon the method and time of collecting the interest. If the interest is discounted at the time the loan is made, the borrower has use of the principal *less* the interest; hence, the actual rate will be somewhat higher than had interest and principal been paid on the maturity date of the loan.

In general, nominal interest rates of from 6 to 9 percent on installment cash loans are common. With these nominal charges, the actual rate of interest paid by the borrower will approximate 12 to 18 percent. Some state laws either imply or permit additional charges, commonly referred to as service charges. Service charges, when permitted, defray the costs of investigation or may be levied to offset the expenses incurred when borrowers are delinquent in their payments.

A rash of interest-rate suits appeared in early 1970 which were aimed at subjecting bank rates to state usury limitations. In answer to the question, "What has caused this rash of interest-rate litigation?" Mr. C. Westbrook Murphy, Director of Litigation, Office of the Comptroller of the Currency, made this reply:[9]

I cannot be sure, but I suspect several factors. First, the widespread use of bank credit cards has increased greatly the number of people indebted to banks.

8 / Joe Sarfati, "Changing Patterns of Consumer Credit," *Banking,* March 1970, p. 41. Reprinted with Special Permission from *Banking,* Journal of the American Bankers Association. Copyright 1970 by the American Bankers Association.

9 / "Bank Rates and Usury Limits," *Banking,* May 1970, p. 43. Also see Irving Scher, "The Consumer Class Action: Federal Law in Federal and State Court," *Quarterly Report,* Summer 1970, p. 76.

Second, the truth-in-lending legislation and regulation, coupled with the current publicity on high interest rates, may have made people more aware of interest rates. Also, there has been a great deal of interest among lawyers in an amendment several years ago in the rules governing class actions in a Federal court.

The class action rule allows one or more persons to sue in certain carefully defined instances as representatives of a large number of persons who have claims involving common questions of law or fact.

The Changing Character of Commercial Banks and Their Customers.

From the viewpoint of the customer, the commercial bank of today is a very different institution than it was two or three decades ago.[10] Historically, the commercial banks have been institutions established to serve the financial needs of businesses for commercial purposes. In their dealings with business, fairly large sums of money are usually involved, and the risk element can be rather accurately appraised. Banks' services to the needs of commerce are still their *raison d'être,* and much change and adjustment to the modern needs of business are characteristic of their growth and overall importance to our economy. Characteristically banks have been conservative financial institutions and are so regarded by most consumers. The conservative nature of their management; the early stigma associated with consumer installment financing; the legal requirements, in some instances, and the reluctance to charge higher rates of interest so as to earn a profit from small loans; and, in general, the bank's preoccupation with commercial needs—all these factors have tended to slow the entrance of banks into the financing of consumer needs.

The following quotation is illustrative of consumer attitudes in the 1950s:[11]

Our relationship with banks is another area where the depth probers have isolated a definite fear factor and have devised techniques for reducing that fear. An ad agency in Rochester, New York, turned to motivation research to try to find out how to broaden the clientele of a leading bank in that city. Its probers turned up in the people sampled a large variety of fears concerning banks: fear of being rejected for a loan, fear of the banker finding out how untidy their family financial affairs really are, or fear of disapproval. The agency concluded that people subconsciously see their bank as a kind of parent, a parent capable of scolding or withholding approval, and constantly scrutinizing. With that subconscious cowering before the parent symbol in mind, the agency designed an ad for the bank, showing a man standing at the bank door saying "How I hated to open that door!" and then relating in the text his story of the warm welcome he got.

Dr. Dichter is another prober who has looked into the problem of the banks

10 / "Recent Changes in the Structure of Commercial Banking," *Federal Reserve Bulletin,* March, 1970, p. 195.

11 / Vance Packard, *The Hidden Persuaders* (New York: David McKay Co., Inc., 1957), pp. 66-67.

in winning friends. His particular interest was in the paradox of the great growth of loan companies in spite of the fact most banks were offering personal loans at lower interest and were more lenient in accepting people for loans. His conclusion was that the loan company's big advantage over the bank is its lower moral tone! The bank's big handicap—and here he concurs with the Rochester findings—is its stern image as a symbol of unemotional morality. When we go to a banker for a loan, he points out, we are asking this personification of virtue to condescend to take a chance on us frail humans. In contrast, when we go to the loan company for a loan, it is we who are the virtuous ones and the loan company is the villain we are temporarily forced to consort with. Here, it is we, the borrowers, who do the condescending. Dr. Dichter explains: "This shift of moral dominance from borrower to lender changes completely the whole emotional undertone of the transaction." We shift from feeling like "an unreliable adolescent to feeling like a morally righteous adult. The higher cost of the loan is a small price indeed to pay for such a great change in outlook." He counsels banks seeking more business to soften their image of righteousness.

Most present-day banks have set out to overcome such negative attitudes and have accepted all kinds of consumer credit as a basic mechanism in our economy. In adopting the policy that consumer financing was sound and aggressively seeking consumer credit customers, they have gradually become one of the dominant sources for consumer installment loans. Much to their good fortune, they have a large customer group which exemplifies stability and a low degree of risk.

In expanding their present-day customer group, banks have had to compete against the other aggressive consumer loan institutions. Much of the increase in bank customers has been accomplished by adopting the sales promotion techniques which were known and proved to appeal to the masses.[12] They have adjusted banking hours to conform with the convenience of the customer; provided friendly, convenient, comfortable, and attractive loan quarters; and used the most effective advertising media and techniques. And, of course, they have become more competitive in the interest rates paid to their depositors.[13] The overall effect of this changed approach has been its success in creating a very different image of banks and bankers than had formerly existed.

A most interesting development has been taking place in Great Britain, where British bankers are being confronted with competition from Britain's General Post Office. Called Giro, the system circulates funds throughout the country's post-office network of some 23,000 post offices. With a small deposit, anyone can open a Giro account and can make arrangements to have his regular bills—such as rent or

12 / For a discussion of some of the sales promotion techniques, see the Suggested Readings at the end of the chapter.

13 / For a discussion of Regulation Q, which governs the interest rates that commercial banks may pay, see Chapter 9.

mortgage installments, telephone and electricity bills, etc.—paid automatically out of his account. If the recipient also has a Giro account, the computer simply will credit the payment to him, with no charge for the service. Business firms also are actively using this system, cutting down on paper work and accounting costs in paying their employees and in collecting bills. The postal giro service now is in use in 40 countries in Europe, Asia, Latin America, and Africa.[14]

The new customer impressions have resulted in a keener appreciation of what commercial banks can and will do for worthy cash loan customers. From the bankers' viewpoint, their entrance and success in the consumer credit field have resolved certain questions for them, namely: Can this type of credit be extended safely to large numbers of consumers? Does consumer credit offer advantages and growth possibilities to commercial banks? The answers to these questions are no longer debatable issues among bankers.

However, the future course of commercial banking is being questioned in many circles and by many observers.[15] For example, Paul S. Nadler, Professor of Business Administration at Rutgers University, made the following comment:[16] "Commercial banks now face some of the worst publicity and adverse legislation in history." As an indication of the current legislative action in the banking field, the so-called bank holding bill was signed into law on December 31, 1970.[17] This legislation requires the breakup of some combinations of banks with nonbanking business. The bill applies to holding companies that number a single bank among their subsidiaries, in addition to other kinds of business. In deciding whether a bank must separate from other businesses, the Federal Reserve Board must decide whether such affiliates are so closely related to banking or managing or controlling banks as to be a proper incident thereto.

Consumer Finance Companies

Consumer finance companies[18] (often referred to as small loan companies, personal finance companies, and licensed lenders) make loans to consumers under regulations enacted by state laws. The

14 / For a fuller explanation, see "Britain's Zipcode Banking," *Directors Digest,* January 1968, p. 13 and Allen L. Appell, "Does the Public Really Want a Cashless Society?" *Bankers Magazine,* Spring 1970, p. 48.

15 / For articles on the future of commercial banking, see the Suggested Readings at the end of the chapter.

16 / H. Erich Heinemann, "Banking's Public Image is Hurting," *Directors Digest,* February 1970, p. 3.

17 / For articles tracing the development of bank holding legislation, see the Suggested Readings at the end of the chapter.

18 / For a very detailed and authoritative account of consumer finance companies, see I. S. Michelman, *Consumer Finance: A Case History in American Business* (New York: Frederick Fell, Inc., 1966).

characteristics of their loans, their customers, their method of operation, and the state statutes under which they do business are the principal distinguishing features of these consumer lending institutions. Consumer finance companies are almost exclusively installment loan institutions, with the average size of their loan being considerably less than that for commercial banks.

A consumer finance business conducted under the Uniform Small Loan Laws may be an individual proprietorship, a partnership, or a corporation. The incorporated company was at first rare, but with the enactment of the Uniform Small Loan Law in most states since 1911,[19] the corporate enterprise has become the dominant form of organization. Typically, the large corporations operate on a national scale, with licensed offices in hundreds of cities of all sizes. The smaller companies are usually regional in operation, while the smallest firms with one or a few offices operate on a local scale.

The rapid growth and present-day position held by consumer finance companies in the lending industry are a direct result of the small loan laws enacted by most states. Prior to enactment of state laws covering the operation of lenders of small sums, this business was characterized by deception with respect to interest charges and abusive collection practices. In 1907 and 1908 the Russell Sage Foundation, a philanthropic organization, financed studies that dealt with existing small loan conditions and the demand for loans of this type. These studies disclosed a large demand for small loans by wage earners and other consumers of small means, the need for legitimate lending agencies to supply the demand, and the necessity of subjecting the business to state supervision. In 1916, the foundation, in cooperation with a group of moneylenders, drafted a model small loan law which has come to be known as the Uniform Small Loan Law. Improved drafts of the model law have been made from time to time by the foundation and by the National Consumer Finance Association.

The first Uniform Small Loan Laws tended to reduce the number of lenders subjected to regulation, because some lenders found it unprofitable to operate at the interest rates permitted by law. It was not long, however, before lenders who formerly shunned this business were attracted to the small loan field and large numbers of new companies were organized to transact small loans under regulation. In all fairness to the small loan industry, it should be emphasized that the industry encourages state regulation as the basis for attracting personnel of high ethical standards and sufficient capital to meet the demand for small loans. The industry's support of the model Uniform Small Loan Law is testimony of its opposition to

19 / In 1911, Massachusetts enacted small loan regulatory laws based on the early recommendations of the Russell Sage Foundation. New Jersey followed with early legislation in 1914; New York, Ohio, and Pennsylvania in 1915.

illegal lenders[20] who prey on wage earners and charge usurious interest rates in those states without effective legislation. Today the National Consumer Finance Association has assumed the role of promoting effective state legislation.

Provisions of an Effective Small Loan Law. An effective small loan law must provide for an interest charge which is sufficient to attract capital to the business and at the same time protect borrowers from abusive practices. Most states have enacted laws which meet this requisite, but unfortunately several states have either ineffective regulation or no small loan law. Many states have modified the model Uniform Small Loan Law to suit local conditions or particular interests. In general, the following are the principal provisions of the Uniform Small Loan Law:

1. Interest Rate. The rate is generally 2 to 3 percent a month computed on the unpaid balance. In recent years some states have provided for the maximum rate to be applied to the first $100 or $200 of the loan and lower rates to loan balances in excess of these amounts. For example, the rate of 3 percent may be on the first $150 or less and 2½ percent on the remaining balance up to $300. Interest is charged only on the unpaid balance and cannot be deducted in advance.

2. Maximum Loan Size. $300 was the original loan size recommended by the foundation. Today, however, this amount is regarded as too restrictive, and the need for larger loans seems apparent. "For example, in California the loan ceiling is $10,000 while in New York the loan ceiling is $1,400. The maximum loan size has been increased in recent years in a number of states so that in 1971, finance companies may make loans of over $1,000 in 42 states."[21] A breakdown of loan ceilings under consumer finance laws in 1971 is shown in Figure 8-1.

3. License and Supervision. The lender must be licensed, and each office operated by a chain company must be licensed by the state in which the business is conducted. Each office is subject to annual and special examinations, must be bonded, and usually must submit to a test of ethical and financial fitness.

4. Other Requirements. Under the disclosure requirements of the Truth-in-Lending act, the lender has to disclose the amount financed, the finance charge, the annual percentage rate, the prepayment procedure and total of payments, delinquency or early payment charges, the rebate calculation procedure, and whether a security interest is taken in connection with the extension of credit.

20 / John M. Seidl, "Let's Compete With Loan Sharks," *Harvard Business Review*, May-June 1970, p. 69.

21 / *1971 Finance Facts Yearbook* (Washington, D. C.: National Consumer Finance Association, 1971), p. 63.

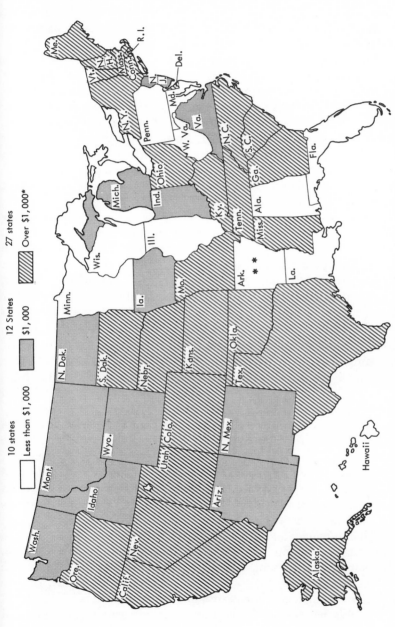

Legend:

10 states — Less than $1,000
12 States — $1,000
27 states — Over $1,000*

*An additional 15 states permit loans of over $1,000 by finance companies under other laws for a total of 42 states.
**Arkansas has no consumer finance law.
Source: Consumer Finance Rate and Regulation Chart.

No fees other than recording fees may be collected by the lender. The licensee must accept payment from the customer in advance of the due date, and interest charged can be only for the time the borrower has had use of the money. Civil and criminal penalties are provided for violation of the provisions of the laws.

While the above are the principal provisions of the Uniform Small Loan Laws (in association with the Truth-in-Lending law), there are many other specific requirements of importance. The states that have enacted small loan legislation have done so with variation from these provisions, but essentially with the same fundamental objectives of effective legislation as cited earlier. Some states prohibit any other business to be operated in conjunction with a small loan office; others permit insurance writing to minimize the degree of risk; and others have stipulated somewhat different methods of interest computation.

The Consumer Finance Customer. Borrowers from consumer finance companies generally come from different occupational groups than do the borrowers from commercial banks. Most of the loans of finance companies are made to two occupational groups: craftsmen, foremen, and kindred workers; and operatives, laborers, and kindred workers. See Table 8-3 for a distribution of the number of loans extended by occupation of borrower in selected years from 1950 to 1969. In other words, a preponderance of skilled, semiskilled, and unskilled workers comprises the customer group of these companies. They borrow funds for the same reasons that other occupational groups borrow, such as consolidation of overdue bills, refinancing existing obligations, payment of medical, dental, and hospital bills, and meeting other emergencies in everyday living.

The services of consumer finance companies are fequently of a different character than those of commercial banks. The finance companies usually are located so as to appeal to the convenience of the customer. Their offices are frequently located in the so-called "high rent" districts, to broaden their customer appeal. Such an office stands ready to accept loan applications, make investigations of the applicants, accept payments by mail and on the premises, and handle delinquencies and other necessary matters.

Individual customers of these companies borrow, on the average, smaller sums than do bank customers. Variations in the average size of loan granted may reasonably be expected by virtue of the dominance of particular occupational groups. Historically, the small loan business has had as its customers wage earners and others of limited means. It is this group that this business has so successfully attracted and served. Generally the customers' income and occupational stability are less than the commercial banks' customers. Despite the fact that the customer groups of consumer finance

TABLE 8-3
Distribution of the Number of Loans Extended
by Occupation of Borrower,
Selected Years, 1950-69
(in percentages)

Occupation of borrower	1950	1954	1958	1965	1969
Proprietors, managers and office workers, excluding farm	8.3	6.6	6.5	5	7
Craftsmen, foremen, and kindred workers	33.2	32.6	31.6	36	34
Operatives, laborers, and kindred workers, including farm and mine	31.0	31.6	29.7	23	23
Clerical and kindred workers . . .	9.4	8.3	8.1	6	8
Sales persons	3.8	3.8	4.0	3	3
School teachers	0.9	0.8	0.9	1	1
Professional and semiprofessional workers, excluding teachers . . .	2.2	2.1	2.7	2	3
Service workers, including government civilian and military personnel	8.3	11.1	13.9	17	16
Occupations not reported and miscellaneous	2.9	3.1	2.6	7	5
Total	100.0	100.0	100.0	100	100

Source: From National Consumer Finance Association survey data as reported by companies which operated 2,243 offices in June 1959, 3,185 offices in 1965, and 3,669 offices in 1969.

Note: Parts may not add to totals due to rounding.

companies and commercial banks have similar reasons for borrowing, the amount borrowed generally is in line with the borrower's income (see Table 8-4) and other existing obligations. Consequently, one can reasonably expect the dominance of a few occupational groups to reflect the character and type of lending services offered by a particular cash-lending institution.

Changing Consumer Attitudes. The widespread change of consumer attitudes and the acceptance of consumer credit of all types during the first half of the 20th century brought with it the general acceptance of the small loan business. Most consumers, at one time or another, experience a temporary need for small loans when income and savings are exceeded by obligations. This need for small loans would exist whether or not the Uniform Small Loan Laws were in existence. Without such laws, however, experience has shown the need has been met by so-called loan sharks or hip-pocket lenders.

An individual who borrows $100 from a consumer finance company at a monthly rate of 3 percent and repays the loan in 12 equal monthly installments will pay a total interest cost of $20.60, or 36 percent true rate of interest. Admittedly, this amount appears high unless the cost of lending small amounts is clearly understood. The cost of capital for these businesses is higher than the cost for

TABLE 8-4
Percentage Distribution of the Monthly Income of Borrowers from Consumer Finance Companies, Selected Years, 1950-69

Monthly income of borrowers	*(Percent of number of loans extended)*							
	1950	1954	1958	1965	1967	1968	1969
$0.00 to 100	0.9	0.4	0.3	0.2	0.6	0.1	0.2
$100.01 to 200	18.9	7.4	4.6	2.2	2.9	1.4	1.1
$200.01 to 300	46.0	30.7	17.6	8.8	6.6	5.6	4.2
$300.01 to 400	20.6	32.1	30.6	16.3	12.6	12.0	10.0
$400.01 to 500	8.7	16.1	22.7	23.1	18.7	18.8	16.1
$500.01 to 750	4.9*	12.0	21.4	33.5	36.1	38.2	38.2
$750-01 to 1,000	—	1.3**	2.3	12.2	15.2	16.9	20.2
Over $1,000	—	—	0.5	3.7	7.3	7.0	10.0
	100.0	100.0	100.0	100.0	100.0	100.0	100.0

Note: Parts may not add to totals due to rounding.

*Over $500.

**Over $750.

Source: National Consumer Finance Association survey data for years through 1965 as reported by companies which operated over 1,800 offices in 1965. For 1967, data as reported by companies that operated 2,638 offices, for 1968 for companies that operated 2,920 offices, and for 1969, companies that operated 2,968 offices.

commercial banks. The alternative to the Uniform Small Loan Law, which has attracted capital and business with high ethical standards to this field, is the fostering of the loan shark and illegal lender. From the standpoint of social necessity, it appears desirable that the customer group served by the consumer finance companies be provided convenient and fair access to small loans rather than be subjected to the lending and collection methods of illegal lenders. It also must be emphasized that for many families the small loan company is their only available cash credit source, whereas the typical commercial bank customer could easily qualify and borrow funds from several sources. Consequently, if a state wishes to make small consumer loans available to its wage earners and lower income borrowers, it must sanction interest charges to cover the high expenses of this kind of business. If it wishes this business to be conducted on a high plane, it must provide for effective regulation and supervision.

The phenomenal growth in both the number of lenders and the number of consumer borrowers is some indication of the widespread acceptance of the small loan business by the American consumer. Today consumer finance companies range from the single-office company to the vast chains which operate hundreds of offices throughout the country. However, not only has competition increased between consumer finance companies themselves but competition for the cash loan business has been greatly intensified over the years as the commercial banks and credit unions have increased their share of the market.[22]

Credit Unions

A credit union is an association of people who agree to save their money together and in turn make loans to each other at relatively low interest rates. In other words, it is a cooperative institution. A credit union is organized by people of a particular group. They may be employees working for the same employer; a group associated with a fraternal order or labor union; or those who live in a closely knit community. At any rate some common bond or factor of homogeneity is characteristic of the members of a credit union. Today, there are more than 23,000 credit unions in the United States and its territories, with approximately 22 million members. Canada has in excess of 4,500 such organizations, with approximately 5.5 million members. More than $12.9 billion in such loans were outstanding in the United States at the end of 1969. Assets are estimated to be in excess of $15 billion.

Origin and Characteristics of Credit Unions. The major impetus

22 / "A Big Change in Small Loans," *Business Week,* June 13, 1970, p. 48.

for the credit union movement came from Edward A. Filene, a Boston merchant and philanthropist. Even though credit unions had their origin in Germany during 1848, and the first credit union in North America was organized in 1900 at Levis, Quebec, it remained for an important United States business figure to head the movement in the United States. Mr. Filene first observed the beneficial aspects of cooperative saving and lending while on a trip to India in 1907. Upon his return to the United States he devoted much time and about a million dollars to the credit union movement. He was particularly successful in getting credit union laws passed and numerous credit unions organized. Much of the growth of the organized credit unions is directly attributable to Mr. Filene and to men whom he influenced to participate actively in the movement.

Today credit unions may be chartered under either state laws or the Federal Credit Union Act of 1934 and its subsequent amendments. Approximately half of the credit unions are chartered under state laws, while the others are chartered under federal law. It is recommended that the organizing group consist of at least 100 persons.[23] The common bond of membership may be reason of employment, church affiliation, residence, labor union membership, and the like. Recently some 18 percent of all credit unions in the United States were owned and operated by associational groups (such as church, labor union, fraternal); 57 percent by occupational groups (such as agriculture, forestry, manufacturing, retail, etc.); 7 percent by educational services; 15 percent by federal, state, county, and local government employees; and the remainder by residential groups.[24]

Credit unions, being essentially cooperatives, adhere to the basic principles commonly associated with other cooperative ventures. The saving and loan facilities are their main function, and they operate only for the benefit and use of their members. Capital is acquired from membership savings which are invested in credit union shares. Additional capital may be borrowed from commercial sources, but such borrowing is subject to legal limitations which are usually relative to the unimpaired assets of the credit unions. Shares usually are in $5 units and amounts deposited which are less than this are applied to the purchase of a share. In turn, a portion of the capital is available for loans to shareholding members. Each member, irrespective of his holdings in the credit union, is entitled to one vote in the election of its board of directors and its committeemen, who manage the organization. Most state laws provide that a dividend, not to

23 / "The Hows & Whys of Credit Unions," *Changing Times,* December 1968, p. 33.

24 / *International Credit Union Yearbook 1970* (Madison, Wis.: CUNA International, Inc., 1970), p. 9. CUNA International, Inc. became the World Council of Credit Unions, Inc. on January 1, 1971.

exceed 6 percent, may be declared on members' shares after expenses are paid and legal reserves are set aside.

Such great variance exists in state laws regulating the operation of credit unions that only the more common requirements and general provisions of the federal law can give an indication of their operating characteristics. The federal law and the state laws may be characterized as emphasizing protection of the members against imprudent management, while still providing the members with a ready source of cash credit at relatively low rates of interest. Loans to officers, directors, and members of committees are limited to the value of their shares in the organization. Further, such persons may not act as endorsers for borrowers. The accounting records of the credit union are subject to regular examination by government authorities. Further protection is afforded the members by surety bond requirements. The treasurer and each officer who handles money are required to be bonded. Most state laws provide for a maximum loan to members on their signature and another limit on secured loans. Under the federal law, interest on credit union loans may never exceed more than 1 percent per month on the unpaid balance. Under the various state laws, the maximum rate may be 1 percent per month on the unpaid balance, or 6 percent per year on the principal amount, discounted in advance. In either case the actual rate of interest on these loans is between 11 and 12 percent. The National Credit Union Administration supervises credit unions operating under federal charter, and in most states the state banking commission supervises the credit unions under state charter.

Character of Loans. A credit union member is one who owns one or more credit union shares. This single share will earn interest and entitle the holder to the lending services of the credit union. Applications for loans, made in writing, tell the purpose of the loan, security offered, and other pertinent information. The credit committee, which is elected by the members, meets as often as necessary to approve and reject loan applications. One type of loan is granted—the installment loan which is to be repaid in equal installments during the time schedule established by the organization. Small amounts may be repaid in 6 months, 12 months, or over longer periods, depending on the amount and requirements of the borrower. Automobile loans typically are made for a maximum of 36 months. The borrower may repay the entire remaining balance of his loan at any time without penalty and hence save interest. As indicated earlier, no credit union loan can exceed 1 percent per month on the unpaid principal balance. Credit unions write life insurance on the life of the borrower through their own Mutual Insurance Society. The premium for this insurance is paid by the credit union out of earnings, at no additional charge to the borrower. If the insured borrower dies before his loan obligation is fully met, the insurance pays off the remaining loan balance.

The reasons for borrowing money from credit unions are essentially the same as for borrowing money from other sources: namely, to pay old bills, taxes, and medical expenses; for home repairs, vacations, automobiles, and education; and to take advantage of various financial opportunities.

Growth and Increasing Importance of Credit Unions.   Since 1921 the growth of credit unions in the United States and Canada has been rapid.[25] In practically every year, except the war years of 1943, 1944, and 1945, credit unions have advanced in number, members, and assets. In addition to the rapid growth of credit unions there has been a gradual increase in their services. The saving[26] and personal loan feature of the business remains its principal function, but in recent years CUNA International has ventured into the insurance field and offers life insurance under several plans.

Much of the growth and present-day soundness of credit unions may be attributed to their relatively low rate of interest. This interest rate is made possible by its low cost of operation.[27] Credit unions frequently enjoy the privilege of free office space provided by the employer; they are exempt from some taxes[28] because of their cooperative nature; and frequently they receive the services of management (except for the treasurer) free, as elected officers serve voluntarily without pay. The very large credit unions which must maintain sceduled and longer hours of operations are staffed with paid employees. Further, many members regard the saving feature of credit unions as advantageous, inasmuch as dividends paid to shareholders are at times higher than interest on savings in commercial banks and savings and loan associations.

Despite the apparent advantages enjoyed by credit unions, there are definite limitations to most ventures of a cooperative nature. It is very difficult to recruit spokesmen and workers for organizations of this type because of the voluntary and free expenditure of time and energy. Another limitation to credit union growth is the number of people with a common bond that are needed before a union can be organized. Groups of this size are not easy to organize in many

25 / For articles tracing the growth of credit unions, see the Suggested Readings at the end of the chapter.

26 / For a discussion of protection against loss in credit unions, see a "Big Share of Safety for Credit Unions," *Business Week,* September 5, 1970, p. 26.

27 / Arthur O'Donogue, "Credit Unions Cooperate in Computer Accounting System," *Credit World,* July 1970, p. 16; Wilbur J. Brown, "Computer Improves CU Services," *Credit World,* August 1968, p. 20.

28 / John D. Chisholm, "Wanted: New Curbs on Credit Unions," *Industrial Banker,* August 1969, p. 14; "The Case for and against Taxation of Credit Unions," *Industrial Banker,* January 1966, p. 9.

professional, trade, and clerical fields. This requirement automatically nullifies development in the many thousands of small business firms in this country. Perhaps the greatest drawback in the credit union movement stems from the credit committee. This committee, which screens all loan applications, is frequently comprised of people closely associated with the borrowers. This fact violates the inherent belief among borrowers that their financial dealings are strictly confidential. Because of this, many credit union members may take advantage of the thrift and savings feature, but they patronize other sources when a cash loan is needed. Despite these important limitations to the credit union movement, it holds an important position as a source of cash loans.

Industrial Banks and Loan Companies

Industrial banks are one of the most complex consumer lending institutions because of the varied nature of their services. They are governed by nonuniform state laws. In some states they are similar to commercial banks in many respects. In others their services are restricted by law, and they operate like small loan companies or the consumer loan departments of commercial banks. The operation of industrial *banks* is permitted by law in more than one tenth of the states. In these states the firm may use the word "bank" in its advertising, contracts, and general literature. The laws of these states authorize the acceptance of deposits and the making of loans, and the banks may become members of the Federal Deposit Insurance Corporation. More than a third of the states do not authorize industrial banks as such, but have legislation which permits the operation of industrial *loan* companies. In these states such firms are commonly known as industrial loan companies or industrial credit corporations, and the use of the term bank is expressly prohibited. Industrial loan companies are not permitted to accept deposits, and hence they take on most of the characteristics of other consumer lending institutions. The remaining states have no specific legislation covering these institutions. If they desire to conduct business in one of these states, they must be awarded a charter under the laws applicable to commercial banks or secure a license and comply with the state small loan law and operate accordingly.

Except in those states which authorize industrial banks to accept deposits, "investment certificates" or "shares of stock" are used to circumvent usury laws. These institutions devised this method because state banking laws, as originally conceived, did not cover interest paid on loans which were repaid in installments. A borrower from an industrial bank is required to subscribe to an equal amount of noninterest-bearing investment certificates. The investment certificates are to be "purchased" by means of a schedule of deposits. When the amount of the deposits equals the value of the investment certificates, the certificates revert to the industrial bank and the loan is thereby paid off. Today industrial banks operate under one of the several methods suggested, depending on the legislative restrictions of the particular state. Some accept deposits from borrowers and nonborrowers and make loans for both consumer and commercial purposes. Others use the investment certificate device so as not to be accused of usurious interest rates. In some states industrial loan companies neither accept deposits nor use investment certificates, but lend money to consumers or businesses in a manner similar to other consumer lending institutions. Whatever the particular method of operation, all industrial banks and industrial loan companies had their origin with Arthur J. Morris during the early 1900s. His original company has evolved into the largest group of industrial banks, now known as the Morris Plan Banks or Companies.

Character of Loans and Interest Rates. Another distinguishing characteristic of industrial banks and loan companies is the amount that can be loaned to any one person. It is not uncommon that the maximum loan may be up to $5,000, with variation between states. The installment type loan is characteristic of operations of these institutions. However, the scope of their lending activities varies greatly. In states which authorize widespread services, industrial banks are almost as diversified as commercial banks in their loan portfolios, making floor plan loans to automobile dealers, automobile loans to consumers, character loans, home improvement loans, mortgage loans secured by first mortgages, and commercial loans. Payment schedules are similar to those of other lending institutions and are relative to the amount of the loan and the degree of risk involved.

Other Types of Lenders

No estimate has been made of the volume of loans made by friends and relatives, philanthropic organizations, church societies, and fraternal orders, but the amount is believed to be sizable. Some persons have the distinct advantage of borrowing from friends and relatives, thereby enjoying less formal contractual arrangements and on most occasions strict secrecy. The interest charge and enforcement of payment depend almost entirely upon the relationship and mutual trust between the individuals.

Philanthropic organizations, church societies, educational institutions, and fraternal orders make loans to individuals under special circumstances. These institutions function to provide financial assistance of a temporary nature to students and other deserving persons. Student loans are frequently made so that they are interest-suspended and payment-free until the student graduates from college. Some loans may take the form of an outright gift, while others are made with the understanding that complete repayment will be made at some future date.

Another source for cash loans to individuals is the pawnbroker, whose interest rates may run as high as 36 percent, but with no inquiry into an individual's credit standing. Insurance companies provide another source; individuals often can borrow on their life insurance policies, paying an interest rate of approximately 5 percent. Some investment houses also provide another source of funds, lending up to 70 percent of the market value on some blue-chip stocks.

In defiance of the state laws, illegal lenders are known to charge interest rates as high as 700 percent. Typically, illegal lenders are more interested in earning exorbitant charges than in actually collecting the principal. They prefer a victim who will obligate himself deeply and be submissive to their collection methods. Collections are enforced by threat of wage assignments, loss of employment, and even physical violence. The debtor is most frequently of limited means and "buys" off the threats, at least temporarily, by paying interest charges; but he seldom has enough to meet the full principal and exorbitant interest charges that these illegal lenders claim he owes them.

RELATIVE COSTS OF CONSUMER LENDING INSTITUTIONS

To appreciate fully the interest rates charged by the various consumer lending institutions, one must examine their costs of operation.[29] Interest rates, or the "price of money," are usually relative to the costs of doing business and the degree of risk assumed by the lender. Costs of conducting a consumer loan activity may be quite high or relatively low. Whether the costs are high or low depends largely on the number and extent of functions performed. Furthermore, the relative costs of capital will importantly influence the rate of interest. Those factors which influence the costs of conducting a cash loan business are discussed in the paragraphs that follow. In these brief discussions no reference is made to the exorbitant rates charged by illegal lenders. Only the legal lenders are considered, and for that matter only the principal factors contributing to costs are explained.

29 / The reader is referred to an excellent study on this subject by Paul Smith, *Cost of Providing Consumer Credit* (New York: National Bureau of Economic Research, 1962); also Robert P. Shay, "The Consumer Finance Industry, Its Cost and Regulation," *Consumer Finance News*, February 1967, p. 3.

Types of Risk Accepted

Lending to wage and salary earners by consumer finance companies is a business in which the average loan is a modest amount. When the amount of the loan is modest, the dollar cost per loan of acquiring customers and then servicing them is relatively high. The type of risk accepted by consumer finance companies is usually one of limited means; in general, the borrower has a limited income and job instability. The greater risk incurred by these companies influences their ability to attract capital, bad debt ratios, and costs of investigation. Commercial banks, in particular, and credit unions accept credit from more stable customer groups, and therefore less risk is incurred. Some occupations have greater income stability than others. The characteristics of the occupation groups attracted by banks and credit unions are qualitatively more acceptable from the credit risk standpoint. This factor alone contributes heavily to the higher cost of credit from consumer finance companies.

Investigation

The cost of investigation by commercial banks and credit unions is generally thought to be less than the cost incurred by consumer finance companies. The types of risk accepted by the latter imply that those who are dishonest, and those who have neither the ability nor will to pay, must be screened out by investigation. The borrower's identity, stability, and general reputation must be verified. His income, expenses, and outstanding obligations must be established. On the other hand, commercial banks and credit unions frequently appraise applicants on whom prior knowledge exists. Each of these institutions accepts deposits, and in many instances the loan applicant is known by someone in the organization. Furthermore, each institution well realizes that the extent and intensity of investigation are governed by the apparent risk. Consequently, consumer finance companies will conduct rather extensive and costly investigations by virtue of the higher risk element characteristic among their customers.

Capital

The cost of capital for commercial banks, credit unions, and some industrial banks is less than that for consumer finance companies. The three former institutions accept deposits, and in each instance their deposits are several times as much as their own capital. In past years these same institutions have been able to attract capital more successfully[30] because of the lower risk nature of their lending operations. Consumer finance companies, on the other hand, cannot accept deposits and must rely on commercial banking facilities or other financial institutions from which to borrow or supply their own funds. Higher rates are thus paid for their capital irrespective of the source. For these same reasons, the operating net profit of these companies must be somewhat higher to attract some investors to the field.

Bad-Debt Losses

The greater degree of risk incurred by consumer finance companies is reflected in higher bad-debt losses. Another factor which contributes to a high bad-debt loss ratio for consumer finance companies is the low average size of loans. Even though a well-managed collection system is in operation, the cost of collecting nominal sums which are about to become bad-debt losses is in all likelihood prohibitive. Furthermore, numerous legal actions against wage earners and others of small means would work against the social acceptance and goodwill which the small loan industry has built. The threat of legal action by a commercial bank or credit union to collect somewhat larger average sums will most certainly bring forth settlement by their type of customers if for no other reason than to avoid embarrassment. The rate to be charged must take into account the relative amount and frequency of bad-debt losses.

It should be recognized, however, that many of the new installment loan plans being adopted by commercial banks may result in a somewhat changing pattern of bad-debt losses in commercial banks. For this reason, these banks undoubtedly will be watching closely for any changes that occur in their bad-debt loss experience.

Collection Costs

The collection costs on an installment account are much higher than costs on a single-payment loan. Commercial banks, it must be remembered, have a large volume of single-payment loans, while consumer finance companies make only installment loans. Other installment lenders are not subject to the same expenses as consumer finance companies. In an effort to protect borrowers from abuse, the Uniform Small Loan Laws of the various states impose costly

---

30 / In Chapter 9 the reader will find material covering the increasing competition between commercial banks and savings and loan associations for deposits of individuals.

procedures on this type of business. Each installment loan must be accounted for in detail; many individual calculations must be made; and detailed informative receipts must be given the borrower. The consumer finance company has its full share of accounts requiring special handling. Again, the modest amount of its loans results in relatively higher costs for the collection function. Delinquencies must be remedied by constant reminders, personal letters, and even personal contact with the debtor.

Services

Consumer finance companies, by the very nature of their business, establish offices for the convenience of their customers. These offices are not generally housed with another institution as are consumer credit departments of commercial banks and credit unions. The services rendered frequently involve more time and relatively more personnel. Most consumer finance companies have gone to considerable expense in establishing programs of debt amortization for their customers. Each borrower who needs this service presents different problems.

Recognition should be given to the fact that many, if not most, of the commercial banks have expanded their services to their customers. They have seen the need to advise and to counsel their customers on money matters, and have made arrangements for debt amortization on a competitive level with the other types of cash-lending institutions. The introduction of the many new installment and loan plans in commercial banks is an illustration of this recognition of the necessity of being more customer conscious.

In this chapter, the attempt has been made to clarify much widespread misunderstanding associated with particular types of lending institutions. Interest charges are simply a pricing matter, similar to the pricing problem confronted by merchandisers of goods and services. We must recognize that interest rates, like prices, must be sufficient to cover the total costs of operation and provide a net profit which is high enough to attract sufficient capital to the field. As the cash-lending industry continues to grow and agressive competition continues to exist among legal lenders, greater efficiency, and hence lower cost methods of operation, can be expected to contribute to the health of the industry in the future.

REVIEW AND DISCUSSION QUESTIONS

1. How does cash loan credit differ from retail credit? From service credit?
2. Discuss the statement, "The borrowing of money by consumers is not of recent origin, but it has occurred in all ages."

3. Why do some consumers borrow money to purchase goods and services when other types of credit could be used to make these purchases?

4. Why do some consumers borrow money to purchase goods and services when they have savings sufficiently large to make the purchases?

5. Distinguish carefully between the different sources of cash loans to consumers.

6. Why were commercial banks so late in.entering the consumer cash loan field?

7. Explain the differences between single-payment loans, conventional installment loans, and the newer types of installment loans.

8. Survey the commercial banks in your community to discover what types of consumer loan plans are in operation.

9. Check the laws in your state to discover the interest rates that may be charged on cash loans to consumers.

10. How do you account for the fact that the commercial bank of today is a very different institution than it was one or two decades ago?

11. What provisions should a small loan law have in order to be effective?

12. Obtain a copy of the small loan law in your state and determine whether it contains these provisions.

13. How do you account for the changing attitude of consumers toward consumer finance companies?

14. Explain the differences in the operations of a small loan company and a sales finance company.

15. Trace the development of the credit union movement in the United States.

16. Why might a borrower go to a small loan company for a loan, even though he was a member of a credit union?

17. How does an industrial bank vary from a commercial bank? From a credit union? From a small loan company?

18. Discuss the reasons advanced to justify the varying interest rates charged by the various consumer lending institutions.

19. What is meant by the postal Giro system?

SUGGESTED READINGS

Sales Promotion Techniques of Commercial Banks

"Banks Go Psychedelic to Lure Customers," *Business Week*, June 21, 1969, p. 78.

"Credit After Banking Hours," *Business Week*, September 14, 1968, p. 37.

Smith, Paul F. "Pricing Policies on Consumer Loans at Commercial Banks," *Journal of Finance*, May 1970, p. 517.

Future of Commercial Banking

"Banks Move into Multipurpose Checks," *Business Week*, February 13, 1971, p. 88.

"Money Goes Electronic in the 1970s," *Business Week,* January 13, 1968, p. 54.
Wallich, Henry C. "Banks Need More Freedom to Compete," *Fortune,* March 1970, p. 114.

Development of Bank Holding Legislation

"Banks Start Banking on Diversity," *Business Week,* July 13, 1968, p. 100.
Cranston, Alan. "One Bank Holding Companies: Good or Bad?" *Business Management,* July 1969, p. 28.
"Fed Acts Cautiously on 'One-Bank' Issue," *Business Week,* January 30, 1971, p. 20.
Nadler, Paul S. "Not Everything Comes Up Roses," *Directors Digest,* March 1969, p. 6.
"Senate Banking Bill Loosens the Reins," *Business Week,* July 11, 1970, p. 16.

Growth of Credit Unions

Bennett, Wallace F. "Credit Unions: Then, Now, Tomorrow," *Consumer Finance News,* July 1968, p. 5.
"Credit Unions and the OEO," *Consumer Finance News,* March 1967, p. 7.
Modley, Rudolf. "Credit Unions Today and Tomorrow," *Credit World,* October 1970, p. 8.
—— "Philosophy Pays Dividends and Makes Outlook Bright for Credit Union Growth," *Industrial Banker,* April 1969, p. 11.
O'Brien, William M. "Credit Unions to Serve Low-Income Families," *Credit World,* January 1969, p. 15.

9

Home Mortgage Loans

The high rate of home ownership in the United States "represents a response to many social, historical, demographic and economic forces, some of which are uniquely American."[1] Home ownership is one of the outstanding characteristics of our society, as illustrated by the fact that in 1970 almost 63 percent of the nation's homes were owner-occupied. For the trend of home ownership since 1890, see Table 9-1.

The proportion of home-owning families varies considerably among the different regions of the nation. For example, it was reported in the *Savings and Loan Fact Book 1971* that in 1970:[2]

Home owners outnumber renters in all but two states—Hawaii and New York—and the District of Columbia. The owner-occupancy rate was 47% for both states, and a low 28% for the nation's capital. States with the highest home ownership rates were Michigan with 74%; Indiana and Iowa with 72%; Minnesota with 71%; and Idaho, Maine and South Dakota with 70%.

TABLE 9-1
Home Ownership, Selected Years, 1890-1970

Year	Owner-Occupancy Rate
1890	47.8%
1900	46.7
1910	45.9
1920	45.6
1930	47.8
1940	43.6
1950	55.0
1960	61.9
1970	62.9

Sources: Bureau of the Census, Department of Housing and Urban Development.

1 / *Savings and Loan Fact Book 1971* (Chicago: United States Savings and Loan League. 1971), p. 44.
2 / *Ibid.*, p. 44.

The meaning of home ownership has been changing over the years, however, with many families today looking upon a home as an investment rather than a family possession. Noneconomic motives still are important, however, as evidenced by consumer beliefs of such things as "children should have a real home in which to grow up," and "when you rent you have nothing but receipts to show for the money."

The mobile home market has been expanding at a very rapid rate. The importance of this relatively new market is shown in the following quotation:[3]

> Here are some up-to-date statistics: It is estimated that in 1968 mobile homes represented 96 percent of all single family homes sold under $12,500; 90 percent of all the single family homes sold under $15,000; and were nearly equal to 60 percent of the 530,000 single family homes sold at any price. How many mobile homes were shipped in 1968? The official estimate is 317,950 with retail sales of just under $2 billion.
>
> It is estimated that over 400,000 units will be shipped in 1969—an increase of 25 percent. For 1970, the Mobile Homes Manufacturers Association estimates 475,000 shipments at an average retail price of $6,000.

Closely associated with home ownership is yet another area of credit involving consumers that has not been covered—that of home mortgage loan credit.[4] Discussion of this type of long-term credit usually is found in books on the subject of personal finance, but not in the books on credits and collections. However, such an omission is regrettable, because the purchase of homes on credit has become an increasingly important factor in the budget of the American family. With almost 63 percent of American families now owning their own homes, a look into this form of consumer credit is important.

INCREASING VOLUME OF HOME MORTGAGE LOANS

Statistics appearing in the monthly *Federal Reserve Bulletin* reflect the steadily increasing volume of mortgage debt outstanding

3 / Norman J. E. Roe, "The Mobile Home Market," *Industrial Banker,* January 1970, p. 5. Also see "Look Carefully at Mobile Home Loans," *Director's Digest,* Part I in January 1970, p. 9, and Part II in February 1970, p. 8; and Charles E. Walsh, "FHA-Insured Mobile Home Loans," *Banking,* October 1970, p. 36.

4 / Entire books have been written on the subject of mortgage lending, whereas in this book only one very short chapter is devoted to the subject. However, the author believes that the student should at least be "exposed" to some of the most important aspects of home mortgage financing, as the majority of the students in the business administration curriculum do not study the field of personal finance.

It is suggested that the prospective home buyer, after having acquired some fundamental knowledge of this subject, rely strongly upon the expert advice of his experienced real estate agent, his banker, his savings and loan executive, his insurance agent, and other experienced executives in this field. Much grief can be saved by following the advice of experts in this complicated field.

on one- to four-family nonfarm houses. Whereas the amount owed at
the close of 1941 totaled $18.4 billion, by the end of 1970 this
figure had increased more than 15 times to $280.2 billion. Of course,
this increasing dollar amount of mortgage debt reflects to some
degree the effect of inflation, but by far the greater influence is
simply that more American families are buying homes. The data in
Table 9-2 show the trend of mortgage debt outstanding for selected
years. Also shown in Table 9-2 is whether the mortgage debt was
FHA-insured, VA-guaranteed (GI), or a conventional type loan. It is
important to note that conventional loans accounted for approximately 65 percent of the total outstanding at the end of 1970.

Before looking at the various sources of financial aid to borrowers,
it is well to understand what is meant by the terms GI loans and FHA
insurance.

TABLE 9-2
Mortgage Debt Outstanding on Nonfarm
One- to Four-Family Properties
(In billions of dollars)

End of Year	Total	*Government-Underwritten*			Con-ventional
		Total	FHA-Insured	VA-Guaranteed	
1941 . . . . . 18.4		. . .	. . .	. . .	. . .
1945 . . . . . 18.6		4.3	4.1	.2	14.3
1950 . . . . . 45.2		18.9	8.6	10.3	26.3
1951 . . . . . 51.7		22.9	9.7	13.2	28.8
1952 . . . . . 58.5		25.4	10.8	14.6	33.1
1953 . . . . . 66.1		28.1	12.0	16.1	38.0
1954 . . . . . 75.7		32.1	12.8	19.3	43.6
1955 . . . . . 88.2		38.9	14.3	24.6	49.3
1956 . . . . . 99.0		43.9	15.5	28.4	55.1
1957 . . . . .107.6		47.2	16.5	30.7	60.4
1958 . . . . .117.7		50.1	19.7	30.4	67.6
1959 . . . . .130.9		53.8	23.8	30.0	77.0
1960 . . . . .141.3		56.4	26.7	29.7	84.8
1961 . . . . .153.1		59.1	29.5	29.6	93.9
1962 . . . . .166.5		62.2	32.3	29.9	104.3
1963 . . . . .182.2		65.9	35.0	30.9	116.3
1964 . . . . .197.6		69.2	38.3	30.9	128.3
1965 . . . . .212.9		73.1	42.0	31.1	139.8
1966 . . . . .223.6		76.1	44.8	31.3	147.6
1967 . . . . .236.1		79.9	47.4	32.5	156.1
1968 . . . . .251.2		84.4	50.6	33.8	166.8
1969 . . . . .266.8		90.1	54.5	35.6	176.9
1970 . . . . .280.2		97.1	59.9	37.2	182.5

Source: Board of Governors of the Federal Reserve System.

GI Loans (VA-Guaranteed)

The original Servicemen's Readjustment Act was passed by Congress in 1944, extending housing benefits to eligible veterans. Under the law, as amended, the Veterans Administration is authorized to guarantee or insure home, farm, and business loans made to veterans by lending institutions. Direct loans may be made in certain areas for the purpose of purchasing or constructing a home or farm residence, or for the repair or alteration or improvement of the dwelling. The most recent amendment, passed in August 1967, extended the period of entitlement for World War II veterans from 1967 to 1970 and continued benefits to Vietnam veterans. A veteran may use his entitlement under the VA loan program for up to 10 years from the date of discharge plus an additional year for each three months of active duty. The final cutoff date for the use of benefits is 20 years from the date of discharge or release from active duty. For a detailed account of eligibility requirements, the reader is referred to the Veterans Administration Pamphlet 26-4, Revised, entitled *Questions & Answers on Guaranteed and Direct Loans for Veterans,* dated February 1970.

Despite a great deal of confusion and misunderstanding, direct loans under the act generally are not made by the federal government. The government simply guarantees loans made by ordinary mortgage lenders (descriptions of which appear in subsequent sections), after the veteran has made his own arrangements for the loan through normal financial circles. The Veterans Administration then appraises the property in question and, if satisfied with the risk involved, guarantees the lender against loss up to 60 percent of the real estate loan for home purposes (i.e., purchase, construction, alteration, improvement, or repair), with a maximum guarantee of $12,500. In order to provide for small monthly payments to conform with the veteran's ability to pay, GI residential loans may be written for a maximum of 30 years and GI farm loans for a 40-year duration. Property cannot carry a GI loan if it sells for more than the Veterans Administration appraisal.

FHA Insurance

As in GI loans, the applicant for the loan makes his own arrangements with a lending institution. This financial organization then may ask if the borrower desires FHA insurance on his loan or may insist that the borrower apply for it. The federal government, through the Federal Housing Administration, investigates the applicant and, having decided that the risk is favorable, insures the lending institution against loss of principal in case the borrower fails to meet the terms and conditions of the mortgage. The borrower, who pays an insurance premium of one half of 1 percent on declining balances for the lender's protection, receives the benefits of a careful appraisal by an FHA inspector and of a lower interest rate on the mortgage than possibly would have been offered by the lender in case the loans were not so protected. The most important provisions of FHA loans to finance proposed or existing residences are as follows:

Maximum loan: $30,000 on one-family house; $32,500 on two- or three-family; $37,500 on four-family. These amounts are for owner-occupied residences and apply to approved new construction, approved existing construction less than one year old, and existing construction over one year old. If housing is not owner-occupied, maximums are 85 percent of loan amounts shown.

Down payment: 3 percent of $15,000 value plus 10 percent of next $5,000 plus 20 percent in excess of $20,000.

The Housing And Urban Development Act of 1968 introduced a wide variety of programs designed to provide housing for low-income families. FHA Section 235 has been called the most significant of these programs and combines mortgage insurance with interest assistance payments made directly to the mortgagee by the FHA on behalf of the mortgagor or cooperative member. Section 236 offers insurance and interest assistance payments for rental projects, while a program of mortgage insurance to finance home ownership for families of low and moderate income who cannot qualify under normal standards because of their poor credit history was established in Section 237.

The Housing Act of 1969 contained a provision for FHA insurance on consumer-type loans for the purchase of mobile homes. The maximum loan is $10,000, with a maturity up to 12 years.

FINANCING A HOME

Of course, the safest and most desirable way to buy a home is to pay cash. But the typical American family[5] is not in such an advantageous position, and thus it must make arrangements for financing its purchase. It probably will be in a position to make only a modest down payment, 25 percent or less, and will be forced to secure the remainder of the purchase price by mortgage from some lending institution. The larger the down payment, the smaller the total interest payment over the term of the mortgage. Buyers are cautioned, however, not to use all of their savings for making the

5 / Glenn H. Miller, Jr., "Some Demographic Influences on the Future Market for Housing," Federal Reserve Bank of Kansas City *Monthly Review,* November 1969, p. 3.

down payment, thus depriving themselves of any reserve on which to fall back if extraordinary expenses arise in the future or if income is reduced.

Sources of These Finances

The family seeking assistance in the purchase or construction of a home generally has several possible sources from which to secure the funds needed to complete the transaction. It should be pointed out, however, that the amount of the loan sought usually is less important than the ratio of the loan to the property value. At certain financial institutions, this ratio is a direct determining factor as to the eligibility of the applying family for the needed loan.

The sources from which a buyer or builder of a home may obtain financial aid include savings and loan associations, life insurance companies, commercial banks, mutual savings banks, mortgage companies, federal agencies, individual investors, and builders. In deciding upon the most advantageous source, a number of factors (such as the size of the loan needed, maturity of the loan, interest rate, method of paying off the loan, and other characteristics) should be considered before actually borrowing the money.

In connection with the financing of mobile homes, it should be recognized that[6]

banks gave up the leadership in this type of financing in 1963, regained it temporarily in 1964, and since 1965 have trailed finance companies. . . . Since 1965, finance companies have been more aggressive in seeking this type of paper. Another reason for doing a more effective job is their broad network of offices which enable them to capitalize on active, regional markets.

Savings and loan associations are the leaders by a wide margin in the total amount of credit provided to home owners and buyers. Their loans exceed the combined holdings of commercial banks, mutual savings banks, and life insurance companies.[7] Table 9-3 contains the percentage distribution of mortgage holdings by type of lending institution from 1940 to 1970.

Savings and Loan Associations. The most important purpose of these institutions is to make mortgage loans on residential property. These organizations, which also are known as savings associations, building and loan associations, cooperative banks (in New England), and homestead associations (in Louisiana), are the primary source of

6 / "Financing of Mobile Homes," *Bankers Monthly Magazine,* November 15, 1969, p. 39.

7 / J. A. Cacy and Linda Moore, "Financial Intermediaries in the Residential Mortgage Market 1966-69," Federal Reserve Bank of Kansas City *Monthly Review,* September-October 1970, p. 3.

(percentage distribution)

Year-End	Savings and Loan	Mutual Savings Banks	Commercial Banks	Life Insurance Cos.	Federal Agencies	Individuals Others	Total
1940 . . .	22.5	12.4	13.6	10.4	12.4	28.7	100
1945 . . .	27.7	10.2	15.5	12.4	4.8	29.4	100
1946 . . .	29.7	8.8	19.9	11.0	2.9	27.7	100
1947 . . .	30.0	8.1	22.4	12.3	2.3	24.9	100
1948 . . .	29.6	8.5	22.2	14.9	2.1	22.7	100
1949 . . .	29.6	9.0	21.1	16.2	3.1	21.0	100
1950 . . .	29.0	9.5	21.0	18.8	3.3	18.4	100
1951 . . .	28.7	10.3	19.9	20.5	4.0	16.6	100
1952 . . .	30.2	10.6	19.2	20.1	4.3	15.6	100
1953 . . .	31.8	11.2	18.2	20.0	4.2	14.6	100
1954 . . .	33.0	11.9	17.6	20.0	3.7	13.8	100
1955 . . .	34.0	12.6	17.1	20.0	3.4	12.9	100
1956 . . .	34.4	13.1	16.4	20.3	3.6	12.2	100
1957 . . .	35.3	13.1	15.3	19.9	4.3	12.1	100
1958 . . .	36.5	13.3	15.0	19.0	3.9	12.3	100
1959 . . .	37.8	12.9	14.7	18.0	4.8	11.8	100
1960 . . .	39.2	13.0	13.6	17.6	5.1	11.5	100
1961 . . .	40.8	13.1	13.1	16.8	4.8	11.4	100
1962 . . .	41.9	13.3	13.3	15.9	4.4	11.2	100
1963 . . .	43.4	13.6	13.7	15.0	3.4	10.9	100
1964 . . .	44.1	13.9	13.8	14.5	3.0	10.7	100
1965 . . .	44.3	14.1	14.2	14.0	3.0	10.4	100
1966 . . .	43.6	14.2	14.7	13.5	3.9	10.1	100
1967 . . .	43.8	14.2	14.9	12.6	4.5	10.0	100
1968 . . .	43.9	13.9	15.4	11.6	5.3	9.9	100
1969 . . .	44.2	13.7	15.5	10.5	6.4	9.7	100
1970* . . .	44.8	13.4	15.1	9.5	7.6	9.6	100

*Preliminary.
Note: Components may not add to 100 percent due to rounding.
Source: Federal Home Loan Bank Board.

financial assistance to a large segment of American home owners. As home-financing institutions, these associations not only give primary attention to single-family residences but also are well equipped to make sound loans in this area.

Some of the most important characteristics of a savings and loan association are:

1. It generally is a locally owned and privately managed home-financing institution.
2. It receives savings of individuals and uses these funds to make long-term amortized loans to purchasers of homes.
3. It has repayment protection through first mortgage security.
4. It makes loans for construction, purchase, repair, or refinancing of houses.
5. Of the more than 5,900 savings and loan institutions, approximately 65 percent are state-chartered and 35 percent are federally chartered.

Under the Housing and Urban Development Act of 1968, federally chartered savings and loan associations are permitted to use the terms "deposit" and "interest" to describe savings accounts and the earnings paid on savings. The lending powers of federal associations also were expanded under the act, which authorized them to finance mobile homes, to make unsecured loans on vacation homes, and to lend up to $5,000 on household equipment for the homes.[8]

Lending limitations on savings and loan associations were relaxed significantly in a broad series of rule changes announced in February 1971 by the Federal Home Loan Bank Board. These changes are designed to make it easier for savings and loan associations to lend on housing, apartments, and commercial projects.[9]

From the data in Table 9-4, it is seen that the conventional type of loan is much more important in the mortgage activity of savings and loan associations than are FHA-insured and VA-guaranteed. At the close of 1970, conventional loans accounted for 87 percent of the $150.6 billion of loans outstanding, whereas VA-guaranteed loans were 6 percent and FHA-insured were 7 percent of the total. In the middle and late 1960s, savings and loan associations faced a tremendous competitive struggle for deposits from other financial institutions. This reduced volume of loanable funds largely accounted for the declining mortgage loan activity on the part of the savings and loan associations shown in Table 9-4 and described in the subsequent section on the competition among lenders of mortgage money.

8 / For articles on this act, see the Suggested Readings at the end of the chapter.

9 / "News and Trends from Washington," *Directors Digest,* March 1971, pp. 16-17. Also see Herbert Bratter, "S & Ls Want To Be Banks," *Banking,* October 1970, p. 44.

TABLE 9-4

Mortgage Activity of Savings and Loan Associations

(in millions of dollars)

Year	Loans Made			Loans Outstanding (End of Year)			
	Total	New Construction	Home Purchase	Total	FHA-Insured	VA-Guaranteed	Conventional
1941	1,379	437	581	4,578	...	...	...
1945	1,913	181	1,358	5,376	...	...	...
1956	10,325	3,699	4,620	35,729	1,486	6,643	27,600
1957	10,160	3,484	4,591	40,007	1,643	7,011	31,353
1958	12,182	4,050	5,172	45,627	2,206	7,077	36,344
1959	15,151	5,201	6,613	53,141	2,995	7,186	42,960
1960	14,304	4,678	6,132	60,070	3,524	7,222	49,324
1961	17,733	5,212	7,317	68,834	4,167	7,152	57,515
1962	21,153	6,115	8,650	78,770	4,476	7,010	67,284
1963	25,173	7,185	10,055	90,944	4,696	6,960	79,288
1964	24,913	6,638	10,538	101,333	4,894	6,683	89,756
1965	24,192	6,013	10,830	110,306	5,145	6,398	98,763
1966	16,924	3,653	7,828	114,427	5,269	6,157	103,001
1967	20,122	4,243	9,604	121,805	5,791	6,351	109,663
1968	21,983	4,916	11,215	130,802	6,658	7,012	117,132
1969	21,847	4,757	11,254	140,347	7,917	7,658	124,772
1970	21,387	4,150	10,239	150,562	10,195	8,507	131,860

Source: Board of Governors of the Federal Reserve System.

Commercial Banks. In the past, commercial banks have not been greatly interested in real estate loans and have placed only a relatively small percentage of their assets in mortgages. As their name implies, these financial institutions have attempted to secure their earning primarily from commercial and consumer loans and have left to others the major task of home financing. However, changes in banking laws and in banking policies have resulted in increased commercial bank activity in home financing.

Changes in banking laws now allow these institutions to make mortgage loans on a more liberal basis than ever before.[10] National banks, for example, now may invest in 25-year mortgages up to 80 percent of the value of the property involved, if the entire amount is to be amortized in the 25 years. Under certain circumstances even this 80 percent figure may be exceeded. They also may invest in 10-year mortgages up to 66 2/3 percent of the value of the property involved, if at least 40 percent of the loan is to be paid off during the 10-year period. This 4 percent per year amortization must take place before such a mortgage can be renewed on the reduced principal. These banks also can loan up to 50 percent of the value if the loan is not amortized and if it is to be paid off within five years. Recent rulings also have liberalized the interpretation of what constitutes "improved realty" on which commercial banks may make mortgage loans.

In acquiring mortgages on real estate, commercial banks follow two main practices. Some of the banks maintain active and well-organized departments whose primary function is to compete actively for real estate loans. In areas lacking specialized real estate financial institutions, these banks become *the* source for residential and farm mortgage loans. The second technique of acquiring mortgages is simply to purchase them from mortgage bankers or dealers. A picture of commercial bank holdings of residential mortgage loans is given in Table 9-5, with a breakdown as to FHA-insured, VA-guaranteed, and conventional types.

Mutual Savings Banks. Mutual savings banks are found today in only about one third of the states, with the majority concentrated in New York, Massachusetts, and Connecticut. These banks receive their charters from the state governments, and the regulations governing their operations have a wide range of variations. In relation to their mortgage-lending programs, for example, the ratio of the maximum loan allowed to the value of the property varies from 50 to 80 percent (except for FHA and GI loans).

Mutual savings bank holdings of residential mortgage loans totaled

10 / Paul S. Nadler, "Fed Tries to Boost Bank Mortgage Lending," *Directors Digest,* October 1970, p. 5.

TABLE 9-5
Commercial Bank Holdings of Residential Mortgage Loans
(in millions of dollars)

End of Year	Total	FHA-Insured	VA-Guaranteed	Conven-tional
1941	3,292	. . .	. . .	. . .
1945	3,395	. . .	. . .	. . .
1950	10,431	. . .	. . .	. . .
1951	11,270	3,421	2,921	4,929
1952	12,188	3,675	3,012	5,501
1953	12,925	3,912	3,061	5,951
1954	14,152	4,106	3,350	6,695
1955	15,888	4,560	3,711	7,617
1956	17,004	4,803	3,902	8,300
1957	17,147	4,823	3,589	8,735
1958	18,591	5,476	3,335	9,780
1959	20,320	6,122	3,161	11,037
1960	20,362	5,851	2,859	11,652
1961	21,225	5,975	2,627	12,623
1962	23,482	6,520	2,654	14,308
1963	26,476	7,105	2,862	16,509
1964	28,933	7,315	2,742	18,876
1965	32,387	7,702	2,688	21,997
1966	34,876	7,544	2,599	24,733
1967	37,642	7,709	2,696	27,237
1968	41,433	7,926	2,708	30,800
1969	44,573	7,960	2,663	33,950
1970	45,640	7,919	2,589	35,131

Source: Board of Governors of the Federal Reserve System.

almost $50 billion at the end of 1970. VA-guaranteed loans accounted for 24 percent of these holdings, conventional loans for 44 percent, and FHA-insured loans for 32 percent.

Life Insurance Companies. Another source of financial assistance to the consumer buying or building a home is the life insurance company. These companies have followed the practice of lending on real estate as one form of investment and have adjusted their portfolios from time to time in order to reflect changing economic conditions. Formerly farm loans were looked upon with favor by life insurance companies. Only in recent years, however, have these institutions gone actively into the market for residential mortgages. Individuals seeking a loan from an insurance company may complete the transaction by dealing directly with a local branch office. Another method is to deal with a local real estate broker who acts as loan correspondent for one or more insurance companies.

Federal Agencies. Under certain conditions and certain fund limitations, the Veterans Administration makes direct loans to veterans who are satisfactory credit risks in housing credit shortage areas designated by the Administrator of the Veterans Administration. These housing credit shortage areas are generally rural areas and small cities and towns not near the metropolitan or commuting areas of large cities, and where GI loans from private institutions are not available to the veterans.

Other Sources. Individual investors constitute a large but a somewhat declining source of money for home mortgage loans. Unfortunately, there are no accurate data reflecting the proportion of mortgage lending provided by individual investors. However, experienced observers claim that a substantial portion of mortgage money originates from this source, which is known to prefer short-term obligations and usually restricts its loans to less than two thirds of the value of the residential property.

Building contractors often are willing to accept second mortgages in part payment of the construction price of a home in those instances where the purchaser is unable to raise the total amount of down payment above the first mortgage money offered by one of the financial sources previously described.

Mention also should be made of mortgage companies which are often known as mortgage bankers or mortgage dealers. In the 1946 constitution of the Mortgage Bankers Association of America, these companies were defined as:

Any person, firm, or corporation . . . engaged in the business of lending money on the security of improved real estate in the United States, and who publicly offers such securities, or certificates, bonds, or debentures based thereon, for sale as a dealer therin, or who is an investor in real estate securities, or is the recognizing agent of an insurance company or other direct purchaser of first mortgage real estate securities for investment only.

These companies were severely hurt by the large decline in real estate values during the Great Depression, and as a result today are not as important a source of home financing as they were during the 1920s. Nevertheless, it is important to know about their operations in order to have a complete picture of the various means by which residential property may be financed for the consumer.

Competition among Lenders for Loanable Funds

To be able to provide home buyers and builders with the funds needed, financial institutions must compete for deposits—and in the middle and late 1960s this competition became intense.[11] Since the

11 / For articles on this topic, see the Suggested Readings at the end of the chapter.

enactment of the Banking Act of 1933, the Board of Governors of the Federal Reserve System has had the power to regulate interest rates payable on time deposits by member banks. This authority is implemented through the Board's Regulation Q.[12] The Banking Act of 1935 extended like authority to the FDIC in regard to nonmember insured banks, and since 1936 this regulation has corresponded to Regulation Q. In effect, then, all insured commercial banks are limited by Regulation Q. In September 1966, a new federal law and regulations issued by the three federal regulatory agencies—the Board of Governors of the Federal Reserve System, the Federal Home Loan Bank Board, and the Federal Deposit Insurance Corporation—attempted to reduce rate competition for funds among the depository-type financial institutions. Before September 1966, the Federal Home Loan Bank Board could influence the rates paid on savings accounts by savings and loan associations only indirectly. Through moral suasion and through withholding borrowing privileges from member associations, the Federal Home Loan Bank Board attempted to hold down rates paid by savings and loan institutions in 1965 and in 1966. In September 1966, however, the Board was granted specific authority to set rate ceilings.

Describing the situation that developed in the late 1960s, Professor Paul S. Nadler pointed out:[13]

> During 1969 and 1970, the Federal Reserve's credit control instruments have been relied upon as the basic weapon in the battle against inflation. Yet the money managers have slowly developed another long-standing power into a second weapon which eventually may have far more significance to the economy and financial institutions than does tight money. This is the Federal Reserve's control over interest rates paid by commercial banks on time and savings deposits under its Regulation Q.
>
> ·
>
> The change that has now taken place and that appears so significant for future financial policy is that, through the use of its Regulation Q weapon, the Federal Reserve has now taken a far more active role in deciding how the funds will be allocated in the economy, instead of just determining how much credit will be available. To use the analogy presented above, "The Federal Reserve has now jumped into the tub and indicated that henceforth it too will play a major role in determining which parts of the bathtub of credit will get soap."

Amortized versus Old-Type Straight Mortgages

Mention has been made previously of an amortized mortgage. While the use of this term is fairly well standardized in financial and

12 / Charlotte ⌐ ng, "The Administration of Regulation Q," *Federal Reserve* Bank of St. Louis *R*. bruary 1970, p. 29.
13 / "Regulation redit Control," *Bankers Magazine,* Spring 1970, p. 17.

credit circles, it is important that a clear distinction be drawn between this newer type of repayment plan and the older type of straight mortgage plan.

When a loan is made on the security of a mortgage, the lender of the funds makes a loan to the home owner in return for a note secured by the mortgage of the property. Formerly, most of the loans made for the acquisition of a home ran for a definite number of years, at the end of which period the entire principal amount borrowed became due and payable. These were known as "straight mortgages" because it was customary to pay only the interest periodically and to make little or no payment on the principal of the loan. Thus most borrowers would meet the interest payments, forget or "try to forget" the principal until the note matured, and then try to renew the loan for another three- to five-year period.

In recent years, however, most of the loans granted by financial institutions have been of the amortized type. All the government mortgage financing institutions, such as the FHA and the HOLC, which were set up during the 1930s, insisted upon the amortized form of mortgage lending. This direct-reduction mortgage provides for a fixed monthly payment which not only covers interest and perhaps taxes and insurance but also provides for a payment toward reducing the principal of the mortgage debt. An amortization schedule is shown in Table 9-6.

The Variable-Rate Mortgage

A term that has recently gained a great deal of prominence in the literature on mortgage lending is the variable-rate mortgage. This

TABLE 9-6
Amortization Schedule

	Monthly Payment to Amortize $1,000 Loan, Including Interest at Rate of:				
	5%	6%	6½%	7½%	8½%
In 5 Years	$18.87	$19.34	$19.57	$20.04	$20.5
In 6 Years	16.10	16.58	16.81	17.29	17.7
In 7 Years	14.13	14.61	14.85	15.34	15.8
In 8 Years	12.66	13.15	13.39	13.88	14.3
In 9 Years	11.52	12.01	12.26	12.76	13.2
In 10 Years . . .	10.61	11.11	11.36	11.88	12.4
In 15 Years . . .	7.91	8.44	8.72	9.28	9.8
In 20 Years . . .	6.60	7.17	7.46	8.06	8.6
In 30 Years . . .	5.37	6.00	6.33	7.00	7.6

variable-rate type of mortgage has been defined as loans carrying:[14]

... interest rates that change by a given amount whenever some other specified financial rate changes in a stated fashion. A variety of arrangements is possible. For example, interest rates may flex only upward, or they may move up and down. They may be tied to an external index such as the discount rate or the interest rate on long-term government bonds. Or they may be tied to an internal index over which the originating lender has some influence, such as the interest-dividend rate paid on savings.

Although only a few institutions have used this type of contract, it is not surprising to note that the variable-rate mortgage has become a subject of very active discussion in recent years, which have seen the exposure of thrift institutions to interest rate levels of such widely varying magnitude.

The "Point" System in Mortgage Lending

Over the years mortgage lenders have in many instances started charging "points" to home buyers. This practice, while generally misunderstood and many times ignored, is vitally important to an understanding of mortgage lending operations. A point is 1 percent of the face value of the mortgage; thus if a home buyer is charged four points on a $20,000 loan, $800 will be deducted and he will receive only $19,200. However, he will have to repay the entire $20,000. This, of course, means that the true annual rate of interest will be more than the stated rate. Because of the difficulty of calculation, Table 9-7 was prepared and published in the *Changing Times* magazine.

Referring to the material in Table 9-7, the following interesting observation was made:[15]

Assume that a $20,000 loan is for 20 years and the stated annual rate of interest is 8½% Then the payment by the borrower of four points would make the actual interest rate 9.066%, assuming—and this is important—that the mortgage runs the full 20 years. The truth-in-lending law requires lenders to state this actual rate over the full term of the loan.

The rate the borrower really pays, however, may be higher than that. If he pays off the loan at the end of ten years (which is about the average life of a mortgage, no matter what the contract term), the actual rate in the example will be 9.185% because the points are spread over a shorter period.

Note here that points may also be charged to the seller. These points,

14 / Robert M. Fisher, *Variable-Rate Mortgages* (Staff Economic Studies No. 30) (Washington: Federal Reserve Board, March 1967), p. 1. Also see "Variable Rate Mortgages: A Way to Ease the Squeeze?" *Savings and Loan News,* August 1969, p. 44; and James A. Hollensteiner, "How to Avoid the 50% Problem on Savings Certificates," *Savings and Loan News,* June 1968, p. 25.

15 / "How 'Points' Hike the Interest Rate on Your Mortgage." Reprinted by permission from *Changing Times,* the Kiplinger Magazine, (June 1970 issue), page 12. Copyright 1970 by The Kiplinger Washington Editors, Inc., 1729 H Street, N.W., Washington, D.C. 20006.

TABLE 9-7

Actual Interest Rate on a 20-Year Mortgage if Paid Off in 10 or 20 Years

No. of Points Paid	6% Paid Off in		6½% Paid Off in		7% Paid Off in		7½% Paid Off	
	10 Yrs.	20 Yrs.	10 Yrs.	20 Yrs.	10 Yrs.	20 Yrs.	10 Yrs.	? Y
1	6.156	6.125	6.658	6.627	7.160	7.130	7.662	7.€
2	6.314	6.252	6.818	6.757	7.323	7.262	7.828	7.∶
3	6.474	6.381	6.981	6.888	7.488	7.396	7.995	7.∶
4	6.637	6.512	7.146	7.022	7.655	7.532	8.165	8.∢
5	6.801	6.645	7.313	7.158	7.825	7.671	8.337	8.∶
6	6.968	6.780	7.482	7.295	7.997	7.812	8.512	8.∶
7	7.138	6.917	7.654	7.436	8.171	7.955	8.689	8.∢
8	7.309	7.057	7.829	7.578	8.348	8.100	8.869	8.€
9	7.484	7.198	8.005	7.723	8.528	8.248	9.051	8.∶
10	7.660	7.343	8.185	7.870	8.710	8.399	9.236	8.€

Source: "How 'Points' Hike the Interest Rate on Your Mortgage," *Changing Times,* June 1970, p. 12.

however, do not affect the interest rate. They simply reduce the amount the seller receives.

The home buyer, therefore, is cautioned to seek expert advice as to the terms of his mortgage and the question of points charged him before making any final decision in the purchase of a home.

REVIEW AND DISCUSSION QUESTIONS

1. Why might home mortgage loan credit be considered as a type of consumer credit? Why might it not be so considered?

2. Why would you want to buy a home? To rent instead?

3. Distinguish between a FHA-insured, a VA-guaranteed (GI), and a conventional type loan.

4. What are the sources available to the American family to finance the purchase of a home?

5. Check with a savings and loan association, a life insurance company, a commercial bank, a mutual savings bank (if there is one in your area), and a mortgage company as to their requirements for home financing.

6. Check the interest rates being paid individuals for deposits in the various types of financial institutions in your area. In which institution would you prefer to place your own deposits? Why?

7. Distinguish clearly between the amortized and the old-type straight mortgage.

8. What are advantages and disadvantages of the variable-rate mortgage to the home buyer? To the lending institution?

8% id Off in	8½% Paid Off in		9% Paid Off in		9½% Paid Off in		10% Paid Off in	
20 Yrs.	10 Yrs.	20 Yrs.	10 Yrs.	20 Yrs.	10 Yrs.	20 Yrs.	10 Yrs.	20 Yrs.
8.135	8.667	8.638	9.170	9.141	9.672	9.643	10.175	10.146
8.273	8.837	8.778	9.343	9.284	9.848	9.790	10.353	10.296
8.412	9.010	8.921	9.518	9.429	10.026	9.938	10.534	10.447
8.554	9.185	9.066	9.695	9.577	10.206	10.089	10.717	10.601
8.699	9.362	9.213	9.876	9.728	10.389	10.243	10.903	10.758
8.845	9.542	9.363	10.058	9.881	10.575	10.399	11.092	10.918
8.994	9.725	9.515	10.244	10.036	10.763	10.558	11.283	11.080
9.146	9.911	9.670	10.432	10.194	10.955	10.719	11.477	11.245
9.300	10.099	9.827	10.624	10.355	11.149	10.884	11.675	11.413
9.457	10.290	9.988	10.818	10.519	11.346	11.051	11.875	11.584

9. What is meant by the "point" system in home mortgage lending? Why might you as a buyer of a home be in favor of the "point" system? Why might you object to it?

SUGGESTED READINGS

Housing and Urban Development Act

"Associations Learn How to Finance with the Help of the '68 Housing Act," *Savings and Loan News,* October 1968, p. 40.
Bratter, Herbert. "S&Ls Want to Be Banks," *Banking,* October 1970, p. 44.
"News and Trends from Washington," *Directors Digest,* March 1971, pp. 16-17.
"What to Expect in Consumer Lending," *Savings and Loan News,* November 1968, p. 30.

Competition for Loanable Funds

"Banks Get More Room to Scramble," *Business Week,* January 24, 1970, p. 29.
"Banks Try to Dodge Fed's Grasp," *Business Week,* April 5, 1969, p. 98.
"Fed Cracks Q Ceiling to Help the Banks," *Business Week,* June 27, 1970, p. 40.
Nadler, Paul S. "Will Small Banks Miss Their 'Q'?" *Banking,* March 1971, p. 37.
Saulnier, Raymond J. "10 Ways to Help the Mortgage Market," *Directors Digest,* July 1970, p. 3.
"The S&Ls Go Slightly Mod," *Business Week,* April 18, 1970, p. 90.
"Where High Interest Rates Hurt: A Look at the Money Squeeze," *Consumer Finance News,* April 1969, p. 6.

PART III

Management and Analysis
of Consumer Credit

10

Management of Consumer Credit

Consumer credit management in today's credit-based economy cannot be considered as a specialized tool or as an isolated function separate and apart from other key functions of business. Instead, consumer credit management must continuously and increasingly familiarize itself with the problems, procedures, and possibilities of its credit function as an integral part of the company's total operations and a path to potential future profits.

Consumer credit management is a developing profession where experience, ability, and education are essential. Opportunities in this field are increasing with our expanding economy, and demands and standards of performance are rising simultaneously.

The management of consumer credit activities involves the fundamental principles of management found in all other types of operations. The term management has been explained as follows:[1]

> Managing is defined here as the design or creation and maintenance of an internal environment in an enterprise where individuals, working together in groups, can perform efficiently and effectively toward the attainment of group goals. Essentially, managing is the art of doing and management is the body of organized knowledge which underlies the art.

For successful credit management, then, it is necessary that planning, organizing, directing, and controlling credit activities take place in an efficient and coordinated manner. The task of credit management will vary depending upon such factors as the type of business, the size of the operation, the organizational framework, the

1 / Harold Koontz and Cyril O'Donnell, *Principles of Management* (4th ed.; New York: McGraw-Hill Book Co., 1968), p. 2. For another excellent book in the management field, see Henry H. Albers, *Principles of Management* (3d ed.; New York: John Wiley & Sons, Inc., 1969); also see Robert Bartels, "Credit Management—An Integrated Approach," *Credit Currents*, May 1967, p. 24.

ownership plan, the authority delegated to the credit executive, and the overall goals and policies of the firm. These will vary, of course, depending upon whether we are discussing a retail firm, a service organization, or a financial institution. Likewise, variations will be found, for example, between a "mama-and-papa" grocery store and a supermarket chain organization.

Consumer credit management involves all activities and responsibilities from the decision as to how credit operations will fit into company objectives, through the consideration of prospective credit "customers," through the decision-making process of whether to accept or reject the credit being offered, through the attention given to the receivables arising from the credit transactions, and finally to the completion of the credit transactions by collections from satisfied customers.

Consumer credit management has come a long way over the years.[2] It has had to face—and still does in some instances—the fact that to some people credit occupies a negative role in business operations. This position in which credit has found itself on various occasions often was the fault of credit people themselves. For a number of years this negative kind of thinking contributed to a lack of fresh and creative ideas, constructive imagination, and positive leadership. When such conditions prevail, rigor mortis tends to set in and aspiring young men and women tend to look elsewhere for positions that offer more opportunities.

Fortunately, in recent years consumer credit management has come to be recognized as the positive and constructive force that it is,[3] and a brand of leadership has appeared that has raised credit management to the status of a profession. More than ever before, credit people as a group are demonstrating technical competence in all the important phases of credit administration. And undoubtedly this will continue in the years to come.[4] In his article on the background of the "new" executive—where he comes from and how he develops—Dr. Robert W. Wald pointed out the following facts as significant:[5]

1. The emerging executive is a product of the American culture.
2. The emerging executive is a product of an above-average socio-economic background.
3. The emerging executive is a product of a happy home and family life.

2 / Allyn M. Schiffer, "Adding to the Credit Man's Dimensions," *Credit World,* September 1970, p. 8.

3 / James F. Benton, "Challenging Credit Management," *Credit World,* July 1967, p. 13.

4 / Lawrence G. Chait, "The Consumer Credit Executive in Tomorrow's Marketplace," *Credit World,* September 1969, p. 7.

5 / "Mr. Executive—A Profile for the Seventies," *Credit World,* April 1968, pp. 13-14.

4. The emerging executive indicates an above-average background of academic training.
5. The emerging executive had an opportunity to serve in leadership capacities before entering the business world.
6. The emerging executive enjoyed good health as a youngster and has continued to enjoy it throughout his working career.
7. The emerging executive enjoys a family life which is conducive to the maximum utilization of his abilities.

He further pointed out the following behavioral tendencies of this "new" executive:[6]

1. The emerging executive is possessed of superior mental and analytical ability.
2. He has the ability to get along well with other people.
3. His predominant interest is also in people.
4. He is adequately aggressive and seeks new work to be done and new methods of doing it.
5. He is at least average in his emotional adjustment and self-confidence.

These characteristics undoubtedly must be shown by the credit executive if he is to take his rightful place in his company's organization.

RETAIL CREDIT MANAGEMENT

Once a retail store has decided to include credit among its selling tools, it then is faced with the task of establishing a credit policy to serve as the cornerstone of sound credit administration, setting up a credit department, securing the services of competent and well-trained individuals to carry out credit activities, and directing and controlling credit operations to attain the functions that may be expected from sound credit management.[7]

Policy Determination

A well-managed organization operates on the basis of sound policies predetermined to guide the courses of action that will be followed. Since a policy is usually defined as a line or course of action to be followed over a considerable period of time, it is imperative that clear thinking prevail and careful appraisal be made of the problems involved and desired results to be attained before a firm decides upon the consumer credit policy that it will follow.

The variety of credit plans now in effect in firms catering to the needs of the American consumer complicates the policy of simply saying, "We sell on credit." What type of credit plan or plans—such

6 / *Ibid.*, p. 14.

7 / Assuming that the retail firm decides to handle its own credit operations and does not turn over all of its credit operations to some outside credit plan, such as BankAmericard or Master Charge.

as revolving charge, installment credit, or open charge—to adopt immediately becomes a vital segment of policy determination. The preceding chapters have been designed to give a word picture of these various arrangements found in the consumer credit field today. Out of this assortment, the firm must select that one type or combination of types which best fits its business and which it believes will produce the results desired. It has been pointed out that there are many factors—effect on profits, amount of capital available, laws, desires of customers, competition, type of goods sold, size and location of community—involved in the firm's choice. These factors vary widely, of course, and must be analyzed separately for each type of credit under consideration.

A credit manager is entitled to a written statement of policy—a policy that should be accepted and clearly understood by the other executives of the firm. Such a spelled-out policy statement should include, at the minimum, an accurate description of the types of credit plans in effect at the retail establishment, the terms of each of these types of plans, the basis for accepting the credit of a customer, the willingness with which it will be accepted, and the relationship of credit to the other major policies followed by the store. Some policy statements on credit will be found to be more detailed and more descriptive than the minimum just described. At the same time, if the facts were known, a surprisingly large number of retail firms attempt to carry on credit activities without any specifically defined policy or with an entirely inadequate policy.

A successful credit policy should strike a definite note for positive thinking, positive creativeness, and positive action. Often the words that are used in carrying out a credit policy can be of great importance in arriving at the desired objectives. Such statements as "dunning," "delinquency," "rejected," "turned down," "problems," and so on have been contributing factors in many instances to negative thinking on the part of credit management. Positive wording can be an influential factor in positive thinking and positive action.

Basic Functions of the Retail Credit Manager

Regardless of the type of retail store involved and the type of organization under which the retail credit department of the store operates, there are certain basic functions that must be performed by the retail credit manager in his efforts to have his department accomplish its duties. These basic functions usually are considered to include the following:

1. Maximizing sales and profits
2. Minimizing bad-debt losses.

3. Efficient utilizing of invested funds.
4. Cooperating with other internal and external departments.

Maximizing Sales and Profits.[8] It should be remembered that credit should be introduced and continued in use in a retail store only as long as it increases the volume of sales and, in turn, profits. Credit is a means to an end, in that a store does not (or should not) accept credit in its operations unless such a policy is to the store's advantage. Of course, if asked, some retailers would reply that they are using credit simply because competition is forcing them to do so. However this is the same thing as saying that unless credit was used, sales and profits in their stores undoubtedly would decline.

Minimizing Bad-Debt Losses.[9] The credit manager not only is faced with the task of using credit as a tool to sell more goods and to make more profit, but he also is simultaneously forced to watch the trend of bad-debt losses that occur. In no way is this to imply that an exceedingly low bad-debt loss automatically is a sign of high sales and profits and of efficient credit management. In fact, it is possible that an exceedingly low bad-debt loss may signify that the store is accepting only the best credit risks and in a sense is operating simply on a "deferred" cash basis. Thus the retail credit manager constantly walks a tightrope. He must determine how much risk he will accept in order to expand his sales and profits to a maximum and at the same time hold a tight rein over his bad-debt losses. This determination will (or should) vary depending upon the type of credit being accepted.

Efficient Utilizing of Invested Funds. Once credit is accepted by a retail store, it automatically becomes an account receivable on the books of the retailer until the account is paid by the customer. In case of nonpayment, it may be changed to a note receivable or charged off as a bad-debt loss. Of course, some accounts may be sold to some financial institution.

The retail store, having invested its funds in its inventory (assuming that the store pays its own bills quickly in order to take advantage of any cash discount) thus finds that these funds are tied up in the accounts receivable representing the goods that have been bought on credit and that still are owed for by the customers. Thus, the retail credit manager has the responsibility of handling and accounting for these invested funds—a responsibility that is just as vital and important as that of a retail buyer in deciding what

8 / Allyn M. Schiffer, "A Management Viewpoint of Credit Extension," *Credit World*, August 1970, p. 12.

9 / Some credit managers may feel that this is only part of the story—that the real attempt should be to minimize all credit expenses, which include bad-debt losses. Such an approach is realistic but it raises the question of what are strictly credit expenses and what are general office operational expenses.

inventory to invest in or that of a financial executive of the firm in deciding upon what kind of securities to buy in order to secure a return on any surplus funds.

Cooperating with Other Internal and External Departments. The day is long past when a credit manager "sits on his credit information" and refuses to share gathered data with the other departments of his retail firm. After all, such credit information can be used to improve the operations of the entire store, as the credit policy being followed should be coordinated and tied in closely with all the other policies adopted by the store management. Thus there is an ever-present need for close cooperation between credit operations and those relating to sales, merchandise returns, financing, accounting, delivery, and so on.

Likewise, the retail credit manager has learned that the sharing of his information with credit managers of other retail firms through the local retail credit bureau or through direct interchange will enable him to make better and more reliable credit decisions than if he works alone in his investigations. Thus directly or indirectly, he more and more is cooperating with his fellow credit people in the mutual exchange of credit data.

Performing These Functions. Performing these functions properly and in an efficient manner will require skilled and competent individuals trained and experienced to keep pace with our increasingly dynamic and complex economy. In an article entitled "Are you the Credit Executive . . . of Tomorrow?" Joseph J. Nugent, former manager of the credit management division of the National Retail Merchants Association, made the following pertinent observations:[10]

However, while we look at this more active role of today's credit manager, we cannot forget that he is still responsible for credit investigation and granting, collections, bill adjusting, maintenance of the accounts receivable, billing and all the other basic areas of credit.

This, in fact, is where the greatest problem for credit originates. The credit manager's prominence and his growth reflect his drive and personality, and not a great deal more. With the rapid growth of credit in the past 20 years, many men have made a full career out of merely meeting its demands. Regrettably, many credit executives perform their duties in a routine, non-creative manner. These individuals are the bookkeepers who looked upon their new field and were unable to recognize it. For several years, these men have been the ones creating the credit manager's image.

Today, however, in order to grow and survive, the credit manager must look to the future. He must recognize and accept the responsibilities of his position and make every effort to project himself into Company Management. He can not

10 / *1967-1968 Credit Management Year Book* (New York: National Retail Merchants Association, 1967), pp. 171-73.

work in a vacuum and console himself with approving new accounts and operating a collection department.

He is going to have to broaden his viewpoint and recognize that in the role of management he must look at the big picture, while at the same time administrating an efficient credit department.

This usually means delegating the detail to assistants and clerks so as to provide time for administrative duties and planning for company profits.

His duties must also extend beyond his immediate surroundings. Now that consumer credit has become the American "way of life," the credit manager is faced with additional challenges and responsibilities of an external nature. He will become involved in the public image of credit, consumer credit counseling, credit legislation, increased competition from banks, finance companies and other industries, as well as many other areas.

The credit men of tomorrow can no longer sit at their desks and concern themselves with happenings only within their own companies. External forces are too great to ignore, and if the men responsible for credit can not handle them, what is to become of the store? When considering that receivables are usually twice or more greater than total company inventory, and that approximately 60% of the sales volume is attributable to credit, it is obvious that the man who can have the greatest effect on the future of a store is the credit man.

It is hoped that much of the additional time needed by the credit man will be brought about by the inventive genius of man. Changes brought about by electronic data processing equipment have opened up new avenues to the credit man, which, in the past, he only dared dream of. And with constant changes and improvements being made in EDP equipment, future programs seem limitless.

Today, many credit men look upon EDP as relieving them of an 8 hour work day and introducing them to a 24 hour work day. This, however, as in any major advancement, must happen in its initial stages. Technological knowledge does not come easily. To develop proper programs to meet today's and tomorrow's challenges, the credit man must accept a new way of life and devote many hours to the mastery of it. A way of life once mastered will prove its value quickly.

Organization of Retail Credit Departments[11]

The particular organization in any store is a product of many factors. Obviously what is suitable for the large store is impractical for the small store. The influence of ownership and personalities also can be responsible for varying types of organizational arrangements.

In the single-proprietorship store, the owner or manager is the jack-of-all-trades. In addition to his other multifold duties, he has supervision of credits and may be assisted by one of his personnel in collecting slow accounts.

In the small department store, the credit activities may become a staff function under the authority of the treasurer-controller.

11 / Adapted from D. J. Duncan and C. F. Phillips, *Retailing, Principles and Methods* (7th ed.; Homewood, Ill.: Richard D. Irwin, Inc., 1967), pp. 179-214.

As the department store becomes larger and more departmentalized, credit activities tend to become the responsibility of the controller, who is the head of one of the four or five major divisions. Often it is he who, in cooperation with the credit manager, has the responsibility of coordinating the objectives of the credit operations with the overall objectives of the firm. If a firm desires to adopt a more lenient credit policy in an effort to stimulate sales, it is often the controller who, in cooperation with the credit manager, translates this change of policy into a changed program of decision making on the credit department level. Of course, the actual operating head of the credit section of the controller's division is the credit manager. The activities of this section may be divided into interviewing, promoting, authorizing, and collecting. The interviewing personnel will gather data about applicants for credit and help determine whether or not credit will be accepted. The authorization people have the responsibility for certain phases of identification and authorization. The promotion of credit may be assigned to one or more people, whereas the collection responsibility is to keep slow accounts on a paying basis or to stop the acceptance of credit from bad risks.

In the typical chain store organization, the controller has responsibilities similar to those of the department store controller. A major one of these responsibilities is credit. However, handling credit today has become such an important function that the top credit manager of a chain organization frequently has a staff of workers (not counting the credit staff in each store) as large as the entire personnel of the controller's division of a few years ago.

Organizations of Retail Credit Managers

It was in 1912 that retail credit managers recognized the need for closer cooperation between themselves and with the organizations that furnished them consumer credit data. As a result, the Retail Credit Men's National Association was formed. In 1927 the name of this trade association for retail credit granters was changed to the National Retail Credit Association. Today this association is known as the International Consumer Credit Association. Through its local, state, and district merchant associations, this association conducts a continuing program of education and service for the personnel of the credit departments of retail firms.

In an effort to raise professional standards and improve the practices of consumer credit executives and their personnel, the International Consumer Credit Association, under the direction of

Executive Vice President William H. Blake, decided to coordinate the many educational efforts of the association into one professional advancement program and in 1958 authorized the formation of the Society of Certified Consumer Credit Executives. The purpose of the society has been stated as follows:[12]

The Society was established to create a professional organization for management level consumer credit granter executives who have a common interest in improving industry operations and to advance the knowledge of its Fellows through a professional journal, formal academic training, research, technical publications, seminars and forums for the exchange of educational information.

To achieve this purpose, the Society will:

A. Provide and promote educational projects consistent with the Society's and the public's good.
B. Develop, expand and improve the professional skills of its Fellows through the exchange of information and experience gained in practice.
C. Maintain an active clearinghouse for the collection and distribution of consumer credit education information.
D. Encourage high standards of ethics and professional conduct among its Fellows.
E. Broaden the knowledge and understanding of consumer credit among its Fellows and others.
F. Make its Fellows available as consultants to government agencies, elected officials and others to assist in the development of consumer credit programs and projects which are fair and equitable to the business community and to the consumer.
G. Publish a professional journal, to be known as the *Journal of Consumer Credit Management,* as the Society's official publication and such other materials as are appropriate to the objectives and purposes herein set forth.
H. Conduct research directly related to policies and procedures in the field of consumer credit independent of, in cooperation with or for other associations, foundations or business organizations.
I. Conduct formal and informal educational programs concerning consumer credit and related activities.
J. Conduct all such other activities as are consistent with the advancement of the purpose and objectives of the Society.

The professional certification program of the Society of Certified Consumer Credit Executives has three phases: first, a Credit Counselor Program designed to meet the needs of the student who desires to enter the credit field, the employee with minimum credit experience who wants to enter credit work, and the credit employee who is preparing for advancement; second, an Associate Credit

12 / *Professional Advancement Program for Consumer Credit Executives and Credit Personnel* (St. Louis: Society of Certified Consumer Credit Executives, n.d.), pp. 2-3.

Executive Program that is designed for the supervisory credit employee; and third, the Certified Consumer Credit Executive phase which deals primarily with the management function of consumer credit department operations. The established requirements permit evaluation of the candidate's comprehension of the basic principles of consumer credit and of his ability to apply these principles. Successful experience, properly substantiated, is weighed most heavily in candidate selection, followed by education and by leadership in community activities and in activities of the International Consumer Credit Association. A minimum of five years of consumer credit management experience is a "must," however, for completion of the third phase of the certification program.

Another organization made up of retail credit personnel is the Credit Women—International. Started in 1934, this active group has grown to a membership of approximately 14,000 women engaged in credit activity in the United States and Canada. Edith Shaw, who was the founder of this association, believed that such clubs would be forums for mutually helpful discussion topics, classrooms for a study and review of changing retail credit techniques, and sororities for social contacts and acquaintances. Such a belief has been borne out by the fact that these clubs have been successful in developing close contact among credit women, in establishing better relations between credit managers and local credit bureaus, and in stimulating an increasing interest in the continuing education of credit personnel.

A third organization of retail credit personnel is the National Retail Merchants Association's Credit Management Division. This association numbers approximately 16,000 department, specialty, dry goods, and apparel stores among its members. Since 1934, when it was established, the Credit Management Division of this association has furnished a special research service to the credit managers of member stores. Through meetings, surveys, and publications (such as the yearly *Credit Management Yearbook*) this division constantly works to keep its members up-to-date on new developments and changing techniques in the retail credit field.

SERVICE CREDIT MANAGEMENT

There really is little basic difference between retail stores and service concerns in the management of credit activities. Usually the size of the service establishment is small, the type of ownership is the independent proprietorship, and the owner is the credit executive, the credit analyzer, and the collector all wrapped up in one person. Generally the credit accepted in the service type of operation is for a relatively short period of time. However, there are numerous instances of installment and revolving credit plans being used by firms and individuals accepting service credit from their customers.

CREDIT MANAGEMENT IN FINANCIAL INSTITUTIONS

Using commercial banks as an example of a cash-lending institution, it should be recognized that in such a bank, whether it be large or small, some one officer is responsible for the installment credit operation. He may be a vice president of a large commercial bank with $100 million or more of loans, or he may be one of the staff of a small bank, who handles only a few such loans along with his many other duties. Whichever is the case, the individual carrying the responsibility is "the management" with respect to that particular bank's installment credit operations.

If there is a separate installment loan department, its activities usually are broken down into three broad categories: acquisition, which includes the duties involved in actually originating the loans; servicing, which includes the disbursement of all loan proceeds and placing the loans on the bank's books, as well as making up the various loan records; and collections, which generally embrace all procedures concerning the follow-up, adjustment, and other related activities involved with troublesome and delinquent accounts. In connection with the activity of collections, the policy established generally will depend on the credit policy followed, the size of the bank, the scope of its installment-lending operation, the size of the community, the competition faced, and the area to be serviced. In addition, the installment credit management must have specific methods for reviewing and checking operations at regular and frequent intervals in order to provide adequate controls on operations.

Likewise, if the commercial bank operates a bank credit card plan, another officer is usually in charge of this operation and is responsible for its management, which includes solicitation of retail and service concerns to become members of the plan, encouragement of consumers to use their bank credit cards at these participating firms, and all the internal operations of approving customers' purchases, billing, collections, legal conformity, and customer satisfaction and goodwill.

Decisions must continually be made as to how bank funds may be used to meet the needs of consumers and businesses and make the most satisfactory return for the bank. Thus division of funds between commercial loans, regular consumer installment loans, bank credit card operations, and long-term home mortgage loans requires constant consideration by executive management personnel. Changes in the banking industry have been widespread in the past decade and more changes are inevitable. The following quotation is helpful in understanding the position bank management is in today: [13]

> Change is inevitable; what does this mean for banking? It means that the needs of the customer are changing rapidly, and that the future of the industry depends on how successfully these needs are met as it faces new competition. The banks have technical financial sophistication; this skill must be transferred to the area of management sciences. There are external obstacles: the regulatory jungle and the bank profit squeeze. There are internal obstacles: the general management gap, an information crisis, an antimarketing paradox, and an organizational dilemma. The author recommends adoption of a marketing concept, truly scientific management, and extensive research—followed by action. The time to move is now, and the future will belong to the banks that seize their opportunities.

Organizations of Financial Institutions

Most of the associations described in this section devote a considerable portion of their efforts to raising the educational background of credit management personnel so that the managers of credit transactions will continue to improve and to recognize and adopt new developments and techniques.

The American Bankers Association (organized in 1875) is a national organization which represents more than 98 percent of the banks in the country and over 99 percent of the nation's banking resources. The ABA operates two important educational activities for bank personnel—the American Institute of Banking (AIB) and the Stonier Graduate School of Banking at Rutgers University. The AIB provides educational services to bank personnel through courses offered by local chapters and study groups in more than 500 communities and through correspondence work. The Stonier Graduate School of Banking has as its educational objective a broad but comprehensive training for bank managerial personnel on the officer level. Graduate schools of banking at other universities, such as the University of Wisconsin and Louisiana State University, offer similar training programs for bank management personnel. In 1940 the American Bankers Association adopted a formal program in consumer credit, and in 1952 this activity became known as the Instalment Credit Committee, which now directs its attention to the many consumer credit transactions of banks.

Other financial associations include the National Consumer

---

13 / David C. Casey, "Bank Management: Problems and Possibilities," *Business Horizons,* June 1970, p. 45. Also see Elliott L. Atamian, "Strategies for Success in the Seventies for Small Commercial Banks," *MSU Business Topics,* Winter 1970, p. 49; and Gordon L. Wadmond, "The Finance Manager of Tomorrow," *Industrial Banker,* November 1968, p. 8.

Finance Association (NCFA), The Consumer Bankers Association (CBA), and the World Council of Credit Unions, Inc. (formerly CUNA International). Some have established schools for the personnel of their member firms, such as the National Institute on Consumer Finance held at Marquette University and sponsored by the National Consumer Finance Association and the School of Consumer Banking run by the Consumer Bankers Association. In total, all of these organizations have worked hard and long to raise the standards of credit management among their members.

REVIEW AND DISCUSSION QUESTIONS

1. What is meant by the term "credit management"?
2. Distinguish between retail credit management, service credit management, and credit management in money-lending institutions.
3. What are the basic functions of the retail credit manager? Describe each function clearly.
4. Explain the term "efficient utilizing of invested funds."
5. How can the retail credit manager cooperate with other internal and external departments?
6. Describe the organization of the credit department of a typical large independent department store.
7. What is the International Consumer Credit Association? Trace its history and its activities.
8. If you were working in the field of consumer credit, why should you be interested in knowing about the Society of Certified Consumer Credit Executives?
9. What are the purposes of the Credit Women—International organization?
10. Explain the activities of the Credit Management Division of National Retail Merchants Association (NRMA).
11. Check with your local bankers and discover the courses being offered by the AIB in your community.

11

Planning the Credit
Investigation

A credit investigation is undertaken to aid in making a sound credit decision; this purpose should be kept in mind constantly when a credit investigation is undertaken. It is not an activity to satisfy curiosity; it has a much more immediate and practical purpose, the guidance of a sound credit decision. The investigation does not seek information for the sake of information; it seeks information pertinent to the specific credit decision and sufficient to assure that the decision will fall within the probability range for payment set by the operating policies. The credit analyst must thus ask himself what he must know in order to make a proper credit decision. The information pertinent to that decision then becomes the guide to the type of information sought. The extent of the investigation should similarly be governed by the degree of certainty necessary for a proper decision.

At all times the credit executive also must weigh the value of additional information about a credit prospect against the cost of obtaining such information. He thus is faced on the one hand with needing sufficient factual information from which to make valid decisions and on the other hand with paying the cost of acquiring these facts. The credit man must carefully decide when enough information is actually enough from the point of view of completeness, accuracy, and cost.

FACTS OR OPINIONS

It is important for the credit investigator to keep in mind the thought that references, informants, and credit-reporting agencies do not create credit information. Credit information is created only by the subject of the credit inquiry, who constantly is creating

218

information about himself through his conduct and activities. Such information becomes credit information when it can be used to predict future behavior of a credit applicant; it is important credit information when, if known, it would influence a credit decision.

Some information may be of that objective and verifiable type known as fact; much is likely to be of that somewhat subjective type known as opinion. Opinions may rest on facts or prejudice or imagination. The opinion may be soundly based on objective facts and be the result of careful and logical analysis of the situation; it indeed may be as sound as or sounder than the opinion the analyst would form after his own analysis, but it is still the opinion of someone else.

The operating credit manager who substitutes the opinions of others for his own judgment has thereby abrogated his position. He has permitted these outside persons whose opinions he accepts to become the credit manager for the department and has himself become merely a credit clerk. Opinion should be given consideration in one respect only, that is, when the opinion of others is itself treated as a fact and so used in the analysis. In effect this happens with that classification of information called "reputation." Reputation is in large part the opinion of others and in fact does have some bearing on the credit analysis. It must be recognized that such opinions, whether soundly based or not, do affect the quality of the credit performance which may be expected and so have a place in the analysis. But these opinions should be regarded as simply a category of facts and in the analysis should be weighed as any other factual category.

When making a credit investigation, the credit executive should do so in a manner designed to collect facts rather than opinions. The phrasing of questions should be such that informants are induced to reply factually rather than with loosely stated opinions or judgments. Specific questions should be selected which draw from each group of informants replies that supply those facts the informant may be expected to know. Asking informants questions about things they are not likely to know is an invitation to reply with opinion rather than fact and is also a temptation not to reply at all.

PREDICTION OR HISTORY

The credit investigation brings together historical information which through analysis is used as a basis for a prediction of future behavior. The prediction desired is a prediction of credit behavior—that is, a prediction of the type and amount of credit obligations that can be expected to be paid and an estimate of the maximum amount of credit which should be accepted from the individual customer. Thus, historical information should be sought which has pertinence to this purpose. The credit analyst by implication necessarily subscribes to the belief that the past can be used to predict the future. The investigation becomes justifiable only because of adherence to this belief.

Not all history is appropriate to this purpose, however. As pointed out, the credit analyst is concerned with what may be called the credit history or credit record. Put in another way, he is interested in historical records which have a bearing on future credit behavior. He is interested in both the past and the present, but he may not be interested in the more remote past nor is he usually concerned with a complete historical review. His interest might be called current, and the things in which he is interested are definitely limited in scope to those items which can be analyzed in terms of prediction of current credit behavior.

WHAT TO INVESTIGATE

When the question of what to investigate is raised, it is easy to repeat the "four horsemen" of credit—character, capacity, capital, and conditions. These so-called four C's of credit have echoed down the ages and through the textbooks, articles, and speeches on credit with a remarkable persistency. However, present-day credit executives are becoming more and more skeptical as to the validity of these famous four C's of credit as direct guides to either the investigation process or the analytical work of the credit department. One reason is that these C's do not form a mutually exclusive classification scheme—it is not possible to separate the facts which bear on character from those bearing on capacity, and those bearing on capacity from those bearing on capital. In fact, then, it is not possible to take the facts gathered during the course of an investigation and sort them into the categories suggested by the general terms of character, capacity, and capital. The same data have to appear several places and be used several times. Another reason is that seldom can these characteristics be best revealed by direct inquiry. If an informant is asked the question,"What is the subject's character?" he is at a loss as to how to respond; similarly with capacity, or even with capital, although the latter is the most tangible and unified of the three.

But what is character? It may be defined as an intangible sum of personal attributes, and these attributes are revealed indirectly rather than directly. What we frequently accept as character is rather reputation, and reputation is really the opinion held by others about a person. Even reputation is a diverse thing, reflecting the opinions of others about behavior in those situations which they have had an opportunity to observe. The elements entering into character may be personal, and thus be concerned with family situation or personal habits and attitudes such as drinking, gambling, and so forth. They may include virtues such as honesty and courage, or the reverse. Character also may be inferred or revealed by business or professional conduct, such as payment of obligations, tendency to make unwarranted claims or to return goods without cause, attitude toward obligations, speculative tendencies, respect for the rights of others. Character being an inward thing, in effect an intangible personal quality, it can be correctly inferred only to the extent that it is revealed. In some respects a reputation for good character may be the result of never having been pressed by adversity.

General questions invite general answers. And one of the most general questions it is possible to phrase is, "What is his character?" Much better credit information will be obtained by seeking the answer to specific questions which, when properly interpreted, can be used to predict personal behavior. These questions may seek to develop facts about past behavior which have credit significance, facts about the current situation which have predictive value, and current information about the opinions of others (that is, a survey of the opinions of those in a position to form an opinion).

"How has he paid his bill with you?" is a better question than "What is his credit reputation?" and it becomes an even better question when the facts are sought even more specifically by asking the year the account was opened, the balance now owing, the highest recent credit, and whether payment is in 30, 60, or 90 days or longer. Attitude toward obligations is better revealed by a question asking whether the person makes unjustified claims or acts in accordance with the contract than by general questions about attitude toward obligations. Family status is revealed in a more meaningful manner by specifics about marriage, number of children, place and length of residence, home ownership, major assets owned by the family, life insurance carried, major savings, and investments than by vague questions concerning personal and family status.

It appears, then, that character is an inward thing which probably cannot be measured or appraised exactly by even those most intimately associated with an individual, certainly not by the measures available during a credit investigation. Nevertheless, the credit investigation can come closer to interpreting this quality correctly when it asks for specifics which can be ascertained and gives each of these specifics its proper weight in the analysis. Although they can be summarized under the heading of character, they are investigated by inquiries about specific and rather tangible elements. Evidence which is largely factual can be gathered about the specifics. Seeking evidence about the general obtains only opinions, often vaguely stated and based on evidence which may be so unsound that were the evidence known, the credit analyst himself might arrive at an opposite conclusion.

Another source of difficulty which arises upon investigating a rather vague characteristic such as character is the tendency of the informant to reply in terms of his own standards and the analyst to interpret in terms of his—and they may well be different. One respondent may interpret good character as associated with church membership and reply in a somewhat derogatory tone when the subject is not an active church member. Another informant may be a foe of alcohol and honestly feel that even temperate social drinking is a mark of poor character. Certainly communication is neither complete nor exact when vague or general questions encourage answers which are value judgments resting on highly variable standards.

Likewise, capacity is a credit quality which rests on a widely diverse group of specific conditions. In a narrow sense, it may mean simply the ability to pay a specific dollar obligation when it is due; but in a much wider sense, it is a measure of the sources of the ability to pay. Such information bearing on an individual's credit capacity is often summarized under the headings of income and of employment While capacity is essentially a question of an individual's earning power, it must be recognized that income by itself should not be the sole determinant of an individual's ability to secure acceptance of his credit. It is generally understood that the average consumer makes his expenditures and meets his contractual payments out of current income rather than from accumulated savings. As a result, unless a fairly complete picture is available of previous commitments, the institution may find that it is dealing with an individual whose income is definitely earmarked for debts previously incurred—and this may be true regardless of the volume of income involved. Thus the relative adequacy of income should be tested by comparing it with the individual's current contractual obligations as well as with his present expenditure pattern.

These comments are in no way designed to deemphasize the fact that the most important evidence of capacity is income, but they are designed to emphasize the fact that credit analysts cannot neglect other evidence that may tend to give an entirely different slant to the value of the income figure than the simple dollar amount.

In the field of consumer credit, it is generally agreed that the credit analyst gives more weight to those specific qualities that reveal the character and capacity of an individual than he does to those specific qualities reflecting the capital of the credit applicant. To the credit manager, capital means the financial strength of the risk that would be available in case of the inability (because of decreased capacity) or mere unwillingness (because of certain traits of character) of the individual to pay his obligations when due. Not only is the quantity of the capital important, but the credit manager also is interested in the nature of the assets in which the capital is invested and the proportion invested in each. While it is true that many consumers have relatively little capital to be used as a backstop, nevertheless information about the capital they do possess (such as home ownership, household furnishing and personal effects, bank accounts, stocks and bonds, real estate holdings, and so forth) may help add to the information already available to the credit manager and give him a better insight into the true character and capacity of the individuals concerned.

CREDIT QUALITIES TO INVESTIGATE

The preceding discussion has illustrated the basic issue raised earlier, that character and capacity and capital are not clearly defined classifications of elements of the credit investigation and that specific bits of information must be sought to have the raw material for proper analysis of each of these. Thus it seems desirable to list the personal credit qualities which appear to be the most essential to investigate. It is not claimed that the credit qualities listed here are all-inclusive of those which might be desirable to investigate. It is not even claimed that they are all of the most important credit qualities, but it is believed that these are the credit qualities which in the great majority of cases are most pertinent to the credit decision. If the investigation reveals information about these qualities, there should be sufficient information at hand to enable the analyst to reach a sound credit decision. And as will be seen later, a method of analysis of the individual's credit is suggested which rests on these very same credit qualities.

Obviously, in certain cases some information will be more important than in others. One should never forget that credit judgments are individual judgments. Although the credit analyst works toward averages and trusts to averages to test his work, there is no such thing as an average credit prospect. A credit prospect—the subject of each investigation—is an individual.[1] The weight given to various credit qualities must necessarily conform to the circum-

---

1 / However in most large firms there is a need to process a tremendous volume of credit requests. In such situations, an attempt is often made at least to categorize credit applicants, however individualistic they may be, simply to handle the tremendous volume of credit transactions. This topic will be discussed in more detail (see Chapter 15) in connection with the numerical pointing plans involved in decision making.

stances of the individual case, so the importance of certain qualities rises and falls in the particular case. The need for and importance of these credit qualities also vary with the circumstances surrounding the credit offered by the consumer—whether it is to initiate the establishment of credit for the first time or to secure added credit on an already existent account.

Payment Record

Many creditors regard the payment record as the most important factor revealed by the investigation. It not only shows the manner of payment and thus is important as a predictor of behavior, but it shows the past payment habits as well. Often creditors feel that the best basis of a forecast of credit experience is the past payment record. While there is no question that such information is important, it should be recognized that in certain instances the payment record may not have the prime importance sometimes attributed to it. In connection with the information sought relative to payment record, the investigation should seek facts as to the type or types of account involved, the amount currently owed, the amount past due, the highest recent credit, and the manner of payment. Manner of payment should be stated specifically—pays in 30 to 60 days, pays in 90 days, and so forth.[2] The adjectives prompt, good, slow can have a variety of meanings; 60 to 90 days may be considered prompt by one firm, slow by another, depending of course on the type of account involved.

The date of the experience also should be established. This is especially important when information is sought about an individual with a varied record which contains some derogatory data. It is important to know whether the profit and loss charge-off, or the collection through judgment, or the paid only after call by collector, or the repossession is in the past or the most recent experience. Certainly a very different conclusion may be drawn from a bad record of some time ago and a good current record than from the opposite sequence.

Income

Since most consumer debts are to be paid from income, investigation of the income of an individual is essential. The amount of it should be ascertained, its regularity of receipt established, and the probability of its continuance estimated. Since income must be evaluated relative to the demands placed upon it, information should

2 / See Chapter 13 for a discussion of the efforts of the Associated Credit Bureaus, Inc. to standardize the reporting of payment experience.

be sought about the demands upon the income brought about by family needs and existing obligations. This seems to be a formidable body of information about the income quality. Actually the discussion has illustrated the nature of the information and the analysis which will be made of it. In the course of the investigation, the specific facts sought should be simply the amount and source of the income.

Employment

Employment is probably the principal source of income, so it should be investigated along with income. Information about employment should seek as a minimum the name of the employer, the type of business, and the position occupied by the subject of inquiry. Additionally an effort should be sought to determine how long he has been employed by his current employer. When employment has been for a comparatively short period of time, less than five years being considered short, it may be advisable to investigate previous employment and to continue the investigation of previous employment until the record has been established for at least a five-year period. In the case of credit prospects who are self-employed, the investigation should be especially extensive, since the employment information also must necessarily be the source of information relative to income.

Residence

Check of residence through the investigation is first of all a routine verification of identity. In addition, the information about residence should show the length of time at that location and if less than five years in duration should reveal the previous residence. These facts can be used as the basis for more intensive investigation in the locality should such be necessary. They also may reveal certain information about the other credit qualities of the credit applicant himself. In addition, the investigation of residence should determine the status of the credit applicant as owner or tenant of the property. If ownership is involved, the investigation should be extended to reveal the amount of the mortgage, if any, and the payment thereon. The amount of the rent and manner of payment should be determined if the property in question is being rented.

Marital Status

The marital status of the individual is a significant quality in most consumer credit transactions, and as a result it should be included as a fact sought through the investigation. In most cases the information is simply married or single. In some cases information may be sought as to whether the person is a widow, widower, or divorcee, as this status often affects the income and obligations against that income as well as the person's attitude toward credit obligations. In certain investigations not only is the marital status significant, but the happiness or unhappiness associated with this status is important to consider. Many difficulties with consumer collections stem from family difficulties, and the investigation may need to be extended to include information relative to the stability of the family situation. A creditor involved in a family which is on the verge of breaking up is almost certain to have collection difficulties. To the extent that such a situation appears imminent, future difficulties can be forecast and perhaps avoided.

Age

With the youthful, the investigation should establish that legal capacity to contract is present. With most investigations, age is not an important credit quality. However, the extremes of youth or age can be of crucial importance, and in these instances this quality becomes the proper subject for intensive investigation. For example, some lenders make it a point not to lend to individuals under 25 years of age[3] nor to individuals over 65 (with certain exceptions in both cases). On the other hand, some retail firms have promoted credit to teen-agers, as long as a parent or some adult guarantees payment.

References and Reputation

The investigation also may seek to develop information about the reputation of the credit applicant and to secure information adequate for evaluating the credit data reported by references. In effect, references and reputation plus payment record are an investigation of character. As previously pointed out, when discussing character, in most instances the credit analyst does not actually appraise the character, which is a complex medley of personal traits and qualities. What he does appraise is the reflection of character as revealed by reputation and references. Thus the importance of these qualities is such that information is needed to make a credit appraisal of them. So the investigation may be extended to develop such information.

3 / Irvin Penner, "The College Credit Market," *Stores,* September 1970, p. 14; C. L. Fagan and T.D. Gover, "Are College Students Good Credit Risks?" *Credit World,* September 1967, p. 20.

Reserve Assets

In only a few instances are reserve assets to be relied upon for payment of a consumer credit obligation. In most cases they are additional surety which both debtor and creditor hope will not be needed. In some cases, especially with aged customers who are living on a pension or income from investments, the investigation of reserve assets may be essential in order to establish capacity to handle the credit obligation. A word of caution is necessary, however, when considering property ownership, to avoid attributing a positive effect to something which, when carefully analyzed, should be given negative weight. Often the ownership of a home may be accompanied by such heavy payments on the mortgage that, instead of being an addition to reserve assets, it is an earmarking of current income to such an extent as to preclude the assumption of any additional commitments. Such a situation should be revealed in sufficient detail to assure that the proper inference is drawn from it relative to the credit decision and that the obligation of meeting a recurring payment is not overlooked.

Equity in Purchase

An additional credit quality, equity in the purchase, is of major concern, especially under the installment method of consumer purchasing. Strictly speaking, this is not an attribute of the individual himself but of the market value of the property. The presence of this market value, as it is available to the creditor through the terms of the lien contract, may raise an otherwise unacceptable credit risk well above the level of acceptability. When the equity is large and is maintained by the amount and frequency of payment, the major question may not be, "Will he pay?" but instead, "Can the property always be found and retaken?" To the extent that the equity is smaller and is not maintained by the amount and frequency of payments, the personal credit qualities should be analyzed more carefully and should be correspondingly stronger to attain equal safety. In addition, the proportion of the initial equity may reflect the attitude of the buyer toward the obligation. When the initial equity or ownership is large, through a significant down payment, it will appear that the buyer fully intends to complete the contract as agreed and by inference this is indicative of character. Conversely, when the initial equity is small, it may reflect an attitude of possession through rental rather than a sense of ownership—by inference, a potential adverse indication of character.

Collateral

While collateral, an element of capital, is lacking in most retail and service credit transactions, it does often appear in those instances in which cash loans are made to the consumer. Thus collateral, in the form of some tangible asset owned by the individual and offered as additional security to the loaning institution, is another credit quality to take into consideration. It is thus another factor to consider when an overall appraisal is made of the individual who is offering the collateral as a way of making himself less of a credit risk.

INFLUENCE OF ECONOMIC CONDITIONS

While it is generally agreed today that a fairly reliable picture can be obtained about an individual's character, capacity, and capital through a series of specific questions, the credit analyst must always be faced with the problem of interpreting this information in terms of the economic environment or conditions in which both his business concern and the credit applicant exist.

Knowledge of the economic environment is not secured by a series of general or specific questions but rather must be part of the general knowledge and makeup of the credit analyst himself. Some of this knowledge is secured by keeping abreast of what is happening in the line of business and the community of which the credit manager is a part. Are there strikes in effect in certain industrial plants, or are such labor curtailments imminent? Is the weather too dry or too wet and is the farmer going to be hurt as a consequence? Are some businesses expanding rapidly in the area and thus furnishing new openings to new residents of the community? In other words, he must know "How's business?" in his own line, other lines, his own town, and surrounding towns. Of course, he will know that some activities are expanding and some contracting—some people are benefiting and some are getting hurt.

Perhaps a knowledge of this short-run economic climate is easier to acquire than the ability to predict the long-run economic picture. The background, experience, and training of the credit man will be vital factors in how he looks at the future. His political beliefs, his international views, his own financial position, and his own experiences in attaining his present position will, of course, color his views as to the future.

Consistent with his short-run and long-run views of economic conditions, the credit man must interpret the information that he has obtained about the credit applicant and make the decision to accept or to reject the credit.

INVESTIGATION AND VERIFICATION

The investigation is a way to develop information not at hand. It is also a method to verify the information supplied. Most credit verifications are initiated because credit has been offered by an individual and the individual has supplied some credit information about himself. Good credit management should conclude that if any investigation is deemed necessary it should have as a portion of its task verifying some of the information supplied by the applicant. Thus the credit executive may find it desirable to confirm some of the most vital and important facts that the credit applicant has supplied by seeking information concerning them from several separate and independent sources. To some degree, the extent of this verification may depend upon the judgment of the credit executive as to the overall quality of the credit applicant as well as upon the manner in which the information supplied coincides with that already known or easily secured.

HOW MUCH TO INVESTIGATE

It has been emphasized that a credit investigation is undertaken to aid in making a sound credit decision. Now the problem must be faced as to just how much investigation is needed to make this sound credit decision, because every bit of information secured through investigation costs money. And it has been pointed out earlier that the credit executive always walks a tightrope in deciding when enough information is actually enough, from the point of view of completeness, accuracy, and cost.

Errors of judgment can arise from not having sufficient information. Inadequate information means that some pertinent fact was not known which, if known, would have caused a different decision. Thus the decision is different than it would have been had the investigation revealed all pertinent information. Even more probable as a cause of error is not giving sufficient weight or the correct interpretation to certain information. The investigation in such cases was adequate, pertinent information was at hand, but the analyst either did not give sufficient weight to certain information or, even worse, interpreted the information incorrectly.

Very extensive investigation costs money and takes time; meanwhile a decision is delayed, with consequent loss of customer goodwill and friction with the sales department. The accumulation of additional bits of information is costly, whether the information is purchased from sellers of credit information or developed by direct inquiry. Unless the information is used and useful, it is not worth what it costs in either time or money. When the extensive investigation develops a mass of factual data, the very mass of the evidence may actually interfere with the analysis and decision. The sheer extent of the evidence may result in its not being correctly weighed or interpreted. The more pertinent evidence may be buried under the mass of nonpertinent detail.

The time when acceptance of credit is requested is the proper time to seek information from the applicant and to decide upon the extent of the investigation. Should the information supplied by the applicant be unusually complete and the case appear on first analysis to be very sound, the investigation may be quite limited, perhaps to payment experience only or to payment experience and verification of employment and residence. Should the information obtained from the applicant be limited, as it sometimes is with retail charge accounts, the investigation should be much more extensive if information sufficient for analysis is to be obtained. Of course, it is quite possible for an account to be accepted without investigation, or perhaps it would be more accurate to say without verification of the information supplied by the applicant. It should be made clear that in some cases the "no-investigation" policy may be advisable. In fact, money often is wasted when investigation is undertaken to verify the obvious. It is far better to save investigation budgets for extensive use with those cases where there is a probability of trouble than to disperse it over those cases in which there is practically no chance of finding cause for rejection.

It is not possible, nor if possible would it be desirable, to gather all possible evidence before reaching a credit decision. The amount necessary is just that needed to reach a decision. Whenever sufficient information is on hand to reach a decision, that is enough. It is here that the judgment and experience of the credit executive appears, as it is he who must decide what is sufficient for a proper credit decision, knowing that excessive information increases the costs to the firm.

WHERE TO INVESTIGATE

What, then, should the investigation do? It should seek specific information from those sources which possess the information desired or which can get the information desired—most accurately, completely, speedily, and at minimum cost. Since information is the raw material of credit decisions, the credit man must keep before himself constantly the thought that he must *give* as well as *get* credit information. The best basis for a full flow of clear credit information is an exchange of information.

The sources available to the credit manager to secure accurate, complete, speedy, and reasonable information are the basis of the next three chapters. In these we will look at the information supplied by the credit applicant himself, data from direct investigation, facts from in-file ledgers, and information from local retail credit bureaus, the Retail Credit Company, banks, Dun & Bradstreet, Inc., specialized credit bureaus, and other miscellaneous sources.

REVIEW AND DISCUSSION QUESTIONS

1. What is meant by the statement, "Credit information is created only by the subject of the credit inquiry?"
2. What is the basic purpose of a credit investigation?
3. Distinguish between information that is subjective and that which is objective.
4. Explain the statement, "The credit investigation brings together historical information which through analysis is used as a basis for a prediction of future behavior."
5. What are the "four horsemen" of credit? Why are they not emphasized in this book as much as they are in other credit texts?
6. How would you explain the term character?
7. When the term conditions is used, does it apply to the conditions surrounding the status of the individual seeking acceptance of his credit or to the general local, national, and international economic conditions? Explain your answer.
8. What credit qualities should a credit executive normally evaluate in his credit determination? Why these qualities?
9. What additional qualities would you recommend be added to the list appearing in the text?
10. Check with several firms (retail, service, and financial) in your community as to the importance they place on each of the credit qualities suggested.
11. Distinguish between collateral and equity in purchase.
12. Why are economic conditions an important factor in a credit executive's determination of credit risk?
13. Why is the question, "How much to investigate?" difficult to answer?
14. What sources are available to the credit manager to secure information on which to base decisions?

12

Basis of the Credit Decision –
Direct Investigation and
Internal Company Data

The credit manager must have information on which to base his decision to accept or reject the application for credit. Certain basic information usually is supplied by the credit applicant through the credit application and the credit interview. Additional data often are gathered by means of the direct inquiry method, to verify certain facts presented by the applicant and to obtain other facts needed in the decision-making process. In-file ledger facts are one of the most important sources of information available to the credit manager. A study of these different informational sources is the subject matter of this chapter.

Perhaps the greatest emphasis in most of the literature on the subject of credit information has been upon the so-called "purchased" information from such organizations as local credit bureaus, specialized credit-reporting agencies, the Retail Credit Company, and other similar credit-reporting sources. But it is necessary, before considering these sources, to recognize that some credit information is obtained internally, within the company itself, and externally through direct interchange of information with other retail, service, and financial concerns that likewise are interested in securing accurate and up-to-date credit data.

The information obtained internally may be for the initial acceptance of credit from a consumer. Undoubtedly, here the credit application and credit interview will come into importance. The extent to which this information is verified or expanded through additional investigation depends upon the judgment of the credit analyst. This information obtained internally also may be used in the determination of whether to accept requests for an increased amount of credit on an already established account. Here the information supplied from the in-file ledgers will come into play, as the credit analyst thus will have readily available one type of evidence, the internal records of his own company, as to how the applicant has paid his bills in the past.

INFORMATION SUPPLIED BY APPLICANTS

Most investigations of consumer credit applicants start with information supplied by the prospect. It is generally agreed that such information should be regarded as a part of the credit investigation. The information thus supplied by the prospect is treated as statements of fact which have not been verified. Certain facts may be accepted as fact without verification; other facts may be verified through further investigation. The first credit determination is to decide whether any facts will be verified. If it is decided to verify certain facts, a second and third determination become necessary: which facts shall be verified through investigation, and what sources shall be used to verify the facts requiring investigation.

The Credit Application

Most credit departments consider some formality desirable before opening a credit account. This formality usually is carried to the point of an application for credit which is signed[1] by the applicant. The extent of the information sought varies considerably, depending upon the policies of the firm, the type of account requested, and the customs of the trade and region (see Figure 12-1 for a type of cash loan application form that has been used by a commercial bank).

The Case for a Formal Application. Those who argue for a rather formal application procedure advance a number of reasons for their view.

Completeness of information can best be obtained by requesting the applicant to fill out a comprehensive application. Certain facts are likely to be known only to the applicant himself and, unless asked for at the time the account is opened, such facts may not be developed through the investigation; in fact they may not even be sought. It is more economical to obtain such leads from the applicant and then simply verify them through further investigation if verification is considered desirable.

1 / The signature becomes a vital factor in those credit transactions (particularly revolving credit) that result in a finance charge being placed on the customer in excess of the state usury law. This point is involved also in those instances in which credit cards were sent unsolicited to customers. Thus, a signature may not be on file, and the legal right to charge a rate in excess of the usury rate is in question.

FIGURE 12-1

DIRECTIONS: Circle the one number on each line that most closely describes you. Write the circled numbers in the appropriate spaces in the code box on the right. Complete form on the right, seal and mail.

A AGE	UNDER 21 **1**	21-25 **2**	26-49 **3**	50-64 **4**	OVER 65 **5**	
B MARITAL STATUS	SINGLE **1**	DIVORCED **2**	SEPARATED **3**	WIDOWED **4**	MARRIED **5**	
C SIZE OF FAMILY (INCLUDING YOURSELF)	FIVE & OVER **1**	FOUR **2**	THREE **3**	TWO **4**	ONE **5**	
D LENGTH OF TIME AT PRESENT ADDRESS	UNDER 1 YR **1**	1-2 YEARS **2**	3-7 YEARS **3**	8-10 YEARS **4**	10 & OVER **5**	
E LIVING FACILITIES	LIVING WITH PARENTS **1**	TRAILER **2**	RENTING **3**	OWN-MORTGAGE **4**	OWN, FREE & CLEAN **5**	
F MONTHLY RENT OR MORTGAGE PAYMENT	0-$75 **1**	$76-$100 **2**	$101-$125 **3**	$126-$200 **4**	OVER $200 **5**	
G LENGTH OF TIME AT PRESENT POSITION	UNDER 1 YR **1**	1-2 YEARS **2**	3-7 YEARS **3**	6-10 YEARS **4**	10 & OVER **5**	
H MONTHLY INCOME (APPLICANT ONLY)	UNDER $300 **1**	$301-$500 **2**	$501-$700 **3**	$701-$900 **4**	OVER $900 **5**	
J OTHER SOURCES OF INCOME	NONE **1**	SPOUSE EMPLOYED **2**	PART-TIME **3**	PENSION **4**	OTHER **5**	
K TOTAL OTHER MONTHLY INSTALMENT PAYMENTS	NONE **1**	$1-$99 **2**	$100-$199 **3**	$200-$299 **4**	OVER $300 **5**	
L PURPOSE OF LOAN	AUTO **1**	PERSONAL **2**	FHA HOME IMPROVEMENT **3**	FURNITURE OR APPLIANCES **4**	OTHER **5**	
M NUMBER OF MONTHLY PAYMENTS DESIRED	12 **1**	18 **2**	24 **3**	30 **4**	36 **5**	

©FIELD PROMOTIONS INC., NEW YORK, N.Y. 1967

SIGN, DETACH, FOLD, MOISTEN, SEAL AND MAIL THIS POSTAGE-FREE MAILER

NB National Bank of Commerce

INSTALMENT LOAN CENTER
12TH & P STREETS
PHONE 477-8911

You can apply for any of these National Bank of Commerce loans quickly and easily. Just use this new high-speed ZIP Loan Application. Confidential because it's in code! Approval good for 90 days.

Auto Loans (L1) For the best deal on new or used car financing, check with your dealer about NBC's fast ZIP LOAN while right on his showroom floor or . . . mail in the ZIP application. You can take up to three years to repay. With a NBC ZIP LOAN you may also use the auto insurance of your choice.

Home Improvement Loans (L3) Enjoy the improvements that make your home more practical for your family . . . more fun to live in. A new kitchen, bathroom, patio or extra bedroom . . . whatever your need, NBC has a plan to suit your budget. Loans up to $3500 . . . with up to 5 years to repay even though ZIP CHART only shows up to 36 months.

Personal Loans (L2) The key to greater comfort and ease of mind. Pay off piled up bills, buy a new color TV, care for your family in an emergency, take advantage of an opportunity, finance a vacation or pay taxes. Repay in instalments tailored to fit your budget.

Furniture-Appliance Loans (L4) A new refrigerator or automatic dishwasher to lighten your kitchen chores . . . a new washer or dryer for your laundry room, new bedroom or living room furniture? No matter what furniture or appliances your family needs, NBC will arrange a loan with convenient repayments while you enjoy the best in modern living.

Your National Bank of Commerce loan can include insurance to safeguard you from worry about payments in the event of illness or disability.

CODE BOX

A
B
C
D
E
F

G $ _____ AMOUNT DESIRED

NAME _____ NAME OF SPOUSE _____

H ADDRESS _____ PHONE _____

EMPLOYER OR BUSINESS _____ PHONE _____

PREVIOUS ADDRESS (if at present address less than 3 years) _____

J NAME AND ADDRESS OF NEAREST RELATIVE (not living with you) _____ RELATION _____

CURRENT OBLIGATIONS (PLEASE LIST ALL)

OWED TO	BALANCE	PYMT. AMT.
K MTG. OR RENT	$	$
L OTHER	$	$
	$	$

M SIGNATURE _____

Courtesy of National Bank of Commerce, Lincoln, Nebr.

Psychological attitudes toward the seriousness of credit obligations are improved when the application is rather formal and complete. When the opening of the account seems a rather minor or routine procedure, the applicant may not be properly impressed with the value of credit nor with the necessity of conforming carefully to the terms established. At the time an account is opened, an unusual opportunity to educate the customer in proper credit behavior exists. First, we are likely to esteem more highly those things which are difficult to get. If we are impressed with the fact that not everyone can receive credit, we are more likely to regard the account as a privilege and not as a right and to cherish it accordingly. Second, the best time to establish sound habits or behavior patterns is when the first of a series of transactions is initiated. Payment in accordance with terms is a habit which should be established early. By making the opening of the account a rather formal process, the first step toward the establishment of good credit habits is taken. Third, the customer is more likely to respect the credit department which operates in a careful and businesslike manner. A casual attitude toward the acceptance of credit is likely to impress the customer as being typical of all operations of the business. It is obvious that to attain the psychological attitude toward credit that has just been described it will be necessary to combine a personal interview between the credit prospect and the credit manager with the completion of the credit application blank.

The Case for an Informal Application. As is to be expected, there are those firms which strongly believe that informality in credit investigation is the more desirable arrangement. They point out that credit is a sales promotional tool just as much as advertising. Advertising is easily viewed and read by customers; thus credit should be made easily obtainable. A brief application form for credit may be made readily accessible to the credit prospect at various convenient points. The prospect simply fills out the short form, mails it to the credit department, and in the majority of such instances never comes into direct contact with any representative of the credit department. In most of the credit accounts established by this technique, the personal interview is not combined with the use of the credit application.

The reasoning often advanced by stores using such a plan or a similar one is that the vast majority of people pay their accounts as they are expected to do. Thus why bother to spend money interviewing such people? To these stores it appears better to conserve these funds to secure proper payment from those people who do not live up to the provisions of the credit arrangement. Of course, such a view presupposes that the credit department will know exactly when and how to go after reluctant payers and that these collection efforts (which cost money) will be successful in securing payment of the indebtedness.

What Information Should Be Requested? Since a considerable range of information might be requested on an application form, it seems best to illustrate the extent of the information to be sought through a discussion of the minimum and the maximum. The bare minimum might be generalized as simply identifying information— merely the name and address of the credit prospect. Since most retail accounts are opened by women, it is necessary in the case of married women for the credit department to get the husband's name. For the sake of accuracy of posting to the account it is desirable to secure the complete given name and at least the middle initial. A retail store handling thousands of accounts often finds itself in a confused situation in this respect; it is quite possible to have a number of Carl Johnsons, or Edward Smiths, and even a considerable number of Mary A. Smiths. A minimum addition to the identifying information is to request the place of employment and the occupation, as well as the length of time the credit applicant has been a resident at the given address or employed by the present employer. Intelligent seeking of credit information will then prompt the question of previous address or previous employment when the current residence or current employment is less than, say, one year. A rule-of-thumb standard often used in retail credit departments is that residence and employment should be known for five previous years. Such information enables the investigation to develop facts or verify information over a sufficient period of time to satisfy doubts as to current behavior. Investigation at earlier places of residence or employment may then be undertaken whenever there is reason to question the consistency of credit behavior. With the widespread movement of population, such caution seems indicated.

Detailed information from the application blank is commonly sought by sales finance companies and cash lenders. Credit institutions of this type may need the additional information because they are entering into credit transactions which are larger in amount and longer in duration than those generally contemplated when a retail account is first opened. These financial institutions may simply be taking advantage of the fact that custom in their line has made it possible to obtain more information without customer resistance. Whether this is opportunistic or simply representative of more careful credit operation, it does remain a fact that more information is commonly sought by the credit analysts in these institutions. Such additional information is likely to extend to questions which seek information as to income received and assets owned. These lenders are likely to ask for statements as to real estate owned, bank deposits and other savings, and insurance carried. They are also likely to seek information as to past credit dealings, by asking for other installment contracts currently open and recently paid and other cash loans currently open and recently paid. They usually ask for a list of references (best asked by the heading, "firms with which you have had recent credit transactions") and also for a list of personal references. A statement as to the name of the customer's bank and the type of account carried also is a natural addition to the list of references.

Some questions may be asked which are precautions against the time when tracing a "skip" becomes necessary. A skip may be defined as a debtor who deliberately disappears and leaves no forwarding address. When a lien has been retained on property purchased on an installment contract or used as collateral for a loan, both the debtor and the property may be sought. In fact when the property under lien is an automobile, it may itself be the means of facilitating the disappearance. Since such a disappearance is deliberate, tracing the debtor becomes similar to a detective act. Certain classes of information supplied when the account is opened can be the leads needed to initiate the search. Such requests as "name and address of nearest relative" are used for this purpose.

Signature and Contract.   It is regarded as good credit practice to have the applicant sign the application. Some credit departments add words above the signature which make the application a rather formal written contract. This clause may be an affidavit that the information is given for the purpose of obtaining credit and that the facts are complete and correct. The clause may also recite the credit terms and be drawn as a contract between creditor and debtor.

The Credit Interview

Obviously the nature of the credit interview should be consistent with the character of the application and the philosophy of the credit department relative to the information to be sought through the application. Opinions differ markedly as to the procedures which are best for conducting the credit interview, especially as to the procedure for completing the application; some prefer to develop the answers to questions through the interview and to record the information on the application form themselves. It would seem, however, that the ability of the credit personnel available for interviewing and the physical facilities available are more important in properly deciding these questions than any principles relative to which procedure is preferable.

Points in favor of having the applicant fill out the form are that fewer skilled credit personnel are necessary and that more customers can be accommodated in the same space. Points in favor of having the credit interviewer complete the form are that a skillful interviewer can secure much more information than can the blank spaces on a form and that the interview can be made a lesson in the rights and wrongs of credit behavior. Even when the procedure calls for the credit interviewer to fill in the application, it is well to provide space on the form for the recording of more information than the minimum asked for and for the interviewer to record this additional information *after* the customer has left. When the customer fills in the application, it is well for the interviewer to look over the form and to provide supplemental information which will assure completion of blanks not filled in or which probes more deeply into questionable areas.

What appears more important is to develop the right attitude toward the credit interview and to accomplish the objectives sought rather than to prescribe a single procedure for completion of the application. The credit interview should be a part of the credit department promotion, in other words promotion of credit sales. It should be regarded as an opportunity for converting a credit prospect into a credit customer. Accordingly the attitude should not be that of an inquisition; rather, it should be that of a business procedure for establishing that the credit offered is equivalent to the goods or services sought. The interview should proceed with the quiet confidence that the prospect has a value to offer which is fully equivalent to the values for which it is to be exchanged. Since the assumption that the vast majority of the credit prospects are honest is reasonably valid, the great majority should not be made to feel uncomfortable by efforts to identify and screen out the very small minority who are not well intentioned.

The credit quarters should be appropriate to the reception of customers. Too often the credit department is located in an area that is difficult for customers to find, is poorly lighted, or is inadequately furnished. Such conditions are not conducive to proper customer reception nor, for that matter, to good work by credit personnel. Since credit interviews are likely to be considered by customers as private affairs, arrangements for privacy should be provided.

Analysis of the Application

It has been suggested that the credit application be considered as a source of credit information which has not been verified. The analysis then should be directed toward the need for verification and the means of verification to be used. Certain information can be verified by confirmation. For example, the address can be confirmed by checking with a telephone directory or a city directory. In some cases the directory also will confirm the occupation of the husband. Date of publication also will give some indication of length of residence. The residence address can give the credit analyst who knows his community some additional information. Certain neighborhoods are known to be upper, middle, or lower income areas. Some addresses can be warning signals indicative of the need for very careful investigation, perhaps because such areas are known to have a heavy concentration of residents of poor morals. On the other hand, other neighborhoods which are known to be beyond the apparent resources and income of the applicant may indicate that he is attempting to live beyond his means. Such inferences will direct the extent of the investigation and the degree of its penetration.

Brevity of residence or brevity of employment may indicate the need for more extensive investigation. Knowledge of the employment policies of certain employers in the community can even help direct the extent of the investigation. Certain employers may have a policy of very careful screening of employees, and employment with such a firm may in itself permit an inference of credit and reliability.

Sometimes an occupation itself may indicate more complete investigation. Occupations which are seasonal in character, which have considerable fluctuations in the level of income, or which have a high turnover of personnel obviously call for more complete investigation than more stable occupations. An interesting, yet rather controversial, bit of retail credit research takes the form of studying occupations[2] and arriving at credit standings related thereto. Recently, some companies have shown an increased interest in this area in their attempts to mechanize some of their decision-making operations. This will be discussed in more detail in Chapter 15.

There are certain characteristics which seem to prevail among the

2 / The study of occupational credit standings dates from 1931, when Professor P. D. Converse, a pioneer in the field of marketing, first made such an analysis. In 1941 he repeated the survey, increasing the size of the sample and the number of occupations studied ("The Occupational Credit Pattern," *Opinion and Comment,* August 12, 1941, pp. 1-9). A repeat of the earlier studies was undertaken in 1951 by Professor Robert S. Hancock and was published in the August 1952 issue of *Current Economic Comment.*

The author made arrangements with the Research Department of the Associated Credit Bureaus, Inc. to study 1,769 copies of actual reports issued by credit bureaus during the months of January, February, March, and June 1966. The reports were coded on the basis of occupations according to the job classifications of the U.S. Bureau of the Census. The reports were further coded on the basis of geographic location of the individual applicant. Four hundred towns were represented in a broadscale geographic coverage. Then the reports were analyzed according to the numerical ratings given on the reports. The results of this study appeared in the June 1967 issue of *ACBofA Management.* The author's final conclusion was that this limited study suggests extreme caution in the use of occupation as an indicator of credit risk.

higher rated occupations, which consist largely of professional and highly skilled workers. Stability of income and better utilization of income are characteristics which are generally apparent among these occupations. These are important factors in the business of accepting credit from these groups. Although there are exceptions among all occupations, the sense of responsibility which an occupational group may have will substantially affect paying habits. This fact may be attributed to the kind and amount of education or training which is necessary to perform these better rated jobs. Some of the training may be of an informal nature and gained over years of experience; on the other hand, many of the better rated occupations represent several years of formal education and personal discipline.

Some occupational groups are made up of transient workers. Such workers have always been regarded as doubtful credit risks because they have little sense of credit responsibility. This is true of those thousands of workers who frequently move from one town to another, such as unskilled factory workers, section hands, common laborers. Until recently, it was a relatively simple matter for a worker to skip his debts and assume another name on arrival in a new community. The network of credit bureaus throughout the nation, strong union affiliations, social security registration, and income tax laws have significantly hampered this practice.

Inasmuch as stability of income is as important as the amount of income in credit risk appraisal, it plays an important role in credit study. Credit selling is most effective when directed toward those individuals who have the financial ability to respond successfully to the series of demands of an installment or revolving credit contract or the recurring amounts due on open account purchases. Selling techniques thus are perhaps best when designed to attract the largest number of people with a reasonably regular income to move the product from the retailers' shelves.

Indicating the Investigation to Make.   The decision of whether to make a further credit investigation and, if so, the extent of the investigation should be a product of the analysis of the application, in the case of an initial request for credit. Of course, a distinction must be made as to whether the decision involves an initial application for credit or the request of an established credit customer for a larger amount of credit than is currently allowed. It has been pointed out previously that the application and interview are the primary sources for determining further action with the initial credit applicants. On the other hand, payment record data from in-file information will play a dominant role in deciding whether to expand the credit base currently being accepted from an individual customer.

What to investigate and what sources of credit information to use should be carefully considered by the credit analyst. Selection must be made between the various sources, and each must be selected on the basis of the type of information desired, the speed and accuracy and completeness of response, and the relative cost of obtaining the information.

INFORMATION SUPPLIED BY DIRECT INQUIRY

Direct inquiry is one of the common methods of obtaining information to verify facts presented on the application or during the interview of an applicant for an initial credit transaction. Likewise, it is commonly used to obtain additional facts needed in the process of deciding whether to accept the credit of an initial applicant or to enlarge the amount of credit being accepted from an established customer. For this reason, this section is devoted to a discussion of obtaining credit information by direct inquiry from sources other than the applicant himself. A careful distinction is made between obtaining credit information directly from the sources having such facts and between buying somewhat similar credit data in the form of prepared reports from credit reporting bureaus and agencies. The latter organizations are discussed in detail in Chapters 13 and 14.

Whereas investigation may be by direct inquiry or by purchase of reports from professional sources of credit information, it should be noted that the term "free" should not be used to distinguish between purchased and direct. Neither is free. Purchased data are obtained upon the payment of a stated fee; direct, through the incurring of costs to obtain it. Actually the purchase fee in some instances may be less than the cost of obtaining the information through direct inquiry. On the side of direct inquiry may be the saving of time, the ability to direct the questions specifically, the chance to develop additional information as needed, and the ability to confine the response to only that information thought pertinent in the current case. It may, for instance, be decided on the basis of preliminary analysis of the application that only employment and its duration need be verified. A telephone call or a letter to the employment office of the employer may suffice to verify the stated facts as to the employment and the length of time so employed, and the case is closed in a matter of minutes. Should inquiry along these lines not confirm the information supplied by the application or raise some additional questions not anticipated at first, the investigation can be extended along the new lines indicated.

On the negative side of direct inquiry[3] is the problem of duplication and the lack of completeness and uniformity of

3 / Another aspect of the negative side of direct inquiry is conformance to the provisions of the Fair Credit Reporting Act. See Chapter 13 for a detailed discussion of this enactment.

information at hand about all accounts. When information is possessed by a number of persons, a middleman usually is the most efficient way to secure complete exchange of such information. For each creditor to know the experience of six other creditors, for example, each must send out six inquiries and each must reply to six inquiries. If each submits his information to a central clearing agency the complete information can be in the possession of each creditor by making only one inquiry and submitting only one reply; a total of only seven inquiries and seven replies. (See Figure 12-2 for an illustration of the economy of centralized clearance.) The economy of such a system of clearance makes the direct exchange of ledger facts a relatively inefficient and costly means of investigation. Despite this, direct inquiry is a source of credit information currently being used and thus should be discussed.

FIGURE 12-2
The Economy of Centralized Clearance

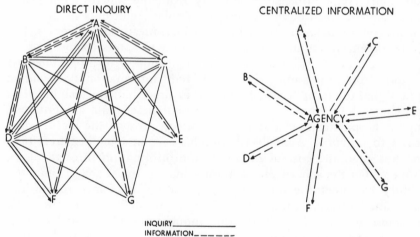

DIRECT INQUIRY   CENTRALIZED INFORMATION

INQUIRY_____
INFORMATION_ _ _ _ _ _

Inquiry by Mail

Direct inquiry by mail may be directed to the employer, firms that have had credit dealings with the applicant, the applicant's bank, attorneys who might have had contact with the applicant, and other references. In each case the reference letter should be carefully framed to solicit information which the informant may be expected to have, which is pertinent to the credit decision, and which the informant may be expected to reveal. The questions should be phrased as specifically as possible and the form designed in such a manner that it is easy for the respondent to reply. In all cases an offer to reciprocate should be made and a self-addressed, stamped envelope supplied for reply. While communication by letter is the more common practice, some firms do use double-return postcards with the name of the applicant shown on the reply card in code to avoid possible legal complications. It is usual to indicate that the information is desired because of a request for credit, and in some cases the nature of the transaction is indicated. Since such information should be and usually is on a give-and-get basis, some firms submit their own experience when asking for the experience of others. It also is usual to state, at least when such is a fact, that the inquiry is directed to a person whose name was supplied as a reference.

As previously mentioned, questions should be phrased in a manner which permits specific and unequivocal answers. So far as possible the questions should invite, in fact require, factual response rather than opinion or judgment. The questions should not indicate or invite bias in either inquiry or reply. The whole tone should be tactful and considerate of the respondent.

Appropriate questions to be directed to the employer are suggested by the following:

Employed since? _____ or How long employed? _____
Position? _____ or Occupation? _____
Salary? $ ___ monthly, or $___ weekly, or $___ per day

And if a former employer, it is appropriate to ask:

Employed? From _____ to _____
Position _____ or Occupation? _____
Reason for separation? _____

Appropriate questions to trade creditors are suggested by the following:

Type of account? _____
When account was opened? _____
Present balance? _____
Highest recent credit? $ _____
Payment experience: Pays when due _____
                        Within 30 days _____
                        In 30 to 60 days _____
                        In 60 to 90 days _____
                        Other _____

(If experience has been unsatisfactory please state the nature of the difficulty, the manner of collection, and if there was a charge to profit and loss) $ __ Date? _____

Appropriate questions to banks are suggested by the following:

Is he a depositor? Yes? _____No? _____Checking? _____ Saving? _____
Approximate amount of the usual balance?_____ (figure)
Have you had lending experience with him? Yes _____ No_____
Was the lending experience satisfactory? Yes _____No_____
Would you recommend?_____

This last question, which violates the precept not to ask for opinion, is suggested because of the desire to conform to bankers' wishes. Some bankers will not answer specific questions as to the amount of the balance, or even as to the lending experience, but will recommend. A question which permits the banker to say whether he would or would not recommend the depositor thus may obtain an answer from a respondent who would not otherwise reply.

Appropriate questions to references who have not had business dealings are suggested by the following:

Is applicant personally known to you?_____ How long?_____
Do you regard him as responsible?_____
Is he of good reputation?_____

When the applicant is of such youth that legal incapacity to contract may be suspected, such references may be asked about his age:

How old is he?_____ What is the date of birth?_____

Developing Additional Informants

It should not be thought that the informants previously listed are the only ones from whom credit information should be sought. Ingenuity should be exercised in order to tap informational sources not supplied by the prospect. It is obvious that when a person is asked for references he will carefully select from the potential list those more likely to give favorable replies; a man must be poor indeed if he cannot select a biased list of references. Although this inherent bias exists, specific questions will develop usable information even from biased sources, since few reputable businessmen will actually falsify credit information. They are more likely to bias their reply by just not mentioning the unfavorable points or by being vague, even overly generous, in response to requests for opinion or judgment. And it is sometimes surprising to the credit analyst—and would doubtless be even more surprising to the prospect—how frank some supposedly biased references are in their responses.

Despite these mitigating factors, the predictable bias should impel the skillful investigator to develop evidence from informants not supplied by the prospect. An added reason for developing such additional sources often is supplied because of the failure to secure a complete list of reference names during the interview or when taking the application. Ingenuity and knowledge of the market often will enable the investigator to add sources. For example, utilities are usually not listed as references, but they do have experience records. A similar situation exists with the local dairies. Public record information also can be used to supplement that supplied. Ownership of property can be checked against tax records. The presence of liens can be determined by examination of the public records. The police records may in some cases be revealing. While it is not suggested that every case be made the subject of such a costly and time-consuming investigation, it should be recognized that when circumstances warrant it, the investigation can be extended in unusual directions.

Inquiry by Telephone

Inquiry by telephone may be directed to the same informants to whom a mail inquiry may be sent. The same or similar questions may be asked. When a telephone inquiry is made, the employee conducting it should have a form upon which the replies can be recorded, and this form should be similar to that used in mail inquiries. Standard questions will attain uniformity of response, but trained telephone investigators should be sufficiently skilled to ask further probing questions as indicated by the nature of the replies.

Telephone inquiry has an advantage over mail: replies are received immediately. The cost per completed inquiry may compare very favorably with a mail inquiry. There is a disadvantage to the respondent, because the reply to a telephone inquiry may be more disruptive of normal work procedures and more time-consuming than the preparation of a reply to an inquiry letter.

Inquiry by Outside Representative

Some firms, particularly cash lenders and sales finance companies, often use their own employees as credit investigators. The employee, or outside representative, may be assigned the dual task of outside or personal collector as well as that of credit investigator. He usually will be supplied with the names of employer, landlord, and business references and is expected to call upon these persons and ask questions very similar to those asked in a mail investigation. Here too, there is an advantage in using standardized questions and a standard form upon which to record replies.

The outside representative should be aggressive in developing additional informants and in extending the depth of the inquiry. Obviously the mail investigation cannot readily be extended on a discretionary basis, but a good outside representative should analyze the information supplied as it accumulates. He thus should extend his inquiries to the point where in his judgment sufficient information is at hand to reach a sound decision to accept or to reject. He may develop, through discreet inquiries, information which no other means of direct investigation can match. He can make inquiries of neighbors and local tradesmen; even the postman or policeman can sometimes supply very pertinent credit information which could only be obtained by careful personal inquiry.

Some cash loan companies, lending on the collateral of household effects, believe that the inferences drawn from personal examination of the home develop useful credit information. Such information as the type and quality of the furnishings, the quality of the housekeeping, the pride or lack of pride in the home can be useful as indicative of the credit quality of the applicant. Also during the interview, the rent or other receipts can be inspected for evidence of payment habits and the insurance carried can be determined.

Inquiry through Credit Group Meetings

Although the technique of group meetings is more common in commercial credit transactions, in some communities it is a convenient method for creditors selling consumer goods to exchange ledger facts and other valuable information. While it is true that such meetings often are held under the auspices of the local retail credit bureau, it still seems correct to classify the action as resulting from direct inquiry.

The purpose of such group meetings, which often are held in conjunction with a social luncheon or dinner, is to provide a quick and easy means of exchanging information about initial applicants for credit, slow-pay customers, and other accounts that are exhibiting an unusual behavior. Usually each participating store is limited in the number of names it can bring up in the discussion. Thus the credit executive is forced to be careful in selecting those customers about whom he believes there exists an important need for an exchange of credit information.

Direct Inquiry—Summary

Direct inquiry has its advantages and its disadvantages. Cost is one of the chief disadvantages, and this may be sufficient to preclude its use by firms which do not specialize in credit work. These comments are in no way designed to discourage direct inquiry. In many instances the direct contact between creditors is extremely valuable and should be encouraged. It is believed, however, that the apparent economy of direct inquiry may be misleading. After all, the true cost is the cost per completed return. Even mail investigation, which appears to be low-cost, can have many hidden costs. The cost per outgoing letter should include the costs of having processed letters prepared, the costs of addressing and filling-in and the costs of the outgoing and return postage. All of the costs of the nonreturns must be added to the cost of the completed usable returns in order to get an average cost per return. Also, one of the large hidden costs of direct inquiry is the high cost of replying to others. If such a system is to work, those sending out inquiries must be prepared to respond and reply to inquiries directed to them. The more the system is used, the larger the number of replies which they must themselves make.

Such a system may lead to a very unequally divided burden upon the larger creditors in a community. Not only do more customers have accounts with the major stores in a market, but they are much more likely to offer the names of such stores as references. Thus investigators are much more likely to direct inquiries to such leading stores. One of the prices of leadership may be the obligation to respond to more than a proportionate share of investigation letters.

INFORMATION SUPPLIED FROM IN-FILE LEDGER FACTS

In-file ledger facts are one of the most important sources of information available to the retail credit analyst who is asked to decide whether to accept or reject a larger amount of credit from an already established credit customer. In these cases, the applicant for a larger credit basis already has been placed on the books as a credit customer through analysis of the application and the interview, through verification of the facts thus obtained, and through investigation to secure any additional facts believed needed at the time of the initial request.

From the in-file records, the credit analyst has at his ready disposal the experience of the concern with the customer. He knows the customer's payment habits, the complaints registered, the collection efforts, if any, needed to keep the customer in line with the established terms. Thus he is in a position to use these data in deciding to accept or reject the request for more credit. In many cases such information is sufficient to enable a decision to be made; in other instances it is necessary for the credit executive to seek more information, which can be called "purchased information," from the professional sources established to supply the additional facts needed before a decision can be reached. Such professional sources are the basis of the next two chapters, Chapters 13 and 14.

REVIEW AND DISCUSSION QUESTIONS

1. Distinguish between direct investigation and internal company data.
2. Explain the statement, "The extent to which this information is verified or expanded through additional investigation depends upon the judgment of the credit analyst."
3. Would you recommend that credit applications be signed? Why or why not?
4. Why is a signature on an application form particularly important in revolving credit transactions?
5. Check with the leading retail stores in your community to determine the type of credit application that is in use in these firms.
6. How would you conduct a credit interview? Why did you include the steps that you did?
7. By what means may the direct inquiry method be accomplished? What are the advantages and disadvantages of each method?
8. Explain the differences between purchased information and free information.
9. Attend a luncheon of retail credit executives in which an interchange of credit information on certain slow-pay customers takes place.
10. When is it desirable to use information supplied from in-file ledger facts?
11. Why is detailed information from the application blank commonly sought by sales finance companies and cash lenders?

13

Basis of the Credit Decision — Local Credit Bureaus

Information about the credit position of individuals may be purchased from many sources. Each source has its own special merits, as well as some disadvantages. For certain types of information, however, one source may be preferable to others. In other localities one source may be particularly strong. Because of special conditions, however, this same source may not hold a preferred position in another locality. Thus, the variation from locality to locality in the quality of the credit reports supplied points up the inadvisability of making dogmatic statements about the superiority of any one reporting organization. Each credit manager should be free to select the source which, all things considered, is best in his own area and which best supplies information of the type he needs.

It will be recalled that the direct method of investigation, as described in the preceding chapter, is "free" only in the sense that a fee is not paid to an outside organization; it is not free in the sense of being costless. Such a technique may in fact be more costly than the fee service, and the product supplied may be inferior. Since the product of the credit investigation is information upon which a sound credit decision can be based, the quality of the information should be a prime consideration. The work of credit investigation has become specialized and, as with any other specialized job, it is usually better entrusted to specialists in that work. In addition, the special agencies avoid unnecessary duplication of effort. Credit information in the files of specialized credit-reporting agencies may be used more than once; in fact, multiple use of the same information is the principle upon which this type of organization is founded. The credit information gathered by direct methods is available only to the firm which has currently made an investigation.

Obviously, for this same information to be available to others interested in the subject, the entire investigation must be repeated, with a greater strain on the contributors because of the duplication of their contribution of credit information.

There are two basic types of purchased informational credit-reporting services when the area over which they operate is used as the basis of classification:

1. Those which serve primarily a local area. Typical of the credit organizations falling into this category are the local retail credit bureaus, both mutually owned and privately owned. These organizations are set up with a primary objective of serving retail merchants, service concerns, professional men, banks and loan companies, and all other types of businesses concerned with the credit of consumers in a localized area. These local credit bureaus are established to provide the latest information in credit reporting and obtain their source data in most instances by centralizing credit information from the ledgers of the principal and most representative credit granters of a local community and by examining the facts contained in public records. They also have a secondary objective in that their membership in Associated Credit Bureaus, Inc. (ACB) extends their services outside their own communities. Thus the credit record of an individual who moves from one area of the country to another is made available to credit businesses in the new community through interbureau reporting arrangements. An examination of the activities of these organizations operating on a local level is the principal subject matter of this chapter.

2. Those which operate primarily on a national basis. Typical of the credit organizations falling into this category are Retail Credit Company and Hooper-Holmes Bureau, Inc. These organizations maintain, in addition to their home offices, extensive branch-office systems over the entire country. They utilize part-time field representatives in the towns and villages which are not of sufficient size to justify full-time employees. These credit-reporting organizations use as their principal method of operation a detailed investigation by their staff of field representatives who gather information in order to fill a specific request for a report. They are in the specialized business of gathering credit information in response to a request from their subscribers or clients. They do not draw from a pool of information contributed by the same people drawing from the pool, as in the case of the local retail credit bureau, but instead develop the information by inquiry or investigation. They too charge fees on the basis of their service agreement or contract and serve those firms that elect to purchase their services. They are in fact specialized independent credit-reporting agencies. The activities of these firms make up the principal subject matter of Chapter 14.

HISTORY AND ORGANIZATION OF RETAIL CREDIT BUREAUS

The local retail credit bureau is generally recognized today as one of the most important sources of consumer credit information. In fact, in thousands of communities it is the most important source for the exchange of ledger information among concerns dealing with consumer credit.

Beginning and Development of Local Retail Credit Bureaus

The local retail credit bureau is primarily a development of the 20th century. Although the 'first so-called credit bureau through which creditors exchanged information concerning their common customers was organized as early as 1860 in Brooklyn, the growth and development of such organizations was slow prior to World War I. In the years prior to World War I, only a very small segment of the total retail business was conducted on a credit basis, and that which was so conducted involved only persons well known to the seller. Movement of people was limited because of the lack of rapid transportation and communication facilities.

Many of the old-time credit exchanges operated on the basis of lists which worked negatively, warning members against known poor credits. In effect, the listing of such risks closed the barn door after someone's horse had been stolen.

From this humble beginning, local credit bureaus have grown to the position of importance that they now occupy. The local retail credit bureaus have become the principal clearinghouses for information furnished by their subscribers and members and other outside sources and are one of the best examples of close cooperation among business firms serving the American public.

Origin and Growth of the Associated Credit Bureaus, Inc. (ACB)

The organized exchange of consumer credit information between local areas appears to have started about the turn of the century. In fact, it was in 1906 that William H. Burr, owner of a "credit company" in Rochester, New York, asked the managers of several other consumer credit-reporting agencies to meet with him to discuss the possibility of forming a national association of credit bureaus. Prior to that time there was no roster of credit bureaus, no system for interchanging reports between bureaus, no standardization of forms. This 1906 meeting resulted in the formation of the first national organization of credit bureaus and was called the National Association of Retail Credit Agencies (now known as Associated Credit Bureaus, Inc.). The need for closer cooperation between credit bureaus and credit granters soon became evident, and in 1912 the

Retail Credit Men's National Association (now known as the International Consumer Credit Association) was formed as a trade association of retail credit managers.

From this 1906 beginning, when six small credit-reporting agencies incorporated and agreed to cooperate in the exchange of credit information, ACB has grown rapidly until today it is one of the foremost trade associations in the credit-reporting industry, offering its members such widespread benefits as interbureau reporting rosters, prepaid interbureau coupons, standardized Factbilt reporting forms, trade publications, national advertising, educational services, credit bureau research, special information reporting service, and annual meetings and conventions. It also serves its members through the affiliation of collection service offices which can be called upon for personal collection effort to collect unpaid consumer accounts. The Collection Service Division may help in locating any skip debtor of a local credit granter, and the Medical Credits Division is especially designed to help physicians, dentists, hospitals, etc., in their collection problems. Another related organization is Credit Bureau Reports, Inc., which was established in 1932 to provide a centralized reporting and collection service to national concerns which use the facilities of nearly all of the local credit bureaus. In addition, ACB has become an international trade association and counts among its members many of the retail credit bureaus located outside the continental limits of the United States.

In February 1971, ACB provided its members with a new marketing service called Credit Services International. The objective of this service is "to secure maximum credit reporting business from national, regional and area credit granters."[1] Credit Services International must approve each new customer brought into the program by a sales agent, who in most instances is a credit bureau operator. This sales agent contracts with the credit granter (national, area, or regional) to furnish him with reports through the system. Reports are ordered from the authorized credit bureaus by the agent or directly by his customer.

Another important service of ACB is the publication of its *Index of Credit Reporting,* which is a measure of the volume of credit reports issued by all the credit bureaus in the United States. Likewise, its *Index of Collections* is a measure of the volume of the collection business of the members of the Collection Service Division.

Organization and Ownership of Local Retail Credit Bureaus

The majority of local retail credit bureaus are merchant-owned; thus they may be considered mutual or cooperative associations. In

1 / "Credit Services International," *Management,* January 1971, p. 4.

most cases ownership by the merchants, which means retail and service firms doing a consumer credit business, is effected through a local credit association. The association elects a board of directors, which in turn employs a bureau manager to operate the bureau. General policies of operation are set by the board of directors. A substantial number of the local bureaus are privately owned. Such bureaus usually are owned by an individual, frequently the same person who originally organized the credit-reporting service in the community. As with any private business, these bureaus may be bought and sold, and, of course, they are operated for a profit. Some bureaus are incorporated, and in some instances a number of them are owned by the same organization and operated as a chain operation. Some bureaus are owned and operated by local chambers of commerce, which run the bureau as a department of the chamber. In effect such bureaus are merchant-owned, but the membership of the chamber of commerce is, of course, wider and not so specifically interested in consumer credit.

Regardless of the ownership, the operation of bureaus is much the same. Most of the local bureaus charge fees for their services based on the use made of the services, and the level of fees charged appears to bear no relationship to the type of ownership. All rely upon cooperation of creditors to contribute credit information to the general pool and to draw credit information from the pool. Whether users of the service are members or customers, they are expected to contribute information if they are to get credit information—thus the bureaus rest firmly on the principle of "give and get."

Bureaus are located in practically every city of over 10,000 population in the United States, and many of the smaller cities which do not themselves have a bureau are covered by the nearby bureau in a larger city. In effect, the bureau service covers every person in the United States and reaches into every city, village, and crossroads. Thus both urban and rural territories are covered. By territorial assignment made by the Associated Credit Bureaus, every portion of the United States has been assigned to a bureau, and that bureau is responsible for supplying credit information on persons residing within the territory assigned it. The bureaus thus constitute a well-organized network of credit-reporting facilities capable of reporting on anyone anywhere in the United States.

OPERATION OF RETAIL CREDIT BUREAUS

Since the local retail bureau usually has more information about the persons and firms of a community than any other one organization, it is imperative that the credit bureau maintain this trust and keep clear control of the facts it has learned through its interchange of information and investigations. The credit bureau has to make a careful and constant check on the identity of the persons and firms receiving its reports. While firms that are not members of the bureau usually may purchase reports, such firms must be identified properly and agree, in writing, to use the furnished information *only* for the purpose of making credit decisions. Such an action prevents this confidential information from falling into the hands of nosy individuals who are seeking information about their friends and neighbors, from being received by firms desiring such data on a nonpay basis, and from involving the credit bureau in costly lawsuits because of the release of data to unauthorized recipients.

Principal Sources of Credit Information

Since the primary activity of a local retail credit bureau is to furnish reports—both written and oral—on consumers desiring to obtain goods, services, and money on credit, it seems best to explore the principal sources that generally are used to supply the data found in the assortment of reports commonly in use today. The most commonly used of the written reports is the ACB Factbilt Report No. 100, which is compiled by member bureaus (see Figure 13-1).

In analyzing form No. 100, it is easy to see that the credit data must be gathered from a large number of persons and firms located in one or more communities and willing to cooperate in the interchange of information on the subject. Thus it is desirable that the local retail credit bureau arrange to secure the necessary information from the following sources of credit information: ledgers of credit granters, employment records, public records, directories, newspapers, landlords, collection services, the post office, other ACB credit bureaus, field investigators, and correspondents. Because of the importance of these sources, it is desirable that they be examined in some detail.

The ledger experiences of credit granters show, in outline form, the exact manner in which an individual meets his credit obligations. Employment records, on the other hand, provide one of the most important facts needed by the credit granter when considering an application for credit, that of a verification of the subject's employment. Public records include such essential facts as property ownership transactions, mortgages, lawsuits and judgments, petitions in bankruptcy, marriages, births, divorces, deaths, arrests, indictments, and convictions. Newspapers contain numerous articles reporting favorable, unusual, and derogatory facts about individuals. Landlords usually are able to furnish a variety of information about

FIGURE 13-1
ACB Report No. 100

NAME AND ADDRESS OF CREDIT BUREAU MAKING REPORT

| ☐ SUMMARY REPORT | ☐ SINGLE REFERENCE | ☐ TRADE REPORT |
| ☐ SHORT REPORT | ☐ FULL REPORT | ☐ PREV. RES. REPORT |

| DATE RECEIVED | DATE MAILED | CBR REPORT NO. |

| DATE TRADE CLEARED | DATE EMPLOY VERIFIED | INCOME VERIFIED ☐ YES ☐ NO |

IN FILE SINCE:

CONFIDENTIAL Factbilt® REPORT   FOR

This information is furnished in response to an inquiry for the purpose of evaluating credit risks. It has been obtained from sources deemed reliable, the accuracy of which this organization does not guarantee. The inquirer has agreed to indemnify the reporting bureau for any damage arising from misuse of this information, and this report is furnished in reliance upon that indemnity. It must be held in strict confidence, and must not be revealed to the subject reported on.

| REPORT ON (SURNAME): | MR., MRS., MISS: GIVEN NAME: | SOCIAL SECURITY NUMBER: | SPOUSE'S NAME: |

| ADDRESS: | CITY: | STATE: | ZIP CODE: | SPOUSE'S SOCIAL SECURITY NO.: |

COMPLETE TO HERE FOR TRADE REPORT AND SKIP TO CREDIT HISTORY

| PRESENT EMPLOYER AND KIND OF BUSINESS: | POSITION HELD: | SINCE: | MONTHLY INCOME: $ |

COMPLETE TO HERE FOR SHORT REPORT AND SUMMARY REPORT AND SKIP TO CREDIT HISTORY

DATE OF BIRTH:				
NUMBER OF DEPENDENTS INCLUDING SPOUSE ⟶		☐ OWNS OR BUYING HOME		☐ RENTS HOME
FORMER ADDRESS:	CITY:	STATE:	FROM:	TO:
FORMER EMPLOYER AND KIND OF BUSINESS:	POSITION HELD:	FROM: TO:	MONTHLY INCOME: $
SPOUSE'S EMPLOYER AND KIND OF BUSINESS:	POSITION HELD:	SINCE:	MONTHLY INCOME: $

CREDIT HISTORY *(Complete this section for all reports)*

KIND OF BUSINESS	DATE ACCOUNT OPENED	DATE OF LAST SALE	HIGHEST CREDIT	AMOUNT OWING	AMOUNT PAST DUE	TERMS OF SALE AND USUAL MANNER OF PAYMENT

PUBLIC RECORD AND/OR SUMMARY OF OTHER TRADE INFORMATION:

AFFILIATED WITH

Form 100   *Associated Credit Bureaus Inc*   *Credit Bureau Reports, Inc.*   Printed in U.S.A.

Courtesy of Associated Credit Bureaus, Inc.

their tenants, including their manner of rent payment, personal habits, morals, number of dependents, and length of residence. Credit bureaus affiliated with ACB are best able to furnish credit information on their former residents because of information in their own master files and a knowledge of the local sources of information. Since all of the sources of credit information cannot be reached by telephone, field investigators provide an efficient method of obtaining certain facts from neighborhood contracts. In addition, there are individuals located in towns and villages throughout the United States who are qualified to obtain and report credit information on residents living in rural areas.

As our population has become increasingly mobile, many purchases are made outside the home trading area. Also, increasing numbers of families are moving from one city to another. Both circumstances usually occasion an interbureau inquiry. Through the facilities of the bureau system, the record of an individual in other markets can be made available to subscribers. ACB has designed and operates a system of prepaid inquiry tickets (see Figure 13-2) which the inquiring bureau can use to draw a report from the files of the bureau which has the subject's prior record. Such a system permits an inquiring bureau to make payment in advance for reports without the bother of bookkeeping or billing and also does away with the need for the bureau to write many checks for small amounts. One difficulty, however, has been that of persuading some bureaus that foreign reports are as important as local reports. Some bureau managers have been more inclined to give local customers preferred service, since they were more easily recognized as the bureau's employers. Another difficulty has been that of educating bureaus to give a uniform high-quality report regardless of recipient. A great help in this matter has been the standardization of reports by ACB under the name of "Factbilt Reports."

Need for Facts—Not Opinions. In using the sources of credit information, it is imperative that the credit bureau distinguish carefully between facts and statements of opinion. This is one of the basic problems of the credit bureau and must be carefully watched in order that the bureau reports may be considered reliable by all users. It is the responsibility of the recipient of the report to use the facts contained in the report to form his own opinion—not that of the bureau—as to the credit applicant, and thus be better prepared to make the "right" decision as to the acceptance or rejection of the credit.

As the sources supply the information needed to complete the reports, the credit bureau must analyze and censor the data, in order to observe any shortcomings, or omissions and, if possible, develop

FIGURE 13-2
Copy of Prepaid Inquiry Ticket of ACB, Inc.

Associated Credit Bureaus, Inc.   OFFICIAL "X" INQUIRY

NOTICE

Use this coupon only for: A—Additional payment for a report submitted upon request, on a non-standard form; or B—For a file search previously requested by telephone, teletype or telegraph, when there was no record in file and when no other service was requested.

Date _____   *Factbilt®* REPORTS   № 315590

1. FULL NAME _____ Age ____ Spouse _____
        (Last)   (First)   (Middle)

2. Present   Residence _____
3. Former   Residence _____
4. Present   Employer _____

Name and Address of Inquiring Bureau

**Credit Bureau of Lincoln
Box 80929
Lincoln, Nebraska 68501**

Please return top of Inquiry Ticket

Associated Credit Bureaus, Inc.   HOUSTON, TEXAS 77036

N O T   N E G O T I A B L E

Standard Inter-Bureau "X" Coupon № 315590

Redeemable only by the Credit Reporting Division member named below, the sum of

FORTY CENTS

This coupon shall be void if not presented to ACB for payment before January 1, 1973.

John L. Spafford
President

Name and Address of Bureau Making Report Must be Inserted Here

2
5
5

The Treasurer may, without prior notice, apply this coupon in payment of past due accounts with ACB.

Courtesy of Credit Bureau of Lincoln, Nebr.

any needed additional information. Such a review also will enable the bureau to determine whether there may be any legal liability involved as to either the content or the form of any derogatory information that has been furnished by these sources. Legal restrictions on bureau operations will be discussed in a subsequent section of this chapter.

Scope of Bureau Operation

The primary purpose of the local retail credit bureaus is to supply information. The ways in which this information is distributed to business concerns will be explained in the following sections, which discuss the reporting and other services rendered to subscribers of the bureaus.

Preparation and Maintenance of Master Card File. It has been said that the heart of the credit bureau records is the master file. This file is close to being the "who's who" for consumer credit in a community and its surrounding trading area. Since the principal task of a local credit bureau is to secure and maintain all available information about consumers, the master file is *the* source of credit information from which data can be obtained quickly and easily and in turn transmitted to inquiring firms. In most bureaus the so-called master card may be either a thin, durable cardboard (4 by 6 or 5 by 8 inches in size) or a heavy paper envelope, or a combination of the two.

Thus, the basic stock in trade of a local bureau is its in-file information, most of which is obtained through ledger clearance among the bureau members. Firms having experience with the subject of an inquiry are asked to supply the bureau with current information covering their recent experience with that subject. New members, upon signing a contract with a bureau, agree to furnish a list of their current customers and supplemental information as to their present and former residences, occupations, business addresses, references, dates accounts were opened, high credit extended, and other pertinent remarks. Data on all new or reopened accounts also are submitted according to the terms of the contract.

As a minimum, the card shows the length of time member firms have had dealings with the subject, the high credit, the amount owing, and the payment experience. If all works as it should, the basic card accumulates automatically and reflects the credit experience of all member firms interested in that person. Most bureaus will institute a new clearance when the date of the last clearance is more than 90 days prior. When a new clearance is instituted, all members listed as interested are contacted and their recent experience is added to the record. Experience of nonmember references is added when available. The experience of members or nonmembers may be sought either by telephone or through written report.

In addition to ledger experience the basic master card usually contains additional basic credit information, such as the address and previous residence addresses, name of wife, occupation, employment, previous employment, and income. Property ownership and public record information may be added. Many bureaus supplement the basic credit information with clippings covering such items as mortgages filed or released, property transfers, births, deaths, suits and judgments, and similar matters. When clippings are added, they may cover matters of direct or indirect credit interest, such as police record, divorce proceedings, engagement announcements, social activities, and business news. In many bureaus, social security numbers have been added to the master card files.

Variety of Reports. While Factbilt Report No. 100 is important, it is by no means the only important report rendered by the local bureau.

A large segment of the activity of a bureau is its oral reporting, in which member firms telephone the bureau, identify themselves by some predetermined plan, and obtain such information as is available in the master card file about the subject desiring credit acceptance.[2] In case the information in the file is out of date, a clearance must be made before the oral report can be given. The oral report usually is the lowest in cost and is furnished quickly and with little effort on the part of the bureau.

Certain groups of creditors desire special reports that are either more detailed or less detailed than the standard credit report and that may cover certain aspects of the credit situation more adequately than a standard report. This demand has led to the development of a number of special reports of various types, one of the most important of which is the CBR Report No. 891 which is used by the Federal Housing Administration, the Veterans Administration, and the Office of Economic Opportunity. A copy of this report is shown in Figure 13-3.

Professional men, such as doctors, dentists, and lawyers, often feel that the complete ledger clearance report overwhelms them with facts which are not especially useful to them because of the different character of their relations with clients or patients. In addition they generally do not have organized credit departments and do not believe that they are doing a standard credit business. Still, they

2 / In view of the cost of reports, a number of lending agencies now have arrangements to call the local credit bureau and for a very small fee ask merely whether there is any negative information on file about the particular customer in question. They receive a yes or no answer. If the answer is yes, they draw a credit report for which they pay the usual fee.

FIGURE 13-3
CBR Report No. 89

CBR CREDIT BUREAU REPORTS inc.
a nationwide service

CBR FHA Standard Factual
Data Report No. 891

CORRECT NAME AND ADDRESS

Name..	Case Number..
Street Address...............................	Property Address....................................
City and State...............................	Date on Order Ticket ....
Zip Code	Date Received by Bureau............................
	Date Report Mailed.................................

(No reference shall be made in this report to race, creed, color, or national origin)

1-A. Do name and address agree with information shown on request for report? If not, explain below.	1-A.
B. Date of Birth -	B.
2-A. Marital status - number of dependents including self	2-A. Dependents:
B. Length of time married -	B.
C. Did you learn of any separation or divorce?	C.
3-A. Name of present employer -	3-A.
B. Position held - length of present connection -	B. Years:
C. Has employment status changed within the past two years?	C.
4-A. If spouse is presently employed, give name of employer -	4-A.
B. Position held - length of present connection -	B. Years:
C. Approximate income -	C. $

REMARKS: 1. Amplify his employment history. (This report shall contain information as to the subject's previous employment status, location and salary, if there has been a change in employment status within the past two years.)

2. The reporting bureau certifies that: (a) ☐ public records have been checked for suits, judgments, foreclosures, garnishments, bankruptcies, and other legal actions involving the subject with the results indicated below: or, (b) ☐ equivalent information has been obtained through the use of a qualified public records reporting service with the results indicated below. (Give details). (The records of real estate transfers which do not involve foreclosure may be excluded).

3. The reporting bureau certifies that the subject's credit record in the payment of bills and other obligations has been checked: (a) ☐ through the credit accounts extended by a combined minimum of 75% of the larger department stores and larger consumer and unsecured credit granters of the community in which the subject resides, with the results indicated below: or, (b) ☐ through accumulated credit records of such credit granters of the community in which the subject resides, with the results indicated below.

CREDIT HISTORY

KIND OF BUSINESS	DATE ACCOUNT OPENED	DATE OF LAST SALE	HIGHEST CREDIT	AMOUNT OWING	AMOUNT PAST DUE	TERMS OF SALE AND USUAL MANNER OF PAYMENT

Report mailed to: _____

Mortgage Stamp Imprint Number (if Applicable)

Prepared by:_____

Name of CBR reporting bureau   City   State

The information in this report is provided under contract between the Federal Housing Administration and Credit Bureau Reports, Inc.

Information furnished on FHA Standard Factual Data Report No. 891, together with related antecedent reports, is furnished upon the express condition that the FHA Approved Mortgagee and/or its authorized agent or FHA Contract Broker and/or its authorized agent or the V.A. Lender and/or its authorized agent agrees to hold such information in strict confidence for its own exclusive use, never to be communicated except to the FHA, or VA (or bonafide purchasers in the secondary mortgage market), and to save Credit Bureau Reports, Inc., and the reporting credit bureaus, their officers, agents and employees harmless from any and all damages which may arise from the violation of the agreement by such FHA Approved Mortgagee or such FHA Contract Broker, or such VA Lender.

TUMBLE OVER. WRITE FROM TOP DOWN.   (SEE REVERSE SIDE FOR COMMON LANGUAGE FOR CONSUMER CREDIT)

Courtesy of Credit Bureau Reports, Inc.

desire some protection against abuse of credit relations. Their true preference may be for an advisory service—a service which in effect makes some outside agency their credit (and collection) department. In some communities this desire has been met by the organization of a special medical or professional credit bureau, in others by the setting up of a special department in the bureau, and in still others by the development of a summary or opinion type of credit report.

Loan companies, especially cash lenders, often want complete information about the contractual obligations of their customers and applicants. To satisfy this desire, the bureau may develop a report which undertakes to exhaust the sources of such information. The loan companies also may work with a special department of the bureau which attempts to make a ledger clearance of all lenders whenever an inquiry is made on a name. Another special need is that of real estate lenders who desire information about other indebtedness, mortgages, and similar public record information. This desire can be met by a property record search or public record search.

Traditionally food retailers, especially the larger chain organizations, have been cash-and-carry firms and have not been considered as prospective bureau members. However, attempts have been made recently to introduce credit into some of these operations, for example by the Kroger Co. and the Great Atlantic & Pacific Tea Co.[3]

Standardization of Terminology. Standardization of terminology within the credit industry has long been a problem. Credit language has been ambiguous, confusing, and sometimes misleading. With the increasing conversion of credit granter operations and credit-reporting services to computers, a common language was vital between these two groups within a given community or across the nation.

For this reason, ACB has developed and put into use a standardized system of terminology and abbreviations for reporting the bill-paying habits of credit users (see Figure 13-4). This common language has been most favorably received and adopted by credit people across the country.

Supplementary Credit Bureau Services. Services of the credit bureau thus far discussed have been custom tailored for the inquiring customer. The bureaus also provide certain services[4] which are not individually tailored in response to an order. The same information is made available to all subscribers to that particular service, and the subscriber selects from the mass of information the portion significant to him.

3 / Lee E. Circle, "Food Retailers Make Excellent Prospective Bureau Members," *Management,* January 1970, p. 6.

4 / James E. Eaton, "Make Selling Your Pathway to Success," *Management,* February 1969, p. 18.

FIGURE 13-4
Common Language for Consumer Credit

TERMS OF SALE

Open Account (30 days or 90 days) ——— O

Revolving or Option (Open-end a/c)——— R

Instalment (fixed number of payments) I

(Where the monthly payment is known it should be shown as in the following example: I$78

USUAL MANNER OF PAYMENT	TYPE ACCOUNT		
	O	R	I
Too new to rate; approved but not used	0	0	0
Pays (or paid) within 30 days of billing; pays accounts as agreed	1	1	1
Pays (or paid) in more than 30 days, but not more than 60 days, or not more than one payment past due	2	2	2
Pays (or paid) in more than 60 days, but not more than 90 days, or two payments past due	3	3	3
Pays (or paid) in more than 90 days, but not more than 120 days, or three or more payments past due	4	4	4
Account is at least 120 days overdue but is not yet rated "9"	5	5	5
Making regular payments under Wage Earner Plan or similar arrangement	7	7	7
Bad debt; placed for collection; skip	9	9	9

KIND OF BUSINESS CLASSIFICATION

Code	Kind of Business
A	Automotive
B	Banks
C	Clothing
D	Department and Variety
F	Finance
G	Groceries
H	Home Furnishings
I	Insurance
J	Jewelry and Cameras
K	Contractors
L	Lumber, Building Material, Hardware
M	Medical and Related Health
N	National Credit Card Companies and Airlines
O	Oil Companies
P	Personal Services Other Than Medical
Q	Mail Order Houses
R	Real Estate and Public Accommodations
S	Sporting Goods
T	Farm and Garden Supplies
U	Utilities and Fuel
V	Government
W	Wholesale
X	Advertising
Y	Collection Services
Z	Miscellaneous

Courtesy of Associated Credit Bureaus, Inc.

Rating Book. The issuance of rating books in the form of blacklists was one of the earliest of bureau services. This has been replaced by the service of providing factual information to be analyzed and interpreted by the subscriber. The written or telephone report is the more complete way of distributing relatively complete factual information. In some markets and among some subscribers, however, there remains a desire for a service which provides a listing of individuals and a summary of their credit standing or credit rating. This desire is met by some bureaus by the issuance of rating books. Such books may either give a rating which summarizes the past credit experience or publish the credit experience in greatly summarized form. Present information indicates that they are now published by a minority of the bureaus, although the number has increased in recent years.

Daily Reporter. Most bureaus now publish a daily reporter through which they make available to subscribers all public-record information. This daily report covers such items as: security agreements recorded or released, transfers of property, judgments, suits filed, bankruptcies, marriage licenses, births, deaths, building permits: in short, all those things which become a matter of public record. Information of this type is picked up daily, often by a special reporter who visits the public offices; organized under the various headings; and distributed to subscribers on mimeographed sheets. Subscribers can check the listings against their own list of accounts and add the information to their credit files or take such action as the information indicates is appropriate. Another use of this information is made by the bureau, which adds the items to its regular credit files at the same time that it is selling such facts in the form of a daily reporter for a subscription fee.

New Account Solicitation Service. A somewhat similar service is provided by those bureaus which distribute lists of moves into, out of, and about town (see Figure 13-5). Such lists enable subscribers to keep their addresses of customers and mailing lists current. Moves into town may be used for account solicitation, out of town for collection attention, and within and about town for keeping addresses current. Such information may be acquired by the bureau from several sources—moving and storage companies, public utilities, and police records. However acquired, it is organized in the form of lists, duplicated, and distributed.

Watch and Warning Service. Most bureaus have a special service in the form of flash or warning bulletins. Such bulletins are a means of putting members on notice of the operations of bad-check artists, credit frauds of one sort or another, and other warnings about things which are important to credit departments.

FIGURE 13-5

DAILY MOVING RECORD

Compiled and Published by The Credit Bureau of Lincoln, Nebraska, Inc.

Credit Reports · Collections

VOLUME   58   NUMBER   19   **Publishers of the BLUE BOOK**   FEBRUARY 2, 1971

126 NORTH 16TH STREET·   LINCOLN. NEBRASKA 68501   TELEPHONE 432-8891

CHANGES

Abboud Linda	From-	1541 S #9	To- 1541 S #2
Allgood Richard C III		3005 So 42	1601 Circle Dr
Armbruster Debi		480 No 16 #11	480 No 16 #18
Baltensperger Barbara		1125 No 16 #316	1125 No 16 #211
Blatchford Dennis		1328 E	1655 Smith
Brown Billy James		2522 So 8	2440 So 10
Burhoop Dave		921 Cobblestone	310 Glenhaven
Buss Jerald		4300 Holdrege #A-101	1418 No 60
Butler Vicki		1747 F	3123 R
Cadwallader Dean J		2211 Dorothy	Rt 3
Carrico Willada		1944 E #1-B	1222 So 14 #1
Crough Genevieve		1503 So 13	2414 No 57
Dulin Michaele Ann		1125 No 16 #308	1125 No 16 #315
Edwards Susan		1601 R	464 No 16 #6
Esch James		2301 A	3636 No 52 #B-B1
Fitzgerald Hilda A Mrs		1327 H #8-C	1327 H #C-4
Garnick Lory Lou		480 No 16 #2	480 No 16 #12
Gibson F E Gene		310 Glenhaven	921 Cobblestone
Greene Molly		4618 Prescott	2442 Vine
Grudzinski Lloyd		1201 West O	1025 J #A-7
Guse John C		2244 Vine	1132 N #304
Hartin Linda		1130 No 14 #923	1130 No 14 #901
Hartsell David		2400 Q	2780 Arlington
Hill Harold		1140 No 25	1502 Garfield #1
Hilligoss Dexter		149 So 29	146 So 28 #3
Klingemann Donald L		1816 Prospect	4600 Briar Park #502
Knox Donald		3902 So 46	5418 Saylor
Kollars Gary P		2023 So 22	1636 Woodsview
Liakus Arthur		1910 J	216 So 29
Liermann Carlene		1600 C	1516 So 13
Magee Oliver		2512 Calvert	7100 South #1
Malone Tom		2501 R	711 No 28
Martell Jack L		1 & Cornhusker	2801 No 1 #252
Mather Marcia		540 No 16 #303	540 No 16 #4402
Murphy Michael		4200 Baldwin	5801 Huntington
Mutthersbough Joseph W		4603 Cleveland	5301 Colfax
Oestreich Wesley		2636 J	620 Capitol #21
Payne Michael		5234 Adams	6719 Aylesworth
Pearson Steve		2834 Stratford	1625 So 11
Shreve Nancy		2000 So 22	2834 Stratford
Skiff Ron G		2202 Washington	1810 So 43
Smartt Howard Austin		5301 Madison #305	5301 Madison #103
Steinheider Dave		1150 No 14	4103 South
Stokes Elmer R		4140 Lewis	3028 South
Trumbley Lucy		2420 So 16	829 W Washington
Turek Charles A		3321 No 44	3205 No 45
Van Ackeren Gene		216 So 29	938 So 16

(OVER)

SUBSCRIPTION RATE - $13.00 FOR 3 MONTHS PAYABLE IN ADVANCE

Courtesy of Credit Bureau of Lincoln, Nebr.

In some communities a new form of telephone alert has recently appeared. Under this plan, a merchant who discovers that a shoplifter or a bad-check artist has been operating in his store can call a predetermined telephone number and have this information recorded. Immediately thereafter, every member who has subscribed for this service will be notified on a specially installed telephone and will be able to hear the recorded message.

Regular Bulletins. The regular bureau bulletins are both a service to members and a part of the educational program of bureaus. They also may be regarded as house organs, customer relations, advertising, or public relations publications. It appears that such bulletins should be considered as a part of the services of a bureau to its members. Through these bulletins, members and their employees are informed of developments in credit work which are in the interest of good credit operations.

Collection Service. Most bureaus, either through a collection department or the organization of an affiliate, offer collection service to their members. A variety of collection services, ranging from the supplying of a series of collection letters to the services of professional collectors, is provided. Since collections are covered in detail in a later chapter, they are merely mentioned here as one of the services available.

Educational Activities. The local bureaus and their national organization have been very active in credit education. The national organization holds an annual meeting and sponsors regional and state meetings. Such meetings are properly considered educational in their purpose, although the fellowship and inspiration generated are considered by-products. The national organization also sponsors institutes or short courses for credit bureau managers, usually held in cooperation with a college or university. The national organization also has published numerous books, periodicals, and bulletins especially directed toward the exchange of information and know-how.

The various local bureaus engage in similar activities but on a local level. They too have meetings of credit department personnel and of owners of the businesses for the discussion of credit matters. In some cases they have organized short courses on credits and collections. Their bulletins and newsletters contain a great deal of educational material. They work to improve the knowledge of credit principles and the proper application of credit procedures both with their own employees and with the employees of retail credit departments.

Cost of Credit Bureau Services

Whether operated as a mutual merchant-owned service or as a private business, the bureau must charge for its services in order to continue to provide them. There are three basic ways of charging for the reporting services:

1. A flat charge for membership, this charge to provide all reports requested. The rate charged members generally varies with their

business classification, and perhaps size, and is a rough estimate of the extent of use anticipated. It has the merit of assuring income adequate to meet the expenses, provided enough members can be secured. It has the disadvantage of not being proportional to use. As a practical matter, it is likely to result in disproportionate charges to a few strong supporters of the bureau and adequate charges to the numerous smaller members.

2. A charge which is metered on the basis of use. Under this method each report is priced and members are charged on a per-report basis. Thus the cost of credit information varies exactly with the extent of its use and the type used. This has the advantage of being strictly equitable, at least equitable on the basis of the extent of not encouraging use by smaller members who are less conscious of the need for credit facts.

3. A combination of the membership charge with the metered charge. Under this method, members are charged a monthly membership fee which entitles them to a specified number of reports. Each report above this number is charged on a unit basis. This method has the advantage of giving some certainty of monthly minimum income and of being reasonably equitable. It also is likely to encourage use up to the maximum, thus enabling all members to get better acquainted with the value of credit facts.

Charges for the special-purpose services usually are established on a subscription basis. Flash and regular bulletins usually are free services. Collection services usually are charged on the basis of a percentage of amounts collected.

LEGAL RESTRICTIONS ON CREDIT BUREAU OPERATIONS

Brief mention was made in Chapter 3 of the Fair Credit Reporting Act (Title VI amendment of the Consumer Credit Protection Act). This Fair Credit Reporting Act, which became effective in April 1971, is the culmination of some three years of research work. Early in 1968, ACB called together credit granters and credit bureau and collection managers, and an Advisory Committee on Protection of Privacy was formed representing all major credit granters and consumer credit associations.[5] By this time the privilege of credit versus the right to privacy had become one of the hottest questions in the credit field, and the problem of how the rights of all parties could be protected while their needs and desires were satisfied had become a topic of concern for legislators, credit bureaus, credit

5 / John L. Spafford, "The 1968-69 ACB Year. . . .Unlike Any Others," *Management* July 1969, p. 2.

granters, and consumers.[6] Working together, these groups produced the Fair Credit Reporting Act.

Provisions of the Fair Credit Reporting Act

The Fair Credit Reporting Act was needed for the following reasons:[7]

1. The banking system is dependent upon fair and accurate credit reporting. Inaccurate credit reports directly impair the efficiency of the banking system, and unfair credit reporting methods undermine the public confidence which is essential to the continued functioning of the banking system.
2. An elaborate mechanism has been developed for investigating and evaluating the credit worthiness, credit standing, credit capacity, character, and general reputation of consumers.
3. Consumer reporting agencies have assumed a vital role in assembling and evaluating consumer credit and other information on consumers.
4. There is a need to insure that consumer reporting agencies exercise their grave responsibilities with fairness, impartiality, and a respect for the consumer's right to privacy.

One of the most interesting provisions of this act is that no consumer-reporting agency may make any consumer report containing any of the following items of information:[8]

1. Bankruptcies which, from date of adjudication of the most recent bankruptcy, antedate the report by more than fourteen years.
2. Suits and judgments which, from date of entry, antedate the report by more than seven years or until the governing statute of limitations has expired, whichever is the longer period.
3. Paid tax liens which, from date of payment, antedate the report by more than seven years.
4. Accounts placed for collection or charged to profit and loss which antedate the report by more than seven years.
5. Records of arrest, indictment, or conviction of crime which, from date of disposition, release, or parole, antedate the report by more than seven years.
6. Any other adverse item of information which antedates the report by more than seven years.

Under the law, it is mandatory for a credit granter such as a retail firm or a service concern to provide the consumer with the name and

6 / For a discussion on the legal restrictions on credit bureau operations, see the Suggested Readings at the end of the chapter.

7 / Sec. 602 of the Fair Credit Reporting Act (Title VI amendment of Consumer Credit Protection Act) effective April 1971. See Appendix B for the complete act.

8 / *Ibid.*, Sec. 605. There are certain exceptions to this provision, depending upon the amount of the credit transaction ($50,000 or more) and upon the annual salary of any individual ($20,000 or more).

address of a credit bureau if the consumer is denied credit (similar provisions of the law apply to the denial of employment or insurance) based wholly or partly on information obtained from that credit bureau. It is recommended by the ACB, Inc. that this be done in writing with a preprinted form. The business concern is not required to give any specific information to the consumer as to what the report contains. In fact, the agreement between the credit bureau and the business concern forbids this kind of disclosure.

Whenever a credit granter denies credit based on information from a source or sources other than a credit bureau (such as a direct clearance from another business concern), the credit granter must inform the consumer, at the time of denial, that he has a right to request in writing, within 60 days, the nature of the information on which the rejection was based. Although the law does not require the credit granter to disclose to the consumer the source of the information received in a direct inquiry, the intent of the law is that the consumer must be given enough facts to be able to refute or challenge the accuracy of the information.

Confusion as to what a consumer reporting agency actually is, under the law, undoubtedly will cause firms to be extremely careful to report only their own factual ledger experience about a consumer. For example, suppose X Department Store receives a call from Y Finance Company about a consumer. If X Department Store tells Y Finance Company of the experience that Z Hardware Store had with the consumer, then that information becomes a credit report and X Department Store is considered to be a consumer reporting agency and must comply with the provisions of the law pertaining to consumer reporting agencies.

One of the most important provisions of the act is the right of the consumer to know what is in his record at the credit bureau.[9] On the question of disclosures to consumers, the act provides that every consumer reporting agency shall, upon request and proper identification of any consumer, clearly and accurately disclose to the consumer the following:[10]

1. The nature and substance of all information (except medical information) in its files on the consumer at the time of the request.
2. The sources of the information; except that the sources of information acquired solely for use in preparing an investigative consumer report and actually used for no other purpose need not be disclosed: Provided, That in the event an action is brought under this title, such sources shall be available to the plaintiff under appropriate discovery procedures in the court in which the action is brought.

9 / "The Importance of the Consumer Interview," *Management,* September 1969, p. 5.

10 / Fair Credit Reporting Act, *op. cit.,* Sec. 609; also see Max A. Denney, "Federal Fair Credit Reporting Act," *Quarterly Report,* Winter 1970, p. 4.

3. The recipients of any consumer report on the consumer which it has furnished—
   A. for employment purposes within the two-year period preceding the request, and
   B. for any other purpose within the six-year period preceding the request.

The law provides that a consumer cannot be charged for an interview at a credit bureau if within the past 30 days he has either been denied credit because of a credit report from a credit bureau or has received a notice from a collection department affiliated with the credit bureau. However, a credit bureau may make a reasonable charge for a consumer interview if the consumer has not been denied credit or has not received a notice from an affiliated collection department.

AUTOMATED CREDIT BUREAU REPORTING

The credit-reporting industry has for some time recognized that the number of reports issued is climbing rapidly to gigantic proportions. As early as 1964,[11]

the credit reporting industry recognized that computer technology had advanced sufficiently to enable economical and "instantaneous" reports to subscribers. This realization has been accelerated toward implementation by a rising volume of inter-city reports caused by increasing mobility of the American public.

The Director of Automation of ACB, Clarke R. Newlin, Jr., has made the following valuable observations on automated credit bureau reporting:[12]

The attached list indicates those cities which have automated at this time . . .

Houston, Texas—operational
Dallas, Texas—operational
New Orleans, Louisiana—operational
Boston, Massachusetts—operational
Denver, Colorado—planned
Kansas City, Missouri—operational
Salem, Oregon—operational
San Francisco, California—operational
San Jose, California—operational
Washington, D.C.—planned
Atlanta, Georgia—operational
Chicago, Illinois—operational
St. Louis, Missouri—operational
Indianapolis, Indiana—planned

11 / Stephen P. Coha, "Automated Credit Reporting," *Bankers Monthly Magazine,* February 15, 1967, p. 20. For additional articles on this topic, see the Suggested Readings at the end of the chapter.

12 / Personal letter from Mr. Newlin, dated February 5, 1971.

Cincinnati, Ohio—planned
Los Angeles, California—operational (not ACB member)
New York, New York—operational (not ACB member)
Detroit, Michigan—operational (not ACB member)

There are plans for other Oregon and California cities to be serviced by the Salem, Oregon computer. There are plans for other bureaus owned by CBI in southeastern U.S. to be tied into Atlanta.

The automated credit reporting agencies in Los Angeles, New York, and Detroit are all operated by Credit Data Corporation.

In the early phases of automation in this industry, there was a fairly high rate of acquisition of major metropolitan bureaus by chains or other companies. Within the last six months, however, there is now beginning to be a processing service approach by some of the chains to other credit bureaus without any acquisition or equity position in such bureaus.

The Credit Bureau of Greater Houston now provides facilities management service to the Credit Bureau of Greater Kansas City and has also signed a contract for such service with the Merchants Association in Indianapolis. The Chilton Corporation is offering a similar service as is Trans Union (Credit Bureau of Cook County, Inc.), Computing and Software (it operates the Retail Merchants Credit Association in Los Angeles), and the Credit Data Corporation has made similar proposals.

It is interesting to note that approximately three years ago we said there was potential for perhaps 23 computer centers in major metropolitan areas in the country. Fourteen of the major centers within 1971 will be automated. Thus, the original projection appears to be valid although the location of computers serving such cities might differ. . . .

EVALUATION OF LOCAL RETAIL CREDIT BUREAUS

As has probably been evident from the preceding discussion, local credit bureaus are a valuable contributor to the work of consumer credit. Their method of exchanging credit information through a pool is sound in principle. The method is one which leads to more complete information exchanged economically. Without the bureaus, credit decisions would be made without the benefit of sufficient facts to verify quality, or the necessary facts would be gathered more slowly and at greater cost.

However, some bureaus fail to some degree in the execution of their tasks.[13] Some of these failings are properly attributable to the lack of complete cooperation from their members.[14] The pool of information can be full only when the members contribute fully; the information in the pool can be fresh only when the members supply current information immediately and when all firms accepting credit

13 / Al G. Bassham, "Today's Credit Bureaus," *Credit Management Year Book 1968-1969* (New York: National Retail Merchants Association, 1970), p. 13.

14 / Duane O. Watkins, "Credit Granters' Relations With the Credit Bureau," *Credit World*, March 1970, p. 6.

in a community are members. To the extent that membership is far from universal and cooperation and participation by members far from ideal, the work of the bureaus suffers. In many markets the bureaus are much poorer than they might be, or indeed than they should be, because they have insufficient members and the members do not properly support their efforts.

Some failings of the bureaus are properly attributable to the failings of bureau personnel. Not all bureau managers are efficient; some are content to be no better than their members demand that they be. In some communities the members do not know what a good report is and continue to accept from their bureaus inferior reports—reports which are incomplete, information which is not verified, and opinions rather than facts. Such failings become especially troublesome when the bureaus attempt to sell their services on a national basis. Delay in reporting also is often troublesome, especially delay in handling interbureau reports.

Some weaknesses of the bureau work may be properly attributable to the effort of retail credit managers to buy reports too cheaply. There is a reluctance to pay enough for credit reports to obtain quality reports. The effort to tailor reports to low costs often leads to poor reports. While economy in operation must be sought, it may be unwise economy to save a few cents on a credit report which is to be the basis for dealings running into the hundreds of dollars.

Some credit bureaus may find themselves in a profit squeeze in the future because of the growth of bank and other private credit card plans. For example if a large number of merchants join a bank card plan and no longer need any, or need only a few, credit reports (the bank being the only party needing the report on the buying consumer), the impact upon credit bureau operations is apparent.

What the future holds in the way of changes in credit bureau operation and organization is highly debatable. Only time will tell the extent to which automated credit reporting will modify the traditional type of operation.

REVIEW AND DISCUSSION QUESTIONS

1. What do you believe will be the effect of the Fair Credit Reporting Act upon credit bureaus? Upon credit granters? Upon consumers?
2. What is meant by a mutually owned credit bureau? By a privately owned bureau?
3. What type is in operation in your community?
4. Trace the beginning and development of the local retail credit bureau.
5. What are the principal activities of the Associated Credit Bureaus, Inc?
6. Describe the principle of "give and get" in credit bureau operation.

7. Explain why credit bureau work must be highly confidential.
8. What criteria would you establish in hiring people for credit bureau work?
9. What are the principal sources of credit bureau information? Discuss each source.
10. What data are reported on ACB Report No. 100? What additional information do you believe should be added to this form?
11. How has the prepaid inquiry ticket helped the operations of the local credit bureau?
12. Explain the statement, "The heart of the credit bureau records is the master file."
13. What does the master card generally show?
14. What additions to and deletions from the master card would you suggest?
15. Review the list of reports available from a local credit bureau.
16. Which of these reports is the local credit bureau in your community providing its subscribers?
17. Describe the methods that credit bureaus use for charging for their services.
18. What is your opinion of the value of the local credit bureau serving your community?
19. Tour your local credit bureau, and discuss with the bureau executives their views on the future of automated credit reporting.

SUGGESTED READINGS

Legal Restrictions on Credit Bureau Operations

"Credit Bureaus Near a Day of Judgment," *Business Week,* August 17, 1968, p. 44.

Mangan, William J. "The Procedures and Practices of Credit Bureaus," *Consumer Finance News,* January 1969, p. 12.

"The Privilege of Credit v. the Right to Privacy," *Stores,* October 1968, p. 23.

Automated Credit Bureau Reporting

Chilton III, J. E. R. "Credit Reporting by Computer," *Credit World,* February 1968, p. 18.

―――― "The Computer Credit Bureau in Action," *1967-1968 Credit Management Year Book* (New York: National Retail Merchants Association, 1967), p. 159.

Newlin, Jr., Clarke N. "The Credit Bureau of Tomorrow," *Credit World,* October 1967, p. 11.

Pinger, Robert K. "Philosophies, Policies and Procedures of the Automated Credit Bureau," *1967-1968 Credit Management Year Book* (New York: National Retail Merchants Association, 1967), p. 156.

Schaffer, Charles A. "Other Automation Activities in the Credit Bureau Field," *1967-1968 Credit Management Year Book* (New York: National Retail Merchants Association, 1967), p. 162.

14

Basis of the Credit Decision – Other Sources

Having examined the sources of consumer credit information which are characterized as local in scope, we turn to those sources which are national in their operations. In contrast with local credit bureaus, which supply valuable credit information to users operating in local markets, the national agencies primarily fulfill the needs of users selling in the national markets. The dominant companies which concentrate in the field of reporting upon individuals are Retail Credit Company, its affiliates, and Hooper-Holmes Bureau, Inc. The firms affiliated with Retail Credit Company are Retailers Commercial Agency; the Credit Bureau, Inc. of Georgia; Credit Bureaus, Inc. of Oregon; and the Credit Bureau of Montreal, Ltd.

RETAIL CREDIT COMPANY

Retail Credit Company of Atlanta, Georgia, has been selected as representative of the national firms which work on the plan of investigation by a staff of field men and which gather information to supply a specific request for a report. Although there may be differences in the operating procedures of the various companies that work on this basis, Retail Credit Company is representative, and a description of its manner of operation and services will permit an understanding of reporting agencies of this type. Retail Credit Company operates nationally, but it does not dominate the field of consumer credit reporting to the same extent that Dun & Bradstreet does commercial credit reporting.

History and Organization

Retail Credit Company was started by Cator Woolford in 1899. His original purpose was to report on the credit of consumers to the retail merchants of Atlanta, Georgia. Developing some reputation for the quality of the information which he was able to supply, the founder soon found himself making reports to insurance companies interested in this sort of information for the purpose of underwriting. Under the impetus of this demand the operation was extended to Dallas, Texas, in 1902 and subsequently to other points, and the methods have been modified until the present techniques were developed as the basic pattern of operation. Although credit reporting was never abandoned, and the name of the company has continued to emphasize credit reporting, the business of reporting to insurance companies for underwriting purposes quickly became more important than credit reporting. However, in 1935 the credit reporting side of the business was again emphasized by the organization of Retailers Commercial Agency, a wholly owned affiliate, which was organized to specialize in credit reporting in major markets throughout the nation. Further expansion of the credit reporting phase of the company has come about through the operations of the previously mentioned wholly owned subsidiaries which own and operate some 120 credit bureaus. In addition to the Credit Bureau, Inc. of Georgia, which operates bureaus in the eastern portion of the United States, Retail Credit Company owns the Credit Bureau of Montreal, Ltd., which operates bureaus in the provinces of Quebec and Alberta, Canada; and Credit Bureaus, Inc. of Oregon, which operates bureaus in the San Francisco Bay area and the Pacific northwest.[1]

In 1968, Retail Credit Company acquired Atwell, Vogel, & Sterling, Inc., a company specializing in premium audits and underwriting inspection reports. Premium audit services involve the formal examination of accounts and records to determine the correct amount of adjusted "earned premium" on expiring or interim policies. In early 1970, Retail Credit Company acquired Gay & Taylor, Inc., an independent multiple-line adjusting company. Gay & Taylor serves the insurance industry through investigation and adjustment of claims and losses which arise under accident and health, life, automobile (all lines), aviation, and casualty policies. They also serve in the fields of fidelity and surety, fire and all marine lines, mobile homes, and workmen's compensation insurance coverages.

The principle guiding the operation of Retail Credit Company differs from that of agencies where credit information is exchanged among members. Retail Credit Company gathers credit information through personal investigation made by field representatives, rather than through the exchange of credit experience among members.

1 / Sarah Dunbar, "Bureau Puts Credit on the Line," *Women's Wear Daily*, January 11, 1971, p. 38.

Retail Credit Company is well organized throughout the continental United States and has branches in Alaska, Hawaii, Mexico, Puerto Rico, and Newfoundland. In 1970, the company had approximately 9,300 full-time salaried employees, of whom about 6,000 were field representatives. Full-time field representatives are located in some 303 branch offices and in more than 1,200 suboffices. Practically all cities of 25,000 or more population and many smaller places are covered by full-time field representatives. Salaried reporters complete the major proportion of the reports rendered by the company. There are, in addition, more than 25,000 part-time reporters, or correspondents. The much more numerous correspondents give coverage in the smaller towns and villages. Correspondents may be bank personnel, local merchants, insurance agents, real estate brokers, retired citizens, or similar persons. Usually they know their communities intimately and have access to excellent sources of information. In the early history of the company, considerable reliance was placed on such persons for the development of reports. The later history of the company has seen a shift toward larger proportions of reports (approximately 97 percent) being developed by salaried personnel who work at credit reporting on a full-time basis.

Users of Retail Credit Company Services

The services are used by subscribers of many types: insurance companies writing life, accident and health, automobile, fire and casualty policies; financing and lending organizations engaged in installment financing, cash lending, and real estate loans; manufacturers who sell on credit themselves or who desire reports to aid in the selection of dealers; merchants, especially those who sell over large territories or on a mail-order basis; oil companies; public utilities; federal agencies; publishers; service organizations; and others. A general listing of the services provided by Retail Credit Company includes insurance underwriting reports (all lines), personnel selection reports, claim reports, claim settlement services, property check reports, management information services, and credit reports. A marketing research service also is available. This service is used by magazine publishers, radio broadcasters, advertising agencies, and manufacturers.

Methods of Investigation

Many subscribers use reports for other than credit purposes, but the nature of the information is similar if not identical to the information pertinent to a credit decision. Although the principal interest here is credit information, a rather complete description of the methods (whether for credit or noncredit use) is necessary to understand the credit aspects of the service. Retailers Commercial Agency was organized to specialize in credit-reporting services and operates in major metropolitan markets. Retailers and other users sign service contracts for credit reports, and if Retailers Commercial Agency has no service in the area, the facilities of Retail Credit Company operate to gather the information and complete the credit report. Conversely, if Retailers Commercial Agency is active in a market, its function is the supplying of credit reports. Thus, facilities of the Retail Credit Company and its affiliates are completely pooled, with the functions of reporting prescribed according to the organization in any particular market. For example, a major market may have a Retail Credit Company office to supply noncredit reports and a Retailers Commercial Agency office to perform the task of credit reporting. The credit bureaus, however, operate as distinct and separate organizations.

Credit and noncredit reports are supplied only to subscribers to the service. When a subscriber enters into a service contract, he is given a subscription code number, a pad of order blanks to be used in requesting reports, and various directories giving him information as to offices covering the territories from which he may desire reports. Subscribers order reports by filling out an inquiry form. These forms cover the necessary identification of the person on whom a report is desired and the type of report requested. The inquiry form is then sent either to the branch office handling the subscriber's account or directly to the office in the territory in which the subject of the investigation resides. The latter procedure, with the territory office replying directly to the customer, saves mail time. Inquiry forms are finally routed to the Home Office in Atlanta, Georgia, from which the subscriber is billed for all reports supplied, thus avoiding duplication of billing and auditing.

The information for credit and noncredit reports is gathered in essentially the same way. The field representatives gather information by means of personal interviews with business associates, friends, neighbors, tradesmen, former employers, and others. Retail Credit Company sets forth the following four steps to be followed by field representatives:[2]

Planning: Determination and location of best logical informants through reference of name of subject to city and telephone directories and other listings that indicate present and former connections. This step includes discussion of field representative's plan with his supervisor who may add suggestions based on a review of any file.

2 | *Retail Credit Company—Description—Principles—Practices* (Atlanta, Georgia: Retail Credit Company, n.d.).

Investigation: Field representatives interview these logical informants. They introduce themselves as representatives of Retail Credit Company and unless permitted do not give the name of company requesting the report. They engage in conversational interviews, leading these over the ground to be covered, briefly, courteously and in a businesslike manner. Unfavorable information is confirmed through two or more sources or through records and is supported by dates and circumstances as far as possible. Field representatives collectively make about 200,000 interviews daily.

Discussion—with supervisor after investigation—to check accuracy and adequacy of information obtained. At this time any file is turned over to the field representative to use as supplementary or confirmatory information.

Writing: Field representatives write their own reports in order to record their findings as directly as possible. They follow two basic principles:

1. Present facts only;
2. Avoid opinion or any coloring of information due to field representative's prejudice or tolerance.

In addition to the personal interview, reports may be verified or supplemented with information on file. Most reports which are entirely favorable are held in file for 13 months; reports containing derogatory information are filed for five years; and any report which is extremely derogatory is held in file seven years and then destroyed. Restrictions on the company's service, as prescribed by law,[3] call for bankruptcies being reported for only 14 years and arrests, indictments, and convictions, for 7 years after disposition, release, or parole; thus, maintaining any files for longer periods would be unnecessary. Current reports are checked against previous reports made within these time intervals to reveal inconsistencies and the relative improvement or deterioration of the subject's record, or to provide a basis for reinvestigation. In all cases the subscriber is assured that the report rendered has been currently checked by a field investigation.

Credit Reporting Services

Regular reports and *special service reports* are the two kinds of services available. Regular reports are somewhat standardized in that they cover specific facts commonly sought by the users of the service. Special service reports are made when a large amount of information is needed on an individual and a period of 10 years or one fourth the lifetime of the subject, whichever is less, is investigated. Regular reports are by far the most frequently requested by subscribers. Facts on these reports are to a great extent supplied by answers to specific questions or the filling in of blanks

3 / Sec. 605 of the Fair Credit Reporting Act (Title VI amendment of Consumer Credit Protection Act), effective April 1971.

which deal with specific types of information. Some reports have space for narrative reporting. Character credit reports on individuals serve as an appropriate example of a regular report. This report on an individual covers employment, income, resources, personal living habits, associates, antecedent history, marital status, and payment record. The character credit report on farmers develops additional facts pertinent to the appraisal of a farmer's credit, such as acreage cultivated, type of crops, equipment, livestock, and local conditions affecting farming. Although Retail Credit Company does not specialize in reports on business firms, such reports are made when requested and develop, in addition to the information on the principal individuals, information concerning the business such as length of time in business, methods of operation, net worth, and general reputation. For some purposes, such as the issuance of a gasoline credit card, reports may be condensed; for others extended.

Retail Credit Company has developed a variety of reports designed to yield the special information needed for subscribers' particular purposes. In credit reporting this has led to variation of reports to cover installment purchases, real estate transactions, and gasoline credit cards. There has also been some special variation to appraise the quality of dealers and agents. In many respects the reports on smaller businesses reflect a desirable blend of personal information about the individuals operating the business and the business itself.

Through this diversity there runs a constant centralizing thread. This is the emphasis on character credit reports and the development of information through interviews with sources who know the subject personally. Thus with all the diversity of special reporting forms, there is certain basic credit information which remains almost a constant. This information may be seen under the various headings of the standard character report: identity, employment, finances, character, and credit record (see Figure 14-1).

Special Credit Services

In addition to the regular reporting services, Retail Credit Company offers some specialized credit services. For example, a sales finance company can have the collateral securing its loans to dealers on floor-plan financing checked by a representative of the credit company. This enables the finance company to assure itself that the collateral is intact and in good condition without the time or expense involved in having an employee physically inspect the collateral. Similarly, a mortgage lender can have reports made showing completion of a construction job upon which it has agreed to lend money, or purchase a record search report to determine properties returned for taxes or ownership of a specified parcel of real estate. A

FIGURE 14-1
Character Credit Report (Individual)

RETAIL CREDIT COMPANY RETAILERS COMMERCIAL AGENCY **CHARACTER CREDIT REPORT** (INDIVIDUAL)	CONFIDENTIAL

Acct. No.   File No.

Report Made By RCC ☐ Retailers ☐ _____ OFFICE

Date

NAME (& Spouse)

REPORT FROM_____ *(If not city in heading)*   *(State whether former addr., etc.)*

Address

Emp-Occ.

Bus. Add.

Transaction:

Amount $

Mo. Notes $

IDENTITY:
1. Time known by each source?
2. Are name and address correct as given above?
3. Is subject known to file?
4. About what is age? (If around 21 verify if possible.)
5. Is applicant married, single, divorced or widowed? No. dependents? (incl. wife)

1.
2.
3. ☐ No   ☐ Yes, for_____years.
4.
5.   No. dependents

EMPLOYMENT:
6. Name of employer? (Give name of firm.)
7. What is nature of business? (State the kind of trade or industry.)
8. Position held—how long? (If less than 1 year, explain.)
9. Work full time steadily? (If not, how many days per week?)
10. Are prospects for continued permanent employment good?

6.
7.
8.   How long?
9.
10.

FINANCES:
11. What would you estimate NET WORTH?
12. Of what does worth consist principally? (Real estate, cash, stocks, bonds, etc.)
13. Does applicant own home, rent or board?
14. What is ANNUAL EARNED INCOME from work or business?
15. ADDED ANNUAL income from investments, rentals, pensions, disability, etc.?
16. If spouse employed, give name of employer.
   a. Position held—approximate ANNUAL INCOME.
   b. Approximate number of years employed.

11. $
12.
13.
14. $_____Exact ☐   Estimated ☐
15. $ Source:
16.
   a.   Income $_____
   b.

CHARACTER:
17. Is reputation as to honesty and fair dealing good?
18. Do you learn of any illegal activities, or domestic troubles? (If so, explain.)
19. Any illness (physical or mental) affecting ability to pay? (If so, explain.)

CREDIT RECORD:
20. Do you learn of any failures; bankruptcies, mortgage foreclosures, suits, judgments or garnishments against him? (If so, state which. Give details.)
21. Do sources recommend doing business with applicant on a credit basis?

17.
18.
19.
20.
21.

22. CREDIT RECORD: Set out CREDIT RECORD in tabular form below.
23. BUSINESS-FINANCES: Comment on present and past business connections, irregular employment or lack of stability. Cover subject's financial position, giving breakdown on worth.
24. PERSONAL: Show how long subject has lived in the neighborhood—how regarded. Amplify any unusual information pertaining to domestic troubles, illness learned or other features that would affect earnings or paying ability.

Date Checked	Kind of Business	How Long Selling	Highest Credit	Terms of Sale	Amount Owing	Amount Past Due	Paying record on: Specify 30, 60, 90 days, etc. (Is this in accordance with terms?) If Contract Acct., so state.

Form 63LE—1-67 U.S.A.

CHARACTER CREDIT REPORT

Courtesy of Retail Credit Company

creditor can also have a special report made on a delinquent purchaser, emphasizing property ownership and other assets held, which will aid in the decision to collect through legal processes.

Another special report is the *personnel selection report,* which emphasizes the type of information especially desired by personnel departments. These are expanded investigations showing a complete record of employment, previous employment, education, health habits, and personal traits. Such reports usually provide a record over a period of at least five years instead of the one-year minimum more common in other types of reports.

Foreign service reports also are available through Retail Credit Company's foreign service department.

The disappearance broadcast is another example of a special service. The extensive files in the various branch offices make this service possible. By subscribing to this service at a cost of $16 to $36.50 per name (depending on the scope of geographic coverage and on whether affiliates are included), a concern can have the name of a skip broadcast to all branch offices. At each of these offices a special notice is placed in the files at the proper alphabetical spot. If and when the person sought appears in any of these files, notice is immediately given the client. Special delinquent-purchaser reports may then be requested, and the creditor can determine what action to take to effect collection from the missing debtor.

Cost of Services

The rate structure of the Retail Credit Company varies depending on whether reports are being made to life and health insurance companies; are being used for credit information, collection information, and record checking by a wide assortment of firms; or are being prepared for personnel selection purposes. Further breakdowns in rate structure also are found. For example, for service to life and health insurance companies there are two types of rates: a basic charge for regular reports in any given locality, and an hourly charge for time required on special investigations. For special speed, all-wire service is available at a slight additional charge plus the cost of the telephone and telegraph expenses incurred.

Automated Services of Credit Bureau, Inc. of Georgia (CBI)

In January 1967, studies made by Credit Bureau, Inc. of Georgia (CBI), a credit affiliate of Retail Credit Company, led to the conclusion that CBI could best serve the needs and wishes of its market by automating an entire trade area. On October 1, 1970, for the first time in the history of CBI, 550,000 current credit records in the Atlanta, Georgia, metropolitan area became instantly available to its members. On January 1, 1971, three additional credit bureaus were put on line with the same Atlanta-based computer, giving members an additional nucleus of 700,000 credit records in the southeastern United States. Other bureaus are scheduled to go on line as rapidly as possible.

The following four-step procedure was described in an article in *Inspection News,* a publication of Retail Credit Company:[4]

1. When a customer calls a CBI bureau for a credit check, the terminal operator "keys" the information he gives her into a video terminal. The information passes through the bureau's terminal control unit and out over a telephone line to a data set receiver and in the regional computer center.
2. From there, the message goes to the "central processor" where it is edited for validity and proper format.
3. The credit requestor's name and address, plus other personal identifiers are used by the central processor to search the "data cell" where the file information actually is stored. The central processor reviews the identifying characteristics and selects up to four similar names, transmitting them back through the system to the terminal operator.
4. She reviews the possible options, and then selects the proper one. She keys her video terminal and the regional computer selects and instantly projects onto her screen the correct credit record. She reads the information to the customer and the transaction is complete. Elapsed time: approximately four minutes, depending on the file depth.

Evaluation of Service

Retail Credit Company and Retailers Commercial Agency and other affiliates supply a valuable addition to the credit informational facilities available to creditors. Their reports are standardized; thus, regardless of point of origin, the quality of the report and the type of information supplied will conform to the standards set by company policies. Supervision is close, and even when reports are submitted directly to the client a copy is filed at the branch office. This copy is reviewed for quality and criticized when not up to standard. Similarly, at the home office, reports are audited from time to time for quality, and offices are criticized or commended on the basis of this review. The form of the report and the operating standards are such that the substitution of opinion for fact is discouraged; the reporter is not supposed to give his personal judgment except in the portion of the report clearly so labeled. The agency attempts to be only a reporter of the record, not the maker of the record. They do not make the record nor do they evaluate it; they simply gather information which their clients may analyze and evaluate.

Costs are standardized. The subscriber knows what each type of report from each point will cost. Because of centralized billing, a single account is rendered regardless of the origin of the reports. This feature is especially appealing to firms doing a national or extensive regional credit business.

That the operation is efficient seems amply demonstrated by the

4 / "Consumer Credit & the Computer," reprinted from the November-December 1970 issue of *Inspection News,* the magazine of Retail Credit Company, p. 13.

remarkable growth of the company. In a half century it has developed from a purely local business into a national, even an international, business. It has enjoyed a constant growth which during recent years has accelerated. The cost of the reports has been held down despite constantly rising expenses, especially wage rates. Considering the amount of information supplied, the cost per report is remarkably low. This in fact may be a disadvantage, because the effort to hold down costs leads to pressure on field representatives to handle a large daily quota of reports, with consequent deterioration of quality or the use of shortcuts in report making. Perhaps creditors who insist on low report charges are to be blamed for these pressures which result in poorer quality reports.

Although Retail Credit Company in its earlier years was diverted from credit reporting into insurance reporting, the company now seems to be once again putting more emphasis on credit reporting, with consequent improvement of this reporting. This has been accomplished especially through the services of its affiliated credit bureaus. For any credit department which does more than a strictly local business, it would seem that this is a credit service designed to be of value and assistance.

SPECIALIZED CREDIT BUREAUS AND OTHER SOURCES

In addition to the retail credit bureaus and the several national credit-reporting companies, there are many specialized credit-reporting agencies throughout the country. Some of these serve particular professional groups, while others are organized to do a highly specialized type of reporting. The medical and dental profession has available the Medical Credit Bureau, which has a collection service as well as a credit-reporting service. Much educational effort has been expended in orientating medical doctors and dentists in the matter of credits and collections. These professions have had a history of poor financial management, but the educational programs of the American Medical Association, American Dental Association, and credit groups have done much to overcome past business practices. In some cities the Medical Credit Bureau is a division of or closely associated with the local credit bureau. In other cities separate bureaus are in operation for the exclusive use of these professions. The services and reports to medical and dental users do not differ fundamentally in character from the types of services rendered businesses. It is thought, however, that this development has had a substantial effect on the adoption of more uniform credit and collection procedures in these professions.

Small loan companies and a few other financial institutions have established what are generally known as lenders' exchanges. These exchanges operate in some metropolitan markets for the express purpose of servicing particular types of lending and financing institutions. It is their function to keep master records of all loans or contracts financed by their members. The records are maintained so that a rapid check can be made on the loans outstanding against a prospective loan customer for whom an inquiry is initiated. Telephone inquiries are made by subscribers and immediate reports received. This service supplies the subscriber with a listing of outstanding loans against a potential debtor and the identity of the lenders. Directing an inquiry to the lenders having had or currently having experience with the subject quickly ascertains their payment record experiences with the debtor. The subscribers or members of the exchange are obligated to disclose their loan activity by individual name, so that a complete record of the subject's similar dealings is available. Exchanges as described here more frequently service the small loan industry of a particular metropolitan area. In some cities, banks and sales finance companies also make use of similar facilities.

The network of credit investigating facilities in the United States conforms to the needs of practically all types of creditors. So complete and highly developed is this phase of credit granting that as a practical matter any credit granter has credit information sources which are easily and rapidly available to him. In those instances where the more standardized sources do not meet the needs of a particular creditor because of some unique requirements, other sources of information are available. Lawyers, bank personnel, and others with intimate knowledge of a community may be valuable sources of credit information. On occasion Dun & Bradstreet services might be used as a source of consumer credit information. Even though Dun & Bradstreet does not purport to gather consumer credit information, its ratings apply to individuals as well as businesses in some instances. Individual proprietorships and partnerships are frequently of such a nature that the credit reputation of the business and the individual is one and the same.

Intelligent selection of a reliable source of consumer credit information contributes to risk minimization. Risk minimization must be gained at relatively low cost. The vast majority of services today are standardized to meet the information needs of creditors. Standardization, which has made possible low-cost credit reporting, may reveal more information than is sometimes needed, and on occasion less information than is desired. However, economical and factual reporting as developed by various information sources has become an indispensable tool to a rational and sound credit decision.

REVIEW AND DISCUSSION QUESTIONS

1. Distinguish between those credit-reporting agencies that are local in nature and those that are national in nature.
2. Trace the history, organization, and development of Retail Credit Company.
3. How do the principles guiding the operations of Retail Credit Company vary from those of agencies in which credit information is exchanged among members?
4. How has the credit-reporting side of Retail Credit Company business been emphasized in the past 25 years?
5. Who uses the services of Retail Credit Company?
6. What methods of investigation does Retail Credit Company employ?
7. What are the four basic steps followed by Retail Credit Company inspectors? Describe each step in detail.
8. Describe the credit-reporting services of Retail Credit Company. The special credit services.
9. If there is a Retail Credit Company branch office in your community, discuss its operations with the local manager.
10. What are advantages of automated reporting of the Credit Bureau, Inc. of Georgia (CBI)? The disadvantages?
11. Describe some of the other types of specialized credit bureaus.

15

Decision Making, Limit Setting, and Transaction Handling

Decisions are the heart of all credit work. Credit is offered by customers for goods, services, and money, and credit managers must decide whether to accept or refuse the credit transaction. Judgment should be based on the information that is readily and economically available and most pertinent to the problem and on an analysis that is sufficiently penetrating to make the available data yield the greatest help possible in arriving at a correct and right decision. Generally the information at hand, or readily available without excessive cost or undue delay, is incomplete. Thus the facts that are obtained through the credit investigation must be used to the utmost in order to offset this common deficiency.

Good judgment is one of the most difficult skills to develop and one of the skills most necessary to the credit manager. Because it is so difficult to develop good credit judgment, too many credit managers have emphasized unduly the negative aspects of credit decisions. Errors of judgment as revealed by bad-debt losses are quite evident, but errors of judgment resulting in lost sales are well hidden. Thus the easy route is to err through excessive refusals of doubtful credit transactions. Sales lost because of refusals to sell accounts which would have paid and which would in turn have contributed to profits are difficult to total.

Errors of judgment may rise from insufficient information, misleading or false information, or improper interpretation of the data on hand. The investigation should be adequate to supply sufficient information on which to base a decision and should at a minimum reveal false information as well as give a basis for properly interpreting data which otherwise would be misleading. Unfortunately the pressures of time and of costs and the desire for sales often cause inadequate investigations and faulty decisions. Faulty investigations tend to increase collection costs and bad-debt losses, whereas excessive investigations tend to increase investigation costs and to lose time as well as to produce customer irritation. The credit manager thus continually attempts to walk the narrow path between extremes, hoping to compensate for the lack of data by more careful analysis.

The credit investigation brings together the raw materials which are processed through the credit analysis in order to get the final product, *the credit decision.* It is this end product which is the objective of all the efforts directed toward gathering information and of all the skill exercised in the analysis of the information.

DECISIONS—THE ESSENCE OF CREDIT WORK

The credit offered must be examined before acceptance and a decision made to accept or reject it. Making these decisions is the single most important credit activity; all other activities of the credit department are contributory to this function. True, these activities support and implement the decision, but unless the decision to accept or reject credit is sound they cannot make the credit operation entirely successful. Thus success of the credit operation rests squarely on the appraisal and acceptance of the credit offered; the activities of the credit department in administering its work and in collecting the accounts may make the operation more successful or less successful, but they cannot by themselves substitute for or replace decisions.

In making credit decisions, the credit executive must appraise or evaluate an individual's credit against the standards set by the general policy established. In order to appraise, he must have information which is supplied by the credit investigation. The analysis of this information is measured against the standards of acceptability set by the credit policy. Analysis and decision are aided by proper operating procedures. These procedures should assure needed and accurate information made meaningful by proper analytical processes. After policy is established and standards set, the subsequent stages are gathering the information through investigation, evaluating and analyzing the information, reaching the decision to accept or reject, and carrying out the credit department operations to reach the ultimate goal—payment by the customer.

Analysis and decision are necessary in every consumer credit transaction, and each transaction is an individual transaction. At the time of acceptance it is expected that this amount will be paid by this individual at some predetermined future date. When a predictable loss account is accepted, it should be called by its proper name—charity, not credit.[1] Of course, some of the accounts which appear safe when they are opened or when additional charges are added to them will eventually fail to pay. Such defaults in payment are inevitable when a forecast of the future is made, especially when it is made on the basis of incomplete information. It should be remembered that the information at hand is generally incomplete, since time and costs do not permit complete information for the usual case. Also the information may not be completely accurate. In the face of sometimes inaccurate and incomplete information, greater analytical skill must be employed. In any event it must be remembered that the goal must not, indeed it cannot, be perfection in the sense of no losses. It must rather be losses within the limits set by the credit policy. Evaluation and analysis can contribute to sounder credit decisions.

Credit information is necessarily somewhat incomplete. It is needlessly costly and time-consuming to try to make it complete. In addition, not all information will be verified; some of the information must be accepted as the basis for decision without verification, and some will be verified only by reasonable inference. Despite these limitations, the first step of the analysis should be to evaluate the credit information at hand. This step of evaluation should be based on a complete review of the credit file and an examination of all information therein. During this examination the two questions, "How complete is the information?" and, "Is the information verified?" should always be in the forefront of the analyst's thinking. The source of the information will lend greater or lesser credibility to certain statements. Other statements may be considered reliable because they are consistent with other facts. By way of illustration, the salary or income claimed by a credit applicant has not been verified through his employer or other sources; we only have the statement on the application. However, we know it is in line with the community level for similar occupations or it is consistent with the amounts paid by that employer. The length of employment has not been verified either, but it coincides with information at hand relative to the period of residence in the community and the stated age of the applicant. Or, as an example of negative evaluation, there is one very favorable reference letter in the file; however, the writer is not personally known to us and from the appearance of the letter it is from an individual, a personal friend of

---

1 / Failure to recognize the distinction between charity and credit causes many doctors to complain of large bad-debt losses. The doctor often feels that he cannot refuse to give a patient the benefit of his skill even though there is no prospect of payment. If such contributions were correctly labeled as charity rather than entered on the books as credit, he would not confuse his charity cases with bad-debt losses.

the applicant. Conversely the information from known informants may be considered more reliable than that from those unknown, or information from a professional credit-reporting source may be evaluated higher than information from personal sources.

It is not suggested that evaluation of credit information be made a separate part of the credit analysis. It is suggested, however, that prior to analysis the entire file be reviewed for credibility and completeness. If sufficient information is not at hand, the investigation should be extended. Under these conditions the specific character of information still needed is known, and the additional investigation can be pointed toward obtaining the exact data desired. When the information is not regarded as reliable or believable, the points in doubt can be cleared up by directing the additional investigation specifically toward these issues. In addition to this review prior to the analysis, the evaluation should be continued during the course of the analysis. As each element of the credit case is examined the judgment of its quality should be mentally tested against the evaluation of the information as to completeness and credibility. Thus when the final credit decision is reached, its reliability or unreliability can be based on the completeness and credibility of the source information.

CREDIT IS RELATIVE

It has been pointed out that a particular credit transaction must be measured against the standards of certainty of payment and found acceptable or unacceptable on the basis of the standards established by the credit policies of the firm. In effect, the determination must be whether or not the particular case falls within the limits established by these credit policies. Obviously judgment is necessarily relative, not an absolute certainty. Judgment is necessarily subject to error and information is necessarily relative, not an absolute certainty. Judgment is necessarily subject to error and information is necessarily somewhat incomplete; accordingly the decision can at best be only a close approximation of reality. If selection is to be confined to only those accounts which will undoubtedly pay under all circumstances, very little extra business will result from the decision to offer the credit service. To put it another way, the soundly operating credit department should have some losses—if it does not, it is selecting its accounts so strictly that some profitable business is not being obtained.

Of course, no policy makers can deal with a concept such as standards with exactness. They can at best adopt policies that seek a high degree of certainty of payment, or they can adopt policies that seek a somewhat lower degree of certainty of payment. From time to time the need for volume, general economic conditions, the nature of the clientele sought, the territorial conditions, or various other environmental situations may cause them to change previous standards.

Credit standards are intimately related to other marketing policies. If selling desires and requirements call for solicitation of trade from preferred customers for a high-quality product, the credit standards can be high indeed. Conversely, when selling policies call for the seeking of patronage from a mass market and for an economy model of the product, somewhat lower credit standards may be indicated.

It is usual to associate stricter terms with lower credit standards. For example, when the credit standards permit acceptance of credit from customers falling in the lower payment-probability ranges the terms might be weekly, or payday terms, for open account sales. For installment sales of durable goods, the lower the credit standard the more necessary it is to obtain down payments which establish a feeling of ownership and monthly payments of an amount and frequency to steadily increase this equity. When credits of lower standard are accepted, it is more important that the time and the amount of the payments be adjusted to the time income is received and the amounts of the income received. Unhappily, easier terms attract lower rated credit risks, and the task of rejecting those which are truly substandard becomes more difficult.

Difficult as it may be to set exact standards and intangible as this concept may prove to be, it is necessary in the daily operations of the credit department to compare specific cases against the standards established and accept those which measure up and reject those which are regarded as substandard. The easy cases are those which are clearly acceptable and those which are definitely substandard. The effort of the credit department can then be concentrated on selecting the acceptable and unacceptable accounts from the minority which are not clearly acceptable. The clearly good cases would not need a credit department—the clearly bad can be detected so easily no great skill is required. The talent must all be exercised upon the number which fall into the probably-good-enough class.

GRADING AS AN ANALYTICAL DEVICE

An aid to careful interpretation is to separate the total quality of the credit into the specifics or elements of the credit. The quality of the whole is, in effect, the net summation of the quality of a number of credit elements or pieces. When each factor of the credit is considered separately, the judgment about each can be arrived at somewhat independently without the reflection or halo effect which certain elements are likely to cast over the whole. When a credit decision is made on an overall basis—the credit is acceptable, or the credit is not acceptable—one or two elements are likely to exercise an undue influence on the judgment. The decision-making process is better when each pertinent element is considered separately and given its proper appraisal. This tends to avoid overlooking items which are pertinent or giving relatively unimportant items excessive weight, and it gives more assurance that all available evidence is brought to bear upon the problem in a properly weighted fashion. Unless the available evidence is carefully analyzed, the decision is apt to be faulty.

Two major points should be recognized: (1) credit quality is a relative evaluation, not an absolute measurement; and (2) measurement of a number of specific factors is likely to be more accurate than a single overall judgment. In the decision-making process these two generalizations may be attained through the device of grading the credit. *Grading the credit is simply the examination of evidence and the recording of the quality judgment drawn from specific evidence bearing on specific factors in an orderly manner.* It is the assignment of a quality grade or rating to each pertinent element of the credit appraisal and finally assigning a summary grade which reflects the combined judgment of the whole credit.

Separate grading of all factors pertinent to the decision permits these specific factors to be appraised independently on the basis of evidence relevant to each. When a quality grade is assigned, the relative evaluation is recorded for that factor. Skilled and experienced credit personnel do this automatically, perhaps unconsciously. A formal grading device assures that the less experienced person will do what the more experienced credit analyst does informally. By working through a rather formal method of grading, the beginner is assured of sound analytical practices and begins to employ good habits of analysis. Thus the product, the credit decision, will be improved and will become more standardized.

If the grading process is formal and systematic, the beginner is assured that all elements pertinent to a decision have been considered; that all available evidence has been used in reaching a decision. He also can have before him the extent to which the information has been verified, and if he is unable to reach a decision because of insufficient verification or inadequate information he can proceed to verify more evidence or to gather additional information. In other words, the process of grading also can indicate the extent of the investigation needed and point to the sort of investigation that will be most rewarding in the specific case.

Elements to Be Graded

Certain classifications of evidence are almost standard subjects for analysis in any consumer credit appraisal. Certainly evidence relative to income, employment, and payment habits would be accepted as essential in any analysis. Some additional qualities such as residence, marital status, age, reserve assets, references, and reputation may be more debatable. Obviously no one list of qualities will be accepted by all credit analysts, nor will any one list best meet the needs of all credit situations. For example, analysis of an installment purchase becomes more meaningful when equity in the purchase is added. When the dealer has some contingent responsibility, as is often the case when such paper is discounted with a sales finance company, the dealer's credit standing attains added importance. Similarly, when analyzing a cash loan the grade assigned to collateral usually has considerable meaning and the purpose of the loan may be a classification of evidence worthy of having a grade assigned to it.

Credit Grading Form

The grading forms which follow (see Figures 15-1 and 15-2) illustrate classifications of information which are important to a credit decision and include those qualities which are sufficient to assure a complete appraisal of the credit applicant. For practical reasons it is suggested that the credit qualities to be graded should be limited in number—too long a list makes the operation unduly time-consuming and also causes difficulty in appraising the evidence sharply. Too brief a list of qualities may not bring all the evidence into sharp focus, since it causes judgments to be formed on the basis of an unrepresentative list of qualities. The items suggested are intermediate between an extended list and an abbreviated list and are about the number which experience indicates to be practical in an operating sense.

The evidence obtained during the course of the investigation does not fall into neat and mutually exclusive classifications consistent with the qualities which it may have been decided to grade. The same items of evidence, or the same factual information, may be used in determining the grade on several qualities. This situation will be apparent as the grading of income is illustrated in the following example.

Let us start with a subject named John Doe, who receives an income of $175 a week. With these limited facts it is difficult to grade the income, for nothing is known of the certainty of its continuance nor of the demands upon it. It cannot be said whether it

FIGURE 15-1
Option-Terms Revolving Credit Account Grading Form

Credit Qualities	Grade			Verified
	Good 1	Fair 2	Poor 3	
Income				
Employment				
Residence				
Marital status				
Age				
References				
Reserve assets				
Payment record				
Reputation				
Summary—overall appraisal				
Limit:	Accept _____ Refuse _____			
Special Conditions:				

is adequate without knowing, Adequate for what? or whether it is certain without knowing, Relative to what? If we obtain the information through a telephone call to the employer that he is employed as a cutter in a local shoe factory, has been so employed for seven years, and is 31 years old, a judgment can be formed that the income is likely to continue based on his age and length of employment. Of course, the judgment becomes better if through knowledge of local conditions something is known of the shoe business and the market position of the local shoe factory. Knowledge is further improved when something is known of the employment policies of the local company. These comments illustrate the value to the credit analyst of general knowledge of local and national business conditions.

With the facts now before us we might be warranted in assigning a grade of 1 on the income quality of the credit although we still would not be able to grade exactly on the issue of relative adequacy of the income. The information about income also is verified and may be so noted on the grading form. Other facts may help us to

FIGURE 15-2
Cash Loan Grading Form

| Credit Qualities | Grade | | | Verified |
	Good 1	Fair 2	Poor 3	
Income				
Employment				
Residence				
Marital status				
Age				
References				
Reserve assets				
Payment record				
Reputation				
Collateral				
Purpose of loan				
Summary—overall appraisal				
	Accept_____ Refuse_____			

grade by forming a judgment as to adequacy. Suppose we add the information that he is married, has one child, and has lived in the community for 15 years. On the basis of the information before us, we now might be willing to assign a grade of 1 to income and to consider the grade verified. Income of $175 a week, which on the basis of seven years' employment with the same company in a skilled occupation is reasonably certain to continue, should be adequate to the needs of a married couple with one child.

To illustrate the sort of information which might cause a change to a lower grade, some facts might be added which would make the income appear somewhat inadequate. Illustrative of this situation would be the existence of other obligations. Let us assume that the credit bureau reports that the John Does have purchased their home and have contracted to make payments on this purchase of $140 a month; they also are buying a Pontiac automobile purchased five months ago upon which they have contracted to make 24 payments of \$115 a month; a department store reports a balance of \$175 with payments slow; a clothing store, balance of \$57, payments 60 days slow; and a men's store reports no balance now, but were slow previously. This family may have assumed commitments which are excessive relative to their income.[2] Because the income may not be adequate relative to the obligations, a grade of 2 may be assigned to the income in the light of these new facts. A grade of 3 would be warranted if the information indicated the continuance of the income to be doubtful; for example, knowledge that the shoe factory was about to shut down for 60 days because of a lack of orders.

Procedure in Using Grading Forms.   When using the grading forms previously illustrated, or similar forms, the credit analyst records his appraisal of each credit quality in the appropriate column. These columns may be considered adjectively: good, fair, or poor. Or they may be given numerical grades, 1, 2, or 3. Only a threefold division is suggested, since finer graduations may confuse the process more than they would contribute to the end result. The description of the general grading standards suggested is as follows:

Good, 1:   Those credit qualities which indicate that the credit will be redeemed with no more than normal difficulty or effort.

Fair, 2:   Those credit qualities which indicate that the credit will be redeemed but only after abnormal difficulties or delays and in response to active collection effort.

Poor, 3:   Those credit qualities which indicate that the credit will not be redeemed.

Although the same information may be used in grading several specific credit qualities, the analyst should attempt to keep the qualities separate in his mind as he works. Thus although existing obligations and manner of payment may be used to qualify the income as adequate for the obligations and family responsibility, they should be used only as they apply to income when that quality is considered. When the analyst considers them under the payment record quality, he should eliminate the income factor from consideration and grade separately on payment record. Only by so doing can the individual qualities be given their proper importance in developing a properly weighted summary judgment.

What grading should accomplish is a prediction of credit experience. This prediction, or forecast, should reflect the best

2 / Undoubtedly, this statement will be challenged by some readers. One commerical bank lender has pointed out that by his rule of thumb of salary alone this customer would be worthy of credit in the amount of \$500 above and beyond the commitments for house and automobile. He also pointed out that although the slow pay might in some instances cause the bank to say no, or in other instances to consolidate the debt or to reduce the amount which might be granted, the bank might be willing to lend as much as \$300 for reasonable purposes.

possible overall judgment considering all the evidence at hand. Earlier, grading was recommended as a device which would assure that all pertinent factors were considered and would avoid undue influence by a single especially favorable or unfavorable piece of evidence. Now caution is suggested against *not* being influenced by a single unfavorable or favorable credit quality. In the final prediction a single highly unfavorable quality (for example, inadequate or uncertain income, a very adverse payment record, or a reputation for very poor morals) might very properly dictate the grade. Any one of the above might well justify a grade of 3 even though all other elements of the credit appraisal were favorable. After all, the end result is a credit decision which, after considering all the evidence and properly analyzing it, forecasts the credit experience that it is reasonable to predict. Although the forecast cannot be 100 percent correct, the orderly and systematic making of it should improve the accuracy of decision making.

The summary grades may be defined as follows:

Good, 1: Predicts excellent to satisfactory experience. Clearly the credit is acceptable.

Fair, 2: Predicts possible unsatisfactory experience but not so clearly predictable as to warrant rejection. Although credit losses and excessive costs will arise from the handling of such accounts, it is not possible to label the one being graded as a certain loss. The maximum investigation and the most penetrating analysis should be lavished on such credits in order to screen out and reject those which should be more correctly labeled 3.

Poor, 3: Predicts unsatisfactory experience with sufficient certainty that it warrants rejection. In other words, rejection does not deprive the creditor of a potential profit nor prevent a worthy customer from having his credit accepted. Instead it saves the creditor from a predictable loss, and it prevents a debtor from adding to his unredeemable obligations.

Use of Credit Grade in Operations

When credit grades are used, their usefulness may be extended beyond the aid they supply to the making of credit decisions.

The summary grade is a prediction of future experience. This prediction may be used to determine the type of collection effort and the time when it is to be applied. When a credit which was highly questionable at the time of acceptance is up for collection, the gentler collection reminders should be abandoned quickly and more severe collection devices applied. Routine and reminder types of collections are not appropriate, and early personal handling is indicated. The cases graded 2 will be pushed to a decision more rapidly than those initially graded 1. Thus the grading guides the intensity of collection effort and will assist in obtaining satisfactory results from lower quality credits.

The quality of business also can be analyzed by means of the credit grades assigned. New accounts currently opened can be compared with accounts opened during past periods and a larger or smaller proportion of 2 credits can be taken as an indication that better or poorer quality credits are being put on the books. Or when the business comes from different areas in a city, the quality generated by various areas can be compared on the basis of the proportion of 1 and 2 quality accounts. Various means of promoting credit sales can be compared on the same basis, and promotion by direct mail, or newspaper advertisements, or solicitation on the floor can be compared as to quality. These various comparisons which grading makes possible enable the credit department to be operated more intelligently and purposefully.

When several people are employed in a credit department, analysis of the grades assigned by each can be helpful in comparing their operations. Comparison of the actual experience of accounts can be made with the grade initially assigned, and more uniform judgments may result from this educational experience.

The development of the grading technique and learning how to apply it is in itself a useful educational device. Credit analysis can become better because of the emphasis on improving the grading skill, and comparison of actual experience with predicted experience will help in self-criticism and self-improvement. Also newer employees will learn the art of making sound credit decisions more quickly when their decision making is directed by the grading system. Consideration of the credit qualities and their measurement relative to payment probability help the new employee develop his analytical skill and improve his judgment.

Grading accomplishes the "easy" part of separating those cases which are clearly acceptable and those which are definitely substandard. It is within the number 2 category that credit decision making faces its greatest challenge. Some credit analysts believe that credit scoring, as described in the subsequent section, may hold a key to solving this problem.

Credit Scoring Plans

In recent years some companies have adopted an operating tool in an effort to improve credit decisions and to gain more control over the decision-making process. This tool is called credit scoring or, sometimes, a numerical pointing plan. The following definition of credit scoring has been given:[3]

Credit scoring is simply a system of numeric values for various credit attributes, e.g., so many points for owning a home, so many for being married, and so on. The point values for each applicant are accumulated and if a pre-determined minimum is attained, credit is granted. Credit-scoring systems are generally designed from a statistical analysis of random samples of "good" credit applicants (those who paid their bills) and "bad" applicants (those who defaulted). Typically, the system is tailor-made for each application. In recent years it has been used for bank consumer loans and mail-order house and retail store accounts.

The requisites of an effective credit scoring system have been outlined as follows:[4]

1. The system should quantify the odds that an applicant will pay as agreed. This enables management to make the decision to grant or not grant credit in accordance with a previously set corporate policy on how much risk management is willing to take. Essential in an effective scoring system are the mechanisms for (a) originally setting the acceptable degree of risk at management level, rather than at sub-unit levels, and for (b) subsequently enabling management to change the degree of risk as circumstances require.

2. Scores should be based on the company's own experience as obtainable from samples of good accounts, bad accounts, and rejects—as in contrast to some generalized system or one borrowed from another company.

3. All the available characteristics of an applicant should be considered in the development phase of the system—as in contrast to preselection of some characteristics found useful elsewhere.

4. Procedures should be readily usable by credit people at field level, with minimum training.

5. The system should lend itself to providing both an early warning on the accounts likely to turn bad, and indications warranting upward revisions in individual account credit limits.

6. The system should provide controls on sub-unit results, indicating where management attention needs to be directed in case of deteriorating sub-unit performance.

7. The operational phase of the credit scoring system (as opposed to the developmental phase) should be designed so that at the proper time it can readily be incorporated into the overall management information system.

8. The system should lend itself both to refinement in the light of on-going experience and to periodic updating.

3 / J. T. Presby and S. R. Simon, "Credit Scoring Can Save Money and Improve Credit Granting Too," reprinted from *Stores Magazine*, October 1969, copyrighted 1969 by National Retail Merchants Association, p. 17.

4 / Herbert J. H. Roy and Edward M. Lewis, "Overcoming Obstacles in Using Credit Scoring Systems," *Credit World,* June 1970, p. 18.

However, there are certain obstacles in the use of credit scoring systems, and these have been well described in the following quotation:[5]

> The last decade has seen a tremendous breakthrough in the improvement of tools available to those who grant credit or make loans. These tools consist of information systems which quantify the risks involved in granting credit to applicants. Such systems, called credit scoring or pointing, use computers to process the astronomically large number of calculations required to determine the predictive values of applicants' individual characteristics. At the same time, despite the sophistication needed to develop these systems, the techniques for actual use in the field can be mastered in a matter of hours.
>
> Yet to date, we know from country-wide contacts that, despite the success experienced by some companies with credit scoring systems, the installation of such systems in banks, finance companies, retail merchandising companies, and credit card issuing concerns is still rather limited.
>
> . . . .
>
> Obstacles to installation and use of credit scoring can be grouped into three categories: (1) obstacles in getting managements to try credit scoring systems in the first place; (2) obstacles in installing a system; and (3) obstacles in later operation. . . .

Although credit scoring systems are not too widely used today, it can be expected that as the volume of new credit applications continues to increase and as more and more firms develop some fully automated system of credit control, an increasing number of firms will begin to experiment with and to adopt some type of numerical pointing plan. Likewise, writing on this subject is bound to increase, explaining the successes attained in the use of this technique.[6]

SETTING THE CREDIT LIMITS AFTER THE DECISION

The term "retail credit limits"[7] is understood by credit personnel to refer to the maximum amount of credit which it is desired to permit the customer to charge. It has been suggested that a better term would be "guide" or "line," since the limits are not considered as absolutes but merely as guides in the handling of the account. They may be changed rather freely or even exceeded should circumstances warrant it. Regardless of what they are to be called, their usefulness in the operation of the credit system should be understood.

At the time an account is originally opened it is subjected to the most complete review and examination which it is likely to have for

5 | *Ibid.,* p. 5.

6 | For a discussion of credit scoring plans, see Suggested Readings at the end of the chapter.

7 | Most of the discussion in this section applies primarily to the retail field.

some time. At that moment it may be possible for the credit manager, or credit analyst, to set a more definite quantitative limit than he is likely to be in a position to fix at any subsequent time. He has just completely analyzed the information available; he has thought more carefully about the payment possibilities of the account than he is likely to do at any future time. Why not, at this point, state specifically the dollar amount for which he thinks the customer is reasonably good? Further, the effort to state specifically the amount which he would accept from the customer will make the credit manager subject the account to a more careful and searching analysis than if he were merely to think of it in general terms. He must commit himself to a specific dollar figure. This necessarily makes for more careful and penetrating analysis than otherwise would be the case.

Are there any other advantages to the use of credit guides in addition to this stimulus to more penetrating analysis? By the use of credit guides, the manager is relieved of the responsibility of passing upon day-to-day transactions. His judgment is exercised at the opening of the account. If the judgment is sound, it will continue to control the account for subsequent use. Thus, during the normal life of the relationship, responsibility for additional charges to the account may safely be delegated to other personnel. This is a safe practice, since they are merely following the routine procedure of approving day-to-day sales within the control limit which has been established by the responsible executive after the exercise of his most careful judgment. This relieves him of much of the routine work of handling daily transactions. Further, being relieved of this routine work, he can more carefully perform the other difficult tasks which fall to his position. If he were to be responsible for routine tasks as well as the major decisions on policy and other difficult problems, it is probable that he would perform the routine rather carelessly, attempting to approve day-to-day purchases from memory or after only a rather cursory examination of the credit file. With set limits, the judgment is carefully reached, and future transactions are maintained in accordance with this original judgment by a rather routine, matter of form, check. In fact, even if a credit manager were to do all the authorization himself, he probably would find it a convenience and an economy in the handling of the routine portion of the task to set limits and follow them.

Further, the use of credit limits permits finer control of the account during day-to-day operations. Suppose a person of rather weak credit desires to open an account. While the credit is not strong enough to convince the credit manager at the time of opening the account that he should carry it on an unrestricted basis, it may be believed that it is not bad enough to reject and that the customer is deserving of a trial period. Without the use of limits it is hard to enforce this period of trial, but with limits those accounts can be easily handled on such a basis. They may be opened with a very small limit, or with no limit, and put on a straight refer basis. This way the account will have every credit purchase scrutinized from a credit standpoint and, during the period of trial, will be very closely supervised. After the period of trial the account may be put on a larger credit limit, or on an unrestricted basis. Or we may have an account which is opened with a reasonable credit limit, but which has behaved in an unsatisfactory manner. Without limits it is hard to correct the handling of the account and approve day-to-day purchases in accordance with the manner the customer has treated the obligation. With limits, this account may be handled on a straight refer basis, or as an overlimit account, and every transaction will be carefully scrutinized.

Possible Techniques to Be Used

Although the use of limits is well recognized and their advantages are quite evident, it is difficult to recommend highly any one method for fixing the limit. Methods are necessarily rather inexact, and in many instances arbitrary. Variations occur between the types of credit plans involved, for example between the option-terms revolving credit plan, the installment plan, and the open charge account plan. Variations also appear between retail transactions, service transactions, and cash loans from financial institutions.

Some credit departments attempt to limit the account to a certain period of time; that is, a month's purchases, a week's purchases, or some definite time. In some lines of trade this makes a normal sort of limit. Thus the milk companies will accept credit equal to about one month's purchases. If they are attempting to control the account a bit more exactly, they may calculate the quantity which would be purchased over a month by a family of the size in question. This would give them a dollar figure rather than just a period of time. The utility companies, such as the water, light, or telephone companies, are likewise almost compelled by the nature of the business to accept as a minimum the quantity which may be used between meter reading and statement time. They may, of course, reduce the risk exposure somewhat by requiring a meter deposit or some protective measure involving advance payment, but in many instances these are being abandoned. A period of time constitutes a rather natural limit for the operator of, say a filling station, or a small retail grocer.

Some credit men, in the course of the credit interview for the opening of a regular 30-day account, will persuade the customer to fix his own limit. Some of them accomplish this by asking, "What do you want as a limit on your purchases?" or, "Do you have any amount you want to place as a limit on your purchases?" Others will approach it a little more tactfully by asking the question, "About how much do you think you will buy in the course of the month?" After the customer has replied a suggested amount, the next statement may be, "Shall we then consider this as being the limit you place on your purchases?" or "Shall we then consider this as being the indicated maximum amount of your requirements?"

In this discussion it is not intended to imply that complete uniformity is to be sought, or is desirable, in connection with the quality standard which the creditor firm follows in determining the quantity of credit desirable to accept from any one debtor. These are matters to be determined by the individual firm and to be enforced through the operation of the credit department. The policy on the quality of credit to be accepted is one which should be adjusted to the general sales policies and it must be consistent with the patronage appeal, the location, the line of goods carried, and the local and general business conditions. The policy on the quantity of credit to be accepted from any one debtor should be adjusted to the financial resources of the creditor, the credit standing of the debtor, and the type of credit plan involved.

HANDLING THE TRANSACTION

After a retail account has been established, some systems must be set up whereby credit management may control the purchases of the individual using credit. There are really two phases—identification and authorization—in connection with this control of the approval of day-to-day purchases. The final step in most credit transactions is billing the customer for purchases made during the previous month. In this final step, consideration will be given to cycle billing, "country club" billing, and descriptive billing.

Techniques of Identification and Authorization

The first phase may be called the identification phase. This is the technique of making sure that the person purchasing is the party who has an account and is not an imposter—namely, someone attempting to buy upon someone else's account or against a nonexistent account.[8] Identification is especially acute in connection with charge-take purchases—that is, purchases which the customer wishes

---

8 / Considerable research work is being conducted in connection with possible new identification techniques, including voice prints, magnetic tapes, code numbers, etc.

to take with him. With charge-send purchases the task of identification is much simpler, because some measure of assurance is afforded through delivery of the purchase to the address of the party having the account. This assurance is, of course, absent when the customer takes the goods with him, and thus it is important to protect the store against possible fraudulent purchases.

The speed element further complicates this activity in that the customer, after having made a selection, does not wish to be delayed in receipt of the merchandise. He may ask to be shown every article in stock and spend hours making up his mind as to what he wants. But after this decision is once reached, he wants the article instantly; therefore, any identification system must be speedy if it is to avoid customer ill will. Further, the problem of identification is one which must be handled with the least embarrassment to the customer. Certain positive means of identification are not readily available because they apparently accuse the customer of lying. He knows perfectly well that he is Mr. John Jones and doesn't see why anyone else should doubt this evident fact. Therefore, the best identification systems are those which do not flatly reveal to the customer that this process is being attempted.

The second aspect in handling the day-to-day charges to customers' accounts is the authorization phase. Authorization is the control of the quantity of credit used by the customers. The account is open, but this does not mean for an indefinite amount of credit. For each customer there must be some quantity of credit which is the maximum the store is willing to accept,[9] and some means of control must be maintained of the day-to-day purchases if the total is to be kept within or near this established maximum point. This quantitative limit may be fixed by the credit line decided for the account at the time the account is opened or by the credit guides used by the store. To enforce this, there must be some checks upon the freedom of use of the credit account.

Identification by Credit Plate. Identification is often combined with authorization. While it is wise to attempt to keep them apart, at the same time it should be recognized that in some systems both identification and authorization are solved at the same time. Identification may be made by issuing credit cards or some similar device. Certain retail stores issue credit cards which, upon being displayed to the sales person, serve to identify the customer.

Identification by Signature. Another technique of identification frequently used is for the customer to be requested to sign the sales ticket. Should the customer claim that he did not make the purchase, the signature on the sales ticket may be sufficient evidence to convince him that he actually made the purchase. If he is not

9 / Albert Williams, "Refusing Credit Privileges," *Credit World*, September 1968, p. 25.

convinced by this, it will be good evidence in case it is necessary to institute legal action. In those stores which return the original sales slips with the monthly statements, the customer is confronted with his signature and generally does not raise any question as to whether the charge is actually his. This has drastically reduced customer inquiries to the credit department as to the accuracy of the amount shown on the statement.

Identification by Personal Recognition. In some stores, frequently the smaller stores, identification is handled by personal recognition on the part of the clerk or manager of the store, and there is no need for more elaborate systems of identification. In some large stores, the department head may perform the identification function and does this by his personal nodding acquaintance with great numbers of customers, supplemented by his judgment in detecting impostors whom he may recognize by their attitude or actions (undue nervousness, for example).

Waiver of Identification. Although it can hardly be called a system, in some stores this task of identification is handled by being waived. Thus on purchases below a certain amount, say $5, the clerk is authorized to accept the customer's own word as complete identification. Only on larger purchases is the signature on the sales ticket transmitted to the credit department for more positive identification. This may handle the identification problem, or at least avoid considering it a problem, in the great majority of purchases.

Sales Floor Authorization. As mentioned earlier, authorization is an attempt to control the use of the account—the quantitative use of it. In stores where many accounts are handled, it would be rather inconvenient for the authorizers to compare the current purchase against the outstanding balance of the account each time a purchase is made. In order to speed up the process of authorization, there are many cases in which it is found advisable to permit authorization in the sales section. This may be done by permitting the department manager to release the merchandise, and he will combine this with the identification function. At other times, or in certain sections of the store, the salespeople themselves may be permitted to release merchandise up to $5 or $10, or above. This often varies depending upon the season of the year; the busier the time, the higher the floor-release limit. In sections where there is a great volume of charge-takes on small purchases—such as cosmetics, hosiery, or some of the other impulse goods—the closing of the transaction is speeded up by permitting the salespeople to release up to some predetermined floor-release limit. This makes for customer goodwill and also increases the flow of traffic through the store. It further saves the credit department the burden of handling a great many small charges.

The credit plate, in addition to serving as a means of identification, also may be used as a device for authorization. The restriction of plate issuance to customers with fairly high credit often permits the release of merchandise upon the presentation of the plate up to fairly large amounts, in some cases as large as $25 or even above. Thus the plate acts both as release and authorization, as well as identification of the customer.

Off-the-Floor Authorization. In those instances in which authorization is accomplished off the sales floor, some means of communication between the sales floor and the credit department is necessary. When using a telephone system, each sales section is connected directly with the authorization section of the credit department. After the sale is made the salesclerk calls the credit department and repeats to the authorizer the name and address of the customer as shown on the sales slip and the dollar amount of the contemplated purchase. If the authorizer finds the account as listed in her files and if the purchase is within the limit which she is permitted to approve, she will furnish an authorization number to the salesperson. This number will then be recorded on the sales slip; in addition, in some firms the automobile license number of the customer will be recorded on the sales slip as well. It should be kept in mind that the increasing number of computer installations has brought about new techniques of credit management which will be discussed in the subsequent section on "Automated Approaches to Credit Control." If the credit is not authorized, the customer usually is asked to step up to the credit department. Generally it is considered unwise to allow the salesclerk to take up questions of credit with customers, since noncredit personnel are not usually competent to do so as tactfully as would be possible in the privacy of the credit department.

Charge-Send Authorization. As with the identification step, it is likewise true with authorization that the time problem is not nearly as pressing with charge-send purchases.

Automated Approaches to Credit Control

Automated systems of credit control are in operation in an increasing number of business firms and are handling paper work of all kinds and varieties. Just what will be the extent of the impact of automation, the so-called second industrial revolution, upon credit transactions, upon the credit office, and upon the credit executive?[10] To give some insight into this developing situation, the following

10 / "Computerized Credit Checking New Retail Tool for Seventies," *Women's Wear Daily,* November 30, 1970, p. 25.

article has been chosen because of the interesting explanation of what is currently being done in this connection:[11]

For profitable growth in today's business climate, the independent retailer must devote a good portion of his attention to two specific management functions: (1) identifying the store's clientele and building their loyalty; and (2) managing the store from an information-oriented point of view, especially as far as credit operations are concerned.

In practice, the two management elements are closly related. The ability of a store to sponsor and control its own credit plan is a major factor today in building customer service and loyalty. Further, a well-run program which the retailer conducts on his own can affect a store's profitability by reducing the cost of extending credit to customers.

One of the outstanding tools available to assist management in meeting these responsibilities is the exclusive store-identity credit card. The same type of card, of course, has been a long-standing tool of the major department and chain stores for establishing customer loyalty, providing customer convenience and realizing high volumes per transaction.

The experience of two greater Los Angeles men's stores has firmly established that these benefits can be realized by independent merchants just as easily as by the retailing giants.

The firms involved are Murray's Custom Clothes, Los Angeles, a downtown operation that emphasizes quality custom tailoring, and Lennard's Men's Store, Lynwood, a suburban outlet featuring quality, ready-made men's clothing. Both Murray's and Lennard's have implemented a system that automatically handles exclusive credit cards, and at the same time captures all of the data necessary for information-oriented management of accounts receivable, basically as a by-product of ringing up the sale.

The credit cards themselves are standard, embossed plastic units. But, in addition to having the customer's name and account number embossed in the lower half, the account number is also encoded in machine-readable punched holes in the heading area.

According to Murray's and Lennard's, these cards go a long way toward building customer loyalty. In fact, they report, the customers are proud of them and many even flash them when they come into the store. And, by issuing the cards themselves, the stores are able to identify their customers and build their computerized mailing lists for special promotions and advertising.

When a customer makes a charge account purchase, the credit card is inserted in the special card reader on one of the NCR 53 sales registers that are the heart of the system. At the same time the cashier keys in the inventory classification number of the merchandise sold, the amount and the sales tax.

Register Records

This information is recorded by the NCR 53 in two ways: first, a standard audit journal is printed for use as an in-store record to balance out the contents

11 / R. A. Knowles, "Clothing Stores Control Credit With Computers," *Credit World*, August 1970, pp. 14-15.

of the cash drawer at the end of the day; second, a duplicate journal tape is printed in National Optical Font (NOF) characters for further processing at the NCR Data Processing Center in Hawthorne, California.

These optical font journals are especially convenient, since they can be read both by people and by the NCR 120 optical scanners at the data center. The scanner, reading numbers and symbols from the NOF tape, operates on-line to an NCR 315 computer which, in turn, encodes the information onto magnetic tape for automatic processing. The data center's computers, in turn, produce customer bills and management reports.

The retailers send their NOF tapes to the center at the end of each week. There: (1) An initial validation run is made on the computer to check for errors. A validation report listing all sales register ringup errors is printed out by the computer and returned to the stores. This enables the stores to correct any errors before they get printed in statements and reports.

And (2) at the end of each month, all of the corrected information is fed to the NCR computer along with the master files which include customer master files (account numbers, names, addresses, credit data, purchase history, accounts receivable status, etc.) and descriptive information on merchandise classifications. The computer prints out management reports, prepares statements for customers and updates the master files to reflect current status.

The statements produced by the computer are in modern, descriptive format. For each item purchased by a customer, the computer picks up from its files and prints a description of the merchandise. Bills are extended automatically—including the computation and adding of service charges on accounts which have balances more than 30 days old. The businesslike appearance of these computer-produced statements helps both to enhance store prestige and encourage prompt payment—since customers soon learn that followup and service charge have been automated by the computer.

Following printing of statements, which are stuffed and mailed by the NCR center, the computer produces a monthly selective analysis report of customer credit. Amounts owed by customers are columnized to pinpoint past-due accounts for guidance in collection followup. A copy of the report is kept in the store as a day-to-day reference in collecting payments against customer accounts.

Other Uses

Besides using the NCR registers to record sales, they can be used as input devices for other merchandising information. For example, the units are used at both Murray's and Lennard's to key in information covering receipts on charge accounts for computer processing. Also, the registers can be used for entries on receipts of new merchandise from vendors. These records would be used to update inventory classification files used in situations where retailers elected to receive merchandise classification information from the computer.

Murray Kafka, owner of Murray's, describes the results this way: "The computer doesn't have any friendships with the customers the way our now-retired credit manager did. If the account is late, a notice and carrying charges are printed on the statement. The results have been surprising.

"Very few customers have expressed any irritation at the reminder (they blame it on the computer) and at the same time, they are paying their bills quicker. In fact, our collection rate has increased at least 15 percent since we started the system."

Murray's and Lennard's are similar as far as the credit part of their operations go. That is, each has about 2,000 active accounts and each has the cards made by the same service in Los Angeles. Also, each store issues only one card to a family, so if the husband has the card and the wife comes in, she must do her shopping on a "no-carry" basis.

This does not present a problem, however, since most of the customers are known to the store personnel. Also, if the customer can identify himself (through a driver's license, for example) as a member of a family with an account at the store, it is a simple matter to look up the account number and key it into the register instead of inserting the credit card in the reader.

Another benefit, according to Jim Ellerman, general manager of Lennard's, is the way in-store routines have speeded up.

"To illustrate," he explains, "before Lennard's went on the system, our salesmen had to make out sales slips to record all the information we needed. We calculated that this took about 25 percent of the total time involved in the sale.

"Now," he continues, "with the cashier simply keying the information into the NCR register, most of this time is saved. And, since starting with this method, our sales have increased a corresponding 25 percent. With the new system, then, we have been able to build our business substantially without adding to our staff."

Another feature of the system that both Kafka and Ellerman point to is that it can be easily expanded to include accounts payable, sales analysis and inventory control simply by asking the NCR center to add these services.

So, both agree, the system puts them in a position to compete with the larger stores, both in terms of services offered, and in terms of management control.

It has been pointed out by various writers[12] that the real value of the new set of computer programs for credit operations lies in helping the credit manager achieve more effective control over operations and better decision making. In addition, a purely objective, carefully customized system enables him to express his credit policy in very concrete numerical terms, to supply his interviewers with consistent evaluation criteria, and to obtain criteria for measuring his interviewers' performance.

The credit area provides many opportunities to revolutionize various outdated and costly manual operations. For example, systems installed in various retail stores are said to have provided faster service, improved the quality of floor authorization for credit sales, strengthened financial control, helped in collection follow-up, and provided useful sales information for soliciting credit accounts, reviewing inactive accounts, and analyzing departmental sales. Nor are the potential benefits of the computer for credit operations

12 / For a discussion of the use of computers in credit authorization, see the Suggested Readings at the end of the chapter.

restricted only to the large firm; computer service centers have been established to enable the smaller firm to have data processed quickly and at reasonable cost. In addition, commercial banks have shown enthusiastic interest in the potential profitability of so-called Automated Customer Services. As a partial solution to mutual problems, over 1,000 commercial banks are now using the excess time on their computers to provide electronic data processing services in handling accounts receivable for physicians and dentists.[13]

Billing the Customer

The final step in most credit transactions is billing the customer for purchases made during the previous month. On a certain date each month, all of the information about an individual's charges, credits, and payments is taken out of his personal file in the credit office of the retail firm, in order that the bill can be made up. Since all of the information from an individual's file has been removed to make up his bill, no charges, credits, or payments made after his bill closing date can be included in his bill for that month.

Cycle Billing. The exact date on which a bill is expected to be paid has been somewhat complicated by the introduction in the early 1940s of the practice of cycle billing. Instead of sending all bills on or around the first of the month, the names in the credit files are divided systematically and statements are rendered to a different group of customers each working day of the month. Thus in stores using a cycle-billing system the statement "accounts are due and payable the tenth of the month following purchase" does not strictly apply; instead, full payment is expected approximately 10 days after receipt of statement. Some retail firms tie in their use of trading stamps with the payment dates and will not give the customer stamps unless payment is made prior to some specified date. The cycle-billing technique has proved extremely valuable to the larger retail establishment, which otherwise would be faced with a tremendous work load on the first few days of each month, thus creating the problem of efficient utilization of personnel during the slack period.

"Country Club" versus Descriptive Billing. The "country club" billing system is generally considered to be a laborsaving device of maintaining customers' accounts and making out statements. Under this plan, the sales slips are kept and are sent to the customer at billing time, along with a statement showing the total amount owed. The store, of course, maintains some type of photographic copy of the sales slips and the statement.

13 / Lewis E. Davids and David A. West, "EDP and Medical Accounts Receivable," *Journal of Consumer Credit Management,* Fall 1969, p. 47.

On the other hand, some stores that have adopted an automated approach to credit control are switching to descriptive billing. Here the customer gets only a machine-produced monthly statement which may show:[14]

(1) previous balance, (2) a dollar figure for each purchase together with a code number indicating the department in which each item was bought (if the customer wants to know the specific item covered by each figure she refers to her original copy of the sales slip), (3) total purchases and credits, (4) service charges, (5) amount due currently, and (6) the due date.

Time and Expense Problems

It should be noted in this discussion of identification, authorization, and billing that emphasis generally is placed on speed and cost of operation and on the maintenance of customer goodwill. At times this necessarily means a relaxation in the credit safeguards. Most stores believe that this is justified, since the savings of time and money may more than compensate for the small number of cases in which advantage is taken of a more lax system. It also should be noted that the systems described here are primarily large-store systems. In many of the smaller stores the same results can be accomplished with much less formal procedure because of the personal acquaintance which will exist between the store manager (or owner) and the bulk of his customers. In any event, whether the system is very formalized and routinized, or whether it is a rather informal and nonroutinized system, the essential features of the task remain the same.

REVIEW AND DISCUSSION QUESTIONS

1. Explain the statement, "Decisions are the heart of all credit work."
2. Do you believe that there really is any difference between bad-debt losses and charity cases? Explain your point of view.
3. Why is it not suggested that evaluation of credit information be made a separate part of the credit analysis?
4. Why is credit a relative matter? Explain your answer clearly in view of the discussion of this point in this chapter.
5. Discuss why credit standards are intimately related to other marketing policies established by a firm.
6. Define the expression, "grading the credit." Is your definition different from that in the text? Why or why not?
7. What qualities are usually graded in the option-terms revolving credit account grading form? In the cash loan grading form?

14 / D. J. Duncan and C. F. Phillips, *Retailing Principles and Methods* (7th ed.; Homewood, Ill.: Richard D. Irwin, Inc., 1967), p. 641.

8. Can you think of any other qualities that should be graded? Any qualities that should be eliminated?

9. What does the grade of 1 or good stand for in the grading forms? In the final summary overall appraisal?

10. Explain the procedure to follow in using the grading forms.

11. Discuss how the use of credit grades may be extended beyond the aid they supply to the making of credit decisions.

12. Discuss the advantages and the disadvantages of setting credit lines or limits.

13. What methods may be used in setting credit limits in a retail store? Can you think of any other techniques? Explain.

14. What is meant by the term, "credit scoring"?

15. Discuss the advantages and disadvantages of credit scoring plans.

16. Distinguish between identification and authorization.

17. What possible techniques might be used for identification and for authorization?

18. Visit the leading stores in your community to discuss what use they are making of automated systems of credit control.

19. Distinguish between "country club" billing and descriptive billing. Which would you as a customer prefer? Why?

Retail Credit Problems

Following are a number of retail credit problems in which you are asked to determine whether to accept the credit or to refuse it. The credit information supplied in some of the cases is quite limited. Despite this limitation you are asked to grade the credit on those credit qualities which the information available permits you to grade, and to indicate the information which has been verified. You also are asked to come to a definite decision as to acceptability or to state the conditions which would make it acceptable.

20. Mr. C. M. has made purchases in a clothing store which amount to $55. He desires to open an option-terms revolving credit account. His application says he is single, a bartender in a local club, 35 years old, and earns $500 per month. He has held this position for six months. For the previous five years he was employed by several nearby hotels and bars. The local retail credit bureau telephone report reveals the following:

   Loan company—I-4.
   Loan company—$122, I-9.
   Department store—R-1.
   Clothing store—H.C. $46, O-5.

21. Mrs. J. F. has selected a new cocktail dress costing $100 and asks to open any type of charge account in a high-fashion women's apparel store. She states her husband's occupation to be an air force first lieutenant, and they have lived in the community two years. Previous resident addresses are a series of military establishments. She appears to be about 30 years of age. The local credit bureau relates the following record:

   Bank—I-1.
   Department store—R-2.

Furniture store—I-3.

Department store—I-4.

22. Mr. B. W. is 29 years of age, married, and works in a Safeway grocery store. He lists his income as $410 a month. He has a balance of $8.50 on an open charge account at a hardware store; this is 90 days past due. Mr. B. W. desires to purchase a $59 power lawn mower from the hardware store. The store has just introduced the option-terms revolving credit plan and has asked all of its old customers to sign an agreement for such an account. Mr. B. W. refuses to sign this agreement and asks to have the $59 purchase placed on his old open charge account. The hardware store obtains the following from the local retail credit bureau:

Doctor—$115, O-9.

Loan company—I-4.

Department store—$15, R-4.

Had automobile accident in 1970 and was convicted of driving while intoxicated.

23. Mrs. M. C. has selected a $30 cloth coat and asks to have it charged to an option-terms revolving credit account. During the credit interview required at the clothing store prior to opening an account, Mrs. M. C. says that she is a widow and is working as a housekeeper. She says she has been employed by the same family for two years. The local credit bureau orally reports the following information:

Department store—R-4.

Dress shop—O-1.

Department store—R-2.

24. Mrs. C. R. has selected a chair in the home furnishings department of a local department store. This chair is priced at $179. She desires to have the purchase charged and delivered during the next three-day period. She desires to pay for it in three monthly installments, with no carrying charges. Mrs. C. R. is the wife of a young medical doctor who has been in the community for the past three years. The credit manager requests a report from the local credit bureau as a basis for a decision before releasing the merchandise for delivery.

Employment—respected and capable young doctor.

Bank—good for $500.

Bank—auto loan $1,300, monthly payments of $70, I-2.

Department store—R-1.

Drug store—O-1.

Clothing store—O-3.

Cash Loan Problems

Following are a number of cash loan problems in which you are asked to determine whether to make or refuse the loan. In some of these problems the credit information is quite limited; still it is all that is available at the present time. You are asked to grade those credit qualities which the information available permits you to grade and to reach a decision.

25. Mr. J. G. requests a loan of $450 from a commercial bank. He states the purpose of the loan is to complete the purchase of a 1963 Chevrolet truck, pickup body. He can buy the truck for $675; the down payment is to be

$225; and he wishes to borrow the balance. Security offered is a lien on the truck. Facts supplied by the applicant: age 22; married, four dependents; occupation, farms part time working 80 acres of land on shares; also works part time for a grain elevator earning about $225 a month. The following credit information is obtained from the local credit bureau:

> Farmer, working mother's land, owns six head of cattle and three hogs. Furniture store—I-1.
> Department store—account approved, credit not used.
> Bank—maintains savings account which is handled satisfactorily.

26. Mr. G. M. requests a loan of $500 from a personal finance company. He states the purpose of the loan is to meet living expenses and to repay a $300 loan from a credit union. Facts supplied by the applicant: divorced, no dependents; occupation, conductor on Burlington Railroad for eight years; income, $700 a month. The following credit information is obtained from the local credit bureau:

> Loan company—high credit $150, loan paid by comaker.
> Credit union—high credit $1,100, applicant owes now $1,100, comaker paying loan; applicant drinks and may lose job shortly.

27. Mr. B. B. requests a loan of $400 from a personal finance company. He states the purpose of the loan is to pay current bills and taxes. Security offered is a lien on household furniture. Facts supplied by the applicant: age 52; widower, two dependents; occupation, laborer at industrial plant, wages of $100 a week; seven years' employment at same plant. The following information is obtained from the local credit bureau:

> Owns home valued at $7,000; balance on mortgage $5,000
> Wife died two months ago.
> Employed as laborer at industrial plant, earns about $400 a month, employed at this plant about four years.
> Grocery store—high credit $22; applicant now owes $5.25 and has bought on credit for 11 years; applicant always pays as agreed and is considered excellent account.
> Arrested in 1970 for carrying concealed weapon, fined $50.

28. Mr. D. W. requests a loan of $125 from a personal finance company. He offers as security a wage assignment. Facts supplied by the applicant: age 26; married, one dependent; occupation, painter, salary $90 a week. The following information is obtained from the local credit bureau:

> Employed as painter, regarded as good worker.
> Furniture store—high credit $100, balance owing nothing, paid $10 a week as agreed, I-1.
> Department store—high credit $30, $30 now owing.
> Jewelry store—high credit $115, balance owing nothing, O-1.

29. Mr. B. P. requests a loan from a commercial bank. He states the purpose of the loan is to pay living expenses. Facts supplied by applicant: age 39; married, separated, no dependents; occupation, chef at Plaza Hotel; income $500 per month; no indebtedness. The following information is obtained from the local credit bureau:

> Cook, income $105 a week.
> Gas company—gave $10 bad check, took three months to collect.
> Clothing store—O-1.

Clothing store—O-1.
Dentist—$65 account, one year old, O-9.
Newspaper clipping, convincted of drunken driving, 1969.

Credit Report Problems

Figures 15-3, 15-4, and 15-5 show ACB Form 100 credit reports (fictitious).

FIGURE 15-3

NAME AND ADDRESS OF CREDIT BUREAU MAKING REPORT				☐ SUMMARY REPORT	☐ SINGLE REFERENCE	☐ TRADE REPORT
				☐ SHORT REPORT	☒ FULL REPORT	☐ PREV. RES. REPORT

DATE RECEIVED	DATE MAILED	CBR REPORT NO.
6/28/71	6/30/71	
DATE TRADE CLEARED	DATE EMPLOY VERIFIED	INCOME VERIFIED
6/28/71	5/31/71	☐ YES ☒ NO

CONFIDENTIAL Factbilt® REPORT   FOR   Any Credit Granter   IN FILE SINCE: 1968

This information is furnished in response to an inquiry for the purpose of evaluating credit risks. It has been obtained from sources deemed reliable, the accuracy of which this organization does not guarantee. The inquirer has agreed to indemnify the reporting bureau for any damage arising from misuse of this information, and this report is furnished in reliance upon that indemnity. It must be held in strict confidence, and must not be revealed to the subject reported on.

REPORT ON (SURNAME):	MR. ✕✕✕✕✕✕ GIVEN NAME:	SOCIAL SECURITY NUMBER:	SPOUSE'S NAME:
DOE	Mr. John M.	494-16-7881	Lulu

ADDRESS:		STATE:	ZIP CODE:	SPOUSE'S SOCIAL SECURITY NO.:
501 N. Elm	Anytown, Anywhere		68501	Don't know

COMPLETE TO HERE FOR TRADE REPORT AND SKIP TO CREDIT HISTORY

PRESENT EMPLOYER AND KIND OF BUSINESS:	POSITION HELD:	SINCE:	MONTHLY INCOME:
Self-employed	Dentist	9/1968	$ 1,200 (est.)

COMPLETE TO HERE FOR SHORT REPORT AND SUMMARY REPORT AND SKIP TO CREDIT HISTORY

DATE OF BIRTH:	NUMBER OF DEPENDENTS INCLUDING SPOUSE			
1938	→ 5	☒ OWNS OR BUYING HOME		☐ RENTS HOME

FORMER ADDRESS:	CITY:	STATE:	FROM:	TO:
At Address since 1968				

FORMER EMPLOYER AND KIND OF BUSINESS:	POSITION HELD:	FROM:	TO:	MONTHLY INCOME:
U. S. Army—3 yrs.				$

SPOUSE'S EMPLOYER AND KIND OF BUSINESS:	POSITION HELD:	SINCE:	MONTHLY INCOME:
			$

CREDIT HISTORY *(Complete this section for all reports)*

KIND OF BUSINESS	DATE ACCOUNT OPENED	DATE OF LAST SALE	HIGHEST CREDIT	AMOUNT OWING	AMOUNT PAST DUE	TERMS OF SALE AND USUAL MANNER OF PAYMENT
D	1/70	6/71	86	53	00	R-2
D	11/69	6/71	347	151	00	R-1
C	12/68	6/71	120	103	00	O-3

PUBLIC RECORD AND/OR SUMMARY OF OTHER TRADE INFORMATION:

AFFILIATED WITH

Form 100   *Associated Credit Bureaus, Inc.*   *Credit Bureau Reports, Inc.*   Printed in U.S.A.

FIGURE 15-4

NAME AND ADDRESS OF CREDIT BUREAU MAKING REPORT	☐ SUMMARY REPORT	☐ SINGLE REFERENCE	☐ TRADE REPORT
	☐ SHORT REPORT	☒ FULL REPORT	☐ PREV. RES. REPORT

DATE RECEIVED	DATE MAILED	CBR REPORT NO.
1/28/71	1/30/71	

DATE TRADE CLEARED	DATE EMPLOY VERIFIED	INCOME VERIFIED
1/28/71	10/30/70	☐ YES ☒ NO

CONFIDENTIAL **Factbilt®** REPORT   FOR   Any Credit Granter

IN FILE SINCE: 1953

This information is furnished in response to an inquiry for the purpose of evaluating credit risks. It has been obtained from sources deemed reliable, the accuracy of which this organization does not guarantee. The inquirer has agreed to indemnify the reporting bureau for any damage arising from misuse of this information, and this report is furnished in reliance upon that indemnity. It must be held in strict confidence, and must not be revealed to the subject reported on.

REPORT ON (SURNAME): MR. ~~XXXXXXX~~	GIVEN NAME:	SOCIAL SECURITY NUMBER:	SPOUSE'S NAME:
ROE Mr.	Richard R.	493-17-9301	Jane

ADDRESS:	CITY:	STATE:	ZIP CODE:	SPOUSE'S SOCIAL SECURITY NO.:
007 Seven St.	Anytown	Anystate	55555	Don't know

COMPLETE TO HERE FOR TRADE REPORT AND SKIP TO CREDIT HISTORY

PRESENT EMPLOYER AND KIND OF BUSINESS:	POSITION HELD:	SINCE:	MONTHLY INCOME:
Title Search Co.	Title Searcher	1964	$ 550 (est.)

COMPLETE TO HERE FOR SHORT REPORT AND SUMMARY REPORT AND SKIP TO CREDIT HISTORY

DATE OF BIRTH:	NUMBER OF DEPENDENTS INCLUDING SPOUSE ➔			
1925	4	☐ OWNS OR BUYING HOME		☒ RENTS HOME

FORMER ADDRESS:	CITY:	STATE:	FROM:	TO:

FORMER EMPLOYER AND KIND OF BUSINESS:	POSITION HELD:	FROM:	TO:	MONTHLY INCOME:
City of Anywhere	Playground Supt.	9 years		$

SPOUSE'S EMPLOYER AND KIND OF BUSINESS:	POSITION HELD:	SINCE:	MONTHLY INCOME:
			$

CREDIT HISTORY *(Complete this section for all reports)*

KIND OF BUSINESS	DATE ACCOUNT OPENED	DATE OF LAST SALE	HIGHEST CREDIT	AMOUNT OWING	AMOUNT PAST DUE	TERMS OF SALE AND USUAL MANNER OF PAYMENT
B			990	00	00	I$50-1
D	yrs	6/70		429	240	R-9
C	11/69	2/70	246	00	00	R-3
D		3/69	136	00	00	R-3
D	yrs	curr.	544	544	00	R-2
B			3588	00	00	I$100-1
O	2/70	12/70	100	50	10	R-3

PUBLIC RECORD AND/OR SUMMARY OF OTHER TRADE INFORMATION:

From 1962 through 1969 various mortgages filed under this name, by various local banks and individuals.

AFFILIATED WITH

Form 100   *Associated Credit Bureaus, Inc.*   *Credit Bureau Reports, Inc.*   Printed in U.S.A.

FIGURE 15-5

NAME AND ADDRESS OF CREDIT BUREAU MAKING REPORT			☐ SUMMARY REPORT	☐ SINGLE REFERENCE	☐ TRADE REPORT

			☐ SHORT REPORT	☒ FULL REPORT	☐ PREV. RES. REPORT

DATE RECEIVED	DATE MAILED	CBR REPORT NO.
6/28/71	6/30/71	
DATE TRADE CLEARED	DATE EMPLOY VERIFIED	INCOME VERIFIED
6/28/71	5/29/71	☒ YES ☐ NO

CONFIDENTIAL Factbilt® REPORT FOR Any Credit Granter

IN FILE SINCE: 1957

This information is furnished in response to an inquiry for the purpose of evaluating credit risks. It has been obtained from sources deemed reliable, the accuracy of which this organization does not guarantee. The inquirer has agreed to indemnify the reporting bureau for any damage arising from misuse of this information, and this report is furnished in reliance upon that indemnity. It must be held in strict confidence, and must not be revealed to the subject reported on.

REPORT ON (SURNAME):	MR., MRS., MISS.	GIVEN NAME:	SOCIAL SECURITY NUMBER:	SPOUSE'S NAME:
HARTZELL	Mr.	Rudolph P.	897-83-2766	Susan

ADDRESS:	CITY:	STATE:	ZIP CODE:	SPOUSE'S SOCIAL SECURITY NO.:
1791 S. Maple	Any City	Anywhere	60101	432-65-3111

COMPLETE TO HERE FOR TRADE REPORT AND SKIP TO CREDIT HISTORY

PRESENT EMPLOYER AND KIND OF BUSINESS:	POSITION HELD:	SINCE:	MONTHLY INCOME:
Stromburg Co.	Prod. Eng.	11/57	$ 950

COMPLETE TO HERE FOR SHORT REPORT AND SUMMARY REPORT AND SKIP TO CREDIT HISTORY

DATE OF BIRTH: 1924	NUMBER OF DEPENDENTS INCLUDING SPOUSE ⟶ 5	☐ OWNS OR BUYING HOME	☐ RENTS HOME

FORMER ADDRESS:	CITY:	STATE:	FROM:	TO:
43 Manor	Any City	Anywhere		

FORMER EMPLOYER AND KIND OF BUSINESS:	POSITION HELD:	FROM:	TO:	MONTHLY INCOME:
Video Mfg. Co.	Lab. Tech.	4 years		$

SPOUSE'S EMPLOYER AND KIND OF BUSINESS:	POSITION HELD:	SINCE:	MONTHLY INCOME:
			$

CREDIT HISTORY *(Complete this section for all reports)*

KIND OF BUSINESS	DATE ACCOUNT OPENED	DATE OF LAST SALE	HIGHEST CREDIT	AMOUNT OWING	AMOUNT PAST DUE	TERMS OF SALE AND USUAL MANNER OF PAYMENT
B		8/69	1839	159	00	I$80-3
D	6/64	6/68	424	64	64	O-4
B		7/70	1473	1068	00	I$35-1
D		1968	84	00	00	R-1
C		1970	16	00	00	R-2
C	yrs	Curr.	27	18	18	O-5
J	yrs	Curr.	102	42	10	O-2

PUBLIC RECORD AND/OR SUMMARY OF OTHER TRADE INFORMATION:

Came from Gramy Park, Anystate, and antecedents in 1957 from that point satisfactory.
No suits or judgments filed against the name locally.

AFFILIATED WITH

Form 100   *Associated Credit Bureaus, Inc.*   *Credit Bureau Reports, Inc.*   Printed in U.S.A.

The new common language for consumer credit has been used in these reports. Based only on the data given in the reports, would you accept or reject the request of the individual on whom the report is written, for:

a. A new 30-day account, with a limit of $100, in a clothing store?

b. A $50 sportcoat purchase in a men's clothing store on an option-terms revolving credit account? The account has never been used before.

c. A purchase of a $500 color television set on a 12-month installment plan from a discount house?

d. An installment loan (to be repaid in 12 months) from a commercial bank to install air conditioning in his automobile?

e. A loan of $500 (single repayment in 90 days) from a commercial bank, signature loan?

Do you need any additional information on which to base your decisions? If so, state what you believe is needed.

SUGGESTED READINGS

Credit Scoring Plans

Biborosch, Rudolph A. "Credit Scoring Systems Have Built-In Bonuses," *Bankers Monthly Magazine,* March 15, 1967, p. 40.

Buel, William D. and Lewis, Gilbert L. "Credit Scoring—and Beyond," *Banking,* February 1969, p. 42.

Caywood, Thomas E. "Point Scoring for Credit Customers," *Banking,* October 1970, p. 42.

Coakley, William D. "Small Loan Credit Scoring," *Industrial Banker,* February 1971, p. 12.

Greer, Carl C. "Deciding to Accept or Reject a Marginal Retail Credit Applicant," *Journal of Retailing,* Winter 1968, p. 44.

Jacobs, E. M. "Point Scoring," *Credit Management Year Book 1968-1969* (New York: National Retail Merchants Association, 1970), p. 25.

Joyce, Jean Ann. "Vulnerability Criteria as Credit Quality Indicators," *Journal of Consumer Credit Management,* Summer 1970, p. 11.

Leavis, C. W. "Statistical Scoring and Credit Limits," *Credit Management Year Book 1967-1968* (New York: National Retail Merchants Association, 1967), p. 104.

"Numerical Risk Ratings Aid Loan Credit Analysis," *Savings and Loan News,* March 1969, p. 52.

Computers in Credit Authorization

Allen, George D. "Credit Authorization Through Computer Service," *Credit World,* June 1969, p. 14.

Blair, David K. "An Automated Approach to Credit Control," *Credit World,* January 1967, p. 15.

Booth, S. Lees. "Data Processing and Consumer Finance," *Consumer Finance News,* November 1970, p. 3.

"Catalog House Speeds Credit OK by Computer and Visual Display," *Stores,* November 1968, p. 14.

"Computer Credit Enables O-Limit," *Chain Store Age,* February 1971, p. E22.

"Credit Authorization," *Department Store Management,* November 1969, p. 34.

Garcia, Joseph P. "What After Conversion," *Credit Management Year Book 1968-1969* (New York: National Retail Merchants Association, 1970), p. 64.

Grinager, Robert M. "What About Conversion," *Credit Management Year Book 1968-1969* (New York: National Retail Merchants Association, 1970), p. 60.

Margolis, Irving. "Application of Automation to Credit Functions," *Credit World,* August 1968, p. 8.

Pipes, Walter H. "The Computer in the Small Store," *Credit Management Year Book 1968-1969* (New York: National Retail Merchants Association, 1970), p. 93.

"Seek Systems to End Boom in Credit Fraud," *Chain Store Age,* March 1971, p. E37.

Sherlock, Earl. "Negative Credit Authorization, an Economical Way to Check," *Stores,* June 1969, p. 31.

"Template and Translator Make Touch-Tone Phone an Input Device," *Industrial Banker,* January 1968, p. 17.

16

Salesmanship by the Credit Department

No magic formula exists for a successful credit sales program. Necessary ingredients include timing, place, message, and form as well as an ample budget to accomplish the job in the proper manner. It should be remembered that credit sales come from just three sources: new account solicitation, which may include brand-new customers or cash customers that are converted; reactivation of accounts that have become inactive; and sales of more merchandise to present credit customers.[1]

Stimulating profitable credit sales is an important but oftentimes neglected function of the credit department. So commonplace is the occurrence of credit transactions that the solicitation which can build the number of profitable accounts may be regarded passively. Little success in this activity can be expected unless the principles of salesmanship are applied to this key function by the credit department. The building of the number of active accounts takes on significance when we evaluate credit customers saleswise and examine the natural causes for loss of these same customers.

Should Credit Customers Be Sought?

The proportion of sales volume which vendors can directly attribute to credit customers varies considerably from store to store. Many of the nation's retail stores do not sell on credit, but is is estimated that from one third to one half of all retail sales are made on credit. Many merchants, particularly those selling very high-quality or prestige merchandise report credit sales as

1 / John F. Horrigan, Jr., "Holding, Regaining and Attracting Customers," *Consumer Finance News,* February 1969, p. 5.

representing 80 percent or more of their total sales volume. Department stores typically account for a heavy volume of credit sales, with many of them known to do more than one half of their volume on credit.

Why is the typical credit customer important to a retail store? Properly used, the selling of merchandise on credit can increase the sales volume of a particular store. Whether or not sales volume increases and a greater dollar profit accrues depends to a large extent on several things. First, if an increase in dollar profit is to result, the costs of opening, controlling, and collecting the accounts must be kept low relative to the merchant's gross margin. Quite obviously, those expenses which accrue at a more rapid rate than the resulting rate of sales may cause losses rather than gains. Merchants who intelligently analyze the pitfalls of consumer credit and wisely adopt credit policies to overcome them can enjoy the benefits generally associated with credit customers. Second, credit customers can increase sales volume because as a group they (1) are closely tied to those stores at which an active account is maintained, (2) have less resistance to price, and (3) have a tendency to buy a higher quality of merchandise.

Credit customers appear to form a habit of buying at those stores where they have credit privileges. Cash customers are restricted in the amount of their purchases and hence can be more easily attracted by offers of other merchants. Conversely, credit customers become well acquainted with the offerings of the stores in which they buy on credit. They become better acquainted with the personnel, are susceptible to the quality of merchandise offered, and are generally regarded as preferred customers of the store. These factors create goodwill and a high degree of loyalty in the customer's mind. The ease and convenience of a credit account and the attitude displayed by the store toward credit customers contribute toward the development of a credit-customer group which habitually trades with the same merchants. The average sale to the credit customer is very likely to be larger than would be the case were he required to pay cash. It is a well-known fact that credit customers are less price conscious. They are not compelled to be as cautious as the cash buyer, who fears the embarrassment of being short of funds. The credit customer can make purchases on any day during the month and, not having to wait for payday, is susceptible to the dictation of his desires and not his cash on hand. Another reason this is true is the fact that the credit customer is a *selected* customer. By means of a selection process, some customers have been preferred to others and the less able customer has been excluded.

In its attempt to maximize credit sales and to minimize losses, a store should closely coordinate its credit operations with the efforts of its advertising program. It is believed by some[2] that the marketing of department store credit, for example, has not kept pace with the credit marketing efforts of other industries; unlike banks and the major credit-card companies, retailing has no credit marketing executives to oversee and coordinate the expansion and promotion of the credit operation. This has created the problem of closing the generation of credit gap between the credit department and the sales promotion department in many stores.

Even though credit customers are a distinct advantage to a store, there are problems which naturally arise. Once having built a profitable credit-customer group, the merchant will soon become aware that accounts become inactive for a variety of reasons. Customers die; go elsewhere to trade; change residence; meet with misfortune; have fluctuations of income; and change from credit to cash customers of their own volition. The proportion of accounts which become inactive each year is conservatively estimated at slightly more than 10 percent. This ratio is in agreement with department store experiences, but may be high or low depending on the type of vendor offering credit. Whether the proportion of accounts is high or low makes little difference, as the fact remains that sales promotion must be applied continuously in order to build a profitable credit-customer group.[3] The remaining sections of this chapter cover some of the more accepted and successful credit sales promotion methods in use.

How to Get New Credit Customers

New credit customers may come from any one of three sources—present cash customers, potential customers presently residing in the store's trade area, and new residents in the community.

Present cash customers are frequently a source of existing credit accounts. A cash customer possibly has already gained a favorable impression of the store, its personnel, and its quality of merchandise and services. Aggressive credit managements have been alert to the possibility of converting cash customers to credit customers. In doing this they adopt methods of account solicitation which make it convenient, pleasant, and complimentary for the customer. Much of the effort in converting these customers is applied in the retail store. Salespeople can be of valuable assistance here and perhaps are the

2 / David Breedon, "Are You Getting a Charge Out of Credit Promotion?" *Stores*, March 1969, p. 38.

3 / Stanley L. Mularz, "Credit Department Communications," *Credit World*, March 1970, p. 28.

principal force in motivating a good cash customer to open a credit account. Salespeople, on the other hand, need to be trained in the art of account solicitation. They must have a thorough understanding of the store's policy with regard to the various credit plans as well as an appreciation of how a credit account can better serve their customers. Trained salespeople can then answer customers' questions more intelligently and approach them with appropriate phrases of solicitation more effectively.

Today it is customary for vendors of goods and services to advertise for credit customers. The letter shown in Figure 16-1 was

FIGURE 16-1
Letter Soliciting New Account

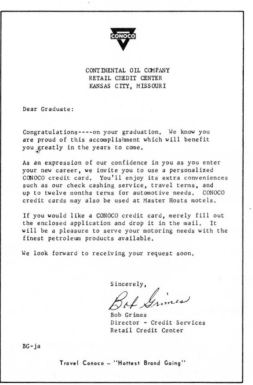

Courtesy of Continental Oil Company

sent unsolicited in an attempt to interest the recipient in becoming a charge customer. Newspapers, direct mail, and credit account promotion within the store play an important role in the sales promotion plans of merchants most successful in this activity. The tone and characteristics of the several methods of advertising for new credit accounts are most effective when patterned after the overall merchandising policies of the store. Very high-quality stores can utilize refined and carefully selected copy which is characteristic of the quality, luxury appeal, and prestige expected. Merchandisers who appeal to a very large cross section of the population invite credit customers with more aggressive and showmanlike devices. The general characteristics of these stores are exemplified further by their account-building methods. Vendors who make no class appeal and promote price to a greater extent than quality usually sell credit terms in the same manner. Of fundamental importance is that the means of account solicitation should not destroy the characteristics and general reputation of the store, for which it may be well known. In recent years many department and specialty stores have placed credit application desks at strategic locations throughout the store.[4] This is an internal form of promotion which attracts passing customers. Application blanks are provided, and an open invitation to apply for a charge account is made. These desks serve the purpose of campaigning for the cash customer who has not taken the time and effort to go directly to the credit department.

The alteration of terms and installments will most certainly add impetus to the sale of some merchandise. Durable good sales are frequently stimulated during periods of low business activity by selling customers through more convenient terms. "No down payment," "no payments until next year," and the extension of installments over more months are typical installment sales-building techniques. Promotions of this type are timed to attract credit accounts when the incentive to enter into a credit obligation might otherwise be low.

Employee campaigns and contests can produce new credit customers. The credit department has the alternative of developing its own employee contest or gaining the assistance of one of the many sales promotion consulting firms. The advantage of professional assistance lies in its ability to overcome contest inequities, set reasonable and profitable goals to be attained, and shift from store management the responsibility for its successful execution. Despite the cost of professional guidance and execution of contests, management benefits from the professional's cumulative experience, and hence the possibility of greater campaign success and the avoidance of most problems associated with promotions of this type.

4 / This practice has been questioned, however. The rejection rate on such applications can run two to two and one half times the normal rejection rate. As a result, are the people being rejected, at least in part, a store's cash and c.o.d. customers? Does it lose their cash business by rejecting them? If so, is this loss offset by the increased business from the customers the store accepted for credit?

New families in the community are perhaps one of the most productive sources of new credit customers. See Figure 16-2 for an example of a letter to newcomers. In recent years the mobility of the American population has become very great. The movement of families into and from a particular community may have great variation. The new family usually has great sales potential. It has immediate and long-run needs for its home, to establish it as a comfortable and convenient place in which to live. Home furnishings, floor coverings, housewares, and small and large appliance departments should be particularly watchful and alert for this new customer. Most communities throughout the country have organized methods which detect the arrival of new families and whether they have purchased their homes or are tenants. In locating and soliciting these customers, it is particularly essential that an early invitation be extended to visit the store and use its services. Otherwise, this valuable source of credit business may be lost to other stores that made their approach soon after the family's arrival in the community. Whatever the method used, it should function to associate the new family with the store before competitors have the same opportunity.

The consumer credit industry also has become increasingly aware of the expanding teen-age market. Long before they acquire full-fledged credit status, teen-agers have woven the actual use of credit (their own or their parents') into their social and economic lives. Thus teen-agers today are an active influence in determining the kind of credit climate in which all of us will live tomorrow.

How to Get More Sales from Credit Customers

A well-organized and successful campaign for the promotion of credit sales must include solicitation of present credit customers. Present credit customers need almost continuous solicitation to keep their accounts active and sufficient in dollar volume.[5]

Inactive credit accounts come about for a number of reasons. The customer may have had an unfortunate experience with the store's merchandise or sales personnel; he may be buying in some departments with apparent satisfaction and not in other departments, going elsewhere to buy the same merchandise; he may have been the subject of an aggressive collection method or be presently overdue on his account; or he may become indifferent for no apparent reason. Of the various methods for increasing credit sales, direct mail and personal solicitation can be effectively employed in some of the above situations. See Figures 16-3 and 16-4 for illustrations.

5 / Mularz, *op. cit.*

FIGURE 16-2
Newcomer Letter

MiLLER ε PAiNE
INCORPORATED
LINCOLN NEBRASKA
68508

Isn't it exciting to move to a new town? We are glad that you have come to Lincoln and we here at Miller & Paine want to extend a cordial welcome to you. We are certain you will enjoy Lincoln's friendly people and its many advantages.

Getting settled in a new home can be rather strenuous and we would like to help make this transition easier for you. An account has been opened for your convenience and a charga-plate token is enclosed. Please feel free to use it at once.

For 80 years, Miller & Paine has had the pleasure of offering its customers dependable merchandise which is style-right and value-right along with prompt and efficient service.

Please use freely all of our store facilities and call upon us for any service which will make your shopping pleasant and enjoyable.

                                        Cordially yours

                                        Credit Manager

FIGURE 16-3
Letter to Inactive Credit Account

Courtesy of Jos. Kuhn & Co., Champaign, Ill.

When the reason for inactivity rests with the collection department, the problem is with the store and not with the customer. If the collection effort is too strict or too lenient, a loss of sales will occur. A very high percentage of customers are concerned about their indebtedness, and particularly so if they are delinquent. The collection policy which has as its sole objective a high collection ratio may very well destroy the goodwill of the store.[6] To achieve the

6 / Philip Sansam, "Importance of Salesmanship for Collection Agencies," *Credit World,* January 1968, p. 20; and George Ntiros, "Collectors Can Be Your Hidden Sales Force," *Credit World,* August 1967, p. 12.

FIGURE 16-4
Letter to Inactive Credit Account

PETROLEUM COMPANY

GEORGE E. PUCKETT
DIRECTOR OF CUSTOMER RELATIONS

Dear Credit Card Holder:

It's been a while since you've used your Champlin credit card. If you haven't been in to see us recently, you may not be aware of the tremendous offer your Champlin dealer is offering on White Dover Ironstone dinnerware.

We call White Dover the everyday dinnerware that treats your family like company. It's that beautiful.

If you could buy White Dover Ironstone in your local stores, a four-piece place setting would cost you $3.95. But you can't buy it anyplace, except at your Champlin service station.

Right now, your Champlin man is offering a four-piece place setting of White Dover for just 99¢ with every fill-up of Champlin gasoline. The enclosed folder has complete details on this outstanding offer.

Naturally, you can charge White Dover Ironstone dinnerware on your Champlin credit card. Just like you can charge tires, batteries, fan belts, radiator hoses, and most other accessories for your car. And when you use your Champlin credit card for these things, you can take up to six months to pay with no interest or carrying charge.

We hope you'll take advantage of your Champlin credit card convenience and start your White Dover dinnerware collection today. We think you'll find it an extremely attractive bargain.

George E. Puckett

CHAMPLIN PETROLEUM COMPANY · P. O. BOX 552 · ENID, OKLAHOMA 73701
A MEMBER OF THE CELANESE GROUP

Courtesy of Champlin Petroleum Co.

goal of a high collection ratio without properly evaluating the result on sales volume is indeed a short-sighted policy. On the other hand a collection policy which is too lenient is likely to result in a large number of overdue accounts. In either case a loss of sales will be experienced. The customer who harbors resentment and ill will is of no greater sales potential than the customer who is overburdened with debt and sensitive to his obligations. The best collection policy to adopt will be one which collects the amounts due and still preserves the goodwill of the store. Great consideration must be given to the collection policy of the store so as not to nullify the sales-creating power held by most customers. There is an optimum type of collection policy for practically all types of creditors without which the value of repeat sales to credit customers may be lost. The collection methods suggested elsewhere in this book are designed to meet collection objectives and yet preserve the goodwill of the customer.

An analysis of credit customer accounts will reveal many interesting facts to management.[7] Some accounts have a large amount of activity, and the average monthly credit purchases contribute importantly to the total sales volume of the store. Some of these same accounts also may be those which reveal trading on a storewide basis. Those customers who concentrate their purchases with a particular store and in many of its departments may be regarded as the "ideal" credit customer. A sizable number of accounts, however, will not measure up to the "ideal" account. Some accounts are used on rare occasions, purchases are few, and amounts charged are small. Still other accounts remain inactive for months and even years for no apparent reason. The task of building credit sales volume through the occasional customer or through those with an inactive account presents a a difficult promotional problem. Direct mail, personal solicitation at the home, and solicitation by salespeople in the store are the most effective methods in these cases. Care must be exercised so that customers solicited are also those which have the credit qualities that make it possible for them to become good credit customers. The small accounts and those used only on rare occasion may best be approached by praise, thank-you letters for past patronage, and the "How can we better serve you?" technique. When the customer is subject to this treatment, he may gain the impression that both his past and future business are of utmost importance to the store. This same customer may need

7 / Peter Wood, "Using Your Computer As a Marketing Tool," *Credit World,* June 1970, p. 10; Eugene F. Drzycimski *et al.,* "Information System for Secondary Uses of Credit Information," *Credit World,* March 1970, p. 10, and April 1970, p. 15.

frequent invitations to visit the store and gentle reminders on how his credit account can function as the means by which purchases can be made.

Well-informed salespeople can be of invaluable assistance in raising the average dollar volume of credit accounts.[8] Customers have their closest personal contact with the store through the sales force. Hence, it becomes imperative that the sales force be instructed in the use of credit as a sales tool. When the sales personnel are completely informed on the offerings of the store and the value of credit as a sales tool, they are well equipped to suggest particular departments and specific merchandise to their customers. Special storewide and departmental sales events, new merchandise arrivals, demonstrations, and shows should always be the subjects of suggestions to credit customers. If salespeople are trained to suggest special events in their own and *other* departments, and such suggestions become a part of their selling, both high-activity and low-activity accounts will be affected in a positive direction.

All too frequently the sales force fails to appreciate the significance of credit as a selling tool. If salespeople understand management's attitudes with regard to credit and the reasons various credit plans are put into operation, they may be more willing to emphasize credit to their customers. They must, however, be told that (1) consumer credit is a selling tool without which the business would suffer;[9] (2) no customer should ever be embarrassed in the use of his credit, but encouraged and complimented on his wise and prudent choice; (3) reasons lie behind all of the various credit plans and a plan is in operation for almost every customer; (4) free and easy credit is not the policy of management, but sound beneficial credit plans are offered to good customers; and (5) salespeople themselves should learn more about the wise use of credit and how different credit plans are coordinated with the store's merchandising policies. While only a few firms are known to do an effective training job with their salespeople, this means of stimulating credit sales, reviving inactive accounts, and increasing the average amount per account cannot be overemphasized.

There are numerous other opportunities to stimulate credit sales. The new account interviewer, the collection clerk, the cashier, the adjuster, and others have a constant opportunity and responsibility to cultivate credit sales through improved customer relations. In particular they should not overlook the sales opportunity when an installment account is completely paid and there is the possibility of

8 / David Jacobs, "Credit Department Communications," *Credit World,* August 1970, p. 28.

9 / Robert P. Shay, "Consumer Credit As a Marketing Tool: Its Present and Future," *Consumer Finance News,* March 1968, p. 4.

using "add-ons" to boost sales. This group, lacking in a credit-sales attitude, can also nullify all the advertising and promotional devices which attracted customers to the store. Their role should be that of building customer relations leading to successful credit-sales promotion. Customer indifference and inactive customer accounts too frequently are traced to the tone of clerical personnel within the credit department. Training programs must be designed and initiated for this important group as well as the sales force.

Goodwill Activities

The credit-sales promotion task, when properly segmented, will include an area of goodwill activities. For the most part these activities can be accomplished by letters and acknowledgments to good credit customers on special occasions.

The credit department has numerous opportunities to compliment good credit customers, say thank you, and praise them for their value to the store. Several occasions on which goodwill letters are particularly desirable are:

1. When the credit customer initially opens an account.
2. During special seasons such as Christmas, Thanksgiving, back-to-school days, Mother's Day, and Father's Day.
3. When the customer's account has its 1st, 5th, 10th, 15th (and so on) anniversary.
4. On a birthday, wedding anniversary, or other pleasant occasion in the customer's life.
5. To acknowledge the payment in full of an installment account.

It should be noted that the above listings emphasize anniversaries and occasions in the life of the *customer* and not events in the history of the retail store. From a psychological standpoint, it is vastly more desirable to place emphasis on events of immediate and personal interest to the customer rather than the anniversaries of the store. Furthermore, goodwill letters should exemplify some prestige element, and it is suggested that the letterhead and signature be that of one of the senior executives of the firm, thus further impressing the recipient.

Special advance sales to credit account customers are another promotional and goodwill activity employed by a large number of retail stores. In addition to the advantages of better selection of merchandise, more pleasant shopping conditions, and the convenience of using his credit at advance sales, the credit customer is imbued with his value to the store. He enjoys the created impression that he has a close association with the merchandiser.

Because customers are restricted to those with credit accounts, he places himself in a distinctive class.

The occasion of customers' misfortunes should not be overlooked in planning goodwill activities. Accidents, sickness, and temporary unemployment frequently set up obstacles to prompt payment of accounts. A sympathetic and understanding attitude toward such circumstances will do much to cement customer relationships. If these circumstances are handled properly, the credit manager can expect that, with the passing of the misfortune, some recipients of this treatment will reciprocate by concentrating an even greater share of their purchases with the store.

It may also be desirable to station credit department representatives throughout the store. Some stores may find this to be impracticable and designate certain key salespeople as "credit sales representatives." In either case this plan can contribute to goodwill and an increased credit volume. The new credit customer, when referred by a salesperson, is more likely to find his way to the credit department when escorted to it. The credit department representative can welcome the new credit customer to the store, carry on a casual polite conversation, and escort the customer to the credit department, where the customer is introduced by name to the credit interviewer and the various credit plans. Some credit representatives are authorized to complete credit applications and other necessary papers on the sales floor. This is particularly important when the sale of high-ticket items is involved. To *send* the customer to the department may result in his finding his way out of the store and into the surroundings of competitors.

Selling Credit to the Organization

To achieve the greatest total benefit from a credit department, its purpose, objectives, and policies must be coordinated with and understood by all segments of the firm. Management must know what contribution the credit department makes to the total firm effort. Throughout this chapter and other sections of this book it has been stated that the credit department can increase sales volume; it can increase the volume from present customers; through promotion it can increase the number of credit customers; and it gives salespeople another selling tool. In accomplishing these objectives, management is going to expect a profit. Profit is one of the aims of a credit department, too, as it functions to increase sales volume at low operating costs. As another store service, credit stimulates goodwill and sales volume. The objectives of management and the aims of the credit executive are one and the same.[10] Credit executives need only to take a positive approach toward their responsibilities and coordinate credit functions with those of management. In such an approach management sees an indispensable service which importantly contributes to the overall aim of the business.

The credit department function must be coordinated with all other departments and personnel. Credit management depends on close cooperation of other departments for the greatest effectiveness. Merchandising, store operations, sales promotion, control, and personnel divisions are interrelated and coordinated to achieve most effectively the objectives of the firm. The total effectiveness can be nullified by malfunctioning of any segment within the various divisions. The credit department is particularly susceptible to malfunctioning because of the false impressions, prejudices, and traditions associated with consumer credit. These problems cannot be overlooked when credit management strives for complete cooperation with other departments. It becomes necessary that sound credit policies be adopted and that the need and impact of such policies be related to all pertinent personnel. In the last analysis, no other department may be as personal as the credit department in the mind of the consumer. This department is one most frequently in contact with the customer in his home. The strategic position of this department relative to the customer's image of the store is a valid reason for credit education and competence of merchandising personnel.

REVIEW AND DISCUSSION QUESTIONS

1. From what sources do credit sales come?
2. Do you believe that credit customers should be sought by the credit department of a firm? Why or why not?
3. Are there any differences between personal salesmanship and credit salesmanship? Explain your position.
4. Why do some stores prefer credit customers to cash customers?
5. Explain why credit accounts may become inactive.
6. What is meant by the expression, "the alteration of terms and installments"?
7. Why are newcomers in a community often one of the most productive sources of new credit customers?
8. How do you suggest getting more sales from credit customers? How are stores in your community doing this?

10 / James E. Locke, "Credit Sales Promotion," *Credit Management Year Book 1968-1969* (New York: National Retail Merchants Association, 1970), p. 155.

9. What procedures are the leading local department stores in your community following to reactivate "dead" credit accounts? Do you believe these have been successful?

10. What can be done to encourage salespeople to appreciate the significance of credit as a selling tool?

11. Discuss the most important goodwill activities in which a retail store may engage. Which ones do you believe are most advantageous? The least?

12. Would these activities be different in a commercial bank? Explain.

13. Why is it necessary to "sell" the credit department to the rest of a retail store's organization? Is this a one-time or a continuous operation? Why?

17

Collection Policies and Practices

Collections are an inherent part of any credit business. Credit has limited acceptance because of the risk and time elements involved, and accompanying these two elements of risk and time is the natural but unfortunate factor of nonpayment of indebtedness in certain instances.

It should be recognized that as its ultimate accomplishment any collection system must get the money. This objective becomes less obvious and much more difficult to attain when the additional requirements of retention of goodwill, rehabilitation of the debtor, promptness of payment, and economical operation are added. If promptness is made the major objective, it may be attained by handling all collections immediately. However, the methods selected and used may be very costly and may simultaneously lose goodwill. On the other hand, if retention of goodwill is made the major objective, the appeals and techniques used will be very gentle, even delicate, and collections will tend to be slow in starting. Which approach proves to be the best for rehabilitation of the debtor will depend in large measure upon the type of individual customer involved.

The word "collections" does not mean the same thing to all people, not even to all credit personnel.[1] There is a so-called intermediate area that is the subject of varying interpretation. Does the collection effort start at the moment that the customer is reminded in some manner of his indebtedness, regardless of whether or not the credit period agreed upon has expired? Advocates of this view consider the statement which is sent to the individual, pointing out that such an amount will be due on such a date, as part of the collection efforts of a firm. It would appear inconsistent to subscribe

1 / Some credit managers state that collections begin when credit is first granted or an account is opened. Under this type of reasoning, collections appear to begin with the clear understanding on the part of the customer regarding the terms of payment.

to such a view, and in this book the word "collections" will refer to those efforts made *after* the credit period agreed upon by the debtor and creditor has expired. Thus, collections will start only in case of nonpayment of indebtedness in the time period established prior to or at the time of sale.

CONSUMER CREDIT INSURANCE

Before discussing regular collection policies and practices, it is important to recognize a collection device followed in certain consumer credit transactions. This type is consumer credit insurance.

During recent years, there has been a very rapid rise in the use of life and disability insurance in connection with consumer credit transactions. This special kind of insurance, called consumer credit insurance, is now offered to debtors by many different types of credit-granting institutions. The insurance names the creditor as the first beneficiary and provides that an insured person's debt will be paid in full upon his death, or that periodic installments will be paid in the event of his disability. It is divided, then, into two major categories: credit life insurance, and credit accident and health insurance.

Credit granters can make the insurance available to their customers by offering individual policies, for which the debtor pays the premium, or by offering certificates of insurance under a group policy. The cost of group coverage may be paid by the creditor, or it may be shifted to the debtors through an identifiable charge.

Nature of the Insurance

Credit insurance is written for the duration of a consumer loan or installment sale contract, and in an amount equal to indebtedness. It is issued to debtors without benefit of a medical examination, with no restrictions for physical impairments or occupational hazards, and with a uniform charge regardless of the insured person's age.

Individual credit life insurance policies may be written either on a decreasing-term or a level-term basis. Decreasing-term coverage provides a benefit that decreases as the installment debt is reduced, so that the protection is always equal (or approximately equal) to the debt. If the coverage is level term, the amount of insurance in force remains the same for the duration of the debt.

There are two basic kinds of credit accident and health insurance policies: those with an elimination period and those with a retroactive period. Under either plan, the insurance company assumes installment payments only after a stated term of disability, which is usually 14 days. The insured debtor, however, is not indemnified for the waiting period if it is "eliminated," while he is indemnified for that time if the coverage is retroactive.

Consumer credit insurance extends benefits both to the insured debtor and to the creditor[2] who makes the insurance available. The debtor benefits from the insurance because it gives him protection and peace of mind, permits him to make greater use of his credit, enables him to get cosigners where needed, and is available without exclusions. The creditor benefits because the insurance serves as an added security device and relieves him of onerous collection duties. In addition, goodwill accrues to the credit granter when the debt is created, since the insurance is desired by large numbers of consumer-debtors, and also when benefits are paid as the result of death or disability.

Origin and Development

Credit insurance was first written in 1917 by the Morris Plan Insurance Society, which was established at that time by Arthur J. Morris, of the Morris Plan banks. During the 1920s and 1930s, credit insurance developed into its present form. Decreasing-term life coverage was introduced in 1922, group credit insurance was first written in 1926, and accident and health coverage was developed shortly before World War II. The charges for credit insurance decreased steadily, many insurance companies began to write it, and a variety of credit granters began to offer it to their customers.[3]

The years following World War II saw an extremely rapid increase in the volume of consumer credit insurance in force and in the number of companies writing it. Group insurance has increased at a faster rate than individual.

The growth of consumer credit insurance in recent decades has been the result of several factors: (1) the public's desire for security, (2) the benefits provided by the insurance, (3) the increased use of consumer credit, (4) the passage of favorable state laws, (5) the great variety of creditors offering the protection, (6) the competitive selling efforts of the insurance companies, and (7) the favorable publicity it has received. Table 17-1 shows the rapid growth of this type of insurance.

2 / "A credit insurance program builds up the volume of preferred business, minimizes collection problems, and creates good will." From *Business Trends* (Lincoln, Nebr.: Journal-Star Newspaper Research Dept., September 15, 1970).

3 / Paul R. Stewart, "Credit Life—Every Man's Insurance," *Industrial Banker,* October 1968, p. 12; and Walter D. Runkle, "Consumer Credit Insurance—Its Future and Effect on the Industry," *Industrial Banker,* January 1968, p. 7.

TABLE 17-1

Credit Life Insurance in Force in The United States, 1949-69

Year	Individual			Group			Total	
	No. of Policies	Amount (Thousands)	Master Policies	No. of Certifi-cates	Amount (Thousands)	Number	Amount (Thousands)	
1949	1,781	$ 482	9	6,170	$ 2,049	7,951	$ 2,531
1950	2,225	720	10	8,609	3,169	10,834	3,889
1951	3,033	1,110	12	9,355	3,708	12,388	4,818
1952	3,596	1,464	14	10,851	4,971	14,447	6,435
1953	4,311	1,851	19	13,550	6,855	17,861	8,706
1954	4,760	2,324	23	16,238	7,917	20,998	10,241
1955	5,001	2,379	27	22,965	12,371	27,966	14,750
1956	6,002	2,844	31	26,123	14,254	32,125	17,098
1957	6,890	3,523	36	27,052	16,225	33,942	19,748
1958	7,271	4,341	43	27,733	17,133	35,004	21,474
1959	7,536	4,949	47	31,354	21,610	38,890	26,559
1960	7,194	5,468	50	36,285	25,715	43,479	31,183
1961	7,188	5,917	53	38,074	27,576	45,262	33,493
1962	7,013	6,091	47	40,607	31,920	47,620	38,011
1963	6,551	6,539	52	46,305	37,016	52,856	43,555
1964	6,885	6,943	56	51,132	42,990	58,017	49,933
1965	6,997	7,690	59	56,181	49,303	63,178	56,993
1966	7,335	8,225	62	62,755	54,447	70,090	62,672
1967	7,978	9,258	62	63,205	57,694	71,183	66,952
1968	8,840	11,725	66	67,020	64,156	75,860	75,881
1969	8,609	12,462	71	70,763	71,326	79,372	83,788

Source: 1970 *Life Insurance Fact Book*, p. 34.

Regulation of Credit Insurance

It appears to be necessary for the state to regulate consumer credit insurance because: (1) the consumer is in an inferior bargaining position and is generally not versed in matters relating to insurance; (2) the insurance companies, as a selling device to creditors, tend to grant higher commissions than necessary; and (3) unscrupulous creditors, in the absence of effective laws, might use the insurance as a means of extracting extra charges from their customers.

If abuses are to be prevented, the following rules should be in effect: (1) charges for individual and group insurance and the compensation received by creditors must be limited, (2) coverage must never exceed the amount of the debt or the term of indebtedness, (3) debtors must be free to acquire the insurance from sources other than the creditor, (4) creditors must give insured persons a statement or a copy of the policy which describes the coverage, (5) insurance must be canceled and unearned charges refunded when debts are prepaid or refinanced, (6) claims must be paid by the insurance company rather than by the credit granter, (7) insurance companies writing the policies must be authorized to do business in the state, (8) creditors selling individual or group coverage must be licensed or authorized by the state insurance department, and (9) all policies must be reviewed and approved by the insurance department.

CONSUMER CREDIT COUNSELING SERVICE

Credit counseling service is discussed before coverage of the more general topic of collection policies and practices. The reason for this sequence is the premise that this service will result in fewer collection problems in the future, rather than being a service called upon after most of the collection efforts have failed.

In describing the activities of credit counseling centers, the following quotation is applicable:[4]

> Credit Counseling Centers provide professional counseling by carefully trained and qualified personnel working under experienced supervision to families needing guidance in the management of their money in family budgeting and in the wise use of credit. In acute cases where over-extension of indebtedness is a major problem the agency attempts to work out a program for orderly debt liquidation recognizing both the needs of the family and the requirements of the creditors and utilizing other public and private resources.
>
> It is intended that the Centers ultimately foster educational programs and

4 / Robert M. Grinager, "Credit Counseling Centers—The Detroit Story," *Credit Management Year Book 1968-1969* (New York: National Retail Merchants Association, 1970), p. 107. For additional articles, see the Suggested Readings at the end of the chapter.

carry on research directed to encouraging constructive use of consumer credit and to avoiding mismanagement of money and the abuse of credit.

Credit Counseling Centers are not collection agencies. They do not lend money. They have nothing to sell. Their sole purpose is to strengthen wise practices in the family handling of money and credit and to rehabilitate through counseling those families whose unwise practices have made them a problem to themselves, their creditors, to the courts, their employers, and the community in general. We believe that with counseling many of these families can again become good credit risks, better customers, better employees, and better citizens than they now are.

It is intended that our counseling be free to debtors with its costs subsidized by the community. For clients needing a program of debt liquidation involving negotiations with creditors and the distribution of funds on a planned basis, a minimal charge sufficient to cover the cost of administering such a program would be made.

The Director of Community Counseling Services of the National Foundation for Consumer Credit has pointed out:[5]

Everyone gains from the community stability offered by a Consumer Credit Counseling Service. Most debtors with troubles are confused and unhappy people, not deadbeats. Most people do not know how they got into their debt problems, and they come to a counseling center seeking an honorable way out.
. . . .
People with credit difficulties come from all levels of all job categories. The only thing they share is a genuine dismay and confusion about their difficulties. The object of a Consumer Credit Counseling Service should be remedial in nature. After all, who looks after the confused debtor? The credit granters have their own local and moral protection systems.

The National Foundation for Consumer Credit entered the 1970s with more than 100 Consumer Credit Counseling Services in 35 states and Canada, with prospects of continued expansion over the future years.[6]

DEVELOPING A COLLECTION POLICY

Since a policy is generally accepted as a course of action to be followed over a period of time, it should be recognized that in developing a collection policy the firm involved should establish a set pattern to be followed in its efforts to collect amounts past due. This does not mean that once a policy is established it cannot be changed. On the contrary, changes are vital to keep any policy alive and face to face with actual operations. But the basic plan of attack should change slowly, so that customers, store personnel, and other interested

5 / A. L. Hackbarth, "How to Establish a Credit Counseling Center," *Management,* February 1969, p. 8.

6 / A. L. Hackbarth, "1970 Program for the National Foundation for Consumer Credit, Inc.," *Quarterly Report,* Spring 1970, p. 40.

individuals are familiar with the general procedure being followed. There are four general policies from which to choose:

1. Liberal credit—strict collection.
2. Strict credit—liberal collection.
3. Liberal credit—liberal collection.
4. Strict credit—strict collection.

Experience has shown that of the four the first two are the most likely policies to be found in effect, especially in retail stores and service establishments. Often the professional man finds himself involved with the third policy, much to his dismay. The fourth policy has appeared most often in credit transactions involving cash loans by commercial banks and by personal finance companies.

It should be recognized by the creditor that as long as his customers regard credit solely as a service rather than a mutual privilege, his collection problems may be troublesome. When the customer begins to think of credit primarily as a business transaction, the collection problems of the creditor tend to become simpler; sentimentality lessens; the creditor is not as afraid to insist on payment for fear of incurring the ill will of his customers. Closely connected with this view is the growing realization on the part of creditors that no credit transaction is complete until cash payment in full is made by the debtor; that payment can be expected more readily if the indebtedness is incurred recently; that terms once established between debtor and creditor must be respected; that slow-paying customers not only cost additional money for collection efforts but also often become reluctant to return to the scene of earlier charging activities until their previous indebtedness is cleared.

Recognizing that unwillingness usually is a more important reason for nonpayment rather than inability, many creditors have come to realize that it is wise to start out any new credit customer with the understanding that prompt payment is expected and that everything possible will be done to collect any indebtedness incurred. It has been shown that "accounts well opened are half collected," and that it is vitally important at the time the account is opened to impress upon the customer the importance of paying promptly.

Factors Affecting Collection Policy

In its decision as to what type of collection policy to adopt, a firm must recognize that there are many factors which should have an influence on policy determination. While they by no means comprise a complete list, at the same time it generally is recognized that capital, competition, type of goods, and class of customers are among the most important and most influential factors.

Capital. One of the most important factors is the amount of capital owned or available to the firm involved. Regardless of how liberal a collection policy a creditor may wish to follow, if he is operating with a limited capital structure he is forced in most instances to adopt a "strict" collection policy in order to keep himself in a position to meet the demands of his own creditors. Most business firms are not blessed with an overabundance of working capital and depend upon the turnover of their goods to provide the funds needed. But a mere turnover of goods is not enough, if these goods are sold on credit. One step is added to the process, and that is completion of the credit transaction by receipt of cash payment. How quickly this last step must be complete is predicated upon how badly the firm is in need of capital. Thus capital availability and need play a vital role in determining just what type of collection policy a firm must adopt, despite the fact that a somewhat different policy might be more feasible in view of some of the other factors which are involved.

Competition. Another influence in the formation and development of a collection policy is, "What is the competition doing?" Of course, size of community plays a role here in that there generally is more room for different policies among large-city competitors than among small-town competitors. Regardless of community size, however, customers in time become cognizant to some degree of widely varying credit and collection policies, and a firm must be aware of what its direct and indirect competitors are offering these mutual customers.

Type of Goods. Another influence in determination of collection policy is the type of goods handled by the retail firm. This factor, however, does not play a dominant role in the policy determination of service concerns, professional men, and financial institutions. It is obvious that the greater the perishability of the good, the greater the need for prompt payment of the account and thus the stricter the collection policy. On the other hand, if the goods involved are of the hard-goods category and repossession (although undesired) is made easier, the need for a strict collection policy is lessened. This is not to say, however, that a strict collection policy is never followed by a firm handling hard goods, but it does point up that such a policy is dictated by some factor other than the type of goods involved.

Class of Customers. Collection work would be easier and the results better if there were some magic way in which each account could be immediately and accurately classified as to the reason for nonpayment and the collection method which would be most effective with that particular debtor. Sorting devices to perform such miracles unfortunately are not yet available, and until such become economically and mechanically feasible the responsibility for any classification, if made at all, rests with the credit personnel involved.

Certain customers regularly and almost automatically pay in response to the simple suggestion that payment time has arrived and that payment is desired. Those who place themselves in this desirable classification—that of prompt payers—solve one part of the problem of classification and remove themselves as possible collection cases. Worries with them cease.

Thus in deciding upon what collection policies and practices to adopt, many firms attempt to decide whether their customers are those persons who pay promptly and who only need slight reminders, if indeed any reminders at all, to make payment. Certainly in these cases if any pressure is ever needed, it will be applied gradually and with exceeding slowness. Included in this classification are those debtors who, although they may be having some difficulty in making payment, respond fully to any inquiry with a complete explanation as to reason for nonpayment and with a careful analysis as to when full payment may be expected.

At the other extreme, if it appears obvious that a mistake was made in accepting credit in the first place, little is to be gained from using gradual and weak devices. Experience has shown that such individuals respect only strong efforts, and immediate threat of legal action may produce results not obtainable by less vigorous attempts.

Between prompt payers and known deadbeats is the group of debtors with whom judgment and experience will have to play a vital role in determining just how strict to be, just how severe a collection method to use, and just when to apply the pressure. Thus it is with these debtors that the problem of classification is most acute.

A GENERAL COLLECTION SYSTEM

The ideal collection system would be one which solves the problem of the volume of work by being largely routine in operation and which operates in such a manner that the problem of classification is primarily solved by causing the debtors to classify themselves by their own actions. When properly adapted to the needs of the creditor firm and when correctly fitted to the characteristics of the customers, such a system should get the money and should do so promptly, economically, and without loss of customer goodwill. The basic question is the design characteristics or principles of such a system. If the principles of design are understood, an actual operating system conforming to these principles can be developed by any competent credit manager.

Promptness and regularity of payment must be built into any system because of the following conditions:

1. A lax collection policy often indicates an incompetent management. This in turn can reflect upon the purchaser's attitude toward the products sold by the firm.
2. Experience has shown that there is a definite correlation between the length of time debts are unpaid and the volume of resulting bad-debt losses.[7]
3. Slow collections tend to result in the loss of future sales to these customers because of their reluctance to attempt to buy from creditors whom they have owed for some period of time. Of course, these creditors may show even a stronger reluctance to sell such customers.
4. Failure to enforce the collection activity tends to aid the imprudent purchaser. Thus, the foolhardy buyer may plunge headlong into unwise buying, knowing that the collection system of the selling firm will permit him an excessively long time before drastic legal action is taken, if it is ever taken at all.

A well-designed collection system may be compared to a series of screens over which the accounts are passed for the purpose of classification. The earlier screens are low in cost and handle the customer gently to preserve goodwill. The later screens are less routine, cost more to apply, may be somewhat sharper in action and thus not preserve goodwill with such certainty, and tend to classify the reluctant debtors into much smaller and more exact assortments.

It is possible to divide a general collection system into four stages, giving emphasis in each stage to the kind of effort associated with that stage. These four stages are:

1. The impersonal routine stage.
2. The impersonal appeals stage.
3. The personalized appeals stage.
4. The drastic or legal action stage.

The collection devices appropriate to each stage and the classes of debtors who may be expected to respond at that stage are indicated in Table 17-2.

7 / The U.S. Department of Commerce appraises the value of accounts receivable as follows:

Current accounts are worth:	100 cents on the dollar
2 months past due are worth:	90 cents on the dollar
6 months past due are worth:	67 cents on the dollar
1 year-old accounts are worth:	45 cents on the dollar
2 year-old accounts are worth:	23 cents on the dollar
3 year-old accounts are worth:	15 cents on the dollar
5 year-old accounts are worth:	1 cent on the dollar

TABLE 17-2
A General Collection System

Stage of System	Collection Devices Available for Use	Debtors Involved
Impersonal routine	Statements—1st, 2nd, 3rd, etc. Statement inserts and stickers Notes on statements Form letters of reminder type (Note: These refer only to devices used after expiration of credit period.)	Those awaiting notice Honestly overlooked Temporarily financially embarrassed Careless or procrastinating debtor
Impersonal appeals	Form letters appealing to: "Anything wrong" tone "Tell us your story" tone Pride in credit responsibilities Sense of fair play Seeking reply from debtor: Telephone Telegram Special letters: Registered Special delivery Trick reply	Honestly overlooked Careless or procrastinator Temporarily embarrassed Overbought Accident or misfortune Disputed account
Personalized appeals	Personal collector: Telephone Personal interview Personal letters to: Debtor Employer Credit bureau	Overbought Eventual insolvents Accident or misfortune Frauds—no intent to pay Disputed account
Drastic or legal action	Extension agreement Composition arrangement Assignment of accounts receivable Collection agency Garnishment or wage assignment Repossession Attorney Suit Other actions	Same as debtors shown in the *Personalized appeals* stage (all should have assets)

Self-classification on the part of the debtors is accomplished in large part at each of the respective stages. The devices suggested for each stage are, of course, much more numerous than would be desirable to incorporate into any one operating system. When developing an actual system to use in a particular situation, the credit manager would select the devices most appropriate to his collection task and would determine the frequency of use and the time to elapse between uses. He naturally would tailor the devices used to his own situation, considering the needs of his firm and the character of his customers. He also would be well advised to conform to the customs of his line of business and territory and to deviate from custom only on the basis of well-informed judgment.

This general system conforms to the principles of effective collection.[8] It assures that lower cost and routine methods will be used for the mass of the accounts and that those customers with more desire and means to pay will meet their obligation during the early stages of the system. After the bulk of the accounts has been reduced by various low-cost methods which also preserve goodwill, the higher cost methods are applied selectively to the remaining small number of accounts which need such higher cost appeals. These stronger and more emphatic methods will have lower percentage returns because the potential of the group to which they are applied is lower, but these harsher devices with their reduced emphasis upon retention of goodwill may be employed since the self-classification process already will have eliminated those accounts whose goodwill is of primary importance. Thus through the four stages suggested, a gradual increase of pressure is consistently built up to such a point that the debtor should (but unfortunately not always does) feel that there is no more desirable alternative than that of payment and that there is no escape from this conclusion.

The general system will give a sound, effective, and logical organization to the collection efforts. The skill in the selection of the devices, the quality of the devices individually prepared, and the appropriateness of the timing should assure that the system is properly adapted to the situation of the firm and the nature of its customers. Thus a specific system developed in accordance with these general principles should be effective for the particular firm.

The Impersonal Routine Stage

It is in this stage that the self-classification of debtors begins. Of course, it should be remembered that many debtors will have paid

8 / E. F. Tyson, D. B. Klein, and E. Novak, *Tested Collection Methods and Procedures* (New York: McGraw-Hill Book Co., Inc., 1966). This book reviews the main causes of delinquency and provides a basis by which the collector can evaluate a specific situation and determine what course of action he should take.

within the credit period established between the customer and the creditor and thus never will appear as persons to be considered in any of the four specified collection stages. This stage does not begin until after expiration of the established credit period.

Some of the more common collection devices available for use in this stage are the various impersonal statements (or bills) sent to customers, statement inserts and stickers, stamped or written notes on the statements, and various form letters of the reminder type (see Figures 17-1 and 17-2). The debtors generally responding to the collection devices of this stage are those who are simply awaiting some notice that the account is overdue, those who have honestly overlooked making payment when due, the careless or procrastinating debtors, and those temporarily financially embarrassed.

One of the most important means of contacting debtors is by mail. Whether use is being made of statements, inserts, or form letters, it is important for the creditor to bear in mind that his collection device is attempting to sell the debtor on the idea that the account must be

FIGURE 17-1
Examples of Impersonal Routine Stage (Stickers for Statements)

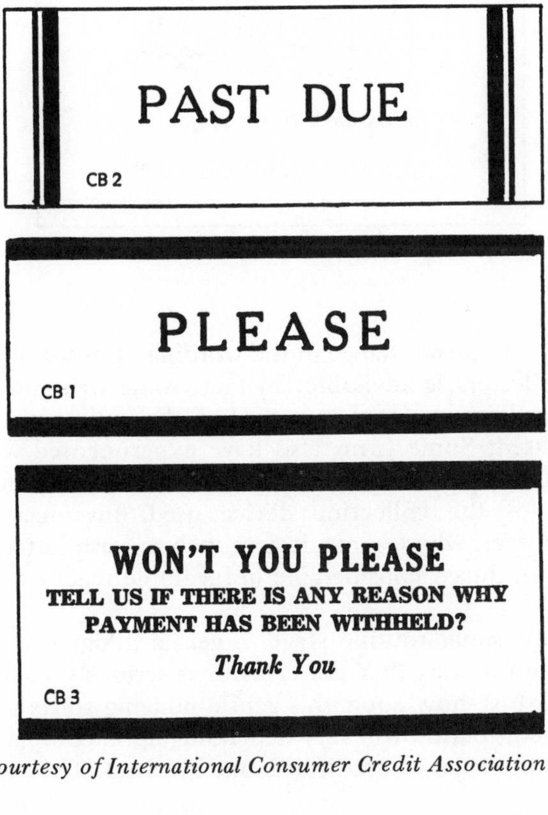

PAST DUE

CB 2

PLEASE

CB 1

WON'T YOU PLEASE
TELL US IF THERE IS ANY REASON WHY
PAYMENT HAS BEEN WITHHELD?

Thank You

CB 3

Courtesy of International Consumer Credit Association

FIGURE 17-2
Example of Impersonal Routine Stage (Form Letter)

paid at once. Frequent change in the wording of notes on statements and of form letters is advisable. In fact, some firms have found it worthwhile to keep a complete record of the pulling power of each form letter used. Some firms also have experimented with colored paper or colored printing to see whether it materially increases the effectiveness of the collection device used. Instances have been reported, however, where some devices such as form letters "edged in black" have produced considerable unfavorable reaction on the part of customers.

In this impersonal routine stage, a gentle nudging is being used without giving the idea that the creditor is seriously concerned over nonpayment. Just how soon this gentle nudging starts after expiration of the credit period will vary depending upon company policy as well as upon the type of credit account involved. Thus with weekly or semimonthly payments, a three-day grace period is common. Since installment accounts generally are paid from current income, a missed payment generally means that the debtor must wait until the next pay period for future payments. Consideration of facts such as these is often overlooked in planning the collection system of a firm.

The Impersonal Appeals Stage

In this stage, the collection efforts are still "impersonal" in nature but have changed from a routine procedure to a nonroutine or an appeals basis. In this stage, the form letters used are no longer of the routine impersonal type but take on more of the character of appealing to "anything wrong?" or "tell-us-your-story" tone, or to the pride of the customer in meeting his credit responsibilities, or to his sense of fair play. If the mild notices in the first stage have failed to produce payment or to gain some response from the debtor, then the time has come for a more forceful means to bring the indebtedness to a speedy conclusion. That is the purpose of this second stage, but the creditor should remember at the same time that the action is yet to be personalized or directed squarely at the debtor involved.

In addition to the form letters suggested, use often is made of the telephone,[9] telegraph, or unusual letters (such as special delivery, registered, or trick reply in which the debtor is given the choice of filling a lengthy questionnaire or paying his bill) in order to secure some indication of receipt of the inquiry on the part of the debtor. After having written to a person who does not respond but who gives every indication of residing at the address used, the debtor has several alternatives which may be more effective but which involve increased costs. These include the use of certified mail, restricted delivery to addressee only, returned postage receipt showing the name of the person who signed for it, and return receipt showing address where delivered.

The debtors involved in this stage generally include those who: have honestly overlooked the amount in arrears; are in a temporarily embarrassed financial position; are careless in making payments or are procrastinators; have suffered a misfortune since incurring the debt and cannot meet their obligation as agreed; have overbought; believe the amount owed is incorrect or raise questions involving some phase of the transaction and thus dispute the amount.

9 / "Through a public notice issued on June 10, 1970 and published June 16, 1970 in the *Federal Register*, the Federal Communications Commission issued a warning to creditors and collection agencies regarding the use of the telephone for debt collection purposes, and put the telephone companies on notice that it expects them to take action against those who abuse the use of telephone service in attempting to contact or collect from delinquent debtors." Quoted from "FCC Warning on Telephone Debt Collection Practices," *Credit World*, September 1970, p. 21.

The Personalized Appeals Stage

This third stage incorporates both the personal aspect and the appeals approach. In other words, all efforts are directed toward the debtor himself on a highly personalized basis—efforts which are the last ones before some type of drastic or legal action is taken. (See Figure 17-3.) Debtors who have forced the creditor to this stage include those who: have overbought; will eventually become insolvents (and may even resort to bankruptcy); have met with some accident or misfortune; are habitual frauds with no intent ever to pay; believe the amount owing is incorrect and dispute the bill as it now stands.

The collection devices commonly in use in this stage include personal letters (usually a series, spaced at different time intervals) to the debtor pointing out the long drawn-out procedure that the creditor has been forced to go through up to this stage. Also included in this stage may be personal letters to the debtor's employer, as well as notification to the local credit bureau of the impairment of the debtor's credit standing. Also commonly used during this stage will be personal collectors, as well as personal contacts via the telephone.[10]

The costs of carrying out the actions in this stage are greater than those involved in the first two stages. Personally dictated letters are one of the main weapons employed. Although personally dictated letters are initially expensive, they permit more varied and persuasive appeals than stock form letters, debtor reaction is generally more favorable, and the end result generally is greater pulling power.

Drastic or Legal Action Stage

In the previous three stages, customer goodwill has been carefully considered before taking any action, but in this last stage the gloves are off and the honeymoon is over. The debtors involved are much the same type as outlined for the third stage, only consideration usually is given here to the ownership of assets on the part of the debtor before undertaking some of the legal actions, such as suit. Mention should be made, however, that many firms would not consider most of the techniques to be discussed in this section because of the possible ill feelings that could be created.

Extension Agreement. Under this agreement an honest and sincere person who is temporarily unable to meet his obligations may

10 / Many credit managers pay particular attention to the advantage of the telephone or the personal visit, which enables them to get an immediate response from the debtor, particularly a promise with regard to the time and amount of a partial or full payment of the obligation. A good article on this topic is George F. Marsh, Jr., "Using an Outside Representative in Hospital Collections," *Credit World,* January 1967, p. 21.

FIGURE 17-3
Example of Personalized Appeals Stage

```
                                                Date


        Mr. John C. Patient
        000 Main Street
        Your City, Your State


        Dear Mr. Patient:

        You expect fairness from us, don't you?

        Our entire collection procedure has been based on courtesy
        and consideration.  We have been willing to cooperate with
        you in every way.

        All, alas, to no avail.

        Now, our last message to you. . . sent in all fairness.

        Your account will be placed with a professional collection
        agency unless you pay it in full, or make satisfactory
        arrangements, within the next five days.

        Be fair to yourself. . . your immediate action will prevent
        serious trouble.

                                      Cordially yours,



                                      (Signature)
                                      Name typed
                                      Title
```

Courtesy of International Consumer Credit Association

be given a longer length of time to pay his debts. The creditor granting this extended length of time may take several simultaneous actions, such as:

1. Addition of a service charge, particularly on 30-day charge accounts on which no finance charge normally is levied.

2. Conversion of a 30-day charge to a revolving credit, with all the accompanying characteristics of such an account.
3. Conversion of an open charge account receivable to a note receivable, with a definite due date and carrying charge.

Composition Arrangement. Under this arrangement a group of creditors agree to accept a reduced amount as settlement of their indebtedness in full. This scaling down is done only in those cases in which the debtor is honest and sincere and entirely free from any taint of fraud. Obviously such an arrangement enables the debtor to recover a debt-free position, while the creditors may have been fortunate in receiving x cents on the dollar of their indebtedness without any more drastic action.

Assignment of Accounts Receivable. Some firms have found it to their advantage to sell their accounts receivable to a financial institution. If this is accomplished and a nonrecourse agreement is made, the firm is relieved of any further responsibilities for collection. Of course, for such a favorable situation the firm must pay the financial institution a fee (or a discount), an action which reduces the profitability of any account receivable. If the sale of the receivable is made on a recourse basis, much of the advantage is lost except for the immediate availability of needed funds. It should be recognized that assignment also may take place much earlier in the collection process, especially if the firm has adopted this as a regular policy in its operations.

Collection Agency. Another of the drastic actions that a creditor may take is referral of an account to a collection agency. Although there are thousands of collection agencies over the country, one of the better known groups is the Collection Service Division[11] of the Associated Credit Bureaus, Inc. Members are located in all parts of the United States and Canada and form what might be termed a network collection service. Each local collection service office may (and does) call upon any one of the other offices for help in locating the debtor of a local credit granter. The account usually is forwarded to any one of the other offices involved, and personal collection effort is expended on the local level to collect the account. These local collection service offices generally have established their own predetermined collection systems, which may closely resemble the four stages just outlined.

The costs of collecting through such an agency vary considerably, although the average will run between one third and one half of the amount collected. See Figure 17-4 for a schedule of charges made by a collection agency.

11 / "Growth of Collections: A City-Size Analysis," *Management,* March 1971, p. 2.

FIGURE 17-4
Charges of a Collection Agency

ACKNOWLEDGMENT

THE CREDIT BUREAU

Established 1889

Telephone 432-6633   126 No. 16 th St.

LINCOLN, NEBRASKA

COLLECTION SERVICE DIVISION

MEMBER
ASSOCIATED CREDIT BUREAU, Inc.

NO COLLECTION — NO CHARGE

THIS is to acknowledge receipt of the claims as indicated upon the enclosed stickers. We suggest you place these on the respective ledger sheets.

Please communicate with this office before accepting any proposition of settlement from debtor. Better yet, refer them to our office in order that we may save you considerable annoyance and render you a far better service.

These claims are accepted upon contingent basis of recovery as follows:

$33\frac{1}{3}\%$ { Net to us on amounts collected —except on claims coming under any of the headings opposite.

50% { Accounts $25.00 or under
Accounts 12 Months past due
Accounts requiring tracing
Accounts requiring litigation
Accounts outside of Lincoln
Accounts for rent
When necessary to receive payments of $5.00 or less.

Once an account is turned over to a collection agency, the debtor should insist that all dealings be made through it, that the collection agency should furnish periodic progress reports, and that definite arrangements should be made as to how and when collections should be remitted.

Garnishment or Wage Assignment. These two actions are combined simply to illustrate techniques available to the creditor to collect amounts due by means of securing part of the debtor's income. The two actions vary considerably, however, in the manner in which they are carried out.

The right of garnishment exists in some form or other in practically every state, although it is called by varying names. It requires a court order, in which a creditor may acquire a right to hold a third party (the garnishee), in whose possession goods, money, or credits of the debtor are found, liable for his debt to the defendant.

On July 1, 1970, Title III, the restriction on garnishment section of the federal Consumer Credit Protection Act, went into effect. The main features of these restrictions on garnishment have been described as follows:[12]

> For the first time in the history of this country, Congress has passed a law that imposes a federal limitation on the garnishment of an employee's wages. To put it simply, the new law limits weekly garnishments to either (1) 25 percent of after-tax pay or, (2) after-tax pay minus 30 times the federal minimum wage, whichever is less.
>
> While it is true that technically the law covers only those engaged in "interstate commerce" the courts over the past few years have established such broad standards for this term that almost every business today can be considered to be involved in interstate commerce in one way or another, and therefore, would very likely be subject to this restriction in the new law.
>
> It should also be remembered that this new federal garnishment law prohibits employers from firing an employee simply because his wages have been subject to garnishment for one indebtedness. . . .

Under a wage assignment, the debtor signs an agreement (usually at the time the credit transaction is made) to the effect that in case of nonpayment of the debt the creditor may seek a certain portion of his wages without the necessity of a court order. Such an arrangement is pertinent only to the employer named in the wage assignment. Generally speaking, when a wage assignment is presented to an employer, he is bound to recognize the terms agreed upon by debtor and creditor.

However, there are exceptions to these provisions. Whether state employees can be bound by garnishment proceedings and by wage assignments will vary by state. On the other hand, generally speaking, federal government and members of the armed forces[13] are not subject to these collection devices.

12 / Max A. Denney, "Restrictions on Garnishment," *Industrial Banker,* March 1970, p. 11. Also see Robert D. Moran, "Federal Restrictions on Wage Garnishments," *Quarterly Report,* Spring 1970, p. 47; and Robert A. Cuccia, "Enforcement of New Federal Wage Garnishment Restrictions," *Quarterly Report,* Winter 1970, p. 34.

13 / DOD Directive on Indebtedness of Military Personnel, dated July 1, 1969, affects any creditor who contacts the military to seek assistance in collecting a past-due account. "Under this new directive, any creditor or claimant desiring to contact a military member about his indebtedness may obtain the member's address by writing to the locator service of

A final word of advice to any firm using these techniques—check with an attorney for the legal provisions of the state involved.[14]

Repossession. Whereas generally the creditor's last desire is to retake the merchandise that is not paid for, this may be the only course of action left to him. The right of repossession is generally found under the right of replevin. If the creditor can show a title or a possessory right superior to that of the debtor, then the merchandise can be retaken in case of nonfulfillment of the terms of the contract. However, the varying state laws set forth widely different provisions as to the circumstances under which replevin is applicable.

Attorneys. Another technique is to turn the account over to an attorney who will act like a collection agency in attempting to secure payment. Two different approaches are found under this arrangement: one, use of the company's own attorney, who probably will contact the debtor as a private lawyer and not as an employee of the company; and two, use of a separate and independent attorney who will attempt to collect the indebtedness on a fee or commission basis.

Suit. Collection by suit generally is considered when all other collection methods have failed and when there are sufficient assets in possession of the debtor against which a judgment may be executed. Suit action, which generally is looked upon with disfavor by the creditors of consumer debt because of the possible resulting bad publicity, accomplishes two things: one, the establishment of the legal fact that the debt does exist and that it is of such an amount; and two, the means of providing the creditor with a legal remedy and aid in collecting the proven debt. However, the mere obtaining of a judgment does not guarantee payment of the indebtedness. As a result, it is advisable to make sure that the debtor has sufficient assets against which the judgment can be entered before instituting suit.

The effectiveness of collection by suit is reduced by two modifications. First, it must be recognized that a debt cannot be held forever and that in every state there are statutes of limitations which spell out in detail the length of time during which a debt may be collected and the provisions for renewal of the limitation period. Second, under the provisions of the various state laws it is stipulated what property and what percentage of earnings are not subject to seizure by suit. These exemptions are allowed because of the

---

the Military Department which is concerned, enclosing a $1.50 fee for service. But no other cooperation will be extended beyond this point to any claimant except under specified conditions." Quoted in Wm. Henry Blake, "New DOD Directives Affecting Credit Transactions with Military Personnel," *Credit World,* September 1969, p. 6.

14 / Lawrence R. Dittelman, "New Questions about Creditors' Remedies," *Stores,* April 1970, p. 32; and Allyn M. Schiffer, "Garnishment Is Not a Table Decoration," *Credit World,* August 1969, p. 20.

traditional belief that an injustice is done both to society and to the debtor if he is stripped of all his assets and all of his income.

Other Actions. No attempt is being made to list all of the possible drastic or legal means available to a creditor. However, in addition to those previously mentioned, consideration should be given to the possible collection of small amounts in the various small claims courts or, as known in some states, justice of the peace (JP) courts. Again, wide variations are found in the state laws governing the actions of these courts.

In connection with all of the collection methods which have been discussed in this chapter, mention should be made of the "Guides Against Debt Collection Deception" which have been issued by the Federal Trade Commission and have been generally accepted as "advice of the FTC to the honest creditor and collection agency."[15] The Commission established the Bureau of Industry Guidance in 1961, with the purpose being "to help the businessman avoid law violation by giving him authoritative advice and guidance as to practices which are questionable under the laws administered by the Commission.[16] Over the years, the long series of FTC and court decisions have resulted in these so-called "Guides Against Debt Collection Deception."

PROBLEM WITH CONSUMER BANKRUPTCY

Another action, this time usually initiated by the debtor, that has the effect of modifying the indebtedness of an individual is the action that can be taken under the federal Bankruptcy Act, as amended.[17] The number of individual bankruptcies being filed under this act poses a problem that can no longer be ignored by anyone engaged in the field of accepting consumer credit. Bankruptcies are today becoming one of the nation's chief domestic problems; the amount of money involved is tremendous. Contrary to common belief, business failures account for only a small percentage of the total bankruptcies, with the bulk being among the wage-earner and salaried worker class.

15 / G. Smith Moreland, Jr., "Preventing Deception in Collecting Debts," *Credit World,* November 1968, p. 18.

16 / *Ibid.*

17 / For the most recent changes in the Bankruptcy Act, see "Recent Amendments to the Bankruptcy Act," *Credit World,* December 1970, p. 12. The law involved is Public Law 91-467, 91st Congress, S. 4247, October 19, 1970. One of the most important changes resulting from the law is that it enjoins "all creditors whose debts are discharged from thereafter instituting or continuing any action or employing any process to collect such debts as personal liabilities of the bankrupt."

The following pertinent observations on the problem of personal bankruptcies were made in the *1971 Finance Facts Yearbook:*[18]

Personal bankruptcies have become a growing concern to credit grantors, the legal profession, legislators and social workers alike. During the fiscal year ending June 30, 1970, there were 178,118 personal (nonbusiness) bankruptcy petitions filed in the United States—an increase of 5.1% from the 169,427 filed in fiscal 1969. In 31 states, there was an increase in the number of bankruptcies per 100,000 population, in 3 states and the District of Columbia no change, and in 16 states there was a decrease (see Figure 17-5). On the average, there were 88 bankruptcies per 100,000 population in the U.S. in 1970, up from 85 per 100,000 in 1969, but still below the 92 per 100,000 population in 1968.

It is unfortunate that too many events and circumstances have conspired to discourage more recourse to Chapter XIII. This chapter, which was added to the bankruptcy statute in 1938, permits the debtor to avoid the stigma of bankruptcy by paying his debts out of future earnings. If the majority of his creditors in number and amount agree, the debtor can make regular deposits with a trustee who uses the money to pay the debts over a three-year period. A Chapter XIII proceeding offers the debtor a variety of other benefits which unfortunately are not well known to members of the legal profession nor their clients.[19]

IMPACT OF A SOUND COLLECTION POLICY

By this time, it must be obvious that collection work is trying and that patience, persistence, and resourcefulness are needed attributes of a collection manager and his staff. How well he performs his job will determine the impact that collection activities will have upon his firm. He always is walking a tightrope, trying to decide just how much effort to make and how much expense to incur in attempting to bring an indebtedness to a satisfactory conclusion.

The collection manager, working usually under the direction of the credit manager, will have the following responsibilities:

1. To aid the working capital position of the firm by securing collections of receivables as quickly, cheaply, and completely as possible.
2. To reduce bad-debt losses. This, of course, involves deciding when an account should be considered a loss. It generally is recommended that any amount that has gone six months past the credit period should be considered as bad and should be

18 / (Washington, D.C.: National Consumer Finance Association, 1971), pp. 53-54.

19 / For articles written on the subject of consumer bankruptcies and Chapter XIII, see the Suggested Readings at the end of the chapter.

FIGURE 17-5
Changes in Personal Bankruptcies per 100,000
Population, 1969 to 1970 (Year ending June 30)

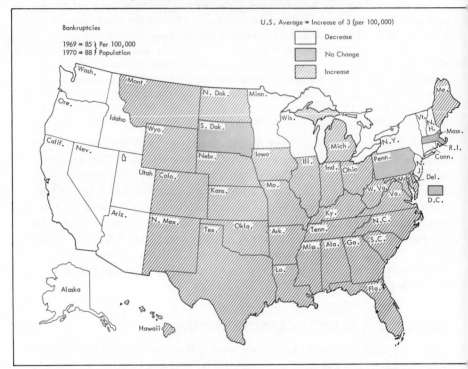

Source: Administrative Office of U.S. Courts and National Consumer Finance Association.

charged off. Of course, this does not mean collection efforts should be stopped at this time, and recoveries of accounts charged off as bad-debt losses may take place.

3. To aid the sales effort, in that an individual who is free from any overdue debt will be much more likely to make purchases there than is the customer who because of a guilty conscience caused by an overdue bill makes future purchases at competing firms.

4. To ease pressure between customer and firm, by straightening out any misunderstanding that stands in the way of payment. In fact, here the collection man doubles as a form of public relations man.

5. To help make policy decisions concerning credit and collections. For example, what policy should be established concerning paid-up slow accounts seeking new credit?

It should be apparent—to repeat the opening sentence of this chapter—that collections are an inherent part of any credit business.

REVIEW AND DISCUSSION QUESTIONS

1. How do you account for the fact that collections are an inherent part of any credit business?
2. Why doesn't the word "collections" mean the same thing to all people involved in the credit and collections business?
3. What is the purpose of consumer credit insurance?
4. Survey the leading stores in your community and see if they are using consumer credit insurance.
5. Explain the two categories into which consumer credit insurance is divided.
6. Why does it appear necessary to have state regulation of this type of insurance?
7. Explain the purposes of Consumer Credit Counseling Services.
8. What four general policies can be followed in collection activities? Which would you recommend?
9. Discuss the factors that are involved in setting up a collection policy.
10. A general collection system is usually divided into four stages. What are these stages? Study Table 17-2 carefully in preparing your answers.
11. How do you account for the types of debtors that are usually involved in each of the four stages?
12. When would you recommend that an extension agreement be used? A composition settlement?
13. Visit a collection agency in your community and compare the charges of this agency with those shown in Figure 17-4.
14. Discuss the new restrictions on garnishment, as set forth in the Federal Credit Protection Act.
15. What is the primary purpose of bankruptcy? How does consumer bankruptcy procedure vary from that of a business firm?

SUGGESTED READINGS

Credit Counseling Centers

Blake, Wm. Henry. "A Report on the Study of Credit Counseling As a Community Service," *Credit World*, November 1967, p. 7.
Lane, Sylvia. "Economics of Case for Credit Counseling Agencies, *Journal of Consumer Credit Management*, Spring 1970, p. 112.
Perlis, Leo. "Criteria for Credit Counseling," *Journal of Consumer Credit Management*, Winter 1970, p. 77.
_____. "Family Credit Counseling—A Community Must!" *Quarterly Report*, Summer 1970, p. 74.

Consumer Bankruptcies and Chapter XIII

Caffrey, Bernard and Capel, William C. "Personal Bankrupts: Psychological Predictors," *Journal of Consumer Credit Management,* Fall 1969, p. 34.

Lane, Sylvia. "Petitioners Under Chapter XIII of the Bankruptcy Act," *Journal of Consumer Affairs,* Summer 1969, p. 26.

Naughton, William S. "Should Referees Have Authority to Exclude Wage Earners from Straight Bankruptcy?" *Consumer Finance News,* December 1967, p. 26.

Stageman, Richard. "The U.S. Bankruptcy Act and the Upcoming Generation," *Credit World,* October 1969, p. 12.

PART IV

Business Credit, Government Credit, and Foreign Credit

18

Business and Governmental
Use of Credit

Credit may be classified, according to the form of the debtor's responsibility, as private or public credit. Private credit has been shown to comprise two major types, *consumer* credit and *business* credit. Private credit, then, identifies any credit employed by individual consumers and businesses, and public credit is the employment of the credit mechanism by political bodies such as federal, state, and municipal governments.[1]

At this point the discussion turns from our comprehensive treatment of consumer credit to a general consideration of the several types of business credit and public credit. Part V is a comprehensive treatment of commercial credit.

BUSINESS USE OF CREDIT

If business is to function properly in the economy,[2] its financial requirements must be accommodated. Not only must the monetary system provide financial assistance to meet the long-term needs of businesses, it must also supply the means whereby intermediate-term and short-term needs are met. Furthermore, business must be accommodated by a variety of credit types to satisfy its complexity of operations. The day-to-day, seasonal, irregular, and even cyclical changes affecting the production and marketing aspects of business demand that flexibility be provided by the nation's financial and credit institutions. Many of the diverse credit needs of business are provided by our modern banking system, while others are provided by other financial institutions, by individuals, and by business

1 / See classification of credit in Chapter 1.
2 / J. Howard Laeri, "Social Responsibility—A Challenge to Business," *Credit and Financial Management,* September 1968, p. 22.

361

enterprises themselves. Regardless of the source, it should be recognized that businesses will need credit at various times.

The Nature of the Demand for Business Credit

Business credit is used to further the production and marketing of goods and services. To a businessman credit is a means to an end. It permits him to engage in the production and marketing of goods and services which yield profits. The expectation of profitable business activity creates the demand for business credit, and conversely the expectation of unprofitable activity depresses this demand. The flow of all forms of business credit into productive activity, then, is a reflection of business opportunity.

This concept of business credit tells us little, however, of the variety of credit needs demanded by business. The variety of credit needs stems principally from the character of the business activity to be financed. Few, if any, businesses are entirely financed by the owner's capital, be they proprietorships, partnerships, or corporations. Even though all businesses have an ownership interest in one form or another, it is seldom large enough to forgo substantial financing of the assets by creditors. With most businesses the ownership interest is an outlay of cash used to purchase only a portion of the current assets and fixed assets. Business credit is used by management to acquire all remaining assets not covered by the owners' investment. Since the total assets of any business comprise current assets and fixed assets, different types of business credit are needed to meet its short-term and long-term requirements. Essentially, short-term financing, as evidenced by the current liabilities section of the balance sheet, is used to acquire current assets for the business. Long-term financing, on the other hand, may be undertaken to acquire both current and fixed assets.

The particular types and magnitudes of credit needed by any business are dictated by its scope of operations, business objectives, and the type of assets to be acquired. This applies, of course, to new businesses just starting operation (see Table 18-1 for a picture of new business incorporations from 1951 to 1961) as well as going concerns. Most businesses throughout their lives have almost a continuous need for cash as well as merchandise and services.

Business credit thus comprises two broad types, namely, *commercial* (mercantile) credit and *cash* (financial) credit.

Commercial (Mercantile) Credit

This type of credit[3] aids businesses in the acquisition of current

3 / Hedwig Reinhardt, "Economics of Mercantile Credit," *Credit and Financial Management,* May 1967, p. 24.

assets. It is created as one business accepts the credit of another business in exchange for goods and services. This is the most frequently used type of business credit by all buyers of goods and services in the various stages of production and marketing. Commercial credit transactions take place from the time goods are sold as raw materials until they reach the industrial consumer or reseller as finished goods. In other words, commercial credit transactions take place between manufacturers, producers, wholesale distributors, and retailers. This type does not include, however, credit which retailers accept from consumers, thus distinguishing commercial credit from consumer credit.

In addition to the above-mentioned characteristics, commercial credit is generally an unsecured short-term type of credit. With the exception of retail firms, most commercial enterprises are both debtors and creditors as the result of commercial credit transactions. A wholesaler, for example, is a creditor as evidenced by his accounts receivable for merchandise sold to his business customers, and a debtor as evidenced by his accounts payable for inventory and services purchased from manufacturers and middlemen. Commercial credit has as its principal purpose the facilitation of the movement of goods through the successive stages of production and distribution.

Cash (Financial) Credit

The sole use of commercial credit would leave most business enterprises short of other working-capital requirements. Hence, to acquire both current assets and fixed assets, most businesses use their credit power to borrow cash. The principal sources of business loans are commercial banks, business finance companies (commercial finance companies, factors, equipment financing specialists), investment companies, insurance companies, the Small Business Administration, and individuals. The issuance and sale of commercial paper is another source through which companies can enter the marketplace and secure funds for short-term needs. The use of one source of funds rather than another, or a particular combination of sources, is mostly determined by the specific financing requirement and the acceptability of the business as a credit risk.

Commercial banks and commercial finance companies usually are the principal sources for short-term loans. In general, short-term loans from these sources are available to businesses for periods of less than one year and frequently for a maximum of two or three months. Businesses use short-term loans for the purposes of acquiring inventory, the payment of current obligations, and the payment of employee wages and salaries. Whereas commercial credit facilitates the acquisition of most inventory needs, the credit terms may be

TABLE 18-1
New Business Incorporations

New business incorporations rise to yearly record in 1969

Monthly Averages*

Thousands

Monthly Averages*

Year	Monthly Average
1951	6,971
1952	7,735
1953	8,545
1954	9,764
1955	11,638
1956	11,731
1957	11,391
1958	12,565
1959	16,089
1960	15,226
1961	15,128
1962	15,171
1963	15,534
1964	16,477
1965	16,991
1966	16,668
1967	17,217
1968	19,470
1969	22,856

Monthly Totals

Month	1968	1969
January	20,438	24,327
February	17,910	20,811
March	19,520	23,089
April	19,641	24,698
May	19,940	23,694
June	18,670	24,128
July	19,733	24,015
August	19,052	20,990
September	19,015	21,498
October	21,636	25,059
November	17,770	19,109
December	20,310	22,849
Yearly total	233,635	274,267

*Series includes data for Hawaii, Alaska, and the District of Columbia beginning with 1958, 1960, and 1963, respectively.

Source: Dun & Bradstreet, Inc., as quoted in *SBA Annual Report 1969* (Washington, D.C.: Small Business Administration, 1970).

unrealistic from the standpoint of some businesses. This type of financing permits a business to meet its obligations until such time as it receives income from products sold. The firm which has a long period of time involved in its manufacturing process or sells products on extended terms of sale will usually require considerable short-term financing. Business enterprises which can finance current operations with owners' investment or by prompt receipt of income from operations have less need for short-term loans.

General Motors Acceptance Corporation, Commercial Credit Company, C.I.T. Finance Corporation, General Electric Corporation, and a large number of similar companies specialize in the wholesale financing of dealers' stocks.[4] Accounts receivable financing and factoring are specialized activities of some of these firms or their subsidiary corporations.[5] Businesses which cannot obtain sufficient working funds from commercial banks may take advantage of this source. These institutions sometimes deal with businesses which cannot qualify for commercial bank loans. A case in point is the financing of automobile dealers' stocks, which frequently are out of balance relative to other balance sheet items.

Long-term financing is usually one of the first forms of financing used by businesses to acquire fixed assets. When a business resorts to borrowing funds for this purpose, the credit involved is known as "investment credit." Evidence of this type of borrowing appears in the fixed liabilities section of the balance sheet. Whereas the fixed liabilities and the owners' interests constitute the total long-term financing, owners' interests are not to be regarded as credit. The ownership of shares of corporation stock does not give the owner a creditor's right, and the purchase of such shares is not a credit transaction nor is the stock representative of a credit instrument. The investment of funds in corporation stock represents ownership equity and not creditor interests.

The typical fixed assets purchased by means of long-term borrowing include land, buildings, machinery, equipment, and other "permanent" items necessary to the operation of the business. In addition to acquiring fixed assets in this manner, a portion of the current assets may be provided by the use of investment credit. Other than many of the technicalities of this type of borrowing, the principal distinction between long-term financing and short-term financing is the time element involved. Whereas short-term loans are expected to be repaid from the conversion of current assets into cash, long-term loans are usually repaid from profits which have resulted from the employment of the additional capital in the business.

4 / This phase of commercial finance companies' operations was covered in Chapter 6.

5 / See Chapter 20 for a detailed treatment of these methods of financing.

It is important to note the growing importance of the Small Business Administration's role in providing both investment and commercial credit to small businessmen.[6] As an indication of this changing role of the Small Business Administration, the following quotation is significant:[7]

The Small Business Administration made more loans in 1969 to aid small businesses than it did in 1968 and nearly doubled its volume of loans to minorities.

During 1969 SBA approved 5,385 loans amounting to $131 million to minorities, compared with 2,739 loans totaling $54 million in 1968.

There has also been a steady upward trend in the volume of SBA loans approved with bank participation or under SBA's loan guaranty plan. In 1969 banks provided $471 million in 10,964 loans approved in these two categories, compared with $403 million provided by banks in 9,037 loans in 1968.

Banks are currently providing 81 percent of the dollars made available through SBA business loans and 41 percent of the dollars made available through SBA economic opportunity loans.

One of the principal sources of long-term loans is the savings of the individual investor. Some individuals may invest their savings directly, whereas most people channel their savings into institutions which perform the investment function for them. Most people are willing to turn their savings over to investment institutions for the following reasons: (1) the small amount an individual has to invest would not attract investment opportunity, (2) the investment structure is complex and not generally understood, and (3) most savers do not have the ability nor inclination to cope with the details of managing their investments. Insurance companies, investment companies, savings banks, commercial banks, and trust companies are the principal channels through which individual savings flow for investment purposes. These institutions are not only more capable of dealing with businesses' long-term financing problems, they also attract the better investment opportunities.

Intermediate-term loans, which may mature in from one to five years, are needed by a large number of business enterprises. The need for intermediate-term loans arises because short-term and long-term loans leave uncovered some important areas of business finance. Plant additions, replacements of machinery and equipment, replenishment of depleted working capital, and financing of temporarily depressed business situations are examples of a few situations calling for intermediate-term loans. For the most part the commercial banks provide this type of capital, although their interest in this type of business credit is of recent origin. Until two or three

6 / Robert C. Moot, "Providing Credit to Small Business," *Credit and Financial Management,* February 1968, p. 17.

7 / *SBA Annual Report 1969* (Washington, D.C.: Small Business Administration, 1970), p. 11.

decades ago, banks held to the theory that their function was to supply to businesses short-term loans of the self-liquidating type.

A more complete treatment of the role of commercial banks, commercial paper, and investment credit in the business area is reserved for Chapter 20.

GOVERNMENT USE OF CREDIT

Public credit, which includes that credit used by all governmental bodies and units, completes the structure of credit in the United States economy. Federal, state, and municipal governments find it increasingly necessary to use credit to meet their expenditures in the many areas of government activity. In recent decades, the increased reliance of governments on credit to finance their operations stems from (1) greatly increased costs, and (2) the expansion of public programs in the areas of military obligations, education, highways, and health and welfare. Governments borrow money for essentially the same basic reason as businesses borrow money; it is simply that their financing needs exceed their incomes. When governments borrow money, it is usually done by the issuance of a credit instrument. State and municipal governments often issue bonds in order to finance their needs. The federal government, on the other hand, may issue bonds or the shorter-term Treasury notes, Treasury bills, and Treasury certificates. Each of these instruments represents government's promise to pay at some future date in exchange for the credit used to acquire money, goods, or services for government use. The issuance of such instruments typically results in the creation of checking accounts in the banking system against which government draws to meet its needs.

The credit capacity of any government is based on the sustained confidence it enjoys and its ability to levy and collect taxes from the public. Insofar as the federal government is concerned, its credit involves little or no risk on the part of lenders.[8] Some other political bodies enjoy this same high rating among lenders, but there are a number of local governments which experience difficulty in fulfilling their credit needs. In recent years it has become increasingly difficult to increase the revenue from existing tax sources and even more difficult to find additional tax sources. As this problem becomes more aggravated in the future, it will have a direct effect upon the

8 / However, changes occur in interest rates and have corresponding effects on the prices of government securities. Purchasers of government securities may find themselves "tied in" until maturity of these securities if purchases are made when interest rates are low and these rates experience a substantial upward movement. Of course, the purchaser may secure the face value of the securities by waiting until maturity, but at the same time there are losses in possible interest return because of the low interest rate established at time of purchase.

services of local governmental units. Because taxation is the local government's principal source of income, which in turn is partly used to meet its credit obligations, it is obvious that a close relationship must exist between the two. Except for the federal government (because it can actually create money), the credit worthiness of political subdivisions perhaps rests more on their tax revenue potential than on the degree of confidence they may enjoy. In this respect local government may be likened to a business enterprise which must assure creditors of its income possibilities relative to its actual and planned expenditures. While governmental use of credit is not of major interest in this volume, it takes on significance when considered relative to business and consumer credit.

THE INTERRELATIONSHIP BETWEEN PUBLIC, BUSINESS, AND CONSUMER CREDIT

If credit executives are to appreciate fully their part in the credit economy, it behooves them to familiarize themselves with the close relationship between public credit, business credit, and consumer credit. The expansion and contraction of any form of credit influences each of the other major types of credit, and hence affects the conditions under which credit management must operate and formulate policies. Monetary and credit conditions help to explain the general level of prices and the overall price-making processes which influence the credit worthiness of credit risks. If a credit manager is to serve his company with the greatest effectiveness, he must be aware of and have a knowledge of monetary matters and how his employer's activity as well as his customers' activities are affected.

While it is not within the scope of this book to consider the detailed workings of our monetary system, a brief summary of its more important aspects will serve to establish the close relationship between public and private credit.

Credit Expansion and Contraction

The monetary system of the United States is a complex mechanism founded on credit transactions. One key to expansion and contraction[9] of bank credit is found in the fact that each bank is required to maintain a fractional cash reserve which is sufficient to

9 / For a more detailed description of these processes, see John A. Cochran, *Money, Banking, and the Economy* (New York: Macmillan Co., 1967), chap. 7; Charles L. Prather, *Money and Banking* (9th ed.; Homewood, Ill.: Richard D. Irwin, 1969), chap. 16; and Charles R. Whittlesey, Arthur M. Freedman, and Edward S. Herman, *Money and Banking: Analysis and Policy* (2nd ed.; New York: Macmillan Co., 1968), chap. 7.

support the bank's deposit liabilities. This reserve must be kept at a specified percentage of its demand and time deposits. The percentage is set by law and regulation. Whenever the bank's reserves are in excess of the minimum requirements, it is in a position to loan or invest the amount of the excess.

The process by which credit expansion and contraction takes place arises from the lending activities of individual banks, operating within the framework of the entire banking system. An individual bank can lend only the money that it acquires (from its depositors, the Federal Reserve, or other sources) in excess of its reserve requirements. After leaving the hands of the first bank, the money continues to do business as it passes into the banking system from bank to bank (in the form of deposits) or from person to person. Each loan or investment results in a series of events that permit a multiple expansion of credit. First, the lending bank increases its earning assets by making the loan. Second, it loses cash to other banks as the money is spent on goods and services, but other banks receive a corresponding increase in deposits. As the series of loans and deposits continues throughout the banking system, multiple credit expansion occurs. On the assumption of a 20 percent reserve requirements, a $100,000 primary deposit can become required reserves for $500,000 of deposits, of which $400,000 can be loaned.

Further expansion of credit in the banking system comes about as the U.S. Treasury, upon receipt of gold, issues an equivalent amount in gold certificates. The gold certificates are issued to the Federal Reserve and permit the Federal Reserve to have four times the value of the gold certificates in commercial bank reserves on deposit with it. With the ability to expand credit 5 to 1, commercial banks may have $20 on deposit for each gold certificate dollar.

The contraction of credit in the commercial banking system can result as the same processes work in reverse. Hence, the credit contraction can take place either with actions of the Treasury or by businesses. As the need for credit from the banking system by businesses diminishes, the repayment of loans occurs faster than the making of new loans, and the contraction of deposit credit takes place. Credit contraction is cumulative, as is credit expansion.

Despite the theoretical aspects of the expansion and contraction processes, they are accurate in the way the phenomena occur. In practice, however, the processes frequently take place in different ways. The importance of the impact of these forces gains significance in that checking account money (credit) is used to settle the great bulk of all business transactions.

Instruments of Federal Reserve Policy

It has been shown that commercial bank reserves are the basis for the volume of credit in the economy. In regulating the reserves of the commercial banking system, the Federal Reserve System relies on three interrelated instruments, all or any of which influence the expansion and contraction of commercial bank credit. *Open-market operations, discount operations,* and changes in the *reserve requirements* are the methods which may be used to effect changes in the capacity of banks to expand or contract the credit supply.[10]

Briefly, open-market operations generally consist of Federal Reserve purchases or sales of United States government securities. These securities are evidence of government borrowing and expenditures. Federal Reserve purchases of government securities add to the reserve balances of member banks and thus result in a greater capacity of member banks to make loans and to acquire investments.

Discount operations permit member banks to obtain additional reserves by borrowing from the Federal Reserve. The proceeds from such loans are credited to the member bank's reserve balance on deposit at the reserve bank. While commercial paper and other business paper of prime quality are eligible for discounting, borrowing against government securities is easier and instantly appraisable. The interest rate charged for this service is known as the "discount rate." The Federal Reserve can either encourage or discourage borrowing by member banks by lowering or raising the discount rate. When the Federal Reserve believes that further credit expansion would be economically harmful, it may raise the discount rate; and conversely when it believes credit expansion may be helpful to the economy. In actual practice member banks may be reluctant to resort to this method of gaining additional reserves which provide the basis for expansion of their loans and investments. The discount rate, however, is typically viewed as the direction of Federal Reserve policy. Furthermore, and more importantly, there is a close interrelationship between the discount rate and other interest rates, because the rate reflects the Federal Reserve judgment on the credit and money supply relative to general economic conditions.

Finally, changes in member bank reserve requirements influence the capacity of commercial banks to expand credit. Changes in the

10 / For a more complete and detailed discussion of these operations, see *The Federal Reserve System, Purposes and Functions* (4th ed.; Washington, D.C.: Board of Governors of the Federal Reserve System, 1961); Charles L. Prather, *Money and Banking* (9th ed.; Homewood, Ill.: Richard D. Irwin, Inc., 1969), chap. 8; and "How Does Monetary Policy Affect the Economy?" *Federal Reserve Bulletin,* October 1968, p. 803.

reserve requirements affect the amount of reserves that member banks must hold as deposits with the Federal Reserve. In other words, a given amount of member bank reserves can be made to support more or less credit and monetary work. If reserve percentages are raised, banks with no excess reserves must sell liquid assets in the market and borrow from other banks or the reserve banks in order to obtain loan and investment funds. If reserve percentages are lowered, on the other hand, banks find themselves with excess reserves which are available for loans and investments or debt repayment. If the required reserve is 20 percent, $1 of reserves will support $5 of deposits, whereas a 15 percent reserve requirement means that $1 will support $6.67 of deposits.

Inasmuch as the banking system has the ability to bring about a greater or smaller amount of credit, the effects on businesses, consumers, and governmental units must be recognized. Since the close interrelationship between credit in our banking system and all other forms of credit is clearly apparent, it is appropriate to examine briefly the widespread effects of monetary actions.

Impact of Credit Expansion and Contraction

It has been shown that the actions taken by monetary authorities are transmitted to the United States economy through the commercial banking system. This same system is the foundation of our monetary and credit structure, and hence the reactions to its changes bear importantly on the credit activities of governmental units, businesses, and consumers. In general, the immediate effect of monetary actions is to influence the cost of credit and the amount available at commercial banks. After a time, the easing or tightening of credit will influence the decisions of businesses and consumers to participate in credit transactions.

If banks begin to restrict credit expansion, many business borrowers can be expected to curtail their spending plans. Insofar as bank financing is relied upon to acquire inventory, expand plant, replace equipment, and perform other financing requirements, a restriction of credit normally will reduce the accomplishment of these business activities. A credit restriction policy also affects long-term financing arrangements, because the willingness of banks to lend for this purpose is also lessened. Financial institutions engaged in taking mortgages on business and consumer durable goods find the likelihood of refinancing through commercial banks lessened. In this way the ability of other lenders is influenced, and in particular mortgage lenders and sales and consumer finance companies will of necessity restrict their operations by becoming more selective (raising their credit standards).

The cost of credit (interest rates) also functions as a brake or release on business and consumer spending. Rates of interest usually move up or down with the availability of credit. A reduced supply of credit will be reinforced with higher rates of interest. Higher borrowing rates alone are frequently enough to discourage and divert some demands for credit. Businesses regard the use of their credit as a device for involvement in a profitable business opportunity, but higher money rates may easily wipe out the attractiveness of the venture. As consumers are confronted with higher real estate mortgage interest or an increase in the cost of financing automobiles, it might be expected that large numbers of households will be discouraged from making the credit-financed expenditure.

When the credit contraction and higher interest rate policies of the Federal Reserve are sufficiently intense to create an atmosphere of business pessimism, secondary effects are likely to occur. Notably, cash expenditures by businesses and consumers are likely to be reduced. This result, coupled with the lessened credit availability, will add to the overall effectiveness of creating depressed economic conditions.

Expansion in consumer and business spending, then, will generally be slowed as the commercial banking system limits the pace at which credit is created and as it adopts policies that make credit-financed purchases more costly. The actual impact on borrowing and spending will differ in timing and degree from one consumer or business to another. The reason for this is that various credit users have different degrees of reliance on credit financing, and some are more sensitive to the increased costs of borrowing than others.

At times Federal Reserve policy attempts to encourage credit expansion and spending. The effects of this policy are the reverse of those briefly described above. With the improved reserve positions of commercial banks, they will undertake the making of loans, thus expanding checking account money (credit). These conditions tend to reduce interest rates, and banks must compete for credit customers. This increased supply of credit and the lower cost of credit-financed purchases will tend to encourage such purchases. As this policy creates a climate of economic optimism, cash expenditures by consumers and businesses will tend to increase.

While this brief description of the impact of credit expansion and contraction is perhaps oversimplified, it suffices to point out the importance of economic forces which are set in motion by a tightening or easing of credit conditions. It should also be noted that Federal Reserve policy is only one factor which influences monetary and credit conditions. The effectiveness of its policies, of course, depends upon the timing and strength given to a particular action and upon its isolation from offsetting influences.

Credit expansion and contraction by the banking system are closely related to the fiscal policies of the federal government. During an inflationary period and if government desires to stem an inflationary tide, one might expect actions designed to reduce government expenditures, increase taxes, and reduce the volume of bank credit. Conversely, in periods of depressed economic activity, the expectation is usually that the government will increase expenditures and ease tax burdens; and banking authorities will take such actions as are necessary to increase the supply of credit.

In actual practice, however, it is not always possible for the inflationary or deflationary measures to effect the results desired, because of the complexity of economic forces at work, the political environment prevailing, the consumers' attitudes and expectations, and the undesirable aspects of monetary, fiscal, and debt management policies exhibiting too high a degree of flexibility. Furthermore, the authoritative powers may be in disagreement as to the soundness of their decisions and the overall impact on the economy. At best, one can expect given monetary and fiscal policies to produce certain economic influences, but one should be aware that offsetting economic forces, poor timing, and the lack of coordinated policy decisions may destroy the possibility of attaining the desired economic results.

PRODUCTIVE NATURE OF BUSINESS AND PUBLIC CREDIT VERSUS CONSUMER CREDIT

Despite the close relationship between business credit, public credit, and consumer credit and their foundation in our modern capitalistic system, there is no unanimity of opinion as to the economic significance of each type of credit. These differences in opinion are partly the result of regarding business credit and public credit as essentially *productive* in use and consumer credit as essentially a *consumptive* type of credit. Some hold the following views: business credit is productive in the sense that this type of credit facilitates the production of goods and services at a profit which in turn liquidates the indebtedness; public credit which is not self-liquidating does, however, give rise to the production of goods and services and frequently sets in motion the wheels which produce the conditions for debt liquidation; and consumer credit is consumptive in that it is used to acquire things for consumptive purposes. This view of consumer credit has led some to regard the use of credit by consumers with reservation and even as ill-advised.

Attempts to compartmentalize the types of credit by the use of the terms productive and consumptive and to regard "productive credit" as beneficial to the economic welfare of the nation often lead to a fallacious reasoning. Unfortunately, this very approach to credit matters is practiced in many circles.

The other view, to which your author subscribes, is that *all* credit is productive, and to view it otherwise is an economic fallacy. Consumer credit, which has been an instrument in raising the standard of living, affording a host of consumer satisfactions and resulting in the creation of utility, cannot be regarded as anything but productive. There is no question that consumer credit has served a need of American consumers, the same as other types of credit serve the needs of governments and businesses.

It is, therefore, desirable and sound reasoning to regard all types of credit as productive. Good economic theory and analysis will not dispute the interrelationships and interdependence of the various types of credit. This chapter is designed to serve as an appropriate basis for a broader and more comprehensive concept of credit in our economy. After all, most credit transactions, whether business, government, or consumer, involve economic activity which has as its aim—consumption.

REVIEW AND DISCUSSION QUESTIONS

1. What is the nature of the demand for business credit?
2. What is the role of commercial credit in the financial scheme of most businesses?
3. Distinguish between the long-term and short-term cash credit needs of a typical business enterprise.
4. Define the term investment credit.
5. What is an intermediate-term loan? How does the need for this type of financing usually arise?
6. What is meant by the statement, "The monetary system of the United States is founded on credit transactions"?
7. Explain how policies of the Federal Reserve System influence credit policy.
8. Are the measures used by fiscal authorities to temper inflationary and deflationary pressures effective? Why or why not?
9. What considerations lead some to regard consumer credit as *consumptive* in character, whereas business credit is more often regarded as *productive*?
10. Is consumer credit clearly a productive type of credit? Justify your answer.

19

Business Use of Commercial Credit

Commercial credit, sometimes referred to as mercantile or trade credit, is the power of a concern to obtain merchandise and services in exchange for its promise of future payment. It is used only in connection with conducting a business enterprise or for the purchase or sale of goods for resale. The fact that the value received includes merchandise and services distinguishes it from cash (financial credit), and because it is accepted by business concerns from other business concerns it does not include consumer credit. Any number of different institutions in the economy use commercial credit, such as manufacturers, wholesalers, retailers, cooperative enterprises, and the like. The services included in commercial credit transactions may be in connection with the goods acquired or may be rendered solely as a service necessary in the conduct of the enterprise. This type of credit is the most important short-term credit used and accepted by businesses, by virtue of the multiplicity of transactions, the policies associated with accepting it, and the accounting procedures necessary to manage it accurately.

FUNCTION OF COMMERCIAL CREDIT

In the preceding chapter it was mentioned that commercial credit facilitates the movement of goods through the successive stages of production and distribution. While this important function is frequently supplemented by other forms of credit, the reliance of businesses upon commercial credit outweighs alternative sources of credit.[1]

1 / Hedwig Reinhardt, "Economics of Mercantile Credit," *Credit and Financial Management,* May 1967, p. 24.

Financing the Movement of Goods

A simple example will be sufficient to illustrate the use of commercial credit in the successive stages of production and distribution. As the producer of raw materials sells to processors and manufacturers, the goods may be financed in several ways. If the original producer of raw materials is financially capable, he may accept the credit of his customers, and hence commercial credit is created. The raw materials supplier may be financially weak, and the burden of financing the goods as they move from hand to hand falls on the purchaser. The purchaser of the raw materials may finance the goods with his own capital, or even by borrowing from a bank or other lending institution.

As the raw materials are processed or converted into semiprocessed goods, they again are sold to manufacturers of finished goods. As these goods are sold the manufacturer will offer his credit in exchange for the goods. This is known as commercial credit because he is acquiring goods for further fabrication or for the operation of his business enterprise. Other forms of credit will, in whole or in part, pay the manufacturer's workers, meet overhead, and cover other manufacturing costs. As the goods are manufactured into finished goods, they are sold to wholesalers or industrial supply houses. The transfer of the goods is again accomplished by commercial credit—the wholesaler offers his credit to the manufacturer in exchange for the goods. A similar commercial credit transaction takes place each time the goods change ownership until such time as the goods reach the retailer, who also gives his commercial credit for the inventory of finished goods he has for resale. As the retailer makes a sale to a consumer, chances are the consumer will use his credit to acquire the merchandise.

Commercial credit, then, is used by all kinds of business enterprises to finance the acquisition of goods or services. The transaction may be very informal, involving nothing more than an order for goods or services by one business and the delivery of goods or performance of services by another business. Evidence of the transaction is an account receivable or a note receivable claim in the accounting records of the seller. The buyer's evidence of the transaction is an account payable or note payable obligation in his account records. Perhaps only a few businesses in the nation are free from the frequent credits and debits to these asset and liability accounts. Furthermore, although there are no precise data to support the point, the vast majority of all goods and services flowing through the productive and marketing processes are financed in this particular way.

The predicament of the medium-sized or small company faced

with liberal trade credit practices on the part of large competitors is at times a very difficult one. This situation was described by Merle T. Welshans in his article "Using Credit for Profit Making."[2]

Dun & Bradstreet has found that receivables difficulties rank first as a fundamental cause of business failure. As a setting for discussing it, consider a typical situation:

The firms in a particular industry have expanded their productive capacity and in the process have increased their break-even points. Furthermore, the fixed-cost component of total costs has risen more rapidly than has the variable-cost component, as a result of investment in labor-saving production equipment. The greater proportion of fixed costs to variable costs causes profits to fall rapidly when sales fail to reach the break-even point. (Conversely, once volume exceeds that point, profits rise rapidly.) So the smaller firms in the industry must do everything in their power to maintain high sales levels.

As a further complication, these companies have drawn down their cash resources while expanding, to a far greater extent than have their large competitors. The latter are in a position to expand sales at their expense by offering more liberal credit terms—an offer most welcome to customers at a time of high money costs and pressure on their own liquid resources.

The predicament of the small firms is obvious. On the one hand, accommodation of credit demands by additional investment in receivables will put extreme pressure on their dwindling cash resources (external sources are no longer readily available). On the other hand, if they fail to meet their large competitors' liberalized trade credit terms, they may expect sales to shrink drastically.

This bleak description of an all too common situation these days offers ample force to the argument for long-range planning before such conditions are created. A carefully paced rate of expansion (compatible with a well-balanced capital structure) may require much managerial discipline during periods of strong economic expansion, but the alternative is often financial disaster.

While there often may be no solution for small firms that find themselves in the plight described above, they may have feasible courses of action to take. Some of these are:

Offering special services to customers. (Their nature cannot here be specified, but smaller companies, by virtue of their size and flexibility, have typically their niche in the nation's industrial complex by competing on the basis of factors other than price or credit terms.)

Guaranteeing supplementary lines of credit between the customer and the customer's bank through "buy-back" agreements or other arrangements.

Selling or otherwise disposing of certain product lines to concentrate financial resources on those that are more productive of profits. (A strategic contraction of activities may free funds to accommodate increasing trade credit demands.)

Entering into "sale and lease-back" agreements, thereby preserving control of company assets and generating substantial increases in working capital to support further investment in receivables.

Accounts receiving financing. (Finance companies that provide funds on the

2 | *Harvard Business Review,* January-February 1967, p. 154.

basis of accounts receivable as collateral can play a strategic role in assisting firms under liquidity pressures. The typical 1% per month interest charge for this service should be regarded as an excessive cost of money only if it worsens the small firm's profit position. But failure to accommodate trade credit demands because of this presumed high cost of receivables financing could result in a serious sacrifice of profits.)

Likewise, recognition should be given to the fact that at times (such as the 1966 and 1969 "credit crunch" periods) some of the largest and best rated companies tend to slow down their payments to smaller and weaker creditors, thus forcing these smaller companies to "carry" them.[3]

It is worthwhile to note that the United States is far advanced in its use of commercial credit as contrasted with other countries throughout the world. Much more credit is offered and accepted by business firms here than in any other nation. Not only is our system simple and informal, it is much more extensive. This is principally due to the informal and well-developed network of interchange of credit information, which is unique among countries of the world.

Essential to a Mass-Distribution Economy

Some method of relieving the financial problem in the various steps of production and distribution is essential to the effectiveness of a mass distribution economy. Other than short-term loans and the ownership interests of businesses, there are few other ways to accomplish the financing task done by commercial credit. Even if businesses of all types were exclusively dependent upon bank loans and their own capital, it is doubtful that enough financial capacity could be marshaled to cover the value of the goods and services handled by means of commercial credit.

The widespread use of commercial credit and much of its importance as a form of business finance stem from the nation's economic developments. As the nation grew, the distances between manufacturers and their customers lengthened. With the development of transportation systems and adequate means of communication, population and businesses became scattered over vast geographical areas. Paralleling these developments, mass-production and mass-distribution methods assumed their place in the economy. Retailers also increased in number, and large-scale retailing became

3 / "Slow Retail Pay Hurting," *Women's Wear Daily,* August 19, 1970, p. 1. Also see Harlan R. Patterson, "What the Future Holds for Accounts Receivable," *Credit and Financial Management,* December 1970, p. 14; Herbert E. Trenning, "Service Charges—Goldmine or Boobytrap?" *Credit and Financial Management,* January 1971, p. 16; James V. McTevia, "How Companies Are Handling Service Charges," *Credit and Financial Management,* February 1971, p. 22.

necessary throughout the nation to meet the wants of a growing population. All these changes resulted in trade being transacted on a more impersonal basis and over greater distances. Speed of commercial transactions became essential as competitive forces became more intense. If the systems of production and distribution, as we know them today, were to be effective in a changed economy, some method of financing goods as they moved through the production and marketing phases was essential. If businesses were required to settle for their purchases with cash, only the imagination could conceive the resulting inefficiencies and delays. Commercial credit, then, has developed alongside economic developments as a means for businesses to finance an important part of their assets. Without this type of credit, a gap in the financing needs of businesses and the economy alike would exist.

Changing Attitudes toward Commercial Credit

It should not be assumed that commercial credit—the giving of goods and services in exchange for a promise of future payment—is of recent origin. The fact is that credit transactions between merchants date back to times of antiquity. In American colonial times, commercial credit was the backbone of trade with England and other European countries. The attitudes associated with credit and the credit instruments used as evidence of the transaction were, however, greatly different.

As compared with the prevailing attitude toward credit only a few centuries ago, the attitude today has undergone marked change. The early laws and attitudes concerning a delinquent debtor were rigid and harsh. Punishments ranged from imprisonment or enslavement to death in some instances. Quite obviously, this state of affairs placed the risk squarely upon the debtor and not upon the creditor. Furthermore, involvement in a credit transaction by a prospective debtor brought about serious consideration of the consequences of nonpayment, and this thwarted the role credit could play in an expanding economy. The abolition of rigorous laws, and hence more lenient attitudes regarding the delinquent debtor, are comparatively recent. Today, only the debtor who perpetrates fraud by means of credit transactions faces the threat of imprisonment. The creditor today who deals with businesses regards himself more as a business partner than one who can ruthlessly enforce his claim. Credit between business enterprises is recognized as mutually profitable, with each seeking to profit from the action of the other. Risk, rather than being placed solely upon the debtor, is now assumed also by the creditor. In a sense then, both have risk capital in the business enterprise, and an attitude of partnership is easily fostered.

Contributing to the changed attitude toward credit has been the different environment in which commercial credit transactions take place. Prior to the Civil War retailers had to estimate their inventory requirements for six months or longer. They took annual or semiannual trips to the market, where they purchased relatively large quantities of merchandise. Because of the large amount of credit needed and the lack of adequate communications systems, the credit was secured with a trade acceptance, promissory note, or draft. As transportation and communications improved, the need to estimate inventory requirements accurately diminished. Supplier's salesmen could now travel to distant points and retailers could visit the market more often. The open-book account, as evidence of the commercial credit transaction, supplanted in most cases the trade acceptance, promissory note, and draft. Retailers no longer had the risk of estimating requirements over an unrealistic period of time; they did not have to obligate themselves so heavily; and the tendency to shorten credit terms prevailed. Shorter terms meant that retailers could liquidate the obligations faster and thereby increase the turnover rate of suppliers' receivables. The adaptability of commercial credit to modern-day business practice has resulted in its becoming commonplace and even a customary means of financing this phase of business operations.

TERMS OF SALE

With each commercial credit transaction, an understanding must exist between the buyer and seller regarding the conditions for payment for the goods and services. The establishment of such conditions is generally known as the "terms of sale," "credit terms," or "payment terms." It is sound business practice which dictates that terms of sale be quoted on all invoices covering the shipment and on all instruments associated with the contract of sale. If specific terms of sale are not quoted, the buyer may legally presume that any terms established by custom for that line of trade may apply. The buyer's obligation to meet the terms of sale arises as the seller delivers the goods or services or meets other specified conditions of the sale. The terms of sale applicable in commercial credit transactions are a characteristic peculiar to this type of credit. Table 19-1, which shows the typical terms of the sale for 67 lines of trade, is a helpful reference for much of the discussion to follow.

Establishing Terms of Sale

The credit terms offered to customers should be determined by the major executives charged with the responsibility of making

TABLE 19-1

Terms of Sale in 67 Lines of Business

Industry (Manufacturers)	*Terms of Sale*
Aluminum windows, doors, and screens	Net 30 days, occasionally 2%-10 net 30 and 1%-net 30. Concerns report growing tendency for customers to take 60 or more days to pay.
Agricultural implements and machinery	2%-10 net 30 on smaller equipment. There are varied terms on heavier equipment such as special datings dependent upon seasons, consignment terms, and floor plan. Many concerns changed from consignment to floor plan terms.
Automobile parts and accessories	Primarily 2%-10th prox.
Bolts, screws, nuts, and nails	1%-10th & 25th net 30, ½%-10th & 25th net 30. Some extend 2%-10 net 30 and 1%-10 net 30.
Castings, nonferrous	Net 30 days. Some extend 1%-10 net 30 and ½%-10 net 30. Several concerns dropped 1% discount because of unfair practices.
Chemicals, industrial	Primary net 30 days. Terms of 1%-10 net 30 also extended. In 1960 some concerns granting 1% discounts discontinued practice because it did not induce customers to improve payments.
Coats and suits, men's and boys'	Most frequent terms are net 30 and net 60 days.
Coats and suits, women's	8%-10 EOM.
Concrete product	2%-10 net 30. Occasionally 2%-15 net 30 and 1%-net 30.
Construction machinery and equipment	On smaller equipment net 30 days. Also use 2%-10 net 30 and 1%-10 net 30. Installment terms extended on heavier equipment as well as progress payments on custom orders during manufacture. Cash discounts lowered or dropped by some concerns to avoid an increase in price. (1961)
Corsets, girdles, and brassieres	8%-10 EOM.
Dresses, rayon, silk, and acetate	8%-10 EOM. Some report extending extra time in 1961 to meet competition.
Drugs	Principally 2%-10 net 30. Also 2%-10th prox.

Reprinted with permission from *Terms of Sale for 1962,* Dun & Bradstreet, Inc., May 1962. Unfortunately, this publication has not been reissued since 1962, and Dun & Bradstreet, Inc., reports that there are no plans to update it. However, it is believed that the figures shown reflect a fairly accurate picture of the terms of sale being used currently in the industries listed.

TABLE 19-1 *(continued)*

Industry (Manufacturers)	*Terms of Sale*
Electrical parts and supplies	2%-15 prox. net 60 days. Also 2%-10 net 30.
Electronic components and accessories	Net 30 days. 1%-10 net 30 and 1%-10 days also used. Some concerns began offering 1% discount to improve customer payments (1960).
Foundries	Principally net 30 days. Terms of 1%-10 net 30 and ½%-10 net 30 also used. During 1959 and 1960 some concerns dropped 1% cash discount because of unfair practices by customers.
Fruits and vegetables, canners.	S.d.-b.l terms. Some canners grant 1%-10 days 1½%-10 days, and 1½%-10 net 30. Some canners report cutting down on sight draft and leaning more to open account.
Furniture	2%-30 net 60 days. Also grant 2%-10 net 30 and 1%-10 net 30 days. A few concerns report dropping 2% discount in 1961 because of unfair practices of customers.
Hardware and tools	Mainly 2%-10 net 30 days. Also 2%-10th prox. net 30, and 2%-10th & 25th.
Hosiery	Net 30 days. Longer terms being extended in some instances to meet competition.
Iron and steel, producers	½%-10 net 30 days. Some also extend ½%-10th & 25th net 30.
Iron and steel fabricators, architectural metal work	Generally ½%-10 net 30 days. Also ½%-10 days and net 30 days.
Lumber	2%-10 days. Also 2%-10 net 30 days.
Machine shops	Primarily net cash and net 30 days.
Machinery, industrial.	Generally net 30 days. Concerns also extend 1%-10 net 30, 2%-10th prox., and ½%-10 net 30 days. Time payment on heavier equipment. Several concerns previously granting cash discounts are reverting to net terms because of unfair practices of customers. Others report dropping discounts to reduce costs. Still others are granting cash discounts to meet competitor terms.
Meats and provisions, packers	Carload lots on terms of sight draft, bill of lading attached. Smaller lots on net 7 day terms.
Metal stampings	Generally net 30 days. Discount terms of ½%-10 net 30 and 1%-10 net 30 days are also granted in many instances. Several concerns granting 1% discounts are

TABLE 19-1 *(continued)*

Industry (Manufacturers)	*Terms of Sale*
	cutting down to ½% to realize more profit. Concerns also report customers requesting discount terms.
Millwork plants	2%-10 net 30 days. Also terms of net 30 days and 2%-10th prox. terms used.
Office and store fixtures, wooden . . .	Net 30 days. Some also grant discount terms of 1%-10 net 30 and also 2%-10 EOM.
Outerwear, knitted	Net 10 days EOM. Some concerns also grant terms of 2%-10 EOM.
Overalls and work clothing	Primarily net 30 days. In some instances 60 days and datings are extended. Several concerns report customers requesting longer terms.
Paints, varnishes, and lacquers	Net 30 days. Terms of 2%-10 net 60, and 1%-10 net 30 days also being granted. Several concerns report dropping 2% discounts to 1% and those granting 1% are discontinuing it. Reasons were to save money, to be in line with others, and customers taking unearned discounts.
Paper	2%-30 net 31. Terms of 2%-10 net 30, 1%-10 net 30, and net 30 also used. Several concerns say customers are requesting longer terms.
Paper bags	1%-10 net 30 and 2%-10 net 30 days.
Paper boxes	Generally 1%-10 net 30 days. Some also use 1%-10 EOM and 1%-15 net 30. Some report dropping 1% discount to cut expenses.
Petroleum, integrated operators	Primarily 1%-10 net 30 days. Load to load or c.o.d. to smaller retail accounts.
Plastic products	Mainly net 30 days. 1%-10 net 30 and ½%-10 net 30 days terms also used. Some concerns report customers pressing for much longer terms.
Printers, job	Generally net 30 days, 2%-10 net 30 and net 10 EOM terms also used.
Shoes	Primarily net 30 days.
Structural steel fabricators	½%-10 net 30 and 30 days. Contract terms for erected materials.
Tanks, steel	Mostly net 30 days. Some also grant ½%-10 net 30 terms.
Toys	2%-10 EOM and 2%-10 net 30. Dating terms also given.
Wire goods	Net 30 days. Terms of ½%-10 net 30, 1%-10 net 30, and 2%-10 net 30 also used.

TABLE 19-1 *(continued)*

Industry (Wholesalers)	*Terms of Sale*
Agricultural implements and machinery	2%-10th prox. and 2%-10th net 30 days. Net 10th prox. terms also used. Many concerns report extending longer terms in order to get business.
Automobile parts and accessories	2%-10th prox. and net 10th prox. Some concerns report dropping 2% discount because of competition.
Construction machinery.	2%-10 days and net 30 days. Seasonal terms and floor plan terms also extended.
Drugs and drug sundries.	2%-10 EOM, 2%-10 EOM 30, and 2%-10 net 30.
Dry goods	2%-10 EOM and 2%-10 net 60 days. Concerns report mills shortening terms and also lowering discounts.
Electrical parts and supplies	2%-10th prox. and 2%-10 net 30. 10th prox. terms also used.
Floor coverings	5%-15/4%-45 net 46 and 5%-15/4%-45 net 71.
Furniture	2%-30 net 60 and 2%-10 net 60. Also 2%-30 days and 2%-15 net 30.
Gasoline, fuel and lubricating oil	Gasoline—load to load and net 30 days. 1%-10 net 30 on lubricating oil and c.o.d. on fuel oil.
General merchandise.	2%-10 net 30 and 2%-10 prox. net 30. Also use 2%-30 days. Concerns report extending longer terms to compete.
Groceries	Primarily net 7 days and also c.o.d.
Hardware	2%-10th prox. and 2%-10 net days.
Household appliances, electrical	Major appliances--net cash on receipt of invoice, net 10 days and net 30 days. Traffic appliances—2%-10th & 25th prox. and 2%-10 days. Some report factory discounts being lowered.
Industrial supplies and equipment	2%-10 net 30 and also net 30 days. Some report dropping cash discount because of customer unfair practices.
Iron and steel sheets, strips, bars, and plates	½%-10 net 30.
Lumber	2%-10 days after arrival, net 30, on carload shipments. 2%-10 net 30 and 2%-10th prox. also used.
Lumber and building materials	2%-10 net 30 and 2%-10th prox. net 30. Also 10th prox. and net 30 days. Customers demanding longer terms at same rate of cash discount.
Meat and poultry	Mainly net 7 days. Also extend net 30 days.

TABLE 19-1 *(concluded)*

Industry (Wholesalers)	*Terms of Sale*
Paints, varnishes, and lacquers.	2%-10 net 60 and 2%-10 net 30.
Paper	1%-10 net 30 and 2%-10 net 30. 2%-30 days and 1%-10 EOM terms also used.
Plate and window glass	1%-10 net 30 and also 1%-10 days.
Plumbing and heating supplies	2%-10th prox. and 2%-10 net 30.
Shoes	Net 30 days.
Sporting goods	2%-10 EOM and 2%-10 net 30. Also net 30 days.

policy decisions. The policy relative to this element of the sale deserves just as careful consideration as any other element of the sales program. While the credit policy and terms of sale may be varied to meet the particular situation at hand, certain general principles are common to most situations. The factors which influence the policy to be adopted will be briefly considered and analyzed.

Two major variables are involved in the establishment of all terms of sale. The first is the *credit period,* also referred to as the net credit period, which is the length of time allowed the buyer before payment is considered past due. The second is the *cash discount* which may be allowed for early payment. Not all firms make a practice of allowing cash discounts, but they are so common in most trades that they should be considered whenever terms are discussed. The cash discount element of terms of sale should not, however, be confused with the trade discount, which is a pricing device and bears no relationship to the time of payment.

In addition to the importance of quoting terms of sale, a clear understanding should exist between seller and buyer as to the credit instrument employed. The most frequent evidence of a commercial credit transaction is, of course, the seller's accounts receivable ledger. In some few instances this is not the credit instrument, and the seller may use the promissory note, trade acceptance, or time draft, all of which require the buyer's signature. If one of these instruments is utilized, its use should be specified. Terms of sale, the credit instrument, delivery dates, and all other details of the credit transaction must be understood by the buyer if sellers are to avoid disputes and eventual loss of customers.

One of the other details of the credit transaction just referred to involves what is known as "anticipation." By contract or by custom most sellers allow their customers an anticipation rate,[4] equivalent to

---

4 / For an article which strongly takes issue with the practice of anticipation, see Eugene F. Drzycimski, "Does It Pay to 'Anticipate'?" *Credit and Financial Management,* November 1969, p. 20.

the "normal going interest" rate, to encourage payment from customers. There is no agreement as to whether this anticipation rate should be given to encourage prompt payment within the cash discount period or whether it should be offered to customers who have let the cash discount period expire and who need an inducement to pay before the end of the net period. Customs of the trade will determine which view will prevail in any transaction.

Factors Influencing Terms of Sale

Even though a great variety of terms of sale are used by American industries, there is a tendency in many trades toward standardized selling terms.[5] Frequently the standardized terms are referred to as "customary" or "regular" terms of sale. This trend suggests that the factors influencing the establishment and adjustment of selling terms similarly affect most sellers and buyers. When conditioning factors influence the members of a trade to adopt similar selling policies over time, such policies become customary or standardized for a trade.

Despite this trend, most companies have several terms of sale that serve as credit department guideposts. Once a company establishes its selling terms, they are likely to correspond to the rest of the trade. Established terms, however, are often subject to adjustment to meet the conditions affecting a particular customer or a circumstance prevailing in the trade. The following factors represent those which most importantly influence the adoption of particular selling terms and which on occasion affect an adjustment in terms for individual customers.

Rate of Stock Turnover. It is rather common practice for the seller to finance the buyer through at least a portion of his turnover period. Accordingly, there is a relationship between the period it takes to convert merchandise into cash and the time allowed for payment of the indebtedness. Those lines of trade having a rapid turnover of merchandise generally have a short credit period, and those lines of trade having relatively slow rates of stock turnover generally have a longer credit period. For example, the short credit period for most food products shown in Table 19-1 and the relatively longer credit period for dry goods and clothing items are illustrative of this factor.

Location of Customer and Transportation Facilities. Sellers in reaching distant markets are often at a disadvantage as compared to local producers. If the time for payment starts from the date of the

5 / For an interesting discussion of the history, development, and trends in terms of sale see Roy A. Foulke, *Current Trends in Terms of Sale* (New York: Dun & Bradstreet, Inc., 1959), Part I, pp. 5-43.

invoice, a distant customer does not have as much time after he receives the shipment as he would receive were he to purchase from a nearby source. To overcome this handicap and bring about more equality, the seller may attempt to equalize the distance and transportation factors by allowing a longer credit period or by allowing terms starting with receipt of goods or receipt of invoice. In this way, the time lost in transportation and the expense of carrying a larger stock by a distant customer are not entirely the loss of the buyer but are in part assumed by the seller through the terms of sale offered.

Regional Differences. When selling in certain sections of the country, it may be necessary to adjust terms to local conditions. While this factor is not as important today as it was in the past, there are many areas today in which this influence is still real. Crop farming, for example, is more seasonal than is dairy farming or farming where products are more diversified. To as reasonable an extent as possible, commercial credit selling terms should be adjusted to this condition. It may also be necessary to make similar adjustment where the nature of a major industry is such that the income of its customers is very irregular.

Character of the Goods. The adoption of terms and their adjustment may be on the basis of the character of the goods. Many concerns sell a wide variety of products, and a single selling term may not apply equally well. Some products on the same invoice may carry no cash discount while a cash discount may be applicable to others. Likewise the credit period may vary from one line of goods to another, even though such goods are sold by the same supplier. Variations in terms of sale thus may be the result of such things as the margin of profit, the perishability of goods, the novelty of the product, and even the seasonal characteristics. For example, goods that are very perishable and those that afford a narrow profit margin usually have a short credit period and little or no cash discount. Conversely, a longer credit period and perhaps a larger cash discount are granted when goods are seasonal, new and novel, and yield a wide margin of profit.

Nature of Credit Risk. The generally announced terms to a particular trade need not be made uniform to all customers. There should be some variation of terms to correspond to the nature of the credit risk. Thus certain buyers who represent poor credit risks may be sold on a cash basis or on c.o.d. (cash on delivery) or c.b.d. (cash before delivery) terms, whereas the better credit risks are given the advantage of more liberal terms of sale. Peculiarly, when most buyers in a particular trade are weak credit risks it may become standard practice to use the above terms, and they may continue even after this reason has ceased to exist.

Class of Customer. Variations in selling terms may also exist because of customer differences. Customers may be classified in numerous ways, as by size of order, type of buyer (wholesaler or retailer), and even by type of wholesaler or type of retailer. Customers making small purchases are frequently allowed shorter terms than the standard terms for the trade. On the other hand, large buyers who represent an important portion of the supplier's total volume may be given terms that are more lenient than customary. Associated with the size of order and the type of customer is the ability of some customers to perform important marketing functions for the suppliers. Large buyers, for example, are frequently in a position to assume the storage function provided the selling terms are adjusted to their requirements and other discounts are made available to them. Usually, as a matter of industry trade practices, wholesalers are given different terms than retailers.

Competition. The competitive influence on selling terms is perhaps the strongest factor to be considered. Since terms of sale cannot be determined without awareness of the action of competitors, the influence of competition frequently causes modification to be made in the customary terms of sale. Because of this we find extra datings or seasonal datings being granted various customers. We may also find certain customers who, because of the competitive pressures which they are able to exert, are granted terms of MOM (middle of month) or EOM (end of month). Too frequently the effect of the competitive influence is a departure from the sound policy which may have been originally determined. Originally some of these modifications of customary terms are made to favored customers and are considered exceptions. Competitors, however, come to adopt the same terms, so generally the more lenient terms become standard trade practice. When this happens, the effectiveness of terms of sale in stimulating sales is lost, and the entire trade may find itself following unsound practices without any one firm deriving any special benefit.

Financial Resources of the Seller. In determining policy relative to the terms of sale, the ability of the seller to carry accounts receivable may force some modification of terms. Obviously, a new business venture which is short of working capital will of necessity sell on shorter terms than might be offered by a well-established business with adequate resources to carry large accounts receivable. If many firms in a particular industry are financially weak, this may cause the policy to be generally adopted. It is said, for example, that the shortage of working capital of the early manufacturers of automobiles led to the adoption of cash terms by the industry. This same policy has persisted long after the shortage of working capital was no longer present as a reason.

Economic Conditions. Business activity is influenced by economic conditions, and hence some business practices are modified in accordance with the business cycle. There is a strong tendency for selling terms to be adjusted in periods of prosperity or depression. Probably the ideal adjustment to cyclical changes would be to tighten terms during prosperity and to liberalize terms during depression. The following quotation illustrates how terms of sale are negotiable and may vary from those commonly accepted in an industry:[6]

> The cutoff date for the payment of invoices gets quite a kicking around from the stores. Traditionally, it's been the 25th of the month. But some stores set the 15th and some the 20th.
> Then too, there's a question about when credit terms become effective. One store covers all bases with "whichever is later, receipt of invoice or goods."
> Special charges are quite the mode with some stores, such as a 1 per cent deduction for central warehouse bookkeeping and distribution expense.
> Problems come up, too, from some stores who use order forms saying "1/10 EOM, 30 days extra." The manufacturers ship on terms of "1/10 EOM" without the 30 days extra.
> There's a statement by one retailer that makes a factor roar with laughter, or maybe curse with gusto. The store gives six long paragraphs of instructions for packing, shipping, and invoicing and then says, "Failure to comply with the terms, conditions and instructions of this order will result in our chargeback to your firm for the added handling costs."
> A further point that burns the factors is when the store refers to the date of its payment check. There's a practice by some to draw up dated checks, but not to mail them for several weeks.

In actual practice, customers demand longer terms during depression or recession and sellers may offer this accommodation. During prosperity, however, there is seldom a tightening of terms as ideally proposed. By tightening terms during the prosperity phase of the cycle the overstimulation of business activity would be somewhat reduced; and by liberalizing terms during the depression phase a stimulus to business would be in operation when it is most needed. This policy has to commend it the arguments that credit would thus be used to aid or abate business stimulation rather than to make it less stable and also that it works with the coming trend rather than against it. Unfortunately, not all business policies are made because of logical reasons, nor can all competitors be expected to be as rational as they might be. Accordingly, and all too frequently, selling terms are not adjusted to changing economic conditions.

6 / "Slow Retail Pay Hurting," *op. cit.,* p. 35.

Attitude of Credit Manager. The credit manager's attitude can influence selling terms. For example, it has been stated that [7]

in the 1970's investment in accounts receivable will require much more attention than ever before. It is up to the financial executive to establish a credit policy which will encourage sales, increase profits, and at the same time keep the investment in receivables at a minimum.

The degree of influence he may register, however, is dependent upon his position within the company relative to other policy-making positions and the relationship he may have established with other selling departments. If the credit manager considers his sole responsibility to be the elimination of bad-debt losses and if he is successful in imposing this attitude throughout the company, the seller may unduly shorten the credit terms. This, and even the opposite extreme of attitude, will abort the function of the credit department, to the detriment of the seller and customers. Such narrow and one-sided concepts on the part of credit managers are in conflict with the role of credit management in our economy.

TERMS OF SALE CLASSIFIED

Terms of sale can be classified into the following groups:

1. Prepayment terms.
2. Cash terms.
3. Ordinary terms.
4. Single-payment or lumped-order terms.
5. Special-datings terms.
6. Consignment terms.

Prepayment Terms

Technically, prepayment terms are not characteristic of a commercial credit transaction. In all instances where prepayment terms are used, the element of risk which is inherent in credit transactions is absent or at least slight. It is necessary, though, to discuss briefly these terms to establish a point of reference. This class of terms includes c.b.d. (cash before delivery), c.o.d. (cash on delivery), c.w.o. (cash with order), c.i.a. (cash in advance), and s.d.-b.l. (sight draft with bill of lading attached).

Aside from a few instances where they are customary in certain

7 / George L. Marrah, "Managing Receivables," *Financial Executive*, July 1970, p. 38. Also see Lester Nelson, "The Courts Look at Credit as a Sales Tool," *Credit and Financial Management*, September 1970, p. 22.

lines of trade, the above terms indicate the seller's unwillingness to accept the credit risk. It may be that the credit risk was never satisfactory or that having once been acceptable, the risk has deteriorated to a point of unacceptability. Not only is the seller unwilling to accept the buyer's credit, he often requires the buyer to submit payment by certified check or cashier's draft, thereby not even assuming the risk of check clearance. It is not advisable to use these terms to ship new orders to customers unless arrangements for prepayment have been made. Furthermore, if the customer has a past-due balance it is wise to reach an agreement on a specific payment schedule for the past-due account.

C.o.d. terms and s.d.-b.l. terms are not entirely free of risk as are the other prepayment terms. The risk involved in the use of these terms centers on the possibility that the buyer may reject the shipment after it has arrived at destination. In such instances the seller has the alternatives of accepting the round-trip transportation costs, entering into a questionable credit arrangement with the original buyer, or, as a last resort, seeking out another possible customer in the immediate vicinity of the merchandise. It is desirable that the seller insist on cash or a certified or cashier's check in payment of c.o.d. shipments.

S.d.-b.l. terms, which are a modification of c.o.d. terms, involve an order bill of lading, properly endorsed, attached to a sight draft. These instruments are sent to a bank in or near the buyer's city. When the buyer is notified of the arrival of the merchandise, he may inspect the condition of the shipment and then pay the sight draft at the bank. In return for his payment of the sight draft he receives the bill of lading, which grants him title and possession of the shipment. Once a shipment is made on s.d.-b.l. terms, the seller should be cautious of the buyer who pleads lack of funds at the time the goods arrive. Coupled with this claim the buyer is likely to encourage the seller to permit the bank to release the shipping papers, promising payment in 10 days. The temptation for the seller to accept this arrangement is strong, for otherwise he is confronted with unattractive alternatives. To accept the arrangement means accepting credit from a customer whose credit was unsatisfactory a few days earlier.

Cash Terms

Cash terms do not indicate the immediate payment of cash, but the acceptance of credit for a period of approximately 10 days from the date of invoice. Clearly, cash terms are a step removed from prepayment terms, as the credit period is very short. The time interval allows the buyer time to inspect and accept the shipment, and the seller's risk is lessened in comparison to more common (longer) terms. These terms do not usually allow the buyer a discount privilege. Since the seller has no special recourse in the event the buyer fails to pay, he is involved with the usual degree of credit risk.

Ordinary Terms

In many lines of trade the terms of sale include only two component parts—the net credit period and the cash discount. Terms involving no other features are referred to as ordinary terms. Typical of the frequently used ordinary terms is "2/10, net 30" (2 percent, 10 days, net 30 days). If a customer receives an invoice for $300, dated March 15, terms 2/10, net 30, he has the choice of paying $294 on or before March 25 or $300 by April 14. By electing to pay the $300 the buyer pays the equivalent of $6 for the use of $294 for 20 days. Buyers are usually well advised to take advantage of the cash discount. In this case the discount is equivalent to 36.7 percent a year.

Single-Payment or Lumped-Order Terms

In a number of industries sellers permit customers to accumulate their obligations over a short period of time. These arrangements are used where there is a high frequency of purchase and repurchase by individual buyers. Rather than bill the customer for each individual order, the multiple number of orders is accumulated, usually for a month, and the customer billed as of one date.

Single-payment terms are in reality a special form of dating. The terms used may be based on EOM (end of month), MOM (middle of month), and proximo (a specified date in the following month). If EOM terms are used, all sales made during a given month are dated as of the first day of the following month. The cash discount period and net credit period commence with this date.[8] Under terms of 8/10 EOM, common in the apparel trades, all deliveries in the month of October would be included in the statement rendered as of the last business day of October, and payment with 8 percent deducted would be due November 10.

MOM terms, a variation of EOM terms, allow for a shorter total credit period. Under MOM terms all purchases made between the 1st and the 15th of any month are consolidated and a statement rendered as of the 15th. Purchases made between the 16th and the

8 / Under EOM terms it is common practice for the end of the month to be considered the 25th day of the month in which the invoice is dated. Thus, on a purchase made on May 26 with terms of 2/10 EOM, the cash discount could be taken through July 10. This is subject to negotiation between buyer and seller.

end of the month are similarly consolidated as of the last day of the month (or as of the first of the next month). Hence all purchases invoiced the first half of a month are to be paid less discount as of the 25th, and purchases accumulated the last half of the month are due the 10th of the following month if cash discount is desired.

Proximo terms specify a date in the month following shipment by which the cash discount must be taken. In many instances of use, there is no distinction between proximo terms and EOM terms, but the use of one or the other terms has become customary in the particular trade. Proximo terms do, however, often provide for a shorter discount period than the net credit period. Hence terms of 2/10 prox., net 30 set the discount date as of the 10th of the month following the shipments and a due date the last day of that month.

Special-Datings Terms

To adjust terms to conditions peculiar to a trade or its customers, special datings are used. The use of special datings functions to extend the credit period. "Season" dating and "extra" dating are two of the common credit terms denoting special dating.

Season dating is used where the demand for a product is seasonal. Hence, an inducement is needed to have a buyer purchase and accept delivery well ahead of his selling season. The seller benefits from these arrangements by being able to plan his production more in accord with his sales curve and also by shifting some of the storage burden to the buyer. The buyer, of course, has the goods on hand without an immediate investment of his own funds. This type of dating compensates the buyer for the storage burden and also brings the payment date closer to the buyer's selling season. Summer wearing apparel, for example, may be purchased in October, delivered in January on terms of 2/10, net 60, but the invoice may be dated May 1. These terms permit the discount on or before May 10 and establish the net due date as no later than July 1. This same arrangement may be accomplished by extending the regular selling terms an additional 30, 60, or 90 days during the preselling season months.

Extra dating is another method of giving long discount and credit periods to customers. Extra dating terms treat the discount period and credit periods as identical, but rather than state the terms as 2/70/70 they are customarily stated as 2/10-60 ex. Under these terms the purchaser is expected to pay the stated amount of the invoice, less 2 percent, 70 days after date of invoice.

R.o.g. (receipt of goods) and a.o.g. (arrival of goods) terms and a few other similar arrangements are used to compensate for disadvantages imposed on distant buyers. The effect of these terms is to adjust the beginning date of the discount period and often of the net credit period. Since terms may start with the date of the invoice, r.o.g. and a.o.g. terms adjust the entire discount period so that the first day of the discount period is in correspondence with receipt of goods or arrival of goods, whichever may be applicable. Terms of this type are often competitively necessary for those sellers dealing with distant customers.

Consignment Terms

Consignment terms are most often used for other than credit reasons. Agricultural products are customarily sold on consignment terms with commission agents; new products, and for that matter *any* merchandise for which a distributing organization refuses to accept the purchase risk, may be handled on consignment terms; and some goods of very high unit value move through marketing channels under these terms. They may also be used when the credit worthiness of the buyer does not justify ordinary terms of sale and when the buyer lacks the resources to satisfy prepayment arrangements such as c.o.d. or s.d.-b.l. Title to consigned goods remains with the seller, while the recipient acts as an agent for the seller. Credit managers must use caution when transactions involve the use of these terms because of the legal implications. The goods must be physically segregated from other goods; proceeds from the sale of such goods must be separately accounted for; insurance on the merchandise, in the name of the consignor, must be carried by the shipper; and periodic sales and inventory reports and remittances by the consignee must be provided for. Credit managers are well advised to seek the services of the legal profession to draw up the consignment contracts and prepare the necessary directions to the consignee.

CASH DISCOUNTS AND EQUIVALENT RATES OF INTEREST

The attractiveness to buyers of taking advantage of cash discounts is indicated by Table 19-2. It is obvious that the equivalent interest rates are substantially above money rates of interest, and hence businesses would do well to borrow money in order to take advantage of discounts rather than forgo this attractive return. In some businesses, particularly retail enterprises, the discounts taken can make the difference between a profit and a loss. Several offices of the National Association of Credit Management have complete tables, similar to this, for distribution to their members, informing them of the advantage of taking all cash discounts.

TABLE 19-2
Equivalent Rates of Interest
to Selected Cash Discounts*

Terms	Annual Rate
½/10, net 30	9%
1/10, net 30	18
2/10, net 60	14.4
2/30, net 60	24
2/10, net 30	36
3/10, net 30	54
3/30, net 60	36
4/10, net 60	28.8

*To compute such equivalents, find the number of days' difference between the cash discount period and the net credit period. This represents the number of days the seller gains in the use of his funds when the buyer remits within the discount period. The potential number of times this is apt to occur in 360 days × the rate of discount = the equivalent rate of interest per year. For example, for terms 2/10, net 30, 360 ÷ 20 = 18 × 2% = 36%.

CASH DISCOUNTS AND FEDERAL LEGISLATION

Terms of sale can be used by sellers to practice price discrimination. When discounts are varied from one buyer of the same class to another, "price discrimination" is said to exist. Credit terms came under the scrutiny of the federal government during the 1930s, when the Robinson-Patman Act became law. Insofar as credit terms are concerned, the purpose of the Robinson-Patman Act is to prohibit price discrimination which results from discriminatory credit terms. If discounts are allowed uniformly to all customers of the same class (i.e., all the manufacturer customers, all the wholesaler accounts, and all the retailer customers), the seller is not practicing price (or terms) discrimination and this is a permissible policy. The giving of larger cash discounts to one buyer than to another of the same class, the acceptance of terms insisted on by "terms chiselers," and the allowance of late discounts when not applicable uniformly to all customers of the same class are generally considered to be illegal practices.

Although it is not entirely clear just what variations in credit terms are prohibited under the law, the Robinson-Patman Act is regarded as lending a legal tendency to greater uniformity of these credit terms. During the past few decades, this tendency appears to be in evidence more and more.

CASH DISCOUNTS OR TRADE DISCOUNTS?

The cash discount as treated in this chapter should be considered as a *reward* to prompt-paying customers for (1) saving the seller additional costs associated with a slower turnover of his receivables, and (2) avoiding the collection difficulties involved in handling slow-paying accounts. It may also be considered a *penalty* assessed against slow-paying customers to compensate for the higher costs and inconveniences of handling their business. In the former case the quoted price may be considered the list price, and the cash discount allowed would then be roughly equivalent to the expenses saved by doing business with prompt-pay customers. In the latter case, clearly, the net price is the true realized price, and the penalty collected from the slow-paying customers is approximately the amount necessary to cover the expense of doing business with them.

It would be very difficult to collect this penalty if it were so labeled, and efforts to enforce payment of "fines" for delinquency would be strongly resisted and cause much ill will. Psychologically, it is better to collect it as a benefit withdrawn. Loss of the discount then appears to the buyer as the withdrawal of a gain which, through his own fault, he did not obtain. Even though stating terms so that the cash discount is made to appear as a reward rather than as a penalty is strategic, we should not allow this strategy to mislead us as to the true nature of the transaction. Considering the cash discount as a penalty assessed against slow-paying customers requires that this penalty, if it is to be equitable, be no larger than necessary to recover the additional costs involved in handling this class of customer. If discount terms are to be logical, these costs should supply the base which determines the amount of the discount.

The costs to be recovered by the penalty are: (1) for the use of the seller's capital during the extra time allowed for payment, (2) for the assumed risk of potential bad-debt losses, and (3) for the increased billing and collection costs. It was previously shown that 1, 2, or even 3 percent is the amount of cash discount usually allowed in many trades. It is generally thought that this amount of discount generally corresponds to the cost savings incurred when doing business with prompt-pay customers. Many discounts under the guise of a cash discount are, however, as high as 6, 7, or 8 percent, and higher. In many instances these larger discounts are not denied even though payment is late. The correct interpretation of large discounts established with a high degree of liberality is that they are *trade discounts* and not cash discounts. It is also proper and sound logic to place a similar interpretation on special-dating terms when the discount is not disallowed because of late payment. Similarly, when the discount period and the net credit period are synonymous, the "cash discount" is considered by some credit managers to be in reality a trade discount.

When discounts offered are so large that all customers take advantage of them, whether paying on time or not, they cease to function as cash discounts. Cash discounts established on some logical basis and allowed or disallowed as specified can function automatically to classify credit customers. When, however, the credit service is taken advantage of by a sizable group of customers because the discount is too liberal, it is clearly a trade discount.

REVIEW AND DISCUSSION QUESTIONS

1. Explain the function of commercial credit.
2. Discuss the statement, "The reliance of businesses upon commercial credit outweighs alternative sources of credit."
3. Why do receivables difficulties rank first as a fundamental cause of business failure?
4. How can the larger companies force small companies to "carry" them during periods of a "credit crunch"?
5. Comment on the changing attitudes toward commercial credit.
6. What are the major variables involved in terms of sale?
7. How do the buyers' rates of stock turnover influence terms of sale? How do other factors exert an influence?
8. Define and distinguish between:
   a) Prepayment terms.
   b) Cash terms.
   c) Ordinary terms.
   d) Single-payment or lumped-order terms.
   e) Special-datings terms.
   f) Consignment terms.
   g) Cash discount.
   h) Trade discount.
   i) Net period.
   j) Anticipation.
9. Why does the rate of anticipation tend to vary directly with the prevailing interest rate at commercial banks?
10. Explain why terms of sale are often negotiable.
11. Explain why a manufacturer might use consignment terms rather than establish price under resale price maintenance arrangements.
12. How do you compute equivalent rates of interest to selected cash discounts?
13. Is there a logical basis to believe that some cash discounts are in reality trade discounts?
14. Explain the relationship between the Robinson-Patman Act and the terms of sale offered by a manufacturer.

20

Business Use of Cash
(Financial) Credit

While commercial credit is used to finance a portion of the current assets of a business in its acquisition of merchandise and services, most businesses require additional financial assistance. It was shown in Chapter 18 that a substantial portion of other business financial needs may be met by cash borrowing. Borrowing of funds may take the form of short-term, intermediate-term, or long-term borrowing. Short-term borrowing is most often undertaken to acquire current assets not covered by commercial credit or by the owners' investment. Intermediate-term and long-term borrowing, on the other hand, may be undertaken to finance both current and fixed assets. Commercial banks, business finance companies (primarily factors and commercial finance companies), and the Small Business Administration are the principal sources for short-term[1] and intermediate-term loans. Long-term loans are available from such sources as insurance companies; investment houses; trust companies; and, to some extent, the Small Business Administration, wealthy individuals, and commercial banks.

COMMERCIAL CREDIT MANAGEMENT VERSUS
CASH CREDIT MANAGEMENT

Commercial credit management is concerned with a highly specialized type of business credit—that of facilitating the sale of merchandise and services in exchange for credit. With a high degree of specialization existing, there is a tendency for the individual managements of the specialized operations to regard their activities

1 / Another source of funds for short-term needs is the issuance and sale of commercial paper. This will be discussed in a subsequent section of this chapter.

399

apart from the entire credit structure. This preoccupation with one's own activities is a natural tendency and has many advantages. Certainly it is of first-order importance that a credit manager conceive, thoroughly understand, and effectively administer the activities of his own company's credit department. He would, however, be seriously deficient in his effectiveness as a credit manager if he failed to gain at least a general knowledge of the more common forms of business credit. Only by having an intimate understanding of his own credit function and a clear concept of the needs and uses of other forms of credit can he best serve his company and its customers. Hence, it is not enough that he recognize the economic impact and interrelationships of all types of credit; nor is it enough that he clearly understand that the very foundation of all credit lies in our commercial banking system. If he is to play the important role of guiding, suggesting, and recommending in regard to the financial aspects of his company and its customers, he must have a clear and concise knowledge of the several classes of business credit.

Whether a credit executive is in a position to be directly concerned with the financial needs of his own company is frequently dependent upon his position in the organizational structure.[2] Organizational structures vary according to the number and type of functions to be performed. A small or medium-sized enterprise may well employ a single executive who is charged with both commercial credit administration and the company's working capital requirements. This person may be designated the treasurer, with a subtitle, credit manager. If this executive is to work both sides of the fence—i.e., customers' credit and his company's credit—he must be intellectually equipped to cope with the several types of business credit. Large business enterprises, on the other hand, often divide financial responsibilities among several executives. Commercial credit management may be established in a separate department headed by a credit manager. The short-term, intermediate-term, and long-term capital requirements of the company may be under the administration of an executive designated as the treasurer, or the treasurer and a select group of company officers. Whatever the policy of the company dictates, it is apparent that these executives need specialized knowledge to perform their tasks effectively. The close interrelationship between credit management and debt management in any company establishes the need for knowledge of all phases of business credit.

Irrespective of titles, organizational structure, and company size

2 / For a discussion of the role of the credit executive, see the Suggested Readings at the end of the chapter.

any executive charged with the responsibility of commercial credit management will be called upon to advise his credit customers on their financial problems. The increased tendency for credit managers to counsel their business customers is fostered by the present-day partnership concept of creditor and debtor. Many commercial credit managers report that they consider the customer-counseling aspect of their credit departments to be one of the most valuable services rendered. Their clear understanding of other sources of working capital and ability to recommend their use have often given new life to a marginal or deteriorating customer. Similarly, cash loan managers must recognize the financial role played by commercial credit in financing a portion of their customers' current assets. Hence, both commercial credit managements and cash loan managements need more than a casual grasp of all types of business credit to serve better their own employer and their debtor customers.

The parts of this book devoted to business credit can be a valuable source of information for cash-lending executives, despite the fact that cash loans to businesses are not a major portion of its content. This stems from the fact that selling merchandise and services on credit and making business loans have a marked degree of similarity. The credit information utilized, the credit decision-making process, and the collection policies of these two fields of credit extension are very similar. The significant differences between commercial credit extension and the making of business loans stem from the dependence placed on various sources of credit information, differences in credit standards, and the methods of controlling customers' accounts.

COMMERCIAL BANK LOANS

As a source for short-term and intermediate-term loans, no other institution is as dominant as the commercial bank.[3] The tremendous financial resources of our commercial banking system make it the largest and most frequently used source for borrowed capital. This is in accord with the basic functions of the American banking system.

Need for Loans

As we saw in Chapter 18, most business enterprises need cash credit to finance a portion of their assets, and the business not requiring such financial assistance is indeed rare. Inasmuch as no one type of business credit normally meets the financial requirements of

3 / For a description of the loaning activities of commercial banks, see the Suggested Readings at the end of the chapter.

a business, commercial bank loans are needed to fulfill a part of business financial needs. Cash loans might be said to equalize the financial requirements of a business with its productive and marketing operations. Cash needs of businesses, though, are seldom constant or regular. At certain times large amounts of working capital are needed,[4] and at other times only small sums.

A retailer, for example, may borrow from his bank shortly after a heavy buying season in order to take cash discounts on merchandise credit obligations. Wholesalers may borrow to acquire inventory and take advantage of suppliers' special offerings. Manufacturers may borrow in order to acquire working capital for current manufacturing operations. These examples serve to illustrate how commercial bank loans are often used to supplement commercial credit. This is only one possible use of bank loans. Realistically, when a business borrows from a commercial bank, it may use the deposit money which is created to fulfill any number of business needs. Whatever the specific use made of the borrowed funds, the fact remains that the need for commercial bank loans stems from the very nature of business itself. That is, the disbursements of the firm do not coincide with the receipt of income insofar as time is concerned.

Credit Policy of Commercial Banks

A business firm can enjoy a long and continuous financial relationship with its commercial bank. Other than acting as a depository for business funds, the bank stands ready to serve its customers by providing an important segment of their financial needs. A commercial bank, however, usually will require borrowers to meet higher credit standards than they are asked to meet in commercial credit transactions. Business houses failing to meet the standards must acquire cash by borrowing from other, frequently less attractive, sources.

Chief among the reasons for the high credit requirements of banks is the fact that they are entrusted with the public's money. A bank acting in this capacity must guard this trust above all else if its confidence and reputation are to be maintained. A Federal Reserve member bank cannot ask for extensions of its obligations without impairing its position in the system. It is said that the liquidity of banks depends largely upon the liquidity of their customers. The requirement that banks always be in a position to meet their obligations places a necessary limitation on extensions granted to

---

4 / At times it is hard to tell the lenders from the borrowers. Manufacturers of countless products are offering customers an increasing number of lease deals, installment credit plans, and trade financing arrangements, and are then turning to lenders to fill their own cash gap.

customers. Banks do grant extensions to borrowers who find it inconvenient to meet their loan maturity, but the number of these cannot exceed a safe limit, beyond which the liquidity of the bank would be impaired.

Another factor which contributes to the banks' attitude is that their stock-in-trade is money and not merchandise. Merchandise creditors generally have a wider margin of profit from the sale of merchandise than banks do from the lending of money. Because of this, merchandise creditors may be more willing to accept marginal risks and grant extensions not considered prudent by a bank. Furthermore, the amount of credit involved in a commercial credit transaction may represent only a small portion of the debtor's total obligations, whereas bank loans frequently represent a major portion of the firm's total debt. These facts clearly indicate that an extension granted by a merchandise creditor has very different implications from the extension granted by a bank.

Finally, banks are subject to the supervision of state and federal banking authorities. They are restricted on the size of loan made to any one borrower; they are not permitted to loan on the security of their own stock; and they are limited in the amount they may lend to an officer of the bank. There are exceptions in one form or another to the above restrictions; but, more importantly, bank loans are periodically examined. Bank examiners and their supervisors have the responsibility of enforcing the numerous administrative regulations affecting bank loan activities. Obviously, if a bank is to be regarded highly in the Federal Reserve System and by its examining bodies, it must not have a record of lending money to a high proportion of weak credit risks. Thus, legal regulations are another factor affecting the standards imposed on business borrowers.

The great majority of bankers operate in accordance with the various state and federal restrictions. Despite the occasional lending abuses which, when publicized, shake the public's confidence in the offending bank, most businessmen experience an atmosphere of conservatism and solidarity when dealing with their bankers.

Kinds of Loans

Traditionally, loans to businesses were made to finance their short-term needs, and the maturities corresponded to the normal terms of sale of 30, 60, or 90 days. During the depression years of the 1930s, commercial banks began to change their policies with respect to loan maturities, and lending was adjusted more to the needs of borrowers. The lending of short-term capital left many business firms with inadequate funds for continuous working capital and sorely needed capital to refinance their bond issues. Since that time banks have been making intermediate-term loans, with maturities from one to five years, and long-term loans with maturities in excess of five years. Hence, when commercial bank loans are classified by maturity they may be referred to as *short-term* loans (maturity less than one year), *intermediate-term* loans (maturity from one to five years), and *long-term* loans (maturity over five years). The trend throughout the last four decades has been toward greater use of the longer term loans.

Bank loans may also be classified according to security. Loans made may be either *secured* or *unsecured.* A secured loan is one which relies not only on the borrower's promise to pay but also on the pledge of some specified property. The bank can exercise its lien upon the collateral in the event of nonpayment by the borrower. Banks prefer security which is readily convertible into cash. Government bonds, for ·example, which are easily converted into cash, represent the highest quality of collateral. Businesses may, and often do, pledge inventories,[5] stocks, bonds, mortgages, equipment, real estate, accounts receivable, and other property of value.

The unsecured loan is one that does not involve the pledge of collateral, but is based solely on the credit worthiness of the business borrower. Evidence of this type of loan is usually the borrower's promissory note. An unsecured loan made on the basis of a single business or a person's signature is known as "single-name" paper.

Another type of unsecured loan takes the form of commercial paper which is discounted at the commercial bank by the borrower. This paper consists of trade acceptances and promissory notes used between buyers and sellers in some lines of business. The seller who holds this paper may endorse it and discount it at his bank. This process gives rise to the terms "two-name," "double-name," or "endorsed" commercial paper. The borrower (seller) by endorsing the instrument assumes a contingent liability, and hence the bank has the specific promise of the buyer of the goods to pay the indebtedness as well as the contingent promise of the seller (borrower). Most American businesses use the open-book account method of selling their merchandise, and therefore this type of paper is relatively scarce.[6]

5 / Financing goods (usually commodities) held by third parties in warehouses is by no means a new or untried method of lending. A very successful record in terms of volume, profitable return, and loss history has been reported by many banks. However, banks face certain risks not generally experienced when they hold the collateral offered by the borrower in their possession on their own premises. For a discussion of the use of collateral in bank loans, see the Suggested Readings at the end of the chapter.

6 / Under certain circumstances drafts or bills of exchange are drawn against the buyer's bank, and upon acceptance the instrument becomes a *banker's acceptance.* Sellers may hold these until maturity or discount them at their banks. In effect, when a bank places its

Double-name commercial paper must be distinguished from that which arises from an *accommodation endorsement*. Some businesses and persons are required, because of a weak credit condition or other circumstance, to bolster the quality of their credit by supplying a comaker or endorser to their promissory note. When this is done the comaker is lending his credit worthiness as an accommodation, and this paper is then referred to as double-name or accommodation paper. In this latter instance the loan is classified as a secured loan, whereas the loan which results from the endorsed trade acceptance or note is classed as an unsecured loan. The endorser of a promissory note as an accommodation guarantees payment and is legally liable for payment in the event of default on the part of the maker.

Bank Interest Rates—Discount Rates

Interest rates on bank loans and discount rates on discounted paper are determined by a number of factors. In contrast to consumer cash credit, an established rate of interest does not apply to all customers. Rather, the rate charged a business customer is determined by the amount and term of the loan, the credit standing of the borrower, the relative tightness or abundance of bank funds, the compensating balance maintained on deposit with the lending bank, the geographical location of the bank, and the demand for loans. In general, small businesses pay higher rates than large enterprises; rates vary inversely with the size of loan; and long-term loans (over five years' maturity) command a lower rate of interest than do shorter term loans.

Commercial banks employ two methods of collecting interest charges. In the case of short-term loans of 30, 60 or 120 days and advances made on customers' discounted paper, the interest charge is deducted at the time the loan (advance) is made. Technically, this charge is referred to as the "discount," "bank discount," or "discount rate." The rate of discount paid by a customer is not the same as the rate of interest paid on other loans. If, for example, a $10,000 note which is to mature in six months is discounted at 6 percent, the discount would be 0.03 of $10,000, which is $300. The business borrower receives $9,700 as the proceeds of the loan, and upon maturity of the note a payment of $10,000 is due the bank. The user has use of $9,700 and not $10,000, and hence the discount

signature on the draft or bill of exchange it is guaranteeing the credit of the buyer. If the bank accepting the instrument is a well-known bank, the instrument is regarded as "prime" paper and as such is sought by other banks for use as a secondary reserve. Acceptances of this type can be converted into cash at a low rate of interest. In banking circles, this and the discounting of notes and trade acceptances are sometimes referred to as "open-market loans."

rate is higher than the interest rate. Interest on other loans is usually calculated on the daily balance of the loan and charged to the borrower monthly.[7]

Line of Credit and Compensating Balances

Once a business has established a relationship with its bank that engenders credit worthiness, a line of credit may be set. A line of credit is the maximum amount the bank is willing to lend. Lines of credit are established after the bank has made a thorough analysis of the customer's needs, credit standing, and frequency of cash needs. Once the line is established, it is much more convenient for the bank and for the customer to borrow needed amounts within the line without the formalities of a new credit investigation, analysis, and credit decision. A line of credit in no way obligates the bank to lend that amount, nor does it obligate the business customer to utilize the entire amount. The bank, however, will normally maintain the line of credit for the firm that preserves its credit standing.

When establishing a line of credit, the bank will usually make two requirements. One is that the customer will be expected to maintain a *compensating balance* on deposit at all times. This balance is a fraction of the line of credit which the borrower is expected not to withdraw. Generally, compensating balance requirements range from 10 to 20 percent.[8] This rule is not uniformly applied, but it is considered a customary requirement among many banks. Some banks have instituted variations of the principle by requiring borrowers to maintain a fraction of the total loans made on deposit. The other requirement is that the borrower may be expected to clean up his loans periodically. This gives the bank the assurance that the loan is fulfilling its proper purpose and is not utilized for investment purposes. The seasonal needs of business are regarded as the basis for the line of credit, and if it is being used for this purpose it should be self-liquidating. Business firms not able to meet this requirement from their own funds must borrow from other banks to clean up their loans and at the same time submit their financial affairs to the scrutiny of the other banks.

7 / In the late 1960s, the high rates of interest being charged by commercial banks and other financial institutions prompted the Federal Reserve Bank of St. Louis to develop an experimental time series for the "real" rate of interest. Such a series deflated the current rates by use of a price deflator. In effect, this work tended to show that real interest rates did not increase nearly as much as the general public imagined. For a more complete story, see *Review* (St. Louis: Federal Reserve Bank of St. Louis, December 1969), p. 34.

8 / For the negative aspects of compensating balances, see John L. Nau, Jr., "Commercial Finance in a Tight Money Atmosphere," *Credit and Financial Management*, December 1969, p. 18.

ACTIVITIES OF THE SMALL
BUSINESS ADMINISTRATION (SBA)

In 1953 Congress created the Small Business Administration as a permanent, independent government agency with the function of helping small businesses grow and prosper. Eligibility for assistance from the SBA is limited to small independent businesses—excepting gambling or speculative firms, newspapers, television stations, and radio stations. For purposes of making loans, the SBA defines a small business as one that meets these general size standards:[9]

Wholesale—annual sales from $5 million to $15 million depending on the industry.

Retail or Service—annual sales or receipts from $1 million to $5 million, depending on the industry.

Construction—annual sales or receipts of not more than $5 million, averaged over a three-year period.

Manufacturing—from 250 to 1,500 employees depending on the industry.

The following quotation describes the type of financial assistance given:[10]

Any small businessman with a financial problem may come to SBA for advice and assistance. Agency loan officers will review his problem and suggest possible courses of action. If a businessman needs money and cannot borrow it on reasonable terms, SBA often can help. The Agency will consider either participating in, or guaranteeing up to 90 percent of a bank loan. If the bank cannot provide any funds, and if Federal funds are available, SBA will consider lending the entire amount as a direct government loan. However, most of SBA's loans are made in participation with banks.

Other activities of the SBA include pool loans, economic opportunity loans (EOL), development company loans, disaster loans, participation in lease guarantee programs and minority enterprise programs, small business investment companies (SBICs), management assistance programs, and advisory council programs. The literature on these diversified programs has been expanding.[11]

ACCOUNTS RECEIVABLE FINANCING

The credit executive needs to have a knowledge of accounts receivable financing. For example, the credit manager's own com-

9 / *SBA: What It Is . . . What It Does* (Washington, D.C.: Small Business Administration, 1970), p. 3.

10 / *Ibid.*

11 / For a discussion of the activities of the Small Business Administration, see the Suggested Readings at the end of the chapter.

pany may at some time find it necessary to engage in such financing, or certain of his suppliers may use this method of financing at various times. Equally important is the fact that customers of his firm may finance certain phases of their operations in such a manner, and familiarity with this type of financing is then necessary for proper analysis and decision making.

Accounts receivable financing has been defined as an "arrangement whereby a financing agency either makes loans or advances to a borrower secured by an assignment of its accounts receivables or purchases the accounts receivables outright."[12] As a firm's sales volume expands, more capital is needed to provide for increased plant and equipment, to carry larger inventories, to support consequent growth in accounts receivable, to meet larger payrolls, and so on. One of the ways now widely used to obtain more operating cash is receivables financing.

There are two basic types of accounts receivable financing—ordinary accounts receivable financing and factoring. So much misunderstanding exists with regard to the ordinary financing of accounts receivable and the factoring of accounts receivable that it is desirable to treat each of these basic types of receivable financing separately. The ordinary financing of accounts receivable is fundamentally different from factoring in the following major respects:

1. Commercial banks and commercial finance companies[13] are the principal sources which finance accounts receivable, whereas specialized companies generally known as factors are the source for factoring.
2. The reasons that a business may enter into the financing of its accounts receivable are fundamentally different than the reasons for factoring.
3. The methods of operation, procedures, costs, and service charges are basically different in each type of financial arrangement.
4. Finally, there is a marked difference in the relationship between the parties involved in accounts receivable financing as contrasted with factoring.

To note clearly the differences and similarities of these methods of financing, the following definitions are suggested:

Ordinary accounts receivable financing involves an agreement under which a financing institution (*a*) purchases its customer's open

12 / *Credit Management Handbook* (2d ed.; Homewood, Ill.: Richard D. Irwin, Inc., 1965), p. 628.

13 / These are companies engaged in commercial financing and serve the business community by making secured loans to manufacturers, wholesalers, and jobbers, just as sales finance and consumer finance companies serve the financial needs of the consumer. For a discussion of the movement of banks into factoring, see Robert A. Klein, "Banks Move into Factoring," *Credit and Financial Management,* December 1970, p. 26.

accounts receivable, or advances him loans secured by the pledge of such receivables, (b) with recourse to him for any losses and (c) without notice to his trade debtors.

Factoring involves a continuing agreement under which a financing institution (a) assumes the credit and collection function for its client, and (b) purchases his open accounts receivable as they arise (c) without recourse to him for credit losses and (d) with notice to his trade debtors.

It is important to emphasize that the above definitions imply the reasons a business may enter into one or the other type of financing arrangement. Businesses use ordinary accounts receivable financing for one major reason, which is to acquire needed capital. Specific reasons for the use of this kind of financing are numerous and varied, but all such reasons can usually be met by short-term or intermediate-term borrowing. Factoring, on the other hand, is entered into for two reasons: first, to acquire operating capital by selling the receivables outright, and second, to shift the entire credit and collection burden to the financing institution.

Ordinary Accounts Receivable Financing

As noted earlier, commercial banks and commercial finance companies are the sources which normally finance accounts receivable. Commercial banks may follow the procedure of making a *loan* on the basis of the accounts receivable as security. Finance companies follow the procedure of *purchasing* the receivables in exchange for some stated amount of cash, or they may accept assigned receivables as security for a loan much as a bank does.

Both lenders will normally make their advances with *recourse* to the borrowing firm, but without notice to the borrower's trade debtors.[14] Recourse gives the lending institution protection against slow-paying accounts and losses which occur due to uncollectible accounts. The recourse provision of the transaction results in the assumption of little or no risk on the part of the lender, for in essence the assigner guarantees payment of all assigned accounts. The lending institution, whether bank or finance company, will examine the quality of the accounts receivable offered. To be acceptable the major proportion (about 75-80 percent) of the assigned receivables

14 / Assignment of accounts receivable may be done either by the *notification* plan or the more common *nonnotification* plan. Under the former plan trade debtors are notified of the assignment or purchase of their receivables and informed that they are to make payment, when due, to the financing institution. Frequently such notification is made on the face of the debtor's invoice. Under the latter plan no notice to trade creditors is given, and the assigned or purchased accounts are borrowed upon without knowledge to debtors. The borrower (assigner) then acts as an agent, accepts collections of the accounts, and in turn pays the assignee.

must have the high or the second-high rating granted by Dun & Bradstreet or some other commercial credit reporting agency. The contract between the parties under the nonnotification plan will: (1) set forth the lender's advances and charges; (2) provide that the assigner act as the assignee's agent in collecting accounts; (3) establish the method and time by which the assigner will transmit collections to the lending firm; (4) provide for the assigner to guarantee all assigned accounts; and (5) provide that the assignee may inspect the accounting records of the assigner at any time. These and other provisions of the contract, as well as other technicalities of the transaction, dictate for the borrower a precise accounting for all funds received which are to be credited to the assigned accounts receivable.

The American Bankers Association recommends that loans based on accounts receivables should be no more than 80 percent of the face value of the receivables, less trade and other discounts allowed to customers and consideration for merchandise returns. Commercial finance companies may advance 70 to 95 percent of the face value of the receivables. Each of the quoted percentages is, of course, dependent upon the quality of the receivables and the standards of acceptability of the lender. The difference between the percentage and the net value of the receivables is a margin of safety against deductions, shrinkages, and bad-debt losses.

Bank rates on this type of lending vary widely. As shown earlier, bank interest rates are determined by a group of complex factors. With regard to this particular type of secured loan the rate may be set on the basis of the risk involved, the credit standing of the trade debtor's accounts which are assigned, the terms of sale of the assigner, the borrower's credit and collection practices, and other factors previously discussed.

There is also wide variance in the rates charged by commercial finance companies. The larger companies generally have lower rates. While the method of computing this rate is quite different from the bank method, it can be said that the two institutions are generally competitive in regard to the rate charged.

A businessman may decide to turn to a commercial finance company for the following reasons: to increase volume by extending longer or more generous credit terms for desirable business; to manufacture and launch a new seasonal product at the right moment; to phase production in advance of peak seasonal demands, thus eliminating overtime and reducing costs; to pay bills promptly or in advance and gain cash discount or price, delivery and service concessions; to increase production and cut costs by purchasing new, more efficient machinery and equipment; to expand production and sales by increasing the number of employees; to help finance the purchase of another company; to buy out a partner; to save on transportation costs by carload-lot buying and to take advantage of favorable prices in raw materials. In addition to financing accounts receivable, commercial finance companies offer a number of supplementary loan services. Loans on inventory; installment financing of machinery, equipment, and other durables; loans on fixed assets and other collateral; and note loans to businesses round out their operations. Many businesses find this source more flexible in its dealings and perhaps more closely meeting their business needs. The wide variety of financial services is in part the reason finance companies enjoy a close working relationship with their customers. Because these companies operate on a branch-office basis, and because they are not hampered by the restrictions imposed on banks, they are able to acquire a more diversified group of risks and hence accept greater risks.

The use of accounts receivable financing by businesses has not always been held a desirable practice, and even today many businessmen and lenders object to this method of acquiring capital. The principal objection seems to be that the assignment of receivables deprives trade creditors from protection against losses. This objection is not as strongly apparent as it was prior to the 1930s. Since that time many creditors have come to recognize the need for this type of financial arrangement and also that the pledging of accounts receivable may be a desired alternative method of acquiring capital. Some evidence of the acceptability of this type of borrowing is indicated by the large number of banks presently making these loans. Furthermore, the American Bankers Association has recognized that: (1) accounts receivable financing is becoming increasingly important, (2) the security is often the most liquid a borrower has to offer, (3) the necessity to borrow arises not from failure but from growth problems in the business, and (4) as a business grows its large volume of receivables places financial stress on the business, and it is only logical that this asset be resorted to for necessary relief.

Borrowing on the basis of accounts receivable may also be considered as an alternative to other financing possibilities. The business that does not have a short-term financial problem is the exception and not the rule. Relief may be had in a number of ways. Rather than gain the necessary relief by increasing its long-term debt, the business is likely to seek an increase in its line of credit at the bank. If this is not possible it may secure an additional loan from the bank by pledging its accounts receivable. Some businesses may not qualify for an additional bank loan, or because of preferences they seek financial aid from a commercial finance company. Whatever the source of the funds, it has secured expeditiously a self-liquidating loan. The self-liquidating feature alone is more attractive than the alternative of a long-term debt burden.

Factoring Accounts Receivable

In contrast to the ordinary financing of accounts receivable by banks[15] and commercial finance companies, the financing aspect of factoring is often secondary to the desire and need to shift the entire credit and collection management phase to the factor.

Factoring involves the purchase of accounts receivable from the client without recourse for credit losses and with the assumption of all credit risks involved. It is the only known institution which completely assumes the entire commercial credit and collection function for its clients. Trade debtors, accordingly, are notified that payments are to be made directly to the factoring company. In addition to these services the factor will advance cash for receivables whenever the client so desires. In other words, he will advance cash immediately for receivables purchased or hold cash in the account of the client until such time as needed by him. This service permits the client to reduce interest charges paid to the factor, because the client pays interest only for cash actually advanced. Factors, in addition to their primary activity, make loans to businesses on their inventory, fixed assets, open accounts, and other security. Most factors maintain an advisory service for their clients which counsels customers on the broad aspects of production, marketing, and financial matters.

Method of Operation.   There may be considerable variation in the factor's method of operation in dealings with individual clients. The specific relationship and the responsibilities of the parties will be set forth in the factoring contract. The following steps indicate the factoring procedure after the assignment of existing accounts on the books is made:

1. Before the client ships any merchandise to a customer as a result of his sales he will submit the list of customers, amounts of the orders, terms of sale, and any other essential information to the factor for approval.
2. The factoring institution will investigate each account and make the credit decision to accept or reject the order. The order

15 / The entry of some leading banks into factoring presages a more general invasion of this historical domain long dominated by firms dealing almost exclusively in factoring operations. For a description of this movement, see Robert P. Shay and Carl C. Greer, "Banks Move into High-Risk Commercial Financing," *Harvard Business Review,* November-December 1968, p. 149.

copies with the proper notations "accepted" or "rejected" are returned to the client. If, at this point, the client desires to ship to the rejected accounts he may do so at his own risk.

3. After shipments are made on the approved orders the client sells the accounts to the factor by signing and transmitting to the factor an assignment schedule supported by a copy of each invoice and shipping order. The assignment schedule provides space for a complete description of the sale and shipment such as customer name, address, terms of sale, due dates, and amounts of invoices. The invoices in turn are stamped before mailing, giving notification to the account that payment is to be made directly to the factor. Sufficient copies of each instrument are made so that the factor and client have complete records.

4. The factor credits the client's account for all accounts receivable purchased. The proceeds are remitted as mutually agreed upon by the factor and the client. If the client does not wish to withdraw the funds immediately, he may do so at regular intervals. The method of payment to the client is normally geared to his working capital needs. The factor pays the client interest on all money which accrues on matured accounts and is not withdrawn.

5. An "account current" is rendered monthly to the client. This instrument reveals to the client the exact financial standing he has with the factor. It is a record of the accounts receivable purchased, the charges for returns and allowances, factor's commission and interest charges, and other items that may affect the account.

Extent of Factoring. Despite heavy concentration and tradition in the textile industry, factoring operations are spreading into many other lines of business. As this method of financing is adopted by other lines, it will result in a continuous growth of the dollar volume supplied businesses.[16]

Factors Terms and Charges. Factoring charges include (1) a commission or service charge and (2) an interest charge. The exact amount of commission is determined by taking into consideration the kind of industry the client represents, the client's annual sales volume, the credit standing of the client's customers, and the like. The commission is based on the face value of the accounts receivable, less cash discounts, merchandise returns, and other normal allowances. The interest charge is computed on the average daily net debit

16 / John F. Stack, "Factoring Volume Tops $10 Billion for New Peak," *Women's Wear Daily,* February 3, 1969, p. 28.

balance. In other words, a 6 percent rate of interest is the true rate of simple interest per year.

In comparing factoring costs with the costs of borrowing funds from other sources, the services rendered by the factor, especially the assumption of the complete credit and collection management operations, should not be ignored.

Use of Factoring Operations by Businesses. Contrary to common opinion the factoring of accounts receivable does not imply a financially weak business concern. It is true that the factoring service may be used by a business whose credit may not be acceptable elsewhere, but many financially strong companies use factoring to good advantage. As implied earlier, other considerations may subordinate the ease of acquiring working capital by financing accounts receivable. The cost of maintaining a commercial credit department is quite obviously determinable and often quite high. Such costs include overhead, investigation costs, accounting costs, collection expenses, and the always present expense of bad debts. The firm that factors all of its accounts receivables, as many textile companies do, can eliminate this important but oftentimes costly business function. Another advantage which is gained is the freedom of business management from credit and collection problems. This permits them to concentrate their efforts more intensely on production and other marketing problems. It should be recognized that in a sense factoring provides a form of complete credit insurance while at the same time it frees the business from its investment in accounts receivable. Finally, factoring increases the client's net working capital provided, of course, the cash received is put to work to pay current obligations.

Perhaps the principal objection to factoring accounts receivable is that the service may be considered too costly. It must be emphasized that only the interest rate should be considered when comparing this method of financing with other possible alternatives. The factoring commission is not entirely a charge for advancing funds, but more accurately also for the assumption of the credit and collection management function, the cost of which must be considered.

COMMERCIAL PAPER AS A SOURCE OF FUNDS

The issuance and sale of commercial paper by business firms[17] is a relatively simple transaction through which businesses can enter the

17 / An interesting development in 1969 and 1970 was the entry of bank-holding company affiliates into the sale of commercial paper as a means of circumventing the impact of Federal Reserve policies. The Federal Reserve System has been confronted with the decision as to whether to put reserve requirements or interest rate ceilings on the commercial paper that bank affiliates issue. For an interesting discussion of commercial paper as a source of funds, see Thomas M. Kruse, "The Rediscovery of Commercial Paper," *Conference Board Record,* April 1970, p. 33.

marketplace and secure funds for short-term needs. Unlike loans, however, such paper is not renewable. Usually, in times of tight money, cash still is available in the money market. The so-called money market is of course the great pool of funds that financial institutions and individuals loan out temporarily. Another reason commercial paper is sold is that it invariably costs less to borrow in the commercial paper market than at a banking institution. This is true even without figuring the cost of keeping cash idle in the "compensating balances" that commercial banks require of borrowers. Furthermore, commercial paper—unlike stocks and bonds—is exempt from registration requirements of the Securities and Exchange Commission.[18]

The favorable aspects of the commercial paper market were highly questioned in 1970 when the Penn Central Transportation Company announced that it could not meet its commitments in connection with the issuance of commercial paper.[19] For decades size had come to be regarded almost as foolproof insurance against bankruptcy; the Penn Central's financial floundering proved just the opposite.

LONG-TERM LOANS

Up to this point, the discussion has been concerned principally with the short-term and intermediate-term financing needs of businesses. Long-term borrowing is often one of the first forms of financing used by a business enterprise. When a business resorts to acquiring funds by entering into long-term borrowing arrangements, it is said to be using its *investment credit.*

The Need for Long-Term Financing

Almost as rare as the firm that does not require short-term financing is the firm that does not need long-term financing. The undertaking of long-term financing may occur for a number of reasons. Frequently the original need for such financing is to provide the costly productive or marketing facilities for an enterprise. In providing such facilities any number of items carried as fixed assets may be acquired on a long-term basis. Land, buildings, equipment, and machinery are a few of the common fixed assets so acquired. If the owners furnish the capital (equity capital), then there may be no need for the use of investment credit.

18 / "More Companies Borrow Direct," *Business Week,* May 18, 1968, p. 80; Robert A. Christie, "New Developments in the Commerical Paper Market," *Industrial Banker,* August 1969, p. 10.

19 / For a good account of this "commercial paper crisis," see "Wall Street's Commercial Paper Crisis," *Business Week,* September 1970, p. 42; "Penn Central—The Unanswered Question," *Forbes,* July 15, 1970, p. 18; "When the Fed Won the Liquidity Battle," *Business Week,* October 24, 1970, p. 50.

Many businesses, after their origin, grow and prosper over the years. This often creates the need for expanded facilities and, at the same time, the replacement of some facilities. Hence long-term financing may be necessary to permit the replacement or expansion of facilities. Corresponding to fixed asset expansion is the need for an increase in current assets. Oftentimes a portion of the needed current asset expansion is financed by long-term methods rather than the previously discussed short-term methods. During periods of rapid expansion it is often more desirable to rely on long-term financing than on short-term financing in order to keep a reasonable balance between current assets and current liabilities. Additionally, such financing may be used to renew existing business indebtedness, to retire some business debts, and to effect the acquisition of assets of another company under merger arrangements.

Forms and Sources of Long-Term Borrowing

As a business has a need for long-term financing and in turn uses its investment credit to acquire the capital, it may take any one or combination of the following three forms: (1) long-term loans, (2) real estate mortgage loans, and (3) the issuance of secured or unsecured bonds. In each instance, the business uses its investment credit as a power to obtain the funds to be used for production or trade in exchange for its promise to pay an equivalent value at some date in the relatively distant future.

Long-term loans are those with maturities in excess of five years. Although not a major lending function of commercial banks, this type of loan is available from that source. Evidence of the transaction is the promissory note, either secured or unsecured. When loans are made over long periods, they are often renewed again and again, thus resulting in a more or less "permanent" obligation on the part of the business borrower. Usually these loans are repaid at specified intervals mutually agreed upon by the lender and borrower. The borrower then gives the lender a series of notes maturing, say, at six-month intervals over the years until the entire loan is repaid. Some borrowers are able to work out arrangements with lenders whereby the payments gradually increase with each succeeding interval. This feature is very attractive to many borrowers because when they use their investment credit, immediate profits are seldom realized.

Real estate mortgage loans for business concerns may be a single-payment type, also known as the "straight-payment loan," whereby the borrower makes no payment on the principal until such time as the entire amount is due. Usually interest on such loans is to be paid at stated intervals and prepayment privileges are provided for in the event the borrower wishes to make part payment or full payment on the mortgage prior to maturity. The direct-reduction mortgage loan, also known as the "amortized loan," is the other common type of mortgage contract. This instrument specifies monthly, quarterly, semiannual, or annual repayments of principal plus interest. Life insurance companies today have taken the lead in erecting stores, shopping centers, and office buildings. They will either finance the building from the construction stage onward, or purchase the property outright and lease it back to the interested parties on favorable terms. Leases under this arrangement run for an extended period of time, such as 99 years.

The corporation that issues bonds as a means of acquiring investment capital guarantees to pay a specified sum at some future date, with interest at a fixed rate. Maturity dates are usually in excess of 10 years such as 15, 20, 25, or 30 years. When borrowing by this method the business sells the entire issue to investment bankers, who in turn sell the bonds to the general public; or the issue may be sold to a single holder, such as a life insurance company.

DIFFICULTIES IN DECISION-MAKING

The material in this chapter has served to illustrate the major problems faced by business executives in handling the problems connected with the business use of cash (financial) credit. Corporate treasurers have gained an increased sophistication in their projections of "cash flow" for their companies,[20] and "the credit executive has never before been so vital to his firm or had such an important role to play in the allocation and efficient measurement of business capital. His decision-making is instrumental in the long-range profitability and perpetuation of his firm."[21]

In addition to the sources of cash credit discussed in this chapter, the business executive also is confronted with a multitude of other alternatives, as illustrated by the following quotation:[22]

Financial managements in recent years have made extensive use of commercial paper, leasing arrangements, convertible debt and preferred stock,

20 / Frederick W. Searby, "Use Your Hidden Cash Resources," *Harvard Business Review,* March-April 1968, p. 71; James R. DeMaioribus and John J. Omlor, "Effect of Accounts Receivable on Cash Flow," *Credit and Financial Management,* September 1968, p. 28.

21 / Wallace W. Reiff, "Capital Allocation in Credit Decision-Making," reprinted from *Credit and Financial Management,* September 1967, p. 20. Copyright 1967 by the National Association of Credit Management, New York, N.Y.

22 / "Changing Styles in Business Finance," reprinted from *Credit and Financial Management,* January 1970, p. 24. Copyright 1970 by the National Association of Credit Management, New York, N.Y.

subordinated debentures, mortgages or other loans with equity kickers (participations in earnings), term loans, revolving credits, Eurodollars, and Eurobonds. The pace of change has accelerated under conditions of monetary restraint and the business boom. The explanation is found in the long-continued high level prosperity and the strengthening of inflation. These have reduced the apparent risks and increased the rewards—current and prospective—of innovation in financial techniques. Significant also has been the slow but steady succession of financial executives in both industrial firms and financial institutions. Those schooled in the adversity of the Great Depression are being replaced by younger men who have known only economic growth and upward pressures on both prices and wages.

REVIEW AND DISCUSSION QUESTIONS

1. Why is it necessary that commercial credit managers be well informed on business needs, uses, and sources of cash credit?
2. In what ways may bank loans be classified? Distinguish each type.
3. Explain: double-name paper and accommodation paper.
4. Distinguish between bank interest rates and bank discount rates.
5. What are the principal reasons commercial banks have high credit standards and requirements?
6. Discuss the activities of the Small Business Administration.
7. What are the principal differences between ordinary accounts receivable financing and factoring accounts receivable?
8. Is ordinary accounts receivable financing a desirable or undesirable business practice? Explain.
9. Under what circumstances can a business use factoring to a good advantage?
10. Explain the use of commercial paper as a source of funds for business concerns.
11. Investigate the financial condition of the Penn Central Transportation Company at the present time.
12. What is investment credit?
13. How have life insurance companies helped business concerns in their long-term financing needs?

SUGGESTED READINGS

Role of the Credit Executive

"Changing Styles in Business Finance," *Credit and Financial Management,* January 1970, p. 24.

Conover, C. Todd. "The Cost of the Costly Credit Agreement," *Financial Executive,* September 1971, p. 40.

Lynch, James R. "The Financial Executive's Role in a Changing Environment," *Credit and Financial Management,* February 1967, p. 14.

Reiff, Wallace W. "Capital Allocation in Credit Decision-Making," *Credit and Financial Management,* September 1967, p. 20.

Loaning Activities of Commercial Banks

Baughn, William H. and Walker, Charles E. (eds.) *The Bankers' Handbook* (Homewood, Ill.: Dow Jones-Irwin, Inc., 1966).

Cochran, John A. *Money, Banking, and the Economy* (New York: Macmillan Co., 1967), chap. 9.

Prather, Charles L. *Money and Banking* (9th ed.; Homewood, Ill.: Richard D. Irwin, Inc., 1969), chap. 13.

Ross, W. Ogden. *Marketing in Commercial Banks: How to Proceed* (Ann Arbor, Mich.: Masterco Press, Inc., 1968).

Use of Collateral in Bank Loans

Campbell, Russell R. "New Trends in Secured Lending," *Credit and Financial Management*, December 1967, p. 16.

Sayer, Stephen F. "How to Corral Your Collateral," *Credit and Financial Management*, February 1969, p. 27.

"The Many Faces of Collateral," *Credit and Financial Management*, February 1970, p. 21.

Activities of the Small Business Administration

The ABC's of Borrowing (Washington, D.C.: Small Business Administration, Management Aids No. 170, 1969).

Parris, Addison. *The Small Business Administration* (New York: Frederick A. Praeger, 1968).

SBA Annual Report 1969 (Washington, D.C.: Small Business Administration, 1970).

Small Business Loans (Washington, D.C.: Small Business Administration, 1969).

21

International Credit
Considerations*

The United States has become the world's leading exporter and importer of merchandise. However, the balance of payments of the United States has shown a deficit for more than a decade, and this has caused the United States government to reevaluate its foreign economy policy and to institute certain necessary adjustments to help reduce these deficits. One of these adjustments has been the enlargement of the existing export expansion program of the federal government, with the aim of encouraging exports by manufacturers not currently engaged in this activity and the expansion of sales among those manufacturers currently exporting.[1]

Another adjustment that took place (in August 1971) was the President's action under the Economic Stabilization Act of 1970 to subject most imports to a surcharge of 10 percent in an attempt to make U.S. goods more competitive in the domestic market with those of foreign producers. Simultaneously, he announced that the United States would no longer convert foreign-held dollars into gold, hoping that the value of the dollar would drop in relation to other currencies and thus make U.S. goods cheaper in world markets. At the time of this writing, the effect of these actions still is uncertain.

Commenting on the causes for an increased interest in export marketing, Dr. A. H. Kizilbash has made the following observation:[2]

Certain other developments in the last two decades have also caused a resurgence of interest in export marketing. For instance, a closer examination of

* / This chapter is not a complete nor an exhaustive coverage of export trade credit. It is intended only to introduce the subject by surveying some of the major considerations of this important and growing area of credit. For a more complete treatment see the Suggested Readings at the end of the chapter.

1 / James C. Baker and Jan B. Verschuur, "The Versatile Combination Export Manager," *Marquette Business Review*, Winter 1969, p. 143.

2 / Askari H. Kizilbash, "A Study of Export Marketing Objectives and Practices of Selected Small Manufacturers with Particular Reference to Their Use of Combination Export Management Firms" (Lincoln, Nebr.: unpublished dissertation, 1970), pp. 2-3.

the international economic picture will show that although the United States has remained a major producer and exporter of goods, its relative importance has diminished. Several Western European countries and Japan have regained some of their prewar markets as a result of post-World War II reconstruction. Their productive capacities have undergone both qualitative and quantitative improvement. They now are major competitors of American products in world markets. In addition to the problem of relatively diminishing exports due to the growth of these major competitors, the United States has become heavily committed in the task of economic and military assistance to many free world countries. These combined factors have contributed to the present unfavorable balance of payments position of this country. In addition they point up the need for improvement in export marketing skills of United States manufacturers.

And of course these export marketing skills include skill in the use of credit. A company's credit policy, or the lack of one, is perhaps one of the most vital determinants of the success or failure of an international marketing program. The fact that a customer trading on his credit is located in a foreign country does not alter the basic principles and procedures of sound credit management. The foreign customers must still be investigated, the risk carefully analyzed, logical credit limits imposed, and collections made. There are, however, some basic differences in practice and some problems encountered not common to domestic credits and collections.

Most of the problems discussed in this chapter are those encountered by firms which sell directly to foreign buyers. Manufacturers who sell in this manner usually do so because of the attractiveness of this alternative. To market products direct to overseas buyers does, however, require that the manufacturer possess the necessary capital, as well as the organizational and manpower requirements. An export credit policy must be developed, capital must be sufficient to finance the slow turnover of receivables, and a host of details and incidental problems create the need for qualified personnel who understand foreign trade credit.

The use of middlemen, or indirect marketing, may be as plausible and advantageous in export trade as it is with some domestic trade. The use of combination export management firms (CEMs),[3] sales agents, factors, export commission houses, export brokers and other export marketing agencies serves to shift the functions and some risks from the manufacturer. In many instances varying export arrangements can be worked out with the export agency so that a major portion of the sales expenses can be shifted to it. Likewise,

---

3 / Kizilbash has divided CEMs into two categories: merchant and agent. "A merchant CEM is defined as one that takes title to the goods and handles all other aspects of export marketing. This allows the manufacturer to have minimal involvement with export trade. The manufacturer sells to the CEM in the same manner as it would to any other domestic account. An agent CEM is defined as one which does not take title to the goods and operates as the export department of the manufacturer. In this arrangement, the manufacturer has a greater involvement in export trade." *Ibid.*, p. 10.

some of these agencies assume all credit and exchange risks. The points to consider when arriving at the decision to market products overseas either directly or indirectly are: (1) the percentage of manufacturing output to be marketed for export, (2) the gross margin, (3) the personnel qualifications versus personnel requirements, (4) the degree of control the manufacturer desires over his product, (5) the need for service and product guarantee maintenance, and (6) financial requirements.

CREDIT PROBLEMS OF EXPORT TRADE

The principal problem area for most credit managers stems from their need to judge the credit risk accurately. A foreign credit customer usually represents greater risk and is more difficult to evaluate. The increased degree of risk and difficulty in evaluation should by no means be construed to mean that credit losses on foreign customers are higher than on domestic customers. On the contrary, the Foreign Credit Interchange Bureau of the National Association of Credit Management reports that "credit losses in foreign trade are consistently below those experienced in domestic operations even when the foreign and domestic credits are handled by the same executive."[4] Risk and evaluation problems are intensified, though, because of the following factors, which must be considered when judging the foreign credit risk: government, economic stability, currency and exchange, business practices, distance factor, status of export credit insurance, and collections.

Government

It should be recognized that "the economy and business climate of any nation is directly influenced by the attitudes and policies of its government. . . . The political orientation of the government whether right or left also affects its economic policy and the degree to which it regulates both the internal commerce and external trade."[5] Textbook familiarity will not be sufficient, since conditions are constantly changing.

One of the basic factors that businessmen have to consider in deciding whether to sell to customers in a particular country is the type of government that has been established. Although the avoidance of politics in international business is desirable, American firms have found that they cannot ignore the role of the government

4 | *Credit Management Handbook,* (2d ed.; Homewood, Ill.: Richard D. Irwin, 1965), p. 727.

5 | *Ibid.,* p. 728.

because of its influence on many phases of business activity. For example, the right to carry on business activities and the extent of foreign investment permitted are determined by government policy.

Economic Stability

Likewise, the export credit executive must be alert to and understand the general economic situation within a foreign country to which his firm is exporting. It has been found that the efficient use of trade credit in a socioeconomic system can lead to further economic progress. Conversely, a poorly developed system is a limitation to economic progress. Thus, American exporters should look to see whether the prerequisites for a good credit system—that is, a system that can advance economic development—are to be found in the importing country.

In addition, business cycles, crop failures, and many other factors must be noted because of their ability to cause fluctuations in a country's standard of living and in the demand for imports or the supply of goods for export.

Currency and Exchange

One of the inherent risks of export trade stems from (1) the instability of some foreign currencies and (2) the inability of some foreign customers to convert their currencies into United States dollars. This risk must be assumed by one of the parties to the transaction. If the exporter bills his foreign customer in the native currency (pounds, pesos, francs, rupees, etc.), he runs the risk that when the bill is paid by the importer the exchange into dollars may yield a smaller amount than anticipated. If the foreign currency should drop in value, the seller will receive fewer dollars as he converts his foreign currency. If, on the other hand, the exporter bills his foreign customer in dollars (this is more common), the risk of devaluation is placed on the importer. If, for example, the value of the dollar rises, the importer will need more of his native currency to make up the difference.

Not only does risk surround the relative value of currencies but each foreign country rigidly enforces exchange regulations. In general, foreign monies can only be obtained from designated exchange authorities, which are usually within the control of the central banking system. Exchange regulations fluctuate with the political and economic conditions of the country. In the past importers in some countries have been prevented from remitting dollars to the United States; or, due to an unfavorable exchange situation, the foreign buyer may delay settlement of the account until more favorable exchange rates prevail.

A credit manager whose firm sells to foreign customers must be a student of international financial developments.[6] The sufficiency of dollar reserves, the likelihood of foreign currency devaluation, and monetary restrictions are all factors which must be considered in evaluating the foreign credit risk.

Business Practices

Management techniques and the tools of efficient business management are not as advanced in most foreign countries as in the United States. This deficiency takes on significance particularly in the area of accounting and the rendition of financial statements. Foreign merchants, except for those in the largest trade centers, do not have trained accountants available to them. Furthermore, many foreign merchants still hold to the archaic view that their "names" and integrity are sufficient evidence upon which to base credit appraisal. Foreign buyers are often highly irritated by unnecessary requests for credit information from United States sellers. Often these foreign firms have been in business many years and have done business with United States firms on an open account basis for fairly long periods of time. Unthoughtful actions in requesting certain information on the part of United States business firms has proved distasteful to some foreign companies. Many also are reluctant to supply financial statements even though they have them, because they fear revealing business secrets. While these arguments have diminished in recent years as more advanced business practices have been adopted, adequate financial information on foreign buyers still remains a problem.

The lack of, or poor quality of, financial data is further complicated by language difficulties. Despite great emphasis on the foreign language requirement for those concerned with foreign trade, it is seldom that either party is well versed in technical terms, commercial definitions, and trade names. Hence there is a greater possibility that misunderstandings, disputes, and rejection of the shipment may occur.

Business practices also are influenced by the diversity of commercial laws of foreign countries. Commonly such things as import restrictions and licenses, laws of contract and title, bankruptcy, commercial arbitration, and patents are highly technical and com-

6 / John W. Knudsen, "International Trade Benefits and Economic Policy," *Monthly Review* (Kansas City, Mo.: Federal Reserve Bank of Kansas City, September-October 1970), p. 11.

plex. Because of the wide variety of such foreign regulations, most creditors are well advised to consult an attorney who is familiar with international law before getting involved with importers of a particular country for the first time.

Distance Factor

The distance between the exporter and importer compounds the problem of risk evaluation. If financial information is inadequate on domestic customers, the credit manager or one of his representatives often has an opportunity to visit his prospective customer's place of business and thereby judge the risk as best he can on nonfinancial factors. Obviously, the opportunity for personal contact with foreign customers is very limited. This is particularly true where small accounts are involved. Consequently, the credit decision must be based almost entirely on data supplied by credit investigation agencies and other sources. In addition, it must be recognized that good credit information cannot always be obtained on customers in other countries, even by well-known credit reporting agencies. Sufficient staff personnel are not always available in the foreign branches offices of these agencies, nor is access to important information always forthcoming.

Furthermore, the distance factor influences the terms of sale. Usually there is a relatively long lapse of time between the purchase or shipment of goods and their receipt by the importer. Because of this, terms of sale are often longer than domestic terms of sale, and hence the accounts receivable remain unpaid for extended periods. Credit managers report that in recent years, as competition for foreign customers increases, their demands for longer credit terms also increase. Inasmuch as the credit manager is not close to the foreign customer, it is extremely difficult for him to know whether such demands are the actual playing of one creditor against another or whether the customer is taking advantage of a plausible situation. Whatever the particular circumstances, the exporter will require greater financial capacity than the amounts needed to carry domestic accounts. The long lapse of time and longer terms granted to compete with other sellers further aggravate the exchange risks and the risks created by the possibility of new import regulations.

Export Credit Insurance

Most of the major exporting nations have adopted either export credit insurance plans or guarantees which protect creditors against defaulting foreign customers. Great Britain, for example, has had such plans since 1920. Export credit insurance was first written in the United States in 1921 by a private insurance company. This company was liquidated in 1932 after a critical export credit situation arose when Great Britain abandoned the gold standard. Another private company succeeded this one, but it operated on a restricted basis until World War II, when the volume of export trade declined and the character of the available risks deteriorated.

The present program is described as follows:[7]

In early 1962, the Foreign Credit Insurance Association was established in collaboration with the Export-Import Bank. The Association is a voluntary group of private insurance compaines that are interested in the insurance of foreign credits. The Association was a response to the invitation of the Export-Import Bank to participate with it in accordance with the directive of the President of the United States. Approximately 75 insurance companies are presently members of the Association.

Under this arrangement, the Export-Import Bank assumes 100 percent responsibility with respect to political risks, and the Export-Import Bank together with FCIA's member companies share the policy obligations with respect to commercial credit risks. Political risks are defined as inconvertibility of foreign currency to United States dollars, expropriation, confiscation, war, civil commotion or like disturbances, and cancellation or restriction of export or import licenses. Commercial credit risks are defined as insolvency of the buyer and his protracted default of any risk in the policy as a political risk.

Two private insurance companies, the Federal Insurance Company and the Continental Casualty Company, have been leaders in offering a private form of export risk insurance.

Collections

Another problem area of concern to the credit manager is that of collections. As with domestic customers, the collection of accounts is an inherent risk of the adoption of a credit policy. The cost of collecting overdue export accounts, the variance in commercial laws from one foreign country to another, and the factors already discussed compound the problem. Because of the greater collection problem, standards of acceptability for foreign accounts are generally higher than for domestic accounts. Even despite the higher standards, creditors should expect to experience some difficulty with collections and some bad-debt losses.

The variety of reasons or conditions which cause export customers to become delinquent and the collection procedures and devices necessary to effectuate settlement are similar to those discussed in

7 / Ronald L. Kramer, *International Marketing* (3d ed.; Cincinnati, Ohio: South-Western Publishing Co., 1970), pp. 327-28. Reproduced by special permission of South-Western Publishing Co. For additional material see the Suggested Readings at the end of the chapter.

Chapters 31 and 32. Due to the nature of the conditions which influence the collection of foreign accounts, it is particularly important that the credit manager establish internal controls which detect overdue accounts at an early date. Prompt follow-up of the account by mail, telephone, or cable will usually bring forth the reason for the delay of payment. Once the specific reason for payment delay is known, future courses of collection action may be planned more intelligently and the effectiveness of such action can then be expected to be greater.

The credit manager is confronted with a particularly knotty collection problem when his collection devices fail to bring results and the export account is eventually classified as "placed for collection" or "legal action." It is at this stage in the life of the account that the credit manager must decide whether it is worthwhile to proceed further. Litigation abroad is not only costly, it is time-consuming, and the effort may well be out of proportion to potential results. Obviously only sizable accounts and large unpaid balances should be considered for legal action. If legal action is necessary the creditor should consult with his bank, his own legal counsel, or an export agency for advice on competent legal counsel in the foreign country. In some countries only nationals are permitted to practice law. American exporters' experiences with foreign counsel have been such that it is often felt that the claimant's rights are not wholeheartedly enforced.

If a foreign account is to be placed for collection (as distinguished from collection by legal action), a number of well-known agencies may be of valuable assistance. Dun & Bradstreet and the Foreign Credit Interchange Bureau of the National Association of Credit Management are two such agencies. Each of these services uses "moral suasion" letters which emphasize the importance of maintaining a good credit standing.

Commercial arbitration also is used in order to try to bring about speedy and inexpensive settlement of overdue accounts. A worldwide system of arbitration, organized by the American Arbitration Association and cooperating trade associations and chambers of commerce, has been in operation for many years.

EXPORT TERMS OF SALE

In recent years competition for foreign customers has become particularly intense in a number of international markets.[8] When this condition exists, considerable bargaining for lenient credit terms

---

8 / Eldridge Haynes, "How to Expand Overseas While Keeping Dollars at Home," *Credit and Financial Management,* May 1968, p. 18.

becomes a normal course of buying action by importers. So prevalent are these practices today that credit managers believe the particular credit terms granted may be a deciding factor in making a sale. The export credit manager must, however, be careful to avoid those risks who take advantage of a competitive situation, but are still marginal or deteriorating in regard to financial condition. Even though the present-day competitive scene magnifies the exporter's credit problems, the future outlook is somewhat brighter. As competition improves some international markets will have overcome their perplexing political and economic situations, and hence the risk of exchange and monetary restrictions are likely to decrease substantially.

Terms of sale used in export trade, to some extent at least, denote the quality of the risk, just as terms of sale in domestic trade classify commercial accounts by risk or unique circumstances. Most writers classify export terms of sale in order of decreasing risk as follows:

1. Open account.
2. Consignment.
3. Draft drawn by the seller on the buyer.
4. Authority to purchase.
5. Export letter of credit.
6. Cash payment before delivery.

Open Account

The open account with terms to compensate for the distance factor and other normal delays is used in a minority of export credit transactions. Again, the utmost confidence in the customer must exist, and the exchange provisions must be favorable to the use of these terms. In some countries priority is given to applications for exchange to settle dollar draft obligations over applications to settle open-account obligations.

Consignment

Consignment sales are not widely used in export trade and are never used when exchange and monetary restrictions are not favorable to converting foreign monies into dollars. Foreign laws on passing title to goods differ in some countries, and this alone may preclude the use of this device. If, however, an exporter is shipping to a customer of long standing in whom he has the utmost confidence or to foreign subsidiaries and sales agents, consignment terms may be desirable. Customers of these types must obviously be located in established foreign markets where the trade and banking facilities are capable of coping with the technicalities of the consigned shipment.

Drafts

Time and sight drafts are widely used credit instruments in export credit sales. Drafts may be either *dollar* drafts or *foreign currency* drafts, depending on the arrangements previously made between the exporter and the buyer.

Usually the drafts (whether time or sight) are *documentary* drafts as contrasted with *clean* drafts. The documentary draft is accompanied by all the title documents and papers essential to the shipment, such as bills of lading, insurance certificates, and shipping documents. The clean draft is free of these attachments. In this case the importer may have already received the shipment, and the clean draft is forwarded through banking channels for the purpose of collecting the amount of money due.

In using a draft to collect the credit accepted, the exporter is well advised to consult the *Credit Manual of Commercial Laws* published annually by the National Association of Credit Management. This volume contains much helpful information on terms of sale, trade definitions, and on the various documentary requirements. Furthermore, the instructions to the bank in regard to collection of the draft, remittance of the funds by the foreign bank, the handling of collection charges and taxes, and other charges must be clearly set forth to avoid misunderstandings, delays, and more complicated collection procedures.

Authority to Purchase

Export sales may involve payment by documentary draft with authority to purchase:

> An authority to purchase is an authorization to a bank to purchase, on behalf of a foreign bank, the documentary draft drawn by the seller on the buyer. The authority to purchase is used mainly by Far Eastern banks to finance exports from this and other countries. Such authority provides a place where the exporter may negotiate a draft with documents attached and thus obtain funds immediately.[9]

Export Letter of Credit

The exporter who desires to have greater certainty of payment, other than cash before delivery, should request the importer to arrange for an export letter of credit.

9 | *Credit Management Handbook, op. cit.*, pp. 744-45.

On a sale that calls for payment by means of a letter of credit, the foreign importer arranges with his bank that a credit for the amount be established in favor of the exporter. Payment generally is made against documents evidencing shipment of the goods. Thus, under an export letter of credit, the importer's bank undertakes to pay the exporter.

A letter of credit issued by a foreign bank and accepted by an American bank is known as an *irrevocable* export letter of credit. An irrevocable letter of credit also may be issued by an American bank, or may be issued by a foreign bank but *unconfirmed* by an American bank. Drafts drawn under this type of letter of credit will be paid by the foreign bank, not by the American bank. A *revocable* letter of export credit may be issued. Because this instrument may be revoked or amended at any time, the exporter has only day-to-day assurance that sight drafts and time drafts drawn against it will be accepted by the issuing bank.[10] The two former instruments are much preferred by exporters and are in widespread use.

The preference of export creditors for the irrevocable export letter of credit stems from their ability to convert accepted drafts into cash almost immediately. All the exporter must do is draw a draft, support it with the necessary shipping documents, and present it to the accepting bank. After verification of the exporter's claim, the bank accepts the draft. Once the bank has accepted the draft on the irrevocable letter of credit, the exporter can in turn discount it on the open market and receive full payment for the shipment less the discount charge. For all practical purposes, then, the irrevocable letter of credit parallels a cash sale. If, however, the exporter desires to save the discount charge he can hold the draft until maturity.

Cash before Delivery Terms

The circumstances under which an exporter may demand c.b.d. terms are much the same as those in domestic sales. When an importer cannot qualify to meet the demand for a letter of credit or when his credit standing is clearly unsatisfactory, it is desirable to ask for cash before delivery. Not all circumstances which call for this arrangement are the responsibility of the importer. Exporters may request these terms when the foreign country's exchange conditions are such that long delays are likely to be encountered if more lenient terms were used. A few products have customarily been sold on c.b.d. terms to domestic customers, and the same terms apply to foreign customers.

10 / For a more detailed description of the types of export letters of credit, see Kramer, *op. cit.,* chap. 16, pp. 279-300.

SOURCES OF FOREIGN CREDIT INFORMATION

The evaluation of the foreign credit customer is much the same as that for a domestic customer. The exception to this, of course, is the close evaluation of those factors peculiar to export trade which were just discussed. Likewise the sources of credit information, the content of credit reports, and their format are much the same as those frequently consulted in domestic credit analysis. However, reasonably good credit information cannot always be obtained on customers in foreign countries. Foreign credit reporting offices are not always adequately staffed, nor do they always have access to all necessary information.

The sources of information on the foreign buyer may be classified as domestic and foreign. Domestic sources may be subdivided into commercial credit reporting agencies, the exporter's bank, United States Department of Commerce, and foreign trade publications. Foreign sources include the buyer, the buyer's bank, and the exporter's foreign sales representative.

Commercial Credit Reporting Agencies

Dun & Bradstreet and the Foreign Credit Interchange Bureau of the National Association of Credit Management are two well-known sources of foreign credit information. Both agencies write credit reports on manufacturers, wholesalers, sale agents, and other commercial enterprises located in most of the free nations of the world.

Dun & Bradstreet maintains offices in foreign countries in order that it may provide a source of credit information to United States business and financial firms. These Dun & Bradstreet offices serve manufacturers, distributors, and bankers whose operations are primarily within the foreign country. Reports (such as shown in Figure 21-1) prepared on customers in foreign countries are of the same general type as those prepared for domestic use, except that more emphasis may be placed on antecedents and less on financial standing. Much of the information shown in the credit reports and rating books (such as the Dun & Bradstreet International Market Guide) is gathered by personal investigations performed by credit reporters operating out of the Dun & Bradstreet foreign offices.

Since 1919 the National Association of Credit Management has operated the member-owned Foreign Credit Interchange Bureau in order to help exporters with the many credit problems inherent in international selling. Like its domestic counterpart, the Foreign Credit Interchange Bureau functions as a clearinghouse for exporters'

FIGURE 21-1
Dun & Bradstreet International Report on a Foreign Customer

(1) **Summary**—Condenses the information needed for a sales or credit decision. Highlights significant facts. Credit Data shows year business started, trend of payments, net worth and composite appraisal.

(2) **History**—Identifies owners and their commerical experience, describes background of the business. Enhances understanding and makes it easier to establish confident business relations

(3) **Finances**—The financial condition and how firm is progressing; capital in use and borrowing record. Analysis covers ability of the concern to meet its obligations.

(4) **Operation**—What the concern does, lines of merchandise and class of trade sold, facilities and equipment. Is it a profitable outlet for your goods and services? Can they supply your needs?

(5) **Trade**—How they pay their bills, the answer to one of your most important questions. A concise record of trade payments, high credits received, amounts owing, terms and pertinent comment from suppliers.

Dun & Bradstreet **INTERNATIONAL** *Report*

ELEKTRON, A. G.

CD 7 855 AUGUST 27, 197
MFR RAD., PHONOS., LOUD SPEAKERS, HI-FI EQUIP.
(15)

MG 1A 2
FRANKFURT/MAIN, GERMANY
Hauptstrasse 14

BOARD OF DIRECTORS
Hans Daniel – President
Robert Peters – Vice-Pres.
Joseph Peters – Treasurer

STARTED: 1929
PAYMENTS: PPT.
SALES: DM. 15,900,000
WORTH: DM. 4,345,000
EMPLOYS: 580

(1) SUMMARY

WELL ESTABLISHED BUSINESS. SOUND FINANCIAL CONDITION WITH OPERATIONS PROFITABLE.

(2) HISTORY

Corporation chartered in 1945 with an authorized capital of DM 4 Million, fully paid in, to succeed a proprietorship established in 1929 by Hans Daniel. Daniel, born 1900, married, an electro-engineer, graduate of the Berlin University. Prior to 1929 employed by the Research Department of a similar firm in Hamburg.

Robert Peters, Vice-President, born 1910, married, graduate of the University of Cologne. Formerly was employed by several import and export houses in the same line of business, prior to 1945.

Joseph Peters, Treasurer, born 1912, brother of the aforementioned, married. Prior to 1945 employed as sales manager by Elektrische Bedarfsartikel A.G., Frankfurt.

Management is well regarded.

(3) FINANCES

Statement December 31, 197
Figures are in DMs quoted at .254 in U.S. Currency.

ASSETS		LIABILITIES	
Cash on hand and at banks	2,235,000	Creditors accounts	2,094,000
Customers accounts	5,730,000	Notes payable	1,284,000
Inventory	4,128,000	Due banks	1,336,000
CURR. ASSETS	12,093,000	CURR. LIABS.	4,714,000
Investments	329,000	Contingencies	1,838,000
Machy. and tools	259,000	General Reserves	2,000,000
Real estate, net	1,447,000	Legal Reserves	1,538,000
Deferred charges	307,000	Capital	4,000,000
		Surplus	345,000
TOTAL ASSETS	14,435,000	TOTAL	14,435,000

Sales DM 15,900,000 (year ending Dec. 31, 197) Net profit DM 825,365 – dividends DM 700,000.

Balance sheet prepared from figures submitted by Hans Daniel, President.

BANKING: Satisfactory accounts maintained many years in four local banks, balances low to medium 6 figures in each account. Accommodations up to low 7 figures have been granted on an unsecured basis with that amount now outstanding .

(4) OPERATION

Manufacturers of radios, phonographs, loud speakers, hi-fi equipment. Sales are on credit terms up to 60 and 90 days. About 580 persons are employed. LOCATION: Owns a three-story concrete building maintained in good condition.

(5) PAYMENTS

August 2, 197

HIGH CREDIT	OWE	P. DUE	TERMS	PAYMENTS	REMARKS
DM 800,000			30/60 days	Ppt.	Sold years to date.
DM 458,000	36,000		30 days	Ppt.	Sold many years.
DM 37,000	29,000		30 days	Ppt.	Sold years to date.
(4)				Ppt.	
8-27 (1)					

PLEASE NOTE WHETHER NAME, BUSINESS AND STREET ADDRESS CORRESPOND WITH YOUR INQUIRY.

payment experiences with overseas customers. This information, rather than being historical and financial in character, is the actual ledger and credit experience of American export creditors. The body of the foreign interchange report (as shown in Figure 21-2) is essentially the same as the domestic interchange report. However, in the foreign report, each member who reports on a particular account also rates the customer as high, good, satisfactory, unsatisfactory, or undesirable by using the respective code letters Q, R, S, T, and U.

Other services of the Foreign Credit Interchange Bureau include: (1) worldwide collection service; (2) free reciprocal copy of all foreign credit interchange reports to which the member contributes experience; (3) weekly bulletins; (4) minutes of monthly round table conferences on foreign credit, collection, and exchange problems, with participation either by mail or attendance; and (5) consultation and market research service.

FIGURE 21-2
Foreign Credit Interchange Report

F C I B CREDIT REPORT
NATIONAL ASSOCIATION OF CREDIT MANAGEMENT
475 PARK AVENUE, SOUTH   NEW YORK, N.Y. 10016

THIS REPORT IS STRICTLY CONFIDENTIAL AND FOR YOUR OWN INDIVIDUAL USE ONLY.
ML WHILE THE INFORMATION GIVEN IN THIS REPORT IS OBTAINED FROM SOURCES DEEMED RELIABLE, THE ACCURACY OF THE INFORMATION IS NOT GUARANTEED AND NO RESPONSIBILITY IS TO ATTACH TO THE BUREAU OR ANY OF ITS REPRESENTATIVES OR AGENTS.

REPORT ON:

JOSE ▇▇▇▇ S. A.   JANUARY 3, 1969
Calle 3, ▇▇▇▇ 425
Colombia

This is a sample of O. B. Report

TERMS OF SALE

1. OPEN ACCOUNT PAYABLE ___ DAYS FROM DATE OF
   (a) INVOICE
   (b) FACTORY SHIPMENT
   (c) EXPORT SHIPMENT
2. OPEN ACCOUNT PAYABLE IMMEDIATELY UPON RECEIPT OF
   (a) DOCUMENTS
   (b) INVOICE
   (c) GOODS
3. ACCOUNT GUARANTEED.
4. VOLUNTARY REMITTANCE WITH ORDER
5. SELL FOR CASH IN ADVANCE ONLY
6. C.O.D. OR S/D R R B/L ATTACHED.
7. CASH AGAINST DOCUMENTS UNDER
   (a) IRREVOCABLE L/C-CONFIRMED
   (b) IRREVOCABLE L/C-UNCONFIRMED
   (c) REVOCABLE L/C
8. AUTHORITY TO PURCHASE OR LETTER OF ADVICE:
   (a) IRREVOCABLE WITH RECOURSE
   (b) IRREVOCABLE WITHOUT RECOURSE
   (c) REVOCABLE WITH RECOURSE
   (d) REVOCABLE WITHOUT RECOURSE

9. BANK ACCEPTANCE OF BANK IN THIS COUNTRY AT ___ DAYS.
10. BANK ACCEPTANCE OF FOREIGN BANK AT ___ DAYS.
11. DRAFT AT ___ DAYS SIGHT D/A.
12. DRAFT AT ___ DAYS DATE D/A.
13. DRAFT AT ___ DAYS SIGHT D/P.
14. DRAFT AT ___ DAYS DATE D/P.
15. CLEAN DRAFT AT ___ DAYS SIGHT.
16. CLEAN DRAFT AT ___ DAYS DATE.
17. CONSIGNED STOCK. TERMS?
18. CASH AGAINST SHIPPING DOCUMENTS, DOCK RECEIPT OR WAREHOUSE RECEIPT.
   (a) AT CUSTOMER'S OFFICE.
   (b) AT PAYING AGENCY OTHER THAN BANK.
   (c) AT BANK.
19. ......

MANNER OF PAYMENT

OPEN ACCOUNT | **GENERAL**
A. DISCOUNTS. | N. ACCOUNT SETTLED BY ATTORNEY.
B. PAYS WHEN DUE. | O. ACCOUNT SETTLED BY ARBITRATION
C. SLOW. | OR COMPROMISE.
D. TAKES UNAUTHORIZED DISCOUNTS. | P. ACCOUNT STILL IN DISPUTE.

DRAFTS
H. ANTICIPATES PAYMENT.
I. ACCEPTS AND PAYS PROMPTLY.
J. ACCEPTS PROMPTLY- DELAYS PAYMENT.
K. DELAYS ACCEPTANCE- PAYS PROMPTLY.
L. DELAYS BOTH ACCEPTANCE AND PAYMENT.
M. MAKES UNJUST CLAIMS.

WE RATE THE ACCOUNT
Q. HIGH.
R. GOOD.
S. SATISFACTORY.
T. UNSATISFACTORY.
U. UNDESIRABLE.

Years	TERMS OF SALE KEY NO.	TERMS OF SALE Days	HIGHEST RECENT ACCOUNT WITHIN PAST YEAR	DATE LAST DEALINGS	AMT. NOW OWING (INCLUDING OUTSTANDING DRAFTS)	AMOUNT PAST DUE	LENGTH OF TIME PAST DUE	MANNER OF PAYMENT (USE CODE)	RATING	REMARKS
5	11	120	4200	12-68	4200			I	Q	
6	11	60	3600	12-68	1500			I	R	
8	16	90	2567	11-68	1156			I	S	
YRS	1A	120	2432	11-68	2000				R	
YRS	12	90	2300	11-68	2150			B	Q	
YRS	S/D	90	1134	11-68	400			I	R	
7	1	90	1102	11-68					S	
4	S/D	90	1264	11-68					Q	
YRS	4		3000	10-68					R	
YRS	12	120	2001	9-68					Q	
YRS	11	90	2347	8-68				I	R	

Note the 9 vital facts supplied by each of the 11 sources reporting. up-to-date complete and authentic data sound judgment

GENERAL INFORMATION

Information received by the Bureau dated December, 1968 indicates that the above is a Corporation which was established on June 1, 1934. They are engaged in the import of drugs and chemicals. This Corporation is well known, has a capable and reliable staff, and they are attentive to the discharge of their financial obligations. The subject firm is considered to be responsible for its business obligations.

Commercial Banks

Oftentimes the bank through which the exporter conducts his international business has credit information on foreign customers.[11] This is in direct contrast to the role of banks as a source of credit

11 / A somewhat different view is expressed by John R. Kreidle and Paul O. Groke, "How to Finance Your Exports," *Credit and Financial Management,* March 1969, p. 14: "Yet many banks, with the exception of the very large urban ones, are wary about giving

information for domestic customers. The reason they have accumulated much foreign information is that they are often directly involved in export credit sales. Drafts and letters of credit are frequently used in export credit transactions, and hence banks have a great interest in the same types of credit information as export credit managers.

The information contained in their extensive files is usually available to clients who request it for credit purposes. In requesting such information the creditor should completely reveal the details of the export credit transaction. Complete information on the transaction will be of much assistance to the bank in making an accurate and most usable reply. Banks will also write or cable for information not in their files. This is possible because their foreign offices and correspondent banks have firsthand experience with importers in the payment of their foreign trade obligations.

Bank information on foreign customers is regarded highly by export credit men. The information available includes the history and antecedents of the importer firm, its financial strength and capacity when available, and its record of the payment performance experienced by the bank's overseas branches and correspondents. In general, this source of information has the advantages of completeness, high quality, and speed.

Other Sources

There are a number of other sources, any one of which may supply valuable information. Foreign trade publications, exporters' associations, and the importer's bank may provide supplemental information of value. The export credit man who is closely associated with foreign trade groups will have little difficulty in picking up essential information on particular markets and the exchange problems encountered by other members. Not to be overlooked are the exporter's salesman, foreign representatives, and, of course, the customer himself.

The U.S. Department of Commerce supplies valuable facts about foreign firms; its *World Trade Directory* also is of value to exporters. United States foreign service offices are in a position to secure information which may be valuable to an American exporter in making credit decisions.

Brief mention should be made of the so-called Edge Law banks. The Edge Law, passed in December 1919 as part of the Federal

---

advice and counsel on international financial matters or on the handling of an export finance transaction. . . . It would appear that banks need to do more to help exporting business firms."

Reserve Act, provides for the federal incorporation of concerns to engage solely in international or foreign banking or in other types of foreign financial operations. These banks are an excellent source of valuable credit information.

REVIEW AND DISCUSSION QUESTIONS

1. How do you account for the fact that the balance of payments of the United States has shown a deficit for more than a decade?

2. How do you explain the increased interest in export marketing among United States manufacturers?

3. Why is a company's credit policy, or the lack of one, a vital factor in determining the success or failure of an international marketing program?

4. Explain what a combination export management firm does.

5. What are the conditions which magnify the problem of credit risk evaluation on foreign creditors? Explain each of the conditions you have listed.

6. What is the present status of export credit insurance?

7. What is the purpose of the Foreign Credit Insurance Association?

8. Explain the activities of the Export-Import Bank in connection with export credit insurance.

9. Under what conditions would you use consignment terms? Open-account terms?

10. What is the difference between a time draft and a sight draft?

11. Discuss the statement, "For all practical purposes an irrevocable letter of export credit results in a cash sale."

12. Do any American industries customarily sell on c.b.d. terms? If so, which ones?

13. How do you account for the differences and similarities between domestic and foreign sources of credit information?

14. Why are commercial banks a source of information on foreign customers?

15. What is the Edge Law? Explain what it attempted to accomplish.

SUGGESTED READINGS

Credit Management Handbook (2d ed.; Homewood, Ill.: Richard D. Irwin, Inc., 1965), chap. 31.

Hess, John M. and Cateora, Philip R. *International Marketing* (Homewood, Ill.: Richard D. Irwin, Inc., 1966), chap. 20.

Kramer, Ronald L. *International Marketing* (3d ed.; Cincinnati, Ohio: South-Western Publishing Co., 1970), chaps. 17 and 18.

Miracle, Gordon E. and Albaum, Gerald S. *International Marketing Management* (Homewood, Ill.: Richard D. Irwin, Inc., 1970).

PART V

Management and Analysis of Commercial Credit

22

Management of Commercial Credit Sales

The position of the present-day commercial credit manager continues to grow in importance. The reasons for this are: (1) commercial credit is heavily relied upon as a means of short-term financing by practically all production and marketing institutions, (2) commercial credit so pervades the industrial and commercial scenes that it is not only a customary means of selling goods and services, it is also the most frequently used type of business credit, (3) the volume of commercial credit is far larger than the other types of business credit, and (4) the emergence of the credit executive as a business advisor[1] has been one of the most dramatic changes in credit management in recent years. The following observations on the role of the credit manager as a business advisor are made in the *Credit Management Handbook:*[2]

> Numerous firms are beginning to realize more fully that their future growth depends to a considerable extent upon the soundness and abilities of their customers and suppliers. When it is considered that marginal accounts have assumed increasing importance in the sales and profit picture of these firms, it is understandable that credit management has expanded its role in the counseling of customers who need guidance to reach their potential. . . .
>
> This development in the credit man's role reflects changing concepts which are being applied at all levels of management. No longer is the credit man adequately fulfilling his function when he simply grants or denies approval to a request for credit. Instead, he is part of a management team, charged with responsibility for increasing both sales and profits. The introduction of new products and the desire for greater sales volume in both new and old products requires the combined efforts of both the sales department and the credit department. With proper help and guidance, small or financially weak customers

---

1 / Stephen F. Keating, "Rx for Success: Think Like an Entrepreneur," *Credit and Financial Management,* August 1970, p. 16.

2 / *Credit Management Handbook* (2d ed.; Homewood, Ill.: Richard D. Irwin, Inc., 1965), p. 372.

can often develop into excellent outlets for a company's products. Only by taking full advantage of opportunities along these lines can a credit man do the constructive job now expected of him.

Some indication of the importance of the commercial credit executive in our economy can be gained from quantitative estimates of the volume of commercial credit. In Chapter 1 it was estimated that 90 to 95 percent of all commercial and industrial transactions between businessmen are made on the basis of commercial credit. While it is very difficult, if not impossible, to estimate the true volume of commercial credit, we do know from U.S. Bureau of Census data that manufacturers' sales, wholesalers' sales, and other middlemen's sales, when multiplied by our estimate, result in a figure far in excess of the volume of any other type of business credit. The receivables item on most manufacturers' and wholesalers' balance sheets is one of their largest and most liquid assets. It therefore must be emphasized that commercial credit management is concerned with a financial aspect of business which, in many respects, is as demanding, important, and significant as many other financial tasks. It is imperative that commercial credit management safeguard the receivables asset with sound, intelligent and effective credit and collection policies.

THE COMMERCIAL CREDIT EXECUTIVE—HIS STATUS, PLACE, AND FUNCTIONS

The commercial credit manager occupies a respected and responsible position[3] in his company's organizational structure. He manages the acceptance of customers' credit and the collection of their debts. As simplified as this may appear at first glance, effective credit management involves several major tasks, all of which are dependent upon numerous routine operations.

One complicating aspect of commercial credit management stems from the fact that a sale of merchandise or services takes place, and as a result of this transaction a credit act takes place. Commercial credit, then, as contrasted with other forms of credit, is not entirely financial in character, but it is directly concerned with both the sales and financial problems of a company.[4] The purpose of any business enterprise is to earn a profit. Profits are derived from the company's sales, which in turn involve a commercial credit transaction. The aim

---

3 / Arthur Atkinson, "Room at the Top for Credit," *Credit and Financial Management,* Part I in January 1968, p. 16, and Part II in February 1968, p. 24. Also *Duties and Compensation of the Credit Executive* (Lake Success, N.Y.: Credit Research Foundation, Inc., 1970).

4 / The problem of specialization in the field of credit management is discussed by Helen Cris, "The Credit Manager: Generalist or Specialist?" *Credit and Financial Management,* May 1970, p. 22.

of credit managers is, hence, the same as the objective of their companies—to earn a profit.[5] With this guiding principle directing the credit manager, the implications of his policies throughout any given company cannot be overemphasized.[6] If his attitude and policies are those which tend to create an ultraconservative atmosphere, customers whose credit is less than prime must go elsewhere to purchase. On the other hand, the attitude and policies of the credit manager may be too lenient, and the company is then involved with an unsatisfactory quality of receivables. In the former instance, sales and the financial gain of the company have suffered; while in the latter instance, sales may increase but the company suffers financial losses on a low-quality group of credit customers. In view of the far-reaching effects of commercial credit management, it would seem that *managing commercial credit sales is the efficient employment of all devices at one's command to create the most profitable balance between company sales and company revenue.*

Changing Status and Qualifications of Credit Management

The major factor contributing to the changing status and qualifications for commercial credit management has been the rapid and tremendous growth of American industry and commerce. When business was largely under the control of a sole proprietor and relatively small in size, the approval of credit was a simple, but personal, matter. It was once customary, 50 to 75 years ago, for buyers to visit markets once or twice a year. After having an opportunity to "size up" the buyer, the proprietor would either approve or disapprove his credit. As commerce developed the personal relationship was lost, and some other basis was needed to manage commercial credit.

It was logical that the task should fall on someone within the company, and hence for a number of years the "bookkeeper" was in control of credit for a large number of concerns. As commerce and industry grew, it became apparent that the work of the "bookkeeper-credit man" would have to be divided. Paralleling the commercial and industrial developments of the present century, a high degree of administrative efficiency was attained through better organization and specialization.

With the organization of the National Association of Credit Management in 1896, the significance of professional credit manage-

5 / D. W. Smith, "Credit Goals as Management Tools," *Credit and Financial Management,* March 1970, p. 16; Karl W. Stockinger, "What Is a Credit Manager Made Of?" *Credit and Financial Management,* February 1971, p. 18.

6 / J. Allen Walker, "What Does a Credit Manager Want from Top Management," *Credit and Financial Management,* May 1967, p. 18.

ment came to be realized. Improved sources of credit information developed; better accounting methods became universal and the techniques of financial statement analysis were refined; management recognized the professional character of credit work and its significant relationship to the marketing and financial operations of their businesses; and an increased number of highly qualified people sought out credit work as a career and profession. The complexities of modern-day business and the need for specialization created the conditions which fostered the status held[7] by today's credit managers. It is well for the aspiring reader to recognize that credit management has moved up to the status of an established business profession, with prerogatives, responsibilities, standards, and ethics.[8]

The changed status and present-day professional character of credit management necessitate changed qualifications for success in this field. It is no longer possible to get along with bookkeeping knowledge, as it was many years ago; nor is it a task which relies solely on accounting principles and financial statement analysis. This latter concept of the qualifications for credit management was held not too many years ago, and it is still entertained by a number of business and educational people. Modern business techniques and the operation of an effective credit department demand that credit management be intimately knowledgeable of the relationships of credit to the financial, production, marketing, and other aspects of the business. All this has entailed a broadening of the base of qualifications, with greater emphasis upon formal training in both the specialized and general areas of credit management.

In recognition of the broader base of qualifications, the National Association of Credit Management (NACM) has done much to make available the types of training needed by credit department personnel and particularly those who aspire to management positions and those already in responsible posts. Specialized training is offered through the National Institute of Credit, which is one of the activities of the Credit Research Foundation of the NACM. The institute offers a nationwide program especially designed for credit personnel from the time they enter the work through their early experience. The main objectives of the institute, which functions through chapters located

7 / Robert Half, "More Recognition for Credit Management," *Credit and Financial Management,* November 1969, p. 24.

8 / "The high honor to be coveted by a credit manager is to be labeled by his top management as the best credit manager in the industry. To stand out among his peers, he should be a good salesman, a good analyst, a good decision maker and a good organizer. He should also be a good developer of men. He should direct his energies and those of his organization in making the credit function help accomplish the total objectives of his firm." J. Allen Walker, "What Kind of Credit Executive Will You Be in the 70's?" Reprinted from *Credit and Financial Management,* January 1970, p. 14. Copyright 1970 by the National Association of Credit Management, New York, N.Y.

in the principal cities of the United States, are: (1) to establish national standards of proficiency and achievement in credit and financial management, and to provide a means for recognition of those who attain the standards; (2) to develop and maintain a sound educational program in credit and financial management; (3) to cooperate with college and university schools of business administration to develop programs of study in credit and financial management; and (4) to make courses of study available to persons who want to use their leisure time for self-improvement. Accreditation for study in the specified fields of credit is given in the form of awards. The Associate Award is given for satisfactory completion of basic education in the field of commercial credit management, provided the student has had work experience in credit, sales, accounting, or financial functions. Each person seeking the Fellow Award must pass an examination which is designed to test his mastery of the fundamentals of credit and financial management and his ability to use these principles in the analysis and solution of current problems. There are two separate plans under which applicants may qualify as candidates for the Fellow Award examination. Under Plan A the student must be a holder of the Associate Award; have six years of business experience in credit, finance, or related fields; and have successfully completed, with an average grade of C, the educational requirements for candidacy under Plan A, or be currently enrolled in courses that will enable him to complete those requirements during the next school year. To qualify as a candidate under Plan B, the applicant must be at least 30 years old and must have had at least 10 years of responsible work experience in credit and financial management.

Graduate schools of credit and financial management of two weeks duration each summer are held at Dartmouth College, Harvard University, and Stanford University. These schools operate in cooperation with the graduate schools of business administration at the respective institutions. The student entering one of these programs is expected to be well versed in credit fundamentals, accounting, finance, and economics. The graduate program includes courses of study and seminars in credit policy, financial management, executive development, and related high-level fields. To complete this program attendance for three summers is required. The credit personnel attending these sessions are nominated by their companies and are expected to possess management capabilities sufficient to qualify them for executive credit positions.

One of the Credit Research Foundation's special projects has been the inclusion of the career category of credit manager among the profiles of the Strong Vocational Interest Test. The foundation undertook this project jointly with Dr. Edward K. Strong of Stanford University to bring credit management as a profession to the attention of college-level guidance counselors and to make available a scientific tool as an aid in credit personnel selection. Vocational interest test blanks distributed to educational institutions throughout the country have now been revised to include credit manager as a specific career.

In the banking field, the American Institute of Banking sponsors similarly excellent programs for commercial bank personnel.

In addition to the above specialized and general educational programs, many of our nation's colleges and universities offer day school and evening school programs designed to help equip the modern-day credit manager. The best equipped to handle the programs seem to be the schools of business administration which offer broad training in the liberal arts and sciences and a specialized training in marketing, management, finance, economics, and accounting. In addition, of course, many firms themselves conduct training programs for their own personnel. There is no cut-and-dried formula for a successful training program. Each concern must determine for itself the type and extent of training best suited to its own needs.

Thus, whatever a person's educational background, it is not too difficult, with the offerings discussed above, to develop the *personal, experience,* and *educational* qualifications necessary for the credit management profession.[9]

The Credit Department in the Organizational
Framework of the Company

A systematic organization will clearly define the lines of authority and responsibility and insure the effective performance of the delegated credit functions. In the organization of the credit department, numerous routine (but essential) activities, decision-making processes, collection phases of the operation, and supplemental services to customers and the company must be provided.

When the commercial credit department is organized, the question of its place in the organizational framework of the company arises. This is not a question that can be easily reconciled, because of variations in size of company, size of department, and the principal business activity of the enterprise. Service companies generally have fewer credit problems and less opportunity to fulfill all basic functions completely. Manufacturers and wholesalers, especially large ones, need a full-fledged effective operational department. Small

9 / Rodman A. Savoye, "How to Attract the Right Candidates to Careers in Credit Management," *Credit and Financial Management,* September 1969, p. 20.

concerns will frequently delegate credit and collection functions among the owners, the salesmen, or accounting personnel.

In large companies where the credit function plays an integral role in accomplishing major objectives, variation is found in the place of the credit department in the sales activity, others with the financial activity, and still others in the accounting activity.

Credit Department in Sales Activity. It is prevalent to have the credit department in the sales activity when the company is in a highly competitive industry, when the policies of the company are almost entirely sales-oriented, and when great emphasis is placed on credit service to customers. The principal arguments advanced for and against this type of organizational plan are:

	For		*Against*
1.	Both sales and credit have the same objective—maximizing sales.	1.	The sales philosophy is too liberal with respect to credit risk.
2.	The gathering of credit information is facilitated by having salesmen perform some of this work.	2.	Overly liberal policies can as easily create ill will among customers as an overly strict credit policy.
3.	Closer cooperation results between sales and credit personnel.	3.	Objectivity in the decision-making process is not free from subjective influences.
4.	Better opportunity exists for the credit manager to build goodwill by keeping alert to weak customers and new customers, as reported by sales personnel.		
5.	The processing of sales orders is facilitated.		

Credit Department in the Financial Activity. A very large number of credit managers are under the supervision of company treasurers. In these companies, great emphasis is placed on the concept and function of utilizing invested capital efficiently. The arguments for and against this type of organizational plan are:

	For		*Against*
1.	The control of funds invested in accounts receivable is improved.	1.	The maximizing of sales function is likely to suffer under the financial-oriented and not sales-oriented department.
2.	A better working relationship between the treasurer and credit manager is fostered.	2.	The treasurer is more importantly charged with management of company debt and not customers' credit.
3.	Current financing of the company mance of the credit department. ance of the credit department.	3.	The credit and collection policies will tend to be conservative and harsh, hence creating poor customer relations.
4.	The total financial plan of the company includes accounts receivables, and the treasurer needs control to forecast financial requirements of the company.		

Credit Department in Accounting Activity. While most credit departments are placed under the sales activity or the treasurer's office, there is much to be said for placing it with the accounting function. Those who argue in favor of this type of organizational setup believe that there are particular advantages to the record-keeping task. Both the accounting and the credit personnel must understand the significance of the accounts receivable ledger. It is usually maintained by accounting personnel to satisfy both activities, and with this apparent advantage there is no reason to separate one activity or the other from the valuable accounting record. The ready accessibility of all pertinent data on current and inactive accounts is then centralized and mutually available. If this arrangement exists, it is desirable that positions of coordinate rank be established for credit management and accounting management. The principal objection to this arrangement is that the credit manager may fail to realize his greatest potential by being *inward* rather than *outward* in his policies and decisions, to the detriment of other departments of the company and its customers.

The Independent Credit Department. If some high degree of independence is not granted the credit department, it may be desirable to create this situation by means of changing the organizational structure. Whether or not this is necessary depends, of course, on the management personalities involved. In some companies it may not be desirable to separate the credit department from the control of another executive because of the incapabilities of the credit manager himself. Conversely, it may be desirable to establish a separate credit operation because of the strong dominance, short-sightedness, and lack of appreciation of credit's role by the sales executive, the financial officer, or the accounting head.

If an independent credit department is organized, it is the responsibility of the senior executives and the credit manager to see that close cooperation between function and operation exists between the various departments in the company. Furthermore, the credit manager should occupy a coordinate place in the structure with other executives. The independent credit department should be able to function more effectively, as it is free of being subject to the supervision of other department managers. Without the onesided dominance of another department, the cooperation between all other departments is unquestionably enhanced.

Basic Functions of Commercial Credit Management

A further understanding of the status and qualification of modern-day credit management may be had by a realization of its basic functions. These functions, believed to be first conceived by Dr. Theodore N. Beckman of Ohio State University, are as follows:

1. To maximize sales and profits.
2. To minimize bad-debt losses.
3. To utilize invested funds efficiently.
4. To cooperate with other internal and external departments.

Maximizing Sales and Profits.[10] The commercial credit manager can accomplish this function in two ways. First, he must work in harmony with the sales personnel of his company, and second, he must lend his knowledge and experience to foster good relations between his company and its customers. If a company is to realize its maximum profit and grow competitively, the volume of sales will be directly affected. The credit department, and for that matter all sales-supporting departments, must lend support to the sales effort. Hence, the credit manager in shaping his policies and departmental operations should avoid hindering the sales and the operations of the sales people. The credit policies adopted and placed into effect should: (1) smooth the path for salesmen by eliminating all nonessential credit and collection duties, (2) handle all orders promptly and speedily so as to assure meeting delivery schedules, and (3) accept all credit when the facts indicate that there is a reasonable certainty of payment.

The credit manager is in an excellent position to create good customer relations for his company and thereby build sales volume. He is in the best position to counsel with marginal or poor customers and oftentimes to suggest remedies which may result in their rehabilitation. If he is alert he can advise the sales personnel on the potential purchases of a customer in his company's line of products. His correspondence to customers can be used to develop customer confidence and goodwill. Finally, to some extent he can propose special terms or special credit services to customers in order to aid the sales-building function.

Minimizing Bad-Debt Losses. It is a very simple matter to operate a credit department with small losses. In operating with the sole objective of minimizing credit losses, only the most acceptable credit risks are taken. Excessive losses, as it was shown earlier in this chapter, can be as destructive to the objectives of the business as no losses at all. It is a difficult and demanding task to accept that quantity and quality of credit which produces the optimum profit at a minimum of loss. To put this in another way, credit department policy should be developed not to avoid *all* bad debts but to insure against *excessive* losses.

10 / For articles on maximizing sales and profits, see the Suggested Readings at the end of the chapter.

Good credit management can do much to minimize losses. It is not only a matter of rejecting the poor risks, but it also requires that management be watchful of the risks that grow weak while on the books. Credit decision making is not infallible; hence some accounts will develop weaknesses and defects. Here again, the counseling services of the credit department should be directed toward the elimination or lessening of these weaknesses and defects.

Perhaps one of the most effective ways to keep losses at a minimum is a good collection policy. This subject is discussed fully in subsequent chapters, but it should be noted here that an effective collection system depends on adequate records, the prompt handling of delinquent accounts, and a series of collection devices and actions. Above all, some credit losses are inevitable. If losses do not occur, then the credit policies and the collection policies of the department are not founded on sound judgment.

Utilizing Invested Funds Efficiently. Commercial credit management is charged with the responsibility of managing accounts receivable.[11] This item is frequently one of the most valuable and liquid assets of a business enterprise. Like all other assets in a business, accounts receivable are financed either by the owner's investment or outside capital. The turnover of the receivables will affect the company's ability to meet current operating expenses. If the turnover is slower than normal, outside sources of financing may be necessary. As turnover increases it yields a higher return on the investment in receivables. As credit management conceives its role as the guardian of the investment in receivables,[12] it follows that it must develop and follow policies best suited for the most efficient utilization of said investment. Credit policies, collection policies, the use of factors, and the assignment of accounts receivable are devices available to credit management to insure or reduce the investment in receivables.

Cooperating with Other Internal and External Departments. It is apparent that credit department activities have a strong impact on the policies and activities of other departments. The sales, accounting, and financial aspects of the business are but a few of the many influenced by the credit manager's policies. Close cooperation with and assistance to all departments are paramount. The day is long past when business enterprises could grow and prosper as a result of the direction of one man. When the credit manager clearly visualizes his responsibility as contributing to the total effectiveness of his

11 / Harlan R. Patterson, "New Life in the Management of Corporate Receivables," *Credit and Financial Management,* February 1970, p. 15; George L. Marrah, "Managing Receivables," *Financial Executive,* July 1970, p. 38.

12 / *Trends in Cash Application and Control of Accounts Receivable* (Lake Success, N.Y.: Credit Research Foundation, Inc., 1969).

company, rather than narrowly regarding his department as segmented from the company's objective, he has taken the major step toward being of greater value to his company.[13]

Cooperation with external departments means that the credit manager can better perform his functions when he works closely and in harmony with other credit-granting institutions, credit-facilitating agencies, and other business organizations. Perhaps no field is as dependent upon mutual exchange of information, cooperation, and collective action as is the credit profession. Credit-reporting agencies, the direct interchange of information among creditors, and the educational ventures undertaken by the profession are widely recognized as dependent upon collective action. When business debtors weaken to the degree of approaching failure, the independent action of a single creditor is censured. Adjustments, assignments for the benefit of creditors, and other settlements in or out of court should be the mutual interest of all interested creditors. Much can be gained from cooperation with external departments and agencies to improve the techniques of the credit profession and lift the quality of the business credit structure.

OPERATION OF THE COMMERCIAL CREDIT DEPARTMENT

The day-to-day operations of a commercial credit department involve a large number of routine functions performed by the employees of the department, plus the handling of special problems, execution of credit policies, and the making of decisions by the credit executive and his assistants. The more or less routine operations of the department are:[14] (1) checking orders for credit, (2) filing credit information, (3) revising credit information, (4) answering credit inquiries, (5) checking credit ratings, (6) checking deductions, (7) collecting accounts, and (8) customer service.

The credit manager and his assistants direct their attention to the following special problems, which often require an authoritative decision:[15] (1) review of credit information, (2) action on special collection problems, (3) consideration of special terms, (4) handling requests for extensions, (5) establishing credit lines for new customers, (6) handling questionable orders, (7) dealing with financially distressed customers, (8) handling credit problems for other departments, and (9) customer counseling. At less frequent

13 / John D. Morrow, "Top Management Sets New Responsibilities for Credit Executives," *Credit and Financial Management,* April 1968, p. 17; Ernest W. Walker, "The Outlook for Credit Management in the 1970s," *Credit and Financial Management,* July 1970, p. 10.

14 / *Credit Management Handbook, op. cit.,* pp 390-91.

15 / *Ibid.,* pp. 391-92.

intervals, the credit manager must review departmental policies in regard to the following matters:[16] (1) reserve for bad debts, (2) credit information services, (3) credit lines, (4) collections, (5) staffing, (6) departmental expenses, (7) marginal accounts, and (8) interdepartmental meetings. In addition to this array of activities, the credit manager will be charged with the responsibility of rendering summary credit and financial reports to higher echelons of management. From such reports the company can evaluate the effectiveness of the department and use the financial data for long-range planning. It is apparent that this department must maintain accurate, revealing, and continuous records.

Handling Orders from New Customers

When an order is received in the credit department, the procedures for immediate processing of the account are set in motion. The first step of the department will be the credit investigation.[17] Whether the order from the new customer will be approved or not depends upon the credit strength of the applicant. It is necessary to conduct a credit investigation so as to marshal the facts upon which a credit decision can be based. The extent of the credit investigation and the types of credit information needed will vary, however, with the size of the order. Small orders may be evaluated on the basis of credit ratings found in one of the several credit reference books of the credit reporting agencies, or they may be evaluated on the basis of the salesman's report and appraisal of the risk. If the limited information available on the small order is favorable, it is likely to be approved and passed on to. the shipping department. Whether additional information will be gathered depends on the creditor firm and the potential of future business from the account.

Large orders from new customers will be investigated more thoroughly. The information needed to make an accurate decision includes: (1) the identity and legal responsibility of the firm, (2) its history and business background, (3) the character and responsibility of the company's management, and (4) its financial ability, strength, and outlook. Unfortunately most credit decisions are made with less information than the credit analyst would like to have. It is more common for the credit man to act without complete information. Although this may lead him into error, it must be remembered that a complete credit investigation takes time and costs money. Too little information, or underinvestigation, results in a scarcity of facts upon

16 / *Ibid.*, pp. 392-93.

17 / For a detailed account of factors to investigate, the sources of credit information, and their significance to the credit decision, see Chapters 23, 24, 25, and 26.

which to base a credit decision. The ideal credit investigation is one which secures just the information essential to a sound credit decision and obtains it from sources best prepared to supply it speedily and at minimum cost. Careful analysis of the risk within the department and an imaginative interpretation of the information at hand will overcome many of the deficiencies of the credit investigation.

Credit executives have tried for years to establish criteria for judging management of firms applying for credit. Some observers believe that a completely satisfactory evaluation of management is not possible at the time of the first order (or of the first loan in a financial institution) but can come about only through a series of business transactions. The American Institute of Management has 10 criteria for judging management from an investment point of view: (1) economic function, (2) corporate structure, (3) health of earnings, (4) service to stockholders, (5) research and development, (6) effectiveness of directors, (7) fiscal policies, (8) production efficiency, (9) sales vigor, and (10) executive evaluation.

If, after the credit investigation and the analysis of the information at hand, the order appears to be a poor risk, judgment may be withheld pending further investigation. If it is rejected at once or after more investigation, the sales personnel should be notified *promptly* so that the action of the credit department can be transmitted to the rejected customer.

In the event the analysis of the credit information proves favorable and the account is accepted, the next step is the assignment of the credit terms and the setting of the credit line. The routines of preparing credit reference cards, opening a credit folder, and recording the information in the customer's ledger are accomplished, and then approval of the new account is sent to the sales department. Similar information is sent to all other interested departments, and an authorized order releasing shipment is sent to the shipping department.

Handling Orders from Established Customers

When an old, established account orders merchandise, the credit department procedures are greatly simplified. In-file information previously recorded and filed in the credit department is referred to in order to determine whether the account is in good standing or not. Most commercial credit departments accumulate credit information and revise credit limits on established accounts periodically. Hence in-file data are usually reasonably current, and this leads to a rapid credit decision. If the order is acceptable and when added to any existing balances is within the assigned credit limit, it is approved and sent to the shipping department, where the order is filled and shipped to the customer.

If, however, the account is not in good standing because of previous balances remaining unpaid or because the credit limit would be greatly exceeded, the order is sent to the credit manager for decision. With all in-file data before him he may revise the credit limit upward; seek out additional credit information from external sources; or, rather than assume greater risk from the customer, notify him of the negative decision. If the account is seriously overdue, shipment may be withheld pending receipt of a check from the customer to defray the previous balance. In this event, the customer must obviously be notified as to the reason for the shipping delay.

Speed—Essential to Handling Orders

In the operation of a commercial credit department, *speed* in the processing and resulting action on orders is imperative. Much of this is accomplished by routinizing the credit-decision task through the maintenance of the department's in-file information. Current in-file information on customers and the use of credit limits safely permit automatic approval of a large volume of orders. New accounts on which no in-file data exist and old revived accounts must be processed quickly, and the credit investigation commenced without delay.

The basis for this contention lies in the strong competitive conditions under which many companies market their products. Speed of action is perhaps one of the most important considerations when customers have the alternative of purchasing elsewhere. Delays, withheld shipments, and unreasonable requests for credit information destroy the desirable customer relationships which were once developed by the sales personnel. Retention of present customers and the gaining of new customers are as much dependent on this point as are the other important considerations of price, quality, service, personalities, and the like.

Automation in the Commercial Credit Department

Credit and accounts receivable departments have felt the impact of the introduction of advanced electronic data processing systems for a number of years. The commercial credit departments of certain major corporations are using the devices, and still other concerns are in the process of making the change or at least contemplating such a change. It is important for the student of credit to be generally aware of the many factors involved in the installation and application of an electronic data processing system in a concern dealing in commercial credit.

In analyzing the reasons for the changeover to computers, it should be recognized that the motivation comes from three needs:[18]

(a) the desire of the company to bring all possible operations into the automatic data information flow which has been started in other departments; *(b)* the desire for more timely and detailed information to use in financial planning and control; and *(c)* the desire to reduce pro rata costs through more intensive use of the computer.

Accounts receivable and credit are not the initial operations placed on electronic data processing but are brought into the feasibility studies very early.

Because a large amount of a company's assets are tied up in accounts receivable at a given moment, the conversion of these receivables to cash requires prime attention and the best available tools. Electronic data processing is one of these tools.

Electronic data processing can: (1) process information faster than any other known means for better and more rapid decisions by management, (2) integrate the data from many business operations and variables, and (3) mechanize practically all routine procedures. These possibilities give business managements the opportunity to consider more departmental relationships in an integrated report and hence study more alternatives. Cost savings may not be attained through the use of electronic equipment, but time savings and other advantages mentioned above may outweigh this consideration.

In a recent, excellent *Staff Report,* the Credit Research Foundation, Inc. of the National Association of Credit Management analyzed some of the problems that small businesses must consider in deciding whether or not to automate their accounts receivable. The highlights of the report are covered by the following quotations:[19]

A main reason that a small business would convert from a manual system to computerized receivables management is the speed and accuracy of the computer in recording daily accounts receivable operations. This makes it possible for the credit manager to obtain analytical and control reports quickly and efficiently.

The final accuracy of a well-run manual system is not being challenged. However, it cannot begin to match the lightning speed of a computer. Consequently, the credit manager of a small business may, on numerous occasions, be forced to make a decision based on insufficient facts—although additional items might very well be in the process of being posted to the customers' accounts.

. . . .

18 / *Credit Management Handbook, op. cit.,* p. 406.

19 / *Staff Report: Small Businesses Must Automate Their Accounts Receivable If They Are to Survive* (Lake Success, N.Y.: Credit Research Foundation, Inc., February 1971).

Most small businesses will realize a cost savings by using an electronic data processing (EDP) system only if *all* costs of their present manual system are considered. These include:

1. *The cost of maintaining office machines.* Having a computer center prepare your receivables records eliminates a given amount of costs involving the maintenance of office equipment. Also, don't forget that when old machines wear out, they must be replaced. This necessitates a cash outlay, whether they are bought or leased. Moreover, bought or leased equipment takes up office space that might be utilized to better advantage.

2. *Payroll expenses.* When a receivables system is converted to a computer, management will need fewer clerical personnel for routine processing. Furthermore, computers do not require costly fringe benefits.

. . . .

The speed and accuracy of a computerized system produce control tools that are indispensable to today's credit managers.

—Payments are quickly posted.

—Slowness in payment is pinpointed.

—Followup collection procedure is accelerated.

—Status of every account is kept current.

When a company speeds up its collections, it also improves its cash flow. It has more funds to run the business and a lesser need to borrow and pay interest.

. . . .

A well-thought-out and carefully planned computerized system will give credit managers a quick, accurate, and concise evaluation of the status of every customer. In addition, the very nature of computer information enables management to make reliable sales forecasts.

Here is a rundown of typical reports prepared for an Accounts Receivable package system by EDP service centers.

1. *The Computer Produces A Transactions Report.* It lists all business transactions. It has a built-in control that checks the accuracy of the input data, thus eliminating human errors. The report replaces the original entry journal, invoice journal, and cash receipts journal, and the computer assigns a sequential control number to each transaction so that, at any given point, immediate reference can be made to the original entry.

. . . .

2. *The Computer Posts Accounts Receivable.* There is an automatic posting of all debits and credits. The posting records all invoices that are added and removed via current transactions. New balances due from each account appear after current postings. In addition, a special note is made on prepaid invoices and payments on account. At the end of the report, there is an automatic printout summarizing all debits and credits posted.

. . . .

3. *The Computer Prepares An Aged Trial Balance.* Aging of trial balances is invaluable to credit managers. They have a list of all open accounts along with aging data, showing open invoices regardless of age, and a total year-to-year sales figure for each account.

. . . .

4. *The Computer Compiles Past-Due Accounts.* Depending on the collection period set by a seller, the computer redflags all invoices that are outstanding for a longer time than the history of average payment. Year-to-date sales are listed for each past-due customer.

. . . .

5. *The Computer Compiles An Analysis Of Every Customer's Sales and Credit Record.* The compilation lists each account's sales and performance record. This covers:
   (a) year-to-date sales
   (b) current month sales
   (c) a ratio that compares current months' sales payments to the average payments during previous months
   (d) the date of the last sale
   (e) the date of the last payment
   (f) the average number of days between receipt of the invoice and payment
   (g) an aging of each account.

. . . .

6. *The Computer Prepares Statements of Account.* Many companies mail statements of account on a regular basis to their customers. Others confine their mailings to past-due customers. These statements can serve as a primary collection tool and, in fact, promote the chance for improved payments.

. . . .

Even if some of the smaller accounts are not ready to automate, a review of their existing systems will allow for immediate improvement and pave the way for future computerization.

The following conclusions were reached in the *Credit Management Handbook* about the present-day status of electronic data processing systems:[20]

The changeover from manual or punched card accounting to electronic data processing has, initially or eventually, an effect on procedures in accounts receivable and in credits and collections.

Functions are integrated, flow of source documents and flow of cash are changed and accelerated, and heuristic programming is being examined to determine which decision processes can be automatically handled by the machine and which must be reserved for human judgment.

Automatic processing causes some dislocation of personnel, especially those in low-rated jobs, but there is an upgrading of the remaining jobs in the credit department once the system is well established.

The credit man is upgraded to purely credit functions such as credit promotion work, credit control, and credit analysis once he is freed, by electronic processing, from routine tasks of sorting, searching through irrelevant information, etc. He can become more valuable to his company than ever before.

20 / *Op. cit.,* pp. 427-28. For additional material on automation in the commercial credit department, see the Suggested Readings at the end of the chapter.

Integrating of functions and removal from the credit department of functions not purely credit in nature result in greater specialization.

An attempt to transfer the ledger system to the computer in its exact form results in delays and disappointments.

Much imaginative and creative thinking about credit functions is being done by advance planning committees. There is a real challenge to credit men to discover ways of utilizing the capabilities of computers so that more and better information is available for their judgment decisions. The machine has a more accurate, although more limited, memory than man. It does not possess judgment. Storing memory data on the computer or tape and bringing it forth as a basis for judgment decisions can free the credit man from extensive detail and permit him to develop the credit area more effectively than ever before.

The exchange of information by credit managers in studies of this type will hasten the breakthrough into new areas of credit management.

REVIEW AND DISCUSSION QUESTIONS

1. Explain why the position of the commercial credit manager continues to grow in importance.
2. Compare the position of the commercial credit executive and the credit executive in charge of installment cash loans in a commercial bank.
3. What is the Credit Research Foundation, Inc.?
4. Comment on the changing status and qualifications for commercial credit management.
5. Discuss the main objectives of the National Institute of Credit.
6. Distinguish between the Associate Award and the Fellow Award of the National Institute of Credit.
7. What are the arguments for organizing the credit department within the sales activity? Within the financial activity?
8. Where do you believe that the commercial credit department should be placed in the organizational framework of a manufacturing concern?
9. Why did you make the decision that you did in question 8?
10. What four basic functions are usually attributed to commercial credit management? Evaluate the probable effects of placing too much emphasis on any one of these functions.
11. What special problems arise at times that require the individual attention of the credit manager or one of his assistants?
12. How would you proceed to handle a sizable order from a new customer?
13. Would your procedure be different in handling a similar order from an established customer? Explain.
14. Visit a firm that has installed an electronic computer for processing its accounts receivable.

SUGGESTED READINGS

Maximizing Sales and Profits

Firstenburg, Irving. "What Does the Sales Department Owe to Credit?" *Credit and Financial Management*, March 1970, p. 24.

Koogle, L. H. "How Good Are Today's Credit Executives?" *Credit and Financial Management*, June 1969, p. 18.
Welshans, Merle T. "Using Credit for Profit Making," *Harvard Business Review*, January-February 1967, p. 141.

Automation in the Commercial Credit Department

Burke, E. T. C. *Electronic Data Processing* (address to Annual Secretary-Managers Conference, National Association of Credit Management, Boston, May 17, 1968).
Cash Application: State of the Art (Lake Success, N.Y.: Credit Research Foundation, Inc., 1970).
Credit Limits Established by Formula and Computer (Lake Success, N.Y.: Credit Research Foundation, Inc., 1970).
Smith, D. W. "Efficient Credit Management with Timesharing," *Financial Executive*, March 1971, p. 26.
Trends in Cash Application and Control of Accounts Receivable (Lake Success, N. Y.: Credit Research Foundation, Inc., 1969).

23

Basis of the Commercial
Credit Decision

Commercial credit management is confronted
with the inherent uncertainties and risks caused by the time element
in the credit transaction. Because of this fact, decision making is the
hard core of commercial credit management, just as it is with credit
management concerned with other types of credit. The decision
maker attempts to improve the quality of credit accepted and to
assure a more profitable relationship by minimizing risk on one hand
and establishing a basis for confidence on the other.[1] Unfortunately
for creditors, there has been relatively little scientific progress toward
the elimination of uncertainty or risk inherent in the credit transaction. But confidence, based upon past and present facts soundly
obtained and appraised, can remove some uncertainty.

To gather the essential facts needed to reduce uncertainty and risk
a credit investigation should be conducted. The credit investigation
should marshal facts of sufficient quantity and quality bearing on the
account so that the credit decision can be rational and sound. It does
not necessarily follow that losses will always occur if creditors accept
credit by the "hit-or-miss" method. There is, however, a correlation
between the quality and amount of credit information and the frequency with which credit losses occur.

Credit information alone is not sufficient to create a credit decision which is based upon rational and sound judgment. The accurate
interpretation of the facts gathered by commercial credit management is the other essential requisite to assure, with a minimum of
uncertainty, a profitable business relationship. Each commercial
account or customer must be considered as an individual problem of
analysis and interpretation. This is true because customers have no

1 / Robert M. Kaplan, "Credit Risks & Opportunities," *Harvard Business Review*, March-
April 1967, p. 83.

fixed value, and the range of risk is likely to have great variation. Additional complications arise for the commercial decision maker because of the unique characteristics of his customers. Accounts are typically some distance from the creditor. Manufacturers and wholesalers frequently distribute their products to unknown customers many hundreds of miles away. These same customers range from the small, individual proprietorship to the complex, vast corporate enterprise. The amount and quality of credit information will vary with the differences in organizational structure, size, and financial strength of the customer. Some customers have many lines of specialized activity while others have a limited scope of operations. Despite the great variation in commercial credit customers and the fluctuations of the house standards, credit management is interested in a reasonably certain affirmative answer to the questions: "Can the account or customer pay?" and "Will the account or customer pay?"

The key to ascertaining the solution to the above queries lies in the credit manager's ability to recognize what he has to know. In other words, he should ask himself, "What must I know before I accept or reject this account?" If the decision is favorable, then the amount of credit must be determined. This brings up the question, "In light of the existing information on this account, what should be the line of credit extended to this firm?" Whether the evaluation is for the purpose of accepting or rejecting the account or for the purpose of setting the line of credit, the factors of appraisal are generally the same.

NEED FOR CREDIT INFORMATION

The questions of whether an account *can* and *will* pay can be answered only after a series of more specific questions about the risk have been raised and answered. Even though no two customers are alike, the same specific questions are likely to arise and the types of information needed to answer these questions will be quite similar. To answer finally the "can" and "will" of paying, credit management is confronted with the task of discovering the answers to the following questions:

1. Can the *identity and legal responsibility* of this account be established so that we can ascertain that this order represents a request from a bona fide business house?
2. What is the *history and business background* of this account and what elements in its background contribute toward making the decision?

3. What is the general *character and responsibility of the management* we will be doing business with? Are these factors of such a quality that we can anticipate a continuous and healthy business relationship?
4. What is the *financial ability and capability* of this customer?
5. What is the *financial strength and outlook* for this account?
6. Does its *past and present payment record* inspire confidence or not, and what are the future expectations in this regard?

To provide the credit analyst with either affirmative or negative answers to these questions, a credit investigation must be conducted. The sources from which credit information may be drawn and the types supplied by the various sources are numerous. Credit management may find it desirable to use several sources or to vary their use depending upon the particular needs of the firm. An experienced and resourceful credit manager will have little difficulty in selecting the most suitable combination of sources to supply useful data quickly, economically, and accurately.

Classification of Sources of Commercial Credit Information

The sources of credit information available to commercial and other business-type creditors may be classified as internal or external as follows:

I. Internal information:
   A. Credit manager's personal knowledge.
   B. In-file information on previously established accounts
II. External information:
   A. Mercantile agencies:
      1. General
      2. Special.
      3. Interchange bureaus.
   B. Trade association bureaus.
   C. Interviews:
      1. By salesmen of the creditor.
      2. By credit manager and other authorized representatives of the creditor.
   D. Financial statements furnished by the account or new customer directly to the creditor.
   E. Banks.
   F. Attorneys.
   G. Public records.
   H. Correspondence with subject, creditors, or references.
   I. Investors' manuals and services.
   J. Newspapers, magazines, trade journals, and other publications.

It is readily apparent that the sources of credit information are not only internal or external, but that they are also commercialized or noncommercialized. The commercialized sources are the mercantile agencies, trade association bureaus, and investors' manuals and services. An organization which has as its dominant function the supplying of credit information in return for compensation may be termed a commercialized source of credit information.

On the other hand, it is obvious that none of the internal sources of information is a commercial venture in itself, and thus they may be termed noncommercialized. The credit manager's personal knowledge and in-file information on previously established accounts are contributory information which is available to most credit analysts. Several of the external sources of credit information are also noncommercialized, such as banks, attorneys, references, interviews, and other creditors who are often willing to supply information because of reciprocity, custom, courtesy, or informal compensation. Most of the noncommercialized sources are available to all credit men on a more or less equal basis. The amount and usefulness of information secured from these sources will depend upon the type of business activity, the creditor's contacts, and the efficiency of the credit department.

It is imperative that credit managers be thoroughly acquainted with the various sources of credit information and the types of credit information supplied by each source. He must know how the available types of information will best serve the needs of his firm, and what value each source can contribute toward a sound credit decision. By having an intimate knowledge of the sources, the credit manager will be able to draw information at the proper time, of adequate amount and quality, and within the cost limits imposed by his budget and the characteristics of each account or customer. The subjects of internal information and direct investigation are treated in subsequent sections of this chapter, whereas information supplied by the mercantile agencies is examined in the next three chapters.

Selecting Sources of Credit Information

The selection of the particular sources of credit information to be used in appraising the credit worthiness of each customer is dependent upon the characteristics of each source. The most important factors which should be taken into consideration are: accuracy of information, content of reports, speed of reporting, cost of the service, trade coverage, geographical coverage, variety and number of reports, and the supplemental services which fulfill particular or occasional creditor needs.

Accuracy of Information. The accuracy of the information supplied to a creditor is obviously of utmost importance. Without this single quality creditors would have little or no basis for relying on credit information to make their decisions. While most of the sources have no other purpose than to report all facts accurately, human frailties cause some errors. Safeguards against errors have been developed in recent years with the advancements made in automatic processing and duplicating equipment. Foremost to take advantage of these technological improvements have been the mercantile agencies. Much information, and particularly financial data supplied to the agencies by firms being reported on, is today duplicated by mechanical means. The adoption of the more reliable methods of recording facts is in stark contrast to the manual operations which at one time were prevalent. It is hardly necessary to point out that to appraise risk adequately and to arrive at a clear-cut credit decision, accuracy of information is paramount.

Content of Credit Reports. Credit report content will vary with the source rendering the report and with the characteristics of the business reported. Comprehensive and detailed reports are required to answer questions raised on new accounts, whereas periodic revision of existing accounts may be accomplished adequately with limited information of a specific nature. In appraising the credit worthiness of most accounts, commercial credit management may find it necessary to have a complete financial picture. If adequate financial data are not available from the mercantile agency sources, such information should be requested from the customer or other sources which have the capability of supplying the information. Because this type of information is essential to the appraisal and decision-making function, reports which contain adequate financial information are regarded most favorably. Each credit instance will dictate the kind and amount of additional information needed to reach a decision. It may be that the situation dictates the aging of accounts payable, the aging of accounts receivable, or even the current status of inventories and other pertinent information. Payment record (ledger) information will be required in most new account instances because it reveals the likely payment pattern which a creditor may logically expect. Whatever the dictated requirements of a particular case may be, there exists a source from which the information can be requested. Prudence, however, will dictate the desirability of obtaining the information within the cost and time restrictions.

Speed of the Reporting Service. Speed is of importance in order to assure the credit decision within a reasonable time. Modern communication systems and duplicating devices have greatly speeded the compilation of credit information. Despite these improvements, some types of information can be gathered only with considerable expenditure of time and effort. Furthermore, it is not reasonable for the credit department to delay a sale or shipment until *all* sources of information have been tapped. Competitive conditions in the market establish the speed requirement to prevent lost sales. While it must be recognized that many credit losses occur when decisions are based on inadequate information, the credit manager must decide at what point he must sacrifice adequacy for speed or vice versa.

Cost of Credit Information.   Credit costs must be evaluated and justified the same as other marketing costs. Creditors dealing with a nominal number of accounts may spend a few hundred dollars a year to acquire credit information, whereas large business enterprises doing business with thousands of accounts may spend tens of thousands of dollars in subscribing to the services of a single credit information source. The cost of the mercantile agencies' service is usually scaled so that the unit cost decreases as the quantity of reports and number of services increase.

The cost of acquiring and maintaining up-to-date information on each individual account is nominal when the unit sale is of sizable proportions. On the other hand, the cost of investigating small orders is frequently out of proportion to their value. To compensate for this relatively high cost, the credit investigation may be relaxed and costs correspondingly reduced. Some business concerns do not investigate exceptionally small orders. Whether or not a credit investigation is warranted depends on the profit in the order, whether the order is a "one-time" customer, and whether overall losses justify the costs.

Another aspect of costs concerns the risk involved. Obviously, the exposure to great risk will dictate more effort, greater costs, and more complete information. It is a generally accepted view that alert and efficient credit management must consider all factors in order to keep costs in line with the risk and profit involved.[2]

Trade Coverage and Geographical Coverage.   Geographical coverage of the credit information source should correspond to the scope of operations and the market geography of the creditor. Business enterprises selling in a number of markets and to different types of customers need sources of information capable of supplying information from these several markets and on the various types of customers. Not all agencies have national and international coverage, nor do all of them report on customers in all lines of trade. Credit managers must have knowledge of these factors in order to select the most effective source to serve their company needs. The variations in these factors become apparent in the next few chapters.

Variety and Number of Reports.   The variety and number of reports supplied by the various sources differ to a considerable degree. Some accounts can be appraised most accurately with

2 / *Credit Management Handbook* (2d ed.; Homewood, Ill.: Richard D. Irwin, Inc., 1965), pp. 155-56.

particular types of reports which are supplied on credit department requests. Other accounts, particularly those where the degree of risk is great and continuous, require a series of reports supplied at specified intervals. Again the characteristics of individual accounts must correspond to the services rendered by the information source.

Supplemental Services. Services such as credit reference books, making of recommendations or decisions, rendering opinions, foreign credit reports, and supplying standardized financial statement forms fulfill particular or occasional creditor needs. Credit reference books are of particular value in making a preliminary credit check and in appraising the reliability of small orders which do not warrant a complete credit investigation. Some sources make recommendations with regard to the acceptability of an account. This service may influence the use of the source when the credit department is staffed by a part-time credit manager or when because of other circumstances it is desirable to shift the decision-making process. It should be quite clear that most creditors' needs are not completely satisfied by the *basic* credit information services. Supplemental services add refinement to the decision-making process and overcome peculiar circumstances which are inherent in trading with a diverse group of customers.

INTERNAL INFORMATION AND DIRECT INVESTIGATION

In some respects there is no better source of information than the internal information on the debtor business itself, or the information gathered by direct investigation. There is, however, an ever-growing tendency toward large-scale production and more complex management. Paralleling these developments has been the tendency for customers to be increasingly removed geographically from their sources of supply. Each of these developments has restricted the ability of creditors to gather sufficient credit information directly. For example, even though it is seldom possible for a credit manager to interview the customer personally, other company representatives may have this opportunity. Typically the creditor's salesmen have direct contact with the account, and it may be mutually beneficial for both the credit department and sales department to cooperate in the gathering of credit information. Credit information available within the creditor organization and by direct means is of such distinct value that it is desirable to examine briefly some of these sources.

Internal Information

The credit office is literally a storehouse of credit facts. Each time a new account is accepted a file on the customer is established. The information contained in these files is known as "in-file information." This source of information and the credit manager's own knowledge represent the principal sources of internal information.

Perhaps the most arbitrary factor affecting the credit risk, and yet a valuable source of information, is the credit manager himself. The information which he has acquired throughout his years of experience in the credit field and what he already knows about his customers will sharpen his decisions and method of operation. Much of what he knows has been acquired through his attention to in-file information in making the difficult decisions, and through the help he has loaned his office associates in making routine decisions.

The customer's ledger record should not be overlooked as a valuable source of information. Each time an active account or inactive account reorders, an opportunity arises to review the recorded data and predicate a decision on the assumption that past experience will be repeated again. The credit analyst may note the size of the new order and make comparisons with previous orders obtained. If radical differences are evident and the time between orders is lengthy, a new investigation may be initiated. An opportunity to review the customer's ledger also presents itself when other creditors request ledger experience. Impressions are made upon the credit manager's mind and his knowledge of the risk is constantly being strengthened. Although not more than a supplemental source of data, it has a modifying influence on the credit decision.

Direct Investigation

The term "direct investigation" is applicable when a creditor is *directly* involved in gathering basic facts from any of the several noncommercialized sources of information. It involves either (1) direct contact with the customer with the aim of acquiring credit information, or (2) direct contact with individuals and institutions who may have some particular type of useful credit information bearing on the account. It does not include information supplied by any of the several commercialized sources.

Customer-Supplied Information. The owners or principals of a business are often the best source of information available to credit management. From this source, the most accurate information about the operation and financial condition of a business can be acquired. Even though the customer is in a position to supply financial data, trade and bank references, and much other pertinent information, there are limitations affecting the use of this source. Direct contact with the customer will depend upon his degree of cooperation, the distance from the creditor, the time available to conduct the investigation, and the amount of the credit requested.

Direct contact with the customer may be made by correspondence, by telephone, and by personal interview. These methods afford the creditor the opportunity to establish goodwill and an enduring business relationship. In addition to gathering the needed credit information, direct contact can be used to clarify credit and collection policies and answer questions posed by the customer. It should be remembered that the first contact with a customer is perhaps the most important. If the creditor's information requirements are firmly, but courteously, stated during the first contact, this will avoid future resistance when larger amounts of credit may be requested. If a customer understands the initial and periodic information requirements, he has little logical basis to refuse releasing the much needed information at later dates.

Correspondence. This is a frequently used, as well as economical, means of direct contact. Letters sent to new and existing accounts should acknowledge the amount of credit; the credit standing of the customer, honestly appraised at the time of writing; and, if applicable, the established relationship which may exist. Financial statements are customarily requested by letter. One of the convenient financial statement forms supplied by the National Association of Credit Management, illustrated in Figure 23-1, can be enclosed with the letter. When completed and returned, this statement provides the creditor with essential financial information.

Personal Interviews. Personal interviews by salesmen or credit department representatives are another excellent means of gathering credit information. Interviews with the customer have the advantage of getting those facts and observing firsthand the important operating procedures which may be closely related to the needs of the creditor. The speed with which information can be acquired and the freshness of the information gained by means of the interview will often offset the cost and time expended in doing so.

Whether the interview is carried on between the customer and the credit manager, or the customer and a credit department representative, the information obtained should be of equal value. Such a desirable result can be obtained only if credit department representatives are trained in the technique of interviewing customers. Interviewing technique should be studied and the questions asked should be planned in order to assure the uncovering of the facts sought. When the interview is conducted by someone who knows how to get adequate information, and by a person who has intimate knowledge of sound credit and collection practices, the quality of the data thus secured is enhanced. In conducting the interview, such vital points as the inventory, sales, and management problems; future plans; capital responsibility; and various aspects of the financial statement can be discussed. This information, combined with

FIGURE 23-1
Financial Statement Form Approved by the
National Association of Credit Management

Form No. 10   This Form Approved and Published by THE NATIONAL ASSOCIATION OF CREDIT MANAGEMENT

FINANCIAL STATEMENT OF   DATE_____19_____

FIRM NAME_____

Address_____City_____

At close of business on_____19____State_____

ISSUED TO_____ ←≪ { NAME OF FIRM Requesting Statement

[PLEASE ANSWER ALL QUESTIONS. WHEN NO FIGURES ARE INSERTED, WRITE WORD "NONE"]

ASSETS	Dollars	Cents	LIABILITIES	Dollars	Cents
Cash in Bank	$		Accounts Payable	$	
Cash on Hand			(For Merchandise)		
			Notes and Acceptances Payable		
Accounts Receivable			(For Merchandise)		
(Amounts Pledged $............)			For Borrowed Money:		
Notes and Trade Acceptances Receivable			Notes Payable—Unsecured		
(Amounts Pledged $............)					
Merchandise Inventory			Notes Payable—Secured		
(Not on Consignment or Conditional Sale)					
			Income Taxes Payable or Owing		
(Amounts Pledged $............)					
Other Current Assets: (Describe)			Other Taxes, including Sales Tax, Owing		
			Rental, Payrolls, Etc., Owing		
			Other Current Liabilities: (Describe)		
TOTAL CURRENT ASSETS			TOTAL CURRENT LIABILITIES		
Land and Buildings (Depreciated Value)			Mortgage on Land and Buildings		
Leasehold Improvements (Amortized Value)			Chattel Mortgage on Merchandise or Equipment		
Machinery, Fixtures and Equipment (Depreciated Value)			Other Liabilities, Unsecured		
			Other Liabilities, Secured (Describe)		
Due From Others — Not Customers					
Other Assets: (Describe)			TOTAL LIABILITIES		
			Net Worth or { Capital Stock $...... Surplus $...... }		
				$	
TOTAL ASSETS			TOTAL LIABILITIES AND NET WORTH		

BUY PRINCIPALLY FROM THE FOLLOWING FIRMS:

NAMES	ADDRESSES	AMOUNT OWING
		$

THE REVERSE SIDE OF THIS FORM MUST BE COMPLETED ⇒→

FIGURE 23-1 (continued)

STATEMENT OF PROFIT AND LOSS FOR PERIOD FROM_____TO_____.

NET SALES FOR PERIOD	$	DETAILS OF OPERATING EXPENSES:	$
Cash $..		Salaries - Officers (or owners)	
Credit $..			
		Salaries - Employees	
Inventory at start of Period $...............................		Rent, Heat, Light	
		(Include Amortization of Leasehold)	
Purchases for Period $_____			
		Advertising	
TOTAL $..............................			
Less: Inventory at		Delivery	
Close of Period $_____			
		Insurance	
COST OF GOODS SOLD.............................			
		Taxes, Including Sales Taxes	
GROSS PROFIT			
		Depreciation (Fixtures, Trucks, etc.)	
Less: Operating Expense			
		Miscellaneous (Other Operating Expenses)	
NET OPERATING PROFIT		TOTAL OPERATING EXPENSE	$
Other Additions and Deductions (net)			
		SUPPLEMENTAL INFORMATION (DETAILED)	$
NET PROFIT BEFORE FEDERAL INCOME TAXES........		If Incorporated, Amount of Dividends Paid	
			$
Less: Federal Income Taxes		Interest Paid (Expense)	
	$		$
NET PROFIT AFTER TAXES		Cash Discount Earned (Income)	

Fire Insurance Carried: On Merchandise $_____ On Furniture and Fixtures $_____ On Buildings $_____

Liability Insurance Carried On Premises $_____ On Auto and Truck $_____Other Insurance (Type and Am't)_____

Name of Bank_____

Title to Business Premises is in the name of_____

If Premises leased state Annual Rental $_____Lease Expires_____

The foregoing statement (both sides) has been carefully read by the undersigned (both the printed and written material) and is, to my knowledge, in all respects complete, accurate, and truthful. It discloses to you the true state of (our) (my) financial condition on the date indicated. Since that time there has been no material unfavorable change in (our) (my) financial condition other than indicated below under "Remarks." The figures submitted are not estimated. They have been taken from (our) (my) books.
    (We) (I) make the foregoing financial statement in writing intending that you should rely upon it for the purpose of our obtaining merchandise from you on credit.

Name of Individual or Firm_____
If Partnership, name partners_____
If Corporation, name officers_____
How long established_____Previous business experience_____
_____where_____

Date of signing Statement_____ Street_____ City_____ State_____

Witness _____ Signed by_____

Residence Address
of Witness _____ Title _____

REMARKS: (Attach separate sheet if necessary)

firsthand observations, can be used in "sizing up" the business ability, credit standing, and financial condition of the customer. Also, but supplementary, the information can be used as a basis of interpreting commercial agency reports. Information that is gathered during the interview should be recorded and filed in the credit office. Filed information eventually results in customer case histories for reference use when accounts are subject to revision.

Salesmen are frequently in an excellent position to furnish the credit department with valuable information pertaining to their customers. Few salesmen, however, are suited to be good credit reporters because their interests, experiences, and temperaments usually are not conditioned toward this aim. On the other hand, it is in their interests to supply information to the credit department when possible, in order that the account may be adequately appraised and credit approved quickly.

A salesman is usually the first contact with the customer, and if all goes well he may be the only company representative who calls upon the account. During these calls the salesman can become acquainted with the business operations and local reputation of the customer. He should be able to furnish information on the following points: business identity and legal responsibility, management ability, habits, local reputation, desirability of location, local conditions, bank and creditor references, and some indication of the financial status of the business.

It is apparent that much of the information furnished by salesmen is in the nature of opinions. Hence, the value of the information must be considered relative to the knowledge, experience, and attitude of the reporting salesman. Another factor affecting the quality of information is the relationship between the credit department and sales activity.[3] E. B. Moran, former executive vice president, National Association of Credit Management, in recognizing the need for close cooperation between credit and sales, wrote:[4]

. . . a salesman is in a position to obtain and pass along valuable information which will help his credit department to better help him. This is particularly true in the case of new accounts. This is why progressive management today requires the closest possible cooperation between the credit manager and the salesmen; why credits and sales are being coordinated as never before; why frequent consultations and conferences between those in sales and those in credits are necessary if the business is to prosper and grow.

3 / Irving Firstenburg, "What Does the Sales Department Owe to Credit?" *Credit and Financial Management,* March 1970, p. 24; and John E. Payne, "What the Vice President of Sales Wants from Credit," *Credit and Financial Management,* January 1967, p. 15.

4 / Edwin B. Moran, *The Credit Side of Selling* (Chicago: Dartnell Corporation, 1947), pp. 13-14.

In view of the foregoing, it should be apparent that both the credit manager and sales manager are justified in insisting upon each other's cooperation. The wisdom of this attitude needs no explanation for progressive sales and credit people. It is desirable that the credit department supply salesmen with printed forms which, when completed, will reveal the types of information previously outlined. Financial statement forms are usually left with the customer for his completion and direct return to the credit department.

Direct Interchange. Other creditors who are known to have had experience with the subject under investigation are another source of credit information. It is common practice for creditors to exchange their experience as evidenced by accounting records and also to give their personal opinion of credit risks. Some credit men believe this source to be one of the most valuable at their disposal.

The direct interchange of ledger information may be effected either by correspondence or personal contact with other creditors, or through trade group meetings sponsored by the National Association of Credit Management. Personal contact is the most costly method and it consumes the valuable time of the credit manager or his representative. Therefore, this method should be limited to those cases in which there is substantial credit exposure for the inquiring creditor, and in which other methods are clearly not practicable. On the other hand, correspondence with other interested creditors is low in cost and obligates a minimum of the credit manager's time. The creditor employing the correspondence method must be prepared to cope with delays caused by the respondents' lack of promptness and delays caused by other contingencies of sending inquiries through the mails.

Trade group meetings sponsored by the National Association of Credit Management take place each month throughout the country. Credit executives in the same or allied lines of business, or selling the same customers, meet to discuss their joint problems and their experience with individual accounts. Some of the trade groups represented are food, drugs and chemicals, hardware and building materials, iron and steel, textiles and ready-to-wear, petroleum and auto accessories, and the electrical industry. At present, several hundred such meetings occur each month in the major metropolitan areas.

Typically, trade group meetings are conducted so that all members have an equal opportunity to request exchange of experiences with individual accounts. Those desiring information submit the names of the accounts on which information is sought to a group chairman or secretary. In some localities, the procedure is quite formalized and the names are circulated among the members in advance of the meeting. Hence, creditors are prepared to reveal the needed information. In some areas the account names are called off at the meetings and those recalling their experiences voluntarily relate them to the group. This method results not only in an interchange of ledger facts, but also an interchange of other confidential facts that could only have been acquired by personal contact with the account in question.

Although the quantity of information supplied by direct interchange may vary with the approach used and the type of creditors contacted, this source can supply the age of the account, the highest recent credit approved, the manner in which the account has been paid, the terms of sale, and an indication of the current status of the account and trade abuses. Furthermore, many credit managers get the responding credit managers' personal opinions regarding the credit worthiness of the customer in question. The advantages of soliciting information from other creditors are:

1. The information is the result of other creditors' experiences. The inquirer can reasonably expect his experience to correspond to that of other creditors.
2. The information is divulged by one who is qualified to recognize the problems confronting a fellow creditor.
3. The inquirer will endeavor to solicit data from those credit managers who have demonstrated their cooperativeness, reliability, and good judgment.
4. The information, under most circumstances, can be obtained more quickly.
5. The information is up-to-date and therefore is of current value.
6. Financial conditions of a mutual customer change from time to time. Contacts with others who are selling the same account prohibit debtors from becoming seriously past due without this being known by other houses.

Banks. The name of the customer's bank can be obtained by direct inquiry, from a commercial agency's report, or by noting the bank on which his checks are drawn. Once this is known another source of useful information is available to the credit manager.

Banks are in a position to be of mutual assistance with respect to the gathering of credit information. This is true because of the large number of banking accommodations used by the typical business enterprise. Similarly, most business concerns are dependent upon commercial credit to meet their inventory, equipment, and miscellaneous requirements. Hence, both banks and commercial creditors have much the same credit information needs. They complement each other in that they both maintain rather extensive credit files.

Despite the help each could be to the other, both banks and commercial creditors fall short in reaching the cooperative ideal. Some banks refuse to reveal some or all of the data requested, and commercial creditors are more inclined to inquire of banks than banks are to inquire of them. To improve relationships with banking institutions it may be well for business concerns to examine their methods of approach and the content of their requests. One of the best ways to get complete information from a bank is by personal contact. Credit managers should make it a point to become well acquainted with the members of their bank's credit department. Furthermore, the credit manager may be able to exert some influence in the placing of his company's deposits. Once this relationship has been cultivated and a higher degree of mutual confidence is developed, the possibility of acquiring more complete information exists. Requests for information should be by a letter which explains clearly the purposes of the inquiry, the nature of the creditor's experience with the subject, and the banking connections of the subject. In general, inquiries should be made to the bank with which the subject does business. Under some circumstances bank credit departments are willing to make inquiries of other banks in behalf of their customer-creditor. The specific procedures to follow should be discussed by the creditor with his bank's credit department.

Commercial banks usually are in a position to supply the following information to commercial creditors:

1. The length of the experience with the depositor or borrower.
2. An indication of the average bank balance on deposit expressed in general terms as "medium four-figure balance," "high five-figure balance," or "low six-figure balance."
3. How the subject meets obligations of which the bank has knowledge, such as notes and trade acceptances.
4. The frequency and form of borrowing as well as other bank accommodations used by the subject.
5. The form of security required if any.
6. An evaluation of the subject's financial condition in general terms.
7. The local reputation of the enterprise and its principals.

When the above facts are furnished by the bank, they contribute importantly to the process of measuring the acceptability of the applicant's credit. These data permit the analyst to verify more closely the reliability of the stated values as shown on the financial statements furnished by the customer. Furthermore, an indication of the local reputation and some idea of the capabilities of the business and its principals are revealed.

Even though the customer under consideration may not be a borrower from the bank, it should be noted that the bank may have had experiences with him in the past. The customer may have made requests of the bank for credit which have been denied; or he may have had overdrafts, or made unusual demands of the bank. Banks will frequently reveal this kind of information as well as the other types already noted.

Attorneys. Attorney credit reports are not used as extensively today as they were in the past. Because the attorney is situated locally, he is qualified to give information based on his professional associations and local observation. But there is little value in seeking the services of an attorney located in a large metropolitan center where it is difficult for him to observe particular business concerns or associate with those who are acquainted with the subject enterprise. Furthermore, it is not possible for creditors to provide sufficient monetary inducement to attorneys who might otherwise be willing to search for credit facts regarding a subject.

When the credit risk operates a business in a smaller community, there is a possibility that an attorney can be helpful in supplying information he already possesses. If this is the case, the compensation for completing a credit report can be quite nominal. Some attorneys will furnish information free in return for the understanding that they will handle any collections and suits in their area at their regular fee.

In inquiring of this source, creditors can use letters or forms so designed that the attorney's report will include an appraisal of business ability, habits, location, local reputation, local conditions, estimated net worth, value of real property and encumbrances thereon, and any claims and suits. Information on these factors would be a substantial addition, in a supplementary way, to the larger mass of data before the credit analyst. The greatest value of the attorney's report lies in the fact that it is up to date, permits verification of some of the stated values on financial statements, contributes a firsthand observation of reputation and business ability, and may inform the creditor of existing local conditions which have a tendency to affect the quality of the risk.

Other Sources. The reading of publications will contribute to the resourcefulness and general knowledge of any credit man. Often, information of a general or of a specific character appears in business magazines and trade publications which help the reader to keep abreast of the times. Articles and data dealing with changing economic conditions and effects of developments upon specific fields of endeavor are valuable types of information.

EVALUATION OF INTERNAL INFORMATION AND DIRECT INVESTIGATION

It is apparent from the foregoing analysis that the noncommercial sources of credit information can be used by most credit managers. The types of information supplied by these sources can be helpful in determining the credit worthiness of new accounts and in revising credit lines of existing accounts. Earlier it was established that the credit analyst needs various types of credit information in order to pass objectively on the acceptability of a customer's credit. Before commercial creditors can adequately appraise an account, they have to reconcile the answers to questions involving an account's identity and legal responsibility, history and business background, character and responsibility of management, financial ability and capacity, financial strength and outlook, and payment record.

By tapping the noncommercial sources credit managers may be able to acquire the needed information to make a logical and sound credit decision. All information, whether acquired directly or indirectly, originates with the account under investigation. Practically, however, it is seldom that a single source of information supplies *all* the data needed to fulfill the creditor's concept of adequate information. Recognizing the deficiencies inherent in contacting one source, credit managers can inquire of other noncommercial sources. They can check the subject's record by examining their own files; they can inquire of other creditors regarding their experiences; they can develop financial information and verify the stated values on financial statements by contacting the customer's bank; or they can tap any other "free" source to obtain needed information.

Despite all these possibilities confronting the credit manager, it is neither good judgment nor prudent to rely entirely on the limited number of noncommercial sources. Accounts deserving of rejection can keep their records clean with a limited number of suppliers. They may even be regarded highly by their banks, by close business associates, and by the creditor's salesmen. In other circles financial deterioration is recognized. It is not unusual practice for businesses experiencing difficulty to channel their remaining strength into those hands which can be most helpful in maintaining their credit reputation.

Of more importance to all credit managers is the fact that they are too concerned with other financial problems of the business to become expert credit investigators. Therefore, the noncommercial sources are best utilized when regarded as a supplemental source of credit information. Even though the credit manager frequently uses the noncommercial sources, he should not fail to recognize that they augment the purchased information which comes to him from a much greater storehouse of credit facts.

Under certain circumstances the facilities of local retail credit bureaus or the Retail Credit Company may be helpful to the credit manager. These agencies, while devoted primarily to consumer credit reporting, perform a number of special investigations. In particular they are useful and valuable sources of information when the identity of a business account and an individual are one and the same. Sole proprietorships, of which there are a great number, are a case in point. One of these sources may also be utilized when company officers or the value of their personal guarantees need further investigation to establish a more accurate appraisal of the degree of risk.

Of all the sources of credit information available to the credit analyst, the most extensive are the reports of the commercialized organizations, which are discussed in subsequent chapters. They have as their major purpose the gathering and reporting of all types of information which affect the quality of the credit of a business firm. This perhaps accounts for the fact that they are also the most frequently used sources.

REVIEW AND DISCUSSION QUESTIONS

1. Why should a credit investigation be conducted in connection with a commercial credit transaction?
2. What is needed other than credit information to create an accurate credit decision?
3. Discuss the general questions that should be answered before a commercial credit customer's credit can be appraised objectively.
4. Explain the classification of sources of commercial credit information.
5. How do these sources vary from those used in consumer credit transactions?
6. What should a credit manager consider in selecting sources of credit information?
7. Which one of these considerations do you believe to be the most important?
8. What is meant by the statement, "The credit office is literally a storehouse of credit facts"?
9. Should salesmen be required to gather credit information? Explain your position on this point.
10. What is meant by the term, "direct investigation"?
11. What is the National Association of Credit Management?
12. What is the purpose of trade group meetings of the NACM?

13. How do you believe that the relationship between commercial credit managers and bank personnel dealing in credit work can be improved?

14. What types of credit information can usually be supplied by commercial banks?

15. Assume you are a commercial credit manager of a manufacturing firm. Would you utilize direct investigation to acquire credit information? Explain your answer.

24

Basis of the Commercial Credit
Decision—Dun & Bradstreet, Inc.

Credit management has at its disposal a variety of commercialized sources of credit information, in addition to the noncommercialized sources discussed in the previous chapter. It will be remembered that a commercialized source of credit information has been defined as one that has as its dominant function the organized supplying of credit information in return for compensation. In this chapter and in several subsequent chapters, a discussion and analysis of the commercialized sources of information at the disposal of commercial creditors and commercial bank creditors is presented. The commercial sources of credit information are of three principal types. For purposes of clarity they may be classified as follows:

1. The general mercantile agency reports on any business enterprise to subscribers in response to credit inquiry (discussed in this chapter).
2. The specialized mercantile agencies report on business enterprises in particular lines of trade to subscribers upon request (see Chapter 25).
3. The Credit Interchange Bureaus of the National Association of Credit Management operate for the systematic exchange of ledger information among members (see Chapter 26).

The services of the commercialized sources of credit information are quite varied and somewhat complex. It is therefore imperative that credit management be thoroughly familiar with these sources, just as it is necessary to be well acquainted with the kinds of information it can obtain internally and by direct investigation. To arrive at a sound judgment of a credit risk, credit managers must have a wealth of credit information at their disposal. One of the most important of the commercialized sources is the general mercantile agency.

THE GENERAL MERCANTILE AGENCY

The activities of Dun & Bradstreet, Inc. are more extensive than any other credit-reporting organization, and it is frequently referred to and classified as the only "general agency." The general agency has a multitude of activities, but its primary function is to supply credit reports on business concerns of *all sizes,* in *all lines* of trade, and *located anywhere* in the United States and many foreign countries. When contrasted with the limited scope of operations of the several specialized agencies, Dun & Bradstreet is appropriately classified as a general agency. Even with the widespread operations and numerous services, Dun & Bradstreet does not occupy a monopolistic position in the field of credit reporting. The various specialized agencies make up part of its competition, and these agencies operate in particular lines of trade in which management may select the services of the general agency or one of the specialized sources of information. In fact, credit management may find it quite desirable to utilize the services of a specialized agency because it may serve the creditor's interests more completely, economically, and effectively. Despite the competitive atmosphere of this field, Dun & Bradstreet has grown and prospered with the commercial development of the country. Its scope of operations is so vast that it is the most frequently used source of credit information, with offices in over 270 principal cities of the United States and leading centers of world trade.

Origin and Development of Dun & Bradstreet, Inc.

The need for credit information developed from the needs of businessmen whose areas of trade expanded with the widening frontiers. A century ago, or even less, there was only a remote possibility of securing organized and factual data with which to make a credit decision. Credit decisions were made by hit-and-miss methods. Terms were long, the relationship was often a personal affair, and some credit transactions were based solely upon references furnished by customers. These methods resulted in large credit losses which had to be offset by greater margins of profit.

During the period of 1820-40, the economic and social pattern of the United States underwent radical changes. The Erie Canal was opened in 1825, and railway building was begun in 1828. Settlers began to pour into the new West to cultivate the fertile lands of the

Ohio-Mississippi Valley. The factory system appeared and expanded rapidly in New England; the growth and movement of the population started the development of new urban areas. This expansion created new markets for the industrial products of New England and the agricultural products of the farmers. This period of expansion was also one of inflation which finally culminated with the panic of 1837. A large number of business firms failed, and credit losses skyrocketed until the end of the depression in 1843.[1]

During the panic, the firm of Arthur Tappan and Company failed. A brother, Lewis Tappan, who was associated with the firm, had gained a wide reputation as an excellent judge of a credit risk. His personal interest in the subject of credit investigation, his reputation in appraising a credit risk, and the steadily growing nation suggested the idea of organizing a central credit reporting bureau. On June 1, 1841, he organized The Mercantile Agency to collect and disseminate information for the benefit of creditors.[2]

The impetus for the development of organized sources of credit information grew out of the uncertainties and losses experienced during the panic of 1837, the rapid changes in the economic structure, and the expansion of trading areas. For manufacturers and suppliers an increase in the use of credit was essential to trade over the wider geographical areas. This meant that no longer could credit judgment be founded on personal relationships, nor could adequate information be gathered in the immediate vicinity of the creditor. Consequently, paralleling the economic development of the nation, there evolved a system of organized credit reporting which was designed to eliminate some of the major uncertainties of trade.

Soon after Lewis Tappan founded The Mercantile Agency at New York in 1841, a branch-office system was developed which penetrated into the major trade centers. Reporters made visits to each community to interview the new and established businessmen. R. G. Dun was employed by The Mercantile Agency in 1851 and became the sole proprietor of the company in 1859. He changed the name shortly thereafter to R. G. Dun & Co. In 1849, John M. Bradstreet, an attorney in Cincinnati, founded The Bradstreet Company. This company operated in a manner similar to The Mercantile Agency and served the same fields of trade for many years. Their coexistence ended in 1933 when the two firms were merged under the name of Dun & Bradstreet, Inc.

The development of organized sources of credit information has

1 / Reginald C. McGrane, *The Economic Development of the American Nation* (Boston: Ginn & Co., 1942), pp. 220-87 and pp. 389-93.

2 / For an authoritative and detailed account of the origin and development of Dun & Bradstreet see Roy A. Foulke, *The Sinews of American Commerce* (New York: Dun & Bradstreet, Inc., 1941).

contributed heavily to greater confidence between debtors and creditors. By virtue of these developments, many of the uncertainties surrounding credit transactions have been eliminated for businesses of all types. Credit judgment thus became more logical. Regardless of the location of the customer, the investigative procedure was speeded. The credit agencies have facilitated the breaking down of the barriers of distance so that a merchant may trade as safely with customers in remote parts of the country as with those situated close at hand.

THE ORGANIZATION, SERVICES, AND ACTIVITIES OF DUN & BRADSTREET, INC., TODAY

The activities and services of the Business Information Division of Dun & Bradstreet, Inc., are more extensive than any other credit-reporting organization. To facilitate the tremendous task of collecting, assembling, analyzing, and disseminating credit information, it employs the services of some 2,000 full-time reporters and approximately 20,000 part-time correspondents who gather credit information from business enterprises throughout the United States and Canada. In addition there are reporters and correspondents in many other parts of the free world. The reporters' activities are supported by a staff of 8,000 analysts, supervisors, and clerks in the various offices located in the principal trading centers of the United States and Canada. To administer and control these activities and services, the United States is divided into 12 regions and further subdivided into 52 districts. Under the supervision of the district offices there are 170 offices located in the larger cities of the various districts. The operations in Canada consist of 17 offices operated by the wholly owned subsidiary, Dun & Bradstreet of Canada, Limited. The files of the mercantile agency contain information on business concerns in the United States and Canada. A complete file on many business houses is maintained in the New York and Chicago offices alike. The entire operation of Dun & Bradstreet in the United States, Canada, and its foreign branches and foreign correspondents is administered and controlled from the general offices located in New York City.

Principal Activities of Dun & Bradstreet

The activities of Dun & Bradstreet in serving the needs of businesses are both numerous and varied. Its principal activity is that of supplying credit information, but over the years it has developed a number of services which are of primary interest to business management and the business community. The diversity of its activities may be shown as follows:

1. *Credit report services*—investigates, analyzes, and edits business information reports on commercial and industrial enterprises and credit reports on municipalities. Reports have the same basic characteristics but are prepared to reflect the varied complexities of financial structure. International reports are prepared to cover the rapidly expanding overseas markets.

2. *Reference book service*—compiles and publishes a credit reference book six times a year which contains the names, line of business, SIC number, and in most instances the estimated financial strength and credit composite credit appraisal rating of business concerns in United States and Canada. The January, March, July, and September revisions also are published in state editions, and city editions are available on several of the larger cities. They are useful to executives and salesmen active in the field. International reference books also are available.

3. *Apparel trades service*—a service designed to meet the special needs of business firms trading in the apparel field. This service is rendered through the Credit Clearing House. This division renders credit reports and recommendations especially designed to fit the needs of the apparel trades. The publication of the *Apparel Trades Book* is revised four times a year.

4. *Commercial collection division*—a service designed to offer account receivables control and collection of past-due accounts where necessary.

5. *Municipal service division*—serves financial and investment enterprises in rendering credit reports on states, counties, cities, and other governmental units. Studies include economic and social characteristics, management of the municipality, the debt record, and current operating data.

6. *Publications*—publishes *Dun's,* a monthly magazine with articles concerning business conditions and techniques that are of interest to business management. Also publishes a wide variety of business statistics, business charts, and business operating ratios which are useful to business management in many phases of their operations.

7. *Education services*—includes correspondence courses, educational films, library, and pamphlets.

8. *Directories*—publishes various directories and other reference books used for credit, sales, purchasing and executive reference, including: *Reference Book of Manufacturers, Reference Book of Transportation, Reference Book of Corporate Managements, Reference Book of Lumber & Wood Products Industries, Market Guide of Mass Merchandisers, Electronic Marketing Directory.*

9. *Marketing services division*—aids business firms in their marketing activities by providing the following: Dun's *Market Identifiers*® (DMI), *Million Dollar/Middle Market Directories,* metalworking marketing service, apparel market identifiers, research services, *D-U-N-S*® (Data Universal Numbering System), Dun's software services, *D-U-N-S Aids* (Account Identification & Description Service), *D-U-N-S AIS* (Account Identification Service), *D-U-N-S Industrial Affiliations Service* (DIAS), and special services.

Of all the activities of Dun & Bradstreet, the one which is generally considered of outstanding importance is the collecting, assembling, and analyzing of credit information. It is this function on which the many other activities are intricately dependent.

Methods of Collecting Credit Information

To accomplish the tremendous task of collecting credit information, Dun & Bradstreet employs personal investigation (both direct and telephone) and mail inquiries. The personal investigations are made by one of the four types of reporters which the general agency has found necessary to gather credit information effectively under all conditions. *City reporters* make credit investigations on businesses located in those cities where Dun & Bradstreet maintains a branch office. They are usually assigned a specific geographical territory within the city so as to become more intimately acquainted with the sources of credit information and with managements of businesses in the section. In the larger cities, businesses are further classified by their common characteristics, and a city reporter will investigate particular types of firms within the specified geographical division. *Resident reporters* operate from their homes located in the important cities or towns near the larger metropolitan areas. For example, resident reporters in the New York City area live in the communities of Hempstead, Middletown, White Plains, and parts of New Jersey. This type of reporter generally receives his lists of concerns to be investigated by mail, and he returns his findings in the same way. *Traveler and city revision reporters* have the task of revising and bringing up to date the credit information currently in the files of the supervising office. This is accomplished on a scheduled basis. Unlike the other reporters, they seldom are called upon to perform immediate investigations. As they go on their schedules, they revise and continually update the reports on an "automatic revision" basis. The information they gather is used to keep the latest available information which the system affords in the files of Dun & Bradstreet offices. Their schedules provide for a new investigation at least once each year, irrespective of the visits that may have been made by other reporters. *Local correspondents* are bankers, attorneys, real estate men, merchants, and others who devote only part of their time to credit investigations. Typically they are located in cities, towns, and villages which do not have Dun & Bradstreet offices. Their task is to perform immediate investigations at locations where there are no resident reporters.

Most credit investigations of business concerns follow a similar pattern. The reporter first interviews the principals of the business, confirms ownership, notes details of its operations and methods, obtains a financial statement, and discusses future plans and sales trends. He may also investigate outside the business concern to gather additional facts or verify existing information. Interviews with bankers, accountants, and other informed sources are typical. The reporter may also check court and other public records. City reporters also analyze the information and prepare the credit report, but local correspondents do not prepare reports. "Report writers" located at branch offices analyze the credit information received from the outlying areas and prepare these reports.

Simultaneously with the gathering of information by personal interview and mail inquiries, the home office has been sending out trade inquiries to the subject's creditors throughout the country. Responses to these inquiries reveal the manner in which the business under review is paying current obligations. This information includes the recent high credit, the terms of sale, amount owing, amount past due, and remarks which reveal the terms and manner of payment. Combined with information gathered by reporters, the report writer has the pertinent data available for analysis and inclusion in the written report.

Principal Types of Credit Reports

Dun & Bradstreet issues several kinds of credit reports, varying on degree of comprehensiveness or adapted to the particular sales and credit needs of subscribers. For commercial and industrial enterprises, the business information report and the analytical report are the most comprehensive and frequently used. The analytical report is written on large, financially complex concerns, and the business information report is prepared on all others, mostly the smaller concerns. The same basic elements are contained in all Dun & Bradstreet reports, but some have been developed in specialized form to fit the credit and sales requirements of various subscribers. Key accounts reports are written to the viewpoint of particular credit and management problems and contain highly detailed information. International reports are written on overseas concerns in principal free world markets. Municipal reports are written in depth on most major governmental units that issue tax-exempt bonds, and appraisal reports are specialized reports written on the fast-growing mass merchandisers' and discounters' market.

Business Information Reports

A typical, though fictitious, business information report is illustrated in Figure 24-1. The heading identifies the standard industrial classification (SIC) code number, D-U-N-S (Data Universal Numbering System) number, buying name and address, ownership, line of business, year business started or came under present management or control, and the Dun & Bradstreet rating.

Also contained in this shaded area of the report is the summary, which is a digest and analysis of the information contained in the report. It consists of seven items: payments, sales, worth, employs, record, condition, and trend. The content of this section of the report depends on the nature and extent of the information obtained during the investigation.

The payments section records the manner in which the subject pays his obligations. It is a reflection of suppliers' ledger experiences, and each line in the payments section represents the experience of one supplier. The six columns of this section show for each reporting creditor the highest amount of credit extended to the subject during the past year, the amount now owing, the amount past due, the terms of sale, the manner of payment, and the length of time sold.

The finance section is included in all Dun & Bradstreet reports. In most reports there is a financial statement. Balance sheet data are usually supplemented by profit and loss information, together with information on leases, fire insurance coverage, and other pertinent financial information. Following this a statement is made regarding the sales and profit trends. When no statement is furnished by the subject, the financial information is prepared by the credit reporter, who may get information from any reliable source that is in a position to estimate financial conditions. When this is done, the financial information is based on interviews with banks, courthouse and realty records, or calls on the "trade" and other informed sources of financial information.

The banking section contains additional independent, or outside, information of credit relevance. This information concerning banking relations includes indications of average balances; previous and current loan experience, including manner of repayment; whether loans are secured or unsecured; and length of time relations have been conducted.

Under the history section, the names and ages of the principals or

FIGURE 24-1
Typical Business Information Report Prepared by
Dun & Bradstreet, Inc. (Fictitious)

PLEASE NOTE WHETHER NAME, BUSINESS AND STREET ADDRESS CORRESPOND WITH YOUR INQUIRY

Dun & Bradstreet ® BUSINESS INFORMATION REPORT   RATING UNCHANGED

SIC	D-U-N-S	© DUN & BRADSTREET, INC.	STARTED	RATING
34 61	04-426-3101	CD 13 APR 21 19--	1957	D 1½
	ARNOLD METAL PRODUCTS CO	METAL STAMPINGS		

53 S MAIN ST
DAWSON MICH   66666
TEL 215 999-0000   SUMMARY

SAMUEL B. ARNOLD)		PAYMENTS DISC PPT
GEORGE T. ARNOLD) PARTNERS		SALES $177,250
		WORTH $42,961
		EMPLOYS 8
		RECORD CLEAR
		CONDITION SOUND
		TREND UP

PAYMENTS

HC	OWE	P DUE	TERMS	APR 19--	SOLD
3000	1500	1	10 30	Disc	Over 3 yrs
2500	1000	1	10 30	Disc	Over 3 yrs
2000	500	2	20 30	Disc	Old account
1000			30	Ppt	Over 3 yrs
500			30	Ppt	Over 3 yrs

FINANCE

On Apr 21 19-- S.B. Arnold, Partner, submitted statement Dec 31 19--

Cash	$ 4,870	Accts Pay	$ 6,121
Accts Rec	15,472	Notes Pay (Curr)	2,400
Mdse	14,619	Accruals	3,583
	------		------
Current	34,961	Current	12,104
Fixed Assets	22,840	Notes Pay (Def)	5,000
Other Assets	2,264	NET WORTH	42,961
	------		------
Total Assets	60,065	Total	60,065

19-- sales $177,250; gross profit $47,821; net profit $4,204. Fire
insurance mdse $15,000; fixed assets $20,000. Annual rent $3,000.
Signed Apr 21 19-- ARNOLD METAL PRODUCTS CO by Samuel B. Arnold, Partner
Johnson Singer, CPA. Dawson
-----0-----
Sales and profits increased last year due to increased sub-contract
work and this trend is reported continuing. New equipment was purchased
last Sept for $8,000 financed by a bank loan secured by a lien on the
equipment payable $200 per month. With increased capacity, the business
has been able to handle a larger volume. Arnold stated that for the first
two months of this year volume was $32,075 and operations continue profitable.

BANKING
        Medium to high four figure balances are maintained locally. An equip-
ment loan is outstanding and being retired as agreed.

HISTORY
        Style registered Feb 1 1965 by partners. SAMUEL, born 1918, married.
1939 graduate of Lehigh University with B.S. degree in Mechanical Engineer-
ing. 1949-50 employed by Industrial Machine Corporation, Detroit, and
1950-56 production manager with Aerial Motors Inc., Detroit. Started this
business in 1957. GEORGE, born 1940, single, son of Samuel. Graduated in
1963 from Dawson Institute of Technology. Served U.S. Air Force 1963-64.
Admitted to partnership interest Feb 1965.

OPERATION
        Manufactures light metal stampings for industrial concerns and also
does some work on a sub-contract basis for aircraft manufacturers. Terms
net 30. 12 accounts. Five production, two office employees, and one salesman. LOCATION: Rents one-story cinder block building with 5,000 square feet
located in industrial section in normal condition. Housekeeping is good.
4-21 (803 77) PRA

owners of the concern and their business experience are revealed. This section emphasizes the length of time the principals have been associated with this business, their past business experience, their other or outside business affiliations, and the financial successes or difficulties which they experienced in the past.

The operation part of the report describes precisely what the enterprise does and its facilities. Considerable detail may be necessary in this section to describe adequately what products or services are produced or marketed, the pricing and credit policies, the character of the operation and its classes of customers, the seasonal aspects of the business, the number of employees, and the like. The physical characteristics are also covered by describing the business location, its physical proportions and characteristics, and the equipment used. In other words, this section details the production and marketing aspects of the business.

Analytical Reports

The subscriber who requests a credit report on a business concern which is large and financially complex will receive an analytical report. A fictional analytical report prepared by Dun & Bradstreet is shown in Figure 24-2. This report has primarily the same basic characteristics as the business information report just discussed. The credit elements needed to arrive at a sound and rational decision are the same whether the business concern be large or small. Typically, larger concerns have more information to reveal, and it may be presented in a more formal style. The more complete accounting reports and the ease with which financial data can be gathered on larger concerns contribute to the completeness of the credit information contained in the analytical report.

Inasmuch as extensive amounts of credit are required by large enterprises, the analytical report expands on those elements most pertinent to the credit analyst. It should be noted that much emphasis is given to comparative analysis of financial statements, ratio analysis of such statements, banking relationships, and other financial aspects. All of this is the result of the more complicated financial and organizational structure of the larger concerns, and the need for a more complete and otherwise more precise analysis of the firm. As the title of the report suggests, it is a more extensive credit report for the subscribers of Dun & Bradstreet services.

Continuous Service

When a creditor subscribes to the Dun & Bradstreet services, he automatically becomes entitled to "continuous service" in addition

FIGURE 24-2
Analytical Report Prepared by
Dun & Bradstreet, Inc. (Fictitious)

Dun & Bradstreet **ANALYTICAL REPORT**   RATING UNCHANGED

SIC	D-U-N-S	DATE OF REPORT	STARTED	RATING
36x62	900-0000	A- AD 13 DEC 20 19-- N		
34 91	ALLIED DEVICES INC	MFG SIGNALING DEVICES	1958	3A 1
	SIGNAL PRODUCTS DIVISION	& STEEL CONTAINERS		Also Branches
	STEEL CASE DIVISION			

77 SHERIDAN BLVD BOX 222
BENSON MICH   48232
      TEL 313 961-3399

ALEX E. FOX, PRES & CHIEF EXECUTIVE

SUMMARY

PAYMENTS	GEN DISC
SALES	$4,410,164
WORTH	$1,640,085
RECORD	CLEAR
EMPLOYS	148 (62 HERE)
CONDITION	STRONG
TREND	UP

PAYMENTS

HC	OWE	P DUE	TERMS	DEC 6 19--	SOLD
26000	14000	1	10 30	Disc	Over 3 yrs
4000		2	10 30	Disc	Over 3 yrs
4000	2000	1	10 30	Disc	Over 3 yrs
3000		-1	10 30	Disc	Over 3 yrs
1000				Disc	
600		1	10 30	Disc	Over 3 yrs
600	100	1	10 30	Disc	3 yrs
5000	400		30	Ppt	Over 2 yrs
2762	943		30	Ppt	Last sale Nov
500			30	Ppt	

HIGHLIGHTS

	Jan 31 19--	Jan 31 19--
Net Working Capital	$ 1,050,616	$ 890,372
Worth	1,427,794	1,640,085
Inventory	535,617	1,063,420
Fixed Assets	275,613	901,258
Total Debt	259,501	1,106,529
Sales	1,914,876	4,410,164
Profit	218,044	301,601

A sizable portion of two acquisitions in Feb 19-- was represented by fixed assets causing a contraction in net working capital. These acquisitions were financed both internally and by bank loans, the latter more than half repaid. The acquisitions contributed to the sharp rise in inventories, fixed assets and total debt at the end of the last fiscal year and were a major factor in the sizable increase in sales and profits. While inventory and debt have increased, condition remains strong with total debt well below net worth.

CURRENT

On Dec 20 19-- F. J. McHugh, Treasurer, stated that the funds borrowed for acquisitions have been steadily reduced. Sales for the 9 months ending Oct for this year were up over 10% and profits were up 12%. At Dec 31 19-- current assets were about $1,700,000 and current liabilities were about $725,000. According to McHugh, sales are expected to exceed $4,800,000 this year.

Banking
A Detroit bank has had the account since 1953 with balances described as strong. Long term loan has been granted to sizable amounts with an amount presently owing which is being retired according to schedule. 12-20-- (922 27) (77)

---

to the business information and analytical reports supplied by the agency. This means that the agency will send the subscriber copies of all reports on the same account for one year from the date of initial inquiry. There is no additional charge for this service during the one-year period, but a charge is made for the successive years of service on any particular account. In this way subscribers can keep

FIGURE 24-2 (*continued*)

```
ALLIED DEVICES INC                                    A CD PAGE 1
BENSON MICH                                           12-20---

Figures of Jan 31 19-- were prepared from a balance sheet signed by Frank J. McHugh,
Treasurer.  Mitchell and Mitchell, CPA's, accountants.

                                          FINANCIAL STATEMENTS

                          Jan 31 19--      Jan 31 19--      Jan 31 19--

Cash                     $   396,666      $   393,818      $   301,802
Marketable Securities        189,128          201,340
Accounts Receivable          154,011          179,342          356,116
Inventory                    452,616          535,617        1,063,420
                         ------------     ------------     ------------
TOTAL CURRENT ASSETS       1,192,421        1,310,117        1,721,338

Fixed Assets                 202,171          275,613          901,258
Investments                   92,000
Prepaid-Deferred               4,916            8,622           38,407
Other Assets                   9,725           92,942           85,611
                         ------------     ------------     ------------
TOTAL                      1,501,233        1,687,294        2,746,614
                         ============     ============     ============
Accounts Payable              44,456           66,587          117,913
Accruals                                        38,301          136,040
Taxes (Exc Fed Inc)                             12,572           18,601
Federal Income Taxes         161,644          126,542          383,412
Long Terms Liabs (curr)                                         175,000
Other Curr Liabs              43,210           15,499
                         ------------     ------------     ------------
TOTAL CURRENT LIABILITIES    249,310          259,501          830,966

Long Term Liabs                                                 275,563

Common Stock                 190,000          190,000          210,100
Capital Surplus               11,313           11,313           11,313
Earned Surplus             1,050,610        1,226,480        1,418,672
                         ------------     ------------     ------------
TOTAL                      1,501,233        1,687,294        2,746,614
                         ============     ============     ============
NET WORKING CAPITAL          943,111        1,050,616          890,372
CURRENT RATIO                   4.78             5.02             2.07

TANGIBLE NET WORTH         1,251,923        1,427,794        1,640,085

At Jan 31 19-- accounts receivable shown net less undisclosed reserves.  Inventory
valued at cost on first in-first out basis.  Fixed assets shown net less reserve for
depreciation $235,612.

                                                      (CONTINUED)
```

their credit files current for one year after showing an interest in an account.

The supplemental or revised reports furnished by this service are prepared for a variety of circumstances. The subscriber may receive a supplemental report because of a "rating change" which indicates a changed credit situation. Another may be issued because it is the "automatic revision" of the file which is accomplished about every six months. Still another report may be issued when a new financial statement has been received by the agency. Finally, a special-notice supplemental report is part of the continuous service. The special-notice report is issued by the agency because of important changes or newsworthy information which has a bearing on the credit standing of the customer.

FIGURE 24-2 (*continued*)

```
         ALLIED DEVICES  INC                              A CO  Page 2
         BENSON MICH                                      12-20---

                      INCOME STATEMENTS AND SURPLUS RECONCILIATION

                       JAN 31 19--        Jan 31 19--      Jan 31 19--

Net Sales              $ 1,825,171       $ 1,914,876      $ 4,410,164
Cost of Goods Sold          922,930        1,129,964        2,932,205
Gross Profit                902,241          784,912        1,477,959
Expenses                    485,933          401,399          768,112

Net Income on Sales         416,308          383,513          709,847
  Other Income                6,427           46,100           19,255

  Other Expenses             37,010                            42,501
  Federal Income Taxes      210,014          119,369          385,000

Final Net Income            201,666          218,044          301,601
                        ==========       ==========       ==========
SURPLUS START               888,925        1,050,610        1,226,480
  Add:  Net Income          201,666          218,044          301,601
  Deduct:  Dividends         39,981           42,172          109,409
SURPLUS-END               1,050,610        1,226,480        1,418,672
                        ==========       ==========       ==========
```

SUPPLEMENTAL DATA Footnotes appended to the Jan 31 19-- statement showed no contingent
        debt. Annual rent shown at $62,000, lease expiring 1985.

According to management, the item other assets represents (1) $50,000 cash held in
escrow by the landlord who pays interest on that sum. (2) Balance consists mostly
of a mortgage receivable on property in Edison Township, Mich. which was sold in 1964.
Management states that more than $2,000,000 in fire insurance is carried on inventories
and fixed assets.

Feb 19-- the company acquired for an undisclosed cash consideration the outstanding
capital stock of Signal Products Corporation and Steel Case and Tube Co. both of which
were established and profitable. A bank loan of $1,000,000 was obtained at that time.
A portion of the loan was voluntarily prepaid and was reduced to $450,563 at Jan 31
19--. $175,000 of that amount is due this year, payable quarterly and the balance is
due over the next two years.

Records show a financing statement entered Feb 15 19-- naming Allied Devices Inc. as
debtor and Saginaw Machine Tool Co. as secured party. Collateral: Specified Machinery.
File #108761. According to F. J. McHugh, Treasurer, the company purchased 2 high speed
Turret lathes at a cost of $28,500 payable over 36 months.

                                                            (CONTINUED)

Key Account Reports

Subscribers who have need for information beyond that found in the business information or analytical report, or beyond that supplied by continuous service, have available to them the agency's key account reports. Each of these reports is designed to furnish comprehensive and detailed information in answer to specific questions for the guidance of individual subscribers. Key account reports provide facts on important credit customers about which specific questions have been raised. Each such report attempts to answer fully the specific point(s) raised. This service continues for one year or until such time as the subscriber's interest in the account is satisfied.

Subscribers in need of these services indicate the nature of their

FIGURE 24-2 (*continued*)

```
ALLIED DEVICES INC                                    A CD Page 3
BENSON MICH                                           12-20---

HISTORY    Incorporated Michigan laws June 30 1920 as Railroad Devices Corp. Name
           changed to present style Feb 1 1960.

Authorized Capital Stock:  1,000 shares no par value common stock, increased to 4,000
shares latter part of 1958.
Outstanding Capital Stock:  $210,000 at Jan 31 19--

Control:  The General Holding Corp., New York City owns 35% of the outstanding capital
stock which is held in voting trust by the Detroit National Bank, Detroit, Mich.  40%
acquired by A. E. Fox in 1958.  Balance owned by Sanborn, Caputo and McHugh.

In early 19-- the company purchased the outstanding capital stock of Signal Products
Corporation, Fairdome, Ky. and Steel Case & Tube Co., Minneapolis, Minn. for an undis-
closed cash consideration.  Late in that year these corporations were merged into
Allied Devices Inc. and their activities are now conducted as divisions.

General Holding Corp., New York City, is an investment and holding company.  It was
formed under New York laws 1900.  At Dec 31 19--, that company had a net worth of
$20,816,112, and a strong financial condition.  According to McHugh there are no inter-
company loans, guarantees, endorsements or merchandise transactions between the two
companies.

OPERATION    Products:  Manufacturers electric signaling devices including crossing
             gates 60% and steel containers 40%.

Distribution:  Sales made to railroads throughout the United States to approximately
100 active accounts.
Terms:  1 10 Net 30 days.
Seasons:  Fairly steady throughout the year
Salesmen:  Six on commission basis.  A. E. Fox and J. S. Caputo are active in sales.
Employees:  148

At headquarters Benson Mich., leases 20,000 square feet in a 3 story brick building
where signal devices are manufactured.  62 employed.

Branches are located at FAIRDOME, KY., MINNEAPOLIS, MINN. and branch sales offices at
New York, N.Y. and Los Angeles, Calif.

Signal Products Division, Fairdome, Ky., leases 12,000 square feet in a 1 story
frame building where railroad crossing signal gates are manufactured.  39 employed.

Steel Case Division, Minneapolis, Minn., leases 15,000 square feet in a 2 story brick
building where steel enclosed containers are manufactured.  47 employed.

                                                              (CONTINUED)
```

question or problem on a special-request form. After a comprehensive investigation and analysis, a report is then prepared to meet the particular need. Because of the comprehensive nature of these reports, the detailed and lengthy investigation, and the time necessary to complete them, these reports are priced higher than the business information and analytical reports.

Use of Credit Reports by Subscribers

Detailed credit reports are used by subscribers for a variety of business purposes. While it is obvious that credit reports are most usually requested to serve credit purposes, much of the same information is valuable for other business activities. Subscribers normally request reports for the following credit purposes:

1. To appraise the credit worthiness of a new account for which no data are on file and the reference book rating alone is not sufficient basis for a rational credit decision.

FIGURE 24-2 (concluded)

```
        ALLIED DEVICES INC                      A CO Page 4
        BENSON MICH                             12-20---

        ALEX E. FOX, PRES                       JOHN S. CAPUTO, V PRES (SALES)
        FRED W. SANBORN, V PRES (PROD)          FRANK J. MC HUGH, TREAS
        HARRY K. LITTLE, SEC                    MARY (MRS. GERALD) LOY, ASST TREAS

        DIRECTORS:  A.E. Fox, F.J. McHugh, Edward Raines and P.J. Walsh.

MANAGEMENT BACKGROUND

FOX born 1908, married.  Employed by the Pennsylvania Railroad latterly as Freight
Operations Manager from 1925 to 1958.  Since 1958 has been with this company as Chief
Executive Officer.  Life is insured for $200,000 with this corporation as beneficiary.

SANBORN born 1913, married.  Princeton graduate 1934 BA Degree.  1935 to 1943 employed
by Ford Motor Company in production control.  Joined this company in 1944, became
General Manager 1951 and elected Vice President in 1958.  Life in insured for $100,000
with corporation as beneficiary.

CAPUTO born 1916, married.  1940 to'1955 employed by Steel Case and Tube, latterly was
General Sales Manager.  Joined this company as a divisional sales manager and elected
a Vice President in 1958.

MC HUGH born 1909, married.  Employed by this company since 1939 as an inside account-
ant.  Elected Assistant Treasurer in 1948 and Treasurer in 1958.

LITTLE born 1932, single.  Served U.S. Army 1951 to 1953.  Employed by this company and
elected Secretary in 1960.

MRS. LOY employed here since 1959 and elected Assistant Treasurer in 1963.  Her husband
is an Associate Professor of Mathematics, University of Detroit.

RAINES is a practicing attorney in Detroit and general counsel.  WALSH is Executive
Vice President of Detroit National Bank, Detroit, Mich.
12-20--- (922 68)
```

2. To review active credit files so as to keep informed regarding the progress and current condition of accounts. Periodic review of accounts is the basis on which customers' lines of credit and terms of sale are adjusted to their financial standing.
3. To determine the underlying causes of slow and doubtful accounts. Current information contributes to alert handling of these accounts, which often may be converted from marginal accounts to profitable customers.
4. To provide a sound basis for decision when customers desire to expand the line of credit or when marked changes in paying habits occur.

In addition to the uses cited above, credit reports should be requested whenever the credit manager's confidence in the debtor has been shaken. A number of circumstances can create this condition, such as radical fluctuations in the buying policies and financial dealings of a concern, suspected fraud or misrepresentation, legal proceedings, and "acts of God."

The use of credit reports by sales departments is of secondary importance but of sufficient value to suggest their use for this additional purpose. Credit reports on new business enterprises and prospective customers are used not only to provide a basis for extending credit in the future, but also to determine the sales potentiality of the prospect. Salesmen are better equipped to sell when they have advance knowledge regarding a prospect's operations, scope of activities, and financial capacity. Similarly, when the periodic appraisal of old accounts warrants an upward adjustment in the line of credit or when it is determined that the full sales potential of a customer has not been reached, it is important that this information be communicated to the salesmen.

The coordinated use of detailed credit reports as suggested above results in the greatest possible advantages to the subscriber. When credit reports serve more than one purpose, it is a simple matter to justify their costs.

THE DUN & BRADSTREET REFERENCE BOOK

The reference book department publishes the *Dun & Bradstreet Reference Book,* which contains the names and credit ratings of nearly three million commercial and industrial enterprises located throughout the United States and Canada. Although the agency is perhaps best known for this single activity, it should be abundantly clear that the preparation of credit reports is the backbone of the business. The information gathered for credit reports contributes to the financial ratings and changes that occur in the reference book. Despite the fact that this function is of secondary importance in the operating scheme of Dun & Bradstreet, reference book ratings are frequently referred to by credit managers. In fact, the credit rating of a business enterprise is frequently the first step in credit risk appraisal. In many instances the rating alone is sufficient to reveal a high degree of credit worthiness.

Contents of the Reference Books

The *Reference Book*, which is prepared in four separate sections, is published every two months and leased to subscribers. It contains a complete listing of most businesses in every city, town, and village in the United States and Canada. Other editions of the reference book are also available in an edition covering only the United States, a *State Sales Guide* for each state, and a number of sectional editions which include listings of several states. These smaller editions are exact copies of the state or metropolitan information contained in the larger volumes and are published in a convenient 9-by-11-inch briefcase size. Company representatives, especially salesmen, use the state editions to appraise customers conveniently, build prospect lists, and gain helpful information about their territories.

The books contain the ratings on manufacturers, wholesalers, retailers, and other businesses on which Dun & Bradstreet has written a business information report. The plan of arrangement is alphabetical by state, then by town within the state. Following the town name is the population, the county in which the community is located, and the name of the local bank or banks. If no banking facilities are available, the nearest community having such facilities is shown. These data are followed by the alphabetical listing of business concerns.

Each business name is preceded by a standard industrial classification code number, which indicates the nature of the business. For example, 52 51 is the SIC code designating retail hardware. All hardware stores have this code number preceding the business name. Following the business name is an abbreviated description of the nature of the business such as Hwr, Dg, Htgsup, which means hardware, drug, and heating supplies, respectively. The numeral immediately after some of these abbreviations indicates that the business was started within the last 10 years. The numeral is the last digit of the year within the 10-year period. To the extreme right, and following this information, appears the rating assigned to the concern. If the business concern's name was added with the current edition of the reference book, the letter A is posted to the left of the business classification code; the letter C appearing in the same place means a rating change has been accomplished with that particular edition.

Explanation of Ratings

A Dun & Bradstreet rating consists of two elements showing (1) the estimated financial strength, and (2) the composite credit appraisal. Figure 24-3 is the Dun & Bradstreet key to ratings. The estimated financial strength is expressed in the letter portion of the rating. These 15 letter codes (5A to HH) designate the range of net worth or pecuniary strength of the risk. The composite credit appraisal is a general credit grade of high, good, fair, or limited, expressed by numerals.

Estimated financial strength is a conservative estimate of tangible net worth of the business. This is arrived at after analysis of the concern's financial statements or other financial data, after allowances for intangible items such as goodwill or patents.

FIGURE 24-3
Dun & Bradstreet Reference Book Key to Ratings

New Key to Ratings
(Effective May 1, 1971)

ESTIMATED FINANCIAL STRENGTH		COMPOSITE CREDIT APPRAISAL			
		HIGH	GOOD	FAIR	LIMITED
5A	Over $50,000,000	1	2	3	4
4A	$10,000,000 to 50,000,000	1	2	3	4
3A	1,000,000 to 10,000,000	1	2	3	4
2A	750,000 to 1,000,000	1	2	3	4
1A	500,000 to 750,000	1	2	3	4
BA	300,000 to 500,000	1	2	3	4
BB	200,000 to 300,000	1	2	3	4
CB	125,000 to 200,000	1	2	3	4
CC	75,000 to 125,000	1	2	3	4
DC	50,000 to 75,000	1	2	3	4
DD	35,000 to 50,000	1	2	3	4
EE	20,000 to 35,000	1	2	3	4
FF	10,000 to 20,000	1	2	3	4
GG	5,000 to 10,000	1	2	3	4
HH	Up to 5,000	1	2	3	4

CLASSIFICATION FOR BOTH
ESTIMATED FINANCIAL STRENGTH AND CREDIT APPRAISAL

FINANCIAL STRENGTH BRACKET	EXPLANATION
1 $125,000 and Over	When only the numeral (1 or 2) appears, it is an indication that the estimated financial strength, while not definitely classified, is presumed to be within the range of the ($) figures in the corresponding bracket and that a condition is believed to exist which warrants credit in keeping with that assumption.
2 20,000 to 125,000	

INV. Shown in place of a rating indicates that the report was under investigation at the time of going to press. It has no other significance.

Not Classified or Absence of Rating. The absence of a rating, expressed by two hyphens (--), is not to be construed as unfavorable but signifies circumstances difficult to classify within condensed rating symbols. It suggests the advisability of obtaining a report for additional information.

Absence of a Listing. The absence of a listing is not to be construed as meaning a concern is nonexistent, has discontinued business, nor does it have any other meaning. The letters "NQ" on any written report mean "not listed in the Reference Book."

Year Business Started. The numeral shown is the last digit of the year date when the business was established or came under present control or management. Thus, 8 means 1968; 9 means 1969. No dates go past ten years. Thus the absence of a numeral indicates ten years or more. This feature is not used in connection with branch listings.

The credit rating or composite credit appraisal is an evaluation of the concern's ability and willingness to pay and its past history in meeting its obligations. It is based on the length of time in business, the abilities of management, general financial condition, the trend of the business, payments record data, and the like. If these factors are judged strong, a concern may be assigned a high credit rating, whereas factors judged to be weak will influence the setting of a lower rating. The exact credit rating used depends on the strength or weakness of all the above factors in relation to each other.

In some instances a capital or credit rating or both cannot be assigned to a business enterprise. The symbols used to denote these more uncommon circumstances are explained in Figure 24-3 in the key to ratings.

Use of Reference Books by Credit Managers

There is no question that the reference books contain a large amount of useful information for credit managers. In general they are regarded highly throughout the credit profession. Experienced credit managers, however, use them with caution because they clearly understand reference book shortcomings. Any publication effort as vast in scope and detail as the general agency's *Reference Book* cannot be accomplished without some errors. Even though the agency exercises great care and has excellent facilities with which to produce such a volume, errors are a natural occurrence in the task. However, advanced printing technology is being utilized and the reference book has been computerized. As a result, improved results are anticipated.

It may be that the more serious shortcomings are not concerned with the publication task but are due to the nature of the investigating task. It is impossible to investigate each name immediately preceding the issuance of each revised edition. Furthermore, the ratings are the result of human judgment based on the information which the editors had available. No rating system is entirely infallible, and it cannot compensate for the deficiencies in human judgment. Credit reporters may gather insufficient information or rely too heavily on certain sources of information. Some business houses will not cooperate in revealing their financial condition and other facts. In such cases the reporter must rely on the best available sources of indirect information that are available to him. When this is the case, *estimates* of financial condition are made, errors in judgment occur, and the actual status of the enterprise may not be fully ascertained.

Despite these limitations, *Reference Book* subscribers can use the book to advantage in:[3]

Credit departments to:
  set up credit lines by ratings
  check small and sample orders
  review continuously important changes in customers and prospects

3 / *How to Use Your Dun & Bradstreet Service Most Effectively* (New York: Dun & Bradstreet, Inc., 1970), p. 8.

Purchasing departments to:
  locate sources of supply
  verify credit standings of suppliers
  determine responsibility of vendors
Sales departments to:
  brief salesmen on accounts
  estimate purchasing power
  build and revise prospect files
  spot new prospects (names prefixed by "A")
  re-classify prospects (rating changes highlighted by "C")
  select prospective distributors
  guide sales research in selected areas

EVALUATION OF DUN & BRADSTREET

In appraising the services of Dun & Bradstreet, it is desirable to examine whether the determinants in the selection of a source of information are met and whether the services supply the information needed by the credit analyst. The important selection factors which should be taken into consideration were set forth in the preceding chapter. These are: accuracy of information, content of reports, speed of reporting, cost of service, trade coverage, geographical coverage, variety and number of reports, and the supplemental services offered. The information needed by the credit manager was also considered in Chapter 23 as follows: identity and legal responsibility, history and business background, character and responsibility of management, financial ability and strength, and payment record experience.

While the agency is not free of limitations and errors, it can reliably be stated that it meets the above criteria. The agency's only interest is to report facts as accurately and completely as possible. Its continuation over the years as the most comprehensive source of credit information depends on its reporting the facts as it knows them. The procedures of reporting are constantly being improved, and Dun & Bradstreet solicits the reporting of known errors from its subscribers.

An old criticism of Dun & Bradstreet was that too much time was necessary to gather current information and finally report it to interested creditors. Slowness in acquiring information resulted in delays and a loss of customer goodwill. Modern communication systems and mechanical devices used to duplicate and process data have met this problem. Today, Dun & Bradstreet leases 16,000 miles of private-wire service. This network connects 89 branch offices from coast to coast. This is one of the largest private-wire systems in the country, and it has greatly speeded the flow of credit information from distant points to the creditor. The agency reports that more than 80 percent of its credit report inquiries are met in the space of one working day.

The trade coverage and geographical coverage of the agency are the most complete in the credit-reporting industry. With its large number of reporters and correspondents gathering information throughout the United States and Canada, the agency can supply a credit report on any business located anywhere in the country. Dun & Bradstreet does not claim to gather information from sources that would be unavailable to creditors. It acquires its information from the same sources available to all credit managers. A direct investigation could be undertaken by the creditor, but Dun & Bradstreet's facilities are tailored to do this for him. Furthermore, in most instances, a direct investigation by the creditor would entail greater costs but would probably result in less effective information.

The content of Dun & Bradstreet reports gives the creditor much of the information which is necessary to make an informed credit decision. If certain types of credit information are not available or the customer has failed to supply financial statements, such shortcomings in the data are clearly apparent to the subscriber. Direct investigation then can be undertaken in an attempt to acquire the data if they are deemed essential to a sound decision. The agency's variety of reports, continuous report service, reference books, and collection services are all designed to fulfill as completely as possible the particular requirements of most commercial creditors. The problems associated with making credit decisions, controlling and collecting accounts, and periodically revising them are greatly eased by the broad scope of the agency's services.

REVIEW AND DISCUSSION QUESTIONS

1. Why is it necessary for a credit manager to have knowledge of a variety of sources of credit information even though he uses only a few?
2. Why is Dun & Bradstreet termed the "general agency"?
3. It is sometimes said that Dun & Bradstreet enjoys a monopolistic position in the field of commercial credit reporting. Discuss the validity of this view.
4. How did economic and business developments of early times influence credit risk and the need for organized sources of credit information?
5. List the principal activities of Dun & Bradstreet and explain each one briefly.
6. Of the various activities of Dun & Bradstreet, which one is the "backbone" of the agency's business? Why?

7. Distinguish between the business information report and the analytical report reproduced in Figures 24-1 and 24-2.

8. Analyze the credit reports referred to in question 7 above. Would you accept credit requests supported by reports containing these qualities? If so, how much credit would you accept? Discuss the basis for your action.

9. Discuss the credit managers' need and usefulness of the agency's Key Account service. The continuous report service.

10. Under what circumstances would you request use of the agency's credit reports? Why would you not request them for each credit decision?

11. What is the basis for the ratings used in the *Reference Book* published by the agency?

12. What credit uses and other business uses do reference book ratings serve?

13. Do the services of Dun & Bradstreet fulfill the credit information needs of credit management? Can you note any deficiencies in the services?

14. How might you as a student find use for D&B's *Million Dollar/Middle Market Directories?*

15. What qualifications do you believe that a city reporter of Dun & Bradstreet should have?

16. What is the standard industrial classification? Why does Dun & Bradstreet use it?

17. Examine carefully the new rating system that Dun & Bradstreet introduced in 1971.

25

Basis of the
Commercial Credit Decision –
Commercial Credit Reporting
by Specialized Agencies

The network of mercantile credit reporting is comprised of an undetermined number of specialized credit-reporting agencies. Some of these agencies are corporate enterprises, while others are operated by trade associations. The specialized agencies may be distinguished from the general agency in the following ways: (1) all of them restrict the credit information which they gather and the reports they render to a single line of trade or to a limited number of allied trades, (2) the geographical coverage by some of the specialized agencies is restricted to a particular territorial region,[1] and (3) some of the agencies restrict their credit information to a special type or concentrate on services which are of particular value to the trade.

Manufacturers, wholesalers, and other suppliers who merchandise their products to business houses in a particular line or to those concentrating in a few allied fields are the users of the specialized agencies' services. As will be shown in subsequent sections, much of the value in using these sources of credit information stems from the specialized nature of their activities.

DUN & BRADSTREET'S INTEREST IN SPECIALIZED
CREDIT REPORTING

While Dun & Bradstreet's interests are principally concerned with the activities of the general agency, it entered the field of specialized

1 / Typically, when this is the case, the territory covered corresponds to the geographical concentration of the trade.

credit reporting upon its acquisition of National Credit Office, Inc., in 1931 and Credit Clearing House, Inc., in 1942. Credit Clearing House now operates as a division of Dun & Bradstreet, while the former functions independently from its New York headquarters and branch offices.

Credit Clearing House

It has long been recognized that the apparel trade is a highly competitive industry permeated with style hazards and a high mortality rate among retail outlets. Because of these characterisitics, business houses selling to the apparel trades are confronted with a degree of risk not ordinarily found in other industries. In recognition of this special need Credit Clearing House, established in 1888 in St. Paul, Minnesota, became one of the largest specialized credit-reporting agencies. Now, as a division of Dun & Bradstreet, Credit Clearing House rates and prepares credit recommendations on concerns in the apparel trades. A few allied industries such as jewelry, notions, and gifts are included in its scope of operations.

A unique feature of Credit Clearing House's operations is the recommendation service. This recommendation service facilitates credit decisions on orders from new and unfamiliar accounts, orders from accounts owing past-due amounts, orders exceeding a previous high credit limit, orders from accounts where a sizable credit exposure already exists, and orders from other types of problem accounts. For each inquiry, there is a specific recommendation taking into account the actual dollar amount of the particular order. For example, if an order is received for $5,000, the recommendation service will indicate whether it is advisable to ship all of the order, part of the order, or whether credit is not recommended for the transaction.

Credit Clearing House analysts, who are familiar with the purchasing habits, trade customs, and seasonal factors of the industry, base their recommendations on Dun & Bradstreet reports and the master buying record maintained on apparel retailers and wholesalers. The master buying record reveals the purchase record and payment experiences of the retailers and wholesalers, as reflected in inquiries made on them by subscribers. From the division's files in New York, information of this type is disseminated daily to all branch offices in the country, thereby making it available to subscribers in markets anywhere in the United States.

This division also supervises the publication of the *Apparel Trades Book*, which is issued every three months in February, May, August, and November, and rates over 110,000 wholesalers and retailers in the apparel industry. The arrangement of the *Apparel Trades Book* is similar to that of the *Dun & Bradstreet Reference Book,* except that the ratings are somewhat more complex. Whereas the Dun & Bradstreet rating consists of two elements, the Credit Clearing House rating consists of three elements. A code letter indicates the estimated financial strength; a number 1, 2, 3, or 4 indicates the payments appraisal; and a letter A, B, C, or D indicates the composite appraisal. Figure 25-1 shows the *Apparel Trades Book* key to ratings, which explains the rating system in complete detail.

National Credit Office

National Credit Office is the largest specialized agency, with executive offices in New York City and branch offices located in Atlanta, Boston, Charlotte, Chicago, Cleveland, Dallas, Detroit, Los Angeles, and Philadelphia. It is a division of Dun & Bradstreet, Inc. Established in 1900, it offers comprehensive services covering manufacturers of textiles, leather goods, paint, rubber products, metals, electronic equipment, and wheel goods; assemblers, converters, and exporters; and soft goods wholesalers.

No retail concerns are covered except large department stores, chain stores, piece goods stores, discount houses, and large furniture stores. In other words, National Credit Office concentrates its reporting services on successive stages of handling, converting, manufacturing, and wholesaling in its several fields of specialization. For example, in the woolen industry this agency investigates and reports on: raw wool dealers, spinners of woolen and worsted yarns, mills which weave woolen and worsted cloth, jobbers of woolen and worsted cloth, manufacturers of ladies', men's, and boys' woolen and worsted garments, and manufacturers and wholesalers of knitted woolen underwear and outerwear. In the final stage, only department stores, discount houses, and chain stores specializing in soft goods are covered. National Credit Office also provides highly specialized reports on concerns offering their commercial paper in the open market.

Credit Reports. Individual departments are operated for each trade line of specialization. All departments of National Credit Office operate in a similar manner, and each performs essentially the same types of services. That is, methods of gathering credit information are the same and the content and structure of all credit reports coincide. Credit investigations by salaried reporters are used primarily in gathering data for credit report inclusion. Individual credit reporters on the staff of National Credit Office are highly trained to specialize in a particular trade line. In fact, many of them not only devote the major portion of their time to one major industry but to a group of accounts within the industry. Such close association with

FIGURE 25-1
Credit Clearing House Key to Ratings

APPAREL TRADES BOOK • KEY TO RATINGS •

		Estimated Financial Strength	Payments Appraisal	Composite Appraisal
⽊ B	A	Over $1,000,000	1 2 3 4	A B C D
	- - -(See Note[1]) - - -		1 2 3 4	A B C D
	C	Over 500,000	1 2 3 4	A B C D
⽊ F	D	Over 300,000	1 2 3 4	A B C D
	E	Over 200,000	1 2 3 4	A B C D
	- - -(See Note[1]) - - -		1 2 3 4	A B C D
	G	Over 100,000	1 2 3 4	A B C D
⽊ K	H	Over 50,000	1 2 3 4	A B C D
	J	Over 30,000	1 2 3 4	A B C D
	- - -(See Note[1]) - - -		1 2 3 4	A B C D
	L	Over 20,000	1 2 3 4	A B C D
	M	Over 10,000	1 2 3 4	A B C D
⽊ S	O	Over 5,000	1 2 3 4	A B C D
	R	Over 3,000	1 2 3 4	A B C D
	- - -(See Note[1]) - - -		1 2 3 4	A B C D
	T			
	V	Up to 3,000	1 2 3 4	A B C D
	W			

(V & W Are Being Phased Out)

X - - Not Classified - - - - - - - - - See Note[2]

§ { The symbol § preceding a rating indicates that an important part of the total worth consists of real estate or other assets not usually considered working capital.

Note[1] { The letters B, F, K, and S in the Estimated Financial Strength column, preceded by the symbol ⽊ indicate in a general way what is considered relative in size. To illustrate: the letter B indicates size comparable to concerns classified in the range A to C inclusive; the letter F, comparable to those from D to G inclusive; the letter K, comparable to those from H to M inclusive; and the letter S, comparable to those from O to V inclusive.

Note[2] { The letter X is not to be construed as unfavorable but, in the column or columns in which used, signifies circumstances difficult to definitely classify within condensed rating symbols and should suggest to the subscriber the advisability of reading the detailed report.

Dun & Bradstreet, Inc.

CREDIT CLEARING HOUSE
SERVING THE APPAREL AND ALLIED LINES NATIONALLY

the same accounts year after year gives the credit reporter an intimate knowledge of each concern assigned to him.

The procedure employed by National Credit Office involves a personal interview with the management of the subject enterprise. During the interview the antecedents, method of operation, and financial data are sought. Externally, the credit reporter endeavors to secure credit information from several sources including trade and credit references, banks, factors, finance companies, accountants, and creditors' ledgers.

The credit reports tendered to all subscribers have three basic sections: (1) current information, (2) management and products, and (3) financial statement. The current information section commences with the name of the concern, its address, and the suggested line of credit. Following this the reports contain new information, a brief synopsis of the antecedents data, a summary of the last three financial statements, a current detailed trade investigation, names of important sources of supply, and an analysis of the financial trend and condition. The management and products section includes the history of the business, the complete business record of the principals, a description of the method of operation, and the names of the subject's banks. In the financial section a detailed current financial statement appears, usually on a National Credit Office form and reproduced photographically. The credit reports of this agency are revised automatically every six months. Figure 25-2 is illustrative of a National Credit Office report.

The most distinguishing feature of National Credit Office reports as contrasted with the reports rendered by other mercantile agencies is the suggestion of a definite line of credit. Statements such as "An excellent risk for requirements," "Reasonable trade needs," or a definite line of credit such as $1,000, $5,000, $20,000 (or no line) are illustrative of the credit suggestions made by the agency's analysts. These appear in the current information section of the credit report.

Guides and Directories.   National Credit Office issues credit rating books or marketing directories in many of the industries in which it specializes. Directories regularly issued include:

The NCO Survey
The NCO Credit Guide of High Fidelity and Sound Specialists
The High Fidelity and Sound Specialists (geographical list)
The NCO Credit and Marketing Guide of Leather Goods Manufacturers
The Electronic Marketing Directory

FIGURE 25-2
National Credit Office Report

---

nco® specialized credit report
MANAGEMENT & PRODUCTS

FEMINA FOOTWEAR CO., INC.   MFR. SLIPPERS & PLAYSHOES
123 West Kerry Ave.   Dept. 964
Buffalo, N.Y. 14020   Analyst: Jeffrey Jones
Phone: 716-477-3602

JUNE 5, 197-

    John W. Sussler, Chairman of Bd.   Edwin W. Delray, Pres.-Treas.
    Peter G. Field, Vice-Pres.   Rosanne S. Dooley, Vice-Pres.
    F. J. Richman, Secy.

DIRECTORS: John W. Sussler, Edwin W. Delray, George H. Lee, and
    Ronald Lockhart.

HISTORY - Established as partnership 1935 as Adorable Shoe Co. Succeeded
    1936 by Femina Footwear Co., N.Y. Corp. 1938 change in control
    occurred and certain of former interests retired. Charter surrendered
    and business re-incorporated under N.Y. laws under present style.
    Plant formerly operated at Manchester, Vt., was discontinued 1949.
    Moved to caption address 1955.

PERSONNEL - Sussler, born 1900, principal financially, maintains general
    supervision over production and purchasing. Long associated with
    line and officer with subject since 1938. Previously Vice-President
    and General Manager of Adorable Shoe Co. Originally employed by
    others as an auditor. $50,000 insurance carried on his life with
    company as beneficiary. Elected Chairman of the Board 1962.

    Delray, born 1911, associated with subject since 1938, is active in
    production. Elected Director 1950. Shortly thereafter elected
    Secretary and assumed the additional office of Vice-President 1959.
    Elected President and Treasurer 1962.

    Richman, born 1930. Employed by subject since 1950. Elected
    Assistant Secretary 1955 and Secretary 1962.

    Field, born 1928. Associated since 1954. Elected Vice-President 1963.

    Dooley, born 1924. Employed as stylist and designer since 1956.
    Elected Vice-President 1959.

    Lee, is a local attorney. Lockhart, is also President of Lockhart
    Gear Works, Buffalo, N.Y. and has been associated with that company
    throughout his business career.

METHOD OF OPERATION - LINE - Manufacture women's and children's turn
    process padded sole and cement process hard sole house slippers and
    playshoes. Retail price range from $3.95 to $10.95 a pair. Approx-
    imately 50% of production is for in-stock and 50% against orders.
    DISTRIBUTION - Direct, nationally, about 75% to department stores and
    25% to individual retailers. Terms of sale 3/10EOM. Use trade styles,
    "Femina", "Kittens", and "Play-Cats".
    EQUIPMENT - Lease quarters on first floor of three-story building.
    Rents 30,000 sq. ft. Output 2,000 pairs daily. Employs about 125.

BANKS - First Marine Bank, Buffalo, N.Y.
    Manufacturers Bank of Buffalo, Buffalo, N.Y.

    cd

The ACS Mobile Home and Travel Trailer Credit Guide
*Mobile Home and Travel Trailer Dealers of the United States and
    Canada* (geographical list)
Mobile Home and Travel Trailer Manufacturers (geographical list)
*The NCO Credit and Marketing Guide of the Chemical Coatings
    Industry*
*NCO Credit and Marketing Guide to the Wholesale and Retail
    Textile Markets*

FIGURE 25-2 (continued)

nco. specialized credit report

FEMINA FOOTWEAR CO., INC.   MFR. SLIPPERS & PLAYSHOES
123 West Kerry Ave.   Dept. 964
Buffalo, N.Y. 14020   Analyst: Jeffrey Jones
Phone: 716-477-3602

JUNE 5, 197-

CREDIT SUGGESTION - (A) - BECAUSE OF FURTHER PROGRESS AND VERY LIQUID
CONDITION, REQUIREMENTS ARE NOW SUGGESTED.

NEW INFORMATION - Management recently advised that sales so far this year
have shown an increase of about 9% over the corresponding period
of last year with profits also ahead of a year ago.

ANTECEDENT COMMENT - Records clear. Originally formed 1935. Present
management in control since 1938. Manufacture general line of
slippers and playshoes. Management experienced and well regarded.

FINANCIAL -	12/31/6-	12/31/6-	12/31/6-
Cash	$ 5,000	$ 12,000	$ 20,000
Receivables	126,000	114,000	134,000
Merchandise	181,000	239,000	184,000
Current Assets	312,000	365,000	338,000
Current Debts	68,000	107,000	65,000
Working Capital	244,000	258,000	273,000
Fixed Assets	44,000	34,000	32,000
Net Worth	353,000	369,000	388,000
Sales	1,234,000	1,336,000	1,423,000
Profit	28,000	32,000	38,000
Dividends	14,000	16,000	19,000

Auditor: Paul D. Hartman & Co., CPA., Buffalo, N.Y.

TRADE - EXCELLENT

HIGH CREDIT	OWING	PAST DUE	TERMS	PAYMENTS
$ 25,000	10,000	0	2/30	ant
15,000	7,000	0	2/15 prox	dis
11,000	5,000	0	2/30	ant
10,000	6,000	0	2/15 prox	dis
6,000	5,000	0	2/15 prox	dis
5,000	0	0	2/15 prox	dis
2,000	2,000	0	2/15 prox	dis
1,000	0	0	2/30	dis

Union Tanning Co., Boston, Mass.   Smith Leather Co., N.Y.C.
Chelsea Heel Corp., Chelsea, Mass.   Fancy Leather Corp., Boston, Mass.

ANALYSIS - This is a well established business which has shown a consistently progressive trend over the years. Steady increases have
been shown in both volume and profits in recent years. Financial
condition has been good for a number of years and was quite liquid on
the last statement which featured all indebtedness covered more than
twice by the total of cash and receivables. Financing is assisted
by unsecured loans from two banks and a small amount was owing to one
bank at recent investigation date.

cd

These marketing or credit directories list concerns, usually showing name and address as well as certain data about each concern. They are arranged either alphabetically or geographically, depending on the purpose of the directory. The data listed about each concern may include: rating, credit line, net worth, volume, number of employees, name of purchasing agent, payments record, trade comments, year established, telephone number, product and distribution breakdown, divisions, and branches.

Commercial Paper Department. The service of this department is not of fundamental interest to commercial credit management, but it is utilized by banks and other commercial paper buyers for which the service was designed. This department writes reports on concerns offering their commercial paper (i.e., unsecured promissory notes maturing in up to 270 days) in the open market. The commercial paper of each company reported upon is graded in one of the following categories: prime, desirable, satisfactory, fair, or not recommended. The reports prepared by this department have a different format from the credit reports of NCO. Major emphasis is placed on the credit responsibility of the company for the maturity of the commercial paper notes.

Other Services of National Credit Office. In addition to the specialization of National Credit Office in a number of important trades, it offers a number of other services for the benefit of its subscribers. The following supplements to the credit reports are included in the service to all members:

NCO News. This publication lists, every month, concerns by industry, showing major changes in principals or financial conditions, changes in credit lines, and financial difficulties.

Group Meetings. Trade groups meet regularly with National Credit Office personnel to facilitate the interchange of information.

Other Specialized Services. In addition there are other specialized services which are offered clients for a separate fee. These include the following:

1. Correspondence and lecture courses in credit and financial analysis.
2. Special line service—designed for lines of credit which are abnormally large or where the risk is a marginal one.
3. Specialized claims service—provides a complete collection service.
4. Management services—assists clients in finding solutions for a wide assortment of management problems.
5. Market planning service—helps establish sales potentials, sales quotas, sales territories; evaluates sales performances; makes special market studies.

LYON FURNITURE MERCANTILE AGENCY

The Lyon Furniture Mercantile Agency, established in 1876 by the late Robert P. Lyon, is the oldest and one of the most important special mercantile agencies. In continuous operation since that date, the Lyon agency has expanded its operations over the years so that today it reports on credit risks in the furniture, interior decoration, major home appliance, contract furnishings, and mobile home trades, as well as on department stores and general stores. Within the mentioned trades, a large number of allied fields are included in the scope of Lyon's activities. For example, in the furniture trade it reports on risk in the carpet, floor covering, upholstery, bedding, bedsprings, juvenile furniture, and baby carriage fields; and in the interior decoration trade the drapery, mirror, picture frame, lamp, lamp shade, gift, and home furnishings fields are covered. Also allied to these trades are the veneer, plywood, and hardwood lumber industries. Although this listing is incomplete, it indicates the extensive coverage of the Lyon agency in its specialized operation.

The subscribers to the Lyon agency's services are manufacturers and wholesalers selling in the several fields of specialization. According to a statement made by management of the agency, more than 95 percent of the units in the industries it serves are subscribers to its services. A credit investigation by Lyon will be conducted on any business concern located anywhere in the United States provided it buys from the specified trades. To provide nationwide coverage, active service offices are located in New York, Chicago, Boston, Philadelphia, Cincinnati, Los Angeles, and High Point, North Carolina. The executive offices of the agency are in New York City.

The principal services rendered to Lyon subscribers are credit reports, the publication of a rating book and weekly supplements, a weekly interchange of trade experience, and a collection service.

Lyon Red Book

As is often the case with specialized agencies, Lyon Furniture Mercantile Agency publishes a rating book known as the *Lyon Red Book*. The organization of the listings in the *Lyon Red Book* is similar in form to that of the general agency. Unlike Dun & Bradstreet, however, the rating system does not include a single key to indicate composite credit appraisal. Instead, the rating system gives a capital rating, which is designated by letters, a pay rating designated by numbers 1 through 9, and a large number of special conditions which are designated by two- or three-digit numbers. Figure 25-3 is a reproduction of the *Lyon Red Book* credit key. Use of this key will show that the rating W 2 should be interpreted to mean that the listed concern has a "small undetermined financial responsibility," and that the pay rating indicates "prompt." The rating 13 L 2 should be interpreted as "inquire for report," a capital rating of $20,000 to $30,000, and the subject's pay rating is "prompt."

FIGURE 25-3
Lyon Red Book Credit Key

LYON RED BOOK — CREDIT KEY

CAPITAL RATINGS	PAY RATINGS
Estimated Financial Worth	Based on suppliers' reports

				PAY RATINGS
A	.............$1,000,000	or	over	1—Discount.
B	500,000	to	$1,000,000	2—Prompt.
C	300,000	to	500,000	3—Medium.
D	200,000	to	300,000	4—Variable, prompt to slow
E	100,000	to	200,000	5—Slow.
G	75,000	to	100,000	6—Very slow.
H	50,000	to	75,000	7—C. O. D. or C. B. D.
J	40,000	to	50,000	
K	30,000	to	40,000	
L	20,000	to	30,000	8—Pay rating not established, but information favorable.
M	15,000	to	20,000	
N	10,000	to	15,000	9—Claims to buy always for cash.
O	7,000	to	10,000	
Q	5,000	to	7,000	SPECIAL CONDITIONS
R	3,000	to	5,000	
S	2,000	to	3,000	12—Business recently commenced.
T	1,000	to	2,000	13—Inquire for report.
U	500	to	1,000	21—Buys small, usually pays cash.
V	100	to	500	23—Sells on commission.

Z-No financial basis for credit reported.

24—Name listed for convenience only.

29—Rating undetermined.

INDEFINITE RATINGS

31—Financial statement declined, or repeatedly requested and not received.

F—Estimated financial responsibility not definitely determined, presumed high.

P—Estimated financial responsibility not definitely determined, presumed moderate.

SYMBOL INTERPRETATION

W—Estimated financial responsibility not definitely determined, presumed small.

● or 12 — Business recently commenced.

Y—Estimated financial responsibility not definitely determined, presumed very limited.

✦ or 116—New statement recently received.

▲—Indicates information of unusual importance.

The omission of a rating is not unfavorable, but indicates that sufficient information is not at hand on which to base rating.

◎—Sells on installment plan.

(?)—Sells from residence, office or catalogue.

CREDIT GRANTORS–NOTE

No system of ratings can ALWAYS convey an accurate summarization of existing conditions. Book ratings reflect conditions believed to exist when assigned, and are based upon information obtained from financial statements, from the trade, special reporters, correspondents, financial institutions and other sources deemed reliable, but the correctness thereof is in no way guaranteed.

Conditions are constantly changing, and changes as made are shown in the "LYON Weekly Supplement and Report", and in Lyon Credit Reports.

Should any error, or inaccuracy in rating be noted, it should be reported only to the Agency, in order that correction may be made.

Inquire for Detailed Credit Report on all NEW ACCOUNTS, and make inquiry at least once a year on old accounts or when change in rating is indicated in the "LYON Weekly Supplement and Report".

To keep the *Lyon Red Book* current between its semiannual publication dates in January and July, the agency publishes the *Weekly Supplement and Report*. This information sheet is distributed to all subscribers to the *Red Book* service and gives them a record of changes in ratings, new businesses, successions, fires, failures, suits, judgments, and claims. The *Weekly Supplement and Report* is a continuous service to the rating book user.

Interchange of Trade Experience

Perhaps the most outstanding feature of Lyon's services is the interchange of trade experience among Lyon subscribers. Each week a national interchange of trade experience is obtained by a "tracer sheet," which is sent to all subscribers. The tracer sheet includes a listing of businesses which have been selected for clearance because of some circumstance affecting their credit position. The subscriber is requested to indicate his ledger experience with the listed concerns by placing a check mark in one of the seven columns opposite the subject's name. The seven columns denote the manner of payment as discounting, prompt, medium, slow, very slow, c.o.d., or c.b.d. The creditor also indicates the "amount owing" and the "amount past due" in appropriate columns. Hence, the manner in which a risk is currently paying his obligations is portrayed by a national survey. The results of the tracer, upon return to the Lyon office, are consolidated and transcribed to a form titled "Result of Tracer," which is made available to all cooperating subscribers. The distinct advantage of this service is that credit men in allied trades and involved with the same credit risks have an opportunity to exchange ledger experiences. A system of this type prevents any risk from becoming seriously delinquent without the cooperating credit men of the trade becoming fully aware of the condition and being in a position to take necessary action.

Credit Reports

The Lyon Agency renders a single type of standardized credit report. The composition of their credit reports is similar to those of Dun & Bradstreet, Inc. The principal sections are heading, antecedents, general information, financial information, summarized statements, analysis, bank information, trade investigation (including interchange results and collection record), and summary. Despite the similarity to other agency reports, the credit analyst should note the detailed and comprehensive nature of the information included in a typical Lyon report. In the analysis section it is common to find the current, net worth, and liquidity ratios, the turnover of inventory, and the average collection period for receivables. At the end of each report a rating is assigned the subject business house as reflected in the *Lyon Red Book* or its supplements. A sample Lyon Mercantile Agency credit report is shown in Figure 25-4.

JEWELERS BOARD OF TRADE

The Jewelers Board of Trade serves as an example of specialized credit reporting conducted by a trade association. This association, as a mutual nonprofit corporation, was organized to promote the interests of the jewelry industry. Throughout the years it has placed increased emphasis on assisting members in matters relating to credit. The credit-reporting activities of the association today are the result of an amalgamation of several credit organizations dating back to 1874, which operated in the jewelry field. The membership of the Jewelers Board of Trade includes manufacturers, wholesalers, and importers of the jewelry and kindred trades. The operations of the association are national in scope.

The services rendered include the issuance of credit reports, the publication of a reference book, and the handling of collections for members. An adjustment department functions to protect members in their actions against businesses that have become financially embarrassed or are bankrupt. Supplementing the credit report services is the continuous service which provides subscribers with all credit reports and special notices on subjects of inquiry for one year from the date of the original inquiry. The *Confidential Reference Book,* which is published each March and September, is supplemented by a weekly *Service Bulletin,* which contains a record of changed ratings, deaths, dissolutions, incorporations, business casualties, and other information of interest to the membership. The methods employed in gathering credit information and the types of credit information supplied creditors have no distinguishing features not covered elsewhere in this and preceding chapters.

In general, however, the costs of credit services provided by trade associations are quite nominal when compared with the costs of credit services provided by private enterprise sources. Typically a given number of credit reports and the early phases of collection are free to members upon payment of the membership fee. After drawing the maximum number of reports a nominal charge is made for each additional report. Similarly, collection cases involving legal action are handled on a cost basis.

FIGURE 25-4
Lyon Furniture Mercantile Agency Credit Report

Form 20

LYON·RED BOOK REPORT

This report is furnished, at your request, in accordance with the terms of your contract with the Lyon Furniture Mercantile Agency. It is to be held **strictly confidential.**   It is for your exclusive use and to be used only as an aid to determine the advisability of granting credit.

(SAMPLE REPORT - NAMES & ADDRESS FICTITIOUS)

DOE, JOHN CORPORATION   FC&Apl 0   NEW YORK 16..........N.Y.
                                                            629 West 34th Street

Morris Doe, President, Age 48, Married
Frank Blank, Treasurer, Age 45, Married
John Smith, Secretary, Age 47, Single

Directors: The officers

REV: (amd-2) November 1, 19

ANTECEDENTS
        Incorporated under New York State laws March 15, 1939, continuing the busi-
ness of the former John Doe Furniture Co., which had conducted business at this
same address as a partnership between Morris Doe and Frank Blank.

        Morris Doe is a son of the late John Doe who started in the furniture
business February 6, 1900 as John Doe Furniture Co., at 1600 Dodge Street, New York,
N.Y. John Doe died May 5, 1935 at which time a partnership was formed between his
son, Morris Doe and Frank Blank, a son-in-law as John Doe Furniture Co. to continue
the business which at that time moved to 629 West 34th Street. Morris Doe had been
assisting his father in the conduct of this business working part time while attending school and after graduating giving his full time to the business. Frank
Blank had been employed by the late John Doe for about ten years.

        The partnership between Frank Blank and Morris Doe continued until December
1, 1938, when they executed an assignment for the benefit of creditors. On December
5, 1938, an involuntary petition in bankruptcy was filed against them and at the
Trustee's sale in bankruptcy the assets were purchased by the present corporation,
the unsecured creditors of the partnership receiving a first and final dividend of
50% on November 28, 1939. The partners received their discharge from bankruptcy
January 12, 1940.

        Control of this corporation is divided equally between Morris Doe, Frank
Blank and John Smith. John Smith joined with Morris Doe and Frank Blank in forming
this corporation to acquire the assets at the sale in bankruptcy, previous to which
time he had been employed for about eight years as a furniture buyer by the New York
Department Store, New York, N.Y.

        On December 16, 1944, a fire which occurred here as a result of the faulty
operation of an oil burner, caused damage to stock of about $10,000, with insurance
adjustment being received in that amount.

FIGURE 25-4 (*continued*)

Form 20

LYON-RED BOOK REPORT

This report is furnished, at your request, in accordance with the terms of your contract with the Lyon Furniture Mercantile Agency. It is to be held **strictly confidential.** It is for your exclusive use and to be used only as an aid to determine the advisability of granting credit.

DOE, JOHN CORPORATION   -2-   NEW YORK.........N.Y.

November 1, 197-

GENERAL INFORMATION

   Principals of corporation experienced and attentive, although the president and treasurer have been identified in the past with an unsuccessful venture.

   Company occupies a three-story building which it owns in a good shopping center, each floor having about 10,000 square feet of display space, the basement being used for warehouse and storage purposes.

   Corporation carries a complete line of home furnishings and has a good sized electrical appliance department handling only major appliances. Deals in medium to low priced lines, with about 90% of sales made on the installment payment plan. Company had enjoyed a fairly good sales volume during the past few years, however, there appears to have been some falling off in volume during the past several months with prospects at this time for a continuance of previous satisfactory sales volume appearing not favorable, local conditions of strikes resulting in unemployment of some weeks having curtailed sales volume in general.

FINANCIAL INFORMATION

   Company has an authorized capital of $300,000, in preferred stock, divided into 3,000 shares with a par value of $100 each. The paid in capital is $150,000, $50,000 each having been contributed by the three principals.

COMPARATIVE SUMMARIZED STATEMENTS

DATE	ASSETS	LIABILITIES & RESERVES		NET WORTH	SALES
Dec. 31, 1958	261,724	101,827	2,428	157,468	
Dec. 31, 1967	317,062	122,674	7,260	187,127	220,647
Dec. 31, 1968	370,085	138,864	14,537	216,683	250,128
Dec. 31, 1969	384,117	147,824	17,027	219,266	270,877
June 30, 1970	371,780	138,473	18,236	215,070	125,608

   The following statement, received by mail, showing condition from books and physical inventory of June 30, 1970.

ASSETS:

Current Assets

Cash on hand & in bank	5,096.28	
Accounts receivable, install.	220,174.05	
Merchandise inventory	50,649.00	
Total Current Assets		275,920.33

Fixed Assets

Real estate	75,000.00	
Furniture, fixtures & signs	15,427.18	
Delivery equipment	4,908.76	
Total Fixed Assets		95,335.94

Deferred Charges

Prepaid insurance & interest		524.51
TOTAL ASSETS		$371,780.78

FIGURE 25-4 (*continued*)

Form 20

LYON-RED BOOK REPORT

This report is furnished, at your request, in accordance with the terms of your contract with the Lyon Furniture Mercantile Agency. It is to be held **strictly confidential.** It is for your exclusive use and to be used only as an aid to determine the advisability of granting credit.

DOE, JOHN CORPORATION   -3-   NEW YORK..........N.Y.

November 1, 197-

FINANCIAL INFORMATION (cont'd)

LIABILITIES & CAPITAL:
Current Liabilities
Accounts Payable	89,452.02
Notes Payable Bank, secured by endorsement	
of president & treasurer	15,000.00
Taxes payable, Federal & State	1,521.87
Total Current Liabilities	105,973.89
Fixed Liabilities	
Real estate mortgage	32,500.00
Reserve for depreciation of Fixed Assets	18,236.20
	156,710.09
Capital	
100 shares preferred stock	150,000.00
Surplus	65,070.69
TOTAL LIABILITIES & CAPITAL	$371,780.78

Sales for six months ending June 30, 1970, $125,608. Insurance on merchandise, $45,000. Insurance on building, $60,000.

(SIGNED) JOHN DOE CORPORATION
By: Frank Blank, Treasurer

ANALYSIS
        Summarized statements show net worth has been steadily increasing from 1958 to 1969, but for the six months there had been some reduction in net worth.

        Comparison of current statement with that of December 31, 1969, shows a reduction in cash of about $47,500, accounts receivable have increased about $25,000, and inventory has increased about $10,000. Accounts payable have increased about $28,000. Bank indebtedness has increased about $5,000, while taxes have been reduced by about $2,400, and an item of about $40,000 previously shown owing to officers no longer appears in the statement, Mr. Blank stating upon interview that this had been paid to officers which also explained a good part of the reduction in cash position.

        Current statement shows a liquid ratio of about .57 to 1, and a current ratio of 1.05 to 1, both of which are well below accepted standard. Sales compared with receivables indicates average collection period of about 313 days which is slower than accepted standard, indicating that some of the accounts are becoming old on the books. Inventory compared with sales indicates a fairly satisfactory turnover of about 2.4 times a year.

FIGURE 25-4 (*continued*)

Form 20

LYON-RED BOOK REPORT

This report is furnished, at your request, in accordance with the terms of your contract with the Lyon Furniture Mercantile Agency. It is to be held **strictly confidential.** It is for your exclusive use and to be used only as an aid to determine the advisability of granting credit.

DOE, JOHN CORPORATION   -4-   NEW YORK..........N.Y.

November 1, 197-

ANALYSIS (cont'd)
        While the current and liquid positions are below accepted standard, the net worth ratio, which is about 1.4 to 1, is satisfactory and there is indicated some margin of ratable worth placed at slightly better than $60,000, after allowing for adjustments and depreciation.

BANK INFORMATION
        Satisfactory account maintained for several years. Balances previously averaging in moderate five figures, but at present average in moderate four to high four figures. Accommodation extended in high four to low five figures, secured by endorsements of principals and cared for as agreed.

TRADE INVESTIGATION
                NATIONAL INTERCHANGE OF TRADE EXPERIENCE

        March 25, 1970 - result - 18 houses reporting

PAYMENTS	OWING	PAST DUE
1-Discount	125	---
2-Discount	---	---
3-Discount	77	---
4-Medium	340	---
5-Medium	260	---
6-Medium	180	180
7-Medium	410	---
8-Medium	---	---
9-Medium	100	---
10-Slow	600	320
11-Slow	390	175
12-Slow	740	650
13-Slow	367	367
14-Slow	239	140
15-Very Slow	842	842
16-Very Slow	726	560
17-Very Slow	163	163
18-Very Slow	639	160

Inquiry of Sept. 16, 1970:

Manner of Payment	Days Slow	High Credit	Owing	Past Due	Date Last Sale
1-Medium	--	400	125	---	11/69
2-Medium	--	725	680	110	11/69
3-Slow	30	667	319	284	10/69
4-Slow	30	981	723	416	10/69
5-Slow	30-60	1,519	1,276	962	10/69
6-Slow	60	724	693	487	9/70
7-Very Slow	90	1,263	981	876	9/70
8-Very Slow	90	1,849	1,547	1,029	8/70
9-Very Slow	120	716	716	616	6/70
10-Very Slow	180	1,057	820	820	7/70

FIGURE 25-4 (*concluded*)

Form 20

LYON-RED BOOK REPORT

This report is furnished, at your request, in accordance with the terms of your contract with the Lyon Furniture Mercantile Agency. It is to be held **strictly confidential.** It is for your exclusive use and to be used only as an aid to determine the advisability of granting credit.

DOE, JOHN CORPORATION   -5-   NEW YORK.........N.Y.

November 1, 197-

COLLECTION RECORD

Mar.	7,	1970 -	Claim (H-35872) $420.50 placed with High Point office for inv. 11/4/69. Collected by Agency 4/1/70.
Apr.	22,	1970 -	Claim (C-48581) $232.60 placed with Chicago office for goods sold 1/70. Collected by Agency 4/26/70.
June	15,	1970 -	Claim (H-36784) $195.80 placed with High Point office for inv. 2/5/70. Collected by Agency 7/7/70.
June	16,	1970 -	Claim (H-36787) $527 placed with High Point office for inv. 1/5/70. Collected by Agency 7/8/70.
June	30,	1970 -	Claim (N-57602) $947.18 placed with New York office for goods sold Dec. through Mar. 1970. Collected by Agency 7/26/70.
July	2,	1970 -	Claim (N-58101) $624 placed with New York office for goods sold 2/21/70.

SUMMARY

    PRINCIPALS EXPERIENCED AND ATTENTIVE, HOWEVER, PRESIDENT AND TREASURER HAVE BEEN IDENTIFIED IN THE PAST WITH UNSUCCESSFUL VENTURE. CURRENT STATEMENT SHOWS SUB-STANDARD WORKING POSITION, ALTHOUGH SOME RATABLE WORTH IS INDICATED. TRADE PAYMENTS DURING THE PAST FEW MONTHS HAVE BECOME SLOW WITH SOME CLAIMS APPEARING FOR COLLECTION.

N: Rate 13-H-5-116   (s.i.)

Other Specialized Mercantile Credit-Reporting Agencies

In addition to the several specialized agencies which have been treated in the preceding sections, a considerable number of similar agencies specialize in other trades. A partial listing of other agencies is as follows:

Name of Agency	Trade Coverage
Shoe and Leather Mercantile Agency, Inc.	Leather and allied trades
Produce Reporter Company	Fruits, vegetables, and other processed farm products
Lumberman's Credit Association	Lumber and woodworking trades
Credit Association of Building Trades	Construction industry
Stationers and Publishers Board of Trade	Stationery, typewriter, and office equipment trades
Credit Exchange, Inc.	Textile, apparel, drygoods, and sporting goods trades

Most of the specialized agencies follow the method of operation of the general agency, except for distinctive features that have been developed to meet the needs of credit management in particular trades. Although major contributors to the field of credit reporting, these agencies have limited their scope of trade coverage even more than National Credit Office or Lyon Furniture Mercantile Agency. Thus, their members or subscribers are somewhat fewer and the completeness of information interchanged among creditors is less. Some of the organizations fall short of having complete coverage in their specialized trades. In general, the services performed by the more limited concerns are highly flavored with trade information such as trade bulletins, advisory information pertinent to the trade, and rating books which serve only those in a specified field of endeavor.

APPRAISAL OF CREDIT SERVICES RENDERED BY THE SPECIALIZED AGENCIES

The extensiveness, particular features, types of credit information, and trade coverage leave little doubt that the specialized agencies are an important source of credit information. The fact that they tailor their services more closely to the needs of their trade implies that their contributions toward better credit judgment cannot be seriously questioned. The specialized credit-reporting agencies, as was shown to be true of the general agency, meet the needs of credit management by supplying data on a subject's identity and legal responsibility, history and business background, character and responsibility of management, financial ability and strength, and payment record experience. These are the criteria established in Chapter 23 against which the credit services of the previously mentioned agencies should be measured. The rather detailed description of the specialized agencies' services lends credence to their value and importance in meeting creditors' needs. The flexibility of these agencies in adapting their services to the particular needs of the trade should not be overlooked as a superior feature when contrasted with the general agency.

It is generally believed that credit investigators and correspondents employed by specialized agencies gain a more thorough knowledge of their particular field. By confining his activities, the specialized reporter frequently has more intimate contact and knowledge which may contribute substantially to a more complete and otherwise more satisfactory type of credit reporting. It seems very plausible that by specialized research in particular trade lines, it may be possible to get more detailed information of broader significance to the credit manager. Detailed information gathered in restricted trade lines, however, is not of credit significance to those credit men whose businesses are selling in a wide variety of markets. There are no specialized credit-reporting agencies in trade lines such as tobacco, coal, eating and drinking places, and many others. Hence the general agency is an indispensable source of credit information for the many marketers selling their products in a large number and wide variety of markets. A common criticism registered by credit managers is that the ledger experiences of the specialized sources are often incomplete insofar as variety is concerned. It is entirely possible that an agency reporter, because of his preoccupation with a particular trade, may fail to investigate those markets in which the subject does the greater proportion of his purchasing. The additional fact that some of these agencies do not cover retailers (or if they do, their reporting is restricted to particular types of retailers), limits the usefulness of the specialized service.

Credit management is particularly aware that the quality of the information in credit reports and rating books is affected by time. That is, information which is intended to be of value and credit significance must be up to date. Somewhat allied to this criticism is the demand for speed in credit reporting. Accurate credit investigating always involves time, and especially so when the information must be concentrated from distant and varied sources. By means of automatic revision systems and the widespread use of wire services by the specialized agencies, their files contain adequate current information to supply the major proportion of all requests. The adoption of such procedures puts current information in the hands of the creditor in a relatively short span of time. To fulfill requests on which current information is not in file, the agency must sacrifice promptness for accuracy. Because of the very nature and character of the work involved, it seems improbable that speed and accuracy can be incorporated into every report.

Some functions of the specialized agencies as well as the general agency are not self-sustaining. A case in point is the trade information which is gathered from credit men who are representative creditors of another credit man's risk. Some credit managers believe a more active interest in the field of credit reporting on their part is necessary, and especially with regard to furnishing ledger experience. How well a system of ledger interchange works is dependent entirely upon credit men who hold the valuable information. The mutual advantage of giving and receiving needs no particular elaboration and should be clear, especially to credit management.

It is quite reasonable to conclude that the advantages of the specialized agencies, as contrasted with the general agency, are for the most part the result of trade specialization. They undoubtedly render very valuable types of information to creditors and are extremely useful to firms trading in a limited number of lines. The general agency, as evidenced by its very wide use and acceptance by credit men, has an undisputed place in facilitating the credit judgment of those who sell in a large number of diverse markets. In the aggregate, the commercialized sources of credit information treated thus far, plus the frequent use of "free" sources of information, provide credit management with an abundance of varying combinations which will help to meet most credit needs.

REVIEW AND DISCUSSION QUESTIONS

1. Explain Dun & Bradstreet's interest in specialized credit reporting.
2. How do specialized agencies differ from Dun & Bradstreet?
3. What are advantages and disadvantages to specialization in the credit reporting field? Discuss.
4. Explain the recommendation service of the Credit Clearing House.
5. What does the master buying record of the Credit Clearing House show?
6. What types of businesses would normally use the services of the National Credit Office?
7. Why is it said that the Credit Clearing House uses a three-legged rating while Dun & Bradstreet uses a two-legged rating?
8. What is the most distinguishing feature of National Credit Office reports?
9. How would this feature benefit a credit manager in his task of decision-making?

10. List the unique features of the services of Lyon Furniture Mercantile Agency. What allied fields does this agency serve?

11. Discuss the advantages and disadvantages of the *Lyon Red Book* Credit Key.

12. List several other specialized credit-reporting agencies and discuss their fields of concentration.

13. What is your appraisal of credit services rendered by specialized mercantile agencies?

26

Basis of the
Commercial Credit Decision—
Credit Interchange Bureaus
of the NACM

The Credit Interchange Bureaus of the
National Association of Credit Management (NACM) are the only
credit reporting organization which renders a single type of credit
information, namely, ledger experience. Since most customers
purchase from suppliers located throughout the country, any direct
attempt to secure a representative number of individual ledger
experiences would involve much time and an unwarranted delay in
making the credit decision. The need for a centralized point of
inquiry from which to obtain such information stems from the
weight given to ledger experience by credit executives and from the
wastes as well as the inadequate results when direct inquiry is
undertaken.

NATIONAL ASSOCIATION OF CREDIT MANAGEMENT

The National Association of Credit Management is the oldest and
largest professional and service association representing commercial
and financial credit personnel in the United States. In 1896, when
the association was formally organized, the climate in which credit
managers operated was vastly different from that of today. The
practice of fraud and misrepresentation by businessmen was common, and creditors were without adequate commercial laws to
prosecute the guilty and protect their businesses. For example, it was
almost impossible to prosecute the debtor who, on the verge of

insolvency, would sell the assets of his business and pocket the proceeds. This type of action on the part of the debtor ignored the interests of creditors and violated the present-day theory that an insolvent business belongs to the creditors. This problem was further aggravated by the rapid growth of interstate commerce and the absence of a uniform federal bankruptcy law to deal with financially distressed businesses. The few state laws at the time were contradictory, complex, and generally failed to protect creditors.[1]

Financial statements, though at the time used infrequently in analyzing the credit worthiness of a risk, could not be relied upon, and no laws protected the creditor. Cooperation among credit men in exchanging credit information was lacking, and many creditors deliberately attempted to deceive by revealing either inadequate data or incorrect information.

Any individual attempt to improve ethical standards of the profession or to raise the quality of the credit structure was recognized as futile. All credit men, however, working together could impose ethical standards on the industry, raise the quality of the credit structure, and develop a scientific approach to the mutural problems of credit management. The National Association of Credit Management realized that cooperation was necessary to cope with the problems which were being intensified by a growing demand for credit. From a humble beginning of less than 600 members, today it numbers more than 36,000 members from the leading manufacturing, wholesaling, and financial institutions of the country.

Organization

Today, with headquarters in New York City, the association is organized into 129 affiliated local chapters representing most of the major and minor markets of the nation. Each local chapter is governed by elected officers, and most chapters employ a full-time administrator of the association activities as well as full-time clerical help. The local units are organized into departments for the various services they render, such as legislation, education, interchange, and collection.

The coordinating unit, of course, is the NACM, which is governed by elected officers and a board of directors. The activities of the national association are directed by a full-time executive vice president and a paid staff. Membership in the association is both local and national by virtue of the fact that dues include membership in both the local chapter and the national association.

1 / *Credit Management Handbook* (2d ed.; Homewood, Ill.: Richard D. Irwin, Inc., 1965), pp. 541-42.

Activities

In addition to operation of the Credit Interchange Bureaus, the association fulfills its objectives and meets the individual needs of its membership by being engaged in the following activities:

1. *Fraud Prevention:* The fraud prevention department detects and prosecutes perpetrators of commercial frauds.

2. *Educational:* The National Institute of Credit offers educational opportunities in the credit, banking, business law, and merchandising fields to members, their associates, assistants, and others desiring to train for a career in credit work. Credit institutes and seminars are conducted at major universities throughout the country.

3. *Legislation:* The legislative department has a continuing program for the correction, modification, repeal, or enactment of both federal and state laws that affect credit and finance.

4. *Adjustments:* Adjustment bureaus of the NACM are maintained throughout the United States and specialize in the orderly administration of distressed businesses. The bureaus function for the benefit of creditors by acting as assignee, trustee, or receiver and by attending creditors' meetings and making recommendations.

5. *Collections:* A nationwide collection service is operated for members.

6. *Publications:* Publishes the *Credit Manual of Commercial Laws* annually and *Credit and Financial Management,* which is a monthly magazine.

7. *Research:* The Credit Research Foundation, founded by NACM in 1949, sponsors and encourages credit research concerned with credit conditions and practices of either a general or specific nature. The foundation also administers the educational activities of NACM. It has prepared and edited the *Credit Management Handbook* and other publications.

8. *Industry and Trade Group Meetings:* Sponsors industry and trade group meetings made up of credit and financial management people who meet regularly to discuss credit problems and economic trends. Trade group meetings also provide the opportunity for discussion of members' experiences with specific accounts.

9. *Foreign Credit Interchange:* The Foreign Credit Interchange Bureau established in 1919 provides a ready source of payment record data on thousands of foreign buyers located throughout the world. Members of NACM may subscribe to its services on a cost basis.

CREDIT INTERCHANGE BUREAUS

Credit Interchange Bureaus were at first operated on a local-market basis. It was soon found that information gathered from one market was insufficient for members' requirements, and a system for the interchange of ledger experience among bureaus was developed. This was accomplished in 1919 by the organization of a central bureau in St. Louis which enabled various bureaus, although independently operated, to exchange their information and reports. It was not until 1921 that NACM took over the central bureau, and with 15 participating bureaus it established the present National Credit Interchange System.

Organization

Today the National Credit Interchange System is entirely an operation of the National Association of Credit Management. The system comprises a coordinating unit, the Central Credit Interchange Bureau, located in St. Louis, and 62 local bureaus (plus bureaus in Hawaii and Canada) covering major and minor markets of the country. Each local bureau operating in the system is member-owned and member-operated under the supervision of the local NACM association. In a few instances bureaus are under the supervision of the national association. Membership is limited to manufacturers, wholesalers, other middlemen, and bankers. There is no restriction by trade line or geographical location. The underlying principles of each bureau are (1) member direction and control, and (2) service charges just adequate to cover the costs of operation. The bureaus serve as mediums for the assembling and dissemination of credit information, which is supplied and used by member-creditors.

The entire system is administered by the Board of Governors, NACM. The board prescribes operating procedures, standards, forms and any changes needed to effectuate a more effective system.

Method of Operation

The successful and efficient operation of the National Credit Interchange System is almost entirely dependent upon the constant cooperation of its members. To encourage member cooperation and to perpetuate an efficient system, the mechanics of the operation have been coordinated and standardized to the extent that a minimum of effort is required of members.

The system operates on the basis of *sources* of information which are accumulated in the local bureaus by requiring each participating member in the service to:

1. Supply a complete list of the active accounts on his ledgers at the time he becomes a member of the service.
2. Supplement that list with new accounts (as they are opened) and reopened accounts after the original list is filed.

3. Furnish the names of all known creditors at the time of making an inquiry for a report on any customer.

Each member of a local bureau is assigned a code symbol which is known only by the member so designated and the officers of the bureau. A code number also designates each local bureau. As the names of members' active accounts and their new and reopened accounts flow into the local bureau, a card is made out showing the name and address of the subject and the symbols of the members doing business with the account. The code number for each local bureau having an interest in the account is also shown on the subject's card. Thus, each local bureau has a ready reference file which shows all local members who have registered an interest in an account as well as information on the other bureaus that have an interest in the account. The constant flow of account names into the bureaus from members assures card files that are up to date.

Each of the affiliated bureaus is allocated a "zone of operation," which is the normal trade territory of the market served by the bureau. Each bureau reports the names of all its members' customers outside its zone of operation to the bureau in whose zone of operation the customers are located. Thus, the files of each bureau contain two types of names: (1) customers located in the zone of operation, whose cards contain the names of suppliers located in that zone as well as a list of other interested bureaus; and (2) customers located in *other* zones but sold by members in the local zone, whose cards contain the names of local suppliers and the other interested bureaus. In other words, the files of the local bureau on all subjects in its zone of operation constitute a record of all local creditors selling a customer, as well as all markets in which he is buying. When a clearance is made, members of all bureaus selling the customer under investigation are canvassed for information without regard to industry or location.

Each member is furnished a supply of inquiry forms (see Figure 26-1). These forms are used by members in requesting a credit report on active accounts or on new and reopened accounts. The inquiring member is required to submit his ledger experience with the subject each time he submits one of these forms. In addition a space is provided for the listing of all known sources of supply. Usually this space lists those business houses that were submitted as references by the prospective customer.

When a member makes an inquiry on a customer located in the same zone as the bureau receiving the inquiry, the files will disclose the names of creditors in the local market and the identity of other interested bureaus. The zone of operation bureau canvasses all creditors who are listed as selling to the customer. This is done by

FIGURE 26-1
Member's Inquiry Form

MEMBER INQUIRY			P.1	IMPORTANT	PRO. NO.
NACM				List other sources of supply below. The bureau will endeavor to obtain their information.	

CREDIT INTERCHANGE BUREAUS
2962 Harney St., Omaha, Nebr. 68131   342-5620

	NAME	ADDRESS

SEND US A REPORT ON   DATE _____

NAME _____

TRADE STYLE. _____

STREET ADDRESS _____

TOWN	STATE	ZIP CODE

TYPE BUSINESS _____

MEMBER	CHECK FOR AUTOMATIC REVISION □ 4 MONTHS □ ___MONTHS	□ SEND PRELIMINARY REPORT □ SEND ONLY COMPLETED REPORT	REVISING FILE □ 1st ORDER □

LIST ADDITIONAL REFERENCES ON REVERSE SIDE

BANKS WITH _____
SUBJECT HAS
BRANCHES AT: _____

sending each known creditor the member's reply form illustrated in Figure 26-2. The local bureau also requests that the same procedure be instituted in other interested markets. When the other markets have accumulated the ledger facts from interested creditors, these facts are forwarded to the zone of operation bureau, where, together with its own local information, the credit interchange report is written. If, on the other hand, the subject of the clearance is located in another bureau's zone of operation, the bureau receiving the request automatically canvasses its local interested creditors for ledger facts, and at the same time forwards the inquiry to the subject's home zone, from which a national clearance is initiated.

The zone bureau is responsible for compiling the information and writing the credit interchange reports on all subjects in its territory. When an inquiry form is received by the bureau from an inquirer, the following actions are taken:

1. The most recent interchange report in the bureau's files is immediately forwarded to the member. Typically, any report older than 120 days is subject to revision, and a canvass of the local markets and other zones is initiated. If this is the case, the inquiring member will also receive the preliminary and final reports noted below. On the other hand, if the credit report on file is not subject to revision, and if it contains sufficiently fresh and adequate information to meet the creditor's requirements, the bureau will take no further action.

2. One or more *preliminary reports* are forwarded to the inquiring member. Preliminary reports contain revised and more current information from the local and nearby markets. Such reports are

FIGURE 26-2
Member's Reply Form

CREDIT INTERCHANGE BUREAUS · NATIONAL ASSOCIATION OF CREDIT MANAGEMENT · ORGANIZED · VIGILANTIA · 1896

Credit Interchange Bureaus
502 THORPE BLDG., MINNEAPOLIS 2, MINN,

PLEASE GIVE EXPERIENCE WITH

HOW LONG SOLD		☐ NO EXPERIENCE WITHIN PAST YEAR
DATE OF LAST SALE		
HIGHEST RECENT CREDIT	$	OMIT CENTS
NOW OWING (Include Notes)	$	
PAST DUE (Include Notes)	$	
TERMS OF SALE (Give Actual Terms)	☐ C.O.D.; ☐ THEIR REQUEST	

TREND OF PAYMENTS	PAYING RECORD
☐ IMPROVING	☐ DISCOUNTS
☐ NO CHANGE	☐ PAYS WHEN DUE
☐ SLOWER	______ DAYS SLOW

COMMENTS:

☐ SEND US COPY OF THIS REPORT

BUSINESS CLASSIFICATION No.

written as sufficient information becomes available in the bureau as a result of its canvassing procedures.

3. Finally, the flow of information into the bureau from other zones of operation is completed and a *final report* is written. Copies of the final report are sent to the inquiring member as well as to each creditor who contributed ledger information to the bureau. As the

final report becomes available, it represents an up-to-date summary of the buying and paying habits of the subject account with all creditors who registered an interest.

CONTENTS AND INTERPRETATION OF A CREDIT INTERCHANGE REPORT

An illustrative Credit Interchange Bureau report is shown in Figure 26-3. It should be noted that unlike many other types of credit reports, this report offers no recommendations or opinions. Personal views that are not based upon actual ledger experience are not included in the report. The report merely presents facts based on the actual ledger experiences of creditors and arranged in an orderly manner for rapid appraisal. The report contains a large amount of information for the credit executive who appraises it carefully and properly. Unfortunately, there are many instances when the only analysis made is a hurried glance at the paying record and comments columns. It should be recognized that the most intelligent appraisal of the credit interchange report involves both the horizontal and the vertical analysis of the columns. Any appraisal which falls short of this technique results in faulty interpretation and failure to uncover the true significance of the data.

Heading

The heading of the credit interchange report identifies the subject account by name, type of business in which it is engaged, its address, and the date the report was written.

Business Classification

This is the first column of the report and it shows *where* the customer buys and *what* types of merchandise he buys. Under each market designation is a code date, which reveals to the creditor the freshness of the information. For example, the code 928-459 under Chicago denotes that Chicago contributors received requests from the bureau and supplied information on or before 928, which means September 28. The last portion of the code is a processing number and is of no significance to the credit analyst.

The proper interpretation of this column reveals the customer's buying practices. Is the customer buying in too many markets? Are these markets his normal sources of supply? Customers who buy in many markets when fewer sources could be utilized to better advantage may indicate creditors' lack of confidence. Or, it may indicate a badly broken stock, which can result when too many

FIGURE 26-3
Credit Interchange Bureau Report

F. 6

 NATIONAL ASSOCIATION of CREDIT MANAGEMENT

Credit Interchange Report

OFFICES IN PRINCIPAL CITIES

JOHN DOE
DOE MERCANTILE COMPANY

ANOKA, MINNESOTA
401 MAIN STREET
ANOKA COUNTY

OCTOBER 11, 197-

The accuracy of this Report is not guaranteed. Its contents are gathered in good faith from members and sent to you by this Bureau without liability for negligence in procuring, collecting, communiccting or failing to communicate the informaiton so gathered. The purpose of this report is intended for use in the extension only of Commercial or Business Credit.

BUSINESS CLASSIFICATION	HOW LONG SOLD	DATE OF LAST SALE	HIGHEST RECENT CREDIT	NOW OWING INCLUDING NOTES	PAST DUE	TERMS OF SALE	DIS-COUNTS	PAYS WHEN DUE	DAYS SLOW	COMMENTS
MINNESOTA 926-142										
#117 GENM						UNFILLED ORDER $310.00				
*236 GENM	yrs	7-70	2100	950	950	note 60			180	
*142 GENM	yrs	9-70	300	165	45	60		x		
138 GROC	1969	9-70	150	85				x		
*137 SHOE	1970	6-70	79	79	79	2-15-60			60	
*153 CLO	yrs	1-70	1350	150	150	60			180	
						in hands of attorney				
239 SHOE	1970	9-70	95	95		60		x		
215 RBR	1969	2-70	114					x		
*240 RBR	yrs	8-70	1000	340	325				60-90	
						UNFILLED ORDER OF $85.00				
165 RBR	2 yrs.	4-70	67			2-15-30			90	
277 SHOE	1970	7-70	284			2-15-60		x		
*320 FDP	3 yrs	8-70	145	95	20	2-10-30		x	30	
*310 PPR	yrs	8-70	475	220	220	30		x	30-60	
323 CONF	yrs	3-70	104			30		x	15	
*347 GROC	yrs	8-70	396	175	145	30			60-75	
453 CLO	yrs	8-70	313			REFUSED IN 12-62			120	
*OMAHA & NEBR 929-20										
418 GROC	yrs	6-70	193						60	
*140 GENM	8-70	9-70	750	750	243	60		no Pay exp.		
264 HFGS	9-70	9-70	325	325		60		no Pay exp.		
*532 ELEC	yrs	1-70	574	477	477	60			150	now cod
*CHICAGO 928-459										
*B120 GENM	yrs	7-70	450	336	120	30			60	
B25 CLO						refused on interchange report				
*ST. LOUIS 929-413										
*730 SHOE	yrs	4-70	249	90	90	45			120	
*624 SHOE	new	5-70	375	325	225	30			90	checks ret
*CENTRAL IOWA 928-24										
*178 GENM	yrs	6-70	165	165	165	2-10-30			60	
BU 5 MS				4822	3254					

CONFIDENTIAL

FOR CREDIT DEPARTMENT PERSONNEL USE ONLY • ANY MEMBER VIOLATING THE CONFIDENTIAL NATURE OF THIS REPORT IS SUBJECT TO SUSPENSION suppliers sell the same line to the same customer. In general, this column should give the credit executive a fair idea of the kind of business and some of the practices in which the risk is engaged. It is not too difficult to appraise the desirability of the risk's buying habits and also to estimate the proportion between total purchases of a line and the purchases made from the credit analyst's company.

How Long Sold

The column "How Long Sold" should be considered as a measure of confidence. When business dealings have continued satisfactorily over the years, it is much more reassuring than dealings of short duration. Credit risks that have recorded satisfactory experiences for many years are usually regarded highly in the credit and sales professions. In addition, the length of creditors' experiences gives a clear indication of the reliability of the information to follow. If, however, an established customer suddenly opens new accounts and forsakes his old established sources of supply, it may mean that his credit is no longer acceptable. One of the early indications of financial difficulties may be the erratic seeking of new sources of supply because of an account's inability to meet current obligations. This same technique may also mean that the risk has overbought in proportion to his ability to pay.

Date of Last Sale

Ledger information which does not disclose the date of last sale is valueless. Credit information not only must be adequate to make a rational decision, it also must be timely. Old information of a derogatory nature has little meaning, because past credit weaknesses may have been overcome and the present-day payment record may be satisfactory. Conversely, former satisfactory performance can easily be nullified by current difficulties which result in slow payment of obligations. Furthermore, this column should be compared with the "How Long Sold" column and the "Paying Record" column; the former to determine whether new sources are being sought by the risk, and the latter to study the trend of the payment habits of the account.

Highest Recent Credit

This column is another measure of the creditors' confidence in the subject. If the figures in this column are large relative to the payments being made on the account, it is an indication that creditors may have an undue interest in the business. There are some other uses of these data which are particularly valuable to the credit executive. For example, the setting of a credit limit may be the average high credit accepted by other suppliers. From the sales viewpoint, it is a simple matter to estimate the proportion of any single line that is supplied by a particular creditor firm.

Now Owing

There is much value in comparing this column with financial statement data. Many credit executives regard the total of the figures in this column to be representative of the accounts payable figure in the customer's balance sheet. There is a strong possibility that this is a valid assumption, provided, of course, both data are of the same date. Although the National Association of Credit Management does not claim that the reports reveal the total indebtedness of the subject, its representativeness can quickly be checked with the balance sheet of the same date. The association does warn its members that if the total of this column is greater than the amount shown on the balance sheet, a complete investigation of the subject should be undertaken. It is also desirable to compare the total amount owing as well as the individual amounts owed with reports over a period of time. This comparison will indicate the improvement or deterioration of the subject's affairs with his creditors. Comparison of this column should also be made with the "Highest Recent Credit" column, as this discloses whether he is currently heavily indebted to all sources of supply or whether most of his accounts with creditors are in balance. The "Now Owing" figures should always be appraised with regard to seasonal variations and other conditions which may affect the activity of the business.

Past Due

Great care should be exercised in appraising the information shown in this column. Under most circumstances relatively large amounts in this column can be regarded as an early indicator of financial difficulties. It should, however, be checked against the "Date of Last Sale" column and the "Paying Record" column to ascertain a clearer concept of the problem. A report that shows little indebtedness, on the other hand, might be an indication of credit refusal and hence must be checked against the paying record column to clarify the condition. A single amount past due may be a legitimately disputed account rather than deterioration of the subject's paying habits, and such isolated amounts should be checked with the "Comments" column.

A large amount shown as past due should not immediately be appraised as an indication of an unfavorable trend. The total amount in this column should be analyzed relative to other things. Oftentimes a comparison of these data with the amount owing, highest credit, and comments columns will disclose that the subject is overcoming a period of adversity.

Terms of Sale

It is necessary that credit executives be well acquainted with the terms and discounts which prevail in various industries. While c.o.d. and c.i.a. terms are sometimes indicative of a lack of confidence, they are also standard terms in some industries and cannot be regarded as restrictive. Restrictive terms may also be the result of the request of the subject and accordingly should be viewed as a favorable factor rather than as an unfavorable factor. The "Terms of Sale" column should be compared with the "Paying Record" column to determine whether the subject is forgoing profitable cash discounts. This latter comparison may also help to explain some of the variations found in the report.

Paying Record

The "Paying Record" section of the report consists of three columns which are subtitled discounts, pays when due, and days slow. These columns are not to be regarded as having separate value to the overall report, but merely represent a summarization and explanation of facts shown in the other columns. An analysis of other columns will help to avoid erroneous assumptions which may be based on an average appraisal of these columns. In other words, the fact that a certain number of accounts are discounting, are paying when due, or are slow is of little significance unless "Comments" and other facts are also evaluated at the same time.

Comments

This column of the report provides a space for information which can lend clarity to the ledger facts recorded in preceding columns. Oftentimes the trend of payments experienced by creditors will appear in this column. In general, data which show no change, improvement, slowness, and the like are valuable in determining the stability of the risk. Any report which shows a large number of unfilled orders in this column should be regarded with pessimism and a signal that further investigation might be advisable. When comments are particularly unfavorable, such as "collected by attorney" or "refused," an appraisal of the general character of the report should be undertaken. Particularly, the date of the transaction involved should be determined so that unfavorable information of long standing is not regarded as current.

When to Use a Credit Interchange Report

The NACM recommends that a credit interchange report be requested each time a new order is investigated, when an unusually large order is received from a customer, and when a large number of direct inquiries are received on a customer. Likewise, a report should be requested on all slow-pay accounts, and when the creditor is anticipating special collection action against the debtor enterprise. Furthermore, the association recommends that creditors keep close watch on important customers, as well as doubtful accounts, by use of the automatic revision service. This service gives the member a series of new, up-to-date reports at regular intervals designated by him. Such a series of reports permits the creditor to keep a close check on the paying habits of his customers and also to determine whether the share of volume secured from good customers is in proper proportion.

APPRAISAL OF THE CREDIT INTERCHANGE SYSTEM

Much of the general worth of the Credit Interchange System is partially indicated by the fact that it is one of the most widely and frequently used sources of credit information. Strength in the system accrues from its operation by NACM, which is one of the nation's largest, most respected and influential trade associations. Each company represented in the association is either an interchange report user or a potential member of the system. The varied services of the association and the high esteem with which these services are regarded by members lend additional support to the strength and overall value of the system.

Perhaps the system's greatest weakness stems from the fact that it is a cooperative venture, and hence of necessity it depends upon its many members' reacting in a like manner in originally supplying ledger information and in answering subsequent inquiries. For the maximum total effectiveness of the system each member must exercise promptness, thoroughness, and exert a high measure of fidelity. Additionally, each credit department member who answers inquiries and analyzes reports affects the quality of the system. Unless these persons are trained to understand the reports and the workings of the system, it cannot be presumed to be of maximum effectiveness. In those sections of the country where communications are easy, and where members of the system are actively interested in using and promoting the interchange system, it seems to work well. In some sections, though, these qualities are not present and the system is unsatisfactory. Despite these weaknesses, a cooperative method of gathering ledger information is the most efficient method known to the industry. To overcome the shortage of trained credit department personnel, the association has developed educational programs and published a great deal of literature, portions of which are designed toward a clearer concept of the Credit Interchange System.

Other than what might be implied from a careful analysis of the credit interchange report, it does not reveal information concerning either the subject's history and business background, nor the character and responsibility of management. These are but two of the six types of information needed by credit management to arrive at a sound credit decision as set forth in Chapter 23. From the preceding discussion it is obvious that the credit interchange report reveals most comprehensively a customer's immediate past and present payment record, and if the recorded data are properly analyzed a fair estimate of the customer's financial condition can be gained. Some credit executives regard the interchange report as supplemental to other types of reports for these reasons.

Despite the apparent weakness of the interchange report in fulfilling all of the needs of credit management, it should be emphasized that ledger information is regarded as one of the most important types of information used in the industry. Following the high importance of ledger information are the financial statement, the creditor's past experience, and then history and antecedents. While credit management needs several types of credit information, there is considerable variation in the value attached to the several types and the frequency with which some kinds of data are needed. The superiority of the credit interchange report stems from the frequency with which ledger data can change as contrasted with other types of information. Antecedents, method of operation, and financial statements do not change frequently, but only in the course of rather extended periods of time. It is the rapidity with which ledger data are observed to change which contributed to NACM's development of the interchange system. The oldest information which a member can receive from a completed credit interchange canvass is 120 days, whereas other agencies normally revise their reports less often. Because ledger data change frequently, each new credit interchange report should assist the creditor in making proper and current revision of his customer's accounts. Finally, the interchange report is not intended to replace financial and operating statements. The best use of the interchange report is in conjunction with these statements. When this is done, credit management has marshaled what many consider to be the most valuable data used in making a credit decision.

REVIEW AND DISCUSSION QUESTIONS

1. Explain what is meant by the term "ledger experience."
2. Compare and contrast the activities of the NACM with those of Dun & Bradstreet.
3. Compare and contrast the activities of the NACM with those of specialized mercantile agencies.
4. Describe the method of operation of the National Credit Interchange System.
5. Analyze the Credit Interchange Report reproduced in Figure 26-3. Would you accept or reject this customer's order for $435 of men's shoes? Why?
6. What is meant by the statement that each of the affiliated bureaus of National Credit Interchange System is allocated a "zone of operation"?
7. Why is it important to analyze fully the interchange report and not arrive at a decision based on one or a few columns?
8. What does the "Highest Recent Credit" column show?
9. What are advantages or strong points of the system? Discuss each you have listed.
10. List the major weaknesses in the system. How would you suggest these be corrected?
11. Would you use other types of credit information to augment the interchange report? If so, what are the other types? Explain.

27

Financial Statements — Analysis and Interpretation

Financial analysis of a credit seeker's condition is one of the processes involved in commercial credit granting. "Such an analysis involves an examination of balance sheet and operating statement details as well as a review of trial balance information, schedules supporting financial statements, and also consideration of economic conditions generally and in the industry in which the possible debtor is engaged."[1]

The balance sheet is a statement of the financial condition of a company as of a moment of time. In other words, it is a photograph of the concern showing the assets,[2] liabilities, and net worth as of the instant of time the "picture is taken." The profit and loss or operating statement, on the other hand, covers a period of time and reflects the sales, cost of goods sold, expenses, and net profit or loss during the interval covered. The statement of source and application of funds is another type of information of increasing significance to the credit grantor. This statement[3] is an outgrowth of recognition that standard methods of statement analysis provide only partial information concerning a company's earning power. The statement of source and application of funds is not new, but it has become more and more popular because of a widening spread between net income or loss and the actual flow of funds.

1 / *Credit Management Handbook* (2d ed.; Homewood, Ill.: Richard D. Irwin, Inc., 1965), p. 188.

2 / It is assumed that the reader will have had a course in the principles of accounting or practical experience covering the accounting field. If this is not the case, the reader is referred to any basic accounting text for definitions of accounting terms used in this and the succeeding chapter.

3 / Larrimore Wright, "How Credit Grantors Can Get the Most from CPAs," *Credit and Financial Management*, August 1970, p. 38.

REASONS FOR FINANCIAL STATEMENTS

In general, the credit manager needs financial statements for the same reason he needs other types of credit information—to arrive at a rational and sound credit decision. Without this type of information, a credit decision would rest upon factors which do not reveal the customer's ability to pay the credit obligation. Because financial data most often reveal this capacity or probability, credit managers rely heavily on financial statements to guide their decision-making processes. No other source can give the credit analyst a clearer insight into the customer's financial condition and capacity or earning ability. Likewise financial statements reflect the integrity of the business management, which is charged with the decision-making functions of the concern. However, statement analysis is not the sole basis of the credit decision; it is only *one* segment of a larger process known as credit analysis. Supplementary data are often required to permit the correct interpretation of what the financial statement reveals.

At this point, a word of caution is appropriate. The credit analyst should not rely too much on those financial statements in which the analyst does not know all the accounting subtleties involved. Some of these can at times be misleading. For example, problems can arise in the analysis of the "pool of funds concept" valuation of goodwill and in the handling of franchise fees as income rather than a footnoted capital payment.

Other problems in the use of financial statements have been pointed out by Dr. Rensis Likert:[4]

> By ignoring a large proportion of their assets, many industries often make sizeable errors in their own financial statements.
> These assets include the loyalty and effectiveness of their human organization. They also include supplier loyalty, shareholder loyalty, customer loyalty, and the firm's reputation in the community. But none of these assets is represented in the balance sheet—and virtually no firms keep rigorous quantitative surveillance over them in order to learn whether they are increasing in value from year to year, and by how much.

Requests for financial statements have increased tremendously in recent years, not only between the cash lender and business borrower but also between the seller of goods and buyer of goods. One of the reasons for this increasing demand for financial statement analysis and interpretation is the growing number of executives who are occupying positions on the credit management level, and who have

4 / Rensis Likert, "Human Resources—the Hidden Assets of Your Firm," reprinted from *Credit and Financial Management,* June 1969, p. 20. Copyright 1969 by the National Association of Credit Management, New York, N.Y. Also see "Why Accountants Need to Tell a Fuller Story," *Business Week,* February 6, 1971, p. 86.

been trained at universities and colleges in this technique of credit determination. Undoubtedly, even greater use of this source of credit information will be made in future years as some of these same individuals occupy an even greater number of decision-making positions.

As more firms and banks call for balance sheets and profit and loss statements from their prospective customers, these credit applicants have come to recognize the necessity of making a good showing in order to obtain on credit the merchandise or money desired. Business enterprises which trade on their credit have been forced to adopt accepted accounting practices and techniques, to keep organized and accurate books of record, and to employ the services of competent and recognized accountants who can certify as to the correctness of the information reported.

The value of the CPA and the increasing quantity of "other information" that he is developing in recent years are brought out in the following quotation:[5]

> Special purpose financial information is thus increasingly being provided by the CPA. Different statement users require different information, and audited financial statements are often directed primarily at investors. Where specific needs of the financial institution diverge, the lender should arrange with his client to have the CPA furnish supplemental financial information. Increasingly, requests are being made for such special purpose financial information as the following [abridged]:
>
> 1. Additional data on specific items in the financial statements.
> 2. Extent of insurance coverage.
> 3. Status of review by the Internal Revenue Service of federal income tax returns.
> 4. Business relationships with other companies.
> 5. Statement of source and application of funds.
> 6. Interim-period financial statements.
> 7. Projections of sources and users of cash.
> 8. Pro forma financial statements.

SOURCES OF STATEMENTS

The question now arises as to where the credit grantor can obtain financial statements reflecting the financial status of the prospective borrower of funds or buyer of goods.

5 / Wright, *op. cit.*, pp. 37-39. A somewhat opposite view is expressed in the quotation, "Today's financial statements are usually prepared 'in accordance with generally accepted accounting principles.' But nobody knows what this phrase means." Harry J. Kane in "What's Your Financial Statement Worth?" *Credit and Financial Management,* August 1969, p. 16. Also see Joseph L. Osberger, "Financial Statements—Help or Hindrance?" *Credit and Financial Management,* January 1971, p. 20.

Directly from Risk

One of the accepted sources is to ask the credit seeker directly to supply financial statements. Some firms have adopted a policy of not only asking for a financial statement prior to the time of initial credit acceptance but also asking for interim and annual statements. Such a practice then becomes almost an automatic procedure on the part of the credit customer. Very often a standardized form, similar to the one illustrated in Figure 23-1, is prescribed and is furnished to the customer for completion.

Commercial banks and accounting firms may also be regarded as a "direct" source of financial statements. Banks often supply the statements rendered to them by businesses for credit purposes. In addition, the commercial creditor may obtain the statement through the customer's bank. Both the bank and the commercial creditors use the statements for essentially the same purpose. Accounting firms that have certified to the correctness of the customer's accounting procedures, as well as prepared the financial statements, may on request from the debtor firm supply statements to creditors.

Indirectly from Mercantile Credit Agencies

The reports furnished by Dun & Bradstreet, Inc. and by most of the special mercantile agencies generally contain financial statements that have been furnished to the agency by the prospective credit customer. These reports often contain financial information covering a period of three to five years, in order to show the financial trends occurring in the business operation. These agencies have made a concentrated attempt in recent years to gather financial statements on as many business firms investigated as possible, thus improving their coverage of the financial aspects of credit information for a subscriber to their services.

PURPOSES OF STATEMENT ANALYSIS

When a credit man approaches the analysis of financial statements, he has some specific goal in mind. The exact nature of his goal depends on the characteristics of the credit case at hand. For example, he may have what appears to be a one-time order to approve or disapprove; or, he may expect this customer to become a repeat buyer and the creditor-debtor relationship to exist over many years to come. Under the former situation he would spend less time evaluating the financial statements and arriving at a decision. If, however, the latter circumstance prevails, much more time will be devoted to the financial analysis, and an attempt will be made to determine the probable continuing profitability of the customer.

Fortunately, the content and structure of financial statements permit flexibility in their analysis, and the precise nature of the analysis can be tailored to the nature of the credit risk.

In general, the analysis of financial statements can uncover three major factors. It can determine a firm's liquidity condition, its solvency condition, and its managerial efficiency. If the credit analyst is only concerned with determination of the liquidity condition of his credit case, then in all likelihood the customer is regarded in terms of a one-time order. When, however, the credit risk appears to be one which will be continuing, the analyst will be more concerned with the long-run financial prospects of his customer. Hence liquidity, solvency, and managerial efficiency may have to be determined in order to arrive at a correct credit decision. The *liquidity* of a business is concerned with its ability to meet day-to-day current obligations. The *solvency* of a business is indicated by its dependence on financial support from creditors as contrasted with the financial investment by its owners. *Managerial efficiency* as revealed by financial statement analysis determines the ability of the firm to operate profitably and successfully over a long period of time. Whether the analyst approaches the credit case to uncover all three financial conditions or only one or two of them depends entirely on the nature of the risk and what the analyst must know to arrive at an objective decision.

In analyzing financial statements, it must be realized that in any line of trade there are certain proportions of assets and liabilities which are more conducive to successful operation than others. There also are certain proportions which are healthy in that they indicate an ability to meet maturing obligations. Thus the proportion of assets to liabilities should be such that the assets supplied by creditors are in no larger proportion than is indicated for safety, for continued operations, and for due division of the risks of the venture between creditors' capital and owners' capital. The debts also should be properly proportioned to the liquidity requirements. In a line of trade where most of the assets are highly liquid, a larger debt structure may be supported by these assets than would be true in a line of trade where a large proportion of the resources is invested in fixed or nonliquid form. There also is a proper proportioning of the assets and liabilities to assure continuation of the business—what might be called the safety factor. Too heavy a debt structure is not a sound financial policy with which to face a period of declining sales. On the other hand, a too conservative borrowing policy may not act to the injury of creditors but may interfere with the profitable operation of the business.

The assets should be distributed in such a way that those which are acquired will result in profitable operations. For example, a common fault in many retail firms is having too large a proportion of the assets invested in buildings. This also may be true of a manufacturing venture; too large a proportion of its resources may be tied up in fixed form. This often interferes with the ability of the business to purchase its desired stock of material. With a merchant, it may interfere with his ability either to carry accounts receivable in sufficient amount to take advantage of the sales potential sought by the offering of credit service or to stock an inventory sufficiently varied and selected to be attractive to his customers. Too large an investment of resources in a fixed form leads to the situation sometimes referred to as "frozen." The firm then may be good, but very slow, in meeting payments. Its resources are invested largely in assets which are not quickly converted into cash during the normal processes of business and, in the event of emergency, converted only at considerable sacrifice of value. In case of an emergency the firm may fail, despite the possession of large resources, because its inability to meet currently maturing liabilities may lead to so much impatience on the part of the creditors that failure will be precipitated by some drastic legal action.

The capital of the business should be in proper proportion to the needs—by this is meant that the resources supplied by the investors, or owners, should be relative to the needs of the business. This may be both a matter of size and a matter of proportion. In connection with the matter of size, sufficient owner capital should be supplied in each type of business to enable it to operate on a scale which is conducive to success. If a business is started without sufficient capital to operate on an efficient scale, it will be hampered in competition and growth. Relative to the proportion concept, a sufficient proportion of the capital should be supplied by outside creditors to distribute the risks properly between owned capital and borrowed capital. Certainly the proportion of the capital supplied by owners should not be so small that creditors are asked to take ownership risks in return for only creditor profits.

The trend, or direction-of-change, concept is slightly different. The credit analyst not only is faced with the question of the financial status of the firm today, but he also is concerned with where the firm has been and where it is going. These latter concepts are as significant as the current financial position. A firm that falls short of the ideal risk, but that has been improving over a period of time, may be a better credit risk than the firm that is above the ideal but has been deteriorating over a period of years. The trend concept also recognizes that what should be thought of as the standard or ideal may change with business conditions. While deterioration may be shown, the fact that business conditions have been difficult would mean that a comparatively small deterioration may be more favorable than would slight improvement under more prosperous conditions.

In analyzing financial statements, the credit analyst should be alert to the success or failure of managerial efficiency in the conduct of the business. Certainly, managerial efficiency over a period of time will affect the ability to pay even current debts. The credit analyst also may test whether the management has been efficient in conducting the business so as to meet new or unexpected conditions. Thus in a period of declining business, it may be seen whether the management has properly adjusted its asset structure to the new situation. In a period of business improvement, questions may be raised whether management has been guilty of expanding too rapidly, though not properly prepared to meet the change which will eventually come; or whether, in a period of improvement, it has strengthened the financial structure so as to be prepared for any future change.

The comparison of these various statement items should be a matter of appraising both the asset and liability structure and earning structure. It cannot be too strongly emphasized that it is the analysis of all the financial statements, not analysis of just the balance sheet, that is sought in order to make a complete, well-rounded analysis of these important business parts. The operating statement should be subjected to close scrutiny. There are a number of specific devices for testing managerial efficiency. For example, the credit analyst may examine the gross profit which the firm earns. He may examine the percentage of particular expense items as compared to the norm for that trade. He may see whether the advertising or selling expense of the credit applicant is too high; whether the firm is spending too much for rent; whether its administrative expense is unduly heavy. The finer classification of the expense items will permit some very exact and detailed examination of operations. Unfortunately, in credit analysis, the credit man is too often content with a balance sheet and sales figure. For this reason, this technique of using the operating statement is not as common in credit work as its importance would warrant.

PRELIMINARY APPRAISAL OF FINANCIAL STATEMENTS

As the credit analyst begins his appraisal of financial statements, his first steps should be those which test the validity of the stated values. The financial statements present certain facts which, if good accounting practices are followed, the accountant will state as accurately as possible. The credit man, on the other hand, approaches the analysis as an outsider. Because of this, he is likely to be skeptical about some features of the statements and hence will examine them critically. Oftentimes, he will try to determine whether the business management has presented a financial statement which overstates financial condition. Some business concerns presenting statements will, for obvious reasons, desire to have them appear as favorable as the circumstances permit. At times, even with no intention of dishonesty, there is an attempt to present facts in a light more favorable than the situation would justify.

Some of the various ways in which financial statements may be adjusted to present a more favorable appearance than the true circumstances warrant include window dressing, undue optimism, inability to reflect current facts, and actual falsification.

Window Dressing or "Putting the Best Foot Forward"

This is not an attempt actually to falsify anything, but merely to present the various aspects in as favorable a light as possible. Knowing that the credit analyst will seek certain relationships in the statement as a test of goodness, the firm may attempt to manipulate its affairs immediately prior to statement time in such a fashion as to make these relationships highly favorable. For example, knowing that a good cash balance and a very liquid current position are considered desirable by creditors, the firm may, for the month immediately preceding the year-end, work strenuously to collect its accounts receivable and accumulate cash for statement purposes. Thus, at the year-end it may have a better-than-normal cash position. It also may defer certain spending which otherwise would take place, to avoid increasing liabilities or draining cash.

A further step in this direction may be taken by following the practice of continuing normal purchases but not entering the goods received in the asset account, Inventory, or the corresponding accounts payable in the liability account, Accounts Payable. This is what might be described as poor accounting practice rather than falsification or deliberate dishonesty.

An effort may be made, just before the statements are prepared, to deposit in the bank a number of items which may be returned unpaid. These may include *N.S.F.* and other bad checks which have been held as collection items; it may even include some drafts or notes which have been previously presented and refused. With the cooperation of the bank, the firm may be able to deposit these and have them included for the last day of the fiscal period as cash in bank, although knowing that within a few days they may be returned unpaid, at which time these items will have to be charged back to the deposit account and again included on their books as unpaid items. There are differences of opinion as to whether this step is to be considered window dressing or actual falsification. Needless to say, it is hard to prove falsification in such cases.

Undue Optimism or "Reluctance to Face Unpleasant Realities"

As with window dressing, this is not usually considered a form of falsification. Instead, it is simply a reflection of a retail firm's natural optimism that certain items on the financial statement will in time return to the value at which they are now being carried. For example, certain inventory items may be carried at a much higher figure than the present market value, thus reflecting the reluctance of this firm to face the unpleasant reality that it has done a poor job of buying or selling, or perhaps both.

Other items of a current nature, while not deliberately falsified, may be treated with undue optimism. It is not at all uncommon, upon investigation, to find that deposits in a defunct bank are still carried as a current asset,[6] or that securities that are not readily converted into cash are continued in a securities account, sometimes at a value considerably higher than their true market value. Because of the difference between the valuations placed upon some of these items by the prospective debtor and by the credit analyst, some credit men refuse to consider these miscellaneous items unless a very definite statement is given as to their true composition.

Inability to Reflect Current Facts

There is a tendency for the beginner in credit work to take the figures shown in financial statements as definite and absolutely accurate. It should be clearly understood, for example, that the depreciated value of certain fixed assets may be quite accurate from an accounting point of view, but from a credit-determination standpoint the actual value of these fixed assets on the present-day market is much more useful and realistic. Not only does such reasoning apply to the fixed-asset item on the balance sheet, but it also has merit in setting a "true" value on accounts receivable (less reserve for bad debts) and on cash on hand (less commitments made but not always shown on the balance sheet).

6 / It would be falsification to include deposits in a bank that has no chance of ever opening. If, however, the closing is of a temporary nature until such time as it is reorganized, then undue optimism is involved.

It might be questioned whether such an entry would not be discovered by an auditor. This is correct *if* the company's books are audited. However, many statements from small concerns are made by the owner, and no outside accountant is involved at all.

Actual Falsification

As a matter of routine procedure, the credit analyst, when first analyzing a statement, should start with a question in his mind as to whether the statement does present any false conditions. The first thing to be done when handling a new statement should be to add the statement to make sure it is correctly totaled; to inspect it to see that it is dated and signed; and if possible, to see that the evidence of mailing is preserved. The statement that has round figures which are clearly estimated rather than book figures should be viewed with suspicion. Notation of this condition should have been made in order to forestall any claims of falsification. The main point to emphasize is not that many false financial statements will be presented, but that a careful credit analyst will view every statement with the thought in mind that the first test to which it should be subjected is one for correctness and honesty in the presentation of statement facts. Obviously, nothing can be gained by analyzing a statement which has been falsified or which has been doctored in such a fashion as to present a more favorable position than would be supported by the true conditions, were they known.

A further exaggeration of statement items may be brought about by even more deliberately dishonest practices. We may consider, item by item, some of the practices of this type.

Cash. If the first of these items, the cash account, is to be properly understood, this account should be divided into Cash on Hand and Cash in Bank. It is possible to exaggerate the Cash on Hand item by including certain items in the cash drawer which are not actually cash. For example, the owner or members of the firm may follow the careless, and probably not approved, practice of taking cash out of the cash drawer and substituting their I.O.U's. For statement purposes these are clearly an exaggeration of the cash item if they are included in Cash on Hand. As a matter of practice, firm members also may include as cash certain advances made to officers of the firm. They would justify this by saying that it is handled just as petty cash would be handled, and that when the expenses are presented these items will be charged to the proper expense account and, of course, taken out of cash. Temporarily, however, this method has the effect of exaggerating the cash item. Advances to salesmen for traveling expenses may be handled in this same fashion with, of course, resulting distortion of the statement values. The credit analyst, in order to check this situation, will note whether cash on hand is unusually large and, if so, be skeptical of it. He also will notice if there has been window dressing practiced in connection with the bank account by observing whether the balance at statement time is in agreement with the normal balance indicated by the bank in the course of the investigation.

Accounts Receivable. This is another item which may be adjusted to show a more favorable situation than the true circumstances warrant. It is possible to be unduly optimistic concerning the collectibility of certain receivables. Continuing to include in accounts receivable those items which are not likely to be collected, or which are very definitely going to become bad-debt losses, clearly exaggerates the value of this asset. Further falsification of this item may be practiced by arbitrarily including certain accounts which are not actually trade receivables, such as amounts due from the business officers and employees. While these are receivables, they are not receivables which will be collected in the ordinary course of business. Including them in the accounts receivables tends to present a more favorable situation than the true circumstances warrant, since this leads the analyst to think of them as current assets when they should be regarded as noncurrent assets and as not contributing to the true liquidity status of the firm.

More deliberate falsification also may be attempted by writing up fictitious accounts receivable. Receivables may be set up with existing firms for imaginary transactions or for imaginary firms. This increases the asset falsely and also increases the sales. Often this device is adopted not only to deceive creditors, but to cover defalcations of employees. In the process of covering thefts, other assets may be falsified and nonexistent inventories created or other unreal assets placed on the books. The outside credit man can, by a careful analysis of the statements, often detect these frauds as soon as or sooner than the owner.

Inventory. Merchandise is a very difficult item to evaluate properly. There are numerous opportunities for honest differences of opinion as to the actual value of the merchandise inventory. Try as one will, it is very difficult to get an inventory valuation which is agreed to by all people concerned. Under these circumstances it is readily apparent that a firm attempting to place more favorable valuation upon the inventory than might be justified would have little difficulty in supporting this valuation on the basis of honest differences of opinion. While taking and valuing the inventory, one can be optimistic or pessimistic. Whichever method is followed will necessarily change not only the assets shown but also the profits for the period. Because of this effect on profits the credit analyst may be deceived as to the true condition. It also may be possible to change the tax which is to be paid by the firm in a particular year. In addition to this unduly optimistic valuation, which may deceive the credit analyst, it is possible to falsify the statements more deliberately by including in the merchandise inventory certain goods, the invoices for which are not included in the liability item of accounts payable. This, of course, has a double effect, that of increasing the assets and decreasing the liabilities, thus making the statement even more favorable than would be the case were just one of these items changed.

Fixed Assets. The fixed assets may be even more difficult to value than the inventory. From a statement standpoint, the credit analyst naturally is desirous of having them properly shown on the statement at their book value, with the depreciation reserve shown separately, rather than having depreciation deducted and only the net value given. For purposes of analysis, it is clearly desirable to know what depreciation policy is being followed by the firm and at least to see whether it is conservative and in line with good practice. Since this is another of those items which directly affect the profit and loss statement, the credit analyst also is anxious to test the profit shown by determining if it is on the basis of proper depreciation policies. Sometimes a check on the valuation placed upon the fixed assets may be made by comparing with the valuation and description given in an agency report or with that arising from the personal knowledge of the credit man.

Accounts Payable. In the previous discussion of the exaggeration of the inventory item, it was pointed out that the liability Accounts Payable may be correspondingly reduced by omitting the invoice as a liability although entering the merchandise received as an asset. A check upon the accounts payable item may be readily supplied by comparing it with the total owing as revealed by a complete trade investigation. Another indication of possible minimization of the accounts payable may be supplied by a very unsatisfactory trade experience report, when compared with a much more favorable current position than is consistent with the payment record. Certainly the possession of a large claimed cash account and a rather liquid position would not be consistent with slowness in the trade, or with the existence of a small accounts payable item. The comparison of accounts payable against purchases to get the turnover should indicate the period of payment; thus, 12 turns of accounts payable would roughly indicate payment in 30 days. With this turnover rate there should be a corresponding trade record of discount and pays when due. If the trade reports do not support the turnover rate, as shown by this calculation, it may indicate that the accounts payable on the statement have been reduced, or it may mean that careful avoidance of purchases just before statement time has resulted in an abnormal lowering of this item.

Other Payables. Notes payable may be checked against the bank letters to see whether the bank report of the notes payable is consistent with the amounts shown on the statement. The mortgages payable may, of course, be compared with the agency reports showing the mortgages, which are matters of public record. If any of them has been omitted from the statement, this should be revealed by comparison with the public record information.

Bonds can hardly be omitted because it is a matter of public knowledge that these are outstanding, and they should be very readily checked against this fact.

Up to this point it has been shown that a hint of possible exaggeration or falsification may be obtained at various points during the process of the analysis. Certain comparisons, or inconsistencies of certain facts with others, should be a warning to the analyst that he should look for some exaggeration or incorrectness in the statement. These indications will be further commented upon in the discussion of the methods of analysis.

The maximum benefit from falsification is, of course, obtained by a minimization of liabilities. In changing a liability item, the falsification must be deliberate rather than a little undue optimism or exaggeration. The falsification of liabilities usually involves deliberate dishonesty, whereas the falsification of assets may be brought about in such a way that it is more difficult to prove deliberate falsification. For this reason firms may be more cautious about changing liabilities than they may be about exaggerating or being unduly optimistic about the assets.

FINANCIAL STATEMENT LEGISLATION

Because the financial statement may be a vital factor in the decision of a firm to sell its goods on credit to a prospective credit seeker, it is imperative that safeguards be provided to prevent the furnishing of false and misleading information to creditors. For this reason, most of the states[7] and the federal government have enacted legislation which holds certain abuses of financial statements to be a misdemeanor subject to civil and criminal prosecution. A comparison of the state and federal requirements for prosecuting credit seekers who have submitted false financial statements is shown in Table 27-1. Although there has been no federal legislation expressly passed for the prosecution of makers of false financial statements, Section 215 of the United States Criminal Code is the basis of controlling those who would use the mails for transmitting false statements in order to obtain credit.[8]

A study of Table 27-1 will reveal that the requirements for prosecution under the various state laws are very similar to those

7 / These are generally known as "false pretense" statutes.

8 / Thomas F. Peckenham, "Keeping the Mails Free of Credit Frauds," *Credit and Financial Management*, September 1968, p. 18.

TABLE 27-1
Prosecution of Makers of False Financial Statements
(state and federal laws)

Requirements	State Laws	Federal Law
In writing and signed ...	Must be proved	Must be proved
Made knowingly	Must be proved	Must be proved
For credit purposes	Must be proved	Must be proved
To be relied upon	Must be proved	Must be proved
Materially false	Must be proved	Must be proved
Fraudulent	Need not be proved	Must be proved
Use of mails	Need not be proved	Must be proved
Place of prosection	Country where statement made	Where statement made or received

under the federal enactment pertaining to offenses against the postal service. Under each set of laws, the burden of proof rests upon the prosecution to show that the financial statement was submitted in writing and was signed; that the maker of the statement knew that the statement was false (under most state laws it is sufficient to show that the maker "should" have known it was false); that the statement was made for credit purposes with the intent that it be relied upon in any credit decision; and that the false part of the statement misrepresented the facts to such a degree that the decision would have been otherwise if the true facts had been known.

It is at this point that the similarities cease and the very important differences begin. In fact, these differences often are the deciding factors as to which set of laws may be best for successful prosecution. The concept of fraud has been the subject of a great many court decisions and legal entanglements. Suffice it to say here that many state laws do not require proof that property was actually obtained on the basis of a false financial statement. Proof that the facts were simply misrepresented has been sufficient for conviction under state laws. On the other hand, in the opinions expressed by some courts (including federal) fraud has been identified with the actual passage of goods as a result of a decision based upon a false and "fraudulent" financial statement. Here again the reader is cautioned to consult competent legal counsel in relation to the conditions prevailing in his situation.

A clearer cut difference is found in the fact that use of the mails is a prerequisite for prosecution under the federal enactment, whereas this is not a condition under the various state laws. To aid the proof that the statement was transmitted through the mails, the self-mailing type of statement form has been developed (see Figure 27-1). The postmark on the back of the statement is thus proof that the mails were used to deliver the form to the prospective creditor.

FIGURE 27-1
Self-Mailing Type of Financial Statement Form Approved by the National Association of Credit Management

THIS FORM APPROVED AND PUBLISHED BY THE NATIONAL ASSOCIATION OF CREDIT MANAGEMENT

Form 1B

FINANCIAL STATEMENT OF

Date_____19____

FIRM NAME_____

Address_____City_____

At close of business on_____19____State_____Zone_____

ISSUED TO_____

{NAME OF FIRM
{Requesting Statement.

[PLEASE ANSWER ALL QUESTIONS. WHEN NO FIGURES ARE INSERTED, WRITE WORD "NONE"]

FOLD IN ON THIS LINE

FOLD IN ON THIS LINE

ASSETS	Dollars	Cents	LIABILITIES	Dollars	Cents
Cash in Bank and on hand			Accounts Payable		
Accounts Receivable			Notes Payable — Unsecured:		
Notes and Trade Acceptances Receivable			Banks		
Merchandise Inventory (Do not include Merchandise on Consignment)			Partners or Officers		
			Other		
Other Current Assets (Describe)			Notes Payable — Secured:		
			Owing to		
			Taxes Payable or Accrued:		
			Withholding and Payroll		
			Federal and State Income		
TOTAL CURRENT ASSETS			Other		
Land and Buildings (Depreciated Value)			Accrued Payroll and Other Expense		
Machinery, Fixtures and Equipment (Depreciated Value)			Other Current Liabilities (Describe) }		
Due from Others — Not Current (Describe)			TOTAL CURRENT LIABILITIES		
			Mortgage on Land and Buildings		
			Liens on Merchandise or Equipment		
Other Assets (Describe)			Other Liabilities (Describe)		
			TOTAL LIABILITIES		
			Net Worth {Capital $ ____ }{Surplus $ ____ }		
TOTAL ASSETS			TOTAL LIABILITIES AND NET WORTH		

SUMMARY OF SURPLUS (or of NET WORTH if not Incorporated)

Surplus (or Net Worth at beginning of period) Dated_____19____ $_____
Add — Profit for Period $_____ and Adjustments $_____ $_____
TOTAL ADDITIONS $_____
Deduct—Loss for Period $_____ and Dividends (or Withdrawals, if not incorporated) $_____
TOTAL DEDUCTIONS $_____

SURPLUS (or NET WORTH) in Statement Above $_____

STATEMENT OF PROFIT AND LOSS FOR PERIOD FROM_____ TO_____

			DETAILS OF EXPENSE		
1. NET SALES ____			Salaries — Officers or Owners		
(Cash $____) (Credit $____)			Employees		
2. Inventory — Beginning $____			Rent		
3. Purchases $____			Heat, Light, Other Occupancy Expense		
4. Total (Item 2 plus Item 3) $____			Advertising		
5. Deduct Inventory — Close $____			Interest		
6. COST OF SALES			Taxes, except Income Taxes		
7. GROSS PROFIT			Depreciation, (Fixtures, Trucks, etc.)		
8. Less Total Expense			All other Expense		
Other Additions and Deductions			TOTAL EXPENSE		
9. Profit Before Income Taxes					
10. Less — Income Taxes					
11. NET PROFIT After Taxes					

LIST PRINCIPAL SUPPLIERS AND BANKS

NAMES	ADDRESSES

Amount you are liable for as endorser, guarantor, surety
$_____

Amount of merchandise held on consignment
$_____

Amount of current assets pledged
$_____

Amount of Taxes past due
$_____

Monthly payment on equipment lease or conditional sale contracts
$_____

Latest year income tax examined_____

Date of latest physical inventory_____

Date of latest audit_____

Date business established_____

If premises leased state annual rental_____

Expiration date of lease_____

Are any of your assets subject to a lien under the Uniform Commercial Code? No_____ Yes_____ (please attach list)

Continued on Reverse Side ➔

FIGURE 27-1 (*continued*)

DETAILS OF LAND AND BUILDINGS

DESCRIPTION & LOCATION	TITLE IN NAME OF	Cost	Accumulated Depreciation	Depreciated Cost	Assessed Value	ENCUMBRANCES	
						Amount	To Whom
					•		

INSURANCE STATEMENT

1. Do you carry fire insurance (including extended coverage) Yes_____ No_____ Total Amount $_____

2. Do you have periodic insurance appraisals and inventories to determine if coverage is adequate to prevent becoming co-insurer? Yes_____ No_____ Date of most recent appraisal_____19_____

3. Have your liability insurance limits been reviewed recently? Yes_____ No_____ Date of most recent review_____19_____

☐ If checked, please complete form below for list and description of all insurance policies.

NAME OF INSURANCE COMPANY	POLICY NUMBER	EXPIRATION DATE	DESCRIPTION OF COVERAGE	AMOUNT OR LIMITS	SPECIAL FEATURES

Name and Address of Agent or Broker_____

This statement has been carefully read by the undersigned (both the printed and written matter), qnd is, to my knowledge, in all respects complete, accurate and truthful. It discloses to you the true state of my (our) financial condition on the date indicated. Since that time there has been no material unfavorable change in my (our) financial condition, and if any such change takes place I (we) will give you notice. Until such notice is given, you are to regard this as a continuing statement. The figures submitted are not estimated. They have been taken from my (our) books and physical inventory taken as on date shown.

Name of Individual or Firm_____

If Partnership, Name Partners_____   _____

If Corporation, Name Officers_____   _____

Signed by_____

Title_____

A last point of difference is the place of prosecution. Under the various state laws, prosecution may be instituted only in the county in which the statement was made. On the other hand, prosecution under the federal law may be started either where the statement was made or where it was received.

The question may be raised at this point as to the true importance of these preventive laws. Because of the large burden of proof necessary under both federal and state laws, it is believed by many that the presence of these laws acts more as a deterrent of false statement submission than it does as a basis of punishment for violations.

METHODS OF STATEMENT ANALYSIS

This chapter has been concerned with only one phase of financial statement interpretation. More often than not, the credit manager will have confidence in his credit customer and rely on the authenticity of the financial statement. After a rapid preliminary appraisal he may, in view of the requirements of the credit problem, proceed to determine the firm's liquidity, solvency, and trend. In general, there are four methods commonly used to determine these factors. They are (1) the simple evaluation method, (2) the percentage comparison method, (3) the source and application of funds method, and (4) the ratio analysis method. In addition to these methods, some credit men also employ a preliminary scaling-down technique. This procedure is simply reducing by some predetermined percentage all the items appearing on the balance sheet before making any comparisons. This procedure is sometimes believed necessary to account for the "optimistic natures" of those people who prepare the financial statement. A discussion of four methods of statement analysis is the subject of the next chapter.

REVIEW AND DISCUSSION QUESTIONS

1. Distinguish clearly between a balance sheet and a profit and loss statement.
2. From what sources are financial statements usually available? What are the advantages of using one source over another?
3. Assume a prospective customer refuses to furnish a balance sheet and a profit and loss statement. How would you proceed to acquire the needed information? Would refusal of this request influence your credit decision? Discuss.
4. Do you think that loyalty and effectiveness of human organization should be included in the assets of a firm? Why or why not?
5. In recent years why has there been an increasing demand for financial statement analysis and interpretation?

6. Do all credit problems require the same degree of financial analysis in order to arrive at a sound credit decision? Why or why not?

7. What is meant by the following terms:
   a) The liquidity position of a firm?
   b) The solvency condition of a firm?
   c) The managerial efficiency of a firm?

8. Why is it said certain proportions of assets and liabilities are more conducive to successful operation of a firm than others?

9. Distinguish clearly between window dressing, undue optimism, and actual falsification.

10. Do you think that window dressing should be a crime punishable by law? Why or why not?

11. What are the most common techniques used to exaggerate or falsify the following: cash, accounts receivable, fixed assets, and accounts payable?

12. Why is it believed that financial statement legislation is primarily only preventative in nature?

13. In what respects do the state laws and the federal law differ in regard to making and issuing false financial statements?

14. What purpose does the self-mailing type of financial statement of the NACM serve?

28

Financial Statements – Analysis
and Interpretation (Continued)

The use of financial analysis basically comes down to a decision on whether or not the customer can pay in the future. Financial statements divulge trends in the business and help the credit manager in his decision-making process. Even though the credit decision is made now, the fruits of this decision will mature in the future. Thus, the preparation made now will affect many in the years to come.

In the analysis of a financial statement, certain fundamental things are sought. One is balance or proportion. If a business is to be successful, the relationship of assets to liabilities must be healthy and sound. Also, the total assets must be invested in such a manner as to form an efficient business machine. Thus inventory must be in proper proportion to sales; receivables in proper proportion to sales and to inventory; investment in plant and equipment must be such that an excessive amount is not frozen in these forms, leaving too little with which to buy raw materials or pay labor; liabilities must be proportional to assets and to owners' investment. This does not mean that there is only one proper proportion or balance for all kinds of business, or for the same business at all times, but rather that there is an ideal or best balance for each business at a particular time. It also means that there are certain disproportions which are dangerous and indicate definitely that trouble is in store for the business.

Another thing sought in the financial statement is the trend or direction of the business. The credit man naturally is interested in the present balance or proportion of the items in the statement, but he is even more interested in knowing what they are going to be in the future. It is advisable, then, to interpret the financial statement in terms of the direction in which the business is moving. Is it moving

553

toward a more correct, healthier proportion of assets, liabilities, sales, and income; or is it moving toward a less correct, an unsound, or dangerous proportion? Perhaps the business has been in difficulty but is working its way out, in which case it may be a good risk. Perhaps it has been sound but is slipping into a dangerous condition, in which case it may be a poor risk. Perhaps, in the face of extremely adverse business conditions, it has managed to hold its own, in which case management has shown ability and the risk is good.

METHODS OF STATEMENT ANALYSIS

The four commonly accepted methods of analyzing financial statements in order to determine a firm's liquidity, solvency, and managerial efficiency are: the simple evaluation method, the percentage comparison method, the source and application of funds method, and the ratio analysis method. It is important to recognize that regardless of the method or methods used, the analyst must carefully conceive and understand the line of trade in which the maker of the statement operates, the location of the business, and the date of the statement in order to make his analysis within the proper framework.

Simple Evaluation Method

This method is the one most closely dependent upon the analyst's experience and judgment. Here the credit manager analyzes the statement by a mere inspection of the dollar items shown. Often this is facilitated by arranging a spread or work sheet. After several statements have been received, the analyst then may have before him at a glance the picture for the last three to five years. Such an arrangement for either the balance sheets or for the profit and loss statements permits a quick appraisal of the company, and to the experienced eye affords an opportunity to spot any obvious changes in the operations of the business. The comparison of dollar items alone, however, is rather dangerous unless the analyst is unusually skilled. Certainly it is not the technique for the beginner. This technique is illustrated in Table 28-1, which shows the consecutive annual balance sheet figures for one company.

Percentage Comparison Method

To facilitate comparison, irrespective of the dollar items, the balance sheet may be computed so that each item in the statement is expressed as a percentage of the total assets, which would be the

TABLE 28-1
Consecutive Annual Balance Sheet Figures for One Company

	1st Year	2nd Year	3rd Year
Current Assets:			
Cash	$ 19,640	$ 20,203	$ 20,620
Notes receivable	6,250	5,075	8,960
Accounts receivable	37,425	43,112	31,177
Inventory	68,115	59,256	70,555
Total Current Assets	$131,430	$127,646	$131,312
Fixed Assets:			
Buildings	27,000	26,100	25,200
Store equipment	4,850	5,200	5,690
Delivery equipment	3,120	3,830	3,412
Total Assets	$166,400	$162,776	$165,614
Current Liabilities:			
Accounts payable	$ 41,170	$ 39,735	$ 42,073
Notes payable	12,300	5,890	11,551
Accruals, interest, salaries, etc.	860	1,430	716
Total Current Liabilities	$ 54,330	$ 47,055	$ 54,340
Long-Term Liability:			
Mortgage payable	21,300	21,300	20,800
Net Worth:			
Preferred stock	50,000	50,000	51,000
Common stock	29,500	29,500	29,800
Retained earnings	11,270	14,921	9,674
Total Liabilities and Capital	$166,400	$162,776	$165,614

same thing as a percentage of the liabilities plus the net worth. Likewise in the profit and loss statements, the net sales figure usually is taken as 100 percent, and the other items are computed as a percentage of this total. This has been called the 100 percent or common size method. When this technique is used, changes are more readily apparent than is the case when only the dollar figures are used. Increases in the dollar items actually may be decreases in the proportion, or vice versa, and this would not be readily apparent except to the very alert and experienced observer.

Source and Application of Funds

Another method of indicating not only the direction of change but also the exact amount of the change is by making a source and application of funds comparison. This technique depends upon the accounting truism that an increase in an asset must be accompanied by a corresponding decrease in another asset or an increase in a liability or net worth. Each of the statement items which has changed is listed as either being plus or minus, and the sum of the pluses is canceled by the minuses. This is based upon the accounting equation, assets equal liabilities plus net worth. The advantage of this method is that not only are changes emphasized, but the policies of the business may be revealed by the increase or decrease in the particular statement items. It may be seen whether the company is increasing its liabilities in order to purchase additional plant, to invest more in inventory, or for other purposes. Unsatisfactory dividend policies and unwise handling of surplus also may be revealed by the analysis of the source and application of the source and application of funds. Thus, if the business has continued to pay out dividends, although suffering losses, this fact will be readily apparent when such an analysis is made.

Ratio Analysis

Another, and perhaps the most publicized, method of statement interpretation is the ratio analysis. One may ask the question, "Is a firm selling a million dollars worth of goods a year a success?" Obviously, to reach a sound answer, more information is needed. A million dollar sales figure accompanied by a loss of $50,000 gives a much different picture than a firm reporting a $100,000 net profit (after taxes) on the same volume of sales.

Certain fundamental relationships of items in the statement are emphasized by stating them in the form of ratios. Interpretation of balanced relationships is easier, and the trend of the business can be easily determined by noting the changes in these ratios: It is not to be thought that the ratios listed and commented upon here are the only ones to be used or even that they are, in all cases, the most significant and are selected to illustrate the method, rather than to give final treatment to the subject of ratio analysis.

The method of ratio analysis received its initial impetus from an article, "Study of Credit Barometrics," by Alexander Wall. This study, which was prepared at the request of the Federal Reserve Board, appeared in the March 1919 issue of the *Federal Reserve Bulletin.* In addition, interest in this field has been taken by Robert Morris Associates, a banking organization which is interested in the analysis of financial statements and which has become active over the years in compiling financial ratios, based on financial statements furnished by the cooperating commercial banks, for the use of the bank members of the organization.

Rather than present a list of ratios and a discussion of how they are computed and what they mean, the following three-way classification will be used: ratios showing liquidity of the firm or its ability to meet debts as they come due, ratios showing solvency of the firm or the division of the risk between owners and debtors, and ratios showing trend and managerial efficiency of the firm. It will be noted that in several instances the same ratios appear under two classifications.

Liquidity Ratios. There are at least seven ratios that generally are considered significant in analyzing the ability of a firm to meet its debts. It should be recognized that many credit analysts do not attempt to compute and interpret all seven, but instead credit executives have developed their own favorites which they follow and on which they base their decisions. However, until one has developed the experienced background from which to pick his favorites, it is well to understand what is involved in each of the seven.

$$\text{Current ratio} = \frac{\text{Current assets}}{\text{Current liabilities}}$$

The current ratio for many years was considered the most important of the ratios. It is computed by dividing the total current assets by the total current liabilities and shows the number of times current assets exceed current liabilities. It is interpreted as indicating the ability of the business to meet its maturing obligations. As the obligations mature, they must be met from the cash item, and an excess of current assets over current liabilities gives promise of having sufficient cash on hand to meet the business obligations without difficulty. The standard most commonly accepted is that current assets should be twice current liabilities, or a 2 to 1 ratio.[1] This ratio is no longer considered of paramount significance because of the growing feeling that the composition of the current assets is more important than the amount by which they exceed the current liabilities. It also is to be noted that many businesses, knowing that the analyst will surely figure the current ratio, strive to make it favorable on their statements and thus artificially bring about a better showing than is justified. Although no longer thought of as being the most important of the ratios, it is still one which must be considered and one with which the analyst should be familiar.

$$\text{Acid-test ratio} = \frac{\text{Current assets} - \text{inventory}}{\text{Current liabilities}}$$

This ratio is computed by dividing the total current assets less inventory by the total current liabilities. Inventory generally is the

1 / This proportion will vary from line of business to line of business and with the various phases of the business cycle.

slowest of the current assets; when it is deducted from the total, the remaining current assets are thought of as already converted or as being very readily converted into cash without shrinkage. The standard commonly adopted for this ratio as a minimum is 1 to 1, although variations are noted between various lines and during different economic conditions.

$$\text{Stock turnover} = \frac{\text{Net sales}}{\text{Inventory}}$$

This ratio may be computed in at least two ways, if the data are available:

$$\text{Stock turnover} \atop \text{(for retailers only)} = \frac{\text{Net sales at retail}}{\text{Average inventory at retail}}$$

$$\text{Stock turnover} = \frac{\text{Cost of goods sold}}{\text{Average inventory at cost}}$$

There is the question of what is meant by "average inventory." Some analysts interpret the term to mean the beginning inventory plus the ending inventory divided by two. Others will attempt to secure figures more often, such as the amount of inventory at the start of each month. Of course, the system of inventory control followed by a firm will determine its ability to supply such detailed information. In any case, this ratio is designed to show the number of times a firm is able to convert its stock of goods into cash or receivables.

Comparison of the results of this ratio from year to year for the same company or for different companies for the same year will show how the subject company is utilizing its investment in inventory to generate sales. This is a very important indication of managerial efficiency and operating results. Declining efficiency, as shown by a declining ratio, forecasts slowness in converting assets into cash, decrease in sales volume, capital investment in less productive inventory, and declining profits. Slow turnover of inventory may be indicative of excessive investment in old and slow-moving stock. This throws doubt on the value claimed for the current asset Inventory. It is, therefore, a test of the current position and may lead the analyst to doubt if the current position is actually as good as the face of the statement may indicate.

$$\text{Receivables turnover} = \frac{\text{Net sales}}{\text{Receivables}}$$

This ratio is computed by dividing the net sales by the receivables. It shows the number of times during the fiscal period that the receivables are turned. This indicates the efficiency with which the receivables are being collected. Comparison of results for the subject company from year to year or for the subject company with other similar companies will show how the subject compares in respect to the efficiency of its conversion of receivables into cash. A slowing down of receivables, shown by a decline in the ratio, shows investment of capital in slow or uncollectible receivables. This, of course, hampers the firm's ability to meet obligations and ties up capital unnecessarily. A more exact showing of conditions is obtained by dividing credit sales by receivables. This shows the true turnover of sales on credit and the average number of days it takes the firm to collect its sales on account. Thus, if the turnover is 6 times a year it collects in 60 days, if 12 times a year it collects in 30 days, and if 10 times a year, in 36 days. From these figures the analyst can appraise the soundness of the value claimed for accounts receivable in the current assets. It is therefore a means of testing the soundness of the current asset position.

$$\text{Sales to net working capital} = \frac{\text{Net sales}}{\text{Current assets} - \text{current liabilities}}$$

This ratio, which is computed by dividing the net sales figure by the net working capital (current assets less current liabilities), shows the efficiency with which the net working capital is being utilized by the firm in producing the desired results—sales.

$$\text{Payables turnover} = \frac{\text{Purchases}}{\text{Accounts payable}}$$

The payables turnover ratio is figured by dividing the accounts payable into the purchases. Interpreting this ratio over a period of years, the analyst is able to tell whether current liabilities are being paid more or less promptly than in prior periods. For example, a firm reporting purchases of $60,000 for a specified period (generally a year) and payables of $12,000 at the end of the period will have a ratio of 5 to 1. Translated into days (360 days divided by 5), this ratio reveals that this company is taking 72 days on the average to pay its accounts payable. This does not mean that some accounts will not be paid in less time than 72 days and some in a longer time, but it simply points out that if a seller is contemplating accepting the credit of this firm the average length of time he can expect to wait for funds is 72 days.

$$\text{Net working capital represented by inventory} = \frac{\text{Inventory}}{\text{Current assets} - \text{Current liabilities}}$$

This ratio, which is not too well known and is not in general use, shows what proportion of net working capital is made up of inventory which may be too hard to sell. In interpreting this ratio, the analyst should recognize that it may be favorably influenced either by an exceptionally low level of current liabilities or by an excessively low level of merchandise relative to the other current assets.

Solvency Ratios. Seven ratios are generally accepted as capable of showing the solvency condition of a firm. In interpreting these ratios, the analyst is answering such questions as: "Is the net worth adequate?" "Is the borrowing proper?" or "Are the fixed assets fitted to the needs of the company, to the capital invested by the owners, and to the demands of outside creditors?" As with the liquidity ratios, the credit manager has favorites which he generally computes and interprets, and does not in most instances analyze all those that are listed and described in this section.

$$\text{Debt to net worth} = \frac{\text{Current debt} + \text{Long-term liabilities}}{\text{Net worth}}$$

The ratio of debt to net worth is computed by dividing the total debt by the net worth. It shows the proportion of investments by outside creditors in relation to capital investment by the owners. In other words, it indicates the proportional relationship which exists between the dollar value of money and goods secured on credit from outsiders and the sum invested by the owners of the business (owners' equity). Obviously the owners should have an adequate equity in the business to protect the investments made by others. A rather general rule is that owners' capital should at the minimum be as great as the outside investments. This is a 1 to 1 ratio. This ratio is not altogether definite but varies with the nature of the business and other conditions. The thing to keep in mind is that as the proportion of owners' capital increases, the business is working into a safer position and the dependence on creditors is lessened. Some analysts also follow the practice of showing the ratio of current debt only to net worth. This is especially valuable when a considerable part of the liabilities is long term.

$$\text{Total assets to fixed assets} = \frac{\text{Total assets}}{\text{Fixed assets}}$$

This ratio is computed by dividing the total assets by the fixed assets. It indicates the proportion of the total assets which are represented by fixed assets. It is of significance only in those lines of trade where fixed assets constitute an appreciable portion of the total assets. The danger to which many businesses are exposed is that they will allow too large a proportion of their assets to become frozen (nonliquid) by being tied up in fixed assets which are not readily disposed of and which may not contribute to earnings. This tendency is revealed by a study of this ratio.

$$\text{Fixed assets to long-term liabilities} = \frac{\text{Fixed assets}}{\text{Long-term liabilities}}$$

This ratio is computed by dividing the fixed assets by the long-term liabilities. The theory of the ratio is that long-term liabilities are created to acquire the fixed assets and are frequently secured by the fixed assets. If this is the case, the comparison of these two items is of significance. It shows among other things the extent to which fixed assets are being carried by means of borrowings. This may indicate the safety margin of the loans, the prospects of renewing maturing debts, and the possibility of acquiring funds by making additional loans. Should the long-term liabilities be large relative to fixed assets, it may be an indication of financial strain and a weakened condition. In some lines of business, however, the fixed assets are so small in proportion to the total assets that this ratio has little significance and may be omitted.

$$\text{Fixed assets to net worth} = \frac{\text{Fixed assets}}{\text{Net worth}}$$

This ratio is computed by dividing the fixed assets (such as plant, machinery, equipment, and other fixed properties) by net worth or owners' equity. A high ratio here generally is interpreted as a danger signal that the firm may have expanded its fixed assets more rapidly than warranted by normal growth. On the other hand, when this ratio materially exceeds the average for a particular type of operation and line of business, a low working capital is indicated. In fact, it may mean an overworking of the working capital of the firm.

$$\text{Sales to net worth} = \frac{\text{Net sales}}{\text{Net worth}}$$

This ratio, which is computed by dividing the net sales by the net worth, shows the number of dollars in sales which are generated by the net worth of the owners. More efficient use of the owners' capital naturally results in a larger ratio. However, this ratio may become "too good." Inadequate investment on the part of the owners for the volume of business being attempted makes this ratio abnormally high. This is known as overtrading. Inefficient use of owners' capital causes a low ratio. Either of these conditions is unsatisfactory, but overtrading is probably more dangerous than undertrading. Inefficient use of owners' capital means that the capital is not being used as productively as it might be. This is likely to cause lower profits or inadequate returns. Attempting to do too much business on the capital invested means that the owners are straining the business. They are relying heavily on borrowed funds; they are able to maintain this pace because of very rapid turnover rates of inventory and receivables. Should something happen to slow down this rate of conversion of assets into cash, they would quickly find themselves unable to pay debts as they mature. Slowing down in debt payment causes anxiety on the part of creditors and hesitancy to accept credit for additional amounts. This is doubly disastrous for a firm in this condition, because the capital supplied by the owners is insufficient to give the creditors much margin of protection and the business is dependent upon continuance of the rate of operations for success. This ratio should be examined with the ratio of sales to inventory, sales to receivables, current ratio, and net worth to debt ratio. The combined review of all these ratios will suffice to reveal the condition. An attempt to do too large a volume of business on insufficient capital may also be revealed by a comparison of sales to net working capital (current assets minus current liabilities).

$$\text{Sales to total assets} = \frac{\text{Net sales}}{\text{Total assets}}$$

This ratio is computed by dividing the net sales by the total assets. It shows the number of dollars in sales which are generated by the total assets invested in the business. More efficient use of the assets results in more dollars of sales, while decreased efficiency in their use is shown by a falling ratio. This ratio may be more significant than the sales to inventory figure for manufacturing firms or other firms which carry only a small inventory but which have a heavy investment in fixed assets. For firms of this type a calculation of the sales to fixed asset ratio is sometimes made to supplement the information given by the other ratios.

$$\text{Sales to fixed assets} = \frac{\text{Net sales}}{\text{Fixed assets}}$$

This ratio shows the dollars of net sales produced with each dollar of fixed assets. When this ratio is low, it may mean that the degree of plant utilization is relatively low; in other words, that the concern is too large for the volume of business transacted.

Trend and Managerial Efficiency Ratios. The nine ratios included in this section are designed to answer such questions as: "How efficient is the firm in the use of its assets?" "What is the ability of management to meet changing conditions?" or "How adaptable and flexible is the firm?" Six of the ratios normally considered as revealing trend and managerial efficiency have been discussed previously. These are the stock turnover, the receivables turnover, the sales to net working capital, the sales to net worth, the sales to total assets, and the sales to fixed assets ratios. The other three ratios in this category involve net profit and are related to the net worth, total assets, and net sales of the firm.

$$\text{Net profit to net worth} = \frac{\text{Net profit}}{\text{Net worth}}$$

This is computed as a percentage of net profit to net worth and shows the earnings made on the owners' capital. This amount is, of course, very important to owners and managers and is often considered one of the most important of the results shown by the statements. It shows the efficiency of the overall operations of the business and may be compared for the subject firm over a period of years or to other similar firms. Clearly the success of operations is summarized here. For purposes of comparison with other firms, however, it is not always the best figure to use. The profit on net worth earned by a particular firm is influenced both by its operations and by its financial policy. To illustrate: Firm A operates extensively on borrowed capital; it has $1,000,000 total assets employed and has $500,000 borrowed at an average interest charge of 6 percent and $500,000 invested by the owners. In a particular year the total profits made before payment of interest are $80,000, and after $30,000 interest is paid they are $50,000, which is 10 percent on the owners' capital and 5 percent of the total assets invested in the business. Firm B operates almost exclusively on its own capital. It has $600,000 total assets employed, with $50,000 borrowed at an average interest charge of 6 percent and $550,000 invested by the owners. In a particular year the profits made before payment of interest are $53,000 and after $3,000 interest are $50,000, which is 9.1 percent on the owners' capital and 8.3 percent on the total assets invested in the business. Looking only at the rate of return on net worth, it would appear that Firm A was the more efficient, but Firm B is actually using the assets employed to better effect than is Firm A. The smaller return made to the stockholders in Firm B may be due to a more conservative policy in the use of other people's money rather than to a lack of managerial efficiency. Therefore to make the most exact comparison, both percentage of return on net worth and percentage of return on total assets should be computed.

$$\text{Net profit to total assets} = \frac{\text{Net profit}}{\text{Total assets}}$$

This ratio is computed by dividing the net profit by the total assets. It is designed to show how efficiently the total assets are being used in producing dollars of profit. Used jointly with the ratio of net profit to net worth, as just discussed, it often will enable the analyst to interpret the true condition and future outlook of the firm more accurately.

$$\text{Net profit to net sales} = \frac{\text{Net profit}}{\text{Net sales}}$$

This ratio, in indicating the efficiency of management, is computed by dividing the net profit by the net sales. It should be recognized that the policies followed by a firm will have a great effect on this ratio. Thus firms employing price-cutting techniques will tend to seek large total profits and high sales volumes and will show a lower ratio than those firms that sell at a high markup and attain a lower volume of sales.

USE OF STANDARDS IN STATEMENT ANALYSIS

The statement analysis procedure gains in importance when the computed percentages and ratios are viewed in light of their trends over several years. These trends may be within the individual company itself or may be within the industry in which the company is included. Commenting on the importance of the use of standards for comparison, the *Credit Management Handbook* points out:[2]

Inherent in any analysis is an expressed or implied concept of the normal or "proper" size and proportions of the objects or items examined. This concept of the normal (not necessarily the ideal) is the premise on which financial statement analysis is based. The normality of the showing, or the degree of variation of an individual statement from the norm, may be established with the statements of other representative concerns in the trade, concerns doing business under similar conditions.

A number of sources provide financial statement averages or norms for almost every field of business in which credit is extended. Credit agencies, bankers, and industry associations, in particular, are in a position to assemble sufficient statements for this purpose. Credit departments of large merchandisers can provide comparable data by careful selection and combining of customers' statements.

Robert Morris Associates

The *Statement Studies* of Robert Morris Associates have been published continuously since 1923. These studies are a collection of "composite" balance sheets and income statements for different lines

2 / 2d ed.; Homewood, Ill.: Richard D. Irwin, Inc., 1965, pp. 220-21.

of business—manufacturers, wholesalers, retailers, and service concerns. Also computed are many widely used financial ratios. A separate section provides information on selling and delivery expense, officers' salaries, and other general administrative expenses, all expressed as percentages of net sales. The statements of each industry or trade are tabulated into groups according to asset size—under $250,000, $250,000 to less than $1 million, and $1 million to less than $10 million. When data are available, information also is presented on larger companies, those with total assets of $10 million to less than $25 million. The statements then are lumped into an "all sizes" tabulation.

Dun & Bradstreet

One of the most comprehensive and current sources for this information is the material published by Dun & Bradstreet, Inc. This company has been one of the pioneers in ratio analysis, and its compilations first appeared in a series of four articles appearing in the *Dun & Bradstreet Monthly Review,* starting in August 1933. The development of the ratio analysis concept since this beginning is outlined in the following quotation:[3]

In 1935 these various studies were brought up to date and with supplemental studies appeared as a brochure entitled *Behind the Scenes of Business.* The median ratios for 27 manufacturing lines of business, 15 wholesale lines, and 7 retail lines were included together with a three year average of each ratio for 1931-1933, a method which would smooth out any unusual yearly variations. In April, 1936, the first revised edition of *Behind the Scenes of Business* appeared with the median and a four year average of each ratio for 1931-1934 for 31 manufacturing lines, 16 wholesale lines, and 7 retail lines. In May, 1937, the second revised edition appeared with the median and a five year average of the medians for each ratio for 1931-1935 for 35 manufacturing lines, 18 wholesale lines, and 7 retail lines. In January, 1953, the third revised edition appeared with the median and a five year average of the medians for each ratio for 1947-1951 for the 70 lines of manufacturing, wholesaling and retailing.

Since 1938 these "fourteen important ratios" have been compiled annually and published in the same form as this current pamphlet. These studies have been undertaken and continued with the sole idea of providing factual information determined from a nation-wide sample of corporations in representative lines of industry and commerce to provide helpful current information of a factual type to managements of businesses, bankers, accountants, industrial engineers, credit men, and analysts. . . .

In Figure 28-1 the *1969 Key Business Ratios* are shown. These are statistics from 125 lines of retailing, wholesaling, and manufacturing

3 / Roy A. Foulke, *The Genesis of the 14 Important Ratios* (New York: Dun & Bradstreet, Inc., 1955), pp. 41-42.

FIGURE 28-1
14 Important Ratios in Retailing, Wholesaling, and Manufacturing & Construction, Prepared by Dun & Bradstreet, 1969
(showing median and quartile ratios)

Retailing

Line of Business (and number of concerns reporting)	Current assets to current debt	Net profits on net sales	Net profits on tangible net worth	Net profits on net working capital	Net sales to tangible net worth	Net sales to net working capital	Collection period	Net sales to inventory	Fixed assets to tangible net worth	Current debt to tangible net worth	Total debt to tangible net worth	Inventory to net working capital	Current debt to inventory	Funded debts to net working capital
	Times	Per cent	Per cent	Per cent	Times	Times	Days	Times	Per cent	Per cent	Per cent	Per cent	Per cent	Per cent
5641 Children's & Infants' Wear Stores (43)	3.98	3.38	16.09	19.33	4.78	7.49	*	7.1	4.0	29.7	83.6	78.0	43.1	27.9
	2.61	2.25	9.12	13.50	4.21	5.18	*	4.8	12.8	51.9	97.3	105.5	64.6	35.2
	1.88	0.73	2.88	4.35	3.20	3.84	*	3.9	28.6	77.9	146.6	146.8	88.9	61.5
5611 Clothing & Furnishings, Men's & Boys' (221)	4.46	4.01	13.31	15.29	4.53	5.19	*	5.3	5.4	26.0	66.8	73.1	38.8	9.0
	2.71	2.40	7.88	8.89	3.33	3.74	*	4.0	10.1	49.2	106.0	97.2	63.4	22.7
	1.85	1.30	3.80	4.64	2.29	2.71	*	2.9	20.1	102.5	190.1	136.4	95.1	46.4
5311 Department Stores (264)	4.28	3.27	10.71	13.78	4.59	5.84	*	6.8	10.7	23.4	46.1	60.9	48.8	13.5
	2.76	2.12	6.46	8.06	3.15	4.16	*	5.5	24.7	41.9	75.7	76.9	72.1	33.4
	2.07	1.19	3.49	4.46	2.44	3.07	*	4.2	46.5	69.4	130.1	106.3	100.0	57.9
Discount Stores (215)	2.41	3.07	18.94	27.76	8.69	11.82	*	7.3	12.9	53.9	82.4	107.1	57.2	12.6
	1.82	2.00	13.19	17.29	6.30	7.68	*	5.2	27.9	90.3	131.6	153.7	78.7	32.5
	1.44	1.25	7.49	9.26	4.52	5.56	*	4.0	48.5	146.7	211.3	220.1	99.8	63.7
Discount Stores, Leased Departments (45)	2.12	2.97	18.94	26.43	9.40	10.11	*	6.4	18.8	83.0	87.2	117.3	63.2	8.4
	1.73	1.79	13.19	16.88	7.10	7.73	*	4.7	28.5	128.4	139.6	182.4	77.6	25.2
	1.37	0.84	5.66	6.93	5.57	5.85	*	3.5	43.3	232.7	222.6	235.8	108.7	41.6
5651 Family Clothing Stores (92)	5.60	4.88	12.35	14.89	4.45	5.47	*	5.8	4.1	15.3	53.0	59.3	30.6	11.3
	3.20	2.61	8.38	10.32	3.11	3.41	*	4.3	11.4	36.9	72.7	82.5	51.4	23.9
	2.22	1.53	5.16	5.58	2.10	2.54	*	3.2	23.0	66.9	129.8	126.2	83.7	40.8
5252 Farm Equipment Dealers (91)	2.57	3.32	15.64	19.50	7.46	8.42	16	4.8	8.1	59.1	126.9	98.9	60.4	16.5
	1.74	1.74	8.75	11.19	5.21	5.82	22	3.4	17.2	121.3	221.9	148.5	82.0	32.3
	1.36	0.56	3.56	4.07	2.72	3.45	46	2.5	27.7	236.1	357.1	283.1	101.0	52.8
5969 Farm & Garden Supply Stores (74)	4.75	4.62	13.25	23.06	4.87	8.06	*	13.3	17.9	16.2	57.0	43.6	50.0	16.5
	2.48	2.46	7.43	13.55	2.92	5.36	*	9.1	38.2	37.4	81.6	67.9	95.3	49.3
	1.68	0.83	2.70	5.53	2.20	4.00	*	5.8	57.7	63.1	121.5	104.3	170.7	127.8
5712 Furniture Stores (188)	5.34	4.52	10.11	11.50	4.18	5.20	54	6.5	4.3	23.2	61.0	30.5	58.6	11.3
	2.87	2.13	6.32	6.85	2.58	2.74	109	5.0	10.3	52.7	104.2	59.4	94.4	20.1
	1.92	0.87	2.11	2.43	1.67	1.75	212	3.7	22.0	98.1	178.6	100.7	146.6	40.0
5541 Gasoline Service Stations (63)	3.27	4.44	11.60	34.23	6.04	13.19	*	27.4	22.8	20.8	46.9	40.0	74.8	11.5
	2.08	2.06	7.50	16.37	3.84	6.83	*	12.0	47.4	38.1	67.5	63.2	159.7	47.2
	1.58	1.11	4.36	6.99	2.31	4.86	*	6.7	69.4	81.4	122.5	99.4	243.2	74.5
5411 Grocery Stores (133)	2.33	1.69	14.44	36.83	13.10	32.70	*	22.3	42.6	35.3	61.7	87.6	69.5	30.7
	1.69	1.06	10.34	24.15	9.72	22.12	*	16.1	66.7	59.2	96.0	135.2	100.0	54.8
	1.26	0.62	5.78	16.23	7.07	13.35	*	13.1	94.2	97.1	146.9	201.9	129.8	186.1
5251 Hardware Stores (96)	9.25	4.35	11.74	16.62	3.82	5.29	*	5.4	5.8	10.7	40.8	58.6	20.7	7.1
	3.52	2.67	7.23	9.40	2.66	3.23	*	4.3	13.0	30.7	54.0	87.0	46.5	19.9
	2.23	1.26	3.45	4.05	1.81	2.34	*	3.0	31.3	60.7	107.6	119.8	77.1	44.5
5722 Household Appliance Stores (86)	3.31	3.53	13.24	19.66	7.19	9.19	18	7.9	5.1	36.8	68.6	59.2	64.9	8.6
	2.20	1.56	8.26	10.10	4.21	5.23	34	5.6	13.1	77.4	128.5	100.3	95.3	32.5
	1.54	0.68	2.96	3.11	3.10	3.52	73	4.2	28.1	127.2	232.9	173.9	112.0	60.9
5971 Jewelry Stores (73)	5.01	6.26	12.54	12.90	3.18	3.65	*	4.0	3.4	24.0	48.2	57.1	37.4	9.0
	2.91	3.81	8.13	8.79	2.11	2.51	*	2.9	9.0	45.6	90.8	77.8	67.3	19.7
	2.04	2.46	4.97	5.59	1.48	1.53	*	2.2	18.2	93.7	154.6	117.9	93.2	40.0
5211 Lumber & Other Bldg. Mtls. Dealers (191)	6.06	3.06	10.59	15.32	4.43	6.35	37	8.3	13.0	16.2	48.5	48.4	35.7	15.3
	3.21	1.98	5.76	7.96	3.07	3.97	51	5.8	23.3	33.1	74.8	67.5	68.1	32.7
	2.21	0.93	2.59	3.57	2.02	2.59	71	4.4	40.3	66.7	127.2	89.0	111.8	57.2
5399 Miscellaneous General Mdse. Stores (84)	6.03	3.25	13.95	18.72	6.00	7.00	*	6.1	8.7	19.7	48.5	64.9	25.9	15.1
	2.97	2.47	7.21	9.08	3.60	4.02	*	4.2	17.1	40.1	91.3	94.8	54.4	24.4
	1.89	1.30	3.44	3.96	1.74	2.48	*	3.2	33.7	86.3	145.5	150.1	91.8	49.1
5511 Motor Vehicle Dealers (98)	2.08	2.07	15.48	26.43	12.76	19.25	*	8.8	11.6	63.5	100.2	124.3	74.4	23.3
	1.61	1.04	7.54	12.86	8.80	13.94	*	7.2	23.6	117.8	147.5	194.5	89.4	40.8
	1.35	0.46	3.54	4.67	5.84	9.18	*	5.9	52.2	170.6	282.9	262.3	103.0	86.3
5231 Paint, Glass & Wallpaper Stores (31)	5.41	5.72	19.55	24.56	4.76	6.11	*	7.7	6.6	14.4	37.2	52.9	33.3	16.1
	3.46	3.76	11.51	15.60	3.38	4.82	*	6.0	18.0	30.1	60.2	77.7	66.6	41.5
	2.54	1.34	4.32	8.17	2.12	2.85	*	4.7	61.4	56.5	100.3	104.9	106.8	110.8
5661 Shoe Stores (91)	5.36	5.06	14.74	19.23	4.51	5.39	*	5.1	4.1	18.5	47.4	67.6	28.4	10.1
	3.48	3.06	9.05	10.88	3.18	3.87	*	3.9	13.0	34.2	81.9	102.3	46.9	18.4
	2.28	1.59	5.77	6.80	2.24	2.77	*	2.9	25.8	66.5	124.9	135.6	64.4	34.9
5531 Tire, Battery & Accessory Stores (68)	3.71	4.48	16.52	25.24	5.29	7.47	*	8.0	9.0	28.0	60.0	57.6	50.5	21.5
	2.58	2.12	8.54	10.64	3.93	4.81	*	6.1	23.6	54.6	85.9	90.1	86.2	34.9
	1.49	1.06	3.96	5.23	2.48	3.31	*	4.5	51.4	113.9	174.1	132.7	147.6	70.3
5331 Variety Stores (65)	4.74	3.72	12.31	15.86	4.89	6.53	*	5.4	14.4	22.7	38.2	96.7	29.5	8.4
	3.00	2.30	9.07	10.91	3.51	4.57	*	4.0	26.1	34.5	64.2	117.0	43.8	29.0
	2.16	1.29	5.00	5.48	2.60	3.62	*	3.2	40.3	59.5	104.9	146.6	59.3	59.8
5621 Women's Ready-to-Wear Stores (196)	4.09	4.12	16.72	22.43	5.75	6.99	*	8.6	6.3	26.8	74.4	50.1	53.0	12.9
	2.50	2.18	8.73	10.92	3.78	4.49	*	6.1	14.7	56.5	125.8	78.3	86.6	30.8
	1.82	1.06	3.30	4.08	2.54	3.25	*	4.7	30.2	102.8	170.0	116.3	135.0	61.6

* Not computed. Necessary information as to the division between cash sales and credit sales was available in too few cases to obtain an average collection period usable as a broad guide.

FIGURE 28-1 (*continued*)

Iow the Ratios are Figured

Although terms like "median" and "quartile" are everyday working guage to statisticians, their precise meaning may be vague to some sinessmen.

In the various ratio tables, three figures appear under each ratio heading. e center figure in bold type is the **median**; the figures immediately above d below the median are, respectively, the **upper** and **lower quartiles**. To derstand their use, the reader should also know how they are calculated. First, year-end financial statements from concerns in the survey (almost elusively corporations with a tangible net worth over $100,000) are alyzed by Dun & Bradstreet statisticians. Then each of 14 ratios is calculated individually for every concern in the sample.

These individual ratio figures, entered on data-processing cards, are segregated by line of business, and then arranged in order of size—the best ratio at the top, the weakest at the bottom. The figure that falls in the middle of this series becomes the **median** for that ratio in that line of business. The figure halfway between the median and the top of the series is the **upper quartile**; the number halfway between the median and the bottom of the series is the **lower quartile**.

In a statistical sense, each median then is the **typical ratio figure** for all concerns studied in a given line. The upper and lower quartile figures typify the experience of firms in the top and bottom halves of the sample respectively.

RRENT ASSETS TO CURRENT DEBT
rent Assets are divided by total Current Debt. Current Assets are the sum cash, notes and accounts receivable (less reserves for bad debt), advances merchandise, merchandise inventories, and Listed, Federal, State and nicipal securities not in excess of market value. Current Debt is the total all liabilities falling due within one year. This is one test of solvency.

PROFITS ON NET SALES
ained by dividing the net earnings of the business, after taxes, by net sales e dollar volume less returns, allowances, and cash discounts). This important dstick in measuring profitability should be related to the ratio which follows.

PROFITS ON TANGIBLE NET WORTH
gible Net Worth is the equity of stockholders in the business, as obtained subtracting total liabilities from total assets, and then deducting intangibles. ratio is obtained by dividing Net Profits after taxes by Tangible Net Worth. dency is to look increasingly to this ratio as a final criterion of profitability. erally, a relationship of at least 10 per cent is regarded as a desirable ective for providing dividends plus funds for future growth.

PROFITS ON NET WORKING CAPITAL
Working Capital represents the excess of Current Assets over Current Debt. margin represents the cushion available to the business for carrying inven- es and receivables, and for financing day-to-day operations. The ratio is ained by dividing Net Profits, after taxes, by Net Working Capital.

SALES TO TANGIBLE NET WORTH
Sales are divided by Tangible Net Worth. This gives a measure of relative over of invested capital.

SALES TO NET WORKING CAPITAL
Sales are divided by Net Working Capital. This provides a guide as to the nt the company is turning its working capital and the margin of operating ds.

LECTION PERIOD
ual net sales are divided by 365 days to obtain average daily credit sales then the average daily credit sales are divided into notes and accounts ivable, including any discounted. This ratio is helpful in analyzing the ectibility of receivables. Many feel the collection period should not exceed

the net maturity indicated by selling terms by more than 10 to 15 days. When comparing the collection period of one concern with that of another, allow- ances should be made for possible variations in selling terms.

NET SALES TO INVENTORY
Dividing annual Net Sales by Merchandise Inventory as carried on the balance sheet. This quotient does not yield an actual physical turnover. It provides a yardstick for comparing stock-to-sales ratios of one concern with another or with those in the industry.

FIXED ASSETS TO TANGIBLE NET WORTH
Fixed Assets are divided by Tangible Net Worth. Fixed Assets represent depre- ciated book values of building, leasehold improvements, machinery, furniture, fixtures, tools, and other physical equipment, plus land, if any, and valued at cost or appraised market value. Ordinarily, this relationship should not exceed 100 percent for a manufacturer, and 75 percent for a wholesaler or retailer.

CURRENT DEBT TO TANGIBLE NET WORTH
Derived by dividing Current Debt by Tangible Net Worth. Ordinarily, a business begins to pile up trouble when this relationship exceeds 80 percent.

TOTAL DEBT TO TANGIBLE NET WORTH
Obtained by dividing total current plus long term debts by Tangible Net Worth. When this relationship exceeds 100 percent, the equity of creditors in the assets of the business exceeds that of owners.

INVENTORY TO NET WORKING CAPITAL
Merchandise inventory is divided by Net Working Capital. This is an additional measure of inventory balance. Ordinarily, the relationship should not exceed 80 percent.

CURRENT DEBT TO INVENTORY
Dividing the Current Debt by Inventory yields yet another indication of the extent to which the business relies on funds from disposal of unsold inventories to meet its debts.

FUNDED DEBTS TO WORKING CAPITAL
Funded Debts are all long term obligations, as represented by mortgages, bonds, debentures, term loans, serial notes, and other types of liabilities matur- ing more than one year from statement date. This ratio is obtained by dividing Funded Debt by Net Working Capital. Analysts tend to compare Funded Debts with Net Working Capital in determining whether or not long term debts are in proper proportion. Ordinarily, this relationship should not exceed 100 percent.

Wholesaling

Line of Business (and number of concerns reporting)	Current assets to current debt	Net profits on net sales	Net profits on tangible net worth	Net profits on net working capital	Net sales to tangible net worth	Net sales to net working capital	Collection period	Net sales to inventory	Fixed assets to tangible net worth	Current debt to tangible net worth	Total debt to tangible net worth	Inventory to net working capital	Current debt to inventory	Funded debts to net working capital
	Times	Per cent	Per cent	Per cent	Times	Times	Days	Times	Per cent	Per cent	Per cent	Per cent	Per cent	Per cent
077	3.49	4.23	19.19	19.23	7.85	8.72	34	11.8	4.7	34.5	42.0	54.9	54.0	8.4
Air Condtg. & Refrigtn.	2.61	1.98	10.64	12.21	4.91	5.56	49	6.9	11.1	51.7	86.0	83.2	105.1	20.8
Equipt. & Sup. (53)	1.69	1.05	7.11	7.30	3.07	3.79	64	4.5	20.7	167.1	267.6	110.2	162.3	40.8
013	3.75	3.44	13.07	15.86	5.26	6.50	28	6.3	5.6	29.2	62.3	70.5	43.9	15.9
utomotive Equipment	2.75	2.13	8.11	9.30	3.80	4.52	35	4.9	12.5	46.3	92.8	94.8	64.3	33.2
(181)	1.93	1.16	4.09	5.41	2.69	3.34	44	3.8	26.5	84.0	151.6	125.9	90.2	59.9
095	2.81	2.26	16.31	22.80	10.82	16.70	9	14.1	7.2	36.5	62.6	76.4	68.3	8.5
Beer, Wine & Alcoholic	1.75	1.35	9.67	12.56	7.45	10.18	25	9.4	20.1	95.4	141.1	118.4	96.1	29.9
Beverages (83)	1.35	0.60	4.76	6.73	5.21	7.69	42	5.8	38.9	184.5	291.3	189.1	138.9	51.3
029	2.94	5.60	13.71	26.54	8.87	12.36	34	17.6	12.2	26.3	90.3	42.0	112.6	15.8
hemicals & Allied	1.95	1.62	8.36	13.62	6.07	9.24	44	12.1	25.6	68.7	167.8	66.6	157.5	40.8
Products (46)	1.52	0.71	3.31	6.05	3.05	5.30	56	8.6	50.5	133.8	268.3	102.7	232.1	124.1
037	2.95	2.58	16.12	19.80	8.28	12.40	28	20.3	1.8	40.5	91.7	45.5	74.0	11.7
lothing & Accessories,	2.09	1.39	8.90	12.39	5.69	6.89	45	8.8	5.4	83.0	118.8	71.3	132.9	23.6
Women's & Child's. (68)	1.58	0.49	3.66	3.92	3.81	4.60	64	5.5	17.8	145.8	188.2	118.0	232.3	43.5
036	3.56	1.92	16.65	16.76	6.69	7.33	24	8.6	1.3	30.7	63.5	62.6	53.1	4.7
lothing & Furnishings,	2.66	1.17	4.68	4.89	5.18	5.44	46	5.6	5.7	58.0	93.1	81.4	77.4	25.2
Men's & Boys' (50)	1.92	0.36	0.92	1.55	2.90	3.08	62	4.2	14.9	93.9	206.0	118.4	111.0	33.6
081	4.05	2.73	16.13	19.09	7.33	9.34	52	10.8	3.6	29.9	88.3	54.0	60.6	3.8
ommercial Machines	2.05	1.45	4.17	10.84	4.61	5.33	65	7.2	9.2	79.6	118.2	81.4	111.5	10.5
& Equipment (34)	1.55	0.22	0.88	1.14	3.51	3.78	92	5.1	22.3	121.1	206.8	109.5	171.3	29.5
045	5.21	1.95	12.19	13.30	17.44	18.44	10	23.1	6.4	21.7	50.6	60.1	35.7	5.0
onfectionery (33)	2.59	0.71	8.21	9.14	10.15	10.80	17	13.9	10.8	49.1	124.8	84.1	69.5	9.0
	2.04	0.35	3.56	3.84	6.24	6.85	26	9.0	29.3	96.6	304.7	114.5	101.7	51.3

FIGURE 28-1 (continued)

Wholesaling

Line of Business (and number of concerns reporting)	Current assets to current debt (Times)	Net profits on net sales (Per cent)	Net profits on tangible net worth (Per cent)	Net profits on net working capital (Per cent)	Net sales to tangible net worth (Times)	Net sales to net working capital (Times)	Collection period (Days)	Net sales to inventory (Times)	Fixed assets to tangible net worth (Per cent)	Current debt to tangible net worth (Per cent)	Total debt to tangible net worth (Per cent)	Inventory to net working capital (Per cent)	Current debt to inventory (Per cent)	Funded debts to net working capital (Per cent)
5043 Dairy Products (61)	2.72	1.68	15.70	35.15	13.10	24.10	21	53.6	9.5	31.6	60.9	21.1	118.8	23.
	1.73	1.03	9.47	20.41	6.83	15.05	29	30.5	39.1	69.9	122.3	50.0	262.6	37.
	1.28	0.18	3.79	4.29	4.80	9.26	36	18.5	67.7	129.4	238.6	92.3	521.0	71.
5022 Drugs & Druggists' Sundries (105)	2.93	2.01	11.46	13.28	8.54	9.60	24	7.6	6.0	44.5	76.7	80.4	60.1	14.
	2.11	1.34	7.38	8.31	5.97	6.91	36	6.3	14.9	71.6	122.5	105.1	78.3	29.
	1.66	0.73	4.60	5.70	4.07	4.82	46	5.4	36.4	130.3	188.2	145.0	111.9	46.
5064 Electrical Appliances, TV & Radio Sets (96)	2.39	1.93	11.25	13.94	7.65	9.28	30	7.9	3.1	55.7	121.0	81.5	82.0	9.
	1.86	1.29	7.98	8.85	6.15	7.41	42	6.0	8.0	92.5	168.9	123.4	99.2	24.
	1.53	0.75	4.21	5.45	4.34	5.46	55	5.0	21.8	151.7	211.4	169.4	133.0	49.
5063 Electrical Apparatus & Equipment (148)	2.90	2.42	12.76	15.77	7.61	8.86	35	10.2	5.1	45.4	71.8	67.8	70.7	10.
	2.17	1.63	8.17	9.44	5.64	6.31	45	7.3	11.7	79.2	114.5	87.3	106.1	20.
	1.69	0.98	4.90	5.69	3.61	4.45	57	5.6	20.9	117.0	160.5	115.8	143.6	33.
5065 Electronic Parts & Equipment (46)	3.16	4.07	16.55	17.40	6.44	6.86	30	5.5	6.1	36.8	76.0	86.9	49.0	11.
	2.32	2.35	8.72	11.34	4.90	5.20	42	4.2	11.8	65.9	135.8	106.7	72.8	22.
	1.83	1.42	3.85	4.94	3.28	3.68	52	3.6	22.5	115.8	192.5	147.1	94.6	46.
5083 Farm Machinery & Equipment (55)	3.75	2.55	12.91	14.06	6.71	7.66	32	7.1	5.2	29.2	64.3	63.6	51.1	10.
	2.29	1.51	8.55	10.23	4.83	5.01	42	5.5	13.5	63.5	126.9	105.5	75.7	25.
	1.64	0.75	4.05	4.42	3.06	3.28	57	3.9	34.2	136.7	184.3	138.9	112.7	49.
5039 Footwear (60)	3.06	2.68	11.27	13.67	6.01	6.94	44	10.2	0.8	44.9	91.0	50.5	65.0	9.
	2.05	1.69	8.03	8.85	4.63	4.94	58	5.8	2.7	82.4	136.5	86.9	111.0	27.
	1.62	0.94	4.65	5.83	2.88	3.28	77	3.8	6.5	139.8	202.8	129.3	182.8	46.
5048 Fresh Fruits & Vegetables (64)	3.55	2.13	15.74	39.14	13.55	22.12	10	103.7	17.3	26.4	66.8	10.8	103.1	22.
	1.79	1.10	10.65	18.10	9.44	13.45	17	47.3	34.5	57.7	102.0	44.3	299.2	35.
	1.35	0.50	5.61	8.15	6.29	9.08	28	20.5	64.0	107.6	144.9	79.8	659.8	72.
5097 Furniture & Home Furnishings (63)	3.55	2.93	12.91	16.26	9.05	9.70	37	12.5	4.6	30.4	75.8	49.9	64.6	17.
	2.12	1.50	7.93	9.09	5.08	5.85	44	7.1	10.5	84.4	156.4	83.0	107.3	28.
	1.42	0.63	3.98	4.23	3.45	4.31	67	4.8	19.6	201.0	236.2	156.3	168.3	39.
5041 Groceries, General Line (217)	3.26	1.12	11.59	17.56	17.68	24.96	7	16.5	9.4	36.3	75.3	89.0	45.7	13.
	2.07	0.58	6.81	9.25	10.72	13.95	13	11.2	24.7	70.7	138.2	119.6	75.1	39.
	1.57	0.23	3.42	3.46	6.72	8.69	20	8.4	59.2	135.8	220.3	170.4	101.9	95.
5072 Hardware (187)	4.32	2.53	9.35	11.62	5.44	6.31	36	6.1	6.5	23.1	47.3	76.2	40.8	5.
	2.89	1.48	4.85	6.59	3.27	4.19	44	4.5	13.8	45.1	83.9	93.4	59.8	15.
	1.90	0.72	2.34	2.71	2.45	3.00	55	3.4	25.5	87.3	163.1	122.1	89.1	38.
5084 Industrial Machinery & Equipment (106)	3.18	2.56	12.36	15.79	6.69	9.88	37	12.3	8.0	38.0	69.8	58.1	63.6	10.
	2.22	1.51	7.05	9.03	4.67	6.12	47	7.4	17.9	69.5	107.2	87.6	100.9	23.
	1.65	0.58	3.55	3.93	3.08	3.81	58	4.4	38.5	121.0	178.5	109.1	173.8	66.
5098 Lumber & Construction Materials (156)	3.54	2.90	14.25	19.60	8.41	10.80	30	13.5	11.0	29.7	61.7	59.8	60.5	10.
	2.47	1.80	8.42	11.16	5.42	6.98	44	7.6	24.0	60.0	118.5	89.9	95.4	28.
	1.63	0.95	4.75	6.55	3.25	4.31	56	5.0	42.8	110.7	195.2	123.4	159.5	51.
5047 Meats & Meat Products (43)	3.81	1.80	25.89	53.82	23.31	35.97	15	88.9	8.2	24.7	67.0	18.8	140.6	22.
	1.80	1.12	12.94	16.57	17.14	23.89	19	44.4	27.5	69.8	104.0	55.8	240.8	34.
	1.37	0.48	5.39	9.70	8.33	14.84	22	24.9	45.7	131.9	175.0	116.3	351.9	69.
5091 Metals & Minerals (72)	3.60	4.00	12.50	14.12	5.90	6.80	33	7.9.	6.5	30.9	61.3	52.5	57.0	13
	2.36	2.09	7.94	9.84	4.02	4.94	45	5.2	26.6	62.1	113.5	91.5	81.9	24.
	1.64	0.93	4.39	5.89	2.64	3.46	59	3.9	42.3	123.0	161.8	125.1	126.5	48.
5028 Paints & Varnishes (38)	5.74	3.96	9.35	18.14	4.50	5.84	28	7.6	8.8	15.3	33.0	53.2	35.4	9
	2.95	1.31	4.67	7.94	3.67	4.77	39	6.2	18.4	33.0	63.4	83.1	62.0	19.
	2.06	0.35	2.02	2.66	2.48	2.98	49	5.1	34.6	72.2	118.0	95.4	113.0	59.
5096 Paper & Its Products (121)	3.43	2.40	12.60	16.65	7.99	10.04	30	12.3	6.0	33.0	59.5	60.9	65.2	10
	2.28	1.29	7.19	9.54	5.64	7.16	39	8.6	14.0	59.2	89.6	80.7	93.3	22.
	1.79	0.74	4.26	4.94	4.10	5.26	51	6.2	30.0	111.0	162.5	105.4	130.3	43.
5092 Petroleum & Petroleum Products (85)	3.16	3.59	14.74	34.20	5.98	12.93	24	26.0	32.0	21.5	36.4	32.2	107.2	21.
	2.12	2.00	8.63	21.10	4.15	8.32	33	17.5	50.0	33.2	66.8	54.7	151.3	46
	1.58	1.09	5.47	10.33	2.71	5.75	49	11.4	74.2	63.6	131.0	75.4	267.3	73
5033 Piece Goods (123)	3.40	2.26	11.34	12.79	8.38	8.83	34	9.9	1.8	41.7	63.9	66.5	56.2	5.
	2.01	1.34	5.71	6.19	5.04	5.19	52	6.1	5.0	88.0	112.2	88.6	89.2	14.
	1.60	0.67	2.75	2.80	3.27	3.68	68	4.1	13.1	144.4	187.6	139.5	137.2	38.
5074 Plumbing & Heating Equipt. & Sup. (184)	3.96	3.13	12.05	13.72	5.90	6.86	38	7.5	6.6	28.4	54.0	64.1	50.1	10
	2.68	1.74	6.91	8.57	3.99	4.99	46	5.8	13.0	49.8	95.7	84.2	78.7	22.
	1.92	0.87	4.00	4.70	3.00	3.81	58	4.4	25.5	89.4	164.4	109.3	107.5	46.
5044 Poultry & Poultry Products (35)	5.77	1.93	12.28	15.89	19.39	23.25	16	72.0	9.5	12.5	64.5	25.2	74.0	3.
	2.44	0.47	8.10	9.62	9.22	12.48	22	47.4	23.6	44.6	98.7	32.0	171.4	38
	1.65	0.27	4.02	6.18	5.97	8.42	27	19.1	41.3	121.9	218.1	71.0	375.5	86
5093 Scrap & Waste Materials (59)	3.77	3.59	13.72	32.83	6.31	11.18	20	23.0	11.5	19.7	34.8	23.7	70.6	11.
	2.45	2.29	8.07	15.81	4.07	6.39	32	13.6	33.9	40.0	48.4	48.5	148.7	31.
	1.55	0.92	4.20	6.17	2.31	4.46	44	8.4	48.2	72.6	108.3	92.0	307.3	67.
5014 Tires & Tubes (38)	2.83	3.78	16.39	20.22	6.18	7.56	34	7.0	15.3	39.6	96.5	75.8	63.7	6
	1.93	2.22	9.33	14.16	4.03	4.88	46	5.3	27.2	80.4	137.0	102.1	106.6	36
	1.66	1.46	5.84	8.40	2.75	3.82	62	4.4	38.3	126.6	253.2	138.5	148.8	73
5094 Tobacco & Its Products (96)	2.64	0.89	9.53	14.20	20.67	26.73	12	35.1	7.0	52.9	79.8	73.3	73.9	15
	1.87	0.46	6.25	7.52	12.72	17.24	17	17.7	13.8	85.6	118.5	100.2	112.6	31
	1.46	0.20	2.77	4.30	8.75	10.97	23	12.4	28.0	144.8	239.7	146.8	164.4	73

FIGURE 28-1 (continued)

Manufacturing & Construction

Line of Business (and number of concerns reporting)	Current assets to current debt	Net profits on net sales	Net profits on tangible net worth	Net profits on net working capital	Net sales to tangible net worth	Net sales to net working capital	Collection period	Net sales to inventory	Fixed assets to tangible net worth	Current debt to tangible net worth	Total debt to tangible net worth	Inventory to net working capital	Current debt to inventor	Funded debts to net working capital
	Times	Per cent	Per cent	Per cent	Times	Times	Days	Times	Per cent	Per cent	Per cent	Per cent	Per cent	Per cent
2871-72-79 Agricultural Chemicals (40)	6.09	4.11	8.29	17.01	3.90	10.69	43	17.2	25.0	16.0	63.5	19.5	80.5	19.2
	1.86	1.45	5.30	7.69	2.78	4.78	57	6.6	43.8	53.2	123.3	76.5	146.3	74.9
	1.25	0.69	1.20	2.31	1.72	2.86	85	5.0	76.7	101.4	178.4	157.9	341.1	130.7
3722-23-29 Airplane Parts & Accessories (58)	3.52	5.22	12.95	24.78	3.71	5.62	28	7.9	36.4	22.3	25.5	67.2	67.9	28.0
	2.16	3.04	9.06	13.32	2.92	4.57	51	5.2	53.6	45.6	72.4	86.6	92.6	54.4
	1.62	1.65	3.19	4.67	2.12	3.41	71	3.8	73.5	75.7	113.7	124.8	117.2	96.2
2051-52 Bakery Products (84)	2.50	4.25	12.97	66.78	5.69	23.38	16	39.6	64.2	18.0	34.6	34.2	152.8	23.7
	1.88	2.54	8.70	41.57	4.08	14.45	22	28.9	80.8	24.9	49.6	57.9	201.9	74.8
	1.46	0.90	5.43	19.36	2.76	10.37	27	21.9	101.5	42.1	99.0	82.6	287.0	150.7
3312-13-15-16-17 Blast Furnaces, Steel Wks. & Rolling Mills (60)	3.13	5.79	11.31	28.70	2.67	5.68	34	7.9	36.4	17.1	24.7	68.8	57.9	38.5
	2.56	3.66	8.66	16.25	1.98	4.23	43	5.4	58.5	26.3	55.9	81.1	80.6	77.5
	1.77	1.88	3.50	6.99	1.52	3.29	50	4.8	84.0	40.7	106.3	98.5	100.0	140.7
2331 Blouses & Waists, Women's & Misses' (62)	2.14	2.62	22.04	25.39	12.76	17.53	34	17.5	4.4	76.2	88.0	61.5	121.3	3.2
	1.67	1.34	12.35	16.63	9.33	12.02	46	12.1	8.3	126.3	144.3	88.7	179.5	12.7
	1.35	0.60	7.13	9.59	5.99	7.73	60	7.4	12.7	234.3	217.1	137.6	309.7	17.2
2731-32 Books; Publishing, Publishing & Printing (46)	3.97	7.56	13.23	20.40	3.32	6.06	43	9.2	9.2	21.0	41.6	47.3	52.3	9.4
	2.52	4.70	8.04	12.04	2.13	3.38	61	4.4	34.8	42.1	52.3	72.0	90.6	29.6
	1.86	2.23	4.98	6.99	1.40	1.87	87	2.8	60.1	75.3	131.5	104.6	184.3	95.3
2211 Broad Woven Fabrics, Cotton (43)	4.77	3.85	7.59	17.38	2.34	6.06	45	7.6	42.1	12.9	27.8	54.3	43.1	34.4
	3.10	2.42	4.88	10.52	1.92	3.84	56	5.1	57.0	21.2	45.9	69.0	63.0	61.0
	2.28	0.92	1.74	2.79	1.42	3.09	64	3.9	70.4	34.8	88.7	111.6	86.0	102.8
2031-32-33-34-35-36-37 Canned & Pres. Fruits, Veg. & Sea Foods (68)	2.19	3.51	11.11	24.40	5.44	12.65	14	8.2	39.1	30.4	61.7	92.0	64.5	14.4
	1.56	1.93	5.79	13.26	3.17	7.59	24	4.5	50.2	70.1	119.7	181.9	91.7	45.8
	1.23	0.28	0.63	3.12	2.21	4.56	36	2.9	76.4	138.1	211.6	327.7	114.3	92.2
2751 Commercial Printing except Lithographic (81)	3.65	4.03	15.49	34.16	4.75	9.04	33	**	37.5	19.4	44.2	**	**	20.4
	2.33	2.35	7.72	15.26	2.98	5.78	46	**	61.3	36.3	89.4	**	**	70.2
	1.70	1.18	2.88	6.14	1.85	3.99	57	**	98.8	62.3	147.0	**	**	140.4
3661-62 Communication Equipment (70)	3.51	4.80	13.73	18.84	3.95	5.88	42	7.5	21.6	26.8	35.0	53.4	60.9	16.6
	2.44	3.78	10.34	11.68	2.70	3.54	61	5.0	37.2	42.6	64.3	75.0	100.0	43.3
	1.37	2.23	5.10	7.73	2.01	2.14	86	3.6	52.2	84.7	152.1	121.8	121.3	66.7
3271-72-73-74-75 Concrete, Gypsum & Plaster Products (81)	4.09	5.87	11.62	37.89	2.88	9.27	40	21.6	45.8	14.7	32.2	36.5	77.7	14.5
	2.35	3.69	7.28	18.59	1.99	5.96	54	11.5	61.6	29.3	58.8	48.9	143.0	67.4
	1.64	1.79	4.18	9.29	1.55	3.42	77	6.5	79.8	47.0	106.0	75.2	254.9	94.8
2071-72-73 Confectionery & Related Products (46)	3.97	3.73	13.02	29.86	5.18	12.07	14	11.7	27.3	18.8	40.2	61.0	48.7	23.5
	2.60	2.17	7.52	17.76	3.24	6.63	20	7.9	44.0	33.3	70.2	84.2	70.5	56.5
	1.98	0.95	3.87	7.19	2.12	4.80	32	5.3	63.8	65.2	161.5	140.1	105.5	139.1
3531-32-33-34-35-36-37 Const., Min. & Handling Machy. & Equipt. (77)	3.74	5.90	15.32	24.35	3.25	5.39	37	7.0	20.4	24.0	37.1	60.2	44.2	14.3
	2.60	4.02	10.32	13.88	2.30	3.46	55	4.6	34.9	38.8	67.2	80.5	68.4	32.7
	1.84	1.96	4.93	6.25	1.81	2.62	77	2.9	49.6	62.0	107.8	112.3	106.8	60.7
2641-32-43-44-45-46-47-49 Converted Paper & Paperboard Prod. (53)	3.27	4.31	13.43	26.13	4.51	11.85	29	9.6	43.7	25.8	60.3	65.9	66.5	40.1
	2.45	3.01	9.36	16.77	2.90	5.69	42	6.8	63.1	43.0	81.4	88.9	92.1	52.4
	1.48	1.59	5.33	9.99	2.43	4.35	53	5.4	85.2	70.7	111.8	140.4	141.6	79.3
3421-23-25-29 Cutlery, Hand Tools & General Hardware (92)	4.13	6.31	14.70	22.30	3.65	4.66	36	6.5	25.8	19.0	29.7	62.7	42.2	8.9
	3.35	4.12	10.05	15.92	2.43	3.63	45	4.6	40.0	28.5	46.7	79.3	62.7	23.0
	2.22	2.41	5.80	6.83	1.69	2.69	61	3.3	51.4	54.4	115.0	99.2	97.5	54.6
2021-22-23-24-26 Dairy Products (121)	2.06	2.24	10.07	52.57	8.47	29.50	16	53.3	39.5	27.8	42.4	36.9	166.7	27.2
	1.54	1.30	7.02	20.52	5.49	17.35	24	31.5	62.7	45.8	73.4	62.8	276.5	64.1
	1.11	0.49	2.93	9.72	3.65	11.81	32	18.5	91.8	86.3	126.4	98.4	407.1	105.4
2335 Dresses: Women's, Misses' & Junior's (108)	2.14	2.31	18.56	24.28	13.18	15.70	40	19.8	2.9	74.9	60.7	49.2	133.0	11.2
	1.58	1.17	10.60	12.85	9.30	11.28	49	13.4	7.4	147.8	179.6	83.3	197.7	27.9
	1.38	0.37	2.47	3.51	6.10	6.29	60	8.4	16.3	218.8	253.0	134.8	265.5	57.8
2831-33-34 Drugs (62)	3.75	8.90	20.10	36.62	3.02	8.21	40	7.5	25.3	23.6	30.9	50.8	67.2	19.1
	2.24	4.76	12.95	15.67	2.12	3.98	55	6.0	40.1	30.0	54.9	78.9	100.0	52.9
	1.42	2.86	6.14	7.42	1.57	2.36	65	4.2	54.4	46.5	87.1	133.9	122.2	92.7
3641-43-44 Electric Lighting & Wiring Equipment (59)	4.43	4.79	14.24	18.89	3.51	5.70	38	7.7	8.7	21.2	48.5	56.3	50.5	18.6
	2.85	2.82	9.22	12.00	2.78	3.97	47	5.0	38.0	37.1	76.6	77.7	65.7	41.3
	2.19	1.25	4.10	6.38	2.03	2.91	60	4.0	65.2	59.5	132.5	98.3	106.4	81.5
3611-12-13 Electric Transmission & Distribution Equipment (59)	3.42	5.70	14.09	21.32	3.88	5.36	51	6.0	20.9	28.8	62.9	69.8	56.9	28.9
	2.70	2.96	8.92	13.71	2.87	3.61	59	4.1	38.5	46.1	93.9	85.6	74.2	48.4
	1.77	1.26	4.59	4.23	1.95	2.62	77	3.2	54.2	74.9	129.8	112.7	102.3	71.3
3621-22-23-24-29 Electrical Industrial Apparatus (52)	3.56	4.63	12.61	18.62	3.75	4.96	43	5.8	33.0	25.5	37.3	67.4	56.2	13.1
	2.56	2.91	7.71	11.93	2.71	3.91	54	4.6	46.8	44.5	83.5	83.9	75.2	41.3
	1.73	1.57	4.90	7.52	2.18	2.81	69	3.8	60.1	74.8	144.9	112.3	121.2	80.9
1731 Electrical Work (139)	2.99	3.57	18.77	28.97	7.51	10.40	**	**	10.6	36.1	58.9	**	**	7.8
	2.06	2.36	10.30	15.93	4.74	6.66	**	**	19.9	68.2	103.2	**	**	17.8
	1.47	1.33	6.16	10.00	3.22	4.62	**	**	33.7	131.9	195.0	**	**	43.4
3671-72-73-74-79 Electronic Components & Accessories (90)	3.03	5.47	16.94	23.27	4.41	5.73	45	7.0	30.3	34.5	55.6	66.5	67.2	21.9
	2.36	3.05	8.46	11.61	3.03	4.09	55	4.7	40.8	53.0	97.4	83.1	90.6	51.7
	1.72	0.96	2.00	2.91	2.21	2.78	70	3.5	77.2	101.9	183.0	111.6	120.9	81.9
3811 Engineering Laboratory & Scientific Instruments (34)	5.42	5.73	15.35	15.04	2.64	3.45	53	5.2	25.1	20.8	48.5	48.2	48.2	15.9
	2.96	4.08	9.76	11.47	2.20	2.82	75	3.7	37.7	37.5	76.1	69.0	72.6	43.0
	2.52	2.35	4.95	8.01	1.93	2.20	89	3.0	55.2	64.7	111.0	88.8	87.5	55.9

** Not computed. Printers carry only current supplies such as paper, ink, and binding materials rather than merchandise inventories for re-sale. Building Trades contractors have no inventories in the credit sense of the term. As a general rule, such contractors have no customary selling terms, each contract being a special job for which individual terms are arranged.

FIGURE 28-1 *(continued)*

Manufacturing & Construction

Line of Business (and number of concerns reporting)	Current assets to current debt	Net profits on net sales	Net profits on tangible net worth	Net profits on net working capital	Net sales to tangible net worth	Net sales to net working capital	Collection period	Net sales to inventory	Fixed assets to tangible net worth	Current debt to tangible net worth	Total debt to tangible net worth	Inventory to net working capital	Current debt to inventory	Funded debts to net working capital
	Times	Per cent	Per cent	Per cent	Times	Times	Days	Times	Per cent	Per cent	Per cent	Per cent	Per cent	Per cent
3441-42-43-44-46-49 Fabricated Structural Metal Products (127)	4.28	3.71	12.36	20.66	4.42	6.96	38	9.6	23.2	21.6	52.8	49.8	57.3	20.1
	2.69	2.23	7.40	11.62	3.13	4.59	54	6.1	38.6	41.8	93.0	73.6	86.9	44.0
	1.69	1.37	3.45	5.80	2.51	3.38	66	4.6	58.8	84.4	147.4	115.1	140.4	71.0
3522 Farm Machinery & Equipment (71)	4.87	4.78	15.13	23.93	4.48	5.25	26	5.0	20.2	18.5	42.9	64.1	34.9	18.0
	2.79	2.42	8.95	12.52	2.45	3.10	43	3.9	38.4	37.2	77.2	85.7	59.2	40.4
	1.61	1.39	3.41	4.10	1.75	2.32	71	3.0	59.3	83.3	146.0	114.0	92.3	57.6
3141 Footwear (109)	3.96	3.66	14.15	17.48	6.16	8.72	38	7.9	12.1	29.6	63.0	63.6	50.2	15.6
	2.41	2.04	8.89	10.73	4.26	4.99	51	5.5	25.0	59.0	101.9	91.7	79.9	25.4
	1.51	1.07	4.30	5.94	3.28	3.36	63	3.5	40.7	130.6	192.6	140.1	126.0	47.1
2371 Fur Goods (54)	2.47	1.18	6.46	8.13	8.48	9.72	27	11.7	1.6	64.9	94.7	61.2	85.3	14.7
	1.83	0.54	2.75	3.16	5.80	6.42	48	5.3	2.9	107.7	205.9	100.3	120.4	28.0
	1.50	0.16	0.81	1.02	3.87	4.17	77	3.5	7.5	193.6	253.4	160.1	172.0	34.6
1511 General Building Contractors (184)	1.95	2.51	16.83	27.05	12.85	22.00	**	**	10.8	63.4	113.8	**	**	11.4
	1.45	1.23	9.66	14.63	8.45	12.69	**	**	25.7	136.4	206.3	**	**	30.7
	1.21	0.58	5.23	8.41	4.33	7.56	**	**	46.8	235.9	325.8	**	**	97.3
3561-62-64-65-66-67-69 Genl. Indus. Machy. & Equipment (107)	3.40	5.82	14.07	24.88	3.90	6.36	42	8.3	28.1	24.9	44.9	60.0	58.6	13.9
	2.49	3.75	10.94	17.22	2.76	4.13	55	4.9	41.8	44.1	72.7	81.9	90.6	37.5
	1.83	2.27	7.32	10.28	1.99	3.04	69	3.9	65.6	74.0	117.1	112.1	128.0	64.4
2041-42-43-44-45-46 Grain Mill Products (67)	3.40	3.31	14.98	31.99	6.24	13.42	20	16.1	32.3	19.1	34.8	52.6	76.8	28.6
	2.24	2.28	9.85	18.50	4.35	9.21	27	11.3	50.2	37.5	58.0	77.6	104.4	51.9
	1.45	1.17	5.68	9.18	3.10	5.52	38	7.9	70.8	69.4	96.2	146.9	126.6	89.5
3431-32-33 Heating Apparatus & Plumbing Fixtures (41)	3.97	4.42	12.17	19.81	3.82	5.98	35	6.5	17.5	19.5	54.1	58.8	55.8	20.9
	2.44	2.28	7.25	10.93	2.83	4.36	48	5.2	42.9	35.9	90.5	85.9	85.1	44.4
	1.81	1.15	4.26	6.28	2.04	3.25	57	4.2	61.5	81.6	128.0	116.6	104.1	71.0
1621 Heavy Construction, except Highway & Street (118)	3.12	5.43	17.32	43.79	6.09	16.49	**	**	34.4	29.1	54.9	**	**	24.9
	1.87	2.67	9.77	22.61	3.74	8.47	**	**	60.0	58.0	88.2	**	**	60.9
	1.37	1.30	5.43	11.91	2.19	3.72	**	**	75.5	95.4	153.3	**	**	169.1
2251-52 Hosiery (56)	4.24	3.91	12.06	27.10	4.82	8.94	37	8.7	32.0	19.7	48.7	62.0	55.3	19.5
	2.39	2.39	7.92	14.02	3.10	5.42	45	5.5	52.8	44.4	81.9	96.0	89.4	37.1
	1.58	1.53	4.67	7.24	1.91	3.34	59	4.0	66.2	80.0	126.4	140.2	127.2	81.9
3631-32-33-34-35-36-39 Household Appliances (44)	3.84	5.19	14.07	24.31	4.99	8.60	28	7.6	17.0	25.7	45.0	67.0	52.7	24.5
	2.37	3.16	9.89	13.28	2.98	4.21	43	4.6	34.7	42.7	77.8	91.4	73.0	42.3
	1.48	1.26	5.69	5.97	2.25	3.17	61	3.7	53.1	81.1	149.1	141.2	94.4	59.7
2812-13-15-16-18-19 Industrial Chemicals (58)	2.92	6.24	13.60	35.14	2.95	10.73	39	11.5	34.8	17.8	26.4	66.5	69.9	48.3
	1.93	4.35	9.68	20.67	2.07	5.27	51	7.1	62.8	34.2	57.6	88.3	100.0	93.5
	1.26	2.33	4.99	8.33	1.67	3.78	63	5.2	90.8	52.8	95.1	136.2	138.4	188.3
3821-22 Instruments, Measuring & Controlling (44)	4.36	6.29	14.37	20.92	3.27	4.38	43	7.2	20.6	22.4	45.3	56.3	47.4	25.8
	2.83	4.42	12.07	15.84	2.65	3.14	57	4.2	36.8	38.9	82.7	70.3	66.0	44.5
	2.12	2.94	6.54	8.56	1.87	2.55	78	3.5	60.1	71.7	147.4	101.2	101.0	76.5
3321-22-23 Iron & Steel Foundries (61)	3.60	4.43	12.65	34.83	3.37	8.82	39	22.7	44.6	19.3	40.2	29.7	87.0	24.7
	2.42	2.87	7.53	16.97	2.62	6.25	46	11.0	59.2	29.9	57.1	68.5	122.5	42.8
	1.73	1.30	3.40	6.56	1.89	3.92	55	6.3	74.5	51.2	102.0	88.8	208.7	92.9
2253 Knit Outerwear Mills (52)	2.60	3.17	15.33	17.93	6.43	8.68	30	10.3	4.4	46.6	71.5	60.0	72.7	17.1
	1.93	1.93	8.86	10.67	4.31	6.33	46	6.0	24.9	73.6	95.5	108.2	91.5	27.0
	1.66	0.35	1.79	2.26	3.05	4.40	59	3.8	45.6	119.8	172.2	153.3	152.8	47.4
2082 Malt Liquors (26)	2.94	5.20	14.32	59.34	3.27	14.60	9	22.3	51.4	18.3	32.2	34.6	121.1	75.6
	2.07	3.74	9.53	36.46	2.65	10.10	16	18.8	67.9	23.1	44.7	54.9	156.0	92.2
	1.62	2.10	5.18	17.27	2.16	4.47	25	14.6	84.9	29.7	76.2	76.7	234.5	200.2
2515 Mattresses & Bedsprings (46)	4.37	3.48	11.28	15.98	5.77	8.98	39	11.7	14.5	24.1	53.5	40.3	72.5	14.2
	2.35	1.96	5.52	8.62	3.31	5.35	49	9.2	23.4	42.3	89.4	67.6	92.0	35.7
	1.83	1.08	3.26	5.92	2.57	4.12	56	6.0	45.6	77.3	158.0	97.8	138.7	75.5
2011 Meat Packing Plants (88)	3.31	1.52	12.43	40.63	17.25	34.29	12	46.5	38.0	20.8	38.1	42.2	84.2	15.9
	2.06	0.91	8.50	19.13	9.33	21.29	15	30.5	58.4	48.0	71.2	68.3	130.3	40.1
	1.35	0.41	4.66	9.51	6.58	12:58	19	19.2	82.9	84.0	116.8	112.9	203.2	93.0
3461 Metal Stampings (100)	3.62	3.75	10.87	23.73	4.18	8.23	28	12.5	35.7	20.9	41.9	49.3	68.5	12.9
	2.32	2.63	7.03	15.40	3.07	5.73	36	8.6	50.0	35.7	76.4	75.7	95.0	44.5
	1.71	1.21	3.88	8.41	2.14	4.05	47	6.4	72.1	64.8	120.8	109.4	165.1	83.2
3541-42-44-45-48 Metalworking Machy. & Equipment (121)	3.26	6.74	14.08	26.50	3.48	7.67	38	11.0	35.0	26.3	44.4	56.4	55.4	12.1
	2.29	3.87	9.79	16.46	2.29	4.43	54	5.5	47.8	38.4	72.9	88.5	100.0	44.8
	1.55	1.50	3.69	6.62	1.68	2.96	69	3.4	68.3	68.4	129.7	118.2	189.2	93.8
2431 Millwork (35)	4.05	2.90	12.51	19.58	6.14	9.27	35	9.8	15.3	19.5	46.5	46.4	58.6	7.9
	2.60	2.06	7.78	11.15	4.01	4.96	46	6.8	40.3	43.3	98.8	74.0	106.5	43.9
	1.66	1.30	4.33	6.26	2.13	3.26	61	4.5	71.7	119.2	208.3	128.2	140.6	84.8
3599 Miscellaneous Machinery, except Electrical (96)	4.34	6.04	17.15	31.55	4.01	7.21	35	23.2	24.5	17.2	49.9	27.9	68.1	16.2
	2.72	3.40	10.02	15.89	2.46	4.74	45	10.9	43.6	34.4	73.7	56.0	128.7	33.6
	1.93	1.37	4.11	7.31	1.79	3.58	59	5.5	72.3	58.3	123.7	89.4	234.6	78.5
3714 Motor Vehicle Parts & Accessories (77)	3.64	5.98	16.60	26.38	3.98	6.27	34	8.7	25.6	22.3	50.3	56.1	55.0	31.6
	2.70	3.99	12.35	18.83	2.80	4.28	42	6.2	43.4	38.2	78.5	82.7	80.4	57.3
	1.75	2.42	7.26	9.85	2.08	2.99	51	4.1	64.3	62.9	145.2	109.4	115.3	83.5
3361-62-69 Nonferrous Foundries (46)	3.72	5.09	11.43	26.90	4.04	9.86	31	18.5	35.5	23.2	47.9	34.5	81.8	18.6
	2.30	2.98	7.72	15.23	3.01	6.56	40	12.5	46.4	39.0	65.8	54.7	140.5	57.4
	1.69	1.13	4.12	7.69	2.28	3.90	52	6.8	77.2	50.8	85.8	109.7	243.7	135.2

** Not computed. Printers carry only current supplies such as paper, ink, and binding materials rather than merchandise inventories for re-sale. Building Trades contractors have no inventories in the credit sense of the term. As a general rule, such contractors have no customary selling terms, each contract being a special job for which individual terms are arranged.

FIGURE 28-1 (concluded)

Manufacturing & Construction

Line of Business (and number of concerns reporting)	Current assets to current debt	Net profits on net sales	Net profits on tangible net worth	Net profits on net working capital	Net sales to tangible net worth	Net sales to net working capital	Collection period	Net sales to inventory	Fixed assets to tangible net worth	Current debt to tangible net worth	Total debt to tangible net worth	Inventory to net working capital	Current debt to inventory	Funded debts to net working capital
	Times	Per cent	Per cent	Per cent	Times	Times	Days	Times	Per cent	Per cent	Per cent	Per cent	Per cent	Per cent
2541–42	3.72	4.88	18.72	29.87	5.27	9.39	36	14.6	18.1	29.3	86.2	45.1	79.2	36.2
Office & Store Fixtures	2.08	3.07	10.80	16.89	3.91	5.86	59	8.6	32.7	59.9	123.0	65.7	141.4	54.6
(52)	1.56	1.37	5.57	8.78	2.43	3.56	72	5.7	66.5	100.3	197.0	122.5	208.3	108.0
2361–63–69	2.01	2.52	18.91	22.02	12.72	18.06	30	16.5	3.8	94.7	102.1	69.8	91.4	6.9
Outerwear, Children's	1.56	1.12	8.96	10.75	10.20	10.58	42	8.7	16.0	157.9	203.5	110.4	179.7	15.0
& Infants' (48)	1.32	0.29	2.75	3.40	5.39	7.21	57	5.4	26.8	244.8	341.6	170.2	238.8	90.9
2851 Paints,	4.40	4.24	11.02	20.93	3.94	6.19	33	8.9	21.2	18.9	36.7	55.6	44.8	13.8
Varnishes, Lacquers	3.14	2.48	7.32	11.90	2.85	4.47	41	6.6	34.3	28.9	64.4	71.3	68.8	28.9
& Enamels (108)	2.23	1.46	4.49	7.15	2.05	3.35	54	5.1	56.1	43.9	98.7	101.2	102.7	57.6
2621	3.49	6.23	10.57	31.90	2.30	6.06	33	9.9	38.7	16.7	22.2	46.4	70.4	41.8
Paper Mills, except	2.57	4.34	8.19	17.96	1.73	4.78	40	7.3	70.9	20.7	48.8	62.7	94.4	104.0
Building Paper (54)	1.51	3.17	5.88	12.59	1.36	3.10	46	5.7	99.0	26.6	89.2	86.3	105.9	192.9
2651–52–53–54–55	4.13	5.85	15.91	38.39	4.40	8.76	30	14.4	34.2	16.6	54.3	35.7	67.7	28.9
Paperboard Containers	2.43	3.36	9.37	19.12	3.00	6.21	38	11.6	45.8	36.2	83.4	61.9	115.8	87.1
& Boxes (48)	1.67	1.97	6.16	11.79	2.27	3.81	49	7.1	89.3	74.3	116.5	110.9	205.2	154.2
3712–13	3.77	3.65	15.58	19.61	5.78	9.78	38	8.3	19.5	30.6	60.6	57.2	62.6	11.3
Passenger car, Truck	2.12	1.82	7.32	11.89	4.12	5.76	48	6.4	38.6	59.5	100.3	83.0	96.4	48.6
& Bus Bodies (48)	1.54	0.66	2.29	4.49	2.56	3.74	57	5.0	62.6	117.0	274.1	121.4	144.3	86.0
2911	1.78	7.45	14.09	95.50	3.14	15.41	17	22.0	7.3	6.8	6.5	45.7	100.0	47.3
Petroleum Refining	1.14	3.76	6.84	30.92	1.78	10.72	30	13.0	41.1	19.1	23.6	117.8	109.3	107.3
(53)	1.00	1.98	3.18	13.07	1.19	3.79	50	8.5	85.5	53.6	97.9	168.3	190.5	249.9
2821–22–23–24	2.55	6.36	14.61	36.27	4.34	10.66	44	9.6	26.3	29.6	45.8	57.0	93.0	21.1
Plastics Materials &	1.88	2.75	8.30	15.45	2.63	5.87	53	8.0	61.0	44.9	60.0	79.0	117.8	86.4
Synthetics (32)	1.26	(1.08)	(2.61)	(4.12)	2.07	4.34	61	6.1	91.9	100.9	142.7	143.1	179.1	128.0
1711	2.59	2.76	19.17	27.47	11.06	14.67	**	**	11.2	45.4	63.0	**	**	4.2
Plumbing, Heating &	1.74	1.71	11.79	16.39	6.07	9.77	**	**	21.8	99.2	114.3	**	**	19.9
Air Conditioning (105)	1.32	1.00	6.91	8.83	4.11	5.64	**	**	41.9	222.3	269.5	**	**	37.4
2421	3.59	7.92	17.90	53.93	3.80	9.02	19	9.8	30.0	15.8	29.8	54.8	58.7	12.8
Sawmills & Planing	2.27	4.04	10.75	28.73	2.46	5.57	31	7.3	58.9	29.1	69.8	84.8	86.0	54.7
Mills (77)	1.52	2.41	4.91	7.96	1.55	3.18	44	4.8	86.4	57.7	116.4	125.5	130.9	126.4
3451–52	3.48	6.29	14.96	31.91	3.44	7.98	29	12.8	39.6	18.6	35.8	55.1	59.1	20.8
Screw Machine	2.53	4.37	11.12	22.31	2.59	5.50	37	7.9	52.0	30.0	54.3	76.8	97.1	29.4
Products (72)	1.82	2.57	6.06	11.67	2.02	3.80	44	5.3	70.8	51.4	95.6	109.7	144.6	86.4
2321–22 Shirts, Under-	2.42	3.01	13.29	15.64	6.87	8.43	37	6.6	3.1	67.3	80.2	82.8	68.8	7.4
wear & Nightwear,	1.93	1.60	7.83	8.20	4.64	5.32	54	5.0	12.4	101.7	112.4	107.2	98.8	11.6
Men's & Boys' (52)	1.50	0.82	3.24	3.48	3.55	3.78	66	3.9	24.0	172.6	175.5	146.0	138.5	43.4
2841–42–43–44 Soap,	3.50	7.27	19.29	33.05	4.07	8.06	37	11.1	22.0	25.7	38.7	46.8	80.8	16.2
Detergents, Perfumes	2.27	3.95	12.36	19.50	3.22	4.45	54	7.8	33.4	41.0	57.5	70.9	103.2	36.4
& Cosmetics (57)	1.71	1.38	5.61	7.54	2.26	3.19	71	5.2	49.6	66.1	119.9	96.3	133.3	72.1
2086	2.66	5.88	17.65	76.78	4.98	19.99	16	25.6	55.3	18.4	56.4	46.9	106.5	53.9
Soft Drinks, Bottled &	1.70	3.91	11.94	39.93	3.20	9.16	21	17.0	83.9	31.9	83.9	83.5	177.7	159.0
Canned (67)	1.31	2.68	7.27	24.58	1.89	5.74	30	9.8	140.2	67.9	221.0	114.1	262.3	326.5
3551–52–53–54–55–59	3.63	6.17	13.04	22.62	3.44	5.99	46	5.6	25.3	26.1	59.9	59.8	58.2	21.7
Special Industry	2.62	3.78	8.86	12.37	2.37	3.30	66	4.3	38.3	41.4	81.6	82.5	82.3	38.8
Machinery (89)	1.74	1.14	3.24	4.82	1.77	2.52	90	3.3	57.0	75.1	144.0	113.0	130.6	78.0
2337	2.52	1.86	11.98	14.93	11.16	12.80	36	20.5	2.9	50.1	120.9	40.5	105.5	8.0
Suits & Coats, Women's	1.81	0.94	7.16	7.84	7.47	8.30	48	9.6	6.0	105.8	191.7	80.8	164.2	24.1
& Misses' (94)	1.44	0.30	2.03	2.54	4.07	5.53	65	5.9	12.0	197.9	358.9	119.0	259.7	50.1
2311 Suits, Coats &	2.56	3.00	13.73	17.62	6.68	8.02	29	7.5	4.2	55.4	82.9	73.1	70.5	7.6
Overcoats, Men's &	2.01	1.39	8.17	9.80	4.59	5.42	56	5.0	10.0	93.2	131.0	105.0	93.3	17.3
Boys' (104)	1.58	0.83	3.85	4.29	3.00	3.73	81	3.5	20.0	146.6	200.5	154.7	133.8	34.4
3841–42–43 Surgical,	5.99	7.19	16.39	25.49	3.08	6.93	37	6.7	14.2	14.3	27.9	55.2	40.5	7.3
Medical & Dental	3.66	4.90	11.65	17.44	2.50	3.23	56	4.3	24.6	27.6	52.4	68.0	63.8	18.9
Instruments (51)	2.12	2.72	4.44	8.42	1.74	2.44	73	3.6	37.6	47.1	84.8	104.9	109.5	51.3
3941–42–43–49	2.59	4.17	13.36	23.40	5.06	6.88	43	6.1	19.3	49.0	86.4	84.8	70.4	27.5
Toys, Amusement &	1.97	2.55	9.22	13.30	3.87	5.22	55	5.0	38.3	73.7	129.9	116.5	104.4	43.8
Sporting Goods (60)	1.47	1.61	5.79	6.03	2.56	3.47	84	3.3	55.5	148.5	195.9	155.5	156.1	77.1
2327	2.88	2.95	16.27	17.19	8.66	9.88	39	9.0	4.0	49.3	80.1	59.6	79.4	13.8
Trousers, Men's &	1.83	1.64	7.37	8.78	5.01	5.91	61	4.9	7.2	124.0	168.7	93.3	112.7	27.8
Boys' (52)	1.49	0.38	1.50	1.66	3.38	3.83	88	3.6	22.4	166.1	246.7	141.8	172.9	43.0
2341 Underwear &	2.72	2.73	13.05	19.88	7.70	10.69	31	8.9	7.6	46.9	68.1	59.5	66.3	13.2
Nightwear, Women's	2.01	1.62	10.22	11.77	5.67	6.60	45	6.2	16.0	82.8	137.4	115.2	105.4	20.2
& Children's (66)	1.44	0.90	4.38	5.03	4.04	4.26	53	4.4	33.0	154.4	198.2	185.6	148.0	60.7
2511–12 Wood	3.93	5.07	14.07	20.60	4.61	6.31	28	9.0	19.1	22.4	44.0	54.6	46.5	9.8
Household Furniture	3.02	3.30	9.99	14.11	2.90	4.31	42	6.4	33.4	35.7	55.7	75.7	66.9	26.2
& Upholstered (108)	2.12	0.81	3.07	5.61	2.29	3.36	56	4.2	49.1	59.7	101.7	107.5	107.5	42.0
2328	4.62	3.87	11.71	12.33	4.03	4.65	35	5.4	3.7	25.5	59.7	68.4	44.1	6.0
Work Clothing, Men's	2.86	2.23	6.80	7.10	3.14	3.48	46	3.8	15.4	50.0	89.8	82.1	67.9	21.7
& Boys' (108)	2.09	1.10	3.28	3.46	2.17	2.21	98	2.9	27.1	81.8	110.6	117.1	95.8	43.1

( ) Indicates loss.

** Not computed. Printers carry only current supplies such as paper, ink, and binding materials rather than merchandise inventories for re-sale. Building Trades contractors have no inventories in the credit sense of the term. As a general rule, such contractors have no customary selling terms, each contract being a special job for which individual terms are arranged.

and construction, developed by the Industry Studies Department of Dun & Bradstreet, Inc.

LIMITATIONS TO STATEMENT ANALYSIS

The techniques of financial statement analysis which have just been discussed involve one very material limitation. They are static in the sense that, at best, they can estimate the apparent ability of a company to meet its obligations as of some *past* date. While it is impossible to estimate future debt payment ability accurately, this lack of skill does not remove the desirability of trying to do so. One tool of credit management directed toward providing some idea of this desired estimate is sometimes available through the use of the cash flow projection.

The Credit Research Foundation of the NACM made the following statement on the topic of cash flow projection:[4]

The flow of cash is an integral part of every business operation. Cash performs a cycle flowing into materials, labor, overhead and inventory; then into receivables and eventually back into cash. The manner and timing within which this cycle is completed determines the operating efficiency of the business. For the credit manager attempting to determine the financial potential of a customer, this short term financial position is important. He must know whether the business has the ability to generate cash through its daily operations within the time necessary to meet its operating expenses and other financial obligations as they come due. Therefore, the technique of cash flow projection is an invaluable tool, not only for the creditor grantor, but for the judicial use by the management of a business which seeks credit as well.

A cash flow projection is a planned program for forecasting estimated cash receipts by various classes, and budgeting cash disbursements according to the obligations and requirements of the business for a specific future period. Ordinarily, a six months' or one year projection is made.

Normally cash is budgeted by month and projected for the forecast period decided upon. However, since actual cash receipts may deviate from the forecast, comparisons between estimated and actual performance should be made periodically. Often such a review is made monthly so that required adjustments in the forecast can be made promptly.

As in the case of any business forecast, the major advantage of the cash flow projection is the development of an intelligent plan. It takes the guesswork out of cash programming by providing a bird's eye view of the cash position in advance. It also enables norms against which adjustments can be made as conditions change and provides a measure for determining the effectiveness of the plan.

4 | *Cash Flow Projection, a Tool of Credit Management* (New York: Credit Research Foundation of the National Association of Credit Management, 1961), pp. 1-2. Also see James R. DeMaioribus and John J. Omlor, "Effect of Accounts Receivable on Cash Flow," *Credit and Financial Management*, September 1968, p. 28.

The cash flow projection assists management by pointing out periods when cash will be plentiful and periods when borrowing will be required. By knowing in advance when funds will be needed, the business manager can plan his loan requirements and take advantage of the least costly source of funds. Furthermore, the cash flow projection provides a definite schedule for the repayment of loans in light of the cash expected to be available each month. In the cash flow statement, borrowed money is included as a particular item under receipts, and cash to repay the loans is included in the cash budget under disbursements.

. . . .

The cash forecast is based to a considerable extent upon a projection of past experience; but it also must take into account changing business influences, general economic environment, internal plans for growth and expansion, sales expectations and spending habits of customers.

While disbursements for capital plant requirements and existing payables of other obligations can be budgeted quite accurately according to the plans of management and in compliance with known payment terms, the sales forecast and collection of accounts receivable require particular analysis and independent projection. Cash receipts generated directly by sales will depend on the amount and regularity of total sales, the percentage of cash sales to total sales, selling terms for credit sales, and collection effectiveness.

Decisions are being reached daily that deviate from the norm and that prove to be profitable to the creditor firm.[5] Thus exceptions to the rule occur, and the area of individual human judgment on the part of credit executives cannot be overlooked. It must be realized that, as a result, most decisions are made by people themselves instead of merely dubbing the given information into a series of ratios and formulas and allowing decisions to result entirely on the basis of the computed results.

ILLUSTRATIVE USE OF RATIO ANALYSIS

Although other comparisons may be made and prove revealing, the ratios discussed above should be more than ample for most cases. The skilled analyst, of course, compares one ratio to other ratios. The object is to compare the condition of the business as a unit. Any one ratio emphasizes and concentrates attention upon highly significant and important details. The interpretation of these details becomes more significant as they are related to others and finally to the entire business unit. The skilled analyst also looks for trends which indicate whether the business being examined is showing progress toward a sounder condition or retrogression toward a less sound state of affairs.

Table 28-2 provides an illustration of statement analysis. These

5 / Ronald W. Melicher, "New Test for Diagnosing Marginal Accounts," *Credit and Financial Management*, September 1970, p. 12.

TABLE 28-2
The Fashion Shop
(retailer of ladies' ready-to-wear)

	19—	%	19—	%
Cash	$ 10,483	6	$ 4,550	3
Receivables	14,977	9	22,657	15
Inventory	60,642	36	45,318	31
Total Current Assets	$ 86,102	51	$ 72,525	49
Fixed assets	82,349	49	74,026	51
Total Assets	$168,541	100	$146,551	100
Current liabilities	$ 25,872	15	$ 23,880	16
Fixed liabilities	38,000	23	30,000	21
Net worth	104,669	62	92,671	63
Total Liabilities and Net Worth	$168,541	100	$146,551	100
Sales	$225,000		$151,688	
Net Profit	7,532		5,221	

Ratio Analysis	19—	19—
Current assets to current liabilities	3.33	3.04
Current assets less inventory to current liabilities (acid test)	0.98	1.14
Debt to net worth	0.61	0.58
Sales to inventory	3.71	3.35
Sales to receivables	15.02	6.69
Sales to net worth	2.15	1.64
Percent net profit to sales	3.35	3.44
Percent net profit to total assets	4.47	3.56
Percent net profit to net worth	7.20	5.63

figures may be interpreted by the credit man as follows:

Both total assets and total liabilities have decreased. The inventory has decreased $15,000, from 36 to 31 percent of total assets. This decline in inventory has, however, been nearly counteracted by the increase in receivables, so that current assets make up almost as large a part of total assets as before. The current assets to current liabilities ratio test shows that current assets are still considerably in excess of current liabilities, indicating that the firm is not in a dangerous condition in this respect.

The acid-test ratio indicates that, even with inventory omitted, the current assets are equal to the current liabilities. For this ratio the minimum for satisfactory conditions is often stated as 1 to 1. The debt to net worth ratio has improved. Despite the decline in net worth, there is a still greater decline in liabilities. It is believed by credit men that owners should have, as a general rule, a larger stake in the business than creditors.

The sales to inventory ratio indicates the efficiency with which the management turns its investment in merchandise into sales. This firm has shown a declining efficiency in this respect, and many firms of this type have a sales to inventory ratio of at least 7 or 8 to 1.

The sales to receivables ratio is alarming. It has deteriorated sharply and shows that the management is not efficient in collecting. Not only has this ratio decreased greatly, but it has reached the point where it is evident that the firm has accepted credit unwisely. (It should be assumed that there has been no change in the type of credit offered.)

The deterioration of both these ratios can be partially explained by the decrease in sales. It must be further said, however, that the firm did not adjust itself to this decline by reducing either its inventory or its receivables to bring them correctly in line with the lessened sales volume. This has kept it from turning these assets into cash and reducing current liabilities accordingly. It has meant the sacrifice of cash and the loss of opportunities to take cash discounts.

The ratio of sales to net worth shows efficiency in the use of owners' capital. Too low a ratio here means that owners' capital is not being used efficiently; too high a ratio shows insufficient capital for the volume of business being attempted. In this case the ratio is too low and is getting worse. Partial explanation of the low ratio here is found in the large investment in fixed assets which are not fully productive.

The three profit percentages are the most encouraging signs in this situation. The net profit to sales appears better than it really is, because adequate reserves against losses on bad debts have not been set up. The ratios of net profit to total assets and to net worth, although not large, are satisfactory.

The credit man reviewing this situation finds some indication of satisfactory conditions and some of very unsatisfactory conditions. He has only the two statements. If he had one or two more, he could better determine the trend. He must determine whether the trend of sales is a result of national and local economic conditions and whether an improvement is to be expected in the near future. Or is this drastic drop a reflection of poor management? There are ample assets to protect creditors· and there appears to be no immediate danger of failure. He might expect payments to be somewhat slow, but would feel safe in accepting a moderate amount of credit if he is able to resolve the declining sales figure. Any decision made involves a compromise.

The future prospects of the firm depend upon what steps the management takes to correct the unsatisfactory conditions. The firm must stage a vigorous selling drive to clean out its surplus stock and at the same time must wage an effective campaign to collect from its customers who are delinquent in their payments. The application of the funds realized from these sources to paying off its own current liabilities would bring them down to manageable proportions and would make the firm liquid enough to take advantage of cash discounts. It also would bring about a proportion of assets to liabilities such that when business conditions improved it could increase its inventory and receivables to keep pace with increased sales. These increases could be managed on credit when accompanied by increased sales, but the wisdom of additional current debt is subject to considerable speculation.

CONCLUSIONS ON STATEMENT ANALYSIS

The methods discussed in the analysis and interpretation of financial statements are obviously not all of the acceptable ones. This does, however, introduce the subject. Other methods are available, and other factors should often be considered in order to make a sound appraisal and interpretation. The major thing to gain in making this appraisal and interpretation is the intelligent understanding of financial statement facts. As the credit manager relates these facts to other significant types of information, the knowledge given him by reading the statement becomes more meaningful and significant.

REVIEW AND DISCUSSION QUESTIONS

1. Explain how financial statements divulge trends in a business and help a credit manager in his decision-making process.
2. Discuss the four commonly accepted methods of financial statement analysis. Explain the most important features of each method.
3. Which method is the one most closely dependent upon an analyst's experience and judgment? Why?
4. Describe the background, development, and reasoning behind the ratio analysis approach to financial statement analysis.
5. What are the most important liquidity ratios? Explain what each ratio reveals.
6. What are the seven ratios most generally accepted as capable of showing the solvency condition of a firm? Explain what each ratio reveals.
7. List the trend and managerial efficiency ratios that appear in the material in this chapter, and explain what each of these ratios reveals.

8. Do you believe it possible to determine accurately the managerial efficiency of a business firm by using ratio analysis? Explain your answer.

9. How are standards used in financial statement analysis?

10. Where might such standards be obtained?

11. Discuss the limitations to financial statement analysis.

12. Explain what is meant by cash flow projection.

13. Study the illustration titled "The Fashion Shop" shown in Table 28-2. Assume you have received an initial order amounting to $1,750. The order is to be made up of women's coats and dresses.

    a) On the basis of the analysis accompanying the illustration would you accept or reject this order? Why or why not?

    b) Would you want additional information on this case? What type of information would be particularly helpful?

    c) If you have rejected the order, would you accept it on c.o.d. terms? Explain your decision.

14. The Happy Shoe Store. *Situation.* Assume you are credit manager for the Royal Shoe Company. Your firm manufactures a complete line of shoes, men's, women's and children's, and distributes them directly to retail outlets. Your merchandising method is to establish the line with one of the better retail stores and attempt to get the major portion of the trade from the selected outlet rather than to sell all possible outlets. Thus the number of accounts handled is small, but each account is rather substantial.

    The Happy Shoe Store has been an outlet for approximately 40 years, becoming a major outlet during the years 1940 to 1945. During these years you favored them by allotting them something more than their share of your production, and they expanded substantially. During the past few years their purchases have been close to $30,000 a year, and the account with you has tended to increase. From a running balance of approximately $3,000, it has mounted until it is currently $10,348. The payments which had been discounted have deteriorated until now the account would be classified as slow, even unsatisfactory.

    You receive a current financial statement direct from the Happy Shoe Store and the receipt of the statement for the year 1971 prompts you to review the account completely and to order a current credit report and a personal character credit report on Walter Green, the proprietor.

    Required:
    a) Make a complete analysis of the financial data.
    b) Make a careful analysis of the credit information on hand.
    c) Recommend the action which would be appropriate and state the reasons for the recommendations made.
    d) What payment experience could the Royal Shoe Company expect?
    e) What collection experience is the Happy Shoe Store having with its accounts receivable?
    f) What additional information, if any, would you like to have to make a more complete analysis?

Financial Information. Copies of standardized financial statements for the last four years are given below:

	12/31/1968	12/31/1969	12/31/1970	12/31/1971
Assets:				
Cash	$ 10,526	$ 8,236	$ 8,684	$ 7,744
Receivables	2,344	2,190	3,172	13,430
Inventory	48,420	47,526	49,946	51,634
Other Current Assets	4,200	4,338	5,190	5,248
Total Current Assets	$ 65,490	$ 62,290	$ 66,992	$ 78,056
Furniture & Fixtures	14,244	13,948	13,462	12,852
Total Assets	$ 79,734	$ 76,238	$ 80,454	$ 90,908
Liabilities:				
Accounts Payable	$ 14,116	$ 13,966	$ 18,438	$ 25,284
Notes Payable (less than 1 year)	7,724	4,230	3,948	4,086
Accrued Taxes & Expenses ...	2,206	1,962	2,234	2,436
Total Current Liabilities ...	$ 24,046	$ 20,158	$ 24,620	$ 31,806
Net Worth	$ 55,688	$ 56,080	$ 55,834	$ 59,102
Total Liabilities & Net Worth	$ 79,734	$ 76,238	$ 80,454	$ 90,908
Sales	$148,534	$140,236	$131,634	$141,232
Cost of Goods Sold	93,504	90,688	85,162	93,226
Gross Margin	$ 55,030	$ 49,548	$ 46,472	$ 48,006
Total Expenses	44,756	42,526	40,238	41,426
Net Profit	$ 10,274	$ 7,022	$ 6,234	$ 6,580

Credit Information. Pertinent information from the credit reports arranged under appropriate headings is presented below.

History and Method of Operation. The Happy Shoe Store was organized in 1933. During the first five years of operation nothing above a bare living was earned, but more rapid progress was made following 1939. In 1941 new quarters were obtained, the store was expanded, and substantial progress was made. It is believed that the rate of progress has slowed down in later years, but the store is considered the leading store in its line.

Operated as a family shoe store, a complete line of men's, women's, and children's shoes is carried. Their principal line is Royal, which is featured in their advertising and display. Fixtures are modern and attractive, windows are attractive, and the stock is orderly and well arranged. They are regarded as a promotional store and frequently emphasize special promotions which are advertised heavily. At the start of 1971, the Happy Shoe Store started promoting quite heavily an option-terms revolving credit plan. They had considered joining a bank credit card plan but decided against such an action.

Walter Green, the owner, is 55 years old, married and experienced in the line. He is active in the business. He employs an assistant manager and two salesmen on a full-time basis, with additional personnel employed on a part-time basis for the weekend and special sales.

The Happy Shoe Store is located in the downtown section of Middleville, a city of 75,000 population. Middleville is an expanding industrial center and also a trading center for the surrounding area.

Ledger Clearance. By direct inquiry of sources the following information is obtained.

HC	Owes Now	Payments
$2234	$2234	$600 not due, balance past due.
294	264	Now on c.o.d. basis.
900	400	Pays when due, formerly discounted.
634	—	Discounts.
2600	736	30 to 60 days slow.
1000	—	Pays when due

Personal. The character credit report in large part repeated the information covered under history. Additional comments were, "Thomas Green did not marry until 1963; his wife is reported to be 20 years younger than he. Since marriage he has become very active socially, and he is an active member of the local country club. . . . He formerly gave close attention to the business but has now left it entirely in the hands of the assistant manager. . . . Some of the plant managers in charge of branch plants of national concerns have incomes well above the community level and are used to living accordingly."

29

Analysis of and Decision
in Commercial Credit and
Setting of Credit Lines

The basic purpose of credit data is to assist the credit executive in making a better analysis of the credit risk and in reaching a sounder decision. In other words, will *profitable* sales and *continuing* sales be the result of the acceptance of the order? A discussion of the role of analysis and decision making in commercial credit transactions and the setting of credit lines is the subject matter of this chapter.

CORE OF THE COMMERCIAL CREDIT TASK

As stated in Chapter 22, many operations are performed in a commercial credit department. Orders are received, investigations are instituted, credit files are opened, accounts are controlled, credit records are maintained, customers are billed, collections are pressed, and adjustments are made. However, as in consumer credit, the really critical core of the commercial credit task is arriving at credit decisions. When credit decisions are formed on the basis of accurate information, properly evaluated and carefully analyzed, they will reflect sounder and more rational judgments. Decisions cannot always be free from error—no prediction of the future can always be correct—but they should be right in a sufficient proportion of cases to conform to the credit policies and objectives previously established.

Establishment of a "House Standard"

In order for a credit manager to accomplish the objectives desired by top management of his firm, it is desirable for management to furnish a clearly defined and understood statement of what is desired of his department. Once this is accomplished, the credit manager is in a better position to establish what might be called a "house standard" or a guide by which he may judge the pertinent qualities of credit risks seeking to purchase from his firm. In determining such a house standard, the credit manager is influenced by various external or uncontrollable factors such as competition, general business conditions, and characteristics of the local market. Certain controllable factors also influence the establishment of this guide. These include profit margin of the seller, type of product, seasonal aspects of the product, use of special terms and special arrangements for marginal and submarginal customers, influence of collection policies and procedures, personality of the credit manager, and other managerial influences. As these factors vary from time to time, so does the house standard by which the credit manager judges whether to accept or reject customer orders. Some of the factors have more weight at certain times than other factors, but no one factor or set of factors is always dominating and all-conclusive.

External Factors. The credit manager, in deciding whether an order is worthy of approval or subject to rejection, must determine the degree of risk connected with the account and then compare this risk to the level the firm is willing to accept. In establishing this level, the credit manager must consider what his competition is doing in the way of lenient or strict credit, type of credit terms, and lenient or strict collections. Regardless of the desire of a company to dictate its own house standard, consideration must be given to the other fellow, who also is eagerly seeking the customer's order.

Attention also must be directed to general business conditions. When the economy is at a high level of activity and the demand for a company's products exceeds its present capacity to produce the necessary supply, the credit manager of the company will have an entirely different philosophy of credit acceptance and rejection from that normally found in periods of reduced business activity and troubled times in moving the company's products. Likewise, firms selling in localized areas will be influenced by local business conditions, and may face problems in disposing of products while the overall economy is moving in the so-called prosperity phase of the business cycle. Such situations may be pointed up by the phrase, "It's a recession when the other fellow's products aren't selling, but it's a depression when our products aren't selling."

Controllable Factors. Although a firm has little or no control over the external factors just discussed, there are other factors which also will influence a house standard and which are largely control-lable within the framework of company policies. Thus the type of product sold, its seasonal or nonseasonal characteristics, the profit margin of the seller—all of these factors will have an influence upon the level of credit acceptance of a company. Generally speaking, the wider a company's profit margin on its sales, the poorer the class of credit risks which it can afford to sell. It is not to be inferred, however, that all firms operating with a high profit picture will sell to poor risks. Such firms simply can *afford* to do so, if they decide such a policy is feasible and consistent with other aims.

It is not always necessary to disapprove orders from marginal and submarginal customers, but there are certain arrangements that might be made that might still permit acceptance of the order at the level of the established house standard. One arrangement is to place these customers on a trade acceptance basis. Such a procedure is aptly described in the following quotation:[1]

> Fairly often the buyers of manufactured articles do not have the ready or liquid cash available to make immediate remittances for the goods purchased. Use of the trade acceptance enables both buyer and seller to consummate their transactions without delay. On many occasions, the buyer needs to sell the goods he is purchasing before he can pay the seller. Therefore the seller makes the instrument to his own order, drawn on the buyer. In effect, the seller is taking the trade acceptance in payment of the goods. At the time the instrument is executed, the actual payment is a fiction. However, since the instrument is drawn upon the buyer, expectation of payment arises. When the buyer accepts this draft drawn upon him, his obligation to pay becomes absolute. The seller may then discount the trade acceptance at his bank for the full amount therein, negotiate it further, or wait until the buyer himself honors it.

Other arrangements with customers who are acceptable only as qualified credit risks include the use of cash terms (generally means payment within 10 days of the invoice date), c.o.d. terms (cash on delivery), or split-shipment terms (part of the goods shipped on cash before delivery and part on regular terms).

The type of collection policy a firm decides to follow is often a determining factor in the level of acceptance that the credit manager may establish.[2] If a firm has a very strict collection procedure, the chances are that the house standard of acceptance level is low or lenient. This is simply saying that the following combinations are found most often:

Strict acceptance—lenient collection
Lenient acceptance—strict collection

Another factor of importance to be considered is the personality and "sales-ability" of the credit manager. Some individuals have the

1 / *Credit Management Handbook* (2d ed.; Homewood, Ill.: Richard D. Irwin, Inc., 1965), pp. 623-24.

2 / Of course, the type of credit acceptance policy adopted in turn influences the decision as to the type of collection policy to follow. In fact, this is the more normal cause-and-effect sequence.

talent to say no to a customer and at the same time maintain his goodwill to such an extent that the transaction still is completed either on a cash basis or on credit terms much more strict than those normally prevailing.

Once all these factors are carefully weighed and analyzed, the credit manager has some guide by which he may judge the credit worthiness of the orders being received.

Automatic and Nonautomatic Initial Orders

A distinction should be drawn between initial orders and follow-up orders. It is particularly essential, whenever possible, that the first order from a new customer be processed as quickly and expeditiously as possible without lengthy and extensive investigation. Here is the first contact between buyer and seller; here is the forming of the initial impression that can often mean the difference between a long-range series of follow-up orders and a one-time, one-order customer. Some firms also follow the practice of considering old customers who have not bought during the preceding year as "new" customers.

Automatic Initial Orders. In order to expedite the processing of initial orders, blanket approval may be given to all first orders below a certain specified amount. This maximum guide undoubtedly will be influenced by the type of product involved, the nature of the company operation, the overall credit policy, general market conditions, competitive credit terms, and prior experience in collecting small credit accounts approved under such a blanket policy. It must be realized, however, that blanket approval should not stop with simply approval, but that a follow-up procedure is a vital necessity for future successful operation. This point is clearly illustrated in the following quotation:[3]

Follow-up work is an important requirement of a blanket approval system. Since the first small order may be a trial shipment which will lead to larger orders, the system should provide for the sales department to supply an estimate of each customer's credit requirements and, if possible, an appraisal of his credit worthiness and importance as an outlet. With that information the credit department is in a position to set up any necessary credit controls or to plan its investigation, thus expediting the processing of future orders. In many cases, no credit investigation at all will be required, if the customer's continuing needs will be within the minimum amount for which referral is required. If this is true, and payment performance is good, the cost of credit investigation is eliminated entirely.

Some concerns follow the policy of appraising initial orders on the basis of ratings given by credit agencies such as Dun & Bradstreet and

3 / *Credit Management Handbook, op. cit.,* p. 281.

the various specialized agencies. The maximum amount[4] of the first order will be specified by the company for each Dun & Bradstreet credit rating, for example, and if the initial order of a customer (with a certain credit rating) falls below that maximum, approval becomes automatic. Of course, each company using such a technique will establish its own first-order limits to meet its own needs and to conform to its own policies.

Nonautomatic Initial Orders. If the company has not established procedures such as blanket and agency-rating approvals, the question arises as to how to handle these nonautomatic initial orders. One suggestion offered is that the decision as to the disposition of the first order may be based on answers to the following questions:[5]

1. Is the dollar value of the order large enough to warrant the cost of investigation?
2. Is the potential for future sales such that the account should be cultivated, or is it immaterial what the reaction may be to a request to do business on other than regular credit terms?
3. Does company policy dictate trying to establish credit terms for *all* customers for the public relations benefit which might result?

Should it be decided to investigate, a further decision must be made as to how extensive the investigation should be. Where present and expected sales potential justifies an intensive and direct investigation, the credit department should seek all available information regarding historic and forecast data, reputation and ability of principals, marketability and competitive forces related to products, and so on.

Credit Decisions as a Routine Operation

The first order has been approved, the complete credit investigation has been made, and every hope now is that the relationship with the customer will prove to be a long and fruitful one, resulting in a series of profitable transactions. The next question to arise is how the subsequent requests for credit may be handled in the most expeditious manner[6] to serve the needs of the customers and at the same time to incur the least possible expense to the company. The credit manager generally is too involved with more pressing matters to have to give the final approval to every order received. Thus, it is

4 / This amount will be changed from time to time, depending upon all the factors affecting company policy.

5 / *Credit Management Handbook, op. cit.*, p. 283.

6 / For a description of how successful use of a computer has been achieved and how it has resulted in a streamlining of the credit department as well as faster order handling, see Morton Reitman, "How a Computer Works for Credit Management," *Credit and Financial Management*, July 1968, p. 34.

necessary that some procedure be established through which the credit manager may delegate authority for credit approval while at the same time retaining the degree of control necessary to protect his department from an excessive bad-debt situation. Such a procedure should act to free the credit manager for really important decisions and to place routine where it rightly belongs in the departmental operation. A common method used today to accomplish this delegation of authority is the technique of credit lines or credit limits.

CREDIT LINES

The two terms "credit lines" and "credit limits" often are used interchangeably. Historically, the term credit limit has been in use for a longer length of time than the term credit line. This is more true in the commercial credit field than in the bank credit field, in which the term credit line or line of credit has always been common terminology.

Some commercial credit managers give a little different interpretation to the two terms. Thus in some companies credit lines are looked at as the maximum amount of credit they are willing to accept from a customer. Used in this manner, the credit line becomes the credit limit.

It appears that the most realistic approach to the use of these terms is to recognize that in most instances a firm will use this figure, indicating the amount of credit to be approved, as a warning signal or as a red flag. It does not mean that orders exceeding this limit will be automatically refused, but that the figure acts as a guide to force a further analysis of the account and another decision as to whether to accept or reject the larger order.

Advantages

As previously mentioned, the use of such credit lines is designed to increase the efficiency of the credit department. If handled properly, they should save the time of the credit manager for really important decisions, should permit delegation of authority but still allow for retention of control of the accounts, and should place routine tasks in the hands of subordinate personnel. In addition, the use of credit lines forces overall consideration of the entire account, not merely consideration on a transaction-by-transaction basis. This should in turn lead to better decisions[7] than a single-order technique would.

7 / C. A. Keen, in "Credit Lines—A Vital Cost Factor" (reprinted from *Credit and Financial Management,* March 1969, p. 16. Copyright 1969 by the National Association of Credit Management, New York, N.Y.) points out: "... in addition to the awesome

Likewise, such an arrangement should protect the buyer from himself, in that it acts as a check on the reckless buyer who for the moment may be unduly optimistic and desirous of buying in amounts greatly in excess of his needs.

Limitations

While the use of credit lines is not universally accepted in all commercial credit transactions, it is believed that somewhere in the neighborhood of two thirds to three fourths of such credit approvals involve the use of some type of credit line control. Unfortunately, the adoption of such a practice carries with it certain problems and limitations.

The firm that establishes a line of credit for a customer and then makes no attempt to keep it up to date immediately defeats the basic premise on which the use of credit lines is predicated. While it is recognized that such revisions are time-consuming and costly, the lines established will not reflect the current ability of the customer to pay for the goods and services purchased until some system of periodic review is installed.

Another limitation involved is that approval of orders within the credit line established will be performed generally by clerical personnel and not by the credit manager himself. Thus in certain instances the credit manager may lose contact with the account and not develop the full potential of future business.

Methods of Setting Credit Lines

Perhaps the credit department will never be in a better position to establish a credit line for a customer than at the moment when the credit investigation is completed. Generally at this time more careful examination of the credit data, more complete analysis of the account, and more thought as to whether to accept future orders will be taking place than at any other moment in the life of the account. It stands to reason, therefore, that the credit manager is in the best position at this time to establish the line of credit which he believes safe to allow the customer on future orders. The question then arises—just how does the credit manager go about setting credit lines? Credit managers generally report that they follow certain techniques, but they are not sure they are the best methods possible.

responsibility of being custodian of the greater part of his corporation's assets, the credit executive now is directly involved in the profit of a corporation. He must be sophisticated in the execution of his duties and fully cognizant of the cost factor in the terms that he extends and the credit lines that he establishes."

Some six methods are found in common use to accomplish this task: (1) allow as much as the customer wishes as long as he pays as agreed; (2) allow as much as the other creditors are allowing the customer; (3) allow a small dollar volume of purchases and raise gradually as the customer proves he is a good risk; (4) allow purchases based upon a time interval; (5) basis of facts (divide the number of creditors of the customer into net worth, current assets, net working capital, and inventory; use of an agency rating); and (6) requirements (or pseudoscientific) method.

As Much as the Customer Wishes. Some firms follow the practice of allowing the customer as much credit as he wishes, just as long as the customer pays as agreed. Such an arrangement stresses the "increasing sales volume" function of the credit department and does not create any real problems for the credit manager unless, at any moment when the indebtedness of a customer is high, he decides he cannot or will not pay as agreed. As long as payment is prompt and automatic, this method is a highly desirable one. On the other hand, some observers believe that this method of setting credit lines should not even be considered as a method, since no definite line is established and the transaction is entirely flexible depending upon the wishes and actions of the customer.

As Much as Other Creditors Are Allowing. This method is based on the premise that a firm can discover the amount of credit that its competitors are allowing the customer in question. While definite and exact figures may be hard to obtain, a firm often is able to acquire approximations through direct interchange of such information and from data appearing in the HC or HRC columns of Dun & Bradstreet and Credit Interchange Bureau reports. Of course, the highest recent credit figure may represent an amount of credit between a seller and his customer in excess of what the seller believes the limit should be. In certain cases, extenuating circumstances such as a desire not to offend a long-time customer may cause the HRC to be more than it ever should have been.

If this method is adopted, the question also should be asked, "How did the competitors decide on what the credit line should be?" Unfortunately, there is usually no good and dependable answer to this question, and many firms decide to rely upon their own analysis and interpretation of the credit information in setting the credit line, using their competitors' experiences only as a guide in some instances or completely ignoring them in other cases.

Start Low and Raise with Experience. Another very common and practical procedure is to start with a small dollar amount, raised gradually as the customer proves to be a good risk. A customer may be started with a low limit, or enough to take care of his first purchase. As experience with the account accumulates, as he proves his ability to pay larger amounts, the limit is raised to take care of his purchases. If the experience is unsatisfactory and he does not prove capable of taking care of the purchases he has made, the limit is held so as to restrain his purchases, or it even may be lowered.

Based on a Time Interval. Some credit departments attempt to limit an account to a certain period of time, that is, a month's purchases, a week's purchases, or some definite time. For example, a line of credit of $5,000 per month would mean that during any one-month period, a credit department clerk could approve without any referral to the credit manager orders totaling $5,000, regardless of the total amount outstanding and owing. This method has been described as follows:[8]

Credit lines stated in this way are particularly useful in companies which process orders at a number of locations but maintain more centralized accounts receivable. Lines for a specific time period provide control with a minimum of referral to a central office and of record keeping at the order-processing point. In assigning such credit lines, the credit man should bear in mind that, since even prompt payment for all invoices billed during the designated period would not necessarily be received during that period, the total credit exposure will often be larger than the amount of the line. Adequate controls must be established to prevent extension of excessive credit to delinquent accounts.

Basis of Facts. This method is based upon certain financial information or facts, such as net worth, current assets, net working capital, and inventory. These data are then related to the number of creditors the customer may have, by dividing the number of creditors into the financial figures chosen by the credit manager. For example, if a firm has a net worth figure of $100,000 and the number of its creditors is 10, then the line of credit may be established[9] at $10,000. Likewise, if this firm has an inventory figure of $80,000, the credit line would be $8,000.

Whereas the financial figures of net worth, current assets, net working capital, and inventory generally are readily available from financial statement information, more of a problem is involved in reaching an accurate estimate of the number of creditors. One method of obtaining this information is simply to ask the customer for a list of the names (and probably addresses) of his creditors. Sometimes, however, this list is discovered to be incomplete, either intentionally or unintentionally. As a check, some firms also follow the practice of obtaining a Dun & Bradstreet report which shows an "owe" column for the customer in question. A similar column, "now

---

8 / *Credit Management Handbook, op. cit.,* pp. 285-86.

9 / Generally, a line of credit is not established on the basis of a single computation. Several of these methods may be averaged to arrive at the final credit line chosen.

owing," appears in the Credit Interchange Bureau reports. Generally these reports do not contain all of the creditors either, and some adjustment must be made to arrive at a fairly accurate estimate of customer count. One method of adjustment is illustrated as follows: XYZ Retail Store is seeking to buy goods from the ABC Manufacturer. This is the initial order. XYZ furnishes a balance sheet which shows accounts payable of $10,000. ABC receives an interchange bureau report that lists 8 creditors of XYZ with an indebtedness of $8,000. Thus if 8 creditors account for $8,000 worth of debt, the $10,000 accounts payable total is probably owed to 10 creditors.

It should be recognized that such a computation or estimate is rough, and no claim should be made that it is 100 or even 90 percent accurate. Critics of this method may point out that one creditor may account for half of the accounts receivable and that any system of proportions based on such a situation would be more misleading than helpful. Any user of this method should consider his estimate of the number of creditors simply as a guide, and it is recommended that these basis-of-facts methods be supplemented with some of the other techniques described.

Requirements (Pseudoscientific) Method. This method usually involves five basic steps in computing a line of credit. These steps are as follows:

1. Secure the total annual volume of sales of the customer. This figure often may be obtained directly from the firm seeking to buy goods on credit, from financial statements if these are prepared for the use of creditors or are published to conform to the various security-issuance regulations, or from educated guesses of the sales activity of the firm in question.

2. Find out what part of these sales is in the line of business covered by you, the seller of the goods. Often this type of information is difficult to obtain with accuracy, unless the customer is willing to cooperate in furnishing it. Otherwise, a "guesstimate" may have to prevail.

3. Decide what proportion of this business you, the seller, can hope to secure. Perhaps this is the weakest link or step in this method, as this figure *has* to be an estimate. Often there is wide variation between the volume the seller actually is furnishing the customer and what he hopes or thinks he will be selling. The accuracy with which this third step is carried out will be a determining factor in the accuracy of the credit limit itself.

4. Determine how many days you will allow the customer in your net credit period. This step is necessary because a customer generally does not buy only once a year, but probably will place an order for goods, pay for them, place another order, and so forth. The line of

credit usually will relate to the total amount of indebtedness that a firm plans to accept from a customer as of any one time, not a yearly accumulation of orders placed by the customer.

5. Adjust the retail limit thus far determined to reflect the cost value of the order. This step, of course, is necessary because the customer's cost price is the seller's selling price. This last step requires that the seller be familiar with the customer's gross margin of profit on which he (the customer) handles the line of goods involved.

For purposes of illustration, dollar figures are substituted for the preceding description and the five steps are followed through mathematically:

1. Customer's annual sales are $50,000.
2. Proportion in the seller's line is $10,000.
3. Proportion the seller hopes to obtain is one fourth or $2,500.
4. Terms of sale are net 60, which means the goods should turn
   . six times a year; $2,500 ÷ 6 equals approximately $416.
5. Gross margin of the customer is 30 percent. Thus, the limit of the seller may be estimated as between $290 and $300.

Caution is urged in the use of this psuedoscientific method. It should be viewed as what it really is—an estimate; and most credit managers who use such a procedure supplement it with one or several of the other methods previously outlined.

To Inform or Not to Inform Customers

There are different schools of thought as to whether the customer should be advised of his credit limit as soon as it is established. Some executives are in favor of notification and claim that such action permits the seller to discuss the entire credit picture with the customer and to offer suggestions as to how to improve the credit standing, if there is need for improvement. Likewise, the customer is not held in the dark as to what amount of credit he can rely on from the seller.

On the other hand, some observers point out that the notification may cause the customer to restrict his buying to the dollar amount of the credit line established, thus strictly interpreting the word "line" to mean an inflexible limit. This damage to goodwill and to expanding sales volume causes some executives to view a credit line only as an instrument of internal control.

There is a similar difference of opinion as to whether the seller's salesmen should be informed of these limits on their customers. Unfortunately, there is no one correct answer to either of these problems. Under certain circumstances, both the customer and the salesman will know when the credit limit has been reached. When an account has reached its limit no further orders will be approved (or at least orders won't be shipped) until payments are forthcoming which reduce the balance below the limit. This condition can exist even though the customer may not have any amount due on outstanding receivables at the time the new order is requested.

REVIEW OF DECISIONS

Business conditions change. The credit standing of customers changes. The outlook of sellers changes. In fact, in credit operations change of many varieties is a certainty, and the successful credit manager recognizes that the decisions he has made and the credit lines he has set must be regularly reviewed to bring them up to date. Otherwise, increasing sales volume, cutting down bad-debt losses, reducing the costs of credit administration, and efficiently managing the investment in receivables will not be accomplished.

Unfortunately, despite all the safeguards of analyzing credit information from a number of sources, making careful and complete credit decisions, setting realistic lines of credit, and constantly reviewing all these steps—still every dollar of credit accepted is not repaid on time and in some instances is never repaid. For this reason, the next three chapters are devoted to a discussion of commercial credit insurance and collection policies and practices.

REVIEW AND DISCUSSION QUESTIONS

1. Why is it desirable for management to furnish its credit manager a clearly defined and understood statement of what is desired of his department?
2. How do various external factors influence a commercial creditor's house standard?
3. Discuss the controllable factors that will influence a house standard.
4. What arrangements might be made to allow approval of orders from marginal and submarginal customers? Discuss these arrangements.
5. Why is it desirable as well as prudent business policy to provide a system for automatic approval of initial orders?
6. What are the advantages and disadvantages of developing a system of credit lines?
7. Describe how credit lines might be set. Can you suggest any others than those found in the text?

8. What data provide the information needed to set limits on a customer's credit buying?

9. Where might these data be obtained?

10. For the Happy Store problem shown in Question 14 of Chapter 28, what credit limit would you set for the account if you were the credit manager of the Royal Shoe Company?

30

Commercial Credit Insurance

Commercial credit insurance may be defined as an arrangement between an insurance company and a business concern under which the insured firm is guaranteed indemnification against abnormal credit losses arising from failure of business debtors to pay their obligations. In addition, the insured firm receives other auxiliary services and benefits from the insurance company participating in the relationship.

Life insurance certainly doesn't eliminate the need for doctors and attention to good health practices, nor does commercial credit insurance eliminate the need for a credit department and credit manager, nor can it ever replace him and his responsibilities. But this type of insurance, which is still unfamiliar to a large segment of the business world, is a valuable tool of management.

Commercial credit insurance is confined to manufacturers, wholesalers, etc., and is not available to firms selling goods and services or loaning money to the ultimate consumer. Transactions involving the ultimate consumer are sometimes covered by what is commonly known as credit life insurance or consumer credit insurance. As described in Chapter 17, this type of risk sharing is predicated on the death or disability of the consumer. Commercial credit insurance is an entirely different field of activity than that of the consumer credit insurance field.

There are two schools of thought as to whether commercial credit insurance should be considered as part of a firm's collection policy or part of its credit determination policy. From the first point of view, when an order is received, the account is investigated through the accumulation of credit information from credit-reporting agencies; the decision is made to accept or reject the order; and, if accepted, a credit line is determined to guide future orders. Now if all accounts paid as agreed, there would be no need to worry about the collection of accounts receivable. But unfortunately, every account does not pay as agreed, and as a result some firms decide to share part of the risk of noncollection with an insurance company and use commercial credit insurance as part of their collection policy. The other point of view is that commercial credit insurance should be used directly in connection with the formulation of credit decisions, as an aggressive weapon rather than a defensive one.

BASIC FEATURES OF COMMERCIAL CREDIT INSURANCE

As previously pointed out, commercial credit insurance is primarily for the protection of manufacturers, jobbers, wholesalers, and certain types of service organizations.

In a commercial credit insurance policy there may be two deductibles, coinsurance and primary loss. The amount of coinsurance (an arrangement by which an insured firm bears a specified percentage of its total losses on all insured accounts) is deducted from the invoiced price of the merchandise shipped. This usually amounts to approximately 10 to 20 percent, although in special instances the amount may vary or even be waived. This amount usually is higher on customers who are not rated in the first or second credit appraisal category of recognized mercantile agencies or who carry no credit appraisal at all.

In addition to coinsurance, a primary loss is agreed upon between the insurance company and the insured as a percentage of the insured's covered sales, with a definite minimum spelled out in the policy. This primary loss percentage varies with the risk covered, the size of the sales volume, and the insured's actual loss experience. If the applicant's loss experience is less than the national average for that line of business, it generally is recognized that he is a better risk and the amount of his primary loss is reduced.

A good description of the most common types of policies written is given in the following quotation:[1]

There are two broad types of policies offered. Either could be used by an average business, depending upon the purpose to be served. One is known as Back Coverage. These guarantee to reimburse the policy holder for losses occurring during the policy term. They pick up the outstanding balances owned by debtors, when the policy starts, and carry them into coverage. The first year policy picks up current accounts only (those not past due when the policy starts). Each renewal policy goes back for a full twelve months and picks up balances owing, whether past due or not. Insolvent accounts must be placed with

1 / J. L. McCauley, *Credit Insurance, A Profit Stabilizer* (Baltimore: American Credit Indemnity Co. of N.Y., 1958), pp. 13-14. This quotation, while a little old, still gives a good description of the present-day policies. Mr. McCauley is the retired president of the American Credit Indemnity Company of New York, which was organized in 1893 and is the leading company writing this type of insurance.

the insuring company. Past due accounts may or may not be handed to the company for collection—this is an optional privilege.

The other type of policy offered is known as Forward Coverage. It guarantees to reimburse the policy holder for losses occurring on shipments made in a twelve-month period. The policy starts fresh each time. No outstanding balances are picked up at the outset of coverage. When the twelve month Shipment Period has ended, that policy continues in effect until the terms of sale have run their course and an additional time allowed for the payment of the bills. This could be for a period as long as seven months after the Shipment Period. The rule followed is to add three months to the longest terms of sale, in order to fix the end of the Policy Term. This type requires the Compulsory filing of all accounts within the policy term.

In 1960, the American Credit Indemnity Company started offering a new standard policy which is available in either the back-coverage or the forward-coverage form. This new policy, which is in addition to the other standard policies offered, eliminates the coinsurance feature. Thus it is now possible for the insured to be reimbursed in excess of the primary loss for the full invoiced price of the shipped goods. As is to be expected, the premium is higher than in those policies that require coinsurance.

Since commercial credit insurance is offered in a wide variety of combinations of policy forms, endorsements, and stipulations, a commercial credit insurance policy may be virtually tailor-made to meet the needs of the policyholder involved. In the past individual account policies, along with general coverage policies, were written. The individual account policies covered only single accounts selected by the insured company. In recent years the writing of individual account policies has been practically abolished because of the possible adverse selection of risk against the insurance company. Practically all policies now being written are of the general coverage type.

Policies may be written with or without a provision for the insurance company to handle all phases of the collection of past-due accounts. When the policy is written on an optional collection basis, the insured firm may turn over any past-due account for collection, no fees being charged on accounts collected within 10 days. In the policy an agreed-upon schedule of fees is listed, usually based upon Commercial Law League rates. Policies also may be written with no collection provision.

PURPOSE OF COMMERCIAL CREDIT INSURANCE

In Chapter 1, credit was defined as a medium of exchange of limited acceptance. It was further spelled out that credit was of limited acceptance because of two elements—time and risk. Thus in every credit transaction there is an element of risk, and the credit manager must decide whether to bear this risk alone or whether to share it with someone else. The firm that factors its accounts receivable has decided to let another institution bear the task of credit acceptance and credit collection without recourse. For this service the firm pays a fee to the factor. Credit insurance is another method of sharing this risk with others, this time with an insurance institution rather than with a financial institution. For a charge, the risk accompanying the credit transaction is shared with a specialist, just as fire, theft, storm, and public liability dangers are passed on to other types of insurance companies.

It is the unusual loss that is insured against, as credit insurance does not protect the insured against the normal (or primary) loss experienced by a particular business firm. The more frequent and important causes of abnormal bad-debt losses are as follows:[2]

1. Concentration of sales in a few accounts, the insolvency of any one of which would inflict an excessive loss on the firm.
2. Concentration of customers in one line of business that could be adversely affected by an unexpected development.
3. Concentration of customers in a particular region.
4. General business recessions and depressions.
5. Custom manufacturing in significant amounts, as where a product custom-made for a certain customer may be difficult to sell if the customer becomes insolvent.
6. Many small accounts, which may make it difficult to obtain credit information on each account.
7. Maintenance of sales volume, necessitating acceptance of greater risks.
8. Shifting to a credit operation with the resulting lack of experience.
9. Conducting a one-man operation under which credit sales may not receive the proper attention.
10. Granting extended terms of sale or larger lines of credit in order to command a market.
11. A series of miscellaneous causes.

With most firms the extent of this unusual or abnormal loss depends on many factors. These include: the highest credit accepted from any one customer, the type of business in which the seller is engaged, the product or products sold (type, stability, diversification, seasonality, obsolescence), the quality and "freshness" of inventories, the geographical location of and competition in the buyer's markets, money supply in the economy, price-level fluctuations, phase of the business cycle, labor conditions, and so forth. Some of these factors are within the control of the seller; others are entirely outside the control area and dependent upon external circumstances.

2 / "Commercial Credit Insurance . . . What's in It for You." Reprinted from *Credit and Financial Management,* October 1965, p. 26. Copyright 1965 by the National Association of Credit Management, New York, N.Y.

ADVANTAGES OF COMMERCIAL CREDIT INSURANCE

Commercial credit insurance offers to the insured the following advantages:[3]

1. Cost basis of products shipped can be better estimated.
2. A large excess bad debt reserve is provided for bolstering the management's own bad debt reserve. Credit insurance supplements normal bad debt loss reserve in the bookkeeping figures.
3. With the guide provided by the policy, a credit department can be more definite. It is surprising that some credit departments frequently limit customers' accounts when no limitation is required.
4. The insurance underwriter's opinion on credit worthiness is available on particular accounts.
5. The sales department can aim to sell up to the limit of protection.

A somewhat different list of auxiliary services and benefits is shown in the following quotation:[4]

1. Assistance in preventing bad-debt losses.
2. Collection aids and an organized collection service on past-due as well as insolvent accounts.
3. Recovering salvage from insolvent accounts for the insured, including cases where the indebtedness on the account exceeds the insurance coverage carried on it.
4. Reduction of the interest costs, collection expenses and other extra costs caused by slow accounts.
5. Creation of an adequate tax-free excess bad-debt reserve.
6. Expansion of sales and profits by safely increasing credit lines allowed present accounts and by adding more customers, including fair and marginal risks.
7. Special investigations, credit granting aids and advice provided by the insurance company.
8. Improvement of the financial position and credit standing of the insured.
9. Provision of more certainty in budgeting and planning ahead.
10. Facilitation of steadier production, particularly in seasonal businesses having to sell on extended dating terms.
11. Improvement of relations between the sales and credit departments of the insured.
12. Peace of mind with regard to the ultimate actual value of the very large part of the insured's working capital that is invested in accounts receivable. Some policyholders call this "sleep insurance."

3 / A. A. Dilworth, "Insuring Accounts Receivable," *Financial Executive,* November 1968, p. 82. The reader is also referred to A. A. Dilworth, "Credit Insurance: the Ace in the Hole," *Journal of Insurance,* July-August 1970, p. 22; Frederick A. Gelderman, "Insuring Accounts Receivable," *Credit and Financial Management,* October 1967, p. 19; A. A. Dilworth, "Credit Insurance: Back-up for Credit Managers," *Credit and Financial Management,* October 1968, p. 31; Irvin D. Shostak, "Credit Insurance as a Sales Tool," *Credit and Financial Management,* October 1970, p. 18.

4 / "Commercial Credit Insurance . . . What's in It for You," *op. cit.,* p. 26.

Balance between Sales and Profits

Advocates of commercial credit insurance point out that a user can have a clear idea in advance of what his costs will be in the form of excessive or abnormal credit losses during the coming year. By combining his normal losses with the premium cost paid for credit insurance, the credit manager will be able to arrive at a fairly accurate estimate of the maximum cost of this item. If its system of expense control is working properly and other expense items are subject to accurate prediction, a firm can then have a fairly good approximation of anticipated profits. This use of credit insurance is dependent upon the type of policy that is written, as some policies do not cover all possible losses on all classes of risks.

Credit insurance also works on the sales side of the credit manager's operations. Some credit managers believe that the purchase of credit insurance has the effect of making them more careful in credit acceptance, in that they have to maintain a strict control over all changes in agency ratings of customers. This is necessary to stay within the provisions of the credit insurance policy. At the same time, others argue that the opposite effect is the result. By shifting extraordinary losses to the insurance company, the insured can afford to take greater risks in credit acceptance and thus can increase his sales volume. Since any increased losses are covered by the insurance company and any increased profits are retained by the insured firm, credit insurance may work for freer credit acceptance on the part of some companies.

Improvement in Collections

It is recognized that the longer an account remains unpaid the more difficult it is to collect. The insurance company usually states that delinquent accounts may be turned over and proved as claims if the placing of the account is in its hands within 12 months from date of shipment or three months past due, whichever is longer. Vigorous collection action generally is taken by the insurance company, thus increasing the chances of early collection and of greater return to the creditor company. The psychological impact of collection by a third party—when the third party is an insurance company—cannot be overlooked.

Improvement in Borrowing Capacity

Most firms find themselves from time to time in the position of having to borrow from a financing source to carry on their operations. Some of these loans are unsecured; some involve the assignment of accounts receivable as collateral to the loan. Credit insurance may act as an aid in the discounting of these accounts receivable with a bank or finance company.

DISADVANTAGES OF COMMERCIAL CREDIT INSURANCE

Some credit executives believe that the weaknesses connected with commercial credit insurance overshadow any benefits that might be obtained from its use. Some even go so far as to say that there is no legitimate place or need for credit insurance in the activities of an efficient and well-run credit department. It should be recognized that despite its widespread use, commercial credit insurance is not coverage which should be bought by all firms able to purchase it. Some types of firms may find credit insurance unnecessary or of little or no advantage.

Some of the most important disadvantages generally listed are cost, false sense of security, restrictions in placing accounts for collection, limiting features of the provisions of the policies, and need for credit insurance as opposed to other types of insurance.

Cost

As in all insurance, premium payments on credit insurance are an expense item for a business concern. Although it is recognized that credit insurance is designed to cover the abnormal or unusual credit loss, some firms have found that recovery from such accounts is frequently less than the premium cost over a number of years. In the instances in which this is true, premiums paid for credit insurance can exceed the return from claims made on the insurance company. Of course, it cannot be overlooked that the company was enjoying *protection* from excess loss during the period under comparison and in one sense was fortunate in the fact that its bad debts stayed within the range normally expected. A somewhat similar situation may be cited in the case of the individual who buys health and accident insurance and who is fortunate enough to stay entirely well for five years. He may reason that the cost of the insurance was just another expense for him and that he would have been ahead at the end of the five-year period if he had not taken out the insurance. His reasoning would be much different, however, if a month's hospital stay had been required during the first year the policy was in effect. Even though no claim was made against the commercial credit insurance (or the health and accident insurance), it must be remembered that *protection* was obtained for the premium paid.

False Sense of Security

Another important objection which has been raised against commercial credit insurance is that it may cause some credit managers to rely more upon insurance protection than upon their own deliberate judgments. Credit insurance thus may cause the credit manager to have a false sense of security in knowing that excessive bad-debt losses are covered, to have less incentive to make a good showing as evidenced by greater sales with lower bad-debt losses, and to exercise a freer hand in credit acceptance in order to receive a pecuniary return from the credit insurance policies purchased.

Collection Restrictions

Under most of the policies being written, accounts that have gone unpaid are turned over to the insurance company within the stipulated time period of 12 months from date of shipment. Previously this time period was only six months, which at times precluded a credit department from exploring all friendly means of collection in an effort to recover the entire amount or an acceptable and fair reduced amount (composition settlement as discussed in Chapter 32) from the debtor firm. The lengthening of this time period from 6 to 12 months recognized the fact that often circumstances prevent a firm from paying within the specified credit period, and a carefully worked out arrangement between seller and buyer may result in complete recovery of the indebtedness and in maintenance of goodwill.

Limiting Policy Features

It will be remembered that credit insurance does not cover all losses. The normal (or primary) bad-debt losses must be borne by the creditor, and some criticism is leveled at the method of computing this primary loss.

Another debatable feature of credit insurance policies is that the insurable risk of any one customer is predicated primarily upon ratings of Dun & Bradstreet and of special agencies. To base credit decisions primarily upon agency ratings fails to give due weight to all the other credit information that normally is available to the credit analyst. While the required limitation is justifiable from the insurance company's point of view, at the same time such a restriction seems to infringe upon the necessity of the credit manager's weighing all the factors involved and of analyzing pertinent sources of information before arriving at a decision.

Commenting on this point, J. L. McCauley pointed out in a letter of June 22, 1967:

> Actually each Credit Insurance policy does have a Table of Ratings and Coverage. We know full well when this Table is inserted in the policy that it will not cover all cases. However, it will take care of the majority of cases, so when the exception occurs and involves a larger amount of credit than is open on the credit rating, we investigate these accounts and give a supplementary credit checking opinion. If it is acceptable then we add the coverage to the policy by endorsement, naming the account for the specific amount. If it is not an acceptable risk we tell our policyholder why it is not and thus perform a credit function which we feel is part of loss prevention.

Commenting further on this point, A. A. Dilworth, Chairman of the Board of the American Credit Indemnity Company of New York, pointed out in a letter of February 26, 1971:

> There are many, many debtors without ratings on whom substantial amounts of coverage are provided through the analysis of their financial condition. Also, as pointed out in Mr. McCauley's comments . . . coverage amounts well in excess of the top open limits of ratings are provided by special endorsements.

Credit versus Other Types of Insurance

Simply to say that a firm needs to protect its accounts receivable by insurance because it protects its inventory, building, and equipment against fire or "acts of God" fails to recognize the differences in the two needs. The company that has all of its inventory and equipment in one building faces the threat that a fire, flood, tornado, or windstorm could completely wipe out these assets in a short period of time. To protect against this calamity, insurance generally is carried. There are companies, of course, whose plants are so widely scattered and whose danger of financial ruin because of fires and "acts of God" is so remote that they have decided to provide their own form of insurance through some system of reserves.

The chances that the accounts receivable of a firm will be wiped out in a single disaster are very remote. Even though the receivables are concentrated industrywise or geographically, it is hard to imagine a firm losing the major portion of its accounts in any one year. Nevertheless, protection against excessive loss in large accounts still has proved desirable in the activities of many firms.

It should be emphasized that the insurance company should never be considered as a replacement for the credit department and the credit manager of a firm. Commercial credit insurance is not intended to make the credit executives careless in credit acceptance.

Its primary purpose is to protect against the unexpected and unpreventable accidental losses which occur at times despite the precautions and safeguards taken by the insuring concern.

REVIEW AND DISCUSSION QUESTIONS

1. What are the advantages of insuring against credit losses?
2. Can the firm with credit insurance accept those credit risks which would be rejected if insurance was not carried?
3. Distinguish between back coverage and forward coverage.
4. Are collections stimulated by virtue of credit insurance coverage?
5. In what ways are the following considered disadvantages of credit insurance:
   a) Premium costs?
   b) False sense of security?
   c) Collection Restrictions?
6. "Credit insurance can be regarded as a substitute for the credit department and the credit manager." Discuss.

31

Collection Policies in
Commercial Credit Management

Collections in commercial transactions are an inherent part of any credit operation, just as noted previously with the collection of consumer accounts. Any collection system to be successful must get the money. This objective becomes less obvious and much more difficult to attain when the additional requirements of retention of goodwill, rehabilitation of the debtor, promptness of payment, and economical operation are added. If promptness is made the major objective, it may be attained by handling all collections immediately. However, the methods selected and used may be very costly and may simultaneously lose goodwill. On the other hand if retention of goodwill is made the major objective, the appeals and techniques used will be very gentle, even delicate, and collections will tend to be slow in starting.

Thus, the purpose of a commercial collection system generally is twofold: maximization of collections and minimization of loss of future trade. Which segment of the purpose is emphasized depends upon the aims and policies of the individual creditor firm concerned.

FACTORS AFFECTING COLLECTION POLICY

In its decision as to what type of collection policy to adopt, a firm should recognize there are many factors which will have an influence on policy determination.[1] While the following by no means comprise

1 / In recent years many credit executives have been spending so much of their time with marginal customers and past-due accounts that they have forgotten the discount customers. There is a definite need to recognize and compliment these customers, since they are responsible for receivables turnover.

On the other hand, for a discussion of how to determine whether or not marginal accounts can be made profitable, see Allan Glubok, "A Second Look at Marginal Accounts," *Credit and Financial Management*, May 1970, p. 18.

a complete list, it is generally recognized that classification of debtors, capital, competition, type of business and type of goods, profit margin, credit policy followed, and type of records used are among the most important and most influential factors. A brief discussion of each of these factors follows.

Classification of Debtors

Collection work would be less involved, time-consuming, and headache-producing if there were some magic formula by which each debtor firm could be immediately and accurately classified as to the reason for nonpayment of its account and as to the collection method or methods which would be most effective in securing payment for the amount past-due. Some firms have developed over the years a classification of debtors somewhat similar to the following:

1. Debtor misunderstood terms.
2. Careless or inefficient customer.
3. Small amount involved and customer therefore ignores.
4. Slow by habit and by nature.
5. Poor business management.
6. Temporarily out of funds but good.
7. Could pay but must be forced.
8. Terms chiseler.
9. A fraud.

Thus, the creditor may classify a past-due debtor into one or more of these categories and from previous experience with similar customers have a predetermined collection policy to follow in his efforts to collect the amount due.

Debtor Misunderstood Terms.   When this is the true situation, the solution is simple. A clarification of what the credit terms exactly are and of what is expected of the debtor should result in prompt payment. The word "should" is chosen because other reasons may be the true causes for nonpayment, and a professed misunderstanding of the terms involved may be merely an excuse. At the same time, however, misunderstandings do occur and care must be taken to handle such cases in a manner that will maintain a maximum amount of goodwill. Firms have at times discovered that certain salesmen, in an effort to make sales, have assured their customers that they can pay "whenever they wish to pay." This lack of coordination between sales and credit can make for customer ill will and require a reselling job on the customer when the true terms are spelled out for him.

Careless or Inefficient Customer.   Again, here is a customer from whom collection should not be a major problem. Pressed with the vast variety of other problems and cares, this businessman has just overlooked making payment. This may be caused by an inefficient system of keeping track of when bills are due or may be the result of the fact that that debtor is just careless or even forgetful. In most cases, a simple reminder that the amount is due and immediately payable will bring in payment with no loss of customer goodwill.

Small Amount Involved and Customer Therefore Ignores. There is the feeling on the part of some accounts payable personnel— fortunately a small number—that if the indebtedness is a small amount they may ignore it for the time being and wait until the account becomes larger to write just one check to cover the entire amount. In such cases there is no attempt on the part of the debtor firm to escape payment; it is simply a delaying action and results in "future" payment to the creditor. In addition to the nuisance and trouble involved in having to start the collection procedure, there is always the problem that what is small to one person may not be small to another. Thus, differences of opinion often arise on this point.

Slow by Habit and by Nature. Some firms—and their accounts payable personnel—are notoriously slow in making payment. Collections are attained, but only after various types of collection devices have been used and various degrees of persuasion have been applied. The firm that sells this type of customer and knows beforehand that the customer is this type should carefully analyze the gross margin on any sale and compare it with the expenses involved in making the sale. Such expenses tend to be high because of the cost of having to invoke certain steps in the collection process used. Even at the risk of losing a customer, the executive to whom the collection task is assigned should adopt a strict policy toward the firm that is slow by habit and by nature. Such firms have a poor conception of what responsibility actually is, and generally are undesirable and unprofitable accounts.

Poor Business Management. Firms falling into this category perhaps account for the largest number of difficulties for the collection manager. Often the operators of these concerns are honest and optimistic but overbuy. Because of poor business management they find that they are not in a position to meet the terms to which they agreed. Whether to follow a strict or a lenient collection policy will be determined largely by the creditor's decision as to whether there is any hope that this poor business manager will ever learn to conduct his activities in a profitable manner. Can he be salvaged and made into a good customer? If the answer is no, the relationship should be short and terminated quickly.

Temporarily Out of Funds but Good. This type of customer is usually delinquent because of conditions outside his control, such as illness, local business conditions, or any one of many other developments. The debtor actually is not attempting to avoid payment, and the delinquency should not be a reflection on his integrity. This should not delay the collection action, however. An amicable adjustment or extension of the credit period should be made as quickly as possible, and the creditor should insist that the terms of the new agreement be carried out to the limit of the debtor's ability.

A different point of view on this classification is expressed as follows:[2]

> An often-quoted rationale for maintaining a continuing trade relationship with a marginal account is the belief that the client is hard pressed for funds and cannot secure the necessary financing to put it on a "current" basis. This can only mean that the account is a risk of such dimensions no other lender is willing to accommodate it. This premise can be disavowed either because the marginal account does not want to exchange the present cost-free financing for interest-bearing financing, or the trade creditor is extending undeserved credit. Again, unless the marginal account is an interim situation, there is no reason to continue the relationship.

Could Pay but Must Be Forced. This type of customer is somewhat similar to the "slow by habit and by nature." However, in dealing with this group more persuasion and even threats must be used to obtain payment. It is here that certain debtors are classified as being the type who must be "forced" to pay their debts. Most of the time unless they are pursued vigorously, payment is unduly delayed or may never take place. Credit standing means very little to this type of customer who has become accustomed to severe collection methods. For this reason, the collection department in its dealings with these chronic delinquents should force the issue immediately and strongly, at the very moment when the account becomes past-due. Less severe actions will prove of little value, with no return for the expense involved.

Terms Chiseler. There are at least two types of chiselers who might be included in this classification. One is the type who regularly deducts cash discounts even though payment is made after expiration of the cash discount period. Firms vary as to their policies in such a situation. The question is raised whether it is best to return the check and request full payment or whether to accept the check and bill the customer for the balance owing. Whichever procedure is followed, the action taken should be accompanied by a clear, concise statement that credit terms are being violated. How strong and

2 / John J. Brosky, "The Care and Feeding of Marginal Accounts," reprinted from *Credit and Financial Management,* December 1965, p. 26. Copyright 1965 by the National Association of Credit Management, New York, N.Y.

threatening the statement should be will depend largely upon how profitable the customer is to the debtor firm and how much his future business is desired.

Another problem facing collection personnel is the customer who makes only a partial, payment, sends a postdated check with deductions for cash discounts, or who dates the check back in order that the date is within the discount period. The chronic offender who operates in this manner should be told "the facts of credit" much more emphatically than the first-time offender who may have been simply careless.

A Fraud. This dishonest debtor should not be shown any consideration, nor should any concerted effort be made to retain his goodwill or possible future business. Just as soon as the creditor firm is convinced that the debtor is dishonest and is engaged in fraudulent actions, the account should be turned over to an attorney or possibly to a collection agency, with instructions to take legal action against the debtor. Time is of the essence in dealing with such offenders, and there is little reason to go through all the steps normally followed in a collection process.

Capital

The discussion that appeared under this topic in Chapter 17 applies equally well to commercial credit transactions and is repeated here. One of the most important factors is the amount of capital owned or available to the firm involved. Regardless of how liberal a collection policy a creditor may wish to follow, if he is operating within a limited capital structure, he is forced in most instances to adopt a strict collection policy in order to keep himself in a position to meet the demands of his own creditors. Most business firms are not blessed with an overabundance of working capital and are forced to depend upon the turnover of their goods to provide the funds needed. But a mere turnover of goods is not enough, if these goods are sold on credit as they usually are in commercial transactions. One step is added to the process and that is completion of the credit transaction by receipt of cash payment. How quickly this last step must be completed is predicated upon how badly the firm is in need of capital. Thus capital availability and need play a vital role in determining just what type of collection policy a firm must adopt, despite the fact that a somewhat different policy might be more feasible in view of some of the other factors involved.

Closely connected with the subject of capital availability is the question of whether a firm should charge its slow-pay customers interest for carrying their past-due accounts. Commenting on this question, Lester C. F. Rothgeb, credit manager of the Foster Auto Supply Company of Denver, stated:[3]

Can a business afford to render free banking service to weak financial accounts? Is it fair to the good accounts, which pay promptly, to carry the weaker ones for 60 to 90 days and more without making some distinction among them?

These are the questions that are pondered by financial and credit management executives as they search for the answer to their constant problem of collection. Many automotive jobbers have concluded a service charge on past-due accounts, while not the ultimate answer, is at least a partial solution.

· ·

Delinquent receivables are related to sales and profits. Collection turnover is just as important as inventory turnover, receivables investment is just as important as merchandise investment. And one of the fastest ways to increase profits is to improve collection turnover. By making a service charge on overdue accounts, however, you stand the chance of attracting some customers who have no bank credit. These people are willing to let you serve as their banker, and are content to pay a service charge for the accommodation. If you have some of these clients on your books, how long would you continue this practice?

If a company calls the charge interest and demands more than the legal rate on delinquent accounts, there is danger of violating the Usury Law and inviting severe penalties. Its application, incidentally, varies from state to state.

· ·

Honest charges, on the other hand, offer several advantages: (1) by not placing a service charge, the good-paying customer is penalized by shorter terms if cash discount is not allowed; (2) with the service charge, you may increase your receivables turnover, and customers pay more promptly; and (3) the service charge partially compensates for carrying past-due accounts and induces better paying habits due to fear of the charge.

Some disadvantages include: (1) reduction in the cash flow of receivables; (2) consideration of service charges as a form of financing, with some companies feeling that this should be left to finance companies or banks; (3) aid to your competitor, that is, if he does not have a service charge; and (4) prohibitive cost of keeping books on small balances.

Competition

The business firm of today does not function in a vacuum, nor in the pure air of "no competition." Rather, the firm attempting to sell its goods and services finds that the actions taken by its competitors are highly influential upon the policies it establishes. And one of the policies influenced is the collection policy. Thus if an active

3 / "Making Past-Due Receivables Pay," reprinted from *Credit and Financial Management,* August 1966, pp. 24-25. Copyright 1966 by the National Association of Credit Management, New York, N.Y. Also see Robert H. Cole, "Service Charge or Interest Charge?" *Journal of Marketing,* October 1958, p. 179, for an early prediction of this present problem. The reader also is referred to "Service Charges. . . . Help or Hindrance on Past Due Accounts?" *Credit and Financial Management,* March 1970, p. 21.

competitor is "selling" its lenient credit and collection policy, a firm cannot simply ignore this policy and indiscriminately follow a very strict credit and collection policy of its own. That is, the firm cannot do this if it wishes to obtain its share of the business. Thus in the decision as to the type of collection policy to establish and to follow, serious consideration must be given to competition as an important factor in policy determination.

Type of Business and Type of Goods

Collection methods and practices tend to vary with the type of business and method of operation of the selling firm and with the type of goods sold. As in consumer credit, it is obvious that the greater the perishability of the product, the greater the need for prompt payment of the account, and thus the stricter the collection policy to be followed.

Profit Margin

With any established collection policy, the ultimate aim of the creditor firm is to collect the amount due and still have a net profit left after all the expenses are deducted from the gross margin. Thus how wide this gross margin is has an important influence upon the collection policy followed. The wider the profit margin on which a firm operates, the more lenient may be its collection policy. On the contrary, narrow profit margins do not permit long delinquencies or extended and costly collection procedures. Thus both the risk and cost involved must be related to the profit margin of the creditor firm. In addition, a collection policy must give consideration to the profitableness of a particular debtor's business, as some portions of a vendor's activities are more profitable than others. Not all lines carry the same profit margin; some sales carry higher selling, delivery, and service expenses than others. A careful analysis of these differences needs to be made.

Credit Policy Followed

The credit policy that has been established and that is followed by a firm has an important influence upon the type of collection policy that is adopted. The chances are that the firm following a liberal credit approach will have a strict collection policy; one with a strict credit approach, a liberal collection procedure. To be liberal in both phases is an invitation to trouble; to be strict in both is to neglect the "increasing sales" aspect of credit activities. It should be recognized by the creditor firm that as long as its customers regard credit solely as a service rather than a mutual privilege, then its collection problems may be troublesome. When the customer begins to think of credit primarily as a joint business transaction, the collection problems of the creditor tend to become simpler; sentimentality lessens; the creditor is not as reluctant to insist upon payment for fear of incurring the ill will of his customers. Terms once established between debtor and creditor must be respected.[4] Slow-paying customers not only cost additional money for collection efforts, but they also often become reluctant to return to the scene of their buying activities until their previous indebtedness is cleared.

Types of Records

While it is not possible to set up a record system that will fit all businesses, it is important to recognize that the type of record keeping that is in use will have a direct effect upon the collection system introduced and the efficiency with which it is operated. Each business concern should carefully study its own requirements and adopt a system that will meet its own needs. It is recommended that the credit and collection manager carefully consider the numerous systems and equipment offered by the office equipment supply houses. These systems and equipment are being revised, modified, and improved constantly, with the aim of providing faster availability of information on which to take the necessary actions to effect collections. But before any decision is made as to the system to introduce and to use, the credit and collection manager should remind himself that the system that *meets the needs* of his business at the *lowest relative cost* is the system for him to adopt.

One of the essential features of an effective collection procedure is the promptness with which the first reminder notice is furnished. If this is not received by the debtor until an extended length of time after the due date has passed, the tendency is for the debtor to feel that he is dealing with an inefficient and indifferent creditor. As a result, collections may drop accordingly. Thus the system used should provide information daily on those accounts which are overdue. And this means every account that is overdue!

PRELIMINARY STEPS IN ESTABLISHING A COMMERCIAL COLLECTION SYSTEM

The reader is referred to the discussion on a general collection system which appears in Chapter 17. While the material in that chapter is slanted toward collection problems and procedures in

4 / C. William Bruder, " 'Selling' Your Collections," *Credit and Financial Management,* June 1967, p. 22.

consumer credit transactions, many of the comments have applicability to commercial credit procedures and practices. At the risk of being repetitive, the following comments are taken from that chapter.

Promptness and regularity of payment must be built into any system because of the following conditions:

1. A lax collection policy often indicates an incompetent management. This in turn can reflect upon the purchaser's attitude toward the products sold by the firm.
2. Experience has shown that there is a definite correlation between the length of time debts are unpaid and the volume of resulting bad-debt losses.
3. Slow collections tend to result in the loss of future sales to these customers because of their reluctance to attempt to buy from creditors whom they have owed for some period of time. Of course, these creditors may show even a stronger reluctance to sell such customers.
4. Failure to enforce the collection activity tends to aid the imprudent purchaser. Thus, the foolhardy buyer may plunge headlong into unwise buying, knowing that the collection system of the selling firm will permit him an excessively long time before drastic legal action is taken, if it is ever taken at all.

In order to bring about promptness and regularity of payment, the following preliminary steps in establishing a sound commercial collection system are suggested:

1. Determination of the length of time for the collection process to run.
2. Selection of appropriate types of collection devices or actions to use.
3. Decision as to the number of actions to be taken.
4. Arrangement of the actions in logical sequence.
5. Schedule of the actions at appropriate intervals.

In the preliminary planning of the collection procedure, the person charged with the responsibility of collecting accounts receivable will have to decide just how long the entire collection process should run. Such a decision generally is controlled by circumstances other than the desires of the collection manager. For example, all the factors (debtor classification, capital, competition, type of business, type of goods sold, profit margin, credit policy, and type of records) previously discussed will have an important bearing upon how long any collection process is to be allowed to run.

Equally important—or possibly even more important—is the selection of the appropriate types of collection devices or actions to take. In Chapter 32 these actions are separated into three categories and are discussed in some detail. The three categories are: (1) actions between a single creditor and a single debtor; (2) actions between a group of creditors and a single debtor; and (3) third-party actions between creditor(s) and debtor. The first grouping includes such actions as invoices, statements, reminders, telephone calls, telegrams, personal calls, personal letters, notes, drafts, trade acceptances, assignment of accounts receivable, attorneys, collection agencies, replevin, extensions, and collection by suit. The second grouping includes extension agreements, composition settlements, assignment, bankruptcy, and arrangements. The third grouping is involved primarily with the Adjustment Bureaus of the National Association of Credit Management.

The third step in establishing a sound commercial credit system involves the decision as to the number of these actions to be taken. In other words, after the decision is made to use collection letters, for example, just how many of these letters will be included in any collection procedure? Undoubtedly, the more lenient the policy, the larger the number of such actions that will be included.

Step four involves the arrangement of these actions in some logical sequence. Since collection efforts have the twofold objective of obtaining the money and of retaining the goodwill, most collection managers bear in mind that generally a successful collection system will use the milder methods first, to be followed by the more intense actions arranged in order of their severity. Exceptions to this arrangement are to be found in those instances in which the debtor was a marginal risk to begin with and the collection manager knows that the milder methods would be a waste of time and money on such firms.

The last step is the determination of the frequency with which the collection actions are to be used, or the interval of time that should be allowed between each action taken. A lenient collection policy calls not only for a relatively large number of collection actions but also a comparatively long lapse of time between the different measures. In all instances, however, the time interval should become shorter as the stage of delinquency advances.

REVIEW AND DISCUSSION QUESTIONS

1. Why are collections in commercial transactions an inherent part of any commercial credit operation?
2. Discuss the twofold objectives of a commercial collection system.
3. Discuss why it is important to classify debtors in commercial collection operations.

4. Explain the nine major classifications of debtors, as outlined in the text.

5. Which of these debtors would you say accounts for a major proportion of slow accounts? Why did you choose the one you did?

6. Under what circumstances and by what procedures does a credit manager have an opportunity to advise and hence possibly aid a debtor in overcoming a relatively bad collection situation?

7. Discuss the importance of capital in establishing a collection policy.

8. What other factors must a commercial credit manager consider in establishing a collection policy? Discuss those you have listed.

9. What should a record-keeping system provide in the way of a "watching" device for a credit manager?

10. What are the possible consequences of a lax and ineffective collection policy? Discuss these consequences.

11. What are the usual preliminary steps in establishing a sound commercial collection system?

32

Collection Practices in
Commercial Credit Management

Selection of the most appropriate types of collection devices and actions that will maximize collections and yet minimize loss of trade is essential in establishing an effective commercial collection system. While the actual choice of the particular action or actions to take in the collection of any commercial account is largely a matter of judgment and experience, it is vital that the person charged with the responsibility of collections understand the benefits and the pitfalls of each of the collection devices at his disposal. In some of the more complicated and legally involved techniques, the assistance of a capable attorney specializing in this area will be well worth the money expended for his services. Some companies encourage their credit managers to study law and hence become proficient in the legal phases of collections.

No attempt has been made in this chapter to cover in detail all the legal ramifications and technicalities that are connected with some of the more involved collection devices. In actual operation, the collection manager must be familiar with the fact that such actions are available, but he undoubtedly will rely heavily upon the legal knowledge of the company attorney or one consulted for this purpose. It is with this idea in mind that the most common collection devices available to the commercial credit and collection manager are discussed in the following sections.

COLLECTION ACTIONS AVAILABLE

Collection actions may be divided into three categories: (1) actions between a single creditor and a single debtor; (2) actions between a group of creditors and a single debtor; (3) third-party actions between a creditor or group of creditors and a debtor. Generally the action between a single creditor and a single debtor occurs before any effort is made to use either one of the other two types. Whether group action or third-party action occurs next in the order of sequence, because single-party actions has not been successful, is dependent upon the circumstances surrounding the particular debtor-firm account.

Single Creditor and Single Debtor

The actions taken between a single creditor and a single debtor are practically the same whether collection procedures are being discussed from the point of view of consumer credit or that of commercial credit. These devices, which generally are well known to both debtor and creditor, include the following:

Invoices
Statements
Reminders
Telephone calls
Telegrams
Personal calls
Personal letters
Notes, drafts, and trade acceptances
Assignment of accounts receivable
Attorneys
Collection agencies (part of the debtor company or separate
    organizations)
Replevin (repossession of merchandise)
Extension agreement
Suit

For a discussion of these devices,[1] the reader is referred to Chapter 17. Mention should be made at this point, however, that the use of notes, drafts, and trade acceptances is common only in commercial credit transactions.

In those instances in which the debtor firm does not meet its obligations on its indebtedness, the creditor may ask that a promissory note be signed. This usually takes place only after a predetermined extension has been worked out and a definite date of repayment can be shown on the note. In addition to the stated repayment date, an interest charge may be agreed upon by the parties concerned.

1 / While the discussion of these devices in Chapter 17 is slanted toward consumer credit, the basic description of such actions applies equally well to commercial credit transactions.

In other instances, a sight draft may be used. Although the sight draft has declined in popularity in recent years, its most common use today is in connection with c.o.d. shipments. In brief, the creditor prepares the draft, which in effect requests the customer's bank to seek payment of the account. Perhaps moral pressure is the greatest asset of the draft in that the debtor desires to maintain good working relations with his bank and to have his banker think highly of his awareness of credit responsibility.

The trade acceptance, likewise, is drawn up in connection with the shipment of goods from seller to buyer. The manufacturer prepares the trade acceptance at the time of shipment. Upon receiving the form, the customer indicates his acceptance of the indebtedness by signing and dating the agreement, and designates the bank at which he will make payment on the noted date. The manufacturer may hold the acceptance until the time of collection and then send it to the bank as a collection item, or he may choose to discount the acceptance with his bank prior to the payment date.

Another action often taken by a single creditor is to assign the early stages of the collection procedure to salesmen. Just as they frequently may be used to do a nominal amount of investigative work on their customers, they also may be called upon to effect collections. Salesmen who call on smaller companies are in a good position to take collection action. It is in the smaller companies that we find relatively simple organizational structures and easy access to the responsible parties. In fact, the salesman can often discuss the collection problem with the proprietor or partner himself. Furthermore, their closeness to the actual business scene and their observations and reasoning as to why a customer is delinquent may be particularly helpful to the collection department in plotting future actions. Past-due and seriously delinquent accounts obviously result in a rejection of future orders written by salesmen; hence their concern for promptness as well as effectiveness in the collection procedures is vital to their welfare.

Group of Creditors and Single Debtor

The most common types of action taken by a group of creditors against a single debtor are:

Extension agreement[2]
Composition settlement
Assignment
Bankruptcy
Arrangements—Chapter XI of Bankruptcy Act

2 / An extension agreement may be a single-creditor action or a group-creditor action.

Extension Agreement. An extension agreement is essentially a moratorium under which the debtor proposes to pay his creditors in full at some future date. This agreement is binding only upon those creditors who sign it, and no creditor is compelled to do so. For this reason, if the larger creditors desire to grant an extension to a debtor but some of the smaller creditors are not in agreement, these smaller creditors sometimes are paid in full by the other creditors to prevent their filing of involuntary bankruptcy proceedings.

Before an extension is granted, however, credit managers have learned to be careful in estimating the extent of the debtor's difficulties. This situation is emphasized in the following quotation:[3]

> ... A debtor may be *solvent* but *not liquid* (unable to pay his debts as they mature), or he may be *insolvent* (his liabilities exceeding his assets). From experience, credit men learn to distinguish between a business which can be salvaged and rehabilitated financially and one in which liquidation for the benefit of creditors, in or out of bankruptcy, is necessary. They also learn to recognize the dishonest debtor, who, although he could be rehabilitated, should instead be liquidated and punished by denial of discharge from his obligations, or even by prosecution. If possible, the dishonest debtor should be prevented from re-establishing a business and repeating the same offenses.

Composition Settlement. This settlement, either with or without an extension of time, is a contractual arrangement under which the creditors signing the agreement offer to accept less than the full amount of their indebtedness and in turn agree to discharge the debtor of any future obligation to make full settlement of the claims.

Again, care should be taken to grant such settlements only to the debtor whose financial position, although serious, is such that he probably could operate profitably in the future if relieved of his excessive debt burden in the present. Also, evidence of fraud should be sufficient to cause any composition settlement to be set aside and the offender to be prosecuted to the limit.

Assignment. When an extension is not warranted and a composition settlement cannot be agreed upon, then "friendly" liquidation of the concern and settlement of the indebtedness may come about through assignment proceedings.[4]

Assignment for the benefit of creditors is generally considered a voluntary, out-of-court action taken by a debtor who usually is insolvent (liabilities exceeding assets). The debtor transfers in trust some or all of his assets to a third party, an assignee, in order that these assets or proceeds from their sale may be applied to payment of his debts. Such an assignment may be made either under common

3 / *Credit Management Handbook* (2d ed.; Homewood, Ill.: Richard D. Irwin, Inc., 1965), p. 334.

4 / Assignment as used here is entirely different from assignment of accounts receivable.

law or under state law, as every state has some form of law that spells out the provisions for an assignment.

At first glance it may appear that assignment prevents all the ills of bankruptcy (described in the subsequent section). Advocates of this method point out that it is fast, relatively inexpensive, free from court restraints, private, and provides more money for distribution to the creditors. On the other hand, critics of the plan point out that assignment constitutes an act of bankruptcy, that the debtor cannot be examined under oath, that recovery of preferential payments is not provided for, that the debtor is not freed of his remaining indebtedness without the consent of the creditors, that there is a lack of uniformity in state laws concerning the procedure,[5] and that there is little or no direct supervision over the assignee in estate administration.

Bankruptcy. The creditor has several duties and responsibilities relative to the action which he must take in connection with bankruptcy cases. The credit man handling bankruptcy matters should be familiar enough with the law to know the rights of his firm and to take the proper steps to protect these rights.[6]

His most important responsibility arises out of the fact that he often has it within his power to decide whether or not to place a debtor in bankruptcy or to attempt other means of working out a bad situation. For creditors to hasten to place every difficult collection into bankruptcy means the overburdening of the bankruptcy courts with unnecessary cases and the liquidation through bankruptcy of many cases which could more economically and advantageously be liquidated by other means. The creditor then should consider carefully whether or not all other possible means of collecting the debt have been canvassed before consenting to being a party to a petition in bankruptcy.

Another consideration is the attitude of the debtor. If the debtor is attempting to give preference to certain favored creditors or if he is dissipating the estate by conveyances, transferances, or concealment of property with the intent to hinder, delay, or defraud creditors, there is no choice but to put the estate into bankruptcy so as to protect all creditors and to secure a fair and equitable distribution of the assets. If, however, the debtor is trying to be fair and is doing everything possible to assist in the protection of the interests of the creditors, there is every reason for the intelligent creditor to help the debtor avoid the stigma of bankruptcy and to find some better way to work out his difficulties.

5 / This constitutes a problem when creditors in several states are involved with the delinquent debtor.

6 / David L. May, "What the Credit Executive Should Know about Bankruptcy," *Credit and Financial Management,* February 1967, p. 28.

Bankruptcy Legislation in the United States. The Constitution of the United States provides in Article I, Section 8, that: "The Congress shall have power . . . to establish . . . uniform laws on the subject of bankruptcies throughout the United States."

The grant of this power to the federal government was not subject to much discussion either in the Constitutional Convention or in the various ratifying conventions. The power was not immediately exercised by Congress, and the first United States Bankruptcy Act was not passed until 1800. This act was repealed in 1803. A second, passed in 1841, was repealed in 1843. A third, passed in 1867, lasted until 1878. The present act was passed in 1898 and has continued in force until the present time. While amendments to the act have been numerous, it was in 1938 that the most thorough revision was made. In fact, the law today often is referred to as the Bankruptcy Act of 1938, or as the Chandler Act.

The year 1966 saw two important changes in the bankruptcy legislation in the United States. On July 6, 1966, the President signed into law bills H.R. 136 and H.R. 3438. These bills were enacted in the hope of providing fairer treatment of general creditors in bankruptcy and of establishing a healthier climate for future credit extensions which are necessary for an expanding economy.

The most recent amendment to the Bankruptcy Act of 1938 was passed by the 91st Congress in mid-October 1970, and was designed:[7]

. . . to permit the discharge of debts in a subsequent proceeding after denial of discharge for specified reasons in an earlier proceeding, to authorize courts of bankruptcy to determine the dischargeability or nondischargeability of provable debts, and to provide additional grounds for the revocation of discharges.

One of the most interesting provisions of this amendment is that it enjoined all creditors whose debts are discharged from thereafter instituting or continuing any action or employing any process to collect such debts as personal liabilities of the bankrupt. While this provision applies more directly to the field of consumer credit, it also is pertinent to the field of commercial credit.

General Purposes of Bankruptcy Legislation. The general purposes of legislation dealing with the relationship of debtors to their creditors have been threefold.

The first and earliest purpose was to provide creditors with some means whereby they might legally possess themselves of the property of the debtor and equitably distribute it among the claimants. In addition to possession of the property of the debtor, creditors

---

7 / Public Law 91-467, 91st Congress, S. 4247, October 19, 1970. The reader also is referred to "Recent Amendments to the Bankruptcy Act," *Credit World,* December 1970, p. 12.

frequently were given control of the person of the debtor to further assist the enforcement of payment from a recalcitrant or unwilling debtor. Some of the more severe penalties of the early legislation on debts had as their underlying motive the belief that severity in treatment of the debtor would stir his relatives to renewed efforts to satisfy the debts or perhaps would dissuade the debtor from attempts to defraud his creditors.

Later, creditors realized that control of the person of the debtor served no useful purpose. Therefore, the later acts of bankruptcy have attempted to provide merely for an equitable distribution of the property of the debtor among the various creditors, and control of the person of the debtor has been relinquished. Provisions for the distribution of property were found necessary to avoid the inequitable division of the debtor's estate which might result from permitting the debtor to continue his full right to pay whomever he chooses after he becomes insolvent. In other words, it prevented the debtor from making preferential payments. It also was necessary to prevent the estate from being apportioned exclusively to the more diligent creditors. To appreciate this necessity, it is only necessary to remember that the condition of insolvency means that the debtor's equity in the estate is entirely extinguished. Under these conditions the entire estate should be used to satisfy the claims of creditors and thus may be said to belong to the creditors rather than to the debtor. Bankruptcy legislation provides a means whereby this property can be prorated among the creditors equitably and economically.

The second purpose was the relief of the debtor from further demands after his confession of inability to satisfy claims against him. The development of more humane notions of the relations of man to man have resulted in fuller realization of the folly of continuing to oppress the debtor by requiring him to continue the struggle to pay debts which are beyond his capacity. It is but common humanity to permit him to be freed from an impossible burden and not be made continually to pay the penalty for past mistakes. This relief from the legal necessity of paying debts is secured by the surrender of the entire estate. This does not necessarily relieve the debtor from the moral obligation, for he may still feel himself morally compelled to repay the unsatisfied debts when he has recovered his fortune. The protection of the law, however, relieves him from the necessity of paying debts which are beyond his capacity.

The third purpose recognized that society has an interest in the rehabilitation of the debtor. As long as he is oppressed by the results of past mistakes, the debtor is lost to society as a useful active producer. Every effort he makes to rehabilitate himself may be defeated by the pressure of creditors, and he is forced to become a drone or burden upon society. Furthermore, the fear of the consequences of debt would inhibit the ambitious man and stifle his initiative. Thus economic development would be slower. Therefore, it is to the interest of society to permit the debtor to recover and to provide an equitable process of so doing. This must not be permitted to go to the other extreme of unduly favoring debtors. When relief from debts is too easy and readily available, the fear of loss inhibits creditors from lending and also slows down social and economic development.[8] Thus the social good requires that legislative control should be exercised in such a manner as to provide full and equitable protection of the rights of creditors and also relief of debtors from impossible burdens, but such control should not make it possible for fraudulent debtors[9] to shield themselves from the consequences of their acts.

In general, bankruptcy legislation in the United States has attempted to strike a balance between the interests of debtors and creditors, while maintaining the social interest at a maximum. At times various changes designed to favor one group or the other have been embodied in amendments proposed to Congress. Associations of creditors have frequently agitated for "reforms" which would afford them more protection or prevent certain "abuses," while associations of debtors have sought "reforms" which would provide them with more certain or readily available "relief."

What Is Bankruptcy? According to the legal definition, in addition to the condition of insolvency there must also be some legal and public recognition of the condition coupled with some specific act or acts on the part of the debtor or creditor or both. Nor can every firm avail itself of the provisions of the bankruptcy act and become legally bankrupt.

Kinds of Bankruptcy. Bankruptcy may be either voluntary or involuntary. As the names imply, voluntary bankruptcy comes about through the conscious desire and initiative of the debtor. Involuntary bankruptcy is brought about through the conscious desire and initiative of the creditor(s).

What Firms May Become Bankrupt? Perhaps the easiest way to answer this question is to list those types or classes of firms that may not voluntarily petition themselves into bankruptcy or may not be forced into it. These are: municipalities, railroads, insurance companies, banking corporations, and building and loan associations.

8 / Evidence of this may be found in the failure of credit to function in certain backward countries whose legislation unduly favors debtors.

9 / Elmer T. Sivertsen, "How to Prevent Credit Frauds," *Credit and Financial Management,* October 1967, p. 30.

The Acts of Bankruptcy. The law sets forth six acts, one of which must have been committed within four months of the filing of the petition. These acts, as set forth in Chapter III, Section 3, of the law are:

1. Concealed, removed, or permitted to be concealed or removed any part of his property, with intent to hinder, delay, or defraud his creditors or any of them, or made or suffered a transfer of any of his property, fraudulent under the provisions of section 67 or 70 of this Act (which deal with Liens and Fraudulent Transfers and Title to Property, respectively); or
2. Made or suffered a preferential transfer, as defined in subdivision (a) of section 60 of this Act (which deals with Preferred Creditors); or
3. Suffered or permitted, while insolvent, any creditor to obtain a lien upon any of his property through legal proceedings or distraint and not having vacated or discharged such lien within 30 days from the date thereof or at least 5 days before the date set for any sale or other disposition of such property; or
4. ·Made a general assignment for the benefit of his creditors; or
5. While insolvent or unable to pay his debts as they mature, procured, permitted, or suffered voluntarily or involuntarily the appointment of a receiver or trustee to take charge of his property; or
6. Admitted in writing his inability to pay his debts and his willingness to be adjudged a bankrupt. (Under this Act it is immaterial whether the debtor is solvent or insolvent.)

Regular Bankruptcy Procedure. It should be recognized that bankruptcy proceedings may take many forms and may become exceedingly complicated and legalistic in nature. However, for the purposes of this text, a brief description of only the so-called "regular" or "ordinary" bankruptcy procedure will be given. For the more complicated procedures, the guidance of a qualified bankruptcy lawyer is a must. The steps generally taken in the ordinary bankruptcy procedure, then, are as follows:

1. The bankruptcy petition is filed with the Federal District Court for the district in which the alleged bankrupt is located. It will be noted that bankruptcy is a federal action.

2. A receiver is appointed to preserve the insolvent estate. The office of receiver is a temporary office which is used only when it is necessary to have someone appointed to take charge of the debtor's property until the election of a trustee. He is appointed only when it is necessary for someone to be in charge to prevent waste or loss during this intervening period. He is supposed, so far as possible, to conserve the property and not to convert it into money. Selling property will take place only when it may be necessary to prevent waste or loss. A receiver is appointed when the creditors request such an action.

3. If proceedings are contested, a jury trial will be held and the debtor will be examined under oath; the court will decide whether the firm is to be adjudged a bankrupt; and if so, the case will be referred to a referee in bankruptcy for legal administration of the case. The referee thus becomes the representative of the court in all subsequent actions. The duties of the debtor are numerous. For example, he is required to comply with all lawful orders of the court, to examine the correctness of proofs of claims filed against his estate, to execute and deliver such papers as ordered by the court, to prepare and file a schedule of his property and a list of his creditors, and to submit to an examination relative to the conduct of the business and the case of his bankruptcy.

4. The referee[10] then notifies the creditors of the adjudication.

5. The creditors then are asked to file proof of their claims.

6. The first meeting of the creditors is held, at which time the election of the trustee occurs, the bankrupt is examined, and allowance of claims occurs. The trustee, who represents the creditors and who replaces the receiver, henceforth administers the estate and keeps a record of all his activities and makes reports to the referee who is representing the court.

7. The trustee, acting in accordance with the instructions and subject to the review of the court, proceeds to convert the estate into money. He takes the same legal position as was formerly occupied by the bankrupt, has the same rights to sue upon the debts due the estate, and can dispose of the assets owned by the estate.

8. From the proceeds of the estate, disbursements (called dividends) are made to the creditors in accordance with the provisions of the act; a final accounting is filed by the trustee with the referee. It is the duty of the trustee to attempt to void any preferences which are voidable and to recover the property for the benefit of the creditors. The order of payment and the priority[11] given certain debts are as follows:

a) Actual and necessary costs of preserving the estate subsequent to filing the petition.

b) Filing fees paid by creditors in involuntary cases and reasonable expenses of recovering transferred and concealed property.

10 / Asa S. Herzog, "The Referee in Bankruptcy—Mr., Master or Judge?" *Credit and Financial Management,* August 1970, p. 12.

11 / H.R. 136, previously mentioned, amends the Bankruptcy Act to restore chattel mortgages and other contractual liens to first priority over other claims, such as administrative expenses, wage claims, and landlord liens. H.R. 3438, on the other hand, limits the previously unlimited priority given to all unsecured federal, state, and local tax claims in bankruptcy to only those claims which have become legally due and owing within the three years preceding bankruptcy, with certain exceptions. The new law also stipulates that all such tax liabilities of the bankrupt legally due and owing more than three years before bankruptcy would be discharged.

c) Costs of administration.

d) Wages (due employees) earned within three months of the commencement of proceedings, not to exceed $600 to each claimant.

e) Reasonable expenses incurred by creditors in opposing the confirmation of an arrangement.

f) All taxes legally due.

g) Debts owed to any person who by the laws of the states or the United States is entitled to priority. Since the trustee's title is only the title previously held by the bankrupt, any valid lien against the property continues and must be paid before the trustee can dispose of the property free of encumbrances. Should a sale of the property fail to pay the entire debt, the secured creditor then becomes a general creditor for the amount of the deficit.

h) Unsecured general creditors.

9. The final meeting of the creditors then is held; the final report is submitted to the court; and the bankrupt is granted his discharge of the indebtedness remaining. However, certain debts are not discharged by bankruptcy action. Debts which are not affected by a discharge are as follows:

a) Taxes levied by the United States, any state, county, district, or municipality.

b) Liabilities for obtaining property by false pretenses, or for malicious injuries to the person or property of another, or for alimony due or to become due, or for maintenance or support of wife or child, or for seduction of an unmarried female, or for breach of promise of marriage accompanied by seduction, or for criminal conversation.

c) Claims not scheduled in time for proof and allowance unless the creditor had notice or actual knowledge of the proceedings.

d) Debts created by a bankrupt's fraud, embezzlement, misappropriation, or defalcation while acting as an officer or in any fiduciary capacity.

e) Wages earned within three months of commencement of proceedings.

f) Moneys of an employee received or retained by employer to secure faithful performance of the terms of a contract of employment.

g) All debts incurred after the petition has been filed.

Responsibilities of Credit Managers in Regard to Bankruptcy.
When becoming a party to an involuntary petition or when receiving notice of the filing of either a voluntary or an involuntary petition,

the credit manager must immediately take steps to protect the interests of his firm. These necessary steps are:

1. Stop all further credit. Mark all records to indicate that credit lines are suspended.

2. Recover as much as can be recovered. Hold up or stop payment on all checks and other remittances going forward to the bankrupt. Issue stoppage orders on goods in transit. Stop work on all goods in process or on order. File suit to recover goods already in the debtor's possession whenever there is legal ground for so doing. Seize and hold all of the debtor's property which is in your possession or which can be placed in your possession lawfully.

3. Start foreclosure proceedings on all secured claims or take possession of all collateral or other property against which you have a lien claim, attempting to reduce this claim to possession wherever possible.

4. File proof of claim with the referee.

5. Attend creditors' meeting; cooperate in the election of a capable trustee; and see, so far as it is in your power, that the estate comes under the influence of a reputable lawyer.

6. Whenever there is the slightest suspicion of fraud, assist other creditors by contributing to an investigation fund to expose further evidence of fraud. Postpone the examination of the bankrupt until such time as the investigation is completed.

7. Assist in the examination of the bankrupt and help other creditors to set aside voidable preferences or conveyances where they are present in the case.

8. Resist the final discharge whenever there are any grounds for opposing the discharge; and if grounds are present, assist in the criminal prosecution of the bankrupt.

Certain of these duties of the credit man are necessary to recover as much from the estate of the bankrupt as is possible. Others of them will pay dividends only over the long run. At times intelligent interest and cooperation in the correction of abuses seems a thankless and profitless task. It is, however, part of the social responsibility which membership in society imposes upon each citizen.

Arrangements—Chapter XI of the Bankruptcy Act. Often a debtor can overcome many of the difficulties encountered in voluntary bankruptcy settlements by utilizing the arrangements proceedings set forth in Chapter XI of the Bankruptcy Act. An arrangement is defined as any plan of a debtor for the settlement, satisfaction, or extension of the time of payment of his unsecured debts, upon any terms. Arrangements proceedings usually are started under one of three sets of circumstances, all involving a debtor who is hopeful of being rehabilitated rather than liquidated but who is financially distressed:[12]

1. If negotiations for an out-of-court settlement break down because of inability to secure the consent of important creditors, perhaps the next best step is for the debtor to file a petition under Chapter XI.
2. The debtor may decide not to undertake an out-of-court settlement, and may proceed at once to file under Chapter XI.
3. If an involuntary petition in bankruptcy has been filed against a debtor, he can avoid this by filing a petition under Chapter XI.

Proceedings under Chapter XI are voluntary only. *No creditor may force a debtor into Chapter XI; the proceedings may be instituted by the debtor alone.* An individual, partnership, or corporation may file a petition. The arrangement will modify the rights of *unsecured* creditors only, although others may be indirectly affected.

In looking at Chapter XI proceedings, it is important to remember that they apply only to unsecured obligations of the debtor. When secured claims are outstanding, such as security agreements or assigned accounts receivable, they may be unaffected by the proceedings under Chapter XI. On the other hand, the debtor is free to arrange privately with the secured creditors for the settlement of their claims. The court, however, usually will require that priority claims, such as taxes, rent, wages, and administrative costs, are covered before approving any arrangement plan for the unsecured creditors.

Before leaving this section on group creditor action, mention should be made of the bulk sales laws. While not strictly a collection device, these state laws generally provide that prior to the sale of a business "in bulk"[13] the seller must give the buyer a sworn list of creditors (name, address, and amount owing), an inventory of the business must be taken, and the creditors must be notified that such a sale is scheduled to take place. Obviously, these laws are designed to prevent debtors from selling out at so many cents on the dollar and leaving the creditors in a precarious position in trying to collect the full amount due them. This was a definite problem before the passage of such laws.

Third-Party Actions

Recognizing the need to speed up the processes of collection, especially in those cases of insolvent and embarrassed debtors, many industries have organized some form of adjustment bureau or agency to aid their members, particularly those in the larger market centers,

12 / *Credit Management Handbook, op. cit.*, pp 340-41.

13 / What is meant by "in bulk" varies from state to state, depending upon the provisions of the law in each state.

in dealing with their overdue accounts. The National Association of Credit Management has been an outstanding leader in the development and widespread use of such an effort, through the establishment of local Adjustment Bureaus within its own organization.

Adjustment bureaus have a long history. The earliest record of merchants organizing to help solve the problems of distressed debtors is in 1868 in San Francisco. Since that time, organizations of credit executives to deal with the problems of firms in trouble have evolved. There is a real need for adjustment bureau intervention in many cases.[14] Adjustment bureau administration usually is less expensive than administration by the bankruptcy court, creditors have a more immediate sense of participation, and often the adjustment bureaus are able to work out long-term solutions not readily done through the courts.

BETTER COLLECTIONS—IS THERE A SOLUTION?

Just as the conditions that lead to collections are due to a number of causes, so the remedy or solution cannot be found in any one change in procedure or any one device.

Part of the remedy may be found in greater care on the part of creditors to accept credit only from those debtors who have good credit to tender and only in such amounts as is justified by the debtors' conditions. This would require of the creditors a more complete and careful investigation and a more penetrating and intensive analysis of the results of the investigation.

Part of the remedy may be found in greater care on the part of debtors in the offering of their credit. Credit should be regarded by the debtor as something of which he has but a limited stock. He should protect his stock carefully and replenish it frequently. He should recognize that acceptance of credit should not be granted indiscriminately and therefore should be cautious to keep his reputation in order that he can offer good credit and be sure of its acceptance.

Part of the remedy may be found in revision[15] of the bankruptcy act itself in such a way as to make it more difficult for fraudulent debtors to avail themselves of its provisions. More investigation should be made before granting discharges. Creditors should take more interest in the protection of their rights under the act and avoid paying undue tribute to unscrupulous attorneys and other parasites and bankruptcy rings.

14 / Donald A. Lewis, "Rx for Credit Woes: Group Therapy," *Credit and Financial Management,* May 1970, p. 16.

15 / Richard P. Matsch, "Bankruptcy: A Study in Functional Obsolescence," *Credit and Financial Management,* April 1970, p. 16.

REVIEW AND DISCUSSION QUESTIONS

1. Why should a credit manager rely heavily upon the legal knowledge of his company attorney or one consulted for this purpose?

2. Explain the three categories into which collection actions may be divided.

3. Which of these actions do you regard as routine devices? Which have at least some aspect of pressure on the debtor? Explain.

4. Which collection actions do you find in the field of consumer credit but not in the field of commercial credit?

5. Which collection actions do you find in the field of commercial credit but not in the field of consumer credit?

6. Explain the essential characteristics of an extension agreement, a composition settlement, and an assignment for the benefit of creditors.

7. Explain how an extension agreement may be a single-creditor action or a group-creditor action.

8. Discuss how assignment in a commercial collection action differs from an assignment of accounts receivable in a consumer collection action.

9. How does early bankruptcy legislation differ from the later acts?

10. How does society in general have an interest in the rehabilitation of the commercial debtor? Explain your answer.

11. What is the legal definition of bankruptcy?

12. What commercial enterprises may not declare themselves bankrupt?

13. Why do you believe that these enterprises may not take such an action?

14. Discuss the most recent amendment to the Bankruptcy Act of 1938.

15. What are the acts of bankruptcy? Of what significance are they?

16. What are the duties of the receiver in bankruptcy? The duties of the trustee?

17. Whom does the receiver represent? The trustee?

18. Why do some costs and creditors' claims have preference over other claims against the proceeds of a bankrupt estate?

19. What debts are not discharged by a bankruptcy action? Why?

20. Explain the provisions of Chapter XI of the Bankruptcy Act. Do you believe that these are desirable? Why or why not?

21. What do third-party actions attempt to accomplish?

PART VI

Control of Credit Operations

33

Measuring Efficiency
and Control of Credit Decisions

Too often in the rush of getting the day's work done the credit manager may tend to lose himself in the mass of the details of his work and never stop to ask himself if he knows exactly what the objectives of his position are or if he still is on the right road to accomplish these objectives. These questions may well be raised, for without clearly defined objectives and the means of measuring his progress the credit executive may waste much precious time, effort, and money in exploring side roads and bypaths which do not lead toward the end desired. In fact there is the possibility he may entirely lose sight of the destination and never arrive.

The credit executive should be prepared to answer the following questions:

1. What are the proper policies of the credit department of my firm in view of the current and anticipated conditions?
2. What measures can I use to determine whether these policies are reached?

Thus enlightened credit management should have constantly before it clearly defined goals or aims. The probability of success in reaching these goals is increased when management is aided by devices and measures which show the progress that is being made toward the final objective—that of satisfying customers and making profits for the business firm.

Although the credit manager constantly is engaged in testing the work of others, it is interesting to note that credit management has paid much less attention to the development of techniques to test its own work. It is not clear whether this situation has resulted because of the difficulty in measuring attainment, because of indifference on the part of management, because of a failure to recognize the importance of evaluating credit operations, or for some other reason.

There is no agreement among credit executives as to *the* best method or technique of judging how efficiently a credit department is operated. This lack of agreement is accounted for partially by variations in size of companies, in credit policies adopted, and in company organization, as well as by the fact that no one statistical measure which attempts to show the results of credit and collection operations is itself an actual measurement of how *effectively* these activities are performed. The person who has the responsibility of judging performance must have some predetermined standard to use as a basis of comparison. It is evident that if this standard has been erroneously set or has not been adjusted to reflect changing conditions, the judgment will undoubtedly be wrong from an overall profit-and-loss view. Thus the establishment of proper standards or targets is a prerequisite to proper judgment of performance.

As credit executives well know, it is easier to voice the need for correct and proper standards than it is to establish them in actual operations. One of the main reasons for this problem is the lack in many organizations of a meaningful, reasonably precise definition of the objectives desired by top management. Until such a definition of objectives is furnished the credit manager or is developed by the credit manager and approved by top management, it is difficult to clarify and to answer the question of how results are to be measured and appraised.

In almost all instances, a business organization attempts to judge the effectiveness of its component parts by how much this part (department, etc.) contributes to the net profit of the operation. Especially in the case of the credit department is this end result very difficult to isolate and measure. As a result, efficiency is more often judged—when it is judged—on the basis of certain figures which are assumed to be correlated closely with the credit department's contribution to the goals previously established by top management—when such goals have been spelled out.

RESPONSIBILITY OF THE CREDIT DEPARTMENT

In setting the proper objectives of his credit department, the credit executive has an implied responsibility to three interests:

1. To the firm which employs him.
2. To the debtor whose credit he accepts.
3. To the business and social community whose well-being may be—and undoubtedly will be—affected by his actions.

The responsibility to his own firm is the most direct and readily apparent of the three mentioned. As previously pointed out, the main objective of business management is to make profits. The intermediate objective of the credit function has long been recognized as being the achievement of a maximum of sales and a minimum of losses. This is its contribution toward the profit objective. At times the emphasis is on the sales portion of the task; at other times, on the loss-avoidance portion. Most frequently, however, the twofold objective has been properly kept in mind. It should be recognized, however, that to accept this statement of the ideal, the phrase "minimum of losses" must be interpreted in the widest possible sense. This must mean more than merely bad-debt losses. By a policy of careful and persistent collections, low bad-debt losses can be attained, but maximum profits may not result because of the high collection costs and expenses involved and the high costs of carrying receivables. The final result may even be considerably less profit and in times of stress may seriously handicap the business operations because of the freezing of capital in slow-moving receivables. Nor can the time element be ignored. Over what period of time shall the minimum of losses and maximum of sales be calculated? Exposure to loss due to the taking of today's substandard business may mean the securing of some customers who will cause losses, but it also involves the securing of some customers who will be the volume buyers of tomorrow. Perhaps a better statement of the ideal might well be to seek a minimum of costs and a maximum of gains in both the present and the future.

The second interest served by the credit manager is that of the debtor. The credit manager has a responsibility to the debtor which is just as definite and exacting as that which he assumes to his own firm. As enlightened sales departments have discovered that "satisfaction" is one of the most vital stages in a sale, so have credit departments recognized the need of customer satisfaction in every credit transaction. When customers find that their obligations are too heavy for them and that the strain of paying on these heavy obligations is severely handicapping them, this final stage of "satisfaction" is not attained, and the credit department has not performed correctly its function to the debtor whose credit has been accepted.

The third interest involved is the interest of society at large. The economic community in general is not a party to the transaction which is arranged between debtor and creditor. It occupies the role of the innocent bystander and as such, society at large is frequently injured by the actions of the immediate participants, unless care is exercised by the debtor in seeking additional credit and by the creditor in making sure that the acceptance of this additional amount is to the benefit of all concerned.

To some extent, credit management should be concerned with the social consequences of policy decisions or operating results. Certainly overextension of credit is not good for the debtor, creditor, or business community. Excessive charges for the credit service not only impose excessive burdens on the debtor and interfere with the expansion of the creditor's market; they also are socially undesirable. Excessive credit losses or long-delayed collections are costly to all parties to a credit transaction and are damaging to the entire business community. They do not contribute to a healthy economic climate.

TESTS OF CREDIT DEPARTMENT OPERATIONS

To serve these three interests—particularly the first one—many elaborate and effective devices for gathering testing material by fact-seeking investigations have been perfected and many highly efficient organizations developed to aid in the accumulation of reliable factual information. Credit executives have been diligent in seeking, and alert in applying, quality tests to the credit which they are asked to accept from day to day. They have discovered that these investigations must be sufficiently complete to uncover all unfavorable information and to permit proper analysis, must be reasonable from a cost point of view, and must be done with sufficient speed to enable a decision to be reached without causing customer dissatisfaction. These are exacting requirements, but credit personnel have discovered the means to meet them well.

The responsibility of credit management to these various interests having been recognized and the objectives of credit department operations having been clearly stated and visualized, the next step should be to measure the attainment of these objectives—the testing of the manner in which the credit department is meeting its responsibility. Some of these measuring devices are fairly well known to most credit personnel; some of them may be familiar only to credit management personnel who have made a study of this phase of credit work. Many credit departments operate without any checks on their operations, other than perhaps that of the bad-debt loss index. Suffice it to say, the tools or indexes described in the subsequent sections are designed to provide credit management with some means to test the efficiency or successfulness of performance of its credit operations. It is with these tools that the credit manager is assisted in determining whether or not his department is succeeding in bringing about maximum sales and minimum losses.

Certain tests of credit department operations have become more or less conventional. To the extent that conventional tests permit comparisons between the subject firm and other similar firms, they are more useful because they have more meaning. Additional tests may be developed to meet the requirements of special situations or to explore further those situations which seem to be significantly important. Some analysis of credit department operating results may be used to test closeness of fit between policies and actual operations or to see whether policy or operation is faulty. On occasion, an analysis of operations should be undertaken as a guide to the formation of new policies.

These tests are valuable in many important ways:[1]

First, the periodic calculation of ratios, percentages, and other figures is necessary to measure credit and collection results. Unless this is done, you have no way of knowing just what has been accomplished and what changes have occurred in each of the various aspects of your firm's credit business.

Second, keeping these statistical records makes it possible to set up standards or goals to shoot at in each phase of your credit and collection activity. Without standards, you have no basis for judging accomplishments. Also, an important stimulus to efficiency will be lacking.

Third, the accumulation of records kept on the same basis from year to year enables you to compare current credit and collection performance with that of previous periods, and to determine the progress made. Credit-sales volume for the current month, for instance, may be compared with the figure for the same month last year, or the preceding month this year, to see whether there has been an increase or decrease.

Fourth, if your firm's credit business is large enough to require the time of more than one person, comparisons often may be made between different individuals. You can calculate separate collection percentages for each person having responsibility for a given section of the accounts. Separate rejection percentages may be computed wherever two or more persons are engaged in granting credit.

Fifth, you may compare results shown by your figures with those reported by other firms. Data for such comparisons are published by the National Retail Credit Association, the Credit Management Division of the National Retail Merchants Association, and many national trade associations in many specific lines of business, as well as by the Board of Governors of the Federal Reserve System.

Sixth, the records you maintain may be used in forecasting future trends in credit sales volume, collections, and other aspects of your credit business. These forecasts can be very helpful in revisions of your general budgets, and they often suggest changes in your credit and collection policies.

1 / Clyde Williams Phelps, *Credit and Collections Controls for Small Marketers,* Small Marketers Aids No. 33 (Washington, D.C.: Small Business Administration, May 1958), p. 1. While this publication is a little out of date, the quotation is still applicable to present-day conditions. The reader also is encouraged to refer back to Chapter 28 and to review the 14 Important Ratios prepared by Dun & Bradstreet, Inc. This material illustrates the fact that there are considerable variations from line to line; thus a low loss ratio in one industry would be high for another.

Bad-Debt Loss

In the past, a credit department's efficiency often has been judged by rule of thumb. Successful operation was assumed to be evidenced by the manager's ability to reduce bad-debt losses to a minimum or to keep them at a minimum. Even now, one sometimes still hears a credit manager boasting of the fact that his concern has lost practically nothing during the year or that losses amounted to a very insignificant fraction of credit sales or of total sales. Such rule-of-thumb judgments are indeed misleading, although unfortunately they often appeal to certain segments of top management. An exceedingly small loss record alone constitutes no indisputable evidence of efficiency in credit administration. In fact, it may be an inferior basis on which to judge performance efficiency, for such a feat may be accomplished with comparative ease by practicing conservatism and accepting only the best risks. Such a policy often results in a diversion of trade to competitors and a loss of possible business profits.

The bad-debt loss index was among the first of the tests to be developed and still is one of the most generally used by credit men. The relationship is generally shown by dividing bad debts incurred during the period under consideration by total credit sales of the period, as follows:

$$\frac{\text{Bad-debt loss}}{\text{Total credit sales}} = \text{Bad-debt loss index}$$

However, there is little uniformity in the calculation of this proportion. It is calculated as a percentage of bad debts to total sales by some firms and as a percentage of bad debts to credit sales by others. There is no uniform practice as to the time when an account is classified as bad, and thus another variable is introduced into the calculation. Some firms leave it to the discretion of some official to decide when an account will be called bad; others so classify accounts after the passage of some definite time without payment; others after the occurrence of some definite act, such as the return of an unsatisfied judgment or similar event. A big margin of error also exists because of the fact that some accounts may be written off as bad debts within a brief period after they have become overdue, while other accounts may be carried for many months before they are eventually written off to profit and loss. Consequently, a substantial portion of the bad debts recorded for a given year may have resulted from credit decisions or collection procedures of the preceding year. Yet they are compared with credit sales of the year just past, and conclusions drawn from the ratio are applied to the credit and collections policies of this year. Furthermore, because of this lag in bad-debt recording, a substantial change in sales volume between two years may introduce a misleading variation into the bad-debt ratio. Thus when sales for credit are increasing while cash sales are remaining fairly stationary, the base on which the index is computed will increase and cause a more favorable apparent showing than is justified.

Percentages of bad-debt losses naturally vary with different lines of business, with competitive conditions, with the month or season of the year, and with general business conditions. Proper interpretation of the figures for bad-debt losses would require comparison between the current year's business, business for previous periods, and results secured by other firms operating under similar conditions. Data for comparison with other firms are becoming increasingly available as a result of the statistical work of the various credit and trade associations and of the federal government. A word of caution should be given, however, on using the bad-debt ratios of other sellers to determine a "sound" ratio for one's own company. The bad-debt ratio of any other concern for a single year would be of little value as a guide because of the lag factor just discussed. Furthermore, if the other concern operates on a higher or lower profit margin, its "sound" bad-debt ratio should be smaller or larger than one's own; if the difference in profit margins is known, an adjustment should be made for it. Trend analysis of a company's bad-debt ratios over a short series of years will not, by itself, indicate whether its credit or collection policies are becoming more strict or more lax. General business fluctuation and particular regional and trade developments are likely to influence the bad-debt ratio more profoundly than changes in the credit and collection policy of a firm.

Too great a reliance on the test of bad-debt losses by the credit department is dangerous since it tends to overemphasize caution in accepting credit. In the proper interpretation of this test, it is recommended that a policy be developed which seeks to hold the proportion within normal limits. These normal limits should be determined, for each firm, on the basis of the profit margin on which it works. An illustration of the fixing of the margin could be drawn from the insurance field. Here the attempt is not to avoid all losses, but to hold the underwriting to the normal loss point in such fashion as to make certain that the profit margin is greater than the probability of loss.

If a firm has adopted a consumer credit plan which includes several types of credit—such as open charge, installment, and revolving credit—it generally is desirable to keep separate data, if consistent with the accounting system used, of the bad-debt losses and credit sales in each type of consumer credit accepted. Such a procedure will enable the firm to pinpoint any troublesome areas as to the particular type of credit involved. In such instances, the additional indexes computed would include:

$$(1) \quad \frac{\text{Bad-debt losses from open charge sales}}{\text{Open charge sales}}$$

$$(2) \quad \frac{\text{Bad-debt losses from installment sales}}{\text{Installment sales}}$$

$$(3) \quad \frac{\text{Bad-debt losses from revolving credit sales}}{\text{Revolving credit sales}}$$

Credit Sales

In all business enterprises, it is important to know what percentage of the total sales is presented by credit transactions. This percentage or index is secured by dividing credit sales by total net sales:

$$\frac{\text{Credit sales}}{\text{Total net sales}} = \text{Credit sales index}$$

Generally, in firms dealing with consumer credit it is advisable to determine the percentage of business done on each type of credit, as for example, installment credit, charge account business, revolving charge account volume, c.o.d.'s, and so on. When comparisons are made from month to month or over a period of years, this measure affords a valuable picture of the firm's credit business and of some of the effects of its conduct regarding its credit policy. Comparisons with similar figures for other firms operating under substantially similar conditions indicate something of the relative success achieved in obtaining credit business.

Of possibly more importance in commercial credit operations is a classification of accounts by risk categories. For example, the following type of breakdown may be carried out within the broader framework of an industry or product-line classification of accounts:

1. *Government.*[2]
2. *Prime*—large, well-established firms involving no real credit risk.
3. *Good*—companies which can be expected to discount but lack the stature of prime accounts.
4. *Limited*—companies which are suspect enough to be held within a definite credit line.
5. *Marginal*—high-risk accounts which bear constant watching.

2 / Certain governmental units are better credit risks than others. Some may pay eventually, but time of payment is predicated on receipt of tax funds.

Such a classification has the advantage of enabling the commercial credit analyst to determine more accurately whether there has been any significant change in the pattern of his company's credit decisions from period to period; whether the change that has occurred will have any effect on the timing of future collections, with an ensuing influence on cash needs; whether certain individuals are doing a better job of accepting credit than are other members of the credit department; and whether marginal accounts are really producing enough orders to make it worthwhile to bother with them. All of these items, plus many others, may be of value to the credit analyst if he is willing and able to justify the expense in order to provide such detailed information on the basis of the suggested or similar classification.

Collection Percentage, Days to Collect, and Turnover of Receivables

These are included under one heading because they simply are different ways of stating a similar fundamental relationship. The collection percentage, which is one of the most commonly used of the credit control indexes, is determined by dividing the total amounts collected during a period (such as a month) by the total receivables outstanding at the beginning of that period as shown in the following formula:

$$\frac{\text{Collections made during period}}{\text{Receivables outstanding at beginning of period}} = \text{Collection index}$$

A derivation of this index is an estimation of the average length of time that receivables are outstanding. If, for example, the net credit period in a particular line of business is 30 days and the collection index is 50 percent, indicating that only one half of the outstanding receivables were collected during the month, receivables would "on the average" be outstanding 60 days. This estimate is made by using the following formula:

$$\frac{\text{Net credit period}}{\text{Collection index}} = \text{Average collection period}$$

$$\frac{30}{50\%} = 60$$

Another criterion of credit management efficiency is the use which is made of the capital invested in accounts receivable. The rate of receivables turnover is found by dividing the total credit sales by the average receivables outstanding, as follows:

$$\frac{\text{Total credit sales}}{\text{Average receivables outstanding}} = \text{Receivables turnover rate}$$

The seasonality of the business is, of course, important in determining how to compute the average of the receivables outstanding. It also is pertinent to point out that the activity of the investment in receivables may be expressed as a rate or in terms of the number of days required for one turn of the accounts. The latter may be computed by dividing 360 days by the receivables turnover rate, as shown below:

$$\frac{360 \text{ days}}{\text{Receivables turnover rate}} = \text{Number of days to collect credit accounts}$$

These measures of credit management have an advantage over the bad-debt loss calculation in that they can be figured earlier in many instances and can help to forecast difficulties in collection sufficiently in advance to permit the application of some corrective measures. Collection percentages, when decreasing, show the accumulation of poor accounts on the books or slackening of collection efforts before the bad conditions have had the opportunity to become inevitable. These measures of credit activity should make it possible to detect the effects of the adoption of unsound policies early. For example, adoption of unduly lenient terms, solicitation of unsound classes of customers, yielding to competitive temptations to outdo the other fellow in credit—all of these will reveal their fruits in a falling collection percentage. In addition, unduly stringent collection activity, overly conservative acceptance of credit, and undue hesitation in taking risks will tend to be detected earlier by study of the trend of collection percentages.

As with the other indexes previously described, these computed figures should be compared for the subject firm with those of the previous months and with the same month of as many preceding years as possible. Such an accumulation of figures over a period of years will permit recognition to be given to possible seasonal trends which should be taken into consideration in any analysis correctly made. Likewise, comparisons with other similar firms will give some indication of the subject firm's activity as contrasted with firms carrying on comparable operations. Like the other indexes, this information is valuable if broken down into the types of credit which are accepted.

These indexes reflect only averages, and it is necessary to realize that certain accounts may be falling behind in payments at the same time that the overall collection tests are reflecting a favorable picture. It is vital that this situation be recognized by credit management personnel and that care be taken to allow for it in any analysis which is based on averages.

An improvement in the collection percentage of a firm may tend to reflect improved economic conditions even before a future increase in credit and cash sales. This situation arises because of the general tendency of consumers to repay previously incurred debts before assuming new obligations. Conversely, a decline in economic conditions is more likely to be reflected first in a decline of credit sales than in a decline of collection percentages. This results from the debtor's reluctance to make additional credit purchases until the way to pay for them is clearly evident. Proper analysis of these pending changes should enable credit management to carry out advantageously its obligation to the firm, the firm's customers, and society in general.

Number of New Accounts Opened

Certainly the activity of the credit department will be reflected by the number of new accounts which it opens during the period in question. This will indicate the extent to which emphasis is being placed upon credit service and whether or not the business concern is alive to its opportunity for attracting new trade. The number of new accounts opened may serve also as a means of measuring the effectiveness of credit publicity. The figure, together with the acceptance percentage, will measure the leniency or strictness of the concern's credit policy.

Acceptance Index

The attitude toward applications as well as the quality of the applicants and the credit policy currently being followed are shown by the number of acceptances. A measure of growing importance is the index or percentage showing the proportion of applications for credit which are accepted. This is computed as follows:

$$\frac{\text{Applications accepted}}{\text{Applications submitted}} = \text{Acceptance index}$$

Of course, this index will vary considerably, depending upon the line of business in which the firm is engaged, the leniency or conservativeness of its credit-granting policies, and the stage of the business cycle.

Past-Due Index

This measure of credit management involves a determination of the proportion of all accounts, in amount or in number, that are past due, as determined by credit personnel. It is computed by dividing the total past due by the total outstanding as follows:

$$\frac{\text{Total past due}}{\text{Total outstanding}} = \text{Past-due index}$$

When this index is computed for several successive periods, it serves as a barometer indicating whether the general trend of poor pay is upward or downward. If this percentage increases faster than it should at any given time, proper steps can usually be taken to curb the trend or perhaps to bring it back to the normal position, which can be ascertained after such a record has been maintained over a period of years.

Aging of Accounts

This is a detailed analysis of accounts—such as not due, 30 days past due, 60 days past due, over one year past due, and so on. This suggestion of aging accounts stems from the fact that there is a direct and important relationship between the length of time that an account has been outstanding and the rate of collection and the probable net loss from bad debts.

This device may be supplemented with a detailed itemized list of overdue accounts, showing both the name and the present status of the account. Such a list is valuable in authorizing additional requests for credit. The introduction of extensive machine operations in the credit department has permitted this type of analysis to be performed easily and quickly.

Slow accounts also call for extra collection effort and expense, additional bookkeeping, extra interest costs in money tied up, and a higher cost of doing business. Knowledge of the exact situation is likely to lead to efforts to remedy it in time.

Aging of consumer accounts is easier to accomplish if a firm is using only one billing date rather than a cycle billing system. Nevertheless, even under a cycle billing arrangement, aging of accounts has been found to be highly desirable, and helpful to better credit operations.

Cost Analysis

Any final summation of the results of credit department activities should include cost figures. Credit management is on much sounder ground in deciding on a policy of instituting a service charge[3] on overdue accounts—and on other important credit and collection

3 / "Service Charges....Help or Hindrance on Past Due Accounts?" *Credit and Financial Management,* March 1970, p. 21.

policies—if accurate knowledge is available concerning the cost of operating on a credit basis and of carrying receivables on the books. To be sure, bad debts afford one such measure, but losses from bad debts are only one item in the operation of a credit department. In addition to bad debts, there are other expenditures the total of which normally exceeds all bad-debt losses. Wages and salaries of persons employed in credit and collection activities are the most important single category of credit expense. This expense—in addition to interest on outstandings, fees and dues for credit information, rentals or purchase of various types of machines, and charges for outside assistance in making collections—constitutes the bulk of the costs incurred. Costing of credit operations may seem needlessly complex, involving a detailed accumulation of data. At the same time, effective credit management cannot be expected to work blindly, nor can policies be intelligently decided on a basis other than of known facts.

ADAPTATION OF NEW MANAGEMENT TOOLS TO TESTING CREDIT OPERATIONS

The tests of efficiency and control of credit decisions discussed to this point are generally measured against past results. This technique of measuring actual results has been in common practice for many years. More recently, truly professional commercial credit managers and a few industry spokesmen have been directing their attention toward (1) forecasting credit department performance and then measuring the periodic results against actual commercial credit activity; (2) measuring costs for various classifications of customers against sales and profitability; and (3) developing methods which explain why certain phenomena occur in credit department accounts or groupings of accounts. Quite obviously these techniques and the more revealing resulting data stem from the current emphasis placed on forecasting and budgeting procedures, cost and distribution analysis, statistical correlation analysis, and the electronic processing of masses of data. Although approaches may appear somewhat sophisticated for the average credit executive, the fact remains that some of the larger credit departments are now utilizing these devices in order to improve their contributions to total company objectives and to plan their operations on the basis of data not previously available. The rapid advancements made in developing more modern tools of management and the rapidity with which they are being accepted certainly indicate that medium-sized and small-sized credit departments will not be insulated from them. Accordingly, students and practicing credit managers will have to be alert to these techniques and be able to adapt to them as these techniques pervade business life more completely.

Cost and distribution analysis affords most credit departments a research tool which can be useful in estimating probable costs, or costs savings, when change in credit policy is contemplated. For example, the functional expense statement (one of the accounting techniques used in the area of cost and distribution analysis) is useful in plotting costs of credit authorization, accounts receivable, invoicing, and the like against credit accounts classified by payment experiences and by sales volume attributable to the various groupings. Credit and collection costs, like all other marketing costs, enter into the determination of the profitability of various classes of customers and hence subject themselves to this technique. In other words, part of the answer to the question, "Is this group of customers (classed by size of order, location, industry type, etc.) a profitable or potentially profitable class of customers in view of our costs of selling them?" can be had by employing devices which are known to be superior to older methods.

Similarly, some credit departments find it managerially desirable to classify their customers according to credit risk and then, at later dates, measure the volume of business conducted, the volume of outstanding receivables, and the past collection efforts expended according to the predetermined categories of risk. One of the most fruitful areas of credit department activity has come from measures which determine to what extent rehabilitation efforts have been helpful in moving a particular group of customers from low classifications to higher classifications. Most of the techniques suggested here are particularly significant when it is realized that decisions in accepting credit are, for the most part, based upon an estimate of other future phenomena such as changes in the nation's economy, trends in an industry, and changes in the individual firm.

PRESENTING THE MEASURED RESULTS

The justification of credit operations as an important division of the business is rendered easier and more certain when it can show definitely and positively the facts relative to its own operations. Consideration might be given to the use of charts in presenting these various measures of the success—or failure—of credit operations. While figures on some things—and people—are very interesting, perhaps use of various types of charts would prove valuable in presenting these credit facts to top management. For example, by using bar charts showing the aging of receivables and line charts illustrating the seasonal influence on collection ratios, the credit manager can give "the boss" much of the story at a glance and be better prepared to present his story justifying the operation and the budget of his department.[4]

The foregoing discussion of techniques to test the success of credit operations should not be considered as final and complete. This is a phase of credit which calls for further refinement of concepts and greater skill in the use of the tests employed. As credit management becomes more and more conscious of the need to measure its own operations, better credit decisions will be made. Such an improvement will benefit the firm, the debtor, and society in general.

REVIEW AND DISCUSSION QUESTIONS

1. Why should enlightened credit management have constantly before it clearly defined goals or aims?
2. What two questions should the credit manager be prepared to answer?
3. It is said that the credit executive has an implied responsibility to three interests. What are these three interests?
4. Why is it necessary for a credit department to have certain tests by which to judge its operations?
5. What is "satisfaction" in a credit transaction?
6. Professor Phelps says that tests of credit department operations are valuable in six important ways. Discuss each of the ways that he lists.
7. How would you define a bad-debt loss?
8. Why are bad-debt losses defined differently by credit managers?
9. How are the following indexes computed and what do they show:
   a) Credit sales index?
   b) Collection index?
   c) Receivables turnover index?
   d) Acceptance index?
   e) Past-due index?
10. Why is it recommended that separate data be kept of the bad-debt losses and credit sales in each type of consumer credit accepted by a firm?
11. Discuss why accounts receivable should be aged.
12. How would you present to top management the measured results of your credit department operations?

4 / Amos Landman, "Increasing the Effectiveness of Financial Reports to Top Management," *Credit and Financial Management,* September 1967, p. 26.

Appendixes

A

Credit Instruments

Credit instruments provide the tangible evidence that a credit transaction has taken place. They specify the obligation which exists between the parties to the transaction, and often they set forth the conditions and terms under which the credit was accepted. Credit instruments vary with the type of credit involved and the purpose it serves for the parties. All instruments, regardless of their form, have the common characteristics of *creditor-debtor relationship, futurity,* and *risk.*

Credit instruments may be classified according to the acceptability of the instrument, the function of the instrument, or the form of the instrument. Instruments of unlimited or general acceptability include all the money of the United States Treasury which is in circulation. Money is the instrument of the United States government and includes the various issues of the authorized monetary authorities (principally the Treasury and the Federal Reserve banks). United States currency has unlimited acceptability and passes freely from hand to hand. In contrast to money, all other credit instruments are said to be of limited acceptability, because their acceptance is contingent on the acceptability of the credit of an individual or business concern.

If credit instruments are classified according to function, they are consumer, business, and government credit instruments. Obviously, such a classification results in some duplication, and needs further subclassification to distinguish between short-term and long-term credit instruments.

To classify by form of instrument, as "promises to pay" and "orders to pay," is the most common method of classification. Promises to pay include open-book accounts, revolving credit accounts, installment accounts, promissory notes, and bonds. Orders to pay include checks and other bills of exchange, all of which are commonly referred to as "drafts." While these are not all the credit instruments in general use today, they do represent the ones with which students and credit managers should be acquainted in order to appreciate more clearly the problems of credit management.

PROMISES TO PAY

Open-Book Accounts

The simplest and most elementary evidence of a credit transaction is the open-book account, or the *open account,* as it is sometimes called. This is the seller's accounting record showing the value (and other descriptive elements) of the merchandise or services delivered to a buyer. The transaction may or may not involve a written instrument signed by the creditor and the debtor. To the creditor it is an account receivable; to the debtor, an account payable.

Despite the lack of written acknowledgment of the debt in certain instances, this record is seldom questioned as evidence of debt but on occasion is questioned insofar as the extent of debt is concerned. In general, books of account are admissible as legal evidence of merchandise sold or services rendered. For example, they serve to support "proof of claim" in bankruptcy proceedings.

Revolving Credit Accounts

Revolving credit accounts involve a contractual agreement between the buyer and the seller. Although a variety of plans have appeared over the years, at the present time the most common arrangement is the option-terms revolving credit plan. All purchases made during a monthly interval are lumped together in one total bill. The customer has the option of paying the total amount due without a finance charge or of electing to pay the obligation in installments over a period of time with a finance charge figured on the unpaid balance. It appears necessary for the firm to have the signature of the customer on file, agreeing to the terms of the revolving credit agreement, in order to be able to charge the interest on a legal basis. No security lien is normally kept by the seller; the legal relationship in this regard is usually that of the seller on open account. The customer is furnished with a monthly statement of charges, and total payment of the outstanding balance may be made at any time without penalty.

Installment Accounts

One of the essential characteristics of an installment account is the written agreement or contract accomplished by the parties to the transaction. A major set of laws governing installment transactions is the Uniform Commercial Code, which is a uniform body of rules designed to deal, from start to finish, with all situations ordinarily arising in the handling of a commercial transaction (including installment transactions). Durable and high-unit-value goods are most often sold under installment agreements. A down payment is normally expected and received by the seller; a set schedule of payments is agreed upon by the buyer and the seller; the right of repossession is retained by the seller; and an interest charge is levied by the seller for the privilege of repaying the amount of credit desired in a series of installment payments. Laws on the state level govern the amount of interest that may be charged by the seller and on the federal level, the disclosure requirements imposed on the seller.

Promissory Notes

As the name implies, the promissory note is a written promise by one party to pay another party a definite sum of money at a specified future time. No specific wording of the promissory note is required, but the wording must acknowledge the indebtedness as due from one to another.

Promissory notes may be either negotiable or nonnegotiable. It is desirable for creditors to require that a promissory note be in a form which will render it a negotiable instrument under the statute. The necessary requirements for this purpose are that the instrument (1) be in writing, (2) be signed by the maker, (3) contain an unconditional promise to pay a certain sum of money, (4) be payable on demand or at a fixed or determinable future time, and (5) be payable to the order of a specified party or to bearer. If the instrument lacks any of these requirements, it is nonnegotiable. For example, the following is a nonnegotiable promissory note:

$1,000.00

Chicago, Illinois
February 14, 197-

Sixty days after date I promise to pay to the Midwest Wholesale Company one thousand dollars ($1,000.00), with interest at 6 percent per year for value received.

(Signature of Maker)

The following is a negotiable promissory note:

$1,000.00

Chicago, Illinois
February 14, 197-

Sixty days after date I promise to pay to the order of the Midwest Wholesale Company one thousand dollars ($1,000.00), with interest at 6 percent per year for value received.

(Signature of Maker)

A negotiable promissory note may be discounted at a commercial bank, and hence both the creditor and debtor are able to use their credit by virtue of the same instrument.

In general, the use of notes in commercial credit transactions is quite restricted. In a few wholesale lines their use is customary when the transaction involves either high merchandise value or high risk for the customer group. Credit managers recommend the use of promissory notes (1) when the transaction is with a concern of inferior credit standing, and (2) when an extension of time is granted in effecting collection of an account. This instrument is very common in connection with bank loans to individuals and commercial houses.

Another form of the promissory note is the collateral note, which is used by commercial banks when making a loan secured by some form of collateral. The collateral note is in all respects a promissory note, with the description of the property pledged as collateral appearing on the face of the form. Commercial banks often use this instrument and prefer that the collateral consist of marketable stocks and bonds, although receivables, warehouse receipts, other securities, and real estate may be pledged.

Bonds

Bonds are written promises to pay a definite sum of money at a specified future date. They are similar to promissory notes except that they are issued in standard denominations. Interest is usually paid semiannually at a fixed rate. Typically, they are issued in series for periods in excess of five years and are used by governments and private corporations to raise large sums of money. Because of these characteristics, bonds are usually classed as investment credit instruments.

Bonds may be secured or unsecured. Oftentimes the security is in the form of a mortgage on some specified property which has been conveyed to a trustee. Collateral also may take the form of securities, in which case the bond is known as a collateral trust bond. Bonds issued as a general credit obligation of the corporation with no specific security are known as debenture bonds. These instruments may be registered both as to principal and as to interest, or they may be registered as to principal only with interest payable to the bearer. Registration provides the owner with protection in the event the bond is lost. Unregistered bonds and bearer securities are generally negotiable instruments, whereas registered bonds may be transferred only if the transferee's name is also registered on the corporation's records. The transfer of a registered bond constitutes an assignment, in contrast to general negotiability.[1]

ORDERS TO PAY

Bills of Exchange

In addition to promises to pay, bills of exchange or drafts are the other instruments which evidence the extension of credit. The Negotiable Instruments Law defines a bill of exchange as "an unconditional order in writing addressed by one person to another, signed by the person giving it, requiring the person to whom it is addressed to pay on demand, or at a fixed or determinable future time, a sum certain in money to order or bearer."

Checks. Checks are the most commonly used bills of exchange in satisfying credit obligations. They are always drawn on a bank and are payable on demand. The drawer of a check may name anyone as payee, including himself, but usually the payee is another person or corporation.

The use of checks has increased to such an extent that oftentimes they are considered as synonymous with money rather than as a credit instrument. The widespread use of checks is accounted for by the great convenience, simplicity, and safety which they afford. In all respects, despite their common use, checks possess the characteristics of credit instruments with limited acceptability.

Certified and *cashier's* checks result in the guarantee of payment of the check by the bank. Cashier's checks are drawn by the bank cashier on his own bank, whereas a certified check is drawn by the depositor, who requests his bank to certify it. Certification is accomplished by the bank officer's stamping the word "Certified" across the face of the check and signing it. This indicates that the

1 / Stock certificates are not credit instruments, as they do not represent a promise to pay and there is no obligation on the part of the corporation to repay the principal.

bank will honor the check if properly endorsed and presented for payment. Certification of a check converts the drawer's order into a bank's promise to pay.

Drafts. There are a number of kinds of drafts, all of which are bills of exchange. Drafts are very similar to checks. They are signed by the creditor and directed to the debtor. A draft directed to a debtor requests the debtor to make payment. When a debtor endorses his acceptance on a draft, it becomes a promise to pay and has the same legal status as a promissory note.

Bank drafts are used between banks to carry on banking transactions. This instrument is simply a draft drawn by one bank against its account in another bank. Usually the bank draft is drawn upon out-of-town banks, where the drawer bank maintains an account. Obviously these drafts facilitate making payments at distant locations.

Commercial drafts may be used in domestic trade or between parties to foreign trade. In the former instance they are classified as domestic drafts, whereas in the latter instance they are referred to as foreign drafts or bills of exchange. Commercial drafts may be drawn payable at sight, in which case the instrument is known as a sight draft, or they may be drawn for payment at some specified future date, in which case they are known as time drafts. The debtor (drawee) has the right to refuse acceptance of a draft, and for this reason the draft is of no value until accepted. The acceptance of a sight draft takes place as the debtor makes payment to the bank of the amount involved. The time draft becomes accepted as the drawee endorses it across the face with the word "accepted." An accepted draft becomes an unconditional promise to pay by the debtor.

Commercial drafts are not widely used in the sale of merchandise except in the case of c.o.d. orders or when the seller desires payment before shipping the goods. These instruments are presented to debtors or buyers through their banks. As the buyer accepts the draft the shipping documents attached to the draft are released, and their possession gives the buyer the right to possess the merchandise. A more common use of the commercial draft is in the collection of past-due commercial accounts.

Acceptances are of two types, the banker's acceptance and the trade acceptance. A banker's acceptance is a written agreement obligating the bank to pay the seller of goods on behalf of the purchaser of such goods. The acceptance stipulates the amount, time, and place of payment. The difference between a banker's acceptance and a trade acceptance lies in the fact that it is drawn upon a bank rather than upon a buyer of goods.

The banker's acceptance comes into existence when a seller refuses to deliver goods on the basis of a buyer's credit alone. To obtain the goods, the buyer requests his bank to underwrite his purchase. For all practical purposes the buyer is requesting a loan. If the bank agrees to the transaction, it may require the buyer to pledge some form of collateral; or, if the buyer maintains an account, the bank will require the buyer to keep a certain amount on deposit. Once the seller has been informed of the buyer's arrangements with the bank, the seller may draw an acceptance upon the bank. The bank in turn will honor such bills as the seller might legally draw upon it. Clearly, most sellers would prefer a bank's acceptance to a trade acceptance, because of its gilt-edged nature and ease of negotiability. Sellers can readily discount such bills and receive their cash immediately. This instrument is used extensively in foreign trade, and to a lesser extent in domestic trade.

A trade acceptance comes into existence as the seller draws the instrument on a buyer. This type of bill is used in the sale of merchandise and never for the collection of past-due accounts. Often a buyer does not have the ready cash to make payment for merchandise purchased. The buyer will, however, be able to pay when he sells the goods he is purchasing. The trade acceptance affords the buyer a means of acquiring the goods, and the seller a means of selling the goods. The seller issues the bill to his own order, drawn on the buyer. The buyer acknowledges the acceptance by affixing his signature across the face of the instrument in the space provided. As the buyer acknowledges the acceptance, his obligation becomes absolute. The seller may now discount the bill at his bank, or hold it until the buyer honors it on the date specified. In general, trade acceptances are more acceptable to banks because they are two-name papers and evidence bona fide commercial transactions.

B

Federal Legislation

TRUTH-IN-LENDING (TITLE I OF THE CONSUMER CREDIT PROTECTION ACT)

The major provisions of the Truth-in-Lending law have been summarized in a clear and understandable publication, *Understanding Truth-in-Lending* by B. L. Kass.[1] The major parts of this summarization are as follows:

Truth-in-Lending Objective

The objective of Truth-in-Lending is simple. It, in effect, puts consumer credit on a more competitive basis. To do this, the law requires you (as a creditor) and your competitors (who do a credit business) to inform customers of all direct and indirect costs they have to pay when they buy on credit. In addition, it requires you and your competitors to let customers know the terms and conditions of credit arrangements. Thus, the customer will be able to compare the cost of credit among different sources and shop more effectively for the "best buy." The law requires that standard terminology be adopted by all credit grantors so that the customer will be able to make meaningful comparisons before he decides to make a purchase on credit.
. . . .

A Disclosure Law

You should know that the Truth-in-Lending Act is a disclosure law. *It does not set maximum interest rates* nor require drastic changes in operating business policies. The law and Regulation Z require that: all disclosures be made in writing, typed, or printed; be clear and conspicuous; and be in terminology specified therein. It specifically prohibits using sales contracts that contain blank spaces.

1 / Washington, D.C.: Small Business Administration, Small Marketers Aids No. 139, November 1969. The reader also is referred to William Henry Blake, "Regulation Z from the International Consumer Credit Association Point of View," *Quarterly Report,* Spring 1969, p. 47.

Perhaps the most important terms to be disclosed to the consumer are the finance charge and the annual percentage rate. These two items will tell the customer at a glance just how much he is paying for credit in dollars and also as a percentage.

The Finance Charge. The finance charge is the total of all costs which your customer must pay for obtaining credit. These costs may be direct or indirect. A finance charge includes—besides interest—other fees involved in granting credit such as carrying charges, costs of insurance premiums (under certain circumstances), and the cost of appraisal or investigation reports required to complete the sale, as well as similar fees. In effect, *the finance charge is the cost of credit.*

On the other hand, costs that would be paid even if credit was not granted can be excluded. Examples of such costs are taxes, licenses, registration fees, and certain title fees. Thus, in some instances, the costs of appraisals and credit reports are included in the finance charge; in others, they are excluded. The determining factor is whether the costs would be paid even if the sale was made for cash. All excluded and included costs must be itemized, however, and clearly disclosed to the customer.

How you disclose information regarding the finance charge will be discussed later in this *Aid* under "open-end" and "closed-end" credit. Regulation Z states that disclosure should be made "clearly, conspicuously, in meaningful sequence . . . in the terminology prescribed. . . ." It further states that the finance charge and annual percentage rate "shall be printed in not less than the equivalent of 10-point type, .075 inch computer type, or elite-size typewritten numerals, or shall be legibly handwritten." The disclosure must be made at the proper time—for example, before the first transaction is made on an open-end credit account.

The Annual Percentage Rate (APR). The Truth-in-Lending Act requires you to disclose to your customers not only the finance charge but also the annual percentage rate. Simply stated, the APR is the relative cost of credit in annual percentage terms. Until January 1, 1971, however, you have the option of disclosing the APR in dollar terms (such as "$11.00 finance charge per year per $100.00 of unpaid balance"). After that date, you must state the rate as a percentage, to the nearest quarter of 1 percent.

An exception is when discounts are granted for prompt payment of bills. You do not have to show single payment discount transactions in terms of annual percentage interest rates if the discount is less than 5 percent.

Figuring the APR for closed-end sales transactions could be a considerable mathematical chore. To assist you, the Federal Reserve Board has published a booklet, *Annual Percentage Rate Tables*, Volume 1, which will help you in your computations. It contains four tables for closed-end credit sales with payment ranging from 1 to 60 months, 61 to 120 months, 121 to 480 months, and 1 to 104 weeks. The booklet is available for $1.00 from your nearest Federal Reserve Bank, or on written request to the Federal Reserve System in Washington, D.C.

Two Kinds of Credit Transactions

You may already offer your customer two kinds of credit, open-end and closed-end (called by Regulation Z "other than open-end"). You will need to know the Truth-in-Lending rules applying to each.

Open-End Credit Transactions. "Open-end" means that your customer may, if he wishes, go on making new purchases under an *original* agreement. Under this agreement, the amount of these purchases is added to the outstanding balances, up to the "ceiling" you have prescribed; the customer has the option of paying the balance in full or in installments; and you may, under the agreed conditions and in the agreed manner, impose a finance charge on any unpaid balance.

Typically, open-end credit covers most credit cards and revolving charge accounts in retail and service businesses where finance charges are usually made on unpaid amounts each month. Today, many retail stores and service shops offer these so-called "revolving" or optional credit accounts.

If you maintain such open-end accounts, the law states exactly what you must tell your customers. There is a two-step disclosure procedure. First, before a new account is opened, you must tell the customer in writing or on a printed form to the extent applicable:

1. Conditions under which a finance charge may be made and the period within which, if payment is made, there is no finance charge (such as "30 days without interest").

2. The method of determining the balance upon which a finance charge may be imposed.

3. How the actual finance charge is calculated.

4. The periodic rates used and the range of balances to which each applies as well as the corresponding Annual Percentage Rate—for instance, a monthly rate of 1½ percent (APR, 18 percent) on the first $500, and 1 percent (APR, 12 percent) on amounts over $500.

5. Conditions under which additional charges may be made, along with details of how they are calculated. (This applies to new purchases, when charges are added to the account.)

6. A description of any lien (secured interest) you may acquire on the customer's property—for instance, rights to repossession of a household appliance.

7. Minimum periodic payment required.

Next, you must send out periodic statements—most retailers do this monthly—on any account with an unpaid balance of more than $1.00, or one where a finance charge is made. (A typical retailer's statement, prepared by a manual billing operation, is shown in Exhibit 1.) You should be sure these statements provide the following information and that it be expressed in the standard terminology (indicated in boldface):

1. The unpaid balance at the beginning of the billing period (**previous balance**).

2. The amount and date of each purchase or credit extension and a brief description of each item bought if not previously given to the customer.

3. Customer payments (**payments**), and other credits, including those for rebates, adjustments, and returns (**credits**).

4. The finance charge expressed in dollars and cents (**finance charge**).

5. The rates used in calculating the finance charge, and the range of balances, if any, to which they apply (**periodic rate**).

6. The annual percentage rate which must be expressed as a percentage after January 1, 1971 (**annual percentage**).

7. The unpaid balance on which the finance charge was calculated.

8. The closing date of the billing cycle, and the unpaid balance as of that date (**new balance**).

Regulation Z requires you to show some of the above items on the actual face of the statement. Others, you may show on the reverse side, or on a separate form enclosed in the same envelope.

Other (Closed-End) Credit Transactions. You may be using the other type of credit transaction: closed-end, or—as described in Regulation Z—"credit other than open-end." Here, you grant your customer credit for a fixed amount over a fixed period of time. The total amount, the number of payments and the due date of each payment are agreed upon by you and your customer. Typically, you use this type of transaction for the customer who buys or finances the purchase of "big ticket" items. This type of credit is usually used for an installment purchase of a washing machine, a television set, or other types of major appliances.

For these credit transactions, the law requires you to disclose certain items to your customers *before* credit is extended. These disclosures must be either on the face of the contract above or adjacent to the customer's signature or on one side of a separate sheet that clearly identifies the transactions.

In closed-end credit, you must provide your customers with certain information just as you do with open-end credit. It must be in writing or on a printed form—usually a sales contract—and must be provided before the credit is extended. Regulation Z differentiates between a credit sale and a loan.

As a merchant giving credit you are required specifically to provide the following information in the required terminology (indicated in boldface):

1. The cash price (**cash price**).

2. The down payment including trade-in (**cash downpayment, trade-in,** or **total downpayment**—as applicable).

3. The difference between the cash price and down payment (**unpaid balance of cash price**).

4. All other charges, itemized but not part of the finance charge.

5. The unpaid balance (**unpaid balance**).

6. Amounts deducted as prepaid finance charges or required deposit balances (**prepaid finance charge**) and/or (**required deposit balance**).

7. The amount financed (**amount financed**).

8. The total cash price, finance, and all other charges (**deferred payment price**).

9. The total dollar amount of the finance charge (**finance charge**).

10. The date on which the finance charge begins to apply (if this is different from the date of the sale).

11. The annual percentage rate which must be expressed as a percentage after January 1, 1971 (**annual percentage rate**).

12. The number, amounts, and due dates of payments.

13. The total payments (**total of payments**).

14. The amount you charge for any default, delinquency, and the like, or the method you use for calculating the amount.

15. A description of any security you will hold.

16. A description of any penalty charge for prepayment of principal.

EXHIBIT 1

```
┌──────────────────────────────────────────────────────────────────────────────┐
│                          ANY STORE U.S.A.                                       │
│                     Main Street — Any City, U.S.A.                              │
│                        (Customer's name here)                                   │
│                                                                                 │
│                                              AMT. PAID $_____         │
│          TO INSURE PROPER CREDIT RETURN THIS PORTION WITH YOUR PAYMENT           │
└──────────────────────────────────────────────────────────────────────────────┘
```

PREVIOUS BALANCE	FINANCE CHARGE 50 CENT MINIMUM	PAYMENTS	CREDITS	PURCHASES	NEW BALANCE	MINIMUM PAYMENT

FINANCE CHARGE IS COMPUTED BY A "PERIODIC RATE" of   % PER MONTH (OR A MINIMUM CHARGE OF 50 CENTS FOR BALANCES UNDER $) WHICH IS AN ANNUAL PERCENTAGE RATE OF   % APPLIED TO THE PREVIOUS BALANCE WITHOUT DEDUCTING CURRENT PAYMENTS AND/OR CREDITS APPEARING ON THIS STATEMENT.

NOTICE

PLEASE SEE ACCOMPANYING STATEMENT(S) FOR IMPORTANT INFORMATION.

PAYMENTS, CREDITS OR CHARGES, RECEIVED AFTER THE DATE SHOWN ABOVE THE ARROW, WHICH IS THE CLOSING DATE OF THIS BILLING CYCLE, WILL APPEAR ON YOUR NEXT STATEMENT. TO AVOID ADDITIONAL FINANCE CHARGES PAY THE "NEW BALANCE" BEFORE THIS DATE NEXT MONTH.

ANY STORE, U.S.A.   MAIN STREET, ANY CITY, U.S.A.

In the above illustration (taken from the Federal Reserve Board's *What You Ought to Know about Federal Reserve Regulation Z—Truth-in-Lending*), the finance charge is determined by a single periodic rate or a minimum charge of 50 cents applicable to balances under a specific amount. Computation of the finance charge is made on the previous balance before deducting payments and/or credits. Separate slips shall accompany each statement and identify all charges and credits and show the dates and amounts thereof. This format is not the only format which will permit a creditor to comply with the disclosure requirements of Regulation Z.

17. How the unearned part of the finance charge is calculated in case of prepayment. (Charges deducted from any rebate must be stated.)

When you offer closed-end credit to your customers, you must include all the above information on the face of the sales contract above or adjacent to the customer's signature or on one side of a separate sheet that identifies the transaction. (A typical retail installment contract is shown in Exhibit 2.) You are not required to send out monthly statements but, if you do, you must show clearly the annual percentage rate and the period in which a payment must be made to avoid late charges.

The Three-Day Rule. While most retailers who do a credit business do not

EXHIBIT 2

Seller's Name: _____   Contract #_____

RETAIL INSTALLMENT CONTRACT AND SECURITY AGREEMENT

The undersigned (herein called Purchaser, whether one or more) purchases from _____ _____ (seller) and grants to _____ a security interest, in, subject to the terms and conditions hereof, the following described property.

PURCHASER'S NAME _____

PURCHASER'S ADDRESS _____

CITY _____ STATE _____ ZIP _____

QUANTITY	DESCRIPTION	AMOUNT

Description of Trade-In:

	Sales Tax	
	Total	

Insurance Agreement

The purchase of insurance coverage is voluntary and not required for credit. ___ (Type of Ins.) ___ Insurance coverage is available at a cost of $_____ for the term of credit.

I desire insurance coverage

Signed _____ Date _____

I do not desire insurance coverage

Signed _____ Date _____

1. CASH PRICE $_____
2. LESS: CASH DOWN PAYMENT $_____
3.   TRADE-IN _____
4.   TOTAL DOWN PAYMENT _____ $_____
5. UNPAID BALANCE OF CASH PRICE $_____
6. OTHER CHARGES:
   - _____ $_____
   - _____ $_____
7. AMOUNT FINANCED $_____
8. FINANCE CHARGE $_____
9. TOTAL OF PAYMENTS $_____
10. DEFERRED PAYMENT PRICE (1+6+8) $_____
11. ANNUAL PERCENTAGE RATE _____%

Purchaser hereby agrees to pay to _____ _____ at their offices shown above the "TOTAL OF PAYMENTS" shown above in _____ monthly installments of $_____(final payment to be $_____) the first installment being payable _____ 19____, and all subsequent installments on the same day of each consecutive month until paid in full. The finance charge applies from ___ (Date)

Signed _____

Notice to Buyer: You are entitled to a copy of the contract you sign. You have the right to pay in advance the unpaid balance of this contract and obtain a partial refund of the finance charge based on the "Actuarial Method." [Any other method of computation may be so identified, for example, "Rule of 78's," "Sum of the Digits," etc.]

Taken from *What You Ought to Know about Federal Reserve Regulation Z—Truth-in-Lending* by the Federal Reserve Board. This format is not the only format which will permit a creditor to comply with the disclosure requirements of Regulation Z.

retain a lien (security interest) on the customer's home as part of the sales contract, a few do. In most instances, the sale would be "large ticket" merchandise such as home improvements requiring installation. For such sales, the Truth-in-Lending Act grants customers the "right of rescission"—cancellation of the sale within 3 days.

In effect, this provision of the law allows the customer to change his mind. If he does, you have to be notified by mail, telegram, or any other form of writing by midnight of the third business day following (1) the date that the sale was made or (2) the date that you supplied the required disclosures, whichever is later. When you supply the disclosure, it is to your advantage to give your customer immediately two copies (required by law) of a "Notice of the Right of Rescission." Moreover, it is just "good business" not to start any installation work, if required, until the cancellation period has expired.

When You Advertise

Advertising of credit terms is also covered under the Truth-in-Lending legislation. In general, you may not advertise that a specific down payment, installment plan, or amount of credit can be arranged unless you *usually* arrange terms of that type.

And "advertising" does not apply only to newspaper, radio and television coverage. As defined in Regulation Z "advertisement" means:

"Any commercial message in any newspaper, magazine, leaflet, flyer or catalog, on radio, television or public address system, in direct mail literature or other printed material, on any interior or exterior sign or display, on any window display, in any point-of-transaction literature or price tag which is delivered or made available to a customer or prospective customer in any manner whatsoever."

In effect, this definition covers all methods of conveying a message to your customers, whether in your place of business or outside.

In addition, no advertisement may spell out a specific credit term unless *all other* terms are stated clearly and conspicuously. For example, a retailer or a business selling service is not allowed to advertise the specific terms "No Money Down" or "36 Months to Pay" unless *all other* related terms are shown. These terms include the cash price, the amount of downpayment required or that no downpayment is required, the number, amounts, and due dates of payments, the amount of the finance charge expressed as an annual percentage rate (which will have to be expressed as a percentage after January 1, 1971), and the deferred payment price or sum of the payment as applicable.

These requirements do not prohibit advertisements that carry no specific terms. You are still allowed to use such phrases as "We welcome credit accounts," "Use our Easy Payment Plan," or "We give you all the credit."

Penalties

The Truth-in-Lending Act provides civil and criminal penalties. It gives the consumer the right to sue a merchant who fails to disclose credit information. In such a civil suit, the customer can recover twice the finance charge from the merchant plus court costs and reasonable attorney's fees. However, the liability shall not be less than $100 or more than $1,000.

If a merchant accidentally overstates a finance charge, he can avoid liability if within 15 days after discovering the error, he notifies the customer and corrects the error. Thus, the law provides for honest error that can be proved in court. However, if the creditor understates the charge, he must live with it.

The criminal penalties apply to individuals who willfully disregard the law. Such persons can be fined a maximum of $5,000 and imprisoned for a maximum of 1 year or both.

FAIR CREDIT REPORTING ACT (TITLE VI OF THE CONSUMER CREDIT PROTECTION ACT)

Sec. 601. The Consumer Credit Protection Act is amended by adding at the end thereof the following new title:

"TITLE VI—CONSUMER CREDIT REPORTING

"§ 601. Short title

"This title may be cited as the Fair Credit Reporting Act.

"§ 602. Findings and purpose

"(a) The Congress makes the following findings:

"(1) The banking system is dependent upon fair and accurate credit reporting. Inaccurate credit reports directly impair the efficiency of the banking system, and unfair credit reporting methods undermine the public confidence which is essential to the continued functioning of the banking system.

"(2) An elaborate mechanism has been developed for investigating and evaluating the credit worthiness, credit standing, credit capacity, character, and general reputation of consumers.

"(3) Consumer reporting agencies have assumed a vital role in assembling and evaluating consumer credit and other information on consumers.

"(4) There is a need to insure that consumer reporting agencies exercise their grave responsibilities with fairness, impartiality, and a respect for the consumer's right to privacy.

"(b) It is the purpose of this title to require that consumer reporting agencies adopt reasonable procedures for meeting the needs of commerce for consumer credit, personnel, insurance, and other information in a manner which is fair and equitable to the consumer, with regard to the confidentiality, accuracy, relevancy, and proper utilization of such information in accordance with the requirements of this title.

"§ 603. Definitions and rules of construction

"(a) Definitions and rules of construction set forth in this section are applicable for the purposes of this title.

"(b) The term 'person' means any individual, partnership, corporation, trust, estate, cooperative, association, government or governmental subdivision or agency, or other entity.

"(c) The term 'consumer' means an individual.

"(d) The term 'consumer report' means any written, oral, or other communication of any information by a consumer reporting agency bearing on a consumer's credit worthiness, credit standing, credit capacity, character, general reputation, personal characteristics, or mode of living which is used or expected to be used or collected in whole or in part for the purpose of serving as a factor in establishing the consumer's eligibility for (1) credit or insurance to be used primarily for personal, family, or household purposes, or (2) employment purposes, or (3) other purposes authorized under section 604. The term does not include (A) any report containing information solely as to transactions or experiences between the consumer and the person making the report; (B) any authorization or approval of a specific extension of credit directly or indirectly by the issuer of a credit card or similar device; or (C) any report in which a person who has been requested by a third party to make a specific extension of credit directly or indirectly to a consumer conveys his decision with respect to such request, if the third party advises the consumer of the name and address of the person to whom the request was made and such person makes the disclosures to the consumer required under section 615.

"(e) The term 'investigative consumer report' means a consumer report or portion thereof in which information on a consumer's character, general reputation, personal characteristics, or mode of living is obtained through personal interviews with neighbors, friends, or associates of the consumer reported on or with others with whom he is acquainted or who may have knowledge concerning any such items of information. However, such information shall not include specific factual information on a consumer's credit record obtained directly from a creditor of the consumer or from a consumer reporting agency when such information was obtained directly from a creditor of the consumer or from the consumer.

"(f) The term 'consumer reporting agency' means any person which, for monetary fees, dues, or on a cooperative nonprofit basis, regularly engages in whole or in part in the practice of assembling or evaluating consumer credit information or other information on consumers for the purpose of furnishing consumer reports to third parties, and which uses any means or facility of interstate commerce for the purpose of preparing or furnishing consumer reports.

"(g) The term 'file', when used in connection with information on any consumer, means all of the information on that consumer recorded and retained by a consumer reporting agency regardless of how the information is stored.

"(h) The term 'employment purposes' when used in connection with a consumer report means a report used for the purpose of evaluating a consumer for employment, promotion, reassignment or retention as an employee.

"(i) The term 'medical information' means information or records obtained, with the consent of the individual to whom it relates, from licensed physicians or medical practitioners, hospitals, clinics, or other medical or medically related facilities.

"§ 604. Permissible purposes of reports

"A consumer reporting agency may furnish a consumer report under the following circumstances and no other:

"(1) In response to the order of a court having jurisdiction to issue such an order.

"(2) In accordance with the written instructions of the consumer to whom it relates.

"(3) To a person which it has reason to believe—

    "(A) intends to use the information in connection with a credit transaction involving the consumer on whom the information is to be furnished and involving the extension of credit to, or review or collection of an account of, the consumer; or

"(B) intends to use the information for employment purposes; or

"(C) intends to use the information in connection with the underwriting of insurance involving the consumer; or

"(D) intends to use the information in connection with a determination of the consumer's eligibility for a license or other benefit granted by a governmental instrumentality required by law to consider an applicant's financial responsibility or status; or

"(E) otherwise has a legitimate business need for the information in connection with a business transaction involving the consumer.

"§ 605. Obsolete information

"(a) Except as authorized under subsection (b), no consumer reporting agency may make any consumer report containing any of the following items of information:

"(1) Bankruptcies which, from date of adjudication of the most recent bankruptcy, antedate the report by more than fourteen years.

"(2) Suits and judgments which, from date of entry, antedate the report by more than seven years or until the governing statute of limitations has expired, whichever is the longer period.

"(3) Paid tax liens which, from date of payment, antedate the report by more than seven years.

"(4) Accounts placed for collection or charged to profit and loss which antedate the report by more than seven years.

"(5) Records of arrest, indictment, or conviction of crime which, from date of disposition, release, or parole, antedate the report by more than seven years.

"(6) Any other adverse item of information which antedates the report by more than seven years.

"(b) The provisions of subsection (a) are not applicable in the case of any consumer credit report to be used in connection with—

"(1) a credit transaction involving, or which may reasonably be expected to involve, a principal amount of $50,000 or more;

"(2) the underwriting of life insurance involving, or which may reasonably be expected to involve, a face amount of $50,000 or more; or

"(3) the employment of any individual at an annual salary which equals, or which may reasonably be expected to equal $20,000, or more.

"§ 606. Disclosure of investigative consumer reports

"(a) A person may not procure or cause to be prepared an investigative consumer report on any consumer unless—

"(1) it is clearly and accurately disclosed to the consumer that an investigative consumer report including information as to his character, general reputation, personal characteristics, and mode of living, whichever are applicable, may be made, and such disclosure (A) is made in a writing mailed, or otherwise delivered, to the consumer, not later than three days after the date on which the report was first requested, and (B) includes a statement informing the consumer of his right to request the additional disclosures provided for under subsection (b) of this section; or

"(2) the report is to be used for employment purposes for which the consumer has not specifically applied.

"(b) Any person who procures or causes to be prepared an investigative consumer report on any consumer shall, upon written request made by the consumer within a reasonable period of time after the receipt by him of the disclosure required by subsection (a)(1), shall make a complete and accurate disclosure of the nature and scope of the investigation requested. This disclosure shall be made in a writing mailed, or otherwise delivered, to the consumer not later than five days after the date on which the request for such disclosure was received from the consumer or such report was first requested, whichever is the later.

"(c) No person may be held liable for any violation of subsection (a) or (b) of this section if he shows by a preponderance of the evidence that at the time of the violation he maintained reasonable procedures to assure compliance with subsection (a) or (b).

"§ 607. Compliance procedures

"(a) Every consumer reporting agency shall maintain reasonable procedures designed to avoid violations of section 605 and to limit the furnishing of consumer reports to the purposes listed under section 604. These procedures shall require that prospective users of the information identify themselves, certify the purposes for which the information is sought, and certify that the information will be used for no other purpose. Every consumer reporting agency shall make a reasonable effort to verify the identity of a new prospective user and the uses certified by such prospective user prior to furnishing such user a consumer report. No consumer reporting agency may furnish a consumer report to any person if it has reasonable grounds for believing that the consumer report will not be used for a purpose listed in section 604.

"(b) Whenever a consumer reporting agency prepares a consumer report it shall follow reasonable procedures to assure maximum possible accuracy of the information concerning the individual about whom the report relates.

"§ 608. Disclosures to governmental agencies

"Notwithstanding the provisions of section 604, a consumer reporting agency may furnish identifying information respecting any consumer, limited to his name, address, former addresses, places of employment, or former places of employment, to a governmental agency.

"§ 609. Disclosures to consumers

"(a) Every consumer reporting agency shall, upon request and proper identification of any consumer, clearly and accurately disclose to the consumer:

"(1) The nature and substance of all information (except medical information) in its files on the consumer at the time of the request.

"(2) The sources of the information; except that the sources of information acquired solely for use in preparing an investigative consumer report and actually used for no other purpose need not be disclosed: Provided, That in the event an action is brought under this title, such sources shall be available to the plaintiff under appropriate discovery procedures in the court in which the action is brought.

"(3) The recipients of any consumer report on the consumer which it has furnished—

"(A) for employment purposes within the two-year period preceding the request, and

"(B) for any other purpose within the six-month period preceding the request.

"(b) The requirements of subsection (a) respecting the disclosures of sources of information and the recipients of consumer reports do not apply to information received or consumer reports furnished prior to the effective date of this title except to the extent that the matter involved is contained in the files of the consumer reporting agency on that date.

"§ 610. Conditions of disclosure to consumers

"(a) A consumer reporting agency shall make the disclosures required under section 609 during normal business hours and on reasonable notice.

"(b) The disclosures required under section 609 shall be made to the consumer—

"(1) in person if he appears in person and furnishes proper identification; or

"(2) by telephone if he has made a written request, with proper identification, for telephone disclosure and the toll charge, if any, for the telephone call is prepaid or charged directly to the consumer.

"(c) Any consumer reporting agency shall provide trained personnel to explain to the consumer any information furnished to him pursuant to section 609.

"(d) The consumer shall be permitted to be accompanied by one other person of his choosing, who shall furnish reasonable identification. A consumer reporting agency may require the consumer to furnish a written statement granting permission to the consumer reporting agency to discuss the consumer's file in such person's presence.

"(e) Except as provided in sections 616 and 617, no consumer may bring any action or proceeding in the nature of defamation, invasion of privacy, or negligence with respect to the reporting of information against any consumer reporting agency, any user of information, or any person who furnishes information to a consumer reporting agency, based on information disclosed pursuant to section 609, 610, or 615, except as to false information furnished with malice or willful intent to injure such consumer.

"§ 611. Procedure in case of disputed accuracy

"(a) If the completeness or accuracy of any item of information contained in his file is disputed by a consumer, and such dispute is directly conveyed to the consumer reporting agency by the consumer, the consumer reporting agency shall within a reasonable period of time reinvestigate and record the current status of that information unless it has reasonable grounds to believe that the dispute by the consumer is frivolous or irrelevant. If after such reinvestigation such information is found to be inaccurate or can no longer be verified, the consumer reporting agency shall promptly delete such information. The presence of contradictory information in the consumer's file does not in and of itself constitute reasonable grounds for believing the dispute is frivolous or irrelevant.

"(b) If the reinvestigation does not resolve the dispute, the consumer may file a brief statement setting forth the nature of the dispute. The consumer reporting agency may limit such statements to not more than one hundred words if it provides the consumer with assistance in writing a clear summary of the dispute.

"(c) Whenever a statement of a dispute is filed, unless there is reasonable grounds to believe that it is frivolous or irrevelant, the consumer reporting agency shall, in any subsequent consumer report containing the information in question, clearly note that it is disputed by the consumer and provide either the consumer's statement or a clear and accurate codification or summary thereof.

"(d) Following any deletion of information which is found to be inaccurate or whose accuracy can no longer be verified or any notation as to disputed information, the consumer reporting agency shall, at the request of the consumer, furnish notification that the item has been deleted or the statement, codifications or summary pursuant to subsection (b) or (c) to any person specifically designated by the consumer who has within two years prior thereto received a consumer report for employment purposes, or within six months prior thereto received a consumer report for any other purpose, which contained the deleted or disputed information. The consumer reporting agency shall clearly and conspiciously disclose to the consumer his rights to make such a request. Such disclosure shall be made at or prior to the time the information is deleted or the consumer's statement regarding the disputed information is received.

"§ 612. Charges for certain disclosures

"A consumer reporting agency shall make all disclosures pursuant to section 609 and furnish all consumer reports pursuant to section 611(d) without charge to the consumer if, within thirty days after receipt by such consumer of a notification pursuant to section 615 or notification from a debt collection agency affiliated with such consumer reporting agency stating that the consumer's credit rating may be or has been adversely affected, the consumer makes a request under section 609· or 611(d). Otherwise, the consumer reporting agency may impose a reasonable charge on the consumer for making disclosure to such consumer pursuant to section 609, the charge for which shall be indicated to the consumer prior to making disclosure; and for furnishing notifications, statements, summaries, or codifications to person designated by the consumer pursuant to section 611(d), the charge for which shall be indicated to the consumer prior to furnishing such information and shall not exceed the charge that the consumer reporting agency would impose on each designated recipient for a consumer report except that no charge may be made for notifying such persons of the deletion of information which is found to be inaccurate or which can no longer be verified.

"§ 613. Public record information for employment purposes

"A consumer reporting agency which furnishes a consumer report for employment purposes and which for that purpose compiles and reports items of information on consumers which are matters of public record and are likely to have an adverse effect upon a consumer's ability to obtain employment shall—

"(1) at the time such public record information is reported to the user of such consumer report, notify the consumer of the fact that public record information is being reported by the consumer reporting agency, together with the name and address of the person to whom such information is being reported; or

"(2) maintain strict procedures designed to insure that whenever public record information which is likely to have an adverse effect on a consumer's ability to obtain employment is reported it is complete and up to date. For purposes of this paragraph, items of public record relating to arrests, indictments, convictions, suits, tax liens, and outstanding judgments shall be considered up to date if the current public record status of the item at the time of the report is reported.

"§ 614. Restrictions on investigative consumer reports

"Whenever a consumer reporting agency prepares an investigative consumer report, no adverse information in the consumer report (other than information which is a matter of public record) may be included in a subsequent consumer report unless such adverse information has been verified in the process of making such subsequent consumer report, or the adverse information was received within the three-month period preceding the date the subsequent report is furnished.

"§ 615. Requirements on users of consumer reports

"(a) Whenever credit or insurance for personal, family, or household purposes, or employment involving a consumer is denied or the charge for such credit or insurance is increased either wholly or partly because of information contained in a consumer report from a consumer reporting agency, the user of the consumer report shall so advise the consumer against whom such adverse action has been taken and supply the name and address of the consumer reporting agency making the report.

"(b) Whenever credit for personal, family, or household purposes involving a consumer is denied or the charge for such credit is increased either wholly or partly because of information obtained from a person other than a consumer reporting agency bearing upon the consumer's credit worthiness, credit standing, credit capacity, character, general reputation, personal characteristics, or mode of living, the user of such information shall, within a reasonable period of time, upon the consumer's written request for the reasons for such adverse action received within sixty days after learning of such adverse action, disclose the nature of the information to the consumer. The user of such information shall clearly and accurately disclose to the consumer his right to make such written request at the time such adverse action is communicated to the consumer.

"(c) No person shall be held liable for any violation of this section if he shows by a preponderance of the evidence that at the time of the alleged violation he maintained reasonable procedures to assure compliance with the provisions of subsections (a) and (b).

"§ 616. Civil liability for willful noncompliance

"Any consumer reporting agency or user of information which willfully fails to comply with any requirement imposed under this title with respect to any consumer is liable to that consumer in an amount equal to the sum of—

"(1) any actual damages sustained by the consumer as a result of the failure;

"(2) such amount of punitive damages as the court may allow; and

"(3) in the case of any successful action to enforce any liability under this section, the costs of the action together with reasonable attorney's fees as determined by the court.

"§ 617. Civil liability for negligent noncompliance

"Any consumer reporting agency or user of information which is negligent in failing to comply with any requirement imposed under this title with respect to any consumer is liable to that consumer in an amount equal to the sum of—

"(1) any actual damages sustained by the consumer as a result of the failure;

"(2) in the case of any successful action to enforce any liability under this section, the costs of the action together with reasonable attorney's fees as determined by the court.

"§ 618. Jurisdiction of courts; limitation of actions

"An action to enforce any liability created under this title may be brought in any appropriate United States district court without regard to the amount in controversy, or in any other court of competent jurisdiction, within two years from the date on which the liability arises, except that where a defendant has materially and willfully misrepresented any information required under this title to be disclosed to an individual and the information so misrepresented is material to the establishment of the defendant's liability to that individual under this title, the action may be brought at any time within two years after discovery by the individual of the misrepresentation.

"§ 619. Obtaining information under false pretenses

"Any person who knowingly and willfully obtains information on a consumer from a consumer reporting agency under false pretenses shall be fined not more than \$5,000 or imprisoned not more than one year, or both.

"§ 620. Unauthorized disclosures by officers or employees

"Any officer or employee of a consumer reporting agency who knowingly and willfully provides information concerning an individual from the agency's files to a person not authorized to receive that information shall be fined not more than \$5,000 or imprisoned not more than one year, or both.

"§ 621. Administrative enforcement

"(a) Compliance with the requirements imposed under this title shall be enforced under the Federal Trade Commission Act by the Federal Trade Commission with respect to consumer reporting agencies and all other persons subject thereto, except to the extent that enforcement of the requirements imposed under this title is specifically committed to some other government agency under subsection (b) hereof. For the purpose of the exercise by the Federal Trade Commission of its functions and powers under the Federal Trade Commission Act, a violation of any requirement or prohibition imposed under this title shall constitute an unfair or deceptive act or practice in commerce in violation of section 5(a) of the Federal Trade Commission Act and shall be subject to enforcement by the Federal Trade Commission under section 5(b) thereof with respect to any consumer reporting agency or person subject to enforcement by the Federal Trade Commission pursuant to this subsection, irrespective of whether that person is engaged in commerce or meets any other jurisdictional tests in the Federal Trade Commission Act. The Federal Trade Commission shall have such procedural, investigative,

and enforcement powers, including the power to issue procedural
rules in enforcing compliance with the requirements imposed under
this title and to require the filing of reports, the production of
documents, and the appearance of witnesses as though the applicable
terms and conditions of the Federal Trade Commission Act were part
of this title. Any person violating any of the provisions of this title
shall be subject to the penalities and entitled to the privileges and
immunities provided in the Federal Trade Commission Act as though
the applicable terms and provisions thereof were part of this title.

"(b) Compliance with the requirements imposed under this title
with respect to consumer reporting agencies and persons who use
consumer reports from such agencies shall be enforced under—

"(1) section 8 of the Federal Deposit Insurance Act, in the case
of:

"(A) national banks, by the Comptroller of the Currency;

"(B) member banks of the Federal Reserve System (other
than national banks), by the Federal Reserve Board; and

"(C) banks insured by the Federal Deposit Insurance Corporation (other than members of the Federal Reserve System),
by the Board of Directors of the Federal Deposit Insurance
Corporation.

"(2) section 5(d) of the Home Owners Loan Act of 1933,
section 407 of the National Housing Act, and sections 6(i) and 17
of the Federal Home Loan Bank Act, by the Federal Home Loan
Bank Board (acting directly or through the Federal Savings and
Loan Insurance Corporation), in the case of any institution subject
to any of those provisions;

"(3) the Federal Credit Union Act, by the Administrator of the
National Credit Union Administration with respect to any Federal
credit union;

"(4) the Acts to regulate commerce, by the Interstate Commerce Commission with respect to any common carrier subject to
those Acts;

"(5) the Federal Aviation Act of 1958, by the Civil Aero-
nautics Board with respect to any air carrier or foreign air carrier
subject to that Act; and

"(6) the Packers and Stockyards Act, 1921 (except as provided
in section 406 of that Act), by the Secretary of Agriculture with
respect to any activities subject to that Act.

"(c) For the purpose of the exercise by any agency referred to in
subsection (b) of its powers under any Act referred to in that
subsection, a violation of any requirement imposed under this title
shall be deemed to be a violation of a requirement imposed under
that Act. In addition to its powers under any provision of law

specifically referred to in subsection (b), each of the agencies referred to in that subsection may exercise, for the purpose of enforcing compliance with any requirement imposed under this title any other authority conferred on it by law.

"§ 622. Relation to State laws

"This title does not annul, alter, affect, or exempt any person subject to the provisions of this title from complying with the laws of any State with respect to the collection, distribution, or use of any information on consumers, except to the extent that those laws are inconsistent with any provision of this title, and then only to the extent of the inconsistency."

EFFECTIVE DATE

Sec. 602. Section 504 of the Consumer Credit Protection Act is amended by adding at the end thereof the following new subsection:

"(d) Title VI takes effect upon the expiration of one hundred and eighty days following the date of its enactment."

And the Senate agree to the same.

Index

*This book has been set in 11 point Baskerville
with Caledonia bold, leaded 1 point, and 9
point Baskerville, leaded 2 points. Part numbers
and chapter titles are in 18 point Bodoni Bold;
part titles are in 24 point Bodoni Bold; chapter
numbers are in 36 point Bodoni Bold. The size
of the type page is 27 x 45½ picas.*